digital media

Concepts & Applications 4e

Tena B. Crews

University of South Carolina
Columbia, South Carolina

Karen May, Retired

Blinn Community College
Bryan, Texas

Contributing Writer: Catherine Skintik

Cengage

Australia • Brazil • Canada • Mexico • Singapore • United Kingdom • United States

Digital Media: Concepts and Applications,
Fourth Edition
Tena B. Crews, Karen May

SVP, GM Skills & Global Product Management:
Dawn Gerrain

Product Director: Matthew Seeley

Product Manager: Jeff Werle

Product Development Manager: Juliet Steiner

Sr. Content Developer: Diane Bowdler

Contributing Writer: Catherine Skintik

Contributing Writer: Cara Norton

Consulting Editor: Jean Findley,
LEAP Publishing Services, Inc.

Product Marketing Manager: Kelsey Hagan

Sr. Content Project Manager: Martha Conway

Media Editor: Tristann Jones

Manufacturing Planner: Kevin Kluck

Production Service: Lumina Datamatics Inc.

Sr. Art Director: Bethany Casey

Internal Designer:
Grannan Graphic Design, Ltd.

Cover Designer: Tippy McIntosh

Cover Image: Steve Rawlings/getty images

Intellectual Property
Analyst: Kyle Cooper
Project Manager: Michelle McKenna

For product information and technology assistance, contact us at **Cengage Customer & Sales Support, 1-800-354-9706 or support.cengage.com.**

For permission to use material from this text or product, submit all requests online at **www.copyright.com**.

 The Career Clusters icons are being used with permission of the States' Career Cluster Initiative, 2011, **www.careerclusters.org**.

ISBN: 978-1-305-66172-1

Cengage
200 Pier 4 Boulevard
Boston, MA 02210
USA

Cengage is a leading provider of customized learning solutions with employees residing in nearly 40 different countries and sales in more than 125 countries around the world. Find your local representative at: **www.cengage.com.**

To learn more about Cengage platforms and services, register or access your online learning solution, or purchase materials for your course, visit **www.cengage.com.**

Printed in the United States of America
Print Number: 04   Print Year: 2024

Media-Driven Marketplace

Digital Media, 4E equips students with the tools and skills to succeed in today's digital-rich workplace by teaching them how to effectively use business-standard software applications to complete projects and solve real-world problems. The text's seven units give students hands-on experience with real-world projects using software from Adobe (Creative Cloud), Microsoft (Office 2013), and more.

A Cut Above

Combine comprehensive coverage with timely real-world applications straight from the marketplace.

▸▸ **Complete coverage** of multimedia applications topics and activities provide a full year of instruction. Extremely thorough, each lesson includes activities and multiple applications covering digital imaging, print publishing, audio and video production, web publishing, presentations, and the changing business environment.

▸▸ **Corporate Capstone** provides real-world projects that integrate concepts learned throughout the course.

▸▸ **21st Century Skills Feature** covers business topics to enhance critical thinking and collaboration. Topics include taking initiative, career planning, communication and active listening, netiquette, organization and punctuality, presentation skills, time management, teamwork, and maintaining ethical standards.

▸▸ **Career Clusters** profile introduces each unit and demonstrates real-life application of multimedia skills to be learned.

iii

Raising the Bar

Lesson structure maximizes student mastery.

» **Lessons** within chapters provide the ideal learning timeframe for students. In addition, practice activities are located in the chapters at the point of learning.

» **CheckPoint** asks critical-thinking questions at the end of each lesson.

» **Portfolio**, a continuing project at the end of each unit, offers students the opportunity to practice skills they have learned and create a portfolio of their work.

Lesson 4.3 Adjusting Settings

Point-and-shoot cameras are designed to make choices for you to help ensure a good photograph. While these choices often result in very satisfactory images, it is helpful to know what changes the camera makes in your camera settings. Many cameras will let you override the choices if you are not getting exactly the shot you want.

Basics LO 4.5

A camera uses three components to capture an image. They consist of the **shutter speed** (how fast the lens opens and closes), **aperture** settings (how wide the lens opens to let in light), and the **ISO** (speed at which the "film" captures an image).

All three of these functions work together in combination to produce an image. Changing any of these three settings will change the way your photograph appears. Point and shoots pick the combination that is likely to give you the best image. Many of these cameras provide pre-set special image types such as a **macro** (close-up) setting, a distance setting, or a sports setting. These special settings use different aperture, shutter speed, and ISO to capture the moment.

shutter speed—Measures the rate at which a camera lens opens and closes.

aperture—Indicates the size of a camera lens's opening.

ISO—A standardized measurement of the speed with which a camera stores an image.

macro—A setting or lens that allows close-ups.

Shutter Speed

You can adjust the shutter speed to achieve specific and desired effects. For example, if your shutter speed is set to open and close slowly while you are taking a picture of a runner crossing the finish line, there is enough time to capture a series of movements, resulting in the runner's blur. If you have the shutter speed set to open and close briefly, then you may catch the specific instant when the runner's foot is coming down onto the finish line.

Portfolio

1. Add your video project from the unit projects to your portfolio folder.

2. Write a summary of teamwork. In your summary, define teamwork, explain what it means to you, and describe in detail at least two experiences you have had in working as a part of a team. Include the advantages of being a part of a team as well as disadvantages.

---

checkpoint

What is color theory and how can you use it in your projects?

ACTIVITY 5.2 ▶ Color Themes

1. Open an image editing program.
2. Create four rectangles of analogous colors to use in a presentation

Setting the Standard

Integrated learning features enhance student engagement and comprehension.

▶▶ Innovative special features such as **History, Think About It,** and **Impact** provide additional information and ask critical-thinking questions for discussion of ethics and related topics.

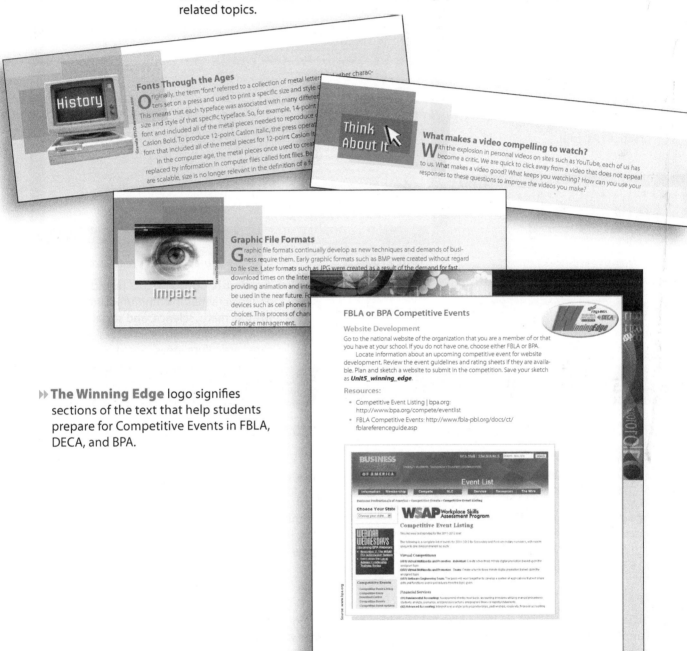

Fonts Through the Ages

Originally, the term "font" referred to a collection of metal letters and other characters set on a press and used to print a specific size and style of typeface. This means that each typeface was associated with many different fonts. So, for example, 14-point size and style of that specific typeface. So, for example, 14-point font and included all of the metal pieces needed to reproduce Caslon Bold. To produce 12-point Caslon Italic, the press operator font that included all of the metal pieces once used to create replaced by information in computer files called font files. Because are scalable, size is no longer relevant in the definition of a font.

What makes a video compelling to watch?

With the explosion in personal videos on sites such as YouTube, each of us has become a critic. We are quick to click away from a video that does not appeal to us. What makes a video good? What keeps you watching? How can you use your responses to these questions to improve the videos you make?

Graphic File Formats

Graphic file formats continually develop as new techniques and demands of business require them. Early graphic formats such as BMP were created without regard to file size. Later formats such as JPG were created as a result of the demand for fast download times on the Internet. providing animation and interactive be used in the near future. For devices such as cell phones choices. This process of changing of image management.

FBLA or BPA Competitive Events

Website Development

Go to the national website of the organization that you are a member of or that you have at your school. If you do not have one, choose either FBLA or BPA.

Locate information about an upcoming competitive event for website development. Review the event guidelines and rating sheets if they are available. Plan and sketch a website to submit in the competition. Save your sketch as *Unit5_winning_edge*.

Resources:

- Competitive Event Listing | bpa.org: http://www.bpa.org/compete/eventlist
- FBLA Competitive Events: http://www.fbla-pbl.org/docs/ct/fblareferenceguide.asp

▶▶ **The Winning Edge** logo signifies sections of the text that help students prepare for Competitive Events in FBLA, DECA, and BPA.

Leading by Example

End-of-chapter features reinforce learning and help students put chapter concepts into practice.

▸▸ **Key Concepts** provides a summary of concepts covered in the chapter that correlate to chapter learning outcomes.

▸▸ End of chapter includes **Review and Discuss** questions as well as applications for hands-on practice (**Apply**).

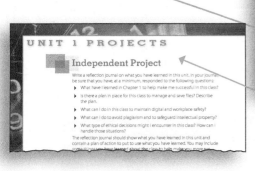

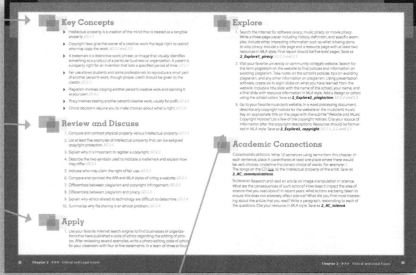

▸▸ **Unit Projects** provide integrated projects to reinforce the topics of several chapters in a unit.

▸▸ **Explore** projects are for reinforcement.

▸▸ **Academic Connections** provide open-ended activities in communications, writing, math, science, and social studies to apply the skills learned in digital media for core curriculum areas.

The Total Package

Additional digital resources ensure student and instructor success.

Instructor's Resource CD

The IRCD includes data files, suggested solutions, evaluation rubrics, teaching notes, and more!
ISBN: 978-1-305-66176-9

Cengage Learning Testing, powered by Cognero®, is a flexible, online system that allows you to import, edit, and manipulate content from the text's test bank or elsewhere, including your own favorite test questions. Create multiple test versions in an instant and deliver tests from your LMS, your classroom, or wherever you want.
ISBN: 978-1-305-66180-6

MindTap

MindTap is a personalized teaching experience with relevant assignments that guide students to analyze, apply, and improve thinking, allowing you to measure skills and outcomes with ease.

- Relevant readings, multimedia, and activities are designed to take students from basic knowledge to analysis and application.
- Personalized teaching becomes yours through a Learning Path built with key student objectives and your syllabus in mind. Control what students see and when they see it. ISBN: 978-1-305-66177-6

Digital Media Companion Website

www.cengage.com/swep/digitalmedia4e

Contents

To the Teacher

Long ago, educators had certain expectations. We knew what concepts students had to master to succeed in the career of their choice. We used textbooks and other resources to reinforce our knowledge.

Then, things changed as computers seemed to take over our lives. We had to teach new things for which we had no preparation, so we used books that taught the topics we did not know. The books provided us with a way to teach skills such as how to open and save a file, how to change a font, how to insert an image, and how to mail-merge a series of addresses.

The books we used looked more like cookbooks than textbooks. One could almost imagine the list of ingredients, followed by the steps, and then the instructions to bake at 350 degrees for 45 minutes for a perfect newsletter. The skills our students acquired with these recipes made it possible for them to learn to use a computer and specific software. We were satisfied that we were meeting the needs of our students.

Along the way, however, we lost something. We lost the idea that we should teach concepts and not just skills. We lost this idea because we were so inundated with the need to learn new and unfamiliar skills that we had no time to worry about concepts. We did what we had to do.

However, the world has changed again. We now know how to use several features in various software packages, create tables, use bulleted lists effectively, yet we strive to learn more. Our cookbooks are still useful, but they should no longer be our only instructional choice.

In today's world, we must teach students a whole new set of concepts. For example, in a business multimedia class, we must address the qualities of a good digital photograph and not just how to take a digital photograph. We must discuss what constitutes a professional PowerPoint design and not just how to add images to a slide show. We must address issues such as what typography can do for a sales proposal instead of limiting our instruction to ways of changing fonts.

As a result, our task has become even more challenging, yet exciting. Instead of relying on cookbooks alone, we now must choose books and materials that respond to this new set of needs. As you are previewing this textbook, look for the concepts. You will notice this book is not a series of recipes. Instead, it is designed to prepare your students for changes they will encounter in their careers. With this book, we can once again begin to feel that we are meeting the needs of our students.

To the Student

Digital media is not about learning everything there is to know about creating graphics, web pages, and PowerPoint presentations. Each of these tasks alone would be enough to fill at least a semester or year-long course. This textbook is instead about learning what concepts drive this field. So, when you enter the world of business, you can understand the jargon, know what expectations are reasonable, and direct in a knowledgeable manner those who do create complex image management tasks.

The course material consists of the student text and supplementary materials found on the Instructor Resource CD (IRCD) and product website (www.cengage.com/swep/digitalmedia4e). Some files will be provided by your instructor. The textbook is software independent and is designed to last through many changes of software. The materials available on the IRCD are software specific, focusing primarily on products from Microsoft and Adobe.

In the text, you will learn about creating powerful presentations, scripting languages, and video editing. You will learn what happens when large graphic files are added to web pages. You will understand the difference between CMYK and RGB color. You will also fully explore what features are available in PowerPoint. In addition, you will develop a keen sense of what is appropriate in a business-oriented document. All these concepts, as well as many others, are addressed in the student textbook.

The activities are designed to lead you through a series of tasks to help you understand and apply the concepts developed in the textbook. You will build simple rollovers, measure graphic file sizes, and experiment with CMYK and RGB graphics. You will build web pages and desktop-published documents. You will explore the options to be found in PowerPoint. The activities will not replace a text devoted to a single piece of software. Instead, they will help you become familiar with the basic functions of a number of software applications and their potential use in the business world.

If you should decide to pursue a career focusing on one or more fields related to digital media, you should find that this course will provide a good foundation. You will have acquired both the concepts and the skills to make it easier for you to pursue an in-depth study of your area of interest.

How to Use This Book

There are a number of ways that these materials can be used in a classroom. One way to is teach a single chapter from the student text, then have students study one of the relevant software programs using the supporting documents. If you have only limited software, you might want to complete all chapters of a given unit and then move on to one of the software packages that you do have. The end-of-unit projects are designed to reinforce and integrate everything the student has learned; therefore, they should be completed after all have been studied.

Student Edition

The student text contains a number of features designed to meet your instructional needs. Each unit opens with a career cluster profile of an actual person engaged in multimedia work. Each chapter contains clear objectives. Within each chapter there are a series of lessons broken up by activities. There are also these special features: CheckPoint for discussion and critical thinking, 21st Century Skills, the Impact of the technology, Think About It critical thinking stimuli, and the History of the technology. Chapters contain callouts of the terms discussed within the body of the text. Each chapter concludes with Key Concepts, Review and Discuss questions, Apply (use your knowledge to apply skills activities), Explore (further exploration material to engage students in critical analysis), and Academic Connections (to tie topics from core curriculum courses). The end-of-unit projects include an independent project and a portfolio project that build through the course, and a Winning Edge activity to help prepare for student organization competitive events.

Resources

In addition to the textbook, the complete instructional program includes Cognero questions, an IRCD with lesson plans, PowerPoint presentations, teaching suggestions, printable grading checklists, and answers to review questions (9781305661769).

There are also available e-book versions of the text. A website (www.cengage.com/swep/digitalmedia4e) provides additional resources.

Digital Media also offers a MindTap personalized learning course. As an instructor using MindTap®, you have at your fingertips the right content and unique set of tools created specifically for your course, in an interface designed to improve workflow and save time when planning lessons and course structure. The control to build and personalize your course is all yours, focusing on the most relevant material for your students. Stay connected and informed in your course through real-time student tracking that provides the opportunity to adjust the course as needed based on analytics of interactivity in the course. Find more information about MindTap at ngl.cengage.com/mindtap.

From the Authors

We are delighted that you are using our book. We have labored long and hard to make it interesting, complete, and useful. If we succeed in our goal of introducing students to the delight of digital media, our task will be complete.

About the Authors

Karen May retired in 2013 as Division Chair and Professor for Business and Information Technology at Blinn College, Bryan, Texas. She has taught Business Education at the high school and community college levels for 40 years. Ms. May earned her Bachelor of Business Education degree from the University of Mary Hardin-Baylor in Belton, Texas. She also holds a Masters of Adult Education degree and in 2013 returned to graduate school to earn 12 hours in Information Systems. She has presented at numerous national, regional, and state conferences and has written eight curriculum frameworks for Texas high schools. She was named the National Post Secondary Business Educator of the Year by NBEA in 2013. Currently, she teaches online for Lonestar College—Montgomery and New Mexico State University. She also serves as a master reviewer for Quality Matters in Online Education.

Tena B. Crews is a Professor of Integrated Information Technology at the University of South Carolina. She also serves as the Director of Online Learning and Program Chair for the Bachelor of Arts in Interdisciplinary Studies for the College of Hospitality, Retail and Sport Management. She is a Quality Matters Peer Reviewer and Master Reviewer. She has taught for 30 years at various levels of education. She previously taught business education and computer science courses at the secondary and technical school levels and served as a Technology Coordinator at the elementary school level. She earned her Bachelor of Business Education and Masters of Secondary Education at Ball State University. She holds a doctorate degree in Business Education with a concentration in Management Information Systems from the University of Georgia. She is also the author of *Fundamentals of Insurance* and *Investigating your Career*.

Reviewers

Tim Burke
College of Hospitality, Retail and
  Sport Management
Production and Design Coordinator
University of South Carolina
Columbia, SC

Doug Cogdell
College of Hospitality, Retail, and
  Sport Management
Director of Information Technology
  Services
University of South Carolina
Columbia, SC

Sally Irons, M.Ed.
Teacher
Southside School
Niles, MI

Cara Norton
Business Educator
Collins Hill High School
Suwanee, GA

Kenny Norton
Senior Videographer
CNN
Atlanta, GA

Mary Wincapaw-White
Consultant, Career and Technical
  Education
Milwaukee Public Schools
Milwaukee, WI

Features

UNIQUE CHAPTER FEATURES	SELECTED PAGES
21st Century Skills CAREER	7, 39, 61, 87, 106, 120, 152, 179, 204, 228, 240, 273, 297, 323, 384, 409, 426, 444, 457, 471, 503, 513
Academic Connections	22, 45, 65, 91, 109, 136, 158, 182, 208, 232, 256, 281, 315, 345, 370, 393, 414, 434, 451, 465, 482, 506, 521
Career Cluster:	1, 49, 163, 235, 285, 419, 487
checkpoint	7, 12, 16, 19, 34, 38, 41, 53, 56, 61, 76, 83, 86, 98, 104, 106, 113, 119, 123, 132, 142, 151, 154, 166, 175, 178, 193, 199, 203, 217, 225, 228, 240, 246, 253, 263, 268, 278, 290, 300, 310, 325, 331, 335, 339, 353, 366, 379, 389, 404, 410, 424, 428, 431, 437, 443, 446, 448, 454, 460, 462, 471, 475, 478, 494, 497, 500, 503, 511, 515, 518
History	11, 32, 52, 75, 100, 114, 143, 167, 187, 227, 241, 242, 277, 308, 355, 374, 396, 423, 460, 472, 491, 516
Impact	4, 33, 53, 71, 86, 96, 133, 155, 176, 190, 220, 253, 264, 293, 380, 406, 427, 438, 454, 469, 495, 511
Portfolio	46, 160, 233, 283, 416, 484, 522
Think About It	17, 29, 54, 84, 102, 123, 144, 166, 176, 192, 211, 246, 267, 296, 322, 348, 377, 403, 431, 446, 462, 475, 499, 518
WinningEdge	48, 161, 234, 283, 417, 485, 523

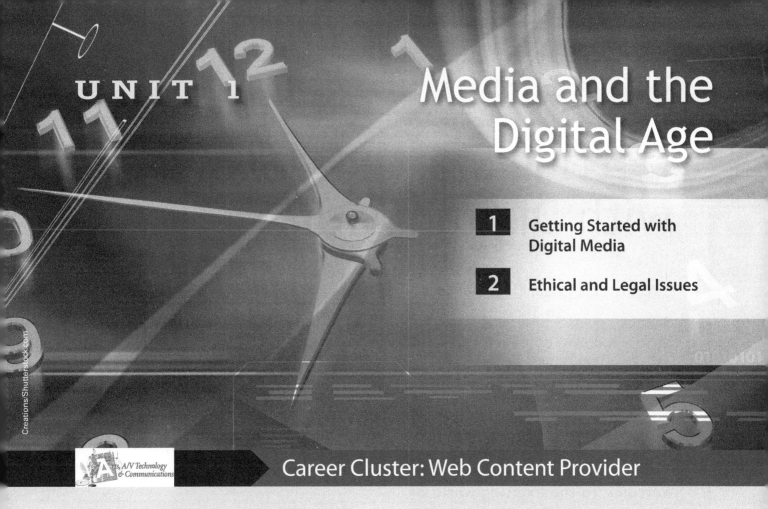

UNIT 1

Media and the Digital Age

1 Getting Started with Digital Media

2 Ethical and Legal Issues

Career Cluster: Web Content Provider

Arts, A/V Technology & Communications

Interview with Laura, Production Editor at eMusic.com

Describe your average day. On most days, I edit music reviews and features, do lots of HTML coding, and post editorial content on the eMusic website. I also write reviews of albums and concerts and sometimes interview musicians. I work with the rest of the editorial team to plan upcoming features. I build marketing newsletters and use Twitter to promote features and communicate with our members.

What is the worst part of your job? In a nutshell, the music industry can be extremely complicated! What I can write about at eMusic is limited by what music we are selling, which isn't all music on every record label.

What is the best part of your job? I get to listen to and talk about music all day, so I'm constantly learning about new and old artists. I can write about and promote bands and musicians I care about, and it directly translates into them selling records and making money.

Employment Outlook In general, average employment growth is expected for writers and editors in the near future, with high competition for jobs, according to the U.S. Bureau of Labor Statistics. However, writers and editors who are knowledgeable about and comfortable working with electronic and digital media tools will have an advantage in the marketplace.

Skills and Qualifications A bachelor's degree or higher in an area such as journalism, communications, or English is sometimes preferred for writing and editing jobs, but good writers from any background can qualify for many positions. Creativity, self-motivation, and a strong sense of ethics in deciding what to publish are important personal attributes for writers and editors. A familiarity with electronic publishing, graphics, Web design, multimedia production, and social networking tools increases employability and is a must to work at a Web-based business.

Job Titles writer, editor, Web content provider, production editor

What About You? You may not have thought of writing as a digital media career, but with the increase in Internet-based businesses, the demand for content providers who are familiar with digital media tools has jumped. Use the Internet to find job postings for Web content writers and editors. Research writing and similar careers using the *Occupational Outlook Handbook* published by the U.S. Bureau of Labor Statistics and available at *http://www.bls.gov/ooh/*.

- What job qualifications are employers looking for?
- What are the most common technical skills and computer programs mentioned?
- How can you best prepare yourself for a career as a Web content provider?

Chapter 1

Getting Started with Digital Media

Welcome to the exciting world of **digital media** or, as it is sometimes called, multimedia. Digital media is about communicating electronically, but it also includes an element of creativity. The Digital Media Alliance of Florida (DMAF) perhaps says it best when it defines digital media as "the creative convergence of digital arts, science, technology and business for human expression, communication, social interaction and education." This text will help you learn how to use digital media tools to communicate creatively.

Learning Outcomes

▶ **1.1** List the characteristics needed to become a skilled digital master.

▶ **1.2** Identify how to name and save a file.

▶ **1.3** Explain how to ensure digital security.

▶ **1.4** Practice the techniques for good keyboarding.

Key Terms

- adware
- cyber predator
- digital media
- encryption
- ergonomics
- hacker
- keylogger
- malware
- naming convention
- online backup
- phishing
- repetitive stress injury
- rootkit
- server
- social engineering
- spyware
- Trojan horse
- virus
- worm

To be successful in the field of digital media requires that you do more than just get a degree. You must be prepared to learn continuously as well as to bring basic work skills to all that you do. Begin by committing yourself to success.

digital media—Any combination of audio, video, images, and text used to convey a message through technology.

Commitment *LO 1.1*

Each year brings interesting changes and surprising additions to the world of digital media. The software you learn today will undoubtedly change dramatically within a few years, requiring you to update your skills and knowledge. In this class, you will learn about current software, but you will also learn *how* to learn. Education is an ongoing process in every field. In digital media, it is an essential skill if you are to remain productive in the field.

Learning new software and computer skills requires the following commitments from you:

- **Be flexible.** In this class, being flexible might mean that you accept that there may not be an exact solution to every assignment.

- **Keep an open mind.** Be willing to accept new ideas. For example, you may have always thought that the subject of every photograph should be in the center of the image. Be open to looking at images in a new way. Or, you may have thought that good software comes only from huge corporations. Become aware of the open source movement. Being closed minded makes it easy to get stuck in a digital rut. Work to avoid that.

- **Use initiative.** Using initiative in class can mean exploring possibilities other than just those given in a list of instructions. It might mean taking a project beyond just that assigned in the text. Learn to explore all the possibilities.

- **Listen and read attentively.** Listening to your instructor and reading the text carefully smooths the path to learning. Reading more than just the text and listening to those with expertise in the field of digital media opens your mind and turns you into an accomplished learner.

- **Seek to acquire new knowledge and skills.** Make a promise to yourself that you will continually seek new knowledge beyond that which is assigned to you. Be an active, engaged learner. Avoid the temptation to say you are finished learning. There is no "finished" in the world of digital media. Keeping current with industry software requires you to know how to learn. You will be seeking new knowledge on a daily basis.

If you keep these five statements in mind at all times, you will become, and remain, a skilled master of digital media technology.

iStockphoto.com/Perkus

Figure 1.1 *Listening attentively will allow you to become an accomplished learner as well as successful in your future career.*

Impact

Software Updates

Eighteen months is about the length of time a version of a software package remains current. The impact of this timeline on digital media experts is that they must be constantly learning new software to maintain their skills. As soon as you have mastered one version, a new one is on the horizon. Avoid the trap of getting too comfortable with today's technology. Anticipate these changes. Be at the forefront instead of the back by paying attention to changes ahead of you.

One way to stay current is to participate in beta trials, which are tests of new versions before their final release. Beta trials let you learn about the changes before they reach most consumers. They also allow you to participate in the process by making suggestions for changes and reporting problems.

Certifications *LO 1.1*

One of the ways to demonstrate your skills to potential employers is to acquire certification from a secondary or post-secondary school or through a provider such as Adobe® or Microsoft. Certification programs provide in-depth training within particular areas and then offer testing—the passing of which demonstrates your proficiency. While such programs cannot ensure employability, they do give you credentials that are quite valuable. It is one way for potential employers to know exactly what skills you possess.

Just as with other educational programs, the cost incurred depends upon the school or the certification program. But do not let cost deter you from obtaining the required certification. You should expect to invest in certification for yourself just as you would with a two- or four-year degree program. Note also that, just as with a four-year program, if you are enrolled in a community college, you may be eligible for grants and other financial assistance.

Digital media certifications generally fall into three categories: Web, print, and video. Graphics, animation, and 3D fall under these groupings. Colleges, universities, your local community and technical colleges, as well as online colleges can be a good place to get the training required for certification. These institutions set up a curriculum with a series of required courses you must take in order to receive a certificate. Certificates are generally broadly defined. For example, you may earn a certificate in Multimedia Studies.

Adobe certifications, called **ACA (Adobe Certified Associate)** and **ACE (Adobe Certified Expert)** certifications, are available online. The ACA credential certifies that you have the entry-level skills to plan, design, build, and maintain effective communications using different forms of digital media. The ACE certifies that you have expert-level skills in the same areas. Adobe provides study materials as part of the testing process, but you must have the motivation to complete them on your own. Each ACE test is for a specific Adobe application, such as Adobe Dreamweaver® or Adobe Photoshop®. You can demonstrate proficiency for a single product to receive a specialist certificate or combine a series of products for master certification. Listed below are the different ACE master certification levels. Notice that the ability to use both Adobe Illustrator® and Adobe Photoshop are required for all three plans. This is because the ability to manage graphical images, as is done with these programs, is the foundation for working in all digital media.

Adobe Systems Inc

Figure 1.2 *The ACE logo on your résumé is proof that you have the skills for which employers are looking.*

Design Master
- Adobe Acrobat® Professional
- Adobe InDesign®
- Adobe Illustrator
- Adobe Photoshop

Web Master
- Adobe Acrobat Professional
- Adobe Dreamweaver
- Adobe Flash® Professional
- Adobe Illustrator
- Adobe Photoshop

Video Master
- Adobe AfterEffects®
- Adobe Flash Professional
- Adobe Illustrator
- Adobe Photoshop
- Adobe Premiere® Pro

Some schools use ACE exams as their final testing products. It is also possible that your school is a testing center for the ACA exam. Check with your instructor for more information on any certifications offered.

Work Skills for Multimedia Careers *LO 1.1*

Beyond becoming skilled in the use of software and hardware, it is important to keep in mind other behaviors that contribute to your ability to acquire a job and grow in the field of your choice, whether it is in digital media or some other profession. These are the same behaviors that ensure success in school. They include the following:

- **Good attendance.** No matter how skilled you are, if you are not at school or at work, you cannot use those skills. Being absent has hindered the success of more students than poor ability.

- **Promptness.** Sliding into work or class late puts you behind before you can begin. Be on time. Plan ahead so no event can prevent you from being on time.

- **Proper attire.** Communication comes in many forms. Words are not the only way to send a message. What you wear can say more about your attitude and respect than you might expect. Choose your clothing so it says that you are a committed employee or student. Wear the clothing that fits the task. Revealing blouses, torn jeans, and sloppy shoes say that you do not consider your work to be important.

- **Clean and safe work environment.** Some jobs require you to keep your work area clean and safe, which usually includes keeping your work space clear of trash. In a digital world, a safe environment is one in which networks are not compromised by viruses and personal identities are not lost through careless passwords. A clean digital world includes maintaining good file structures and updated software. Regardless of your job, safety and cleanliness are essential.

- **Appropriate voice.** In some work environments, such as those that require employees to use the telephone or to talk to customers, appropriate voice means avoiding harsh words and inappropriate language. Electronic language has the same restrictions. Emails and text messages written in anger or carelessly can end the career of even the most talented. Electronic content that includes inappropriate language or topics can be just as damaging. In a world of digital social networks, that means monitoring all content to ensure that your voice is always appropriate.

- **Pride.** No matter what task you are assigned in school or at work, always perform it in such a way that you can feel pride in your accomplishment. That means caring about the most minor detail as well as the larger components. In digital media, for example, that pride shows when you crop an image carefully to remove the slightest imperfection. It shows when you verify the spelling of a simple one-line caption. It shows when you assign descriptions to Web images for use by the visually impaired. Pride means you care that your work is good. Pride shows.

Figure 1.3 *The clothing you choose communicates a lot about your attitude toward yourself, others, and your work.*

Taking Initiative

Probably the best way you can advance your career is to take initiative at work. You should not stand around with nothing to do. If you complete an assignment, go to your supervisor and request something else to do. Do not wait to be given a new task—ask for more work and responsibility. Supervisors notice and respond favorably to employees who do so. One good way to take initiative at work is to find small ways to improve the way a job is done. Or consider doing a job in a slightly different way. Taking initiative on the job can be a bit tricky, though. Employers are not necessarily looking for workers to come in and start "running the show." Taking initiative does not mean insisting that things be done your way. It means determining what your employer wants and needs and then doing it the best way possible.

Skills in Action: Think about ways you can take initiative in a classroom. Check with your instructor and follow through with at least one of them.

checkpoint
What are the keys to success in digital media?

ACTIVITY 1.1 ▶ Creating a "Commitment to Learning" Presentation

1. Using presentation software such as Microsoft PowerPoint, create a slide show with **Commitment to Learning** as the title and your name as the subtitle.

2. Create a slide for each of the five commitments to learning discussed in this lesson. For example, the first slide will have the title **Be Flexible**.

3. On each slide, add a bulleted list of three to five brief statements expanding on the commitment in the title. You may want to do some research to create the best statement on what this commitment means or how it can best be accomplished.

4. Save the presentation as *1_Activity1_commitment*.

Lesson 1.2 ▶ Reviewing the Computer System and File Management

Before moving on to the study of multimedia software, it is necessary to make sure you have a clear understanding of basic file management. While much of this material will be a review, it is easy for details, such as naming conventions, to have been omitted from your previous instruction. This lesson makes sure that these gaps, wherever they might be, are filled in.

Managing Files *LO 1.2*

Managing digital media files is an essential part of creating a good work environment. Digital media projects often include multiple components as part of the final product. These may include image, text, audio, and video files. All must be saved in such a way and in such a place that anyone involved in the project can find the most current versions. Horror tales abound of products that appear finished until someone discovers that a wrong version of one of the component files has been used.

Naming Files

naming convention—A set of rules used in the naming of files and folders.

The first step in managing files is deciding on a naming practice, or **naming convention**. It is easy to assign a filename quickly, without much thought. However, that often means you cannot find the document in a maze of files when you look for it later. Choose a name that clearly identifies the contents of the file. If files are to be shared, the author's name or initials and some numbering method should be used to make sure that correct versions are apparent.

If a filename includes more than a single word, one of two formats is generally used to connect the words. One method links words with an underscore, as in Book_revision.doc. The other format links multiple words using upper and lower case, as in BookRevision.doc. While you can separate words with spaces in standard filenames, empty spaces are discouraged because they can lead to problems down the road. Avoiding blank spaces in filenames is especially important for files used in a web page because the linking process replaces empty spaces with "%20," making the URL address appear confusing when it is cited or referenced. There are other characters that should also be avoided in file or directory names as shown in Table 1.1.

Table 1.1 *Characters to avoid in file and directory names.*

SYMBOLS			
#	%	&	?
$	!	@	{ or }
< or >	' or "	+ or =	:
`	|	/ or \	

Saving Files

The second consideration in managing files is making sure you have saved your file to the correct location. There should be a designated place to save project files, and everyone on a project team must know where that is. Network locations or shared Internet locations are often used to allow everyone access to the same material. Make sure you know where the shared folder is located. If you are responsible for creating folders, make sure they are clearly identifiable. Develop the habit of saving files into folders so that similar documents or files that are all associated with the same project are gathered together.

Many programs, such as Adobe Photoshop, offer several file type options such as .jpg or .psd when you save a file. Make sure that you know what file type should be selected for your project. You will learn more about image file type choices in Chapter 3, but this is not just an image issue. It also applies to word processing, spreadsheet, and database files. In some programs, such as Microsoft Word, you can choose to save as a certain file type based on software version compatibility. For example, if you need to share a file with someone who does not have the most current version of the software you are using, you must be sure to save in a format that is readable in the earlier version.

Choosing Storage

A computer hard drive is the internal storage space for files on your computer. While a computer's hard drive is installed inside the machine, it is also possible to have external hard drives that are used to expand storage space. The size of hard drives has increased dramatically over the last few years even as the prices have dropped. In the past, a hard drive of 500 gigabytes (GB), or "gigs," would have been considered large. Today, drives are often measured in terabytes (TB). The next generation of drives will be measured in petabytes (PB). See Table 1.2 for descriptions of storage sizes. As the size of these drives increases and the cost drops, it becomes easy to ignore the size of files you store on your hard drive. However, video and audio files are so large that they can consume the space of even very large hard drives. It is important to pay attention to file sizes and understand what demands they are making on your system.

Table 1.2 *A summary of storage descriptions.*

kilobyte	1000 (or 1024) bytes
megabyte	1000 (or 1024) kilobytes
gigabyte	1000 (or 1024) megabytes
terabyte	1000 (or 1024) gigabytes
petabyte	1000 (or 1024) terabytes

Organizations often store files on dedicated servers. A **server** is one or more large hard drives stored in a location separate from the desktop

server—A computer designed to store files from multiple computers.

computers used by employees. (For safety and security, this location is often a physically different address.) This hardware "serves" one or more computers on a network. Just as with a personal computer, you must be aware of the size of the digital media files you are storing on a server. While their storage capability is far greater than your computer's hard drive, it is not unlimited.

Another means of storage can be a writeable CD or DVD. CDs can store about 700 MB while DVDs can store 4 to 15 GB, depending upon the method of recording. CDs and DVDs are useful as a means of archiving files that you want to store for retrieval on a later date. They are also used to share files with someone who does not have access to your computer or network. Because of their much larger capacity, DVDs are often used to store digital media files. While the disks appear to be permanent, the length of time you can trust the reliability of the data stored on them is a subject of discussion. Some reports have shown that the plastic used to create the disks begins to break down in as little as five years. Some of the reliability issues are based on the manufacturing process used. If you are archiving files that need to be stored for long periods of time, investigate different brands before you choose which one to use.

Figure 1.4 *The flash drive has had many names since it was introduced. Originally it was known as a thumb or key chain drive, but as users became more familiar with the concept, the term* flash drive *became more widely used.*

Flash drives (also called thumb drives or USB drives) are not hard drives. Instead of a spinning platter on which data is stored, these small devices store information electronically on a circuit board. This means there are no moving parts to break. They are attached to a computer through the USB port, making them easy to use as a means of transferring data from one machine to another. Flash drives come in many sizes from a few hundred MBs to several GBs.

Storage Methods

The history of the personal computer (as compared to mainframe or business computers) can be tracked according to the different storage methods used at each point along the timeline. Early computers had no hard drives. All the data was originally stored on tape cassettes, but soon moved to "floppy" disks (so named because they were bendable). These disks had a paper covering and were 5.25 inches square. In time they were replaced with 3.5-inch floppy disks with a hard plastic covering. Each year brought changes in the storage capacity of these disks. Eventually a larger hard plastic "zip" disk with 10 times the storage came on the market, although floppy disks remained the primary means of transferring data.

During the time in which floppy disks of various sizes were being used, hard drives or hard disks were added to computers, dramatically increasing their storage ability.

CD-ROM (compact disks–read only memory) drives, which originally could only read information, were added to computers. In time these disks became writeable.

Disk storage has always served two purposes: to provide information to a computer and to store the information for archival or transfer purposes. The need to physically transfer files has nearly disappeared with the use of networks and email to send documents. Floppy disks have become obsolete, replaced by CDs and DVDs. We may see even these disappear as flash drives become larger and cheaper. And many people now store a great deal of information in the "cloud"—a network of servers that you can access from any location with an Internet connection. It will be interesting to see what the next point will be on the history timeline.

Making Backups *LO 1.2*

Digital media files represent hours of work. Losing this work through a hardware failure or virus attack is a concern to every designer. Backups can be made to hardware such as a flash drive or another hard drive. Backing up over a network means that the information is stored on another computer within the network. A third option is an **online backup**. With this process, files are transferred over the Internet to a computer in a distant location. All three of these methods may be used to ensure that files are not lost. Whatever method you choose, backing up or saving your work is another means of maintaining a good working environment.

Some organizations have systems in place that automatically back up files at a set interval. Others require you to save only when you believe it is appropriate. Whenever you are working on a project, whether for yourself or someone else, it is important to consider backups. Make sure you have a plan in place. Short-term, more frequent backups can be made to removable media such as a flash drive. Long-term backups may be sent to an online server.

online backup—A means of backing up or storing data using the Internet.

checkpoint

List four areas that are important to understand when using computers.

ACTIVITY 1.2 ▶ Planning File Management

With a partner, write a brief file management plan for your class. Ask for any special instructions from your instructor before getting started.

1. Include naming conventions and a folder structure in your plan. Consider the following:
   - Include some examples of both good and bad folder names. Show different folder levels to demonstrate organizational structure.
   - Give some filename examples and include several bad filename examples with each good example.
2. Indicate where folders and files will be stored.
3. Develop a plan to back up files.
4. Join together with another team and compare your plans.
5. Adjust your plan as needed.
6. Submit the written plan to your instructor in a word processing document saved as *1_Activity2_planning*.

Lesson 1.3 ▶ Maintaining Digital Safety

Safety at school and in the workplace is not limited to physical safety. It also includes using the Internet safely. There are two areas of concern: yourself and your computer.

Personal Security *LO 1.3*

Protecting yourself means not revealing personal information unnecessarily or providing any information to sites you do not trust. It goes without saying that personal safety also includes never meeting in person anyone whom you have met on the Web unless you have a trusted adult with you. This is true regardless of your age. Online **cyber predators** who hunt for victims are dangerous to everyone. Be skeptical; not everyone is as they appear online. Even the most seemingly harmless exchange can turn into a dangerous situation.

Another danger to you is identity theft (stealing someone's information to use for illegal purposes). This is an issue that applies to anyone who uses the Internet to register at a website, purchases items on the Web, emails or texts others, or uses social network sites. It is easy to feel invisible on the Web and just as easy for others to be invisible to you. Part of your commitment to digital learning requires you to read and listen attentively. That includes keeping current on the most recent Internet security issues, which might include the latest **social engineering** scams or **keylogger** tricks.

cyber predator—A person who uses the Internet to make contact with others (usually with children and teens) in order to harm them.

social engineering—Tricking users into providing information in the belief that a request is legitimate.

keylogger—Software that tracks keyboard use and transmits it to be used for illegal purposes.

Susan Lake

Figure 1.5 *Social security numbers, driver's license numbers, and credit cards are some of the most frequently stolen forms of identity.*

Computer Security *LO 1.3*

Keeping your computer and network safe requires you to be attentive to dangers from information carried on disks, on flash drives, and over the Internet. There are countless ways for these delivery methods to bring unwanted changes to your computer. These include viruses and other malware. **Malware**, or malicious software, is a general term that covers any software installed on a computer without the consent of the owner. It is usually designed to damage the computer or steal information. Malware includes products such as spyware, Trojan horses, adware, and rootkits. One of the first ways to keep your computer secure is to install virus and malware protection software and keep it up-to-date.

malware—The abbreviation for malicious software, designed to damage a computer or steal information.

It is helpful to understand the distinctions between each of the hazards mentioned above. Table 1.3 describes several different types of malware.

Table 1.3 *Different types of malware.*

virus	A program that infects a computer without the permission or knowledge of the owner. A virus usually attaches itself to executable programs, allowing it to travel to other computers. Viruses require action by the computer user in order to activate them.
worm	A form of a virus that does not require any action by the computer user. It spreads by using the email functions of the computer. A worm's action overwhelms Web servers, often shutting them down.
spyware	Malware that captures information from a computer without the user's knowledge or consent.
Trojan horse (also called Trojan)	Software that appears to be useful but instead allows access to a computer without the user's knowledge or consent.
adware	Software that delivers advertising without the user's knowledge or consent.
rootkit	Software designed to keep a computer user from knowing the computer system has been infected by malware.

Although a computer can be protected using specialized software packages, no virus protection is foolproof. The computer user has a responsibility to be vigilant. That means if you download software and images from the Internet, make sure they are from secure sites. It means not opening suspicious email or unexpected attachments. And it means staying current on the latest Web security issues.

Networks are everywhere: businesses, homes, coffee shops, airports, and even fast food restaurants. As soon as you log in to one of these networks, there is a potential risk to your computer. Some networks are more secure than others, meaning they have passwords and **encryption** (means of disguising information) to prevent outsiders from using them. Networks that are open to the public are far less secure. If your computer is using one of these networks, your information can be captured even as you send it. Be very careful what information you share over a network, and remember that no software protection can prevent a network **hacker** from stealing information shared over an open network.

encryption—Converting text into an unreadable series of numbers and letters to protect information. Digital encryption uses software that can scramble and unscramble the data.

hacker—A person who finds an electronic means of gaining unauthorized access to a computer.

Password Security *LO 1.3*

One of the most effective ways to protect your computer and its information is through wise use of passwords. Passwords are an important barrier between your computer and the outside world. If your password is easy to figure out, code hackers can easily gain access to your computer and its files. Strong passwords are those that meet a set of rules designed to make it difficult for others to figure out. Some basic requirements for strong passwords consist of the following:

- Have a minimum of eight characters.
- Use both upper- and lowercase letters.
- Use at least one number.
- Use at least one special character such as ! @ $ % ^ & * ( ) - _ = + [ ] ; : ' ", <. > / ? (note that passwords may not begin with the exclamation or the question mark).

Passwords can be challenging to remember, and it is tempting to use the same one in every case. Unfortunately, that means one broken password opens up all your computer, network, and Web logins at once. Using sticky notes attached to your computer creates the same set of problems. One of the best ways to create strong but easy-to-remember passwords is to create a statement and then to use the first letter from each word as your password. For example, the login for this text might be **L**earning **a**bout **D**igital **M**edia **i**n **2017**. The password would be LaDMi2017. Notice that the lowercase "i" and "a" break up the other uppercase letters, and the date provides a series of numbers.

Another way to make sure you can easily remember your passwords is to use a password manager. Password managers allow you to store not only your passwords but also user names and other important login information. Passwords are encrypted in a database for which you must provide a strong password. Using a password manager makes it easy to keep track of many strong passwords without having to write them down.

Figure 1.6 *A secure password may be all that prevents others from gaining access to your computer and its data.*

As users have become more adept at creating good passwords, those seeking unauthorized access to passwords have become more creative by sending out realistic-appearing emails asking for the information. These emails and other such actions are called **phishing**, and they convince users to reveal confidential information. Once again, caution and suspicion are important ways of helping your computer and its information remain safe.

Hardware Security *LO 1.3*

Another consideration when thinking about security is maintaining the physical security of your actual computer, particularly laptops and portable devices. Laptops, smartphone, and other devices are portable and easy to use away from your desk. Unfortunately, that very portability creates problems because these items are no longer secured by the locked windows and doors of an office. Laptops are often stored in cars; taken on public transportation; and used in restaurants, hotels, and countless other public places. Consequently, they can be easily picked up and removed without the owner's permission. Loss of the actual hardware is an obvious problem, but often more important is the loss of the information that is stored on the device. If proper backup techniques were not employed, whole projects can be lost. The information contained on the portable device may also be proprietary or confidential, and a theft could lead to that data being used in an undesirable way.

Maintaining the security of your equipment is your responsibility. Carelessness with physical property is just as much a problem as carelessness with a password. As a member of a digital project, it is your obligation to pay attention to any situation that might endanger your equipment, whether it is a risk of theft or the risk that comes from spilling drinks into a keyboard. Protecting equipment and data require you to be diligent and forward-looking.

Figure 1.7 *Portability has many advantages for users. Unfortunately, it also means easier targets for opportunistic criminals.*

Acceptable Use Policy (AUP)

One of the tools organizations use to encourage both digital safety and appropriate use of hardware and software is an Acceptable Use Policy (AUP). These AUPs are written agreements that all system users must agree to and acknowledge that agreement with a signature. These policies are designed to ensure safety for everyone who uses a network. They are also designed to discourage inappropriate use of equipment. AUPs generally outline acceptable behavior and also establish consequences for not following the rules.

AUPs may include the following:

- Password selection requirements, including frequency of change.

- Software usage restrictions to ensure that users adhere to intellectual property laws.

- Netiquette rules (social network etiquette) including prohibition of inappropriate emailing or texting subjects (such as racist or sexist jokes).

- Limits on the use of systems or items that overtax the network (such as online game playing or downloading of videos).

AUPs are documents that should be taken seriously. Businesses may monitor computer usage to verify that all computer users are adhering to the policies. Networks may also have software that alerts the administrator when certain words or even images are posted by users. Consequences can range from restriction on the use of computer systems to loss of employment.

checkpoint

What is the single most important means of ensuring your personal or computer security?

ACTIVITY 1.3 ▶ Researching Computer Security

1. With a partner, write a one-page report with a separate reference page researching one of the keywords in this lesson: identity theft, phishing, keylogger, malware, virus, worm, spyware, Trojan horse, adware, or rootkit. Get your topic approved by your instructor.

2. Research to get a better understanding of that specific topic and the latest information on issues concerning the topic.

3. Cite at least two references with appropriate documentation.

4. Save the document as *1_Activity3_computer_security*. If time permits, share your research with your classmates.

Lesson 1.4 ▶ Practicing Workplace Safety

ergonomics—A science that studies the best way to design a workplace for maximum safety and productivity.

Ergonomics is the study of the best way to design equipment to ensure safety and productivity. As it relates to computers, this involves the design of the workstation, use of correct posture, and finding ways to prevent computer-related injuries. Ergonomics raises awareness of all parts of your body as you use a computer in order to maintain a safe and healthy workplace.

Avoiding Repetitive Stress Injury LO 1.4

repetitive stress injury—Muscle or joint injury that results from performing actions repeatedly.

Those who work in the field of digital media find themselves in front of a computer and keyboard for long periods of time. It is important to develop good keyboarding practices to reduce the risk of injury. **Repetitive stress injury** (RSI) results from repeated movement of a particular part of the body. For example, graphic artists use their "mouse hand" more than some other workers do. Everyone who works at a computer is at risk for developing a form of RSI called carpal tunnel syndrome (CTS). CTS is a painful inflammatory disease that affects the wrists, hands, and forearms. Symptoms include numb or tingling hands and wrists; pain in the forearm, elbow, or shoulder; and difficulty in gripping objects.

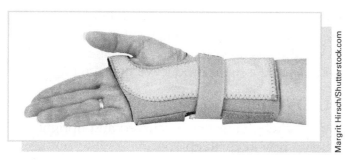

Figure 1.8 *Carpal tunnel syndrome is a type of repetitive stress injury and often requires surgery or at least a brace to protect the injured hand.*

Margrit Hirsch/Shutterstock.com

Who Is Responsible?

One of the expectations that we all have in our modern world is that we will not come to any harm in our workplace. That is true if your "workplace" is school, home, or a business. Some items, such as safe drinking water, are not even given a second thought. Others, such as knowing that no one will physically attack us, should be another item that is not given a second thought. But what about issues such as repetitive stress injury? Who is responsible for ensuring your safety? Is it the employer who should provide ergonomic chairs and keyboards? Is it a personal responsibility that requires you to pay attention to how you are using your hands? What happens if you identify a problem, and your employer does not allow you to make changes to improve the situation? The Occupational Safety and Health Administration (OSHA) is the federal agency charged with assuring safe and healthful working conditions. Explore the OSHA website and then discuss what protections they provide to workers.

Creating Effective Workstations *LO 1.4*

Ergonomics teaches that proper workstation arrangement is vital. Considerations include the following:

- Your keyboard should be at elbow height and even with the front edge of your desk.
- Your monitor should be positioned to avoid glare and be located at least an arm's length away.
- Your chair should have a good backrest.
- Your back should be touching the backrest at all times.
- Your feet should be flat on the floor (or use a footrest).
- You should sit up straight, keeping your head and neck as straight as possible.

Arrange your work material so you can see it easily and maintain good posture. Some experts recommend positioning whatever you look at most often (the monitor or documents) directly in front of you so you do not have to turn your head frequently.

Low levels of light are recommended if you are working on the computer; turn up the lights if you are examining paper documents. Keeping these guidelines in mind will let you become a more productive digital media artist.

© franksiteman.com 2007

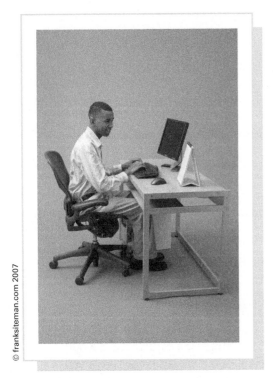

Figure 1.9 *Sitting up straight with feet flat and your back touching the chair helps make you more productive and less likely to be injured.*

Correct Keyboarding Technique

When you key, keep your fingers curved and upright over the home row keys. Keep your wrists low, but not touching the keyboard. Lightly tap each key with the tip of your finger, snapping the fingertip toward the palm of your hand. Your hands and arms will not be as tired at the end of the day if you follow these simple techniques.

As with any muscle, it is often helpful to warm up your fingers by performing a series of actions that allow the body to remember movements. The following two exercises can be used for that purpose.

Key each of these lines twice to exercise your fingers and to improve your keying techniques. The sentences were constructed to give you practice in all letters of the alphabet.

1. Zack and our equipment manager will exchange jobs for seven days.
2. Next week Zelda Jacks will become a night supervisor for quality.
3. A man in the park saw a fat lizard quickly devour six juicy bugs.

Or

1. Jack Faber was amazingly quiet during the extensive program.
2. Dixie quickly gave him two big prizes for completing a jump.
3. Jordan placed first by solving the complex quiz in one week.

Ergonomic keyboards are designed to improve hand posture and make keying more comfortable. They usually have a split design with left and right banks and the ability to tilt or rotate the keyboard for comfort. You may find that using such a keyboard reduces the strain on your hands and wrists while you work.

© Cengage Learning

Dmitry Melnikov/Shutterstock.com

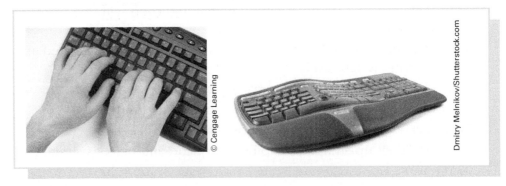

Figure 1.10 *If you learned to use a keyboard without proper instruction, you might not know that there are techniques you should follow.*

Figure 1.11 *An ergonomic keyboard looks strange, but it can speed up your productivity and protect you from injury.*

Mouse Techniques

Those who work in multimedia often have strong preferences for using a certain type of mouse. Regardless of the mouse you select, the most important thing you can do when using a mouse is to hold it gently. Keep your wrist straight and use your elbow as the pivot point rather than "flicking" your wrist to move the mouse. Do not use a wrist rest (it actually increases the pressure inside the carpal tunnel). Consider using a large mouse, which encourages arm rather than wrist movements. Whatever you use, keep your arms, hands, and fingers relaxed.

Taking a Break

While working with multimedia, it is easy to become so immersed in a project that time passes quickly. You may find it hard to remember to take a break. Develop a plan to make sure you take breaks automatically, perhaps by setting a timer.

Get up from your workstation at least once an hour and move around a bit. Get a drink or snack. Rest your eyes occasionally by focusing on an object at least 20 feet away. Stretch your muscles to relax and strengthen them. You will actually be more productive if you step away from your work from time to time.

Figure 1.12 *Breaks do not have to be extended. Even taking the time for a quick drink of water or a cup of coffee can be enough to reduce strain.*

iStockphoto.com/killerb10

checkpoint

Why is it important to be aware of your body while using a computer?

ACTIVITY 1.4 ▶ Evaluating Keyboarding Technique

1. Using a word processing document, create a table with three columns and seven rows. In the first row, key headers for each column: Criteria, Points Possible, and Self-Evaluation. In the first column, list the six criteria for proper workstation arrangement as discussed in the lesson.

2. In the second column, assign points to that item so that there are 100 points total. Right-align the point amounts in the second column.

3. Using the checklist that you have created, evaluate yourself. Then ask a student near you to also evaluate you. Compare the two evaluations. Make a commitment to yourself to improve any area that falls short of top scores.

4. Save the document as *1_Activity_keyboarding_technique*.

Key Concepts

▶ The five commitments to learning include: be flexible, keep an open mind, use initiative, listen and read attentively, and seek to acquire new knowledge and skills. *LO 1.1*

▶ The six behaviors that contribute to your ability to acquire a job and grow in the field of your choice include good attendance, promptness, proper attire, a clean and safe work environment, appropriate voice, and pride. *LO 1.1*

▶ You can demonstrate your digital media skills by seeking certification from a secondary and/or post-secondary school or through a provider such as Adobe or Microsoft. *LO 1.1*

▶ Managing digital files is an essential part of creating a good work environment. *LO 1.2*

▶ Strong passwords are those that meet a set of rules designed to make it difficult for others to figure out the word. *LO 1.3*

▶ Repetitive stress injury (RSI) (including carpal tunnel syndrome) results from repeated movement of a particular part of the body. *LO 1.4*

Review and Discuss

1. Define digital media. *LO 1.1*

2. List the five commitments to learning that will help you to become successful in a digital media field. *LO 1.1*

3. What are the six behaviors that make you more employable? *LO 1.1*

4. What software tests are covered by an Adobe Certified Exam? *LO 1.1*

5. List some options for backing up files. *LO 1.2*

6. How can you protect yourself in an electronic world? *LO 1.2 and 1.3*

7. How can you protect your computer and network? *LO 1.2 and 1.3*

8. Explain what describes a strong password. *LO 1.3*

9. What is the purpose of ergonomics? *LO 1.4*

10. What steps can you take to prevent repetitive stress injury? *LO 1.4*

Apply

1. With a team of four students, create a do's and don'ts list for social networking. List at least five items for each. Each student should then create an individual flyer to post in the classroom. Save the document as **1_Apply1_social_networking**. *LO 1.3*

2. If there is an ergonomic keyboard in the classroom, use the keyboard to key the practice sentences in the chapter. Use a regular keyboard to key the same sentences. Discuss in class the differences in the two keyboards and your experience in using each of the keyboards. Take notes about the discussion and save them as **1_Apply2_keyboarding**. *LO 1.4*

3. Make a list of all the software or sites you visit that require a password. Think about your passwords. How secure are they? Using the information in this chapter, change passwords so they follow the criteria for security. Be sure to make a plan for how to remember those passwords. Write an evaluation of how secure the passwords are and a plan for how to remember them. Save the evaluation as **1_Apply3_passwords**. *LO 1.3*

4. Go to a social network site. Search for pages on topics related to information in this chapter. Select a page and add it to your profile. Review the postings over the last few weeks. Ask your friends to comment on the page you have added. Write a 150-word summary of what you learned from that page as well as what you have learned from comments made by your friends. Save the summary as **1_Apply4_social_networking**. *LO 1.1 and 1.4*

Explore

1. Meet with a team of four students to plan the following project. The team should plan different places for each student to call or visit, what information is expected from their visit, and a timeline for completion. Each student should call or visit an ACE (Adobe Certified Expert) certification center as planned in the team meeting. If you can't call or visit in person, visit a website. Ask questions to learn more about getting certified in the Adobe products. What is the cost? How long is the certification valid? When are the tests? Are there study materials? Brainstorm more questions. Make a list of the questions that you want to ask before you call or visit. Follow the timeline as planned in your team meeting. Meet with your team to compare notes and compile all the information that you have learned. Summarize the information for all places visited in a word processing document. Save the document as **1_Explore1_certification**. If time permits, present your team findings to the class. *LO 1.1*

2. Using your favorite search engine, research a specific security breach (case) associated with identity theft. Create a slide show with information from your research that covers information about the specific case, how it could have been prevented, and how it was resolved. The slide show should contain a title slide, a summary slide, eight slides with identity theft information, and a resource slide with at least two resources. Save the slide show as **1_Explore2_security**. *LO 1.3*

3. Write a 250-word article on ergonomics. Include an image that would enhance your report and submit it with your article. Include at least two resources with your article. Work with a partner to edit your article. Save the document as *1_Explore3_ergonomics*. LO 1.4

Academic Connections

Communications: Using a blog, create a brief entry each day about what you accomplished or learned in your digital media class. Share your blog with other classmates and commit to reading at least two other classmates' blogs each day. Continue this for a minimum of two weeks or until your instructor gives instructions to stop.

ARENA Creative/Shutterstock.com

Figure 1.13 *Blogs provide a forum for people to share their thoughts and ideas.*

Science: Who is considered the father of WiFi or Wireless LAN? Locate the name of the individual and create a storyboard on his life and what led up to his being named the father of WiFi. Save your work as **1_AC_science**.

Storyboard for _____ , page _____

Figure 1.14 *The use of a storyboard similar to this can help when organizing your thoughts and plans for a report, a story, a video, or a website.*

Chapter 2

Ethical and Legal Issues

Lesson 2.1 Safeguarding Intellectual Property

Lesson 2.2 Avoiding Plagiarism

Lesson 2.3 Making Ethical Decisions

Before the Internet era, finding information often required hours of research, and copying had to be done by hand. Copies of photographs, records, and movies were of far lower quality than the original work, making them less desirable. The Internet has changed all of that, making it easy to find and copy text as well as images, recordings, and video. However, just because it is now easy to capture the work of others does not make it right to do so without permission. Digital media specialists have to be very aware of the pitfalls that arise when using work done by others. Understanding concepts such as intellectual property is the first place to start in building this awareness.

Learning Outcomes

▶ **2.1** Explain the concept of intellectual property, including copyright and trademarks.

▶ **2.2** Identify the difference between copyright violations and plagiarism.

▶ **2.3** Demonstrate proper use of citations and fair use.

▶ **2.4** Discuss the ethical challenges facing digital media, including piracy and file sharing.

▶ **2.5** Explain how licensing applies to software.

Key Terms

- copyleft
- copyright
- deep linking
- digital rights management (DRM)
- end-user license agreement (EULA)
- ethics
- fair use
- file sharing
- GNU General Public License
- intellectual property
- open source
- patent
- piracy
- plagiarism
- proprietary
- public domain
- royalty
- royalty free
- social media
- trademark

One of the ways creative works are protected is through the concept of **intellectual property**. Laws treat the creative works of a mind as real property even if you cannot see their physical presence.

intellectual property—A legal concept that protects a creative work just as if it were physical property.

For example, when you buy a CD, it is easy to identify the product as property. Once you buy it, the disk belongs to you and you can use it as you like. If someone takes it, you can say, "That's my property, give it back." You own it, so you control who can physically use it. The songs on that CD, however, are a different story. While you may own the physical CD, you do not actually own the sound. Instead, the sounds belong to the person who created the music. The songs that are played using the CD are considered intellectual property.

Because the sound itself is intellectual property, musicians and music companies object to the illegal copying and distribution of digital recordings. When a song is copied and distributed without their permission, their intellectual property is stolen. The sound is the intellectual property of whoever produced the CD. While laws allow you to copy the sound for your personal use, they do not allow you to share that sound with others without permission from the intellectual property owner.

Blend Images/Shutterstock.com

Figure 2.1 *When you purchase a CD or DVD, you own the plastic disk but not the music recorded on it. The purchase allows you to listen as often as you want but not to give or sell the music to someone else.*

The idea that something invisible is actually a piece of "property" can be confusing. To identify an intellectual property, it's helpful to think about creativity. If someone creates something using their mind that is not likely to be created in the same way by another person, then that piece of creativity is an intellectual property. If you take a photograph, the image itself rather than the print is intellectual property. If you write a term paper, the words you use to complete the project are intellectual property as soon as they appear on the page. No special action must be taken to establish protection for those words. If you compose a song, the notes and the words as they are joined together are the property of the composer regardless of the form the song takes. The song is yours whether you perform it or merely write it down.

If you are working on your own as a freelancer to design and complete creative works, you can ensure that you retain rights to your work by completing an intellectual property agreement with anyone who might want to use your work. Such an agreement clearly spells out who owns and has the rights to use the intellectual property asset.

A company can safeguard its intellectual property by requiring employees or consultants to sign non-disclosure agreements. A non-disclosure agreement specifies information that cannot be shared with persons outside the company.

Copyright *LO 2.1, 2.2, and 2.5*

copyright—The term literally means restricting the right of others to copy.

Copyright is a legal means of establishing ownership of an intellectual property. The term **copyright** actually comes from the two words "copy" and "right." It means that the owner of a creative work has the legal right to restrict who may copy the work. Copyright does not prevent others from using the work, but instead it requires permission from the copyright owner in order to be used.

To qualify for copyright protection, an idea must be converted into a physical form. Physical form has been broadly defined by law to mean even the briefest of presence, including a digital media presence. If a speech given before an audience is recorded, then it has presence even though the words may only be heard for the time it takes the sound to register on the human ear. The recording becomes the physical form. However, an impromptu speech that is not recorded or written down is not eligible for copyright. Basically, as soon as the creative idea is shared with the world in some physical way, it becomes eligible for copyright. That means a poem in your head that is never shared with anyone is not eligible for copyright, but if you scribble it on a napkin for someone else to read, it is (see Figure 2.2).

iStockphoto.com/Chriskocek

Figure 2.2 *An original work scribbled on a napkin is eligible for copyright protection.*

A copyright notice follows this format: Copyright © *[date] [Name of Copyright Holder]*. It is not necessary to place a copyright notice on a creative work to make it legally protected from use by another without permission. However, a copyright notice serves several useful purposes.

1. It reminds users that the work is protected.

2. It clearly establishes the date when protection begins.

3. It makes it easier for someone to seek permission to use the work because the owner is named.

Since it is impossible to attach a copyright notice to sounds, you will often find a notice in a concert program that no recordings may be

iStockphoto.com /Warchi

Figure 2.3 *As soon as a creative idea is shared with the world in some physical way, it becomes eligible for copyright.*

made of a performance without permission from the artist. This serves as a form of copyright notice.

As noted previously, copyright registration is not required to provide protection. However, registration is usually done when a work is to be widely distributed to the public domain. It establishes, without question, ownership of the creative work. Registration of a copyright requires submitting a form and paying a fee to the U.S. Copyright Office.

Copyright laws are quite complex and can vary depending on the date when a work was created and the method used to create it. The extract below, taken from the government site www.copyright.gov, highlights some of the more general copyright information. Visit this website for more detailed information about copyright.

> Copyright is a form of protection provided by the laws of the United States (title 17, U.S. Code) to the authors of "original works of authorship," including literary, dramatic, musical, artistic, and certain other intellectual works. This protection is available to both published and unpublished works.
>
> Section 106 of the 1976 Copyright Act generally gives the owner of copyright the exclusive right to do and to authorize others to do the following:
>
> - To reproduce the work in copies or phonorecords
> - To prepare derivative works based upon the work
> - To distribute copies or phonorecords of the work to the public by sale or other transfer of ownership, or by rental, lease, or lending
> - To perform the work publicly, in the case of literary, musical, dramatic, and choreographic works, pantomimes, and motion pictures and other audiovisual works

- To display the work publicly, in the case of literary, musical, dramatic, and choreographic works, pantomimes, and pictorial, graphic, or sculptural works, including the individual images of a motion picture or other audiovisual work
- In the case of sound recordings, to perform the work publicly by means of a digital audio transmission

Copyright protection subsists from the time the work is created in fixed form. The copyright in the work of authorship immediately becomes the property of the author who created the work. Only the author or those deriving their rights through the author can rightfully claim copyright.

Copyright protects "original works of authorship" that are fixed in a tangible form of expression. The fixation need not be directly perceptible so long as it may be communicated with the aid of a machine or device. Copyrightable works include the following categories:

- Literary works
- Musical works, including any accompanying words
- Dramatic works, including any accompanying music
- Pantomimes and choreographic works
- Pictorial, graphic, and sculptural works
- Motion pictures and other audiovisual works
- Sound recordings
- Architectural works

Figure 2.4 *Many forms of expression fall under copyright protection, including literary, musical, dramatic, artistic, and architectural works.*

These categories should be viewed broadly. For example, computer programs and most "compilations" may be registered as "literary works"; maps and architectural plans may be registered as "pictorial, graphic, and sculptural works."

A work that is created (fixed in tangible form for the first time) on or after January 1, 1978, is automatically protected from the moment of its creation and is ordinarily given a term enduring for the author's life plus an additional 70 years after the author's death.

Works originally created before January 1, 1978, have been automatically brought under the statute and are now given federal copyright protection. The duration of copyright in these works will generally be computed in the same way as for works created on or after January 1, 1978: the life-plus-70 or 95/120-year terms will apply to them as well. The law provides that in no case will the term of copyright for works in this category expire before December 31, 2002, and for works published on or before December 31, 2002, the term of copyright will not expire before December 31, 2047.

Think About It

Are Copyrights Needed?

If there were no protections for creative work, would people still produce movies, publish music, or create software? Would artists paint and would writers write? Would you be more or less willing to be creative if you knew that your work could be used without your permission?

Permission

One of the phrases that continues to appear in any discussion of copyright is "without permission." As discussed earlier, an important element of copyright is the owner's right to grant permission for someone else to use his or her creative property. You might wonder how to get permission to use copyrighted material that you plan to include in a work of your own. The answer is simple: Ask. A phone call, a letter, an email, perhaps even a text message, can be used to seek permission to use someone else's intellectual property. Depending on the size of the organization that owns the copyright and how you want to use the borrowed material, permission may be readily given. Often authors are so delighted to be asked permission that they will quickly grant it.

Royalties

Sometimes, copyright holders grant permission to use their material for free. Other times, they charge a fee. When you pay to use someone's copyrighted material, you are not paying for the object itself but rather you are paying for the permission, or license, to use it. Some copyright holders charge a fee for each use of the material. This fee is referred to as a **royalty** (see Figure 2.5). You may see websites that advertise **royalty free** images or music. These are images and audio files that you may purchase and use more than once without having to pay a fee each time they are published or used. Note that they are not necessarily free, despite the name. You will read more about licenses and specifically how they relate to purchased images in Chapter 9, "Print Graphics."

royalty—A fee paid to the person who owns the copyright on a creative work when it is used by someone else.

royalty free—A type of licensing agreement that gives the buyer almost unlimited permission to use a copyrighted image for a one-time fee.

proprietary—A term used for software code that has restricted rights of use.

end-user license agreement (EULA)—A contract software purchasers must agree to before using software.

Software Licenses

Software programs written by companies such as Microsoft are considered **proprietary**. This means that the software is owned by the company that created it. When you purchase proprietary software, you are licensed to use it. You do not own it. When you install software on a computer, you must accept licensing limitations before installation can proceed. This is called the **end-user license agreement (EULA)**.

Jim Arbogast/Getty Images

Figure 2.5 *Although there are questions about the legitimacy of its copyright, "Happy Birthday to You" is a protected work and any time it is performed in public for profit—as in a movie or on television—a royalty is due to the song's copyright holder. However, no royalty is due if you sing the song to friends or family at a private birthday party.*

open source—Software that allows others to use its code without cost.

copyleft—A licensing protection used by those who create open source software.

GNU General Public License—The standard open source contract or license.

public domain—Creative works whose copyright restrictions have expired. The term may also be used for open source software.

trademark—A word, phrase, or image used to identify something as a product of a particular business.

patent—A property right for an invention that lasts a specified period of time.

Some software is developed as **open source**. This means that the code used to create the software is open to anyone who wants to make changes to it. Open source software is free but not without copyright protections. In a play on the word *copyright*, the term **copyleft** has been used to describe the legal protections for open source. The open source license allows users to use, study, copy, share, and modify the software. The most commonly used open source license is the **GNU General Public License**.

File formats can also be considered proprietary if they were created using licensed code. Microsoft Word creates files as .docx. While other word processing software can often open and save files as .docx, the extension is proprietary to Microsoft. (In order to encourage its widespread usage, Microsoft has agreed to let others use this format without risk of legal action.) Other software file formats are not proprietary and are considered part of the **public domain**. For word processors, this would be a .txt file that can be opened and saved by any word processor. In the next chapter you will learn about the file extensions used by digital media software.

The productivity software used by most digital media artists is usually proprietary; however, there are open source choices available such as the GIMP and Inkscape. Adobe products (such as Photoshop, Illustrator, Dreamweaver, InDesign, and Premiere) are the most commonly used digital media software packages, but both Microsoft and Apple have their own. You will learn about these in detail in later chapters.

Trademarks and Patents

One way of establishing intellectual ownership is to create a trademark. A **trademark** is a distinctive word, phrase, or image used to identify something as a product of a particular business or organization. A trademark automatically conveys the identity of the organization it represents. For example, the Golden Arches outside a fast food restaurant immediately tell the viewer that this is a restaurant that makes a certain hamburger. The publisher of this text has a trademark that appears on this book. Notice the small TM symbol next to the Cengage logo on the cover. Just as with copyrights, trademarks do not need to be registered to be protected from use by others without permission. Trademarks that are registered carry the ® symbol while unregistered ones use the ™ symbol. While copyrights are administered by the U.S. Copyright Office, trademarks are handled by the U.S. Patent and Trademark Office because they represent a business function.

To make the ownership of intellectual property even more binding, a person can patent his or her invention. A **patent** gives the patent holder a property right to an invention for a specified period of time and prevents others from using that invention for commercial profit without permission from the patent holder. Like trademarks, patents are administered by the U.S. Patent and Trademark Office. There are three types of patents: utility (covering inventions of processes, machines, and manufactures, for example), design (covering original ornamental design of a manufactured item), and plant (covering new and distinct plant material). Utility and plant patents last for 20 years from the date the patent application was filed in the United States. Design patents last 14 years.

A person or company that makes use of or sells a patented product or design without permission of the patent holder is said to violate or infringe that patent. If the infringement was unintentional, the person or company can sometimes resolve it by a licensing agreement, whereby the violator agrees to pay the patent holder for the right to use the patented invention. If licensing is not an option, the patent holder may file suit against the alleged violator, which can lead to long and costly legal procedures to hash out whether the invention described in the patent application has actually been used by another individual or company.

Illegal File Sharing *LO 2.2*

The development of technology has complicated the traditional understanding of copyright violation. One particularly confusing area involves file sharing. File sharing is a useful means of transferring information from one computer to another. However, the term **file sharing** has come to mean the illegal transfer of copyrighted material between computers. This is a form of copyright violation. Websites and software have been developed to make it easy to share files, but that does not make it okay. The ease of sharing files and ignorance about copyright law can lead some otherwise law-abiding people to violate copyright rules without knowing it. If you receive payment for stolen DVDs, it is easy to see that this is considered stealing since you are selling something that is not yours.

However, where many people violate legal boundaries is when they "share" a digital product that they have purchased. They assume that since they have paid for the product, they can share it with anyone they choose just as they might share a candy bar with a group of friends. This is untrue.

In recent years, federal courts, including the U.S. Supreme Court, have consistently ruled that uploading or downloading copyrighted material without permission is against the law. Groups that represent music recording, motion picture, and television companies have successfully pressed

file sharing—Use of a network to move files between computers, often for illegal purposes.

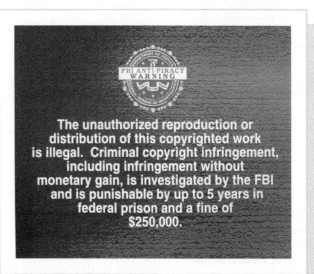

Figure 2.6 *You are probably familiar with the Federal Bureau of Investigation (FBI) warning at the beginning of DVDs and other digital recordings. The FBI is charged with investigating charges of intellectual theft, including illegal file sharing.*

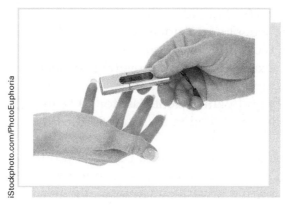

Figure 2.7 *Sharing copies of copyrighted material, even if you did not know you were acting illegally, is a prosecutable offense.*

charges against file-sharing networks and individuals who illegally share copyrighted material. Even first-time offenders can face hundreds of thousands of dollars in fines and possible imprisonment if they illegally share files. This is true even if they did not know they were acting illegally or if they did not profit from the file sharing. It is important, therefore, that you learn the rules about sharing files before you upload or download anything.

Digital Millennium Copyright Act

In 1998, the U.S. Congress passed the Digital Millennium Copyright Act, which attempts to address some of the legal issues that advancing technology has created. Basically, the act gives protection to digital rights management systems. The law prohibits software that makes it possible to illegally copy other software. It also makes it illegal to "break" antipiracy protection built into software. In addition, it makes "webcasters" pay fees to record companies for music played over their Internet sites. Laws such as this will continue to be written as technology evolves.

Piracy

piracy—Copying a product (often digital) for profit without authorization from the owner. Music and video products as well as software are frequently subjects of pirating.

Making a copy of a software package, a video, a music CD, or a digital book is sometimes referred to as **piracy**, especially when the illegally copied item is sold for profit.

Piracy of digital products is an ongoing issue causing much frustration in the various industries that support artists of all kinds. Some experts estimate that music companies, publishers, motion picture producers, and other businesses lose billions of dollars per year because of piracy.

Figure 2.8 *Pirates of an earlier age stole jewels and other forms of wealth. Digital pirates steal software, music, and videos by making copies and then selling them. If you buy a DVD or CD from a street vendor, you may be buying a pirated item.*

Richard Levine / Alamy

Digital Rights Management

One method that businesses have used to prevent unauthorized copying is to control how a digital work can be used. **Digital rights management (DRM)** is a form of technology that controls digital copying by inserting a software program into the CD (or other media) that restricts copying. It often prevents the purchaser of a CD or video from making copies of the audio or video work even as a backup. DRM is a direct result of piracy. It is unfortunate that unethical copying impacts even those who have legitimately purchased a product.

digital rights management (DRM)—Technology that prevents unauthorized copying of a digital work.

lavitrei/Shutterstock.com

Impact

Digital Rights Management

While it might seem obvious that companies should be able to protect their products from piracy, digital rights management raises some serious questions about the rights of copyright owners versus the rights of consumers who legitimately pay for copyrighted material. The issue has been that in order to keep the pirates at bay, the rightful owners have sometimes been harmed. Some early DRM software downloaded files directly to a computer without the permission of the user. This software inadvertently allowed malware to be installed. While companies are no longer following that path, there are other problems. Today the biggest frustration is that the technology may prevent music or videos from playing on the user's computer or smartphone. The solution to finding a balance between the consumer and the artist has yet to be found.

ACTIVITY 2.1 ▶ Researching Intellectual Property Lawsuits

1. Research five intellectual property lawsuits relating to digital media.

2. Create a table in a word processing document with three columns and seven rows. Merge all cells in the first row and add a title. In the second row, add a column heading in each cell: **Name of Case**, **Description of Case**, and **Comments on Case**. Format the column headings.

3. In the next five rows, add the information you gathered in your research, citing at least five different cases that involved digital media. Add your comments and thoughts on the cases in the last column. Adjust column widths as needed.

4. Save the document as *2_Activity1_intellectual*.

Lesson 2.2 ▶ Avoiding Plagiarism

Fair Use Guidelines *LO 2.3*

fair use—The right to reproduce a small part of a copyrighted work for educational or other not-for-profit purposes without having to obtain permission or pay a royalty fee.

Students are taught in school that they can use excerpts from another person's work provided they give proper credit or documentation. This use of copyrighted material is called **fair use**. Fair use is generally limited to educational copying and is very limited in the commercial or business world. Some professionals may use it in situations such as criticism, comment, news reporting, teaching, scholarship, and research.

Fair use is determined using the guidelines shown below. These guidelines are part of Title 17 of the U.S. Code, the federal law covering copyright.

Section 107 in the United States copyright law outlines the four factors to consider when deciding on fair use.

Section 107 contains a list of the various purposes for which the reproduction of a particular work may be considered fair, such as criticism, comment, news reporting, teaching, scholarship, and research. Section 107 also sets out four factors to be considered in determining whether or not a particular use is fair:

The purpose and character of the use, including whether such use is of commercial nature or is for non-profit educational purposes

The nature of the copyrighted work

The amount and substantiality of the portion used in relation to the copyrighted work as a whole

The effect of the use upon the potential market for, or value of, the copyrighted work

The distinction between fair use and infringement may be unclear and not easily defined. There is no specific number of words, lines, or notes that may safely be taken without permission.

Acknowledging the source of the copyrighted material does not substitute for obtaining permission.

Notice that the guidelines do not give a specific number of words or lines that can be considered fair use. Instead, you must consider the overall work. For example, copying three lines from a five-line poem might not be considered fair use since it represents over half the work itself.

Defining Plagiarism *LO 2.2*

Plagiarism means using someone else's work as your own and not giving the original author credit. Plagiarism in the digital world is an easy trap to fall into. Copying words, capturing images, and adding someone's YouTube clip to a website are all done so frequently that we often do not think about the plagiarism this may involve. Plagiarism is different from copyright infringement. Schools and the academic world punish plagiarism. Courts address copyright issues. Schools administer harsh consequences for plagiarism. Courts administer their own consequences for copyright infringement. However, regardless of whether or not it is a legal issue, using someone else's creative work and calling it your own is wrong.

plagiarism—Copying or otherwise using someone else's creative work and claiming it as your own, usually in an academic or journalistic work, but also more recently in social media.

Ritu Manoj Jethani/Shutterstock.com

Figure 2.9 *Plagiarism can have serious consequences in school and in professional life. In 2003, a* New York Times *reporter had to resign after he plagiarized material from other newspapers.*

The way to avoid plagiarism is to document the source of your material. For a formal school paper, you will be given guidelines for the proper citation style to use. In less formal situations, sometimes a link to a website or a mention of the source can be sufficient. Note that, unlike avoiding plagiarism, it is not enough to cite the source of copyrighted material to avoid copyright infringement. You cannot use copyrighted material in your own work (except under the guidelines of fair use) without the owner's permission, even if you properly attribute authorship.

Using Proper Website Citations *LO 2.3*

Several pieces of information are usually required for a proper citation of material you get from a website. Unfortunately, websites often lack the information you need to properly document a source. If that is the case, you may need to do some research to make sure you are giving credit to the author of material you use. The five basic components of a proper website source citation are as follows:

- **Author.** You may not find an author listed on a website, but you may find the Web administrator's name located on the home page. It may be possible to contact the Web administrator to find out the author of the information found on a particular page. Take the time to search rather than just leaving the author's name unlisted in your document.

- **Date.** Often the only date you will find is the date the site was last updated. This may not be the date the original material was written. Make a distinction between updates and actual dates of the original material in your source citation.

- **Title of article.** Sometimes titles are not given. You may need to use the heading that appears as part of the page.

- **Access date.** This is the date on which you retrieved the site during research. This is important because information may change or the page itself may be removed. Including an access date establishes the point in time when the information appeared.

- **URL.** This is the Web address of the site you used. If you used a page within a site, the URL will include slashes to lead the reader to the exact page (see Figure 2.10). Moving past the home page in an address is called **deep linking**. The problem with citing any web page is the frequency with which sites disappear, and deep links disappear even more often than the sites themselves as changes are made to the website. Also be aware that if information was retrieved from a website storing information on a database, the address may not provide a link to the actual material. You should

deep linking—Citing a Web address that goes beyond the home or entry page.

http://school.cengage.com/k12/search/totalresults.do

Figure 2.10 *Deep linking allows the reader to go directly to a specific page. Often deep links are so long that it's difficult to key them accurately, making the link difficult to access.*

check with your instructor to determine whether you should include the URL and how deep it should go.

There are two major organizations that define what information should be included in formal Internet source documentation. Both of them require similar information, but use slightly different capitalization, order, and punctuation. You will need to follow the style assigned to you for your project.

American Psychological Association (APA)

The American Psychological Association (APA) requires the following style for its citations of websites:

> Author [last, first]. (date [year, month day]). Article title. Retrieved from URL

An example of this would be:

> Peterson, E. (1993, March 15) *Weather prediction as an unstudied art.* Retrieved from http://www.weatherscience.org/peterson/article.html

Modern Language Association (MLA)

The Modern Language Association (MLA) requires the following style for website citations:

> Author [last, first]. Article Title. Date. Publisher. Date retrieved. <URL>.

An example of this would be:

> Peterson, Emil. "Weather Prediction as an Unstudied Art." *Weather Science.* 15 Mar. 1993. Web. 22 May 2017. http://www.weatherscience.org/peterson/article.html.

Note that in the seventh edition of MLA's style guide (the most recent edition when this book was written), MLA style no longer requires a URL in a citation. It is only needed when the reader would be unlikely to locate the source without its inclusion or when required by a publisher or instructor. Again, consult with your instructor to determine the needs of your specific project.

Online Bibliographies

There are a number of websites (such as EasyBib and BibMe) that help you create bibliography entries. On these sites, you enter the Web address or the name of the print document and fill in detail boxes. Once the information is complete, you can then copy and paste into your research document a pre-formatted bibliography entry. With a site such as EasyBib, you can enter each site that you use, compiling a complete list as you write your paper. Most online sites also allow you to designate the desired style, such as MLA. Tools such as these make it easy to document your research.

checkpoint

What can you do to avoid being accused of plagiarism?

ACTIVITY 2.2 ▶ Citing Websites Properly

1. Create an annotated bibliography of at least 10 Web resources on plagiarism and piracy. If necessary read about an annotated bibliography or participate in a class discussion before getting started.

2. Use MLA style for your annotated bibliography.

3. Save the document as *2_Activity2_bibliography*.

Lesson 2.3 ▶ Making Ethical Decisions

ethics—Moral choices between right and wrong actions.

Ethics is about making the right choices. The problem is knowing what is *right*. New advances and possibilities in technology mean that the old rules may no longer apply or that new rules need to be developed. Ethics is involved in the answer to a question such as "Is it ethical to text while you drive?" In some states, there are no laws against texting while driving. And texting itself is not wrong. But it has been clearly shown to make an individual more likely to have an accident. Is it right to risk not only your own safety but the safety of others by texting while driving?

Some ethical questions are even trickier because the consequences are not as serious. For example, is it ethical to text your friends while at work? Again, texting is not wrong. Depending upon your job, you may or may not be putting anyone's safety at risk. But do you owe your employer your complete attention while you work?

Your task as a member of society is to think about these types of questions and make ethical choices. Part of the ongoing learning process requires you to pay attention to changes and think about the ramifications. What was impossible only a few years ago suddenly becomes not only possible but easy. Once that change occurs, you must be prepared to make ethical decisions when choices arise.

Maintaining High Ethical Standards

Business and ethics are not mutually exclusive terms. Most businesses work hard to maintain high ethical standards and to present a good public image. A few, regrettably, do not. The temptation to skirt the law regarding multimedia applications can be particularly strong. For example, many graphic images are copyrighted and require permission (and fees paid to the owner) before they can be used in brochures or other documents. Sound files are often illegally pirated and used. It is easy to assume that nobody will find out about such activities. The bottom line is this: You do not have to do something unethical just because your employer tells you to. Maintain your integrity. If your employer repeatedly asks you to act unethically, you are in the wrong place. Your next employer will likely highly value your honesty.

Skills in Action: Suppose your supervisor asks you to create a series of graphs using financial data you know has been falsified. A coworker was fired last month for refusing to do this. What will you do? Discuss in class.

Ethics and Photo Editing *LO 2.4*

Digital media is a field filled with ethical questions and dilemmas. For example, photo editing software makes it easy to substantially change an image. But just because it is easy, is it right? Consider these image editing questions.

- Is it ethical to make a model look thinner than she is in real life?
- Is it ethical to change a sky from cloudy to bright blue?
- Is it ethical to add a missing family member to a group photo?
- Is it ethical to remove someone from a photo because you no longer like that person?
- Is it ethical to use a photo taken by someone else and distort the image, making the subject appear ridiculous?

It is clear that some of these questions have more serious consequences than others. If the photo with the newly blue sky is one you display on your desk, it is considered harmless editing. If that same photo is used to advertise a resort, it may be misleading to vacationers trying to decide whether they want to stay at that location. At the moment, there are no laws against changing a sky from cloudy to blue. However, as readers become aware of the often blatant disregard for truthful images, that is beginning to change and new rules are being established to address these issues. Until such laws are made, you must make your own ethical decisions about the proper use of the technology.

You will learn more about specific ethical challenges in digital media throughout this book.

Susan Lake

Figure 2.11 *Can you see the slight modifications made to the first image? Have there been any other changes? Is this an ethical use of technology?*

Ethical Decision Making *LO 2.4*

There is an ethical element to all the topics discussed in this chapter. If you decide to load a pirated version of Illustrator on your computer, you are making an illegal choice as well as an unethical one since piracy is theft and stealing is ethically wrong. Similarly, plagiarism is stealing someone else's work, and while it may or may not be illegal, it is morally wrong and therefore unethical. However, not all ethical dilemmas faced by digital media students and professionals are a clear choice between legal and illegal or right and wrong. There is some gray area. When making an ethical decision, you must think about what harm you are doing others. For example, when you share software or digital media (i.e., music, videos, or images), you must ask yourself:

* Does my action hurt someone?
* Does my action act as a form of stealing?
* Does my sharing prevent someone from earning a living?
* Does my action encourage another person to hurt someone else?

social media—Websites that allow users to create and exchange information.

Users of **social media** must be especially careful in answering these questions. A user may, for example, post a photo to his or her social media site without the permission of those in the photo; some of these photos may violate the privacy of the people in them. A user may also post remarks that are hurtful or damaging to others. And the fact that social media make it possible to disseminate information swiftly and widely compounds the harm that may result from compromising photos or inflammatory statements.

Living in a global digital world makes ethical questions much harder to answer. When thinking about these questions, keep in mind that the Internet has such a broad impact that your actions might touch someone you will not ever meet, possibly thousands of miles away. Try to consider all the possible consequences of your choices.

For example, if you share a music file with hundreds of people, will someone in Bangladesh lose her job producing CDs with that music? Will the composer of that music no longer publish musical works because too few copies of the music are bought? On the other hand, will that composer suddenly reach worldwide fame because so many people have heard the notes? The answers are seldom obvious.

checkpoint

How do changes in technology make it challenging to know what is ethically correct?

ACTIVITY 2.3 ▶ Discussing Ethics

1. In a team of three or four students, brainstorm some situations in which you have had to make a decision that was difficult because of how it impacted others.

2. In a word processing document, list at least four of these situations that your team has discussed. Under the first situation, add the four questions to ask when deciding if something is ethical. Copy and paste these questions under the other three situations.

3. Respond to all the questions and then write a statement regarding whether the situation was ethical as determined by your team. Include the rationale for your response.

4. Save the document as *2_Activity3_ethics* and submit it to your instructor.

Key Concepts

▶ Intellectual property is a creation of the mind that is treated as a tangible property. *LO 2.1*

▶ Copyright laws give the owner of a creative work the legal right to restrict who may copy the work. *LO 2.2 and 2.5*

▶ A trademark is a distinctive word, phrase, or image that visually identifies something as a product of a particular business or organization. A patent is a property right for an invention that lasts a specified period of time. *LO 2.1*

▶ Fair use allows students and some professionals to reproduce a small part of another person's work, though proper credit should be given to the creator. *LO 2.3*

▶ Plagiarism involves copying another person's creative work and claiming it as your own. *LO 2.2*

▶ Piracy involves stealing another person's creative work, usually for profit. *LO 2.4*

▶ Ethical decisions require you to make choices about what is right. *LO 2.4*

Review and Discuss

1. Compare and contrast physical property versus intellectual property. *LO 2.1*

2. List at least five examples of intellectual property that can be assigned copyright protection. *LO 2.1*

3. Explain why it is important to register a copyright. *LO 2.2*

4. Describe the two symbols used to indicate a trademark and explain how they differ. *LO 2.1*

5. Indicate who may claim the right of fair use. *LO 2.3*

6. Compare and contrast the APA and MLA styles of citing a website. *LO 2.3*

7. Differentiate between plagiarism and copyright infringement. *LO 2.2*

8. Differentiate between plagiarism and piracy. *LO 2.2*

9. Explain why ethics related to technology are difficult to determine. *LO 2.4*

10. Summarize why file sharing is an ethical problem. *LO 2.4*

Apply

1. Use your favorite Internet search engine to find businesses or organizations that have published a code of ethics regarding the editing of photos. After reviewing several examples, write a photo editing code of ethics for your classroom with four or five statements. In a team of three or four

students, review each of your codes and compile one code to take to the entire class. Share your team codes with the class and collaborate to produce a single photo editing code of ethics for the class. Finally, create a flyer with the final code of ethics to submit for posting in the classroom. Save as **2_Apply1_ethics_code**. *LO 2.4*

2. Using an Internet search engine, find and save 10 image trademarks of businesses that you frequent or recognize because of their trademark. In a word processing program, create the following table:

TRADEMARKS		
Name	**Trademark**	**Attention-Getter**

For each trademark you find, insert the business name in the first column and the corresponding trademark from the website in the second column. Use the third column to explain what it is about the trademark that captures your attention. Save as **2_Apply2_trademark**. *LO 2.1*

3. Key "paraphrasing" into your favorite Internet search engine. Read about paraphrasing to gain an understanding of the skill. Choose three quotes from the online material and copy them into a word processing document. Format the quotes in bold. Below each quote, paraphrase the quoted material. Format the paraphrased material using a red font color. Below each paraphrased section, cite the source of each quote in MLA style. Format the citation with a green font color. Save as **2_Apply3_paraphrasing**. *LO 2.2 and 2.3*

4. Create a fair use survey of 12 questions. The survey can cover fair use as it pertains to a number of different types of media: software, books, CDs, music, etc. If needed, use the Internet to get some ideas for questions. Sample question: Is it within the rules of fair use to burn a CD to give to

a friend? Use a table in word processing software to create your survey. The response columns can be as simple as Yes or No, or be more complex with a rating system. Be sure to title the survey. Save the document. Work in teams and then as a class to create one survey to use. The survey should then be given to a different class. The class should work together to poll the results. Save as **2_Apply4_fair_use**. *LO 2.3*

5. Read the case study below. In a team of three or four students, discuss the case. Consider the following questions:

    1) Would you have used the photographs in the first place? Why or why not?
    2) What can the person in the case use in the newsletters instead of someone else's images?
    3) How can the person get permission to use the photographs?
    4) What other thoughts do you have or other lessons did you learn from this case?

    Write an individual summary of your team's responses to the questions. Save as **2_Apply5_case_study**. *LO 2.1, 2.2, and 2.3*

    I recently had a reader comment on how they missed seeing the animals I promoted last year to support conservation and help prevent species extinction. In my newsletter each month I would pick an animal from a national nonprofit conservation organization to promote and support, make a donation, and encourage my readers to do the same. In fact, from that comment, I intended to donate again this year and announce the animal being sponsored each month. Unfortunately, two weeks later, I received a letter from an image company saying that I had used one of their photographer's photographs illegally.

    Unfortunately for me, I used pictures off of the website of the conservation organization without thinking that using those photographs could be in violation of copyright laws. I've since contacted the organization and was informed that using photographs found on their site, even to promote their organization, is not permissible. The image company informed me that I owed them $450.00 even though I was promoting the same charity! I wish the image company had sent me a "cease and desist" letter before fining me.

    I also tried contacting the photographer, but she stated that her contract with the image company is so limiting that her "hands are tied." I was able to negotiate a decreased fine of $350.00, which I paid to the image company, and I removed all the graphics/photos from any past newsletters promoting the organization. Please, learn from my mistakes. Don't use graphics to illustrate your point, be it for charity or not, without receiving permission to do so in writing!

Explore

1. Search the Internet for software piracy, music piracy, or movie piracy. Write a three-page paper including history, definition, and specific examples. Include other interesting information such as what is being done to stop piracy. Include a title page and a resource page with at least two resources in MLA style. Final report should be five total pages. Save as **2_Explore1_piracy**. *LO 2.3 and 2.5*

2. Visit your favorite university or community college's website. Search for the term *plagiarism* on the website to find policies and information on avoiding plagiarism. Take notes on the school's policies, tips on avoiding plagiarism, and any other information on plagiarism. Using presentation software, create six to eight slides on what you have learned from the website. Include a title slide with the name of the school, your name, and a final slide with resource information in MLA style. Add a design or colors using the school colors. Save as **2_Explore2_plagiarism**. *LO 2.2 and 2.3*

3. Go to your favorite musician's website. In a word processing document, describe any copyright notices for the website or the musician's music. Key an appropriate title on the page with the subtitle "Website and Music Copyright Notices." List a few of the copyright notices. Cite your source of information after the copyright descriptions. Resources should be formatted in MLA style. Save as **2_Explore3_copyright**. *LO 2.1, 2.2, and 2.3*

Academic Connections

Communications: Write 10 sentences using terms from this chapter. In each sentence, place in parentheses at least one place where there would be verb choices. Underline the correct choice of words. For example: 1. The songs on the CD (<u>are</u>, is) the intellectual property of the artist. Save as **2_AC_communications**.

Science: Research and read an article on image manipulation in science. What are the consequences of such actions? How does it impact the area of science that you read about? In recent years, what actions are being taken to ensure this does not adversely affect science? What did you find most interesting about the article that you read? Write a paragraph, responding to each of the questions. Cite your resource in MLA style. Save as **2_AC_science**.

UNIT 1 PROJECTS

Independent Project

Write a reflection journal on what you have learned in this unit. In your journal, be sure that you have, at a minimum, responded to the following questions:

▶ What have I learned in Chapter 1 to help make me successful in this class?

▶ Is there a plan in place for this class to manage and save files? Describe the plan.

▶ What can I do in this class to maintain digital and workplace safety?

▶ What can I do to avoid plagiarism and to safeguard intellectual property?

▶ What type of ethical decisions might I encounter in this class? How can I handle those situations?

The reflection journal should show what you have learned in this unit and contain a plan of action to put to use what you have learned. You may include some things you have learned about the class to help make you more successful for the rest of the class. Using word processing software, write at least 500 words in this journal.

Save the journal as **Unit1_independent_project**.

Portfolio

Following the instructions from your instructor, prepare the folder structure for your portfolio. This should include a decision about where you will store the portfolio as well as a plan for a backup place. How often the folder should be backed up should also be established. Consider saving in several ways, including as a web page.

Write a brief account of your short- and long-term goals. After your instructor approves it, add this to your portfolio.

Add your edited and corrected reflection journal to the portfolio.

Creating an electronic portfolio for employment purposes gives you an edge over a job applicant who may not have one. This gives your potential employer a glimpse of your abilities, training, and experience with actual samples of what you can do for them.

iStockphoto.com/Pashalgnatov

When looking for employment, it is important to have both a physical portfolio and a digital portfolio.

In each unit of this text, you will add a variety of projects and assignments to the portfolio folder. In a future unit, you will begin the creation of a PDF portfolio, which will put the portfolio together for you so you can burn it to a CD and/or upload it to a website. This will also enable the viewer of the portfolio to navigate the documents easily. Consider adding samples of your ability to write and communicate as well. The creation of this portfolio will also demonstrate your skills with a variety of software.

Portfolios should be prepared in several formats to provide to the employer, depending on the situation. Prepare the portfolio items for print publishing as well as digital publishing. For print publishing, when the portfolio is complete, it is recommended that you take it to a print shop to have it bound with a cover. As you do web pages in future units, you can set your work up as web pages or, if available, you can use PDF portfolio creator to save it as a web page. Follow instructions from your instructor on how to proceed with saving your portfolio for each unit.

If available, use PDF portfolio creator to keep your portfolio for electronic and Web purposes as well as storing the files for print publishing at a later date. Using the PDF format enables the viewer of the portfolio to navigate the documents easily. Be sure to archive each folder and file added to the PDF portfolio in a separate place. The creation of this portfolio will demonstrate your skills with a variety of software.

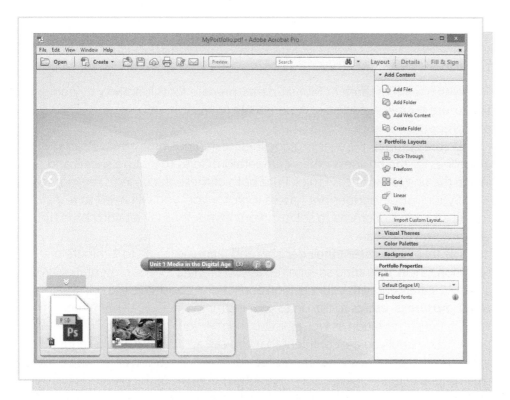

PDF portfolio creator allows for the easy organization of files.

Business Ethics

Knowledge of what constitutes good business ethics and making ethical decisions is an important part of being successful in today's business world as well as sometimes being successful in personal relationships. Basic starting points in making ethical decisions include the following questions:

1. Could this decision cause damage to someone?
2. Is this issue about more than what is legal?

You will find opportunities to sharpen your business ethics skills in units and activities in all your business courses as well as in student organizations such as the one you will experience in this activity.

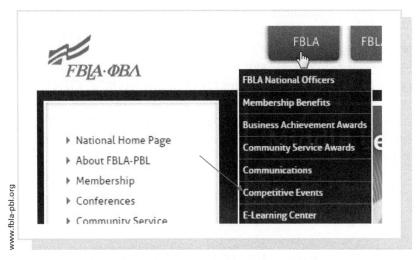

The Future Business Leaders of America is one organization in which you can sharpen your business ethics skills.

With a team of three or four students, prepare for this activity by going to the Future Business Leaders of America site (www.fbla-pbl.org) and clicking on Competitive Events.

On the competitive events guidelines, search business ethics. Read the guidelines for the business ethics competition. Go to the rating sheets and locate the one for Business Ethics. Print both of these documents for your team.

If your instructor does not have a topic for you, you will need to research to find an ethical dilemma to solve or your instructor may let you come up with your own scenario.

The team will present their decision and rationale in a 5- to 7-minute presentation. Check the rating sheet often as you prepare for the presentation. Write a written statement with your decision and rationale and save the document as **Unit1_business_ethics** to turn in to your instructor. Include all members of the team in the presentation as well as listing them in your document. Practice the presentation until you are confident that you can achieve the results required on the rating sheet. Suggestions for practice could include: using an iPhone or other smartphone with a voice recorder to practice your part of the presentation; using an iPad with apps such as Evernote to practice your part of the presentation; and using a camcorder or other video recording device to video the team's practice.

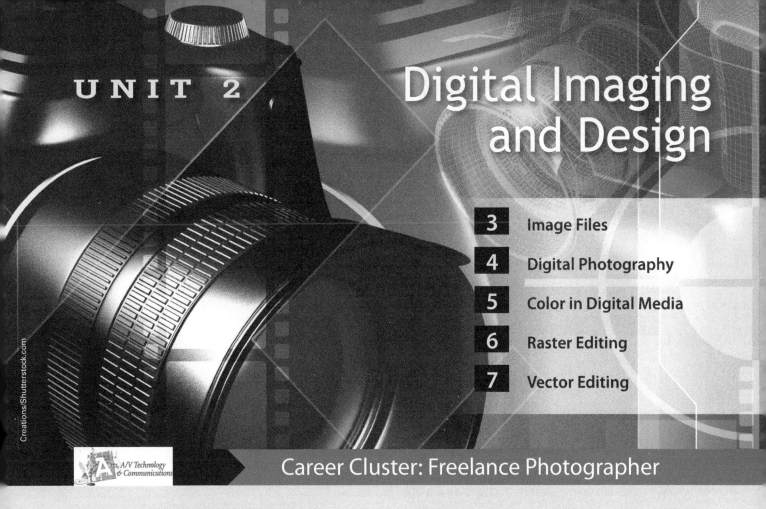

UNIT 2

Digital Imaging and Design

Arts, A/V Technology & Communications

Career Cluster: Freelance Photographer

Interview with Bridgette, freelance portrait photographer and small business owner of BDphotography

Describe your average day. I may be shooting at an outdoor location, editing photos at home, or updating my website/blog. I shoot all of my photos on a digital camera, process them with an Adobe Photoshop product called Lightroom, prepare online digital sneak peeks for clients to preview, archive final images, share snippets from sessions on a WordPress blog site, and send all final digital images to clients on CDs.

What is the worst part of your job? I don't enjoy the back end work of having a small business, like keeping records, filing taxes, and so on.

What is the best part of your job? I love meeting new people and families, recording a part of their lives, enjoying the creative process myself while putting a smile on their faces, and delivering memories that are preserved forever in a unique style!

Employment Outlook In general, average employment growth is expected for photographers, with high competition for jobs, according to the U.S. Bureau of Labor Statistics. More than half of all photographers are self-employed, and salaried positions will continue to become scarcer since affordable digital photography equipment and access to photo editing software mean it's easier for people to enter the field. News agencies and other companies that traditionally have hired staff photographers are increasingly contracting these positions instead.

Skills and Qualifications Photojournalism and some specialty photography positions require a bachelor's degree. Some photographers obtain an art degree before launching their careers. Apprenticeships, internships, and assistant positions offer the type of hands-on training that is valuable in the field. Above all, creativity and technical proficiency are important skills for a photographer.

Job Titles Portrait photographer, commercial and industrial photographer, scientific photographer, photojournalist, fine art photographer.

What About You? Photography is an appealing career to many people who like to take pictures, which is why the competition for jobs is so high. Search the Internet to find job postings for photographers.

- Is it difficult to find an open position?
- Can you find any opportunities for internships or apprenticeships that would prepare you for a career in photography?
- What are some things you can do in your own school or community to gain experience in this field that would help you land a job later?

Image Files

Creations/Shutterstock.com

Learning Outcomes

▶ **3.1** Convey the difference between painting and drawing programs.

▶ **3.2** Demonstrate an understanding of file extensions and file types.

▶ **3.3** Recognize the role that compression and resolution play in file sizes.

Key Terms

- aspect ratio
- bandwidth
- compression
- drawing program
- GUI
- paint program
- pixel
- pixel dimension
- resampling
- resolution

Almost anyone with a digital camera knows the value of being able to digitally crop images and remove redeye before printing or posting photos. In most cases, the average person does not need to develop skills beyond these simple tasks, but as a digital media professional, you will. In this unit, you will learn not only how to make the easy fixes but also how to use image software in sophisticated ways. But first you must understand the basic technology behind electronic images, become familiar with software that is used to produce and modify images, and learn how to manage image sizes.

Reproduced by permission.

Graphic programs fall into two categories: painting and drawing. **Paint programs** create images by using **pixels** (or *picture elements*). Pixels are small squares (usually) with each pixel assigned a color (see Figure 3.1).

paint programs—A general term for graphics software that uses pixels to create an image.

pixels—Consist of a specific color at a specific location in a matrix or grid. A collection of pixels produces an image on a computer screen or on a printed page.

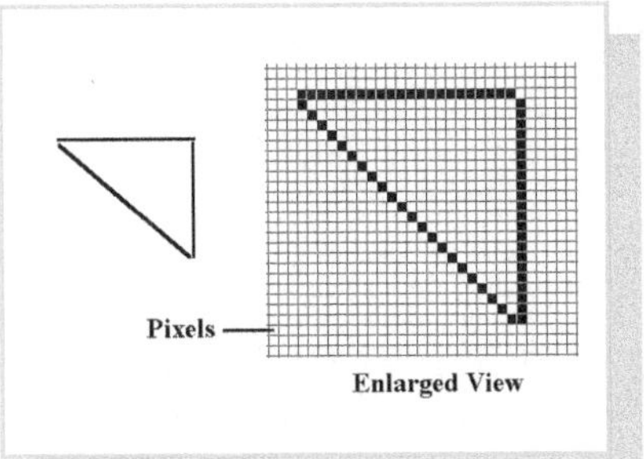

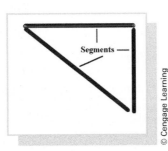

© Cengage Learning

Figure 3.1 *While an image may appear smooth, if you enlarge it, you will find that it is made up of a series of small squares or pixels.*

Figure 3.2 *Vector images are smoother than bitmaps and print without jagged edges because they are made up of individual lines, not pixels lined up next to one another on a grid.*

Drawing programs use vectors, or lines, to produce an image (see Figure 3.2). These lines are created using a series of mathematical points that can be changed without distorting the drawing. It is important to understand the difference between the two types of imaging programs because the software you choose to produce and edit images will impact the quality and usefulness of the final product.

drawing programs—A general term for graphics software that uses mathematically defined lines to create an image.

Raster-Based Paint Programs *LO 3.1*

Paint programs create images by assigning each pixel to a point on a grid of x and y coordinates. This grid is called a raster, and images created using this grid are sometimes referred to as raster images or raster graphics. More commonly, these images are called *bitmaps*.

Raster graphics are used to create images such as photographs because of the wide range and variations of colors possible. Unfortunately, because of the nature of pixels, enlarging raster images can result in pixelation, or jaggies (jagged edges), as each individual pixel is made bigger. Reducing images can also produce images that lose sharpness. Notice in Figure 3.3 (on the following page) the jaggies created when enlarging the image.

Many software programs are available to create and manage raster (or bitmapped) images. The most widely used program in the professional world is Adobe Photoshop. However, you have many choices beyond Photoshop available to you. Some programs, such as Microsoft Paint, are provided with the operating system you buy for your computer.

Figure 3.3 *Pixels can show up in an image as jagged edges.*

Others, such as Corel PaintShop Pro, are stand-alone programs that you purchase separately. Still other programs, such as the GIMP (GNU Image Manipulation Program), are open source, which means they are free and work across a wide range of computer platforms.

A more recent use of technology called cloud computing offers access to imaging software through the Internet. Many cloud computing services are free, but some charge a per-use fee or even require a subscription to use them. You may have already used cloud computing imaging software such as Picasa or Flickr to upload and edit photos. Use of cloud software may provide a less expensive option than purchasing software for your computer, but it also means that you must have Internet access in order to use it.

GUI—An acronym for graphical user interface. The GUI makes it possible to use a device, such as a mouse, to interact with a computer.

First GUI

The introduction of image creation software was the beginning of the use of computers for artistic purposes. Apple Computer, Inc. marketed the first **GUI** (graphical user interface) programs as MacPaint and MacDraw.

These early graphics software applications were quickly replaced with products such as Corel Draw (1989) and Adobe Photoshop (1990). These newer software programs increased the user's ability to fine-tune artwork and to create renderings that had never been possible in the world of paint and pen. Today we take for granted the ability to create an image or edit a photograph using a computer, but that was not always the case.

checkpoint

Which type of graphics program is better, vector-based or raster-based?

ACTIVITY 3.1 ▶ Researching Cloud Computing Graphics Programs

1. Using your favorite search engine, search for a list of drawing and paint programs that would be considered cloud computing. (Do not use any that were mentioned in the lesson.)

2. Using Google Docs (or another word processing program), create a document giving the names of at least two vector and two raster programs, their Web addresses, and a brief explanation of the programs' capabilities and limitations.

3. Save the document as **3_Activity1_cloud_graphics**.

Lesson 3.2 ▷ Determining Image File Formats

A file extension is the two to four letters following the dot at the end of a computer filename. For example, if a file is listed as "picture.jpg," *picture* is the name of the file and *.jpg* is the extension. The extension indicates the file format, which determines, among other things, what program(s) open the file. Becoming familiar with the most common image file extensions is useful because each file format offers advantages and disadvantages depending on how you intend to use an image. You can adjust your computer's settings to display extensions so you can easily determine file types (see Figure 3.4).

lavitrei/Shutterstock.com

Impact

Graphic File Formats

Graphic file formats continually develop as new techniques and demands of business require them. Early graphic formats such as BMP were created without regard to file size. Later formats such as JPG were created as a result of the demand for fast download times on the Internet. Flash formats have continued to evolve as a means of providing animation and interactivity on the Web. What is current today will likely not be used in the near future. For example, the movement to small screens on portable devices such as cell phones has already caused designers to rethink their graphic choices. This process of change will continue to impact all those who work in the field of image management.

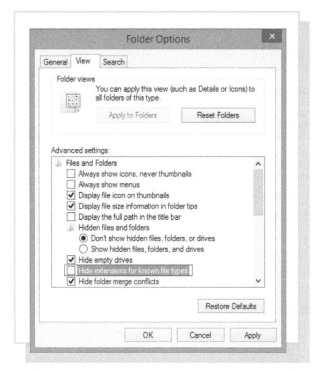

Figure 3.4 *To see extensions on your Windows-based computer, make sure the box indicated by the highlight is cleared.*

Nonnative Raster File Types *LO 3.2*

Adobe Photoshop is one of the most widely used raster-based graphics programs, but you will also see many other types of files used in digital media projects. Often, you will encounter one of the following nonnative raster image extensions that each have different characteristics and uses.

BMP

One of the earliest image file types is a BMP (bitmap) file. BMP images are usually placed in word processing documents. BMP file sizes are often quite large even though they are usually limited to 256 colors (rather than the millions of colors possible in a photograph) because they are created without using any compression.

JPG

JPG or JPEG (pronounced *jay-peg*) was developed by the Joint Photographic Experts Group. Using up to 16 million colors, JPG images reproduce the quality, color, and detail found in photographs or graphics using blends and gradients. Most digital cameras save photographs as JPGs to conserve memory space on the camera's storage device. JPGs are the most common nonnative raster file format in use today.

GIF

GIF (pronounced with either a hard or soft "G") is an acronym for Graphics Interchange Format and was developed by CompuServe. Because GIFs are compressed and use only 256 colors, the file sizes

Licensing Fees

In 1994, CompuServe, the developer of the GIF file format, caused a stir when it announced its intention to require that all commercial software companies using GIF compression in their programs pay licensing fees.

Was CompuServe correct in its decision to charge a licensing fee? Why or why not?

are quite small. Because photographs require greater color depth, they lose much of their quality if they are saved as GIFs. However, GIFs are suitable for line drawings, images with transparent backgrounds, and animated figures. Because they are small and work on many platforms, GIFs are commonly used in web page design.

TIF

A bitmap file type that works well in all environments is a TIF or TIFF (Tagged Image File Format). Like BMP files, these files are quite large. TIFF files can show 16 million colors and are often used in print documents. Some digital cameras can save photographs in TIFF format as well as the standard JPG.

PNG

Another choice for use on the Internet is the PNG (Portable Network Graphics) format. It retains 16 million colors and supports transparency much like GIF files. The graphics world has been slow to adopt PNG, but it is becoming more common. Today it is often used to replace GIF files partly because of the increase in available colors while remaining a small file size.

Nonnative Vector File Types *LO 3.2*

The most common native vector file format is AI (from Adobe Illustrator). These files may be converted to a PDF, EPS, or SVG depending upon the intended output. The following are some common nonnative file formats and their characteristics.

EPS

EPS (Encapsulated PostScript) is a general-purpose vector file format that has both the vector image data and a screen preview in the same file. It is most commonly used for printing purposes.

SVG

SVG software is an example of an open source image. SVG (Scalable Vector Graphics) is a vector graphic format designed specifically for use on the Web. SVG images are created using HTML code. Programs such as Adobe Illustrator can be used to create an image and then convert it to SVG. SVG is a popular choice for mobile devices because of its small file size.

Format Conversion *LO 3.2*

Once a copy of an image has been saved in its native format, you can change to another file format by using the drop-down arrow next to the Format or Save as type box as shown in Figure 3.5 (on the following page). From the list that appears, you can then choose the appropriate file format.

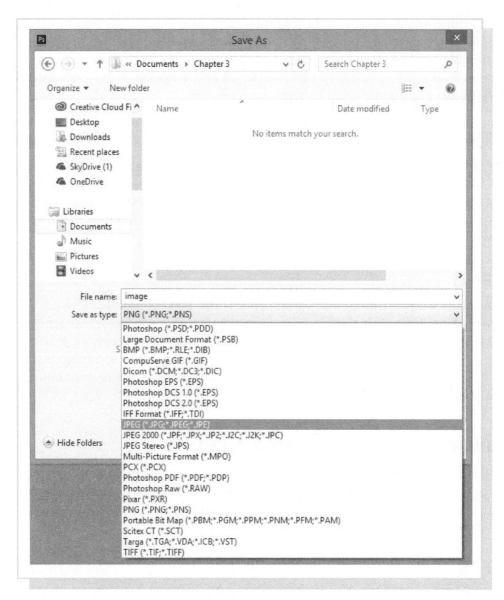

Figure 3.5 *Once an image has been saved in its native format, you can then choose Save As, click the Format drop-down arrow in Photoshop (or Save as type in other programs) and select another format.*

Different file formats are appropriate for different situations, so it is important to understand the distinctions between the various file formats. For example, some programs can import only graphics with specific file formats. Some images look better saved as one format rather than another, and some images need to be small in order to load quickly on the Internet. Knowledge of file formats enables you to make the best choice.

checkpoint

Why is it important to save an image file in a native format?

ACTIVITY 3.2 ▶ Exploring Image File Types

1. Search Google images or use another source and download and save an image of each of the following file types: BMP, JPG, GIF, TIF, PNG, and EPS.

2. Open a word processing document and key the title **File Types** at the top.

3. Create a table with two columns and six rows.

4. In the first column, insert each of the files you downloaded. Resize if needed as long as it does not distort the image. Images should be approximately 1 inch × 1 inch in size.

5. In the second column, state the file type and give a short description of it, including advantages and disadvantages.

6. Resize the columns and center the table horizontally.

7. Save the document as *3_Activity2_file_types*. Turn in all saved images with this activity.

Lesson 3.3 ▶ Managing Image Sizes

There are two ways to look at image sizes. One is the file size or the amount of storage space an image requires. The other is the visual image size. The two are connected because raster images that are visually large take up more storage than smaller ones. (Recall that vector images do not change their storage requirements based upon size.)

As hard drive, flash drive, and other storage device capacity has increased, the size of image files has become less of a concern. However, it is still important to keep file size in mind. Many websites and email services restrict the size of image files that can be uploaded. At a minimum, huge attached images can slow email delivery.

File size is also a consideration when adding images to a website. The time it takes to download a graphic on the Internet and display it in a browser depends on both the size of the file and the type of Internet connection. Dial-up connections that require a modem and a telephone receive data over a narrow **bandwidth** and are very slow. Broadband connections using DSL, cable, or wireless connections are much faster because they have a larger bandwidth. The narrower the bandwidth, the longer it takes to display images in a browser. So the smaller the file size, the faster an image will load on a computer accessing a website with a narrow bandwidth. Once you have a high-speed connection, it is easy to forget that not everyone has a fast connection, but it is an important consideration for Web developers. Fortunately, there are a number of ways to reduce image file sizes without giving up quality.

bandwidth—The speed at which a computer can transmit information along a network.

Compression LO 3.3

compression—The process of reducing the size of the image. *Lossy compression* reduces the size of an image file by removing information that is not essential. *Lossless compression* does not change any pixel data.

To reduce image file sizes, several algorithms (a sequence of steps used to perform a function) have been written to reduce, or compress, the size of image files. The two types of **compression** are lossless and lossy.

Lossless compression reduces the file size without losing any pixel information. Files saved as .gif, .png, .tif, and others use a lossless compression algorithm to produce smaller file sizes than those created when an image is saved in native formats.

The .jpg file format uses lossy compression. Lossy compression deletes or changes some pixels when saving. Since lossy compression removes unneeded pixels from within an image, this might appear to degrade the quality of the picture. However, this is not usually the case. When you save a file as a JPG, you select an image quality ranked from 1 to 12 (see Figure 3.6). This number represents the amount of compression, which determines the final size of the file. The higher the number, the more image quality is preserved and the bigger the file size. A lower number means a lower quality image but a smaller file size. If you will be using a large version of a JPG image, you might want less compression to ensure a better image.

It is important to know that each time you change a lossy image and then save it, the file is compressed again. If you save several times in this way, you will see your image begin to degrade, or become less acceptable. If you make all your changes in a native format and then save the last copy as a JPG, you will not encounter this problem.

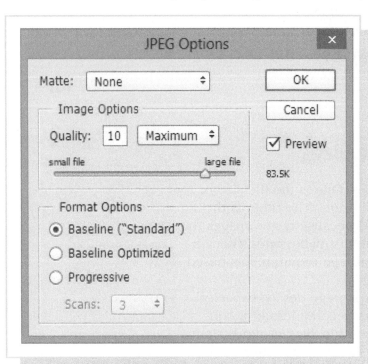

Figure 3.6 *It's easy to choose the amount of lossy compression that is applied to a JPG file.*

Resolution, Resizing, and Resampling LO 3.3

pixel dimension—The number of pixels in a row and column of a raster grid.

resolution—The density of pixels in an image.

Bitmap images have visual sizes measured in two ways: the physical size (such as a photograph printed as a 4- × 6-inch image) and the number of pixels in each inch. Physical sizes are also measured in **pixel dimension** such as 640 × 480. In Figure 3.7, you can see two images. Each one has a physical size of a 1-inch square. If each colored block represents a pixel, then the first image has a pixel dimension of 4 × 4 and the second is 16 × 16. The first contains 16 pixels per inch and the second has 64. The size of the pixels is much smaller in the second one and the pixels are much denser. The **resolution** of an image is measured in pixel density or pixels per inch (ppi). You can see that an image with 64 ppi will give you a better image.

If you are sending an image using email or posting it to a social networking site, you will want to use a lower resolution. If you are printing an image, you will want the highest resolution possible to improve the final print.

Different devices such as digital cameras produce images with different pixel densities. Image software allows you to manipulate these images by changing the physical size as well as the pixel density.

When you resize an image, you can choose whether to maintain the same amount of image data as in the original image. Photoshop and other image software provide you with an option called **resampling** that makes it possible to add or remove pixels when you resize an image. When resampling is on, changing the size of the image will not change its resolution, but it will become larger or smaller. If you turn off resampling, changing the physical dimensions of the image will change its resolution, and vice versa, in order to maintain the same amount of data that was in the original image. Figure 3.8a shows the image size of the first sample in Figure 3.7 and what happens if you change the resolution with resampling selected (Figure 3.8b). The actual dimensions of the image stay the same, but the pixel density changes as pixels are added to increase the resolution, and the object appears larger in the preview area. If you turn off resampling and increase the resolution (Figure 3.8c), the image size decreases in order to maintain the same amount of image data. It is important to keep in mind how both physical size and resolution work in tandem to determine your final product.

Special formulas are used in resampling to determine what colors each new pixel should be, based upon the colors around it. Different resampling formulas are used depending upon the desired outcome as can be seen in the Photoshop drop-down menu in Figure 3.9.

When changing the height and width of an image, it is important to keep in mind the **aspect ratio**. This is the ratio of the width of the image

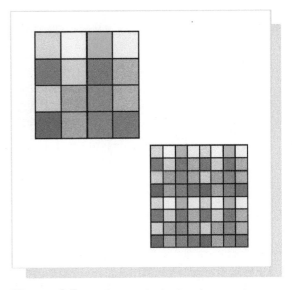

Figure 3.7 *The first block of colored squares has a resolution of 16 ppi, while the second block shows 64 ppi. The square on the right will be a larger file size but a more accurate reproduction of the image.*

resampling—Adding or deleting image pixels during the process of resizing.

aspect ratio—The ratio of the width to the height of an image.

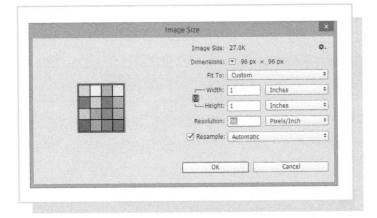

Figure 3.8a *Images can be resized with or without resampling.*

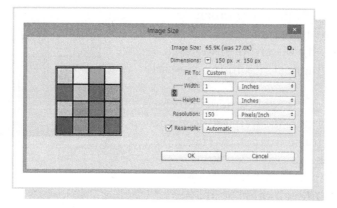

Figure 3.8b *Images can be resized with or without resampling.*

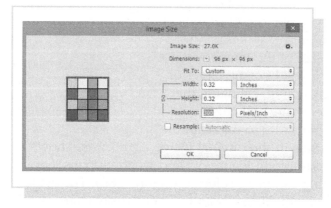

Figure 3.8c *Images can be resized with or without resampling.*

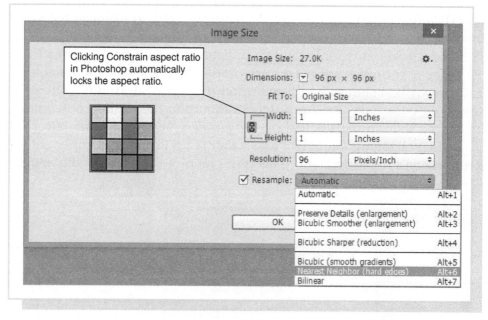

Figure 3.9 *Resampling allows software to add or remove pixels in an image to improve the appearance of an image when it is resized.*

to its height. If you change one number without changing the other, you will get a distorted image. Image software sometimes allows you to lock the aspect ratio (see Figure 3.9) to keep this from occurring.

ACTIVITY 3.3 ▶ Comparing Image File Size Management Methods

1. Choose a topic and then locate and save five images related to your topic. Use Google images or another source to locate the images.

2. Using photo editing software, resize each image three times: at 75%, 50%, and 25% of the original size. Save the image with a different name each time you resize it.

3. In a word processing document, create a 3-column, 15-row table with the title **Image File Sizes**.

4. Insert the images in the first column of the table. In the second column next to each image, key the size of the image (in pixels) and the size and space it will use if uploaded to the Web.

5. In the third column, merge the three rows that contain the same image. Discuss any noticeable changes to the size and quality of the three images.

6. Save the document as *3_Activity3_image_file_sizes*. Turn in your saved images with the document.

Career Planning

The first step in finding the job that is right for you is to target specific jobs and careers. Decide what you want—not just now, but five or ten years into the future. Have a career plan. One way to know what you want is to try out a wide range of jobs through part-time work, volunteering, and so forth. Then research potential employers that can offer you the kind of job or career you seek.

Skills in Action: Research some local digital media–related companies. Develop a list of people you might approach within the companies for a brief informational interview. Arrange and follow through with an interview. Discuss your impressions in class.

Key Concepts

▶ Image programs can be categorized into two groups: paint programs and drawing programs. *LO 3.1*

▶ Paint programs produce images using pixels. Each pixel consists of a specific color. Images produced by paint programs are called raster images or bitmapped images. *LO 3.1*

▶ Drawing programs use vectors or lines to produce an image. The vectors are created using a series of mathematical points. Images produced by drawing programs are called vector images. *LO 3.1*

▶ Extensions for the most common raster file types are *.bmp, .tif, .gif, .jpg,* and *.png. LO 3.2*

▶ Extensions for the file formats that are typically used for the Web are *.gif, .jpg,* and *.png. LO 3.2*

▶ Extensions for the most common vector file formats are *.svg* and *.eps. LO 3.2*

▶ Different file formats are appropriate for different situations. *LO 3.2*

▶ JPG image file sizes are reduced using a lossy compression algorithm that removes unnecessary pixels. GIF, PNG, and TIF use a lossless compression. *LO 3.2*

▶ Resolution and pixel density help determine the size of a file. *LO 3.3*

▶ Resizing is best done maintaining the aspect ratio. *LO 3.3*

Review and Discuss

1. Name the two types of digital imaging programs and differentiate them. *LO 3.1*

2. Identify the advantage of using a raster graphic. *LO 3.1 and 3.2*

3. Identify the advantage of using a vector graphic. *LO 3.1 and 3.2*

4. Describe the advantages and disadvantages of cloud computing. *LO 3.1*

5. Explain why it is important to understand file extensions. *LO 3.2*

6. List at least four types of bitmap image extensions. *LO 3.2*

7. Differentiate between an AI vector file and an SVG or EPS one. *LO 3.2*

8. Explain why images are compressed. *LO 3.3*

9. Differentiate between lossy and lossless compression. *LO 3.3*

10. Explain what happens to an image if you resize it with resampling selected. *LO 3.3*

Apply

1. Use the table function in a word processing document to create a table similar to the one below. Insert sample images found from the Web for as many of the file types as possible. Save the completed table as **3_Apply1_file_formats**. LO 3.2

File Format	Acronym Stands For	Extension	Type of Program	Sample
BMP	Bitmap	.bmp	Paint (raster)	
TIFF or TIF	Tagged Image File Format	.tif	Paint (raster)	
GIF	Graphics Interchange Format	.gif	Paint (raster)	
JPG or JPEG	Joint Photographic Experts Group	.jpg	Paint (raster)	
PNG	Portable Network Graphics	.png	Paint (raster)	
SWF	Shockwave Flash	.swf	Drawing (vector)	
EPS	Encapsulated PostScript	.eps	Drawing (vector)	
SVG	Scalable Vector Graphic	.svg	Drawing (vector)	

2. Keeping in mind the advantages, disadvantages, and uses of each file format, choose one file format and write an original slogan advertising the file format and its usefulness. Keep the slogan to eight words or fewer. Use an available paint program to effectively communicate your slogan. Save the slogan as **3_Apply2_slogan**. LO 3.2

3. Use a Web-based image editing software to upload and edit a photo. (You can also use a sample photo provided on the website of the software.) Save the original photo as **3_Apply3_original**. Resize the image to approximately 200 pixels × 200 pixels. Save the edited photo as **3_Apply3_web_based**.

   Write a reflection journal in a word processing document explaining what changes you made to the image. Insert both images somewhere in the document using the text wrapping feature to wrap text around the image. Include in your journal a description of your experience in using the Web-based software. Did you find it easy? Was it difficult or limiting? What do you think was missing that you would have normally used in editing an image? Save the journal as **3_Apply3_journal**. LO 3.1, 3.2, and 3.3

4. Key the table below into a word processing document. For each project scenario, respond to the questions in the columns next to the scenario. Save the completed table as **3_Apply4_scenarios**. LO 3.2

Scenario	What file types should be used?	Why?
Website using black and white clip art or line drawings.		
Website using all photographs created with a digital camera.		
Printed brochure with images of a construction site taken with a digital camera.		
Slide show for a wedding containing images only on each slide.		
Image that will need to be edited in the future many times.		

5. Key the table below into a word processing document. In the last column, answer the following questions: Should the file be used as is? Does it need to be saved as a different file type, and, if so, what file type? Should it be compressed? Save the completed table as **3_Apply5_ editing_files**. LO 3.2 and LO 3.3

File Type	Size of File	Use of File	Needed Edits
JPG	60KB	Insert on a web page.	
TIF	5MB	Insert on a web page.	
BMP	2MB	Animated graphic on a web page.	
PNG	15KB	Print in a brochure that will be sent electronically.	
GIF	1MB	Place in a slide show.	
BMP	2MB	Print catalog.	

Explore

1. Survey the home pages of your favorite websites (at least five) to determine what file formats the sites are using for their images. To determine the type of file format, right-click on the image and choose Properties. The Properties dialog box will show the extension. *LO 3.2 and 3.3*

   a. Create a table showing the address of each site and the number of each type of image file used on each site.

   b. Do you disagree with the sites' choices of file formats? How long did it take for pages to load? What can you suggest be done to increase the speed at which the pages appear? Write an explanation summarizing your comments.

   c. Save the table as ***3_Explore1_favorites***.

2. Explore the code needed to create an SVG graphic. What are the basic shapes that are used to create SVG graphics? What problems are there using SVG graphics on the Web? Include your resources in MLA style. Write a summary of what you found and save it as ***3_Explore2_svg***. *LO 3.2*

3. Create a three-column table in a word processing document with the title Web-Based Image Editing Software. In the first column key the name of the software, and in the second column cite the resource in MLA style. The last column will be used to write your review on at least two of the software applications. Create the list for the first column of Web-based image editing software by searching the Web and talking with family, friends, and others who may have used this type of software. Use at least two of the software applications to edit or create images. Write a review of the two that you explored. What did you like about them? What did you find frustrating? What do you think could be done to improve either software? Would you use each software again? Save your table as ***3_Explore3_software_review***. *LO 3.1*

Academic Connections

Communications: Using a poem from one of your favorite poets, key the poem in a document. Add appropriate formatting to the poem. Write a summary of what the poem means to you and what makes the poem your favorite. Use a drawing or paint program to edit an image that enhances and adds to the message of the poem. Insert the image into the document with appropriate placement. Save your work as ***3_AC_communications***.

Math: Read and study how to calculate the photo resolution needed for an image to get the best print quality possible. The following website may be of assistance: *http://www.photoshopessentials.com/essentials/image-quality*

Using the method of calculation given on the website, create a table similar to the one shown below in a word processing document and fill in the print size for the best image.

Megapixels	Photo Pixel Count Setting	Printer Resolution	Print Size
5	1944 × 2592	300 ppi	
8	2448 × 3264	300 ppi	
10	3648 × 2736	300 ppi	
12.1	4000 × 3000	300 ppi	
14.6	4680 × 3120	300 ppi	
18	5000 × 3240	300 ppi	

Save the completed table as **3_AC_math**.

Digital Photography

Learning Outcomes

▶ **4.1** Demonstrate knowledge of camera basics

▶ **4.2** Transfer images from a digital camera to a computer

▶ **4.3** Use good composition skills to take photographs

▶ **4.4** Photograph images with several different techniques

▶ **4.5** Use camera settings to modify an image

▶ **4.6** Adjust camera's white balance to improve an image

Key Terms

- aperture
- back lighting
- candid photograph
- color temperature
- cropping
- depth of field
- digital zoom
- DSLR
- focal point
- framing
- front lighting
- illusion of depth
- ISO
- jog dial
- Kelvin
- leading lines
- macro
- megapixels
- metadata
- mode dial
- optical zoom
- perspective
- photographic composition
- point and shoot
- rule of thirds
- shutter speed
- side lighting
- white balance

If a picture is worth a thousand words, then its power to communicate is indeed great. Digital photography makes it easy to use this power. Most of us like to take photographs and do so frequently. This chapter should help you get better at that. However, even if you do not see yourself as a photographer, it is important to know what constitutes a good photograph. This chapter will provide you with these skills.

In an earlier time, almost all cameras used film to capture images. To produce a photograph, the film had to be developed using special chemicals and then printed on photographic paper. Even in the early days of digital media, to convert images into a digital format, you had to scan hardcopy photographs using an optical scanner connected to a computer. But advances in technology and the introduction of digital cameras dramatically changed the process. In digital cameras, electronic image sensors capture images and built-in computer processors digitize image information, saving it to a memory device such as a flash memory card (see Figure 4.1).

Susan Lake

Figure 4.1 *Digital memory cards come in many different types and storage capacities.*

Digital cameras offer many benefits over conventional film cameras. Digital cameras allow you to review your images immediately on a preview screen instead of waiting for film to be developed and printed. Also, a typical memory card can store many more images than a roll of film, can be erased and reused many times, and eliminates processing costs to produce photos. Therefore, taking a lot of pictures with a digital camera is far less expensive than with a film camera.

But perhaps most significantly to a digital media professional, moving images from a camera to a computer is as simple as connecting the camera or the memory card to your computer, making it much faster and easier to use photos in digital media projects. Some professional photographers, especially fine art photographers, still use film cameras, arguing that film offers image quality that even the most advanced digital cameras can't provide. However, digital cameras are far more common these days, especially when images are destined for a digital media product such as a website or an electronic presentation.

DSLR Versus Point and Shoot *LO 4.1*

Digital cameras fall into two basic categories: **DSLR (digital single lens reflex)** and **point and shoot**. Generally, DSLR cameras are designed for the professional or serious amateur photographer who is most interested in image quality (see Figure 4.2). Point-and-shoot cameras are designed for the more casual photographer who is looking for ease of use and convenience. Even simpler to use than point-and-shoot cameras are the cameras built into the smartphones and tablets that have become ubiquitous in the past few years. These cameras do not allow for the adjustment of many settings, but they can record a scene quickly and conveniently, and the resulting image can be easily transmitted using the phone's message or email feature. People who choose DSLR cameras over point-and-shoot cameras commonly note the following advantages:

- **Better image quality.** DSLR cameras include larger image sensors than point-and-shoot cameras and therefore produce higher quality photographs. This is an important factor for many photographers who choose DSLRs over point and shoots, especially if images will be significantly enlarged or if photos are intended for certain print media.

- **More adaptability.** DSLR cameras are designed for interchangeable lenses and other accessories like special flashes and filters (see Figure 4.3). This means a DSLR camera can be fitted with anything from a super-zoom lens, to a close-up lens, to a wide angle lens, depending on what kind of photograph you are taking. A point-and-shoot camera with a zoom lens or other automatic features that mimic different lenses is just not as flexible and customizable as a DSLR camera.

- **Faster performance.** DSLR cameras power on faster, focus faster, and offer faster shutter speeds than point-and-shoot cameras. This means fewer lost shots waiting for a camera to power up and focus and fewer blurred images due to "shutter lag," the delay between pressing the shutter release button and the actual recording of the image.

Digital single lens reflex (DSLR)—A camera that uses a mirror system to capture an image. DSLR cameras have interchangeable lenses.

point and shoot—A camera designed to be easy to use with preset functions.

Susan Lake

Figure 4.2 *DSLR cameras have detachable lenses, which usually make them larger than point-and-shoot cameras.*

Susan Lake

Figure 4.3 *DSLR lenses come in many sizes depending upon the photographer's needs. This is a lens designed to zoom to capture images at great distances.*

- **More manual control.** Point-and-shoot cameras are designed to be used mostly in auto mode where the camera automatically determines what settings are appropriate based on shooting conditions. Generally, auto mode will produce a decent or even great image; but in certain conditions, auto mode can't fine tune the settings enough to produce the very best image. DSLR cameras offer more direct control over the various camera settings, so a photographer can fine tune the camera for every situation. DSLR cameras are especially good for adjusting to a wide range of lighting conditions. Manual mode is optional on some point-and-shoot models, but the settings are usually more limited than on a DSLR camera. Also, on a point-and-shoot camera, you sometimes need to search through complicated menus on the LCD screen to change manual settings. On a DSLR camera, you can more quickly access and change manual settings with dials and knobs at your fingertips on the camera body.

- **"What you see is what you get."** One of the major distinctions between DSLR and point-and-shoot cameras is that a DSLR camera uses a mirror to reflect light coming through the lens into the view finder. When you look through the view finder of a DSLR camera, you are essentially looking through the lens of the camera and what you see through the view finder is exactly what the image sensor will record when you press the shutter release. In contrast, point-and-shoot cameras display a digital preview of the image on an LCD screen. The preview is not always an exact representation of what the lens is seeing. For instance, it is difficult to determine focus based on an LCD screen. Many photographers prefer composing their images through the view finder on a DSLR camera rather than on a point-and-shoot LCD screen because they can be more confident that what they see is what they will get.

There is no doubt that DSLR cameras have the potential to deliver excellent image quality. However, point-and-shoot cameras are perfectly suitable for many digital media applications, especially if images will ultimately be viewed on a computer screen. Furthermore, point-and-shoot cameras are evolving rapidly (see Figure 4.4), and many of today's point-and-shoot cameras provide advanced options, making them more than just

Susan Lake

Figure 4.4 *An advantage of point-and-shoot cameras over DSLRs is that they are easy to carry.*

a beginner's camera. Point-and-shoot cameras offer several advantages over DSLR cameras:

- **Less expensive.** Point-and-shoot cameras are more affordable than DSLR cameras. A DSLR camera may be more adaptable with a wide range of lenses and accessories, but these items are additional costs beyond the price of the camera itself.

- **More portable.** Point-and-shoot cameras are compact, light, and easy to carry. They fit into a pocket, bag, or glove box so they are always at hand. DSLR cameras are bigger and heavier, not to mention any specialty lenses you may need to carry with them.

- **Easier to use.** Probably the most important advantage of a point and shoot over a DSLR camera is how simple it is to use. The versatility and manual control offered by a DSLR camera means that you need to know a lot more about photography to take full advantage of its features.

In the end, whether you use a DSLR camera or a point-and-shoot camera will come down to personal preference, circumstances, and experience.

Camera Features *LO 4.1*

Each brand of digital camera has its own features. The best way to learn about your camera's particular features is to read the owner's manual or search the Web for additional information. If you are buying a new digital camera, consider the following general features when making your selection.

lavitrei/Shutterstock.com

Impact

Photo Printing and Online Photo Albums

Before the digital age, it was necessary to print photos before you could see them. Polaroid cameras catered to people who wanted to see their prints immediately, but most other cameras required owners to send film away and receive prints later. With digital cameras, users can see their images right on the camera screen, and if the picture is acceptable, it can be printed using a desktop photo printer or a service at locations such as office supply stores and pharmacies. And rather than store and share printed photos using physical photo albums, people use applications such as Shutterfly, Snapfish, and Flickr to create custom photo albums, cards, and other types of illustrated documents and share them via the cloud. Storing photos in the cloud can be an added form of security for images you may never be able to capture again.

Critical Thinking: Do you think photos you print yourself on your desktop printer display the same quality as photos printed in the pre-digital age from film on professional-quality photo stock? How important is it to have a good-quality photo that will stand the test of time when you could easily print another version from images you have stored in an online album?

Shooting Modes

As noted earlier in the chapter, point-and-shoot cameras with automatic settings appeal to people who want to take good pictures without learning all of the complexities of photography. Most point-and-shoot cameras offer several shooting mode options beyond auto mode. Depending on the shooting mode you choose, the camera automatically adjusts the settings to capture the best possible image.

The different shooting modes are often represented by icons on a small dial called a **jog dial** or **mode dial** (see Figure 4.5). Table 4.1 lists just a few of the common shooting modes offered on many digital cameras. If you plan to take pictures in a variety of situations but don't want to learn about adjusting settings manually, choose a camera with a wide range of shooting modes and read the camera's manual to discover how to use each mode.

Your digital camera may offer more options than the modes detailed in Table 4.1. Again, the best way to learn about your camera's features is to read the owner's manual or research them on the Internet.

jog (or mode) dial—A type of wheel or dial on a camera that makes it possible to scroll through setting options by rotating. There is an indicator for the current selection.

Susan Lake

Figure 4.5 *A jog dial similar to this one is often found on a digital camera. It is used to change the camera functions.*

Megapixels

The image sensor in a digital camera is made up of millions of pixels that react to and record light to capture a digital image. In fact, there are so many pixels on an image sensor, they are referenced in terms of megapixels (1 **megapixel** = 1 million pixels). The number of megapixels on the image sensor directly impacts the potential resolution of the photos a camera captures. In general, the greater the number of pixels, the higher the level of detail and the better the quality of the photograph. The first popular digital cameras had 2 or 3 megapixels. These cameras were fine for viewing images on a screen or even for printing up to 4- × 6-inch prints. However, if you printed anything larger than that, the lack of resolution showed. In the early days, the number of megapixels in a camera was an important consideration when deciding what model to buy.

megapixel—A unit of measure equal to one million pixels. On a digital camera, the megapixels on an image sensor react to and record light to produce an image. The number of megapixels indicates the maximum image resolution of a camera.

As higher megapixel cameras became available, consumers had to weigh their need for higher resolution photos against higher price tags. Fortunately, technology advanced rapidly, megapixels went up, and camera prices came down. Now, a 3-megapixel (or lower) camera is rare, except perhaps in a cell phone. (Although even the

Table 4.1 *Common shooting mode icons and functions.*

ICON	FEATURE OR MODE	FUNCTION
or Auto	Auto mode	Use this default mode for shooting general images. The camera will select all of the settings for you.
M	Manual mode	Select this mode to control all of the camera settings.
(tulip icon)	Macro (or Close-Up) mode	Use this mode for shooting close-ups of small items, such as flowers or insects.
(mountain icon)	Landscape mode	Use this mode for shooting wide scenes, such as a field or a skyline.

cameras in cell phones are improving rapidly—it's not uncommon for a smartphone to include a 5- or 8-megapixel camera.) In fact, the question these days may be how many megapixels is too much. More megapixels mean bigger file sizes. If you don't intend to make large prints of your photos, you probably don't need a high megapixel camera. For instance, a photo from a 3-megapixel camera looks fine on a web page. An image taken with an 8-megapixel camera will probably not look a whole lot better, but it will have a bigger file size and take longer to load.

Optical Versus Digital Zoom

Most digital cameras offer some type of zoom feature so that you can get "closer" to a subject without actually moving closer. With **optical zoom**, the camera lens physically moves to magnify your subject and make it appear closer, similar to the function of lenses in binoculars. Optical zoom has no impact on the resolution of the image—the pixels are unchanged by zooming. In **digital zoom**, the digital image sensor crops the area around your subject and digitally enlarges the subject to fill the frame. To make the subject bigger, the camera (Figure 4.6) interpolates (or makes up) pixels based on the information in existing pixels and adds them to the image. The result can be fuzzy or distorted, especially if you eventually enlarge and print the image.

Newer cameras offer what is sometimes referred to as intelligent or smart digital zoom. With intelligent zoom, instead of interpolating

optical zoom—The actual magnification of an image through the movement of a camera lens.

digital zoom—The digital enlargement of an image on an image sensor through interpolation of pixels.

Rafal Olkis/Shutterstock.com

Figure 4.6 *A digital zoom camera interpolates pixels based on existing pixels.*

pixels and enlarging the image to fill the entire available image space, the camera simply crops the information around the subject and does not enlarge it. This means that you can digitally zoom in on a subject without losing the photo quality, but your finished image will be smaller than the normal picture size. So, for example, if your camera normally produces 4- × 6-inch images and you use intelligent zoom to capture a subject, the resulting image will be smaller than 4 × 6 inches.

If you enlarge the image up to or beyond the normal size with photo editing software, the software will interpolate the pixels to enlarge the subject just as a camera does with regular digital zoom. So if you want to use your images at the regular size or larger, you are no better off with smart zoom than you are with regular digital zoom. Many photographers simply turn off the digital zoom, smart or otherwise, and rely solely on optical zoom for their photographs.

File Types

The default file format for most digital cameras is JPEG (.jpg). JPEG files are often the best file type for digital photographs because they are relatively small and widely accepted by photo editing and printing software and hardware. In addition, many digital cameras allow you to set the quality of the JPEG as high, medium, or low. Higher quality JPEGs take up more memory but give you better results.

One drawback of JPEG files is that they use lossy compression, meaning they lose a little bit of digital information each time they are manipulated and saved. Also, JPEG images are processed inside the camera—the camera's processor determines all kinds of settings for color, light, saturation, etc., when creating the JPEG. Because these settings are determined by the camera before you even open a JPEG in photo editing software, your editing choices are limited to a certain extent.

For these reasons, some professional or serious amateur photographers prefer cameras that can save an image in a raw file format. Raw image files include all of the image data without any compression or processing. Raw image files must be processed by the photographer using conversion software on a computer. Although this means an extra step before a photo can be edited or used, some photographers prefer having full control over the settings and levels of the images they capture. Raw file formats are not standardized; each camera manufacturer uses its own file extension and specifications. Therefore, cameras that offer a raw file format feature normally come with software specifically designed to process the raw files, although, these days, many photo editing software packages can convert the raw files from most manufacturers. Some photographers will always prefer the higher level of control over their images that raw file formats offer, but for most digital media projects, small, easy-to-use JPEG files are a good choice.

History of Digital Cameras

Digital cameras, so popular with the average consumer today, were actually developed by the U.S. space program to capture images from space and send them back to Earth. The chip, similar to the one used in most digital cameras today, was developed in 1969 by Bell Laboratories to meet this need. The chip recorded an image of only 100 × 100 pixels (far smaller than today's images that can store photographs in thousands of pixels). By the late 1980s, digital cameras had moved into the world of the professional photographer, but they were too expensive for most photographers. In the 1990s Kodak, Apple, and Olympus introduced cameras that had much lower costs. With the introduction of the Sony Mavica that stored images on floppy disks (making it easy to store and access images), the world of photography changed dramatically. Since these early years, each year has brought cheaper, faster, and more powerful digital cameras with more features.

Camera Care and Safety *LO 4.1*

Digital cameras are sturdy, but they are carefully designed technology and you should treat them with care. Follow these rules to keep your camera in good working order:

- Keep the lens area clean by using a soft cloth designed especially for camera lenses.
- Keep the lens cap on or the shutter closed (usually by turning off the camera) when not using the camera.
- Beware of dropping the camera even from a short distance such as onto a counter.
- Never force a memory card in or pull it out if there is resistance.
- Never force an uncooperative switch; instead find out why the latch or door is unable to function.
- Never throw rechargeable camera batteries in the trash: They can leak toxins into the environment. Do a simple search online to find out where you can recycle rechargeable batteries.

Follow these safety procedures when using digital photographic equipment:

- Don't shoot directly into the sun, to avoid damaging your eyes through the viewfinder.
- Don't walk while looking through the viewfinder, to avoid tripping over or running into obstacles.
- Be careful with a camera's batteries; don't store them where they can come in contact with each other, and don't handle batteries that appear to be leaking.
- Don't try to fix a digital camera yourself by opening the camera; some components in digital cameras are capable of delivering an electrical shock.

checkpoint

Why is it important to understand the relationship of megapixels to cameras?

ACTIVITY 4.1 ▶ Exploring a Camera

1. Spend some time getting to know the camera that you will use in this class. Examine the camera itself and review the user's manual (either in print or online). If you do not have a camera available, alternatively, research the basics and options of a camera that you would like to use.

2. If possible take a picture of the camera.

3. Using image editing software, create a new 8.5- × 11-inch document.

4. Place the image of the camera and a layer of text in the blank document. Text should include, at a minimum, the following information about the camera: megapixels, optical or digital zoom, flash technology, image editing options, and any other options special to that camera. You may add any other information you learned about your camera as you were exploring.

5. Save as *4_Activity1_camera_exploring* with a JPG extension.

Lesson 4.2 ▶ Taking Photographs *LO 4.2 and 4.3*

candid photographs—
Non-posed, usually informal pictures.

photographic composition—
The selection and arrangement of design elements within a photograph.

Most likely, you've used a digital camera of some sort, even if just to take snapshots or candid images. **Candid photographs** are unplanned photographs taken with little or no preparation or posing. While these are fun to take and post on a social networking site, taking good photographs requires some thought and preparation. With a little bit of knowledge, even your candid shots can improve significantly.

Taking great photographs requires an understanding of the elements of design and the principles of **photographic composition**. These are complex subjects. But learning and applying just a few basic design elements and composition principles can greatly improve your photographs. Elements of design include line, shape, color, and lighting. Principles of composition include unity, balance, perspective, and emphasis. You can think of elements as the building blocks and composition as the arrangement of the blocks to create a final product. Throughout the centuries, artists, designers, and photographers have followed some simple rules of composition to arrange the elements in their work and turn out visually pleasing products. This section describes how some very basic elements of design and principles of composition work together to create pleasing photographs.

Focal Point *LO 4.3 and 4.4*

A good photograph begins with a strong focal point. A **focal point** is the most important element on which you want a viewer to focus. Once you choose a focal point, you can use some simple principles of composition to organize the other elements in the image to direct your viewer's attention to the focal point of the image.

focal point—The element within an image on which the viewer's eye focuses.

Rule of Thirds *LO 4.3 and 4.4*

You may think that placing the focal point in the center of a photograph is the best way to draw attention to it. Surprisingly, this is not necessarily true. On a rectangular surface, the human eye naturally focuses on an off-center spot. This is related to a phenomenon known as the golden mean. The golden mean is an interesting, complicated mathematical problem well beyond the scope of this book. However, you do not need to be a mathematician to take advantage of this natural tendency and use it to direct a viewer's eye to your focal point. You can use a composition principle called the rule of thirds.

The **rule of thirds** states that an image should be divided into an imaginary grid of nine equal parts and that the focal point should be placed at or close to the point where the lines of the grid intersect (see Figure 4.7). To apply the rule of thirds, imagine a tic-tac-toe grid placed over a scene, dividing it into three columns and three rows. Place the focal point along the imaginary lines, preferably at or near the spot where a horizontal and a vertical grid line meet—that is, off center. Following the rule of thirds produces an effect similar to the golden mean; your viewer's eye naturally moves to an area slightly off center and rests there. Because it feels natural, the viewer finds the image pleasing.

rule of thirds—Principle of imposing an imaginary grid of nine equal spaces (like a tic-tac-toe grid) over a scene to be photographed, then positioning the most important elements of the image along the gridlines, most preferably at or near the intersection of two imaginary gridlines.

It's difficult to understand the impact of the rule of thirds just by reading about it. The best way to appreciate how the rule of thirds can affect your photographs is to experiment. Take some pictures using the rule of thirds. Move your focal point to the left, to the center, and to the right. How does the positioning change the image and the feeling the image gives? Turn the camera vertically and photograph a subject in the bottom, middle, and top third of the imaginary grid. Which picture

Susan Lake

Figure 4.7 *The grid on the image makes it easy to see how the rule of thirds applies to this photograph. The flower has been intentionally positioned to the side and the rocks fill the bottom third of the image.*

Susan Lake

Figure 4.8 *Placing the horizon in the lower third of a photograph gives importance to the sky. Notice how the prominent sky in this photograph dwarfs the items below.*

Susan Lake

Figure 4.9 *The gate entrance to this backyard acts as a frame drawing your eye into the garden.*

framing—The use of elements within a scene to visually surround the subject and draw attention to it.

leading lines—Actual or suggested lines in an image that draw a viewer's eye through an image in a specific direction, usually to the focal point.

best portrays your subject? Go outside and photograph a landscape. Position the horizon in the top, middle, and then lower third of the frame. Notice how the impact and focal point of the image change. When the horizon is in the middle of the image, the picture is probably a bit boring. Is the picture more interesting when the horizon is in the lower or upper third of the frame? How does the focal point change between these two images (see Figure 4.8)?

Framing *LO 4.3 and 4.4*

Another composition technique you can use to draw attention to your focal point is framing. **Framing** is using elements in a scene to visually surround your subject and make it stand out. So, for example, a wedding photographer might photograph the bride and groom in the doorway of a church. The outline of the doorway forms a visual frame around the happy couple and makes them stand out. Almost anything that creates a visual border around your subject will emphasize it and draw the viewers' attention. Trees, rock formations, arches, doorways, windows, and buildings are just a few elements that can be useful for framing a focal point, but the possibilities are really endless.

One key to framing is to make sure that the frame does not draw too much attention to itself since the objective is to focus on your subject. Figure 4.9 is a good example of how framing can draw the eye to a focal point in a photo. Again, the best way to understand framing is to experiment. Next time you are taking pictures, look for other elements in the scene that you can use to frame your subject. Keep in mind that you might need to move around to get the framing right.

Leading Lines *LO 4.3 and 4.4*

As the name suggests, **leading lines** are visual elements in a photograph that draw a viewer's eye through an image in a specific direction. Because the human eye naturally follows a line, whether literal or suggested, you can use lines in your photo composition to draw a viewer's eye through the photograph and to the focal point. When taking a photo, look around to notice if anything in the scene forms a line that you can use in composing your picture. The lines can be straight, curved, vertical, horizontal, or even diagonal. They can be composed of almost anything at all: fences, roads, shorelines, train tracks, river beds, rows of street lamps, or forest paths are just some of the elements that can be used as leading lines.

You can use leading lines in a photo not only to direct focus to your main subject, but also to control how a person's eyes move through a photograph. Figure 4.10 is an example of leading lines drawing the eye through a photograph. When you look at it, notice where you look first and how your eyes move through the photo. Do you look first at one end of the photo and then follow a certain element through the image to another end?

Cropping *LO 4.3 and 4.4*

Cropping in photo composition means including all of the elements you want in the picture and excluding anything you don't want. When you take a picture, you may be so focused on the main subject that you do not notice other distracting elements in the viewfinder. Before you release the shutter, take a moment to look at what else your picture will capture. Is there unnecessary clutter in the background or surrounding your subject that will distract from your focal point (see Figure 4.11)? If so, move closer, zoom in on your subject, or change your position around the subject.

Photographers sometimes talk about "filling the frame," meaning that the subject—and only the subject—occupies the limited space of the photo. Cropping means you are filling the frame, eliminating unwanted elements, and allowing your subject to occupy more space. This can make a photo more interesting and dramatic and leaves no doubt about what you were trying to capture when you took the picture. Definitely experiment with cropping by moving closer, zooming in, changing the angle, or rotating the camera vertically or horizontally to see how different crops impact the composition. But be careful not to crop out essential elements. A photo of a person playing tennis just doesn't look right if the arm holding the racket is cropped out of the picture!

Directional Lighting *LO 4.3 and 4.4*

Lighting is perhaps one of the most important elements of a photograph and also one of the most complicated to explain. The color, direction, amount, and quality of light all have an impact on photographs. If you intend to develop your photography skills, it is well worth your time and effort to seek out books, websites, and classes to learn all you can about how light affects your photos and how you can control it to your advantage. But a good place to start learning about light in photographs is to consider how the direction of light falling on your subject affects

Susan Lake

Figure 4.10 *The curving lines of the creek bed draw the eye from the bottom of the image to the top.*

Susan Lake

Figure 4.11 *The clutter in this image detracts from the main subject of the photo, a flower pot sculpture. How could cropping improve the image? What else could improve the image?*

cropping—In photo composition, including all wanted elements in a photo and excluding all unwanted elements.

Figure 4.12 *Directional lighting can help an image appear three-dimensional.*

photo composition by contrasting light and shadow. This contrast helps a viewer perceive a subject as three-dimensional and interesting. There are three basic types of directional lighting: front, side, and back lighting. (See Figure 4.12.)

front lighting—When light shines from behind the camera and illuminates the front of the subject, producing few or no shadows.

Front lighting comes from behind the camera and illuminates the front of the subject. It can come from many sources, including the sun, indoor lights, and the flash on your camera. Photos shot with front lighting are generally bright and well lit, but this type of lighting produces the fewest shadows and can make your subject look flat in photographs. It is a good choice, however, when you want all of the details of a scene to show up in the final image with no shadows, as in certain nature shots or architectural photos where each detail should be equally illuminated.

side lighting—Light that shines from the right or left of the camera and illuminates the subject from the side, creating more defined highlights and shadows.

In **side lighting**, the light is directed at a subject from either the left or the right side, creating lots of shadows and highlights. Side lighting emphasizes texture and gives depth to your subject, so you may find it the most useful for delivering high-impact, interesting photos. The light can come from any source such as the sun at dusk or dawn, a window, or a lamp. To use side lighting, simply position your subject so that light is coming from one side and take the photo.

back lighting—When light shines from behind the subject toward the camera, often casting all of the front details of a subject in shadow or silhouette.

In **back lighting**, the light shines from behind the subject, toward the camera. It emphasizes the shape and outline of a subject, but other details are mostly lost in shadow. At its most extreme, back lighting produces a silhouette of your subject. If you've ever photographed someone in front of a window (without a flash) only to have him or her show up as a black shadow in the final image, you are familiar with the perils of back lighting. Although back lighting is a tricky technique to master, it can produce dramatic results when done right.

Experiment with directional lighting to see how it changes your photos. If you have a pet, photograph it in front of a window to see the effects of back lighting. Is the background bright but the animal lost in shadow? Then shoot the picture with the light from the window at your back, illuminating the front of the pet. How is this photo different? Finally, try moving so that the light streams in from the window and illuminates the pet from the side. Can you see more detail in its fur, feathers, or scales?

Depth *LO 4.3 and 4.4*

The brain uses many different visual clues to perceive depth in a three-dimensional world. The term *depth* is used a lot in discussions about photography. In fact, it's been mentioned a few times in this chapter already! The previous section described how directional lighting can affect the depth of your photos. The contrast between light and shadow is one of the clues the brain uses to perceive an object as three-dimensional. Another clue is the size and relative position of items, or perspective. In photography, the camera takes three-dimensional scenes and records them on the flat, two-dimensional surface of a photograph. Even though there is no third dimension of actual depth in a photograph, the brain uses the same visual clues in a photograph to perceive the **illusion of depth**. The more a viewer perceives depth in a photo, the more lifelike and interesting it is.

Perspective

Perspective in photography is what makes items look bigger, smaller, closer, and farther. (See Figure 4.13.) You can manage perspective in your photo composition to give an image depth. Perspective in a photo can be affected by special lenses if you have a DSLR camera. Even some point-and-shoot camera settings can mimic different lenses to change perspective in photos. If you intend to take your photography to the next level, you should investigate how different lenses or settings impact perspective. However, an easy way to get started learning about perspective (especially if you have a point-and-shoot camera with limited shooting modes) is to physically change the position of the camera in relation to your subject.

Moving closer, farther away, or even to the side of your subject changes its perceived relationship to the other items in the scene and the perspective of the image. Note that this is not the same as zooming in on a subject. To change the perspective, you have to change the physical position of the camera in relation to the subject. Experiment with perspective by taking pictures of a person in front of a row of trees. How does the image change when you move closer, farther away, or to the side? Do the trees look bigger or smaller in certain shots? Do they appear closer together in some shots?

Angles

Just as you can change the perspective of an image by moving closer, farther, or to the side of your subject, you can impact perspective and depth by changing the angle of the shot. Beginner or casual photographers often shoot their subjects from a standing, eye-level position. This position is considered the normal perspective, but it often lacks depth. However, simply changing the angle from which you shoot a subject can completely alter the perspective and the impression your photo makes on a viewer.

illusion of depth—In photography, the effect of visual clues that make a viewer perceive an image as three-dimensional in a two-dimensional image.

perspective—In photography, what makes items look larger and closer or smaller and farther away; can be used to create depth and express a story about a subject.

Elena Elisseva/Shutterstock.com

Figure 4.13 *Perspective creates depth in an image.*

Figure 4.14 *The low angle of this shot of a windmill emphasizes its size even more than a shot from a more traditional angle would.*

Shooting from a low angle makes subjects appear bigger and more important (see Figure 4.14). Shooting from an extremely low angle can even make a subject appear menacing or threatening. In contrast, shooting from a higher angle diminishes a subject. A higher angle can also bring harmony to a busy scene and reveal patterns and textures not normally seen from eye level. For example, in a photo of a crowded farmers market shot from street level, the people, produce, and other elements can jumble together in a confusing display. But if the same market is photographed from an upper-story window of a nearby building, you may be able to capture harmonious patterns, textures, and colors someone doesn't see at eye level.

To capture images from different angles, you have to physically move around. This means you may need to kneel, lie down on the ground, stand on a chair, or climb a flight of steps to capture your subject from a different viewpoint. You may feel silly at first, but the impact of shooting from different angles will make you feel proud of your final results (see Figure 4.15).

Shooting from different angles can improve your photos and make them more interesting. However, when shooting from different angles, keep in mind the concept of a level horizon. This means that in any scene with the horizon in it, the horizon should be straight. A crooked horizon can make a viewer feel uneasy since a level horizon and other objects' relation to it is one of the visual clues that helps the brain understand the three-dimensional world. On the other hand, if you want to convey a sense of unease, you may intentionally make the horizon crooked in your images.

Figure 4.15 *The angle of this photo emphasizes the wood pattern and adds interest and depth that it might not have if the trellis had been photographed straight on.*

The same is true about other objects that people normally experience in a certain orientation: a tree appearing diagonally in an image is a good example of how you can present a normally vertical subject in an abstract way to produce a certain feeling in your viewers. As with all of the other techniques described in this chapter, the best way to learn about different angles and how they change the impression your photos make is to experiment. Try photographing a friend from different angles and then review your photos. Which one best matches how you see your friend as a person? How does the impression he or she makes change depending on the angle of the photo? Does the low angle picture of your friend make her seem strong and confident? How does a high angle shot make her look?

Foreground, Middle Ground, Background

Another easy way to create depth in your photos is to make sure you have elements in three dimensions: the background, the middle ground, and the foreground. (See Figure 4.16.) Most snapshots have just two dimensions: the subject and whatever is behind it. It's easy to add depth to these shots simply by adding another element in front of your main subject. Doing so creates the illusion of three dimensions: the elements behind your subject are in the background, the subject is in the middle ground, and the elements in front of your subject are in the foreground.

Studio and portrait photographers use this trick all the time. You've probably seen something like a picture of a baby leaning on a rocking horse with a country backdrop behind him, or an outdoor shot with a family posed behind a split rail fence and a pretty wooded scene at the back. In these examples, the horse and the fence make up the foreground, the people make up the middle ground, and the scenery is the background. The images have more depth than they would without the props in front. This trick works for all types of photos and not just portraits.

Pressmaster/Shutterstock.com

Figure 4.16 *Depth can also be created through the use of foreground, middle ground, and background elements.*

checkpoint

What decisions must you make when composing an image?

ACTIVITY 4.2 ▶ Perfect Photograph

1. Find three objects of various sizes to use in experimenting with the techniques you have read about in this lesson.

2. Decide which object will be your focal point, and which will be a background for your images. Take several pictures, rearranging the objects each time. Take the pictures from different angles by moving the camera slightly and moving yourself around the objects. Use the rule of thirds when moving yourself or the camera by looking at the whole image in the camera's LCD as if it were divided into thirds. Consider both vertical and horizontal thirds.

3. Move away from the objects and take pictures at various distances from them. Do not worry about the number of pictures you are taking.

4. View all your images on a computer. Save the images you judge to be the top six images as: *01photo, 02photo, 03photo, 04photo, 05photo, 06photo*.

5. Create an 11- × 17-inch document image. Insert the six photos as a collage in your image editing software. Save in JPG format as *4_Activity2_best_photos*.

6. If time permits, compare collages with those done by other students. Pick the image you believe to be the best in your collage as well as in the collages of other students. See if they choose the same photograph as you to be the number one photograph. Discuss why you each chose the selected photograph.

Film Manufacturers

The rise of digital photography meant business challenges for film manufacturers. Research the challenges faced by Kodak, Fuji, and Polaroid. How did they each respond differently and what was the outcome? What can other industries learn about being ready for technological advances?

Lesson 4.3 ▶ Adjusting Settings

Point-and-shoot cameras are designed to make choices for you to help ensure a good photograph. While these choices often result in very satisfactory images, it is helpful to know what changes the camera makes in your camera settings. Many cameras will let you override the choices if you are not getting exactly the shot you want.

Basics *LO 4.5*

shutter speed—Measures the rate at which a camera lens opens and closes.

aperture—Indicates the size of a camera lens's opening.

ISO—A standardized measurement of the speed with which a camera stores an image.

macro—A setting or lens that allows close-ups.

A camera uses three components to capture an image. They consist of the **shutter speed** (how fast the lens opens and closes), **aperture** settings (how wide the lens opens to let in light), and the **ISO** (speed at which the "film" captures an image).

All three of these functions work together in combination to produce an image. Changing any of these three settings will change the way your photograph appears. Point and shoots pick the combination that is likely to give you the best image. Many of these cameras provide pre-set special image types such as a **macro** (close-up) setting, a distance setting, or a sports setting. These special settings use different aperture, shutter speed, and ISO to capture the moment.

Shutter Speed

You can adjust the shutter speed to achieve specific and desired effects. For example, if your shutter speed is set to open and close slowly while you are taking a picture of a runner crossing the finish line, there is enough time to capture a series of movements, resulting in the runner's blur. If you have the shutter speed set to open and close briefly, then you may catch the specific instant when the runner's foot is coming down onto the finish line.

Aperture

Changing the aperture settings determines the **depth of field**. Aperture settings are measured in f-numbers (often referred to as f-stop or f-ratio). A larger f-stop value allows less light in. A smaller f-stop value lets in more light. If you are photographing a squirrel in your yard with a narrow (large f-stop) aperture, you will see clearly the squirrel as well as the grass and trees behind. If your aperture is wide (small f-stop), the trees and grass will appear fuzzy. Your depth of field will be limited. Figure 4.17 uses a wide depth of field to establish a focal point.

ISO

Even though digital cameras have no film, ISO is still used to indicate how the image is captured to the storage media. Low ISO settings capture an image sharply with few extra pixels or graininess. Low ISOs are used when there is plenty of light. High ISO settings work hard to capture an image in low light but the result is an image that has artifacts. (Artifacts are irregularities in digital images, such as jagged edges or pixelation.)

Susan Lake

Figure 4.17 *The background of this image appears blurry, allowing the butterfly to stand out from the image. The depth of field was intentionally reduced to create this effect.*

depth of field—Indicates how much of the image is in focus.

color temperatures—Measures the type of light shining on an image.

Kelvins—The measurement, in degrees, of the color temperature of light.

white balance—Adjusts an image based upon the color temperature present when an image is photographed.

White Balance *LO 4.6*

Light comes from many sources, including the sun, incandescent bulbs, and florescent bulbs. Sunlight on a cloudy day is different from that seen on a bright sunny day. Photographs taken under each of these conditions will appear different. Light is described as having various **color temperatures** (measured in **Kelvins**, which are outlined in Table 4.2) depending upon the source. Incandescent bulbs generate a warm, yellow light with a low Kelvin measurement. Overcast days generate cold blue light with a higher Kelvin rating.

Cameras attempt to establish settings based upon the temperature of the light coming in, but it is not always accurate. As a result, one of the functions cameras provide is the option to set the white balance. **White balance** means that the camera attempts to make white look truly white without the yellowness of a candle or the blue of an overcast day. White balance settings ask you what type of light you are photographing in so that the camera does not have to guess.

Table 4.2 *Kelvin measurements.*

COLOR TEMPERATURE	LIGHT SOURCE
1000–2000 K	Candlelight
2500–3500 K	Incandescent bulb
3000–4000 K	Sunrise/sunset
4000–5000 K	Fluorescent bulb
5000–5500 K	Camera flash
5000–6500 K	Clear day
6500–8000 K	Moderately overcast sky
9000–10000 K	Shade or heavily overcast sky

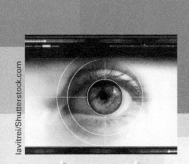

lavitrei/Shutterstock.com

Impact

metadata—Information about a photograph stored within the image file.

Metadata

Digital photographs have information "hidden" in their file structure that can be viewed in some editing software. This information, called **metadata**, records a number of valuable details about the photograph, including the date and time when the image was taken, the type of camera used, and the various settings such as aperture and shutter speed (see Figure 4.18). Some editing programs allow you to modify the metadata or add information such as the name of the photographer and copyright details. Note that, if you want to use a photograph and are unsure of the source, the metadata would be a good place to look to determine who holds the copyright and how to contact them to obtain permission to use.

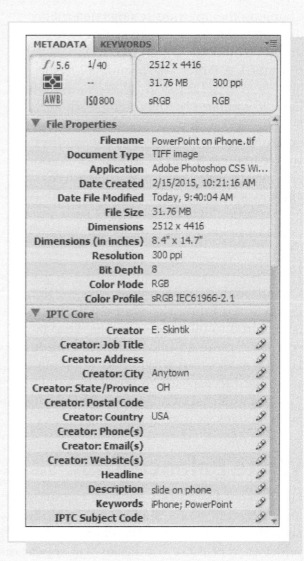

Figure 4.18 *The metadata for this image tells you when it was shot as well as the file size, dimensions, and resolution. The photographer's name and location have been added along with a description of the photo and keywords.*

Figure 4.19 shows you an example of a camera that lets you set ISO and white balance.

checkpoint

What three settings determine the way an image is photographed?

ACTIVITY 4.3 ▶ Camera Settings

1. Attend a school sports activity, or with a partner in class, take some images of each other with movement. Adjust the camera to appropriate speeds, using what you've learned from this lesson and the options available on your camera.

2. Experiment with shutter speed, aperture, ISO, and white balance options as available on your camera.

3. Save four of your best photos as: **01settings**, **02settings**, **03settings**, and **04settings**.

4. Insert the photos into a word processing document. Write a brief explanation of what you learned about the settings of your camera while taking the pictures. Save as **4_Activity3_camera_settings**.

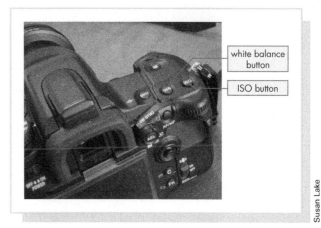

Susan Lake

Figure 4.19 *This camera provides easy access buttons to change the ISO and the white balance.*

Maintaining Perspective

Once you have been working for a while, you may begin to notice a few things about a job that rub you the wrong way. Maybe you think some of the work rules are unnecessary, or perhaps you do not like the way a job assignment has been delegated. Few workplaces are perfect. Some of your grievances may be legitimate. But not every "problem" is truly serious or a cause for complaint. Do not become the type of employee who finds fault with every little thing. Always maintain perspective. One good way to do this is to find out if you are the only one who thinks a situation is a real problem. Discuss the matter with more experienced coworkers whom you respect. Does the situation really prevent you from doing your job well? Do not overreact. Your employer and coworkers will appreciate your relaxed attitude, and you will be less likely to suffer from on-the-job stress or burnout.

auremar/Shutterstock.com

Skills in Action: What are some common challenges faced by people who work in multimedia-related fields (such as tight deadlines or changing technology)? Which of these would you classify as serious problems? Which are simply minor annoyances? Discuss in class.

Key Concepts

▶ Digital cameras fall into two categories: point and shoot and DSLR. *LO 4.1*

▶ Some people choose DSLR cameras for high image quality, more adaptability, faster performance, and more manual control as compared to point-and-shoot cameras. *LO 4.1*

▶ Point-and-shoot cameras are generally less expensive, less bulky, and easier to use than DSLR cameras. *LO 4.1*

▶ A wide range of shooting modes on a point-and-shoot camera can help you take better pictures in a bigger variety of situations. *LO 4.1*

▶ Cameras measure the possible image size by using megapixels. You should consider how you will use images when determining how many megapixels you need in a camera. *LO 4.1*

▶ In optical zoom, the camera lens actually moves to magnify a subject. It has no impact on the image resolution. In digital zoom, the image processor crops the area around the subject and uses interpolation to make it appear bigger. This can affect resolution in the final product. *LO 4.1*

▶ Most digital cameras save images as JPGs, which are relatively small and easy to use in a variety of settings, but use lossy compression. Some cameras offer a raw data file option, which is stable and offers more control over settings, but must be converted before images are editable and usable. *LO 4.2*

▶ Digital cameras must be treated carefully to prevent damage and maintain safety. *LO 4.1*

▶ Photographic composition requires the photographer to consider the focal point, the rule of thirds, framing, leading lines, and depth. *LO 4.3 and 4.4*

▶ Shutter speed, aperture, and ISO determine the way a photograph is captured. *LO 4.5 and 4.6*

Review and Discuss

1. Identify what has replaced film in storing images on cameras and state the advantage of this new storage medium. *LO 4.1*

2. Explain how digital cameras increase your chance of taking the perfect picture. *LO 4.1*

3. Explain the difference between an SLR camera and a point-and-shoot camera. *LO 4.1*

4. Define a jog dial. *LO 4.1 and 4.5*

5. Differentiate between digital and optical zoom. *LO 4.1*

6. Define a megapixel and explain why it is important for a camera. *LO 4.1*

7. Describe why a photograph that will be used for a web page would be saved as a JPG with a resolution of 640 × 480. *LO 4.1 and 4.2*

8. Explain the advantages in setting a camera so it saves an image as a raw file type. *LO 4.1 and 4.2*

9. List three rules for keeping your camera in good working order and three procedures for maintaining safety while working with a digital camera. *LO 4.1 and 4.2*

10. Describe what composition has to do with taking a good photograph. *LO 4.3 and 4.4*

11. Define focal point and explain how this can be changed in an image. *LO 4.3 and 4.4*

12. State why the rule of thirds is important when taking a photograph. *LO 4.3 and 4.4*

13. Assess what makes a background that frames the subject effective in an image. *LO 4.3 and 4.4*

14. Cite how the use of lines within a photograph can help to unify elements in an image. *LO 4.3 and 4.4*

15. Consider how the ability to catch action shots has changed photography. *LO 4.5*

16. Explain briefly the three components that a camera uses to capture an image. *LO 4.5*

17. Give an example of how the settings of shutter speed would affect a photograph. *LO 4.5*

18. Define an f-number. *LO 4.5*

19. Differentiate between a photograph using a low ISO setting versus one with a high ISO setting. *LO 4.5*

20. Describe white balance on a camera setting. *LO 4.6*

Apply

1. Open each of the following images from your data files: ***01movement***, ***02movement***, and ***03movement***. Analyze what settings were used to take the photographs with movement. Was this done effectively? What could have been done more effectively? Access and use metadata information to assist with your analysis. In your analysis include specifics about the ISO settings and flash used. Also include an analysis of depth of field. Write a summary in your word processing program and save it as ***4_Apply1_movement***. Include the images in the summary. Crop the images so that the focus is on the moving object and resize the images to an appropriate size for a document. *LO 4.3 and 4.5*

2. Take some pictures focusing on each of the principles of photographic composition listed below. Choose a good example and a bad example of each composition principle to submit. The following table shows the list of files that you should have when you have finished. Create this table in

Composition	Saved file name	Saved file name
Focal Point	**4_Apply2_good_focal_point**	**4_Apply2_bad_focal_point**
Rule of Thirds	**4_Apply2_good_rule_of_thirds**	**4_Apply2_bad_rule_of_thirds**
Background	**4_Apply2_good_background**	**4_Apply2_bad_background**
Unifying Elements	**4_Apply2_good_unifying_elements**	**4_Apply2_bad_unifying_elements**
Distance	**4_Apply2_good_distance**	**4_Apply2_bad_distance**

a word processing document. Replace the image name with the actual image. Crop and resize appropriately for a word processing document. Save as **4_Apply2_composition**. *LO 4.1, 4.2, 4.3, 4.4, and 4.5*

3. Edit images **01edit**, **02edit**, **03edit**, **04edit**, **05edit**, and **06edit** using image editing software. Use cropping, light, and color adjustment on each image. Resize each image. When finished, using image editing software, create an 800- × 800-pixel artboard for a collage. Insert each image to form a collage. When you have finished placing all six images on the artboard, crop the collage to an appropriate size. Save as **4_Apply3_edited** in JPG format. *LO 4.3*

4. From your data files, open **01flower** and **02flower**. Study the images and then answer the following questions about each image:
   Was the rule of thirds applied?
   Is the focal point obvious?
   Is there a good background or is it distracting?
   Are there any unifying elements in the image?
   Is the distance from the focal point appropriate?

   Include a summary for each of the images that answers the following questions:
   What made it a good image?
   What could be done to make it a better image?

   Save as **4_Apply4_critique**. *LO 4.3*

5. Using image editing software, make light and color adjustments to the following data files: **01light**, **02light**, and **03light**. If a histogram is available in your image editing software, use the histogram to adjust shadows and highlights. Change the brightness and contrast on at least one image. Practice adjusting image colors by changing from RGB to CMYK or grayscale. Adjust the saturation of at least one of the images. When you are satisfied that you have improved the image, place the images in a 4- × 16-inch artboard and save as **4_Apply5_light_adjustment** in the native format of your image editing software. *LO 4.3*

6. Open **horizon.jpg** from your data files. Adjust the image using channels and curves four different times. Each time you have finished making an adjustment to your satisfaction, save the image and start again with the original image. Before saving each of the images, resize to half the original size. Save the adjusted images as **4_Apply6_adjusted_horizon1**, **4_Apply6_adjusted_horizon2**, **4_Apply6_adjusted_horizon3**, and **4_Apply6_adjusted_horizon4**. Use the default file format of your image editing software. While making the adjustments, consider how the adjustment might make you feel if used in business in a presentation, report, web page, or other document. Insert the four images and the original image into a document that is 4 x 6 inches. The images can overlap. Save the image as **4_Apply6_horizon_collage**. *LO 4.3 and 4.4*

Explore

1. Visit a camera store or a local store that carries cameras. Compare three SLR cameras and three point-and-shoot cameras. Collect brochures on each if you can or take notes. Compare the following: megapixels, lens size, ISO settings, aperture, white balance, cost of the camera.

   Organize your information in a word processing document. Include an image of each of the cameras that were compared. Save as **4_Explore1_ camera_comparison**. *LO 4.1*

2. Research storage media for cameras. Include in your research the type of storage media, storage capacity, cost, and where you found the media. Include at least ten items on your list. Organize your information into a report, table, or slide show. If time permits, present what you have learned to the class. Save as **4_Explore2_storage_media**. *LO 4.2*

3. Read at least two articles on camera care and safety. Create a list of basic camera care and safety practices from the information found in this chapter. Add at least ten more statements about camera care found in your reading. Cite your resources in MLA style. Save as **4_Explore3_camera_care**. *LO 4.1*

Academic Connections

Communications: Choose a topic from this chapter to research. Read an article on the topic. Paraphrase the article with a citation in MLA style. If needed, read a review of paraphrasing tips or discuss paraphrasing tips with your instructor. Save your paraphrased article as **4_AC_communications**.

Science: Open **aquatic_science** from the data files for this chapter. Briefly answer each question in the left column. Insert an appropriate image in the top row. It can be an image you have taken or one that you have found on the Internet. Include a title in the first row. Save as **4_AC_science**.

Chapter 5

Color in Digital Media

Lesson 5.1 **Understanding RGB, CMYK, and HSB**

Lesson 5.2 **Recognizing Color Theory Terms and Concepts**

Lesson 5.3 **Using Color Matching Systems**

Color is an essential element of many different types of digital media projects from website designs, to business presentations, to high-school textbooks. Color can grab attention and it can set a mood. This chapter will give you a foundation of knowledge about color that will be useful whether your digital media projects are online or in print.

Creations/Shutterstock.com

Learning Outcomes

▶ **5.1** Understand the difference between RGB, CMYK, and HSB color models.

▶ **5.2** Specify the appropriate color mode based on output.

▶ **5.3** Become familiar with basic color terminology.

▶ **5.4** Identify and use basic color theory to choose colors.

▶ **5.5** Recognize the advantages of color matching systems.

Key Terms

- additive color mixing
- analogous colors
- brightness
- CMYK color model
- color harmony
- color mode
- color model
- color theme
- color theory
- color wheel
- complementary colors
- gamut
- grayscale
- HSB color model
- hue
- neutral color
- out of gamut
- Pantone Matching System (PMS)
- primary color
- RGB color model
- RGB triplet
- saturation
- secondary color
- shade
- spot colors
- subtractive color mixing
- tertiary color
- tint
- tone
- Web-safe colors

Reproduced by permission.

Lesson 5.1 ▶ Understanding RGB, CMYK, and HSB

One of the first things to decide when working with color in a digital media project is what color model to use. A **color model** is a group of colors identified in a way that computers can understand. So, instead of names like "red" or "blue," a color model identifies colors with a combination of numbers, kind of like a code. There are several different color models to choose from, but the three most common color models in digital media are RGB, CMYK, and HSB. Which color model you work in depends mostly on your final product. If you are making something that will be viewed on a screen, such as a website, you will use RGB. If you are creating something that will be sent to a printer, like a book, you should choose CMYK. But it is not enough to know only which color model is suited to which task. You will also need to know how the color models work so that you can use them effectively in your projects.

The RGB Color Model *LO 5.1*

To understand how the color models work, you'll need to recall some concepts from art and science classes. At some point, you likely learned that **primary colors** are basic colors that cannot be created by mixing other colors. You also learned that mixing two primary colors creates a **secondary color**. You may recall this in terms of something like "red + yellow = orange." If you remember this, you are familiar with the basic idea of color mixing: Combining colors creates new colors. In science class, you may have learned about the nature of light and how it can vary in terms of brightness or intensity.

Light is made up of different wavelengths, and, in what is called the visible spectrum, some of these wavelengths are associated with colors. All of these wavelengths combined create pure white light. But if certain wavelengths are blocked, humans perceive different colors. If all of these wavelengths are blocked, humans see black. This is called **additive color mixing**. These are the basic ideas behind the RGB color model. In the **RGB color model**, three primary colors of light—red, green, and blue—are mixed at different intensities to create a range of other colors and display them on a computer screen.

How a computer uses additive color mixing to display color on a computer screen is a complicated process, but to understand how RGB color works, you just need to know a few basics. Each pixel on a computer screen includes a red, a green, and a blue element. (See Figure 5.1.) Light shines through these elements to create red light, green light, and blue light. When the three colors of light mix in different combinations, they create different colors. Varying the intensity of the light coming through each color produces an even wider range of different colors. But how does the computer know how much light to shine through each primary color to create the color you want?

color model—A group of colors identified in a way that computers can understand.

primary color—A basic color that cannot be created by mixing other colors.

secondary color—A color created when two primary colors are mixed.

additive color mixing—Combining three different colors of light at different intensities to produce a whole range of other colors.

RGB color model—A color model that uses red, green, and blue primary colors plus different intensities of light to create colors on an electronic display like a computer screen.

© Cengage Learning, 2013

Figure 5.1 *Computer monitors display pixels that can be seen in photo enlargements.*

As mentioned earlier, the colors in a color model are identified not by names but by a combination of numbers that a computer can interpret. In the RGB color model, each primary color is assigned a number between 0 and 255. This number tells the computer how much light should come through that primary color; 0 indicates no light at all and 255 indicates full light. Together, the numbers assigned to the three primary colors make up what is called an **RGB triplet**. For example, R=155, G=109, B=214 is an RGB triplet. The RGB triplet is the "name" of a color in the RGB color model.

RGB triplet—The combination of numbers indicating light intensity for the red, green, and blue primary colors in the RGB color model and representing a certain color within the model. Can be considered the "name" of a color in the RGB color model.

For instance, a computer reads the RGB triplet in the previous example, adjusts the amount of light coming through each primary color element in the screen, and displays what we might call "lavender." Figure 5.2 shows the relationship between the RGB triplet in the previous example and the color it represents on the computer screen. Changing the value for any of the primary colors changes the color on the screen. In different combinations of light, the three RGB primary colors mix to create more than 16 million colors.

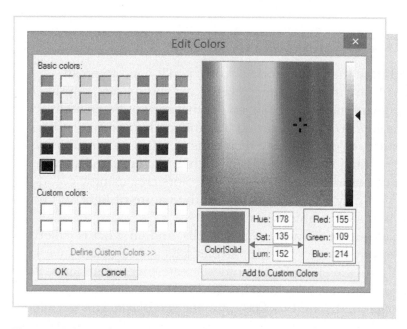

Figure 5.2 *The numbers for each primary color in the RGB triplet tell the computer how much light to project through each color. The result is a certain color from the RGB color model, in this case, lavender. Changing any of the values for red, green, or blue changes the color on the screen.*

You can get a better idea about how RGB color works by experimenting. If you have access to a Windows-based computer, open the drawing program Microsoft Paint and select Edit Colors on the Home tab to display the Edit Colors dialog box. (This is what appears in Figure 5.2.) Experiment with changing the values for red, green, and blue. Remember, the values for each primary color can vary between 0 and 255, with 0 being none of that color in the mix and 255 being the most of that color in the mix. Notice how the sample color box changes as you enter different values for each primary color. What values do you need to enter for each primary color to create black? How can you create white? Knowing what you do about how the numbers in the RGB triplet relate to light, do you know why a certain combination of values creates black and another creates white?

The CMYK Color Model *LO 5.1*

Like RGB, the CMYK color model uses primary colors to create a whole range of other colors. However, instead of mixing colors of light, the CMYK color model produces colors by mixing color pigments, like ink or paint. When printed on material such as paper, ink actually absorbs light, blocking certain wavelengths from being reflected back to your eye. You see the reflected wavelengths as color. Mixing pigments together in different amounts changes how much light is absorbed and creates a whole range of colors. This is called **subtractive color mixing**. You can think of the difference between additive and subtractive color in this way: additive color is created when light comes from inside a source; subtractive color is created when light comes from outside a source.

In the **CMYK color model**, three primary pigment colors—cyan, magenta, and yellow—plus black mix in different combinations to create all of the CMYK colors. (The "K" in CMYK stands for "key"; the key color to which the other colors align during printing is black.) The scale for each pigment is 0 to 100 percent, with 0 percent being none of that color and 100 percent being the maximum amount. Similar to an RGB triplet, a CMYK color is expressed like this: C=49, M=63, Y=28, K=15, where each number indicates a percentage of that color. This particular CMYK combination represents a purple color (see Figure 5.3). Varying the percentage of any primary color or black in the mix changes the color.

You can experiment with CMYK colors the same way you experimented with RGB colors. Find a program that provides a CMYK option such as Adobe Illustrator, Adobe InDesign, or a free, Web-based program. Navigate to the color palette or color picker and practice

subtractive color mixing— Mixing primary pigment colors to absorb different amounts of light and create a range of colors.

CMYK color model—A color model based on cyan, magenta, yellow, and black pigments used to create full color on printed materials.

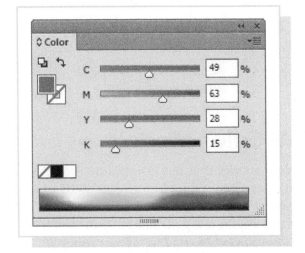

Figure 5.3 *This color picker from Adobe Illustrator shows how the percentages of each CMYK color mix to create the color in the sample box toward the top left of the image.*

changing the percentages of each primary color and black to see how the mixed color changes. What values do you need to enter to create black? What values do you need to enter to create white? Can you guess why these values make these colors?

Impact

Four-Color Printing

CMYK is not only the name of a color model; it is also the name of a color printing process. CMYK printing is also sometimes called four-color printing because it uses the four basic colors of the CMYK color model to print full color on a medium such as paper, canvas, or even plastic. These days, CMYK printing usually begins with a digital file that includes an image to be transferred to the printed material. (In this context, an image refers to the words, graphics, photographs, and other elements that make up whatever is to be printed.) The color information in the file is divided into what are called separations. In four-color printing, there is one separation for each color: cyan, magenta, yellow, and black. Think of this as "unmixing" the colors in a four-color image. (Figure 5.4 shows a CMYK image and its corresponding separations.)

Each of the four separations is transferred to one of four individual printing plates. On the press, the corresponding ink color is applied to the plate: cyan is applied to the cyan plate, magenta to the magenta plate, and so on. The ink "sticks" to the image on the plate. As paper (or whatever is being printed) runs under the plates, the ink from each plate is layered on the paper. The result of the layered inks is a full-color image. It is like "remixing" the colors.

Figure 5.4 *In the CMYK printing process, electronic files are separated into the four main CMYK colors and then reassembled on a press.*

HSB, HSL, and HSV Color Models *LO 5.1*

As indicated above, RGB is a color model that lets computers read and display colors. But humans don't perceive colors in terms of RGB triplets or even in the combinations of CMYK inks, for that matter. When you want to adjust the color of the sky in a digital image, you don't think, "It should really be more R=23, G=174, B=232." You probably think it should be brighter or darker or it should be more colorful or less colorful. Humans perceive color based on a combination of three qualities: hue, saturation, and brightness. To make it easier to adjust colors on a computer screen according to the way people perceive color, software engineers developed a color model based on these qualities. In some software applications this is named the **HSB color model** for hue, saturation, and brightness. Some programs name it HSV for hue, saturation, and value. And others name it HSL for hue, saturation, and luminance. Unfortunately, the definitions for brightness, value, and luminance are not standardized across software and there can be some slight technical differences among the three. But for the purposes of this class, you can think of them as roughly the same. This chapter will use the HSB color model terminology.

In the HSB color model, **hue** refers to the general color of an object. Within the HSB model, hue is expressed as a degree between 0 and 360. **Saturation** refers to the intensity of a hue. Saturation varies on a scale from 0 to 100 percent, beginning with no color at all (gray) and ending with full color. **Brightness** refers to how light or dark a color is. Brightness varies on a scale from 0 to 100 percent, beginning with black and ending with white. The combination of these elements is what defines a color in the HSB color model.

HSB color model—A color model based on human perception of color that uses hue, saturation, and brightness to define a color.

hue—In the HSB color model, the general color expressed by a value between 0 and 360 degrees.

saturation—In the HSB color model, the intensity of a hue on a scale from 0 to 100%.

brightness—In the HSB color model, the measure of how light or dark a color is on a scale of 0 to 100%.

Selecting the Appropriate Color Model *LO 5.2*

As mentioned earlier, the color model you work with for your digital media project will depend on the type of project. Now that you've learned a little more about how RGB and CMYK colors are produced, it should be clear which color model matches which type of project. You use RGB for projects that will be viewed on an electronic screen such as a website, a slideshow presentation (Figure 5.5), or a video because RGB uses light to create color and an electronic display has a light source. You use CMYK for any project that is destined to be printed on a commercial press, such as a book, a magazine, a poster, or a brochure because CMYK uses pigments like ink or paint to apply color to a printed material like paper, canvas, plastic, etc. It's important to make the right choice for a few reasons:

Figure 5.5 *For a presentation, you would choose the RGB color model.*

- As you read in the Impact sidebar on the previous page, a printing press uses only CMYK ink colors to reproduce images on paper. If you send a file that uses RGB colors to the printer, it won't work. The colors in the file will have to be converted to CMYK to be printed. (Note that this does not apply to sending files to a desktop printer.)

- The range of colors that a color model can produce is called a **gamut**. There are many more colors in the RGB gamut than in the CMYK gamut. This means it is possible to produce RGB colors that do not exist in CMYK. This is called **out of gamut**. If you choose RGB colors and later have to convert them to CMYK, you risk having colors that are out of gamut. In that case, you would have to choose new colors. In addition, RGB colors and CMYK colors are

gamut—The range of colors that can be produced by the primary colors in a particular color model.

out of gamut—Refers to colors that are part of the range of one color model but not another.

not exact matches. So if you convert an RGB color to CMYK, the color may not be what you were expecting. You can avoid these problems by selecting and working with the proper color model in the first place.

- Choosing RGB color for files that will be viewed on a screen is important, too. RGB files are normally smaller than CMYK files and load onto screens faster.

Once you determine which color model best suits your project, you indicate your choice by selecting the color mode in the digital media software you are using to create your piece. The **color mode** tells the computer which color model to use to represent colors. Your computer then stores that data (the RGB triplets or the CMYK percentages) in your project's electronic file. Logically enough, color modes are named for the color models they represent. So if your project will use the RGB color model, you select RGB mode in your software. Similarly, if you want to use the CMYK color model, you select CMYK mode. (Note that HSB is not a color mode. It is used mostly to make editing color easier and can be used in either RGB or CMYK mode. The computer links the HSB values to RGB and/or CMYK values as you adjust the color using HSB.)

color mode—A way to indicate to a computer what color model to use when representing colors.

checkpoint

What are the differences between RGB, CMYK, and HSB?

ACTIVITY 5.1 ▶ RGB vs. CMYK

1. Open an image editing program and then open *lake* from your data files.

2. Create a word processing document with the title **RGB vs. CMYK**. Insert a table with five rows and three columns. Label the three columns with the column headings: **Color**, **RGB**, and **CMYK**.

3. Using the Eyedropper tool, choose four colors from the lake image. Key the RGB and CMYK numbers shown on the Color Picker for each of the four colors with a description of the color in the first column.

4. Save the document as *5_ Activity1_lake*.

5. Use one of the RGB numbers that you wrote down and the Text tool to label the photograph with a title.

6. Save the photograph as *5_Activity1_lake.jpg*.

Lesson 5.2 ▸ Recognizing Color Theory Terms and Concepts

As mentioned in the previous lesson, there are more than 16 million possible colors in the RGB gamut and, although more limited, millions of potential colors in the CMYK gamut as well. With so many to choose from, how do you select the best colors for your project? A good place to start is with some basic knowledge of color theory. **Color theory** is a set of guidelines about how colors communicate feelings and how they can be combined to create the best look and feel for a project.

color theory—A set of guidelines about how colors communicate feelings and how they combine to create the best look and feel for a project.

The Color Wheel and Basic Color Terminology *LO 5.3*

You can begin exploring color theory by thinking about the color wheel. A **color wheel** begins with three primary colors. As mentioned earlier in the chapter, when two primary colors are mixed, the result is a secondary color, which is placed between the primary colors on a color wheel. When a primary color and secondary color mix, the result is a **tertiary color**, which is placed on the color wheel between the primary and secondary colors used to create it. Figure 5.6 shows a color wheel based on the RGB color model.

color wheel—A visual representation of primary, secondary, and tertiary colors that can be useful for understanding and using basic concepts in color theory.

tertiary color—The color created when a primary and a secondary color are mixed.

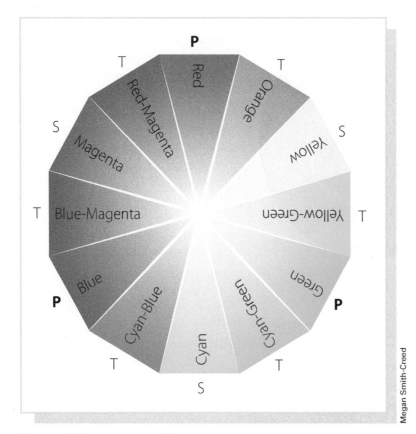

Megan Smith-Creed

Figure 5.6 *A color wheel based on the RGB color model. "P" stands for primary color, "S" stands for secondary color, and "T" stands for tertiary color.*

hue—In color theory, another word for color.

neutral colors—In color theory, black, white, and gray used to change the nature of hues, creating shades, tints, and tones.

shade—A hue mixed with black.

tint—A hue mixed with white.

tone—A hue mixed with gray.

grayscale—A range of grays from white to black with all the variations in between.

In color theory, colors on a color wheel are referred to as hues. **Hue** is basically just another word for color and you can use the terms interchangeably. (This is just slightly different than a "hue" in the HSB color model.) However, it's important to note that black, white, and gray are *not* hues in color theory; they are **neutral colors**. Neutrals are mixed with hues to change the nature of a color. For instance, a hue mixed with black creates a **shade** of that color. Navy blue is a shade of blue. A hue mixed with white produces a **tint** of that color. Pink is a tint of red. Gray is an interesting neutral because it can be a tint of black or a mixture of two complementary colors. When gray is mixed with a hue, the result is a **tone** of that color. A range of grays, as in a black and white photo for example, is called **grayscale**.

The Traditional Color Wheel

In art class, you probably learned about the traditional color wheel that was developed by artists before the RGB and CMYK color models were created. The traditional color wheel starts with red, blue, and yellow as the primary colors. Figure 5.7 shows a traditional color wheel.

Notice that the complementary colors on the traditional color wheel are different than on the RGB color wheel in Figure 5.6. Although the complementary colors may vary on different color wheels depending on what color model the color wheel represents, the principles of color theory involving general categories such as complementary colors work the same. In this chapter, the RGB color wheel is featured as an example because it is the main color model in the digital world. However, many artists and designers still use the traditional color wheel and you may find it helpful for developing color themes in your projects as well.

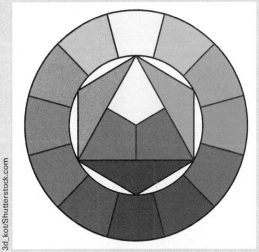

Figure 5.7 *The traditional color wheel is based on red, blue, and yellow as the primary colors.*

The color wheel in Figure 5.6 can be useful for understanding the relationships between different colors. Hues opposite each other on the wheel are called **complementary colors**. As you can see in Figure 5.6, this means that in the RGB model, blue and yellow are complementary colors,

complementary colors— Colors that are opposite one another on a color wheel.

for example. Hues next to each other on a color wheel are called **analogous colors**. In the RGB example above, red and orange are analogous colors. You'll read more about these terms a little later in this lesson.

analogous colors—Colors that are next to one another on a color wheel.

Color and Its Meaning *LO 5.4*

Colors can produce different impressions on the people who view them. Just what impression a color makes on a person can vary based on age, gender, culture, and personal experience. However, color theory indicates certain colors and color combinations seem to cause similar reactions in most people. For example, people often view orange, red, and yellow as warm colors. This could be because humans associate these colors with elements that are actually warm, like sunshine and fire. But color associations go beyond just the "temperature" of a color. Certain hues are also associated with certain emotions or states of being. Table 5.1 includes just a few colors and some examples of what they can communicate.

Table 5.1 *Colors have many associations with moods, emotions, and states of being.*

SAMPLE	COLOR NAME	A FEW ASSOCIATIONS
	Red	Stimulating. Suggests anger, excitement, or danger.
	Orange	Increases mental sharpness; associated with autumn.
	Yellow	Creates harmony or anxiety, depending on the brightness; sunshine.
	Green	Gives a soothing feeling; associated with nature.
	Blue	Creates tranquility or peacefulness, but also sadness; associated with water.
	Purple	Suggests royalty; creativity.
	Black	Denotes elegance or evil. In some cultures, mourning.
	White	Represents purity, cleanliness. In some cultures, mourning.

Table 5.1 is far from complete, but as you can see, a single hue can suggest a wide range of feelings both good and bad. What a color suggests can change depending on tone, shade, tint, or context. For example, think about the different impression a shade of blue such as navy has compared to a tint such as pastel blue. What do you associate with each color? Which shade would you more likely see on a baby announcement and which one on a graduation announcement? The Internet is full of websites detailing color associations. Write down your impressions of your favorite color and then use a search engine to see if color theory matches your ideas. Make a chart of colors and

their associations to use as a reference when choosing hues for different projects. Once you learn more about what colors "say," you can choose the hues that will help your digital media projects have the impact you want.

Think About It

Color Preferences

How do you respond to color? Are you more likely to buy a product because it is a certain color? Does the background color of a website make it more interesting? What makes you choose one color over another?

Color Themes *LO 5.4*

color theme—A combination of different hues that work together to create color harmony.

color harmony—A cohesive and pleasing combination created by a group of colors.

Normally when you design something using color, you will use a color theme. Very simply put, a **color theme** is a combination of colors. The goal of a color theme is to create color harmony. **Color harmony** occurs when a group of colors create a cohesive and pleasing combination. But randomly grouping colors doesn't always create color harmony. Fortunately, you can rely on some traditional formulas to create harmony in your color themes. These themes are covered in this section. As you become more experienced working with color, you'll learn more complex ways of combining colors to create harmony in your designs. But these basic formulas will help get you started. Keep in mind that all of these color themes can be improved by including a neutral color such as black, white, or gray in addition to the hues you select.

Monochromatic Color Theme

A monochromatic color theme includes a single color combined with shades and tints of that color. It is the most subdued color theme and doesn't offer a lot of contrast in a design. (Contrast in a design is what draws attention and makes certain elements stand out.) But a monochromatic color theme is easy to create and can make designs look elegant and calm.

Complementary Color Theme

At its simplest, a complementary color theme includes two colors that sit directly across from one another on a color wheel. For example, yellow and blue from the RGB color wheel in Figure 5.6 form a complementary color theme. To make a design more interesting, you can expand a complementary color theme by using different shades, tints, and tones of the two complementary colors in the theme. The contrast between complementary colors makes these themes vibrant and gives a sense of excitement to a design. However, complementary color themes work best if you choose one main color and use the other color for smaller details, especially if there are only two colors in your theme and no shades or tints. (See Figure 5.8.)

Analogous Color Theme

The analogous color theme includes colors that are next to one another on a color wheel. For example, blue, blue-green, and green from the traditional color wheel in Figure 5.7 are an analogous color theme. Because the colors are similar hues, analogous color themes create a sense of calm and unity. However, they don't have as much contrast as complementary color themes. To get the best effect, you can choose a main color and use the others as accents and/or vary the shades and tints of the hues in the theme to create contrast and energy in your designs.

Triadic Color Theme

The triadic color theme is a little trickier to create, but also a little more unexpected than the other traditional color themes. The triadic color theme includes three evenly separated hues from a color wheel. For example, the primary colors red, yellow, and blue are a triadic color theme because they are each separated by three other colors on the traditional color wheel. Likewise, violet, green, and orange are a triadic color theme. These themes have a lot of contrast and energy. As with the other color themes, you can expand a triadic theme by using different tints and shades of the hues you've selected. This can also help calm a triadic color theme if it is too high-contrast or "loud."

Color Theme Tools

While you can develop your own themes manually in many digital media software programs, you can also automatically generate color themes using online tools. For example, Adobe Color is a free, Web-based color tool you can use to automatically generate a color theme by selecting a base color and then selecting a color rule such as complementary or triadic. Adobe Color can also extract a color theme from a photo based on a mood you designate such as "bright" or "muted," or you can use the Adobe Color app with your smartphone or tablet to pick up colors in a room or other location and create a theme from them. Alternatively, you can browse through color themes created by other Color users.

Once you have selected the colors for a theme, you can save that theme in the cloud. It then becomes available in Adobe Creative Cloud applications such as Illustrator and InDesign. Explore Adobe Color or look for similar online tools to learn more about how color themes work.

Figure 5.8 *Choosing an appropriate color theme can make a design more interesting.*

ACTIVITY 5.2 ▶ **Color Themes**

1. Open an image editing program.
2. Create four rectangles of analogous colors to use in a presentation that will deliver bad news.
3. Save as *5_Activity2_bad_news.psd*.
4. Create two rectangles of complementary colors to use in a presentation that will deliver good news that may generate excitement.
5. Save as *5_Activity2_good_news.psd*.

Lesson 5.3 ▶ Using Color Matching Systems

As you select color for your projects, keep in mind that a carefully selected color or set of colors may not appear the same in different viewing situations. You may have noticed how color seen outside in sunlight appears quite different from color seen under fluorescent or incandescent light. The same is true in digital media where colors can look different depending on many factors such as the kind of screen someone is using to view a website or the kind of paper that is used for printing a magazine. There are some very sophisticated tools in digital media design software to help make sure that the colors you select are the colors your ultimate viewers will see in a project. These color systems help you predict how the colors you choose will look in the finished product. This section covers just a couple of simple ways to ensure that the colors you select come out the way you envision them.

Web-Safe Colors *LO 5.5*

Web-safe colors—216 colors that all users can see, regardless of their computer displays.

At one point, Web designers were very concerned about color matching because not as many computer displays were able to show the wide range of colors that most are able to display today. This meant that colors chosen on a more powerful computer system would look much different when viewed on other less advanced systems. To address this concern, designers and developers experimented with RGB colors and came up with the **Web-safe color** set. Designers could rely on the 216 Web-safe colors in the set to be accurate even on the most limited computer screen. As computer video cards became more powerful and as displays using true color (32 bit) or high color (24 bit) became more common, the use of "safe" colors became less of a concern. Still, some digital media design programs have a feature that automatically limits the color choices to Web-safe colors. Figure 5.9 shows a selection of these Web-safe colors.

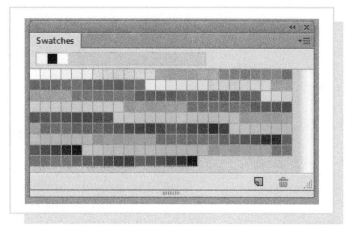

Figure 5.9 *Web-safe colors provide a limited palette of colors.*

Pantone Matching System *LO 5.5*

While concern about color accuracy is subsiding somewhat in the Web design community, it's still an issue for print media designers. Colors on a computer monitor (which are represented by RGB colors) may not match what is produced on a professional printing press using CMYK inks. In certain situations, it is important that the color on the printed material matches exactly what the designer intended—on a company logo, for example. To address concerns like this, standardized color systems and associated ink formulations have been developed to identify and label specific colors in the design and printing industry. The colors in these systems are called **spot colors**.

spot colors—Colors that are generated by a single ink, rather than created by blending ink colors.

Pantone Matching System (PMS)—A standard set of colors and associated inks that make it easy to reproduce a color in printed material consistently.

The most widely known color matching system is the **Pantone Matching System**, more commonly referred to as PMS color. There are more than 1,000 PMS colors. When you designate a spot color based on a Pantone color, a printer uses a single ink that matches that color rather than creating the color using the CMYK process. This means that a plate specifically for that ink color is added to the press to print anything that was created using that PMS color. Most major digital paint, drawing, and design programs, like those from Adobe Creative Suite, allow you to designate PMS color in your projects. Here are a couple of things to keep in mind when choosing to work with spot colors:

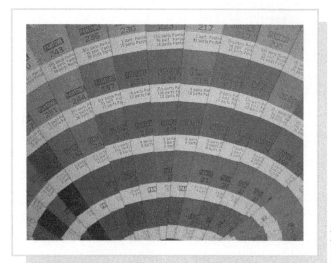

- Use a printed PMS swatch book to choose your colors (see Figure 5.10). One of the reasons to use spot color is that the monitor makes it difficult to determine how a printed color will look. You can't rely on the monitor to show PMS colors accurately.

- Because a printer has to add a specific plate to print spot color, it can be expensive.

Susan Lake

Figure 5.10 *Pantone charts or sample cards allow you to select an exact color for use by a printer.*

ACTIVITY 5.3 ▶ Web-Safe Colors

1. Use image editing software to create a 5- × 10-inch document.

2. Use the Rectangle tool to draw a 2.5- × 2.5-inch square, starting in the upper left corner of the document. Choose any color to fill the rectangle.

3. Repeat the square on the right side next to the first square. Use the tools available to change the color to a Web-safe color, allowing the software to make the adjustment.

4. Repeat steps 2 and 3 until you have four square samples of color on the left and, on the right, a very similar color that is Web-safe.

5. Note the very subtle differences in color between some of the squares and that, in some cases, there is no visible difference at all.

6. Save as *5_Activity3_web_safe.psd*.

De-Stressing

It can sometimes be difficult to manage the demands of a job, family, friends, and your personal life. Everyone has a bad day every now and then, but sometimes the pressure can get to be a little difficult to handle. If you get too stressed over your job, unfortunately your work can suffer—which in turn will simply increase your anxiety.

It is possible to take your work seriously but not become overly stressed about it. When you feel overburdened, try a few simple tactics to relieve the pressure: Keep your sense of humor, take a coffee break with a coworker, go for a walk, or listen to music. Try to stay focused and use your time wisely. Above all, make sure to eat right and exercise daily; good nutrition and physical fitness are great stress-busters.

Skills in Action: What do you do to relieve stress? Create a collage of calming images you can look at when you're stressed. Choose a calming color theme for your collage.

Key Concepts

▶ The RGB color model uses red, green, and blue and different intensities of light to create a range of colors. It's used to show color on an electronic display. *LO 5.1*

▶ The CMYK color model uses cyan, magenta, yellow, and black pigments to create a range of colors. CMYK is used to reproduce colors on printed materials. *LO 5.1*

▶ HSB is a color model based on human perception of color (hue, saturation, and brightness). It is used to make adjusting colors easier and can be used in either RGB or CMYK mode. *LO 5.1*

▶ The color mode tells the computer which color model data to use to represent colors. *LO 5.2*

▶ The two main color modes are RGB and CMYK. You use RGB mode for projects that will be viewed on a screen and CMYK mode for files that will be printed. *LO 5.2*

▶ Using a color wheel and understanding concepts such as complementary and analogous colors as well as terms such as shade, tint, and tone can help you recognize and use color theory in your projects. *LO 5.3*

▶ You can use different colors to set different moods in your projects. *LO 5.4*

▶ Using color themes such as monochromatic, complementary, analogous, and triadic can create color harmony in your projects. *LO 5.4*

▶ Color matching systems such as Web-safe colors and PMS make it easier to accurately reproduce colors no matter where they are viewed or where they are printed. *LO 5.5*

Review and Discuss

1. Explain the difference between complementary and analogous color themes. *LO 5.3*

2. Define the triadic color theme. *LO 5.4*

3. Summarize the three most common color models in digital media. *LO 5.1*

4. Explain the scale for RGB colors. *LO 5.1*

5. Describe how the color mode is useful. *LO 5.2*

6. Explain "out of gamut." *LO 5.3*

7. Define RGB and CMYK and explain the differences in the use of the two. *LO 5.1*

8. Detail how Adobe Color helps to generate a color theme. *LO 5.4*

9. Describe the HSB color model. *LO 5.1*

10. Cite the determining factors in what message is communicated by color. *LO 5.4*

11. Summarize the relationship between different colors and how those relationships are determined. *LO 5.4*

12. In your own words, explain Web-safe colors. *LO 5.2*

13. Differentiate between the ways in which a computer screen and paper send color images to our brain. *LO 5.2 and 5.3*

14. Detail how color is reproduced on a printed page in the CMYK printing process. *LO 5.1 and 5.2*

15. Describe the Pantone Matching System. *LO 5.5*

 Apply

1. Create a default size image with a background and foreground color and with the text *Health Insurance Rates on the Rise*. Consider an audience's likely response to this topic in determining colors. Save as **5_Apply1_health_insurance.jpg**. Create a second image with the text *Pay Increase Highest Ever*, again considering the audience when selecting colors. Save as **5_Apply1_pay_increase.jpg**. *LO 5.4*

2. Use image editing software to create a new document that is the default size. Draw a variety of six shapes on your document. They can be different shapes and sizes. Use a color theme, as discussed in the textbook, to fill each shape. Label the image with an explanation of your theme. Save as **5_Apply2_themes**. *LO 5.4*

3. Use image editing software to create an 8.5- × 10-inch document. From your data files, select and place **mountain.jpg** in the middle of the document. Consider that this image will be used on a web page to advertise a wedding destination. Draw some rectangles around the image filled with colors that could be used for text, objects, and other accents. In each rectangle, add text explaining briefly why the color was chosen. Consider Web-safe colors only. Save as **5_Apply3_wedding**. *LO 5.2 and 5.4*

4. You have been asked to give ideas for colors to use in a brochure for the opening of a new podiatry clinic. Find a local clinic on the Web, and using their logo to get started, create a set of three complementary colors. Reference the website at the bottom of your images. Create another set of three analogous colors. Use image editing software to insert the logo into the middle of the document. Draw shapes around the image and fill with the color. Use text in the middle of each shape to document the RGB color number for each color. Save as **5_Apply4_analogous** and **5_Apply4_complementary** using the default file type of the image editing software. *LO 5.1, 5.3, and 5.4*

Explore

1. Visit a favorite website. On the homepage of the website, determine what two or three colors are used most often. You can right click on the website and choose View Source to write down the exact RGB numbers. Determine what colors capture your attention on the website before looking at the actual RGB numbers. Create a rectangle with text that explains why you think the designer used these colors and whether it was a good choice. What would you do differently? Include a reference at the bottom of your image to the website. Save as **5_Explore1_color_use** with the default file type of your image editing software. *LO 5.3 and 5.4*

2. Explore the Adobe Color website. Write a 200-word summary of what you learned about color themes. Include the resource at the bottom of your summary in MLA style. What did you learn from using the interactive color feature? What are some of the color rules of Adobe Color? How do you think those rules could apply to your projects? Save your summary as **5_Explore2_color**. *LO 5.4*

3. Search for color trends. Read and summarize what you have learned about color trends. This can be in a specific area, such as fashion, or generally used colors and how trends affect what is being used. Use at least two resources that are cited in MLA style. The summary should be at least 200 words. Save as **5_Explore3_color_trends**. *LO 5.3 and 5.4*

Academic Connections

Communications: Write a letter, in correct personal business letter format, to your instructor. Include at least three paragraphs. Summarize the important points of what you have learned in this chapter about communicating with color. Save as **5_AC_communications**.

Writing: Write a journal reflecting on what you have learned in this chapter. What did you find the most interesting? What did you find the most difficult? What would you like to learn more about? Use color in your reflective journal to demonstrate how you felt while learning the material. You can use a variety of colors by changing the color of a word, phrase, or entire paragraph. Explain why you used the color that you used. Save as **5_AC_writing**.

Chapter 6

Raster Editing

Creations/Shutterstock.com

Raster editing is an essential skill for many digital media professionals. This chapter introduces some common photo editing concepts and features that are useful whether you end up designing websites, books, smartphone applications, or any other media that incorporates photos. If you've used photo editing software before, even just the software that came with your camera, some of what is covered in this chapter will be familiar since so many raster editing programs include similar tools. On the other hand, if photo editing is entirely new to you, the material in this chapter may help as you start exploring raster editing software, whether free cloud software or a full-blown digital editing package such as Adobe Photoshop.

Learning Outcomes

▶ **6.1** Be familiar with a basic raster editing workspace and common tools.

▶ **6.2** Select portions of an image for editing by using selection tools.

▶ **6.3** Recognize common settings for certain selection tools.

▶ **6.4** Make and refine selections by using Quick Mask mode.

▶ **6.5** Adjust levels, brightness, and contrast in photos using curves.

▶ **6.6** Use a cropping tool to adjust photo composition.

▶ **6.7** Edit a photo by using retouch tools.

▶ **6.8** Understand the usefulness of layers and layer masks in nondestructive editing.

▶ **6.9** Use layers and layer masks to edit digital images.

▶ **6.10** Manage file size in files with multiple layers.

Key Terms

- anti-aliasing
- background color
- background layer
- contiguous
- feathering
- flatten
- foreground color
- hand tool
- highlights
- layer mask
- layers
- midtones
- nondestructive edit
- quick masks
- retouch tool
- selection tool
- shadows
- tolerance
- zoom tool

Chances are if you own a digital camera, you've used some sort of raster editing program to manipulate your pictures. Perhaps you've used editing software that came with your camera or cloud software. These user-friendly software programs are handy for the most common photo editing tasks. They are also cost-effective since many are free to the public or available for a small subscription fee. However, if you continue to develop as a digital media artist who will work with raster images professionally, it is essential that you become familiar with full-blown raster editing software such as Adobe Photoshop. Programs like Photoshop are extremely powerful and offer a wide range of editing tools that you just can't access in most free raster editing programs.

As you progress in your digital media studies and career, you'll likely take classes entirely devoted to the ins and outs of raster editing programs . . . and even then you may not learn everything these programs can do! This chapter will introduce a few editing tools and features, but it will cover only a small fraction of what is possible with the powerful raster editing programs. It will be important for you to seek out other sources to learn more about how to use these particular programs.

Lesson 6.1 ▶ Becoming Familiar with the Raster Editing Workspace *LO 6.1*

The workspace is the window where you edit images in a raster editing program. Most raster editing programs include some combination of a main viewing area and a selection of tools, menus, panels, and dialog boxes. The user interface differs from program to program and sometimes can be customized to suit your needs. But many photo editing programs use similar tools and techniques, so your familiarity with one program will be useful when you work in a new program for the first time. Figure 6.1 shows an Adobe Photoshop workspace. The Application bar houses drop-down menus with options and features you can use to alter the workspace and perform a huge variety of tasks in Photoshop.

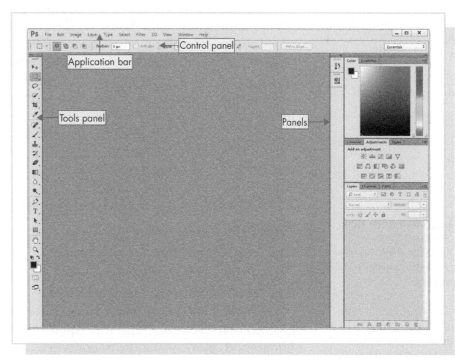

Figure 6.1 *The workspace in many raster editing programs will include elements like those in the Adobe Photoshop workspace shown here, although each program will have a different user interface.*

Figure 6.2 *You can use a zoom tool like this one in Photoshop to magnify or reduce the view of an image.*

Figure 6.3 *You can use a hand tool like this one in Photoshop to move an image around the viewing area.*

zoom tool—Navigation tool that magnifies or reduces the view of an image.

hand tool—Navigation tool that moves an image around in a viewing area.

foreground color—The color that appears when one paints, draws, or fills an image in a raster editing program.

background color—The color "behind" a raster image that appears when one erases or cuts a selection from the background layer of an image.

The Tools panel groups the most common tools used in Photoshop. Each time you select a different tool, the Control panel below the Application bar changes to reflect the settings for that specific tool. In Figure 6.1, three different panels with editing options are displayed on the right side of the workspace: the Color panel, the Adjustments panel, and the Layers panel. You'll learn more about using specific tools and panels to edit images later in this chapter. But before you learn about editing images, it may be helpful to become familiar with some common navigation tools and with the concept of background and foreground, which so many raster editing programs use, in conjunction with tools, to manipulate images.

Navigation Tools *LO 6.1*

Navigation tools help you move around the workspace. A zoom tool is a useful feature available in most raster editing programs. Frequently represented by a magnifying glass, a **zoom tool** (Figure 6.2) enables you to magnify or reduce the view of an image. In Photoshop, when you click the Zoom tool on the Tools panel, options for that tool appear in the Control panel. Select the Zoom In tool (magnifying glass with a plus sign) or the Zoom Out tool (magnifying glass with a minus sign) from the Control panel as necessary. The pointer changes to match your selection. Click or click-and-drag to zoom in or out of the image. You can also toggle between the Zoom In and Zoom Out tools by holding down the Alt key (Windows) or the Option key (Mac OS).

Another fairly common navigation tool in many raster editing software programs is a **hand tool** (Figure 6.3). A hand tool (many times represented by a small hand icon) moves an image around in the viewing area. If you've used an application such as Google Maps before, you're very likely familiar with how this tool works. In Photoshop, simply click the Hand tool in the Tools panel and then click-and-drag the image to move it around in the viewing window. This tool is useful for viewing different parts of a magnified image.

Foreground and Background Color *LO 6.3*

Raster editing programs normally include a foreground and background color feature. For instance, toward the bottom of the default Tools panel in Photoshop are two slightly overlapping squares (see Figure 6.4). These squares indicate the background and foreground color settings. The top square is the foreground color. The **foreground color** is what appears when you paint, draw, or fill in part of an image. The bottom square is the background color. The **background color** appears when you select and delete an area of an image on the background layer (which you will learn about later in this chapter). The default color for the foreground is black and the default color for the background is white, but you can change either of them by clicking the one you want to change and selecting a new color in the color picker dialog box that appears. You can also use the Color panel to do the same thing: click the foreground or background square in the Color panel and set a new color using the panel options (the Color panel is in the upper right portion of the workspace in Figure 6.1).

Notice the smaller version of the foreground and background color squares in Figure 6.4. To reset the default black and white colors, simply click this smaller version of the overlapping squares. To swap the foreground and background colors, click the double arrow just above the main foreground and background squares.

The background and foreground color feature is common in many different raster editing programs. Understanding how this feature works will be helpful for learning about other editing tools and special effects that use the background and foreground colors such as the Quick Mask mode, which is covered in the next section.

Figure 6.4 *The foreground and background color area of the Photoshop Tools panel.*

checkpoint

What are some common features found in many raster editing workspaces?

ACTIVITY 6.1 ▶ Familiarizing Yourself with the Raster Editing Workspace

1. Create a new 700 × 600 pixel image.

2. Place **pattern.jpg** from your student data files onto the bottom part of the new image.

3. Use the Eyedropper tool to set the background color to a dark color from the pattern image and set the foreground color to a light color from the image.

4. Use the Paint Bucket tool to fill the space outside the pattern.jpg placed on the image.

5. Use the Lasso tool to trace one of the middle squares, then delete that selection.

6. Switch the background and foreground colors. Fill the cut out square with the lighter color.

7. Use the Text tool to place a title at the top of the image: **Possible Pattern for Seat Covers**.

8. Save as **6_Activity1_pattern**.

Photo Manipulation before Photoshop

Digital photography and raster editing software make it possible and easy to create practically any image a person can dream up, whether realistic or fantastic. But the phenomenon is not new. The truth is, photographers were using a variety of methods including staging, lighting, and darkroom techniques to manipulate images long before the advent of digital files and editing software. Sometimes, photos were manually enhanced for publication. For example, airbrushing was used to remove an awkward-looking pole behind the main subject of John Filo's Pulitzer prize–winning photo of the Kent State University shootings.

Other photographers have manually manipulated photos to stage a hoax, for example, to prove the existence of UFOs or ghosts. Some fine art photographers have used manual photo manipulation to create surreal images. For example, Jerry Uelsmann has been creating fantastical photo montages using darkroom techniques since the 1960s. Raster editing software may make it easier, but the idea of changing photo images is an old one.

Lesson 6.2 > Using Tools to Make Selections *LO 6.2*

selection tool—A type of tool used to select a portion of a raster image before modifying it.

For certain tasks in many raster editing applications, including Photoshop, you must first select a portion of an image before you modify it. You designate the portion of the image you want to modify by using a **selection tool**. Figure 6.5 shows the default selection tools on the Photoshop Tools panel.

Notice the small triangles next to some of the tools on the Photoshop Tools panel shown in Figure 6.5. These small triangles indicate a group of similar tools hidden below the default tool. (This applies not just to selection tools, but to all tools with this triangle on the Tools panel.) You can view and select hidden tools by clicking and holding (or right-clicking) the small triangle and then clicking one of the tools on the menu that appears. For example, right-clicking the Quick Selection tool reveals another tool called the Magic Wand tool, as shown in Figure 6.6.

When you use a selection tool, the area you select is outlined with a moving dashed line, sometimes called "marching ants." Once an area is selected, you can use other tools and features to make changes to only that portion of the image. So, for example, once an area is highlighted with the marching ants, you can use the Brush

Figure 6.5 *This figure shows the main selection tools on the Photoshop Tools panel.*

Figure 6.6 *Clicking and holding (or right-clicking) the small triangle next to a tool on the Photoshop Tools panel reveals additional similar tools.*

tool to color just that area—you don't have to worry about "coloring outside the lines." Or, you can move or delete just that portion. The unselected portion of the image stays the same.

Photoshop Selection Tools *LO 6.2*

Table 6.1 describes the main Photoshop selection tools. You may find tools with similar functions in other raster editing programs. The tool names in bold are the default tools on the Photoshop Tools panel; the others are hidden.

Table 6.1 *Photoshop selection tools.*

TOOL	TOOL NAME	FUNCTION
	Move	Use to move selections or other elements (for example, layers described in a later section of this chapter).
	Rectangular Marquee	Rectangular selection area forms as you click and drag in an image.
	Elliptical Marquee	Elliptical selection area forms as you click and drag in an image.
	Single Row Marquee	Selection area forms around a single row of pixels as you click and drag in an image.
	Single Column Marquee	Selection area forms around a single column of pixels as you click and drag in an image.
	Lasso	A freehand selection line forms as you click and drag in an image.
	Polygonal Lasso	Straight-edged selection lines form as you click; then move the insertion point around an image and click again to change directions of the straight line.
	Magnetic Lasso	Selection line snaps to the edges of an object as you click and drag to trace it.
	Quick Selection	Selection line appears on the outside edges of an object as you "paint" it.
	Magic Wand	Selection line forms around an adjacent area of pixels that match a pixel you click.

Making a selection with one of the marquee tools like the Rectangular or Elliptical Marquee tool is easy if the area you want to select is a clearly defined shape. You simply click the tool and then click and drag around the item you wish to select.

However, choosing just the pixels you want to work with in an irregularly shaped item can be more challenging. For these areas of

Figure 6.7 *The lasso allows you to broadly define a specific selection area.*

an image, you can use the Lasso tool to draw freehand around the item you want to select, as shown in Figure 6.7.

If you want to be more precise, you can make your selection using the Magic Wand, Magnetic Lasso, or Quick Selection tools. These tools detect where colors in an image begin to change and use that information to establish a selection line. Each tool works in a slightly different way. The Magic Wand, for example, selects an adjacent area based on the color of the pixel you click with the tool. Simply click an area and all of the pixels with similar colors (within a certain range) are selected.

With the Magnetic Lasso tool, the selection line snaps to the edge of an object as you trace around it. In contrast, the Quick Selection tool finds the outside edges of an object as you paint the inside of it. (You "paint" by clicking and dragging with the tool.) In Figure 6.8, the flower was selected using the Quick Selection tool. Notice how much more refined the outline is compared to the selection in Figure 6.7.

Tips and tricks for using these tools (and all of the others introduced in this chapter) are detailed in Photoshop books, online tutorials, and within the Photoshop Help system. The same is true for tools in any raster editing program. The best way to learn how these tools work is to do some research and experiment with the tools on a test image. Through trial and error, you'll soon get the hang of how each tool works. As you experiment, it may be helpful to know that you can cancel a selection in Photoshop by selecting Deselect from the Select menu on the Application bar or by using the keyboard shortcut Ctrl + D (PC) or Cmd + D (Mac).

Figure 6.8 *The Photoshop Quick Selection tool makes it easy to select specific, irregularly shaped objects in an image.*

Selection Settings *LO 6.3*

As mentioned earlier in this chapter, when you click a tool, the Control panel toward the top of the Photoshop window displays settings for that particular tool. It is impractical to describe all of the various settings in this book, but because some of these settings appear in many different raster programs, it may be helpful to learn what a few of these options mean as you begin learning about image editing.

Anti-Aliasing and Feathering

Because bitmap images are created using square pixels, the edges of a selection can be ragged when you make a selection with a curved line. This is particularly problematic when you ultimately cut or copy and paste a selection. To soften the edges of a selection, select the **anti-aliasing** option. Anti-aliasing works by softening the color of the pixels along the edge of the selection. This option is available for several Photoshop selection tools, including all of the lasso tools as well as the Elliptical Marquee tool and the Magic Wand tool. You may also run across anti-aliasing options in other raster editing programs.

Feathering is another way to soften harsh edge lines in a selection. Feathering works by creating a border along the edges of a selection that fades gradually into the background (see Figure 6.9). The result is a soft blur at the edges of the selection. You set the width of the feathering effect in pixels. In Photoshop, this option is available for the marquee tools and the lasso tools. Feathering differs from anti-aliasing in a couple of ways. First, you can only apply anti-aliasing if you select the option before using a selection tool; you can apply feathering before or after actually making a selection. Second, you may lose some detail at the edge of a selection when you use feathering, but using anti-aliasing softens without sacrificing any detail.

anti-aliasing—A raster-editing feature that softens the hard edges of a selection by adjusting the color of the pixels along the outside edge.

feathering—A raster-editing feature that softens the hard edges of a selection by adding a border along the outer edge that gradually fades into the background, creating a soft blur.

tolerance—A setting that determines the range of pixels affected by a raster editing tool's action. In Photoshop, this is a setting for the Magic Wand tool.

Additional Magic Wand Tool Settings

In addition to anti-aliasing, the Magic Wand tool in Photoshop includes a couple of other settings that you may see for similar tools in other raster editing programs. The **tolerance** setting determines how precisely the Magic Wand tool does its job. The tolerance determines how many pixels are affected when you use the tool. The higher the tolerance, the higher the number of pixels affected. As mentioned earlier, the Magic Wand uses similarities and differences between pixel colors to determine what to include in a selection. The tolerance setting tells the Magic Wand tool

Photo courtesy of Susan Lake

Figure 6.9 *The fuzzy edge around this flower is the effect of feathering applied with the Elliptical Marquee tool in Photoshop.*

the range of color differences to consider in its selection process—in other words, where to literally draw the line between what is included and what is not. The default tolerance for the Magic Wand tool is 32 pixels. This means that in addition to all of the pixels that match the first pixel you click, the Magic Wand tool will also select any pixels that are 32 shades darker and 32 shades lighter than the original. If you increase the tolerance, more pixels will be included in the selection. If you decrease it, fewer pixels will be included. Sometimes you have to try different tolerance settings to get the results you want.

contiguous—Linked or touching each other (in reference to parts of an image).

Another Magic Wand tool setting to consider is the contiguous option. **Contiguous** refers to pixels that "touch." If the contiguous setting is selected (indicated with a check mark), only pixels that are touching will be included in the selection when you click an image with the Magic Wand. Any other pixels within the tolerance but not linked to the original pixel selection will not be included in the selection. However, if the contiguous setting is not selected, all pixels within the tolerance will be included in the selection no matter where they appear. This can be useful if you want to select a lot of similarly colored but not adjacent items within an image. Figure 6.10 shows the Control panel for the Magic Wand selection tool with a tolerance setting of 30 pixels and with anti-aliasing and contiguous options selected. Figure 6.11 demonstrates the resulting selection.

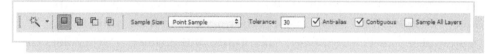

Figure 6.10 *Tolerance, contiguous, and anti-aliasing are three settings to consider before using the Magic Wand tool in Photoshop.*

Photo courtesy of Susan Lake

Figure 6.11 *The settings shown in Figure 6.10 were used to make this selection using the Magic Wand tool.*

Quick Mask Mode *LO 6.4*

Near the bottom of the Tools panel in Photoshop is a rectangular icon with a small circle in the center. When you click this icon, you access a special selection feature called Quick Mask mode. Quick masks are not to be confused with layer masks, which you'll learn about later in this chapter. **Quick masks** enable you to make and refine selections using the Brush tool. As indicated above, when you make a selection, you are essentially protecting the unselected area of the image from any changes you make to the selected area inside the marching ants. This is called masking. If you make a selection using one of the selection tools and then click the Quick Mask mode icon on the Tools panel, a ruby-colored overlay appears over the entire image *except* the selected area (see Figure 6.12).

quick masks—A temporary mask used to make or refine a selection.

The ruby area is the mask formed by the selection. To adjust what is covered by the mask, click the Brush tool and paint with black to cover more area with the mask or with white to reveal more area. Click the Quick Mask mode icon again and the marching ants will reveal the selected areas as indicated by an updated selection outline. Quick Mask mode is useful for refining a selection of an irregular shape in an image, especially if you use the Zoom In tool to magnify the area before you use the Brush tool to adjust the quick mask.

Photo courtesy of Edward Skintik

Figure 6.12 *In Quick Mask mode, Photoshop displays a ruby-colored screen over the nonselected areas of an image. In this picture, the flower was selected using the Quick Selection tool and then Quick Mask mode was selected. The selection can be refined by painting with black to cover more area or white to uncover other areas.*

checkpoint

Why do you need to be able to use different selection tools and their settings?

ACTIVITY 6.2 ▶ Using Selection Tools

1. Open *lily.jpg* from your data files.
2. Experiment using the Magic Wand, Quick Selection, and Magnetic Lasso tools (or similar tools in your image editing software) to select the most prominent bloom. Try selecting using the different options under each tool.
3. Use the Magnetic Lasso tool with feathering set to **50 px** and **Anti-alias** checked to select the most prominent bloom. Once you have the bloom selected, copy the selection.
4. Create a new image and paste the selection into the new image.
5. Save the image as *6_Activity2_lily_edited* in the native format of the software. Do not save the changes to your original data file.

Problem-Solving Skills

Employees who can solve problems on the job are more valuable than those who are easily stumped by difficulties or new situations. So learn to approach problems in an organized and efficient way. Avoid quick fixes; they rarely solve problems in the long run. Take the time to consider the problem thoroughly. Be creative when you consider solutions; do not rule out ideas just because they're new or have never been tried.

You must first identify what's causing a problem before you can solve it. (For example, bad color in a scanned photo is a symptom of the problem; the cause might be faulty software or a missed step in the scanning process.) Then explore many possible solutions before selecting the best one. Input from your supervisor and coworkers can be very valuable at this stage. Finally, implement your solution and determine whether it will work; if not, select another from the alternatives you considered earlier. Be persistent.

Skills in Action: Use the Internet to research further the steps to take in solving a problem. Create a slide show to communicate your findings.

Lesson 6.3 ▶ Digital Photos: Fixing Common Problems and Enhancing Images

Sometimes you capture a great image with your digital camera but something just isn't right. Perhaps it is a little dark or the composition is off. Luckily, raster editing programs offer easy-to-use tools for fixing common problems. In fact, you can so drastically alter a problematic photo it might not even look like the same picture when you're done! The editing possibilities with a program like Photoshop seem almost unlimited. This section covers just a tiny (but useful) fraction of the fixes you can make with a powerful raster editing program.

Adjusting Brightness and Contrast *LO 6.5*

Brightness and contrast in raster images are sometimes referred to in terms of levels. Levels fall into three basic categories: highlights, shadows, and midtones. **Highlights** represent the lightest part of the image; **shadows**, the darkest; and **midtones**, the middle range. Adjusting the levels of any of these three areas can dramatically improve a picture.

Most advanced image editing software, and even some basic software, offers features to adjust the brightness and contrast levels. Some software offers several techniques. One of the easiest and most common methods is to adjust the curves. A curves feature in a raster editing program represents the three levels on an interactive graph, meaning you can click and move the lines on the graph to change the levels in

highlights—The lightest part of an image, which is usually white.

shadows—The darkest part of an image, which is usually black.

midtones—The middle range of colors in an image.

your image. In very basic terms, moving the line on the graph in one direction or another adjusts the overall levels. Grabbing the midpoint, as shown in Figure 6.13, and moving it toward the light or toward the dark will automatically adjust your image.

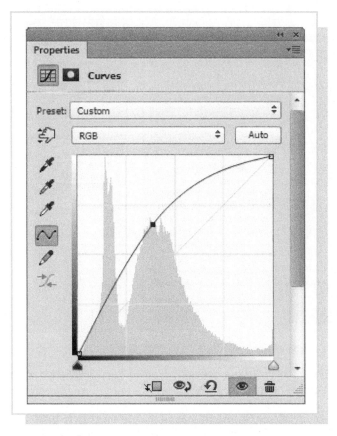

Figure 6.13 *You can adjust the levels of an image in several ways. Using the curves function is one of the best ways. In this example from Photoshop, the curves line can be adjusted to achieve the effect you want.*

Another simple way to adjust the levels with the curves function is to use eyedroppers like those shown to the left of the graph in Photoshop's Curves panel (Figure 6.13). Use the black-tipped eyedropper to select the darkest (blackest) point in the image to set as the shadow. Use the white-tipped eyedropper to select the lightest (whitest) color in the image to set the highlights. Use the gray-tipped eyedropper to select and set a midtone. The image will automatically adjust the overall levels based on these measurements. The best way to use the curves function is to play around with the options until you see the desired effect in the image.

Cropping *LO 6.6*

In Chapter 4, "Digital Photography," you read about cropping an image in the camera's viewfinder before you take a photo. If, however, you didn't compose the shot properly at first, all is not lost. You can easily use the cropping tool in raster editing software to achieve good composition in your images. Most, if not all, raster editing programs include a cropping tool similar to the tool in Photoshop (see Figure 6.14). You use the tool by clicking and dragging around the area you would like to include in the final image.

Figure 6.14 *You can use a cropping tool in raster image editing software to achieve good photo composition even after a picture is already taken.*

In Photoshop, the Crop tool automatically lays a rule of thirds grid over the image so that you can crop using those guidelines. The area inside the crop outline is highlighted and the area outside is dimmed. You can adjust the selection area by using the arrow keys on the keyboard or by clicking and dragging the handles on the outline. When you commit the change, the outside area is cropped out of the picture, leaving just the highlighted part of the image. Use caution when cropping. Once you crop an image, then save and close the file, the cut information is discarded. Revisit the section on good photo composition in Chapter 4 for more information about the importance of cropping in photo composition.

Using Retouch Tools *LO 6.7*

Sometimes you'll want to change the content in your images, perhaps to remove a distracting element or enhance a person's appearance in a portrait. Raster editing software features **retouch tools** that enable you to make changes like these. Table 6.2 details some of the common photo retouch tools in the main Photoshop Tools panel. The tool names in bold are the default tools on the Photoshop Tools panel; the others are hidden by default. You'll find similar tools in other raster editing programs. To learn more specifically how these tools work in your raster editing program, consult the help feature and, as always, experiment on a sample image.

retouch tool—A tool used to alter the content of an image.

Table 6.2 *Common Photoshop retouch tools.*

TOOL	TOOL NAME	FUNCTION
	Spot Healing Brush	Removes objects and unwanted elements like blemishes.
	Red Eye	Fixes red eyes in people and animals caused by a camera flash.
	Clone Stamp	Paints with a sample color from another area of the image.
	Eraser	Erases pixels from a layer. Effect is different depending on layer.
	Background Eraser	Erases to transparency when you drag it on an image.
	Magic Eraser	Makes solid color areas transparent with a single click.
	Blur	Blurs hard edges as you drag.

Think About It

Retouch Ethics

Retouch tools are often used in advertising to make models and products more appealing. Is it ethical to drastically change a person's or product's appearance for marketing purposes? What about using photo editing tools to enhance your profile picture on a social networking site?

checkpoint

Are you stuck with a bad photo if it doesn't come out as you expected?

ACTIVITY 6.3 ▶ Editing an Image

1. From the data files, open and then edit the following files, adjusting as described:

   a. ***01red_eye***: edit to remove the red eye

   b. ***02cropping***: crop so that most of the door is not in the image and the focus is on the larger bloom

   c. ***03light***: make light adjustments

2. Insert the three edited images into image editing software, creating a collage. You decide the size of the artboard. You may want to use the software's help system to learn about the artboard.

3. Save the collage as ***6_Activity3_image_edits*** in JPG format.

When you first start working with raster editing programs, your tasks may be simple, like making adjustments similar to the changes covered in the previous section. However, as your tasks become more complex, you'll likely begin using more powerful features called layers and masks. The following section is a brief introduction to the concepts of layers and masks. To take full advantage of these powerful features, you should spend some time learning more from online tutorials, design classes, and books devoted to your raster editing software. You might be amazed at what layers and masks can help you achieve in your images.

Understanding Layers *LO 6.8*

Layers are often described as a digital version of a stack of clear plastic sheets, where printed material from lower layers is visible through the clear areas of upper layers. In a program that offers the layers feature, each new file—whether you are opening a digital photo file or creating a new raster document—begins with a single layer. You add **layers** as needed to do the following sorts of things:

layers—A raster-editing feature used to layer editable images individually, make changes, add effects, and make nondestructive edits.

- Combine and overlap multiple images
- Draw vector shapes on a raster image
- Add text to an image
- Change the order of overlapping items (move from front to back or vice versa, for example)
- Adjust the position of different elements independently
- Apply special effects and filters

Layers help you achieve all sorts of results in your images, but one of the most significant advantages of layers is that they enable you to edit an original image without actually changing the image's pixels. This is called **nondestructive editing** because no part of the original image is altered in the process. Nondestructive editing gives you great freedom to experiment and also allows you to create multiple and varied final images from one initial image. More on this a little later in the chapter.

nondestructive editing—A change made to an image that does not actually alter the original image's pixels.

Background and Normal Layers *LO 6.8*

You manage layers in Photoshop by using the Layers panel, which opens by default along the right side of the Photoshop workspace. Figure 6.15 shows the Photoshop Layers panel for a document with two layers.

As mentioned above, new raster documents in applications with a layers feature begin with a single layer called the **background layer**. (There is one exception, but that is beyond the scope of this book.) You can see this layer in the Photoshop Layers panel in Figure 6.15. Likewise, if you open a digital photo with Photoshop, it automatically becomes the background layer. The background layer is a special kind of layer with certain restrictions:

- It is always the bottom layer no matter how many other layers you add.

- It cannot be renamed.

- It cannot be transparent.

- It cannot be moved or deleted. (Notice the small lock icon next to the Background layer in Figure 6.15. This icon indicates that a layer is locked and cannot be moved or deleted.)

Figure 6.15 *The Layers panel in Photoshop is where you manage layers in your document.*

These restrictions also apply to objects and changes you make on the background layer. So, for example, if you add a shape, such as an arrow, to an image on the background layer and then want to reposition it using the Move tool, you can't. The background and its objects are locked. Likewise, if you try to select and delete the arrow using a selection tool such as a marquee tool or the Magic Wand, the selection area will fill with the background color. For maximum flexibility, it's best to make changes and adjustments on a "normal" layer.

New normal layers are added above the background layer and are labeled with numbers in the order you add them (Layer 1, Layer 2, etc.). By default, new layers are transparent, as indicated in Photoshop by a checkerboard pattern in the Layers panel (see Figure 6.15). Normal layers and their objects have none of the restrictions of the background layer: You can reorder them, rename them, move them, delete them, or lock and unlock them as much as you like or need to. You can also change the transparency of a layer by adjusting the Opacity or Fill percentages in the boxes at the top of the Layers panel in Photoshop (see Figure 6.15 again); you can use the sliding scale that appears when you click the arrow next to either of these settings to adjust the transparency between completely see-through (0%) and completely solid (100%).

Also notice the drop-down list at the top left of the Layers panel. This is the Blending Modes menu. Blending modes affect how a layer blends into the layers below it. The default blending mode is Normal as shown in Figure 6.15, but you can achieve many different effects by choosing from the list that appears when you click the list arrows to the right of the option box, as shown in Figure 6.16. The best way to learn about these different blending modes is to experiment with them.

background layer—
A special kind of layer in raster programs such as Photoshop that is always at the bottom of the layer stack and cannot be renamed, moved, or deleted or contain any transparency.

| Normal |
| Dissolve |

| Darken |
| Multiply |
| Color Burn |
| Linear Burn |
| Darker Color |

| Lighten |
| Screen |
| Color Dodge |
| Linear Dodge (Add) |
| Lighter Color |

| Overlay |
| Soft Light |
| Hard Light |
| Vivid Light |
| Linear Light |
| Pin Light |
| Hard Mix |

| Difference |
| Exclusion |

| Hue |
| Saturation |
| Color |
| Luminosity |

Figure 6.16 *Photoshop offers a wide variety of blending modes allowing you to modify the appearance of objects on a normal layer.*

Sometimes, you may find it useful to create a new layer by duplicating an existing layer. You can do this by right-clicking the layer in the Layers panel and selecting Duplicate Layer from the menu that appears. Note that you can create a duplicate layer from a normal layer or a background layer using this method.

As mentioned earlier, one of the biggest advantages of layers is that they allow you to make nondestructive changes. Adjustments and edits you make on normal layers added over the background will show up on the image, but will not change the original image data. This means that editing on normal layers not only gives you the flexibility to easily change your designs, it preserves the original image on the background layer. This is especially important if you are working with photos.

The results you can achieve with advanced layer techniques and tools is amazing, but as you get started working with raster images, you may find that the aspect you like the most is being able to try different effects and techniques without risking your original data. However, if for some reason you need to edit the background, you can turn it into a normal layer by double-clicking it.

Basic Layer Actions *LO 6.8 and 6.9*

Table 6.3 describes some of the most basic layer actions you can achieve with the Layers panel in Photoshop. Some of these tasks are associated with icons on the small toolbar that appears at the bottom of the Layers panel in Photoshop, which you can review in Figure 6.15. (You may find basic tasks work similarly and share similar icons in other raster editing programs.) You'll revisit this toolbar later in the chapter when you read about a few slightly more advanced layer options.

Layer Styles and Adjustment Layers *LO 6.8*

Once you've created a new layer, the first thing to do is rename it using a logical and understandable name. As you work with images and add more and more layers, you will find that it is often difficult to keep track of what changes you have made and where elements of the image are located if you have not labeled the layers sensibly.

Once a layer is created and renamed, you can add color and other details just as you would to any image. You can also take advantage of any shortcuts your raster editing program offers for adding special effects to a layer. In Photoshop, for example, you can use the Layer

Table 6.3 *Common Photoshop Layers panel actions.*

ACTION	PROCEDURE	ASSOCIATED ICON (IF APPLICABLE)
Create a new layer	Click the Create a new layer icon	
Rename a layer	Double-click the current name of the layer and key a new name	
Select a layer to work with	Click the name of the layer in the layers panel	
Delete a layer	Select the layer and then click the Delete layer icon or drag and drop the layer name over the Delete layer icon	
Move a layer up or down in the stack	Click the layer name, drag to the new position, and drop	
Hide or show a layer	Click the eye icon to the left of a layer name to hide a layer; click the blank space again to show the layer	

Styles feature to add special effects to your images. Layer styles are special effects such as drop shadows and glowing edges that you can add to specific layers in your image.

Access Layer Styles by clicking the Add a layer style icon (a small "fx" on the toolbar at the bottom of the Layers panel shown earlier in Figure 6.15), choosing a style from the menu that appears, and then adjusting settings in the Layer Style dialog box that opens. When you add a layer style, "fx" appears next to the layer name in the Layers panel and the name of the style is indented below (see Figure 6.17). Since layer styles are applied to layers, they are nondestructive: The changes show up in the image view, but your original image is not impacted by them.

Another nondestructive Photoshop shortcut feature is Adjustment Layers. Adjustment layers allow you to change elements like the lighting, color, and tones of an image without actually changing the pixels in the original image. You add an adjustment layer by clicking the *Create new fill or adjustment layer* icon (the half white, half black circle on the toolbar at the bottom of the Layers panel) and choosing an adjustment from the menu that appears.

Figure 6.17 *The special effect layer style Bevel & Emboss has been added to the text layer for this image, as indicated by the "fx" next to the layer name and by the name of the style indented below.*

Two things happen: A new layer appears in the Layers panel showing the name of the adjustment, and the settings selections for that adjustment appear in the Adjustments panel on the workspace. (Normally, the Adjustments panel opens in a tab above the Layers panel in the Photoshop workspace. See Figure 6.1 at the beginning of the chapter.) The layer just above the Background layer in Figure 6.17 is an adjustment layer. Adjust the settings as much as you like and watch how the changes are applied to your image in the viewing area.

If at any time you want to change the adjustment, even if you've closed and then reopened the file, simply click the adjustment layer in the Layers panel and make your changes in the Adjustments panel. Instead of adding an adjustment layer and changing the settings manually, you can also choose from a selection of common image adjustments listed in the Adjustments panel and Photoshop will automatically apply the adjustment layer and settings to your image.

Understanding Layer Masks *LO 6.9*

Recall from earlier in this lesson that you can adjust the transparency of normal layers using the tools on the Layers panel. Layer transparency can vary from completely see-through (0%) to completely solid (100%) and every level in between. Using these tools to adjust layer transparency affects everything on the layer equally. But what if you want to adjust the transparency of just a certain part of the layer? In that case, you use something called a mask.

A layer mask is not too different from a Halloween mask: it hides everything except where holes are cut out. Similarly, a **layer mask** can hide everything on a layer except what you tell it to reveal. In Photoshop, you add a mask to a selected layer using the Add layer mask icon (the gray rectangle with a circle in the center on the toolbar at the bottom of the Layers panel). A rectangle appears next to the layer thumbnail in the Layers panel connected by a chain link. This is the layer mask.

Photoshop and many other raster editing programs use black, white, and gray to indicate what part of the layer is hidden by a mask (anything black), what part is shown by a mask (anything white), and what is a level of transparency in between (different levels of gray). By default, when you add a new mask to a layer, the mask thumbnail in the Layers panel is pure white, meaning everything on the layer is showing. To hide an area on a layer, make sure the foreground color on the toolbar is black, select the Brush

layer mask—A raster-editing feature used to control what is visible on a layer.

tool from the main toolbox, and "paint" (click and drag) the area you would like to hide.

As you paint, whatever is under the layer with the mask will show through and your "brushstrokes" will appear in black on the mask thumbnail in the Layers panel. (See Figure 6.18.) If you make a mistake or change your mind, simply swap the foreground and background colors and paint with white. What was hidden on the layer will re-emerge as you paint it. You can also select an area to hide with a selection tool, select Fill from the Edit menu on the Application bar, and choose Black from the options that appear.

Figure 6.18 *You can use a layer mask to hide parts of a layer that you don't want to show in the final image. In this example, a layer mask is applied to the image of the red plane and everything except the plane is hidden. Note that the mask thumbnail in the Layers panel is pure white in A, indicating that everything is showing. In B, part of the mask thumbnail is black, showing what part of the image is hidden by the mask.*

Although the default is to add a white mask that shows the entire layer, you can add a mask that hides everything on the layer by holding down Alt (PC) or Option (Mac) before clicking the Add layer mask icon. In that instance, the mask thumbnail next to the layer thumbnail will be black and nothing from that layer will be showing on the main image in the workspace viewing area. If you set white as the foreground color and use a paintbrush, you can reveal areas of the layer by painting.

You can also use a mask in combination with an adjustment layer to apply an effect to only a specific area of a layer. In fact, when you add an adjustment layer, Photoshop automatically attaches a mask to the layer. To apply an adjustment layer to just a section of a layer, use a selection tool to select the area you would like to adjust, then click the *Create new fill or adjustment area* icon and choose the adjustment you would like to make.

Layers and Layer Masks in Action *LO 6.9*

This lesson covers the most basic concepts behind layers and masks. Even so, you may be having a hard time picturing how the features actually work. To give you an idea of how these elements come together to create a single image, the following example describes how some of the tools and features described were applied to a sample image. Notice that each image reflects the actions described in the step because the layer is showing, as indicated by the eye next to each layer in the Layers panel.

1. Opened original image in Photoshop. It was automatically set as the background layer.

Photo courtesy of Edward Skintik

2. Used the Quick Selection tool to select the flower, then added a Vibrance adjustment layer by clicking the *Create new fill or adjustment layer* icon (half white, half black circle) at the bottom of the Layers panel. Used the Vibrance settings to increase vibrance and saturation.

Photo courtesy of Edward Skintik

3. Drew a text box using the Text tool. (This automatically added a text layer to the image.) Keyed "Yellow Hibiscus" and adjusted font, color, size, alignment, and style by using settings on the Control panel. Positioned the text using the Move tool. Added a layer style by clicking the Add a layer style icon (fx) at the bottom of the Layers panel and selecting Bevel and Emboss from the menu that appeared. Adjusted the style settings in the Layer Style dialog box.

Photo courtesy of Edward Skintik

4. Duplicated the Background layer and hid the Background layer. Used the Healing Brush, Spot Healing Brush, and Clone Stamp tools to remove the shadow of the stamen on the petal to the left.

Photo courtesy of Edward Skintik

Layers, File Size, and File Format *LO 6.10*

If you save a layered image in a file format that is native to the image editing software, such as PSD for Photoshop, the layers will remain available to you even after you have closed the file. If you save your image as a JPG or other nonnative file format, the layers will be merged into a single image and you will no longer be able to edit them individually. However, layers contribute to large file sizes, so the benefit of merging multiple layers into a single layer is a smaller file.

If you intend to use your file in another medium, such as posting it to a website or placing it in another design program file, you'll probably want to minimize the file anyway, and using a file format such as JPG is a good way to do so. But what if you need to edit the image later? To address this issue, when you elect to save as certain nonnative file formats, Photoshop (and perhaps some other raster programs) automatically prompts you to save as a copy. You should see this prompt as a reminder to also preserve the version of the file with layers in a native format.

flatten—To merge multiple layers into a single layer. Flattening can reduce file size, but should only be done after all editing is complete and is best done on a copy of the original file.

Even if you intend to keep your files only in a native format and never save them as a nonnative format such as JPG, you may want to minimize file size for one reason or another. In these cases, you can **flatten** the image, which merges all of the layers into a single layer and reduces the file size. In Photoshop, you can flatten an image by choosing Flatten Image from the Layers menu on the Application bar. However, if you do this, remember that you will no longer be able to adjust individual layers, so it is good to develop the habit of saving a copy of a file before flattening it.

Reading about layers, masks, and other raster editing features gives you an overview of the tools available and introduces raster editing terminology, but there is no substitute for hands-on learning. Open some raster images in your software and experiment with the tools described here. If you run across a tool or feature you can't seem to make work, use the software help system or look up a solution using an Internet search engine.

checkpoint

Why are layers and masks useful?

ACTIVITY 6.4 ▶ Layering Basics

1. Create a new 4- × 4-inch image and name it *6_Activity4_layers_practice*.
2. Unlock the Background layer and then change the opacity of Layer 0 to 0%. Rename the layer **Background**.
3. Create four new layers named **Blue**, **Red**, **Green**, and **Yellow**.

4. Using the rulers to guide your sizing and placement, draw a 1-inch diameter circle on each of the new layers, filling each circle with the color of the layer. Draw the first circle starting at 0 inches on the horizontal ruler and 3 inches on the vertical ruler. Draw each remaining circle 1 inch higher and 1 inch to the right of the circle below it.

5. Move the four shapes in a semicircle as shown so there is room for a text layer.

6. Add a text layer (named **Text**) with the text **Registration Today at Noon!** Apply the Bevel and Emboss layer style to the Text layer.

7. Create a new layer named **Gradient** and apply a **linear gradient** fill of **red** at **50%** opacity.

8. Move layers as needed so that the Background layer is the first layer in the list (on the bottom) followed by the Gradient layer, the Text layer, and then the shapes.

9. Save the image (as *6_Activity4_layers_practice*) in the native format of your software and save it again as *6_Activity4_layers_practice.jpg*. Use any default save options. Note that the layers will merge when you save as a JPG. You will need to open the PSD version in order to make changes to the image.

lavitrei/Shutterstock.com

Photo Manipulation and Photojournalism Ethics

Photo manipulation is not a new phenomenon. Even before the introduction of raster editing software, photographs were altered using special darkroom techniques. However, easily accessible and powerful software such as Photoshop and GIMP make altered photographs more common than ever. People who work with digital images and editing software have a special responsibility for preserving the integrity of a photo as much as possible when it really matters that the image represents reality.

This is especially true for photojournalists. In fact, the National Press Photographers Association (NPPA) adopted a specific statement against photo manipulation as part of its code of ethics in 1995. Nevertheless, photo manipulation scandals occasionally surface in the news. Since it is often impossible to tell if an image has been manipulated, it is up to individual photographers to uphold the ethical standards of their field when editing images.

Critical Thinking

Use the Internet to research several famous photo manipulation scandals. In each case, how and why was the image changed? How was the fraud discovered? What were the consequences (if any) for the person responsible? In your opinion, are some cases more serious than others? What sorts of changes are okay for a photojournalist to make when editing photographs? Break into groups to discuss your findings.

Key Concepts

▶ Many raster editing programs have similar workspaces and basic tools. *LO 6.1*

▶ For certain tasks in raster editing, you must first select a specific area to edit by using a selection tool or a feature like Photoshop's Quick Mask mode. *LO 6.2*

▶ Some selection tools include settings such as anti-aliasing, feathering, tolerance, and contiguous options that enable you to enhance the effect or precision of a selection. *LO 6.3*

▶ Quick Mask mode helps you refine a selection. *LO 6.4*

▶ You can adjust levels, brightness, and contrast in photos using curves. *LO 6.5*

▶ A cropping tool in a raster editing program can help improve photo composition. *LO 6.6*

▶ Retouch tools make it possible to alter large and small imperfections in an image. *LO 6.7*

▶ One of the most important uses of layers and layer masks is nondestructive editing. *LO 6.8 and 6.9*

▶ Since layers add to file size, you can choose to merge several layers into one by saving in a nonnative format or by using a flatten image feature in a raster editing program. *LO 6.10*

Review and Discuss

1. Define the Zoom tool and briefly explain how it works. *LO 6.1*

2. Explain the purpose of the Hand tool. *LO 6.1*

3. Explain the difference between the foreground and background color and how each is used. *LO 6.3*

4. Describe the Selection tool, "marching ants," and the purpose of using the Selection tool. *LO 6.2*

5. Describe the selection tool that is best used when you want to select an irregularly shaped area. *LO 6.1 and 6.2*

6. Describe the selection tools that would be used when more precise selections need to be made, and how these tools make more precise selections. *LO 6.1, 6.2, and 6.3*

7. Identify the option that is used on images when the edges are ragged. Describe how it works. *LO 6.1 and 6.2*

8. Explain how the Magic Wand tool settings affect the selection of an image. *LO 6.1, 6.2, and 6.3*

9. Explain the purpose of Quick Mask mode, and how to use it. *LO 6.4*

10. Explain the differences between the three levels of brightness and contrast: highlights, shadows, and midtones. *LO 6.5*

11. Identify and describe one of the most common methods of adjusting brightness and contrast levels. *LO 6.5*

12. Explain the purpose of using the Cropping tool. *LO 6.6*

13. Discuss some of the retouch tools that may be found in a raster editing program and their purpose. *LO 6.7*

14. Describe uses of layers. *LO 6.8*

15. List the restrictions of the background layer. *LO 6.8*

16. Discuss the differences between the background layer and a new layer. *LO 6.8*

17. Explain blending modes. *LO 6.8*

18. Discuss the advantages of using layers. *LO 6.8, 6.9, and 6.10*

19. Explain the use of Layer Styles. *LO 6.8*

20. Define Adjustment Layers and the purpose of using them on your image. *LO 6.8 and 6.9*

Apply

1. Create an image that is postcard size, 3.5 × 5 inches. The image should announce the Grand Opening of *An Eye for You Optometry* on Saturday, June 20, 2XXX from 10 a.m. to 2 p.m. The image should have a minimum of three layers with text and shapes and two to three colors used. Be creative with the use of shapes! Save as **6_Apply1_eye_for_you**. *LO 6.8*

2. Open **texan.jpg** from your data files. Use any selection tool to select an area around the central star. Use Quick Mask mode to refine the selection as necessary, and then invert the selection. Select a yellow foreground color and then delete the content in the selection (with the selection active, tap Delete on the keyboard) and choose to fill the deleted area with the Foreground color. Use the Polygonal Lasso tool to select the star, and then choose a blue foreground color. Delete the content in the selection and fill the star with the Foreground color. Save as **6_Apply2_texan**. *LO 6.1, 6.2, and 6.4*

3. Open **three.jpg** from your data files. Use a marquee tool to select parts of one or two of the images. Apply a free transform to your selections of the image. Crop the images to focus on the new image that you have created. Save as **6_Apply3_free_transform**. *LO 6.1 and 6.2*

4. Open **windmill.jpg** from your data files. Add text to the image advertising The Windmill Restaurant. Be sure that the text is on a new layer that is named **The Windmill Restaurant**. Change text to an appropriate size, placement, and color for the background. Add a stroke effect to the text that is an appropriate color to help make the text stand out on the background. Save as **6_Apply4_windmill_restaurant**. *LO 6.1, 6.8, and 6.9*

5. Create an image that is 8.5 × 11 inches. Place the **sunset** image from your data files at the top of the image. Name the layer **sunset image**. Promote the background layer and name the layer **sunset background**. Add an

appropriate layer style to the background. Using the Text tool, key a 100-word story about the image with your name right-aligned at the end of the story. Format all text appropriately in color, size, and spacing. Add another layer and name it **sunset title** with appropriate text formatting and a layer style added. Place both text boxes appropriately on the image for a balanced image. Save as **6_Apply5_sunset_story**. *LO 6.1 and 6.9*

Explore

1. Using a favorite search engine, locate a photo editing tutorial that relates to one of the concepts learned in this chapter. Follow the tutorial to create or edit an image. Write a summary of what you learned and how you think you will use it. Cite the location of the tutorial in MLA style. Save the image as **6_Explore1_tutorial**. Save the summary as **6_Explore1_tutorial_summary**. *LO 6.4, 6.5, 6.6, and 6.7*

2. Using a favorite search engine, search for information on cropping an image. Find information on the following:

   • Why crop an image?

   • Best tips on cropping an image.

   • How to crop an image effectively.

   Write a one-page summary of the best tips and ideas that you found in your search, providing at least two image samples that you have created by following the tips. Save the image samples as **6_Explore2_image1** and **6_Explore2_image2**. Save the summary as **6_Explore2_cropping_summary**. *LO 6.6*

3. Research to improve your understanding of raster graphics. Write a ten-question quiz with a variety of question types (multiple choice, true/false, fill in the blank, short answer) to test yourself on what you learned about raster graphics. Cite at least two references using MLA style or the style given by your instructor. Save your work as **6_Explore3_raster_quiz**. *LO 6.1*

Academic Connections

History: Create a photo collage of a famous historical event or era using images from the Library of Congress, http://memory.loc.gov/ammem/index.html, or the National Archives. Save your collage as **6_AC_history**.

Communications: Search using one of the following key word searches:

   • Visual communication

   • Communicating with graphics

   • Making graphics that communicate clearly

Write a one-page summary of the articles that you have read, focusing on tips for effectively communicating with graphics. Cite at least one resource using MLA style. Save your work as **6_AC_communications**.

Chapter 7

Vector Editing

Learning Outcomes

▶ **7.1** Recognize the essential elements of a vector object and use vector terminology.

▶ **7.2** Draw simple shapes and lines using vector drawing tools.

▶ **7.3** Draw straight or curved paths segment by segment.

▶ **7.4** Transform objects using a selection tool and a bounding box.

▶ **7.5** Adjust curves.

▶ **7.6** Stack and reorder objects.

▶ **7.7** Create a clipping mask.

▶ **7.8** Convert a raster image into a vector object using a tracing feature.

Key Terms

- anchor point
- bounding box
- clipping mask
- closed path
- corner point
- endpoint
- fill
- line tool
- open path
- path
- scale
- segment
- shape tool
- smooth point
- stroke

Before you began the previous chapter on raster images, you may have been somewhat familiar with the image editing possibilities of raster images. As you begin this chapter, you may not be as familiar with vector images. But if you intend to pursue a career in digital media, you should get to know vector editing software, especially if you will work with logos or generate three-dimensional graphic renderings, which are both almost always created in a vector format. The lines and curves used in vector rendering make it easy to create drawings that look quite professional, even if you are not particularly artistic. And if you are an artist, vector programs offer a way to move your hand-drawn artwork to a digital drawing format.

Creations/Shutterstock.com

One of the most widely used vector editing programs in the professional graphic arts world is Adobe Illustrator. This chapter will introduce general vector editing terminology, tools, and concepts using Illustrator as the main model. The names of some tools and features will vary from program to program, but this introduction to vector editing will show you some basic capabilities of vector programs in general.

This basic knowledge should help as you explore whatever vector drawing program you decide to use, whether it is a free, open source program such as Inkscape or another popular for-purchase program like CorelDRAW. There is much more to discover about these powerful drawing programs than is covered in this chapter. Vector editing programs are just as complex as raster editing programs, so if you intend to enter a field like graphic design, you'll need to explore more resources to become proficient in vector editing and design across many platforms.

Lesson 7.1 > Understanding Essential Vector Terminology

As you learned in Chapter 3, "Image Files," the essential difference between raster and vector graphics is that raster images are composed of pixels whereas vector graphics are made of mathematically defined lines. (Revisit Chapter 3 for more information about the differences between raster and vector graphics.) However, when you first launch a vector editing program, the workspace may seem familiar if you have worked in a raster program. For example, most if not all vector editing programs include a main viewing area and a selection of tools, menus, panels, and dialog boxes to edit images (see Figure 7.1).

Also, some tools look the same and function similarly. For example, the Zoom tool and the Hand tool in Photoshop and Illustrator are identical. However, because of the fundamental difference between raster and vector images, using vector editing software means learning a new set of concepts, tools, and techniques. The best way to start learning is by becoming familiar with some vector-specific vocabulary.

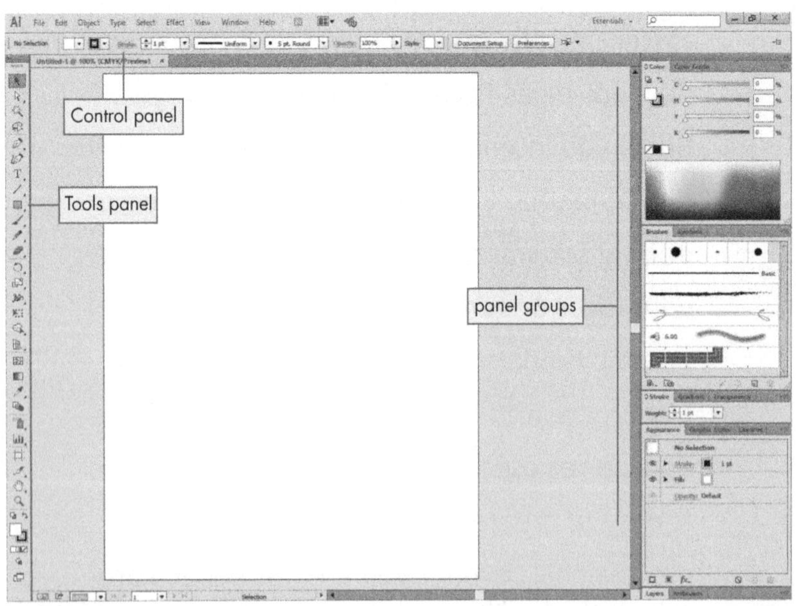

Figure 7.1 *A vector editing workspace, such as the Adobe Illustrator workspace shown here, is similar to a raster editing workspace in some ways. However, they are not identical because of the different functions and tools needed to work with raster and vector graphics.*

Anatomy of a Path *LO 7.1*

If you've ever taken an algebra or geometry class, you may have practiced graphing linear equations by plotting points on a graph and connecting them with lines. If so, you are familiar with the math behind vector images. In vector software, lines connect points to form an object. You can think of a vector object almost like a connect-the-dots puzzle where lines connect dots to form an outline. The lines in a vector image are usually called **paths** by most vector applications. "Path" doesn't refer to the physical line you see in an object; it refers to virtual lines. For example, in Illustrator a path is represented on screen as a blue line that does not show up when you print an object. (The visible lines you see in a vector object are called strokes, which are covered in the next section.)

A **closed path** refers to objects without a clear beginning and end such as a circle, square, or other shape. An **open path** refers to a path with a distinct beginning and end such as a single straight, curved, or wavy line. Each path includes one or more **segments**, which can be either straight or curved. The beginning and end of each segment on a path is marked by **anchor points** (sometimes referred to as *nodes* in certain vector programs). Distinct anchor points at the beginning and end of a path are referred to as **endpoints**. There are two types of anchor points. Anchor points along the path where the angle changes are called **corner points**. Anchors along a curve are called **smooth points**.

That is a lot of vocabulary to learn! It may be helpful to look at a couple of vector drawings to really picture all of the elements of a vector object. Figure 7.2 shows a simple vector drawing of a star. This vector object is a closed path because there is no distinct beginning or end.

path—A line that makes up a vector object.

closed path—A path with no distinct beginning or end, for example a circle, square, or other shape.

open path—A path with a distinct beginning and end; for example, a straight line.

segment—A distinct portion of a path that connects two anchor points.

anchor point—A point defining the beginning or end of a segment along a path.

endpoint—A beginning or end anchor point on a path.

corner point—An anchor point along a vector path where the direction changes.

smooth point—An anchor point along a vector curve.

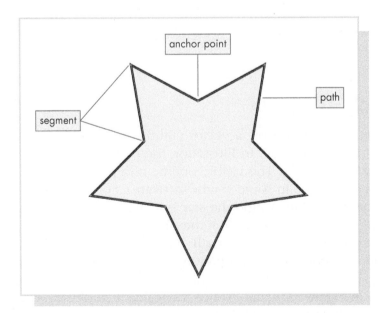

Figure 7.2 *This star was created in Adobe Illustrator. If you look closely, you can see the blue anchor points and lines that represent the path on screen. These blue guides do not show up when the image is printed.*

It is made up of ten segments and ten anchor points. All of these anchor points are corner points because they mark a clear change in the direction of the path.

Figure 7.3 is another simple vector drawing. This spiral is an open path because there is a distinct beginning and end that do not connect. Ten curved segments and 11 anchor points make up this vector path. In this case, all of the segments are curved and all of the anchors are smooth points because they fall along a vector curve. Note, however, a vector path can include a mix of straight and curved segments and corner and smooth points.

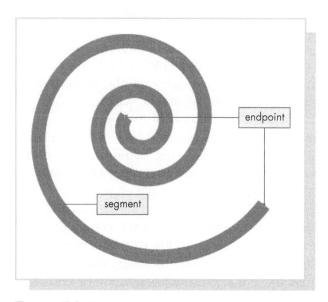

Figure 7.3 *This spiral was created in Adobe Illustrator. It is an open path object with 10 curved segments and 11 smooth points. The blue lines and dots representing the path and anchor points are easier to see in this image.*

Strokes and Fills *LO 7.1*

stroke—The visible outline of a path.

As mentioned in the previous section, a vector path is not a visible line in a vector object; it is a virtual line. In Illustrator, the path is represented on screen by blue guides. The visible outline of a path is called a **stroke** (also called an *outline* in some vector software). So, for example, in Figure 7.2, the black line around the star is a stroke and the blue guidelines represent the path. In Figure 7.3, the pink line is the stroke and, again, the blue guides represent the path. A stroke can vary based on width (also called weight), color, and pattern (solid or dashed, for instance).

fill—A color or pattern applied to the inside area of a path.

Refer to the star in Figure 7.2 again. Notice the inside area of the star is yellow. This is called the fill. A **fill** is a color or pattern applied to the inside area of a path. Now look at the spiral in Figure 7.3 again. The inside area of the path is empty. This is because there is no fill applied to this object. Any vector object can have a fill or no fill, a stroke or no stroke, or any combination. However, strokes and fills are what make paths visible, so if there is no fill and no stroke on an object, the path will be invisible when printed or placed in another program. See Figure 7.4 for variations of the fill and stroke on the star and spiral examples.

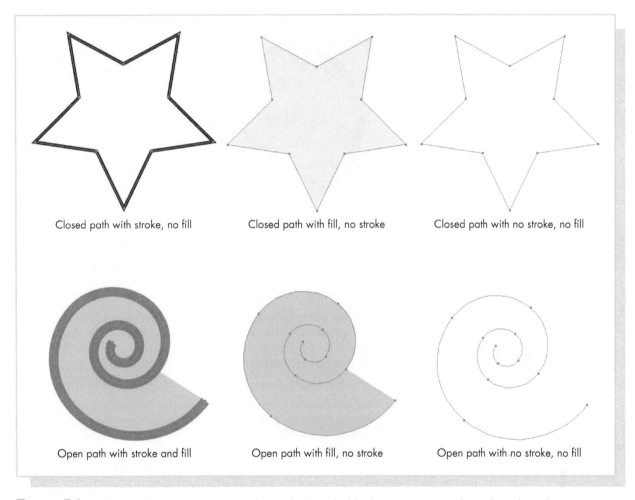

Closed path with stroke, no fill   Closed path with fill, no stroke   Closed path with no stroke, no fill

Open path with stroke and fill   Open path with fill, no stroke   Open path with no stroke, no fill

Figure 7.4 *Strokes and fills are what make paths visible. Since the blue lines representing the paths in these Illustrator vector objects do not print, the star and spiral with no stroke and no fill would be invisible if printed or placed in another design program.*

In Illustrator, you can set the stroke and fill options many different ways, but one of the easiest methods is to use the options on the Control panel (refer to Figure 7.1 to see where the Control panel is located in the Illustrator workspace). By default, the Control panel shows (among other settings) the fill color, the stroke color, and the stroke weight. When an object is selected, the Control panel changes to reflect the settings for that object (see Figure 7.5 on the following page).

Table 7.1 (on the following page) details how to use the Control panel in Illustrator to adjust fill and stroke options. Other vector programs use similar methods for adjusting the fill and stroke of an object. Since strokes and fills are what make objects visible, it is worthwhile to learn how to control them in any vector program you use. Using these types of controls, you can change the color and weight of fills and strokes of a selected object or you can set the options for new paths by clicking a tool and choosing settings before you begin to draw, which is covered in the next section.

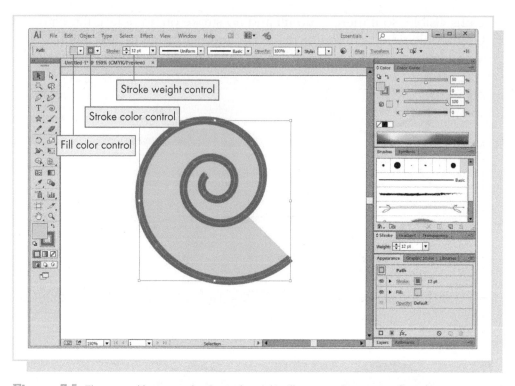

Figure 7.5 *The control boxes on the Control panel in Illustrator change to reflect the settings of a selected object. Notice that the fill and stroke colors are also reflected on the Tools panel to the left of the workspace and in the Color panel to the right of the workspace. You can adjust fill and stroke color settings by clicking the icons at either of these locations as well.*

Table 7.1 *Setting stroke and fill options on the Control panel in Illustrator.*

TO	DO THIS
Change the fill or stroke color options	Click the small arrow to the right of each control box and make a selection from the panel that appears.
Switch from the color swatch panel to a manual color settings panel	Press the Shift key and click the arrow next to the fill or stroke color control box.
Adjust the stroke weight	Click the arrow next to the stroke weight control box and make a selection from the menu that appears.
Access additional stroke settings beyond weight	Click the word "Stroke" to the left of the stroke weight control box and make selections from the stroke panel that appears.

checkpoint

What are the main parts of vector objects and what makes them visible?

ACTIVITY 7.1 ▶ Using Drawing Tools

1. Using Adobe Illustrator or another, similar vector editing program, create a new image named **7_Activity1_tool_practice** that is 8.5 × 11 inches.

2. Choose a fill and stroke color. Use the Rectangle tool to draw a rectangle at the top left corner. Deselect the rectangle. Change the fill and stroke color. Hold down the Shift key and use the Rectangle tool to draw a square next to the first rectangle drawn.

3. Turn on the rulers and guides. If your software has shortcuts to the rulers and guides, you may want to learn them!

4. Select the rectangle with the Selection tool. Experiment with the stroke and fill options on the Control panel. Repeat this with the square.

5. Below the rectangle, draw an ellipse using the Ellipse tool. Next to the ellipse, draw a circle by holding down the Shift key while using the Ellipse tool. Select each of the objects and choose a fill and stroke color. Experiment with options.

6. Use the Line Segment tool to draw some lines underneath the ellipse. Underneath the circle, hold down the Shift key to draw a straight line. Adjust stroke colors and options.

7. Underneath the line on the left side, draw a spiral using the Spiral tool. With the spiral selected, choose to copy the spiral. Paste the spiral and drag it so it is next to the first spiral. Add a different stroke color and stroke weight to each spiral.

8. Using the ruler, drag all the objects as needed so that they do not extend beyond a 1-inch margin at the top, bottom, left, or right of the image space.

9. Save **7_Activity1_tool_practice** in the native file type.

Granata1111/Dreamstime.com

Early Vectors

It might be surprising to learn that vector drawing preceded raster drawing. Early computers relied upon mathematicians to create graphics software. These mathematicians understood the use of geometry to create images and incorporated these tools into graphic functions. Sketchpad was the first such drawing system. Vector software went on to be used extensively in computer-aided design (CAD) programs used by architects and others who were less interested in color variations and more concerned with creating linear images such as buildings.

Vectors also were used to create 3-D drawing programs because a linear framework was possible. With a framework, a figure such as a human hand could be created and made to move. More recently, the field of scientific visualization has developed vector applications to render scientific data in graphic ways that allow for easier analysis of data. Because of the widespread use of digital cameras, the general population is more familiar with raster images and the editing that is possible, but vectors are used just as widely in other environments.

Raster Versus Vector Software

Why is it important for a graphic artist to be familiar with both raster and vector editing software? Is one graphic format easier for you to grasp than the other?

Lesson 7.2 ▶ Working with Objects

As indicated at the beginning of the chapter, vector editing programs are extremely complex and capable of a huge range of tasks. In addition, most vector programs provide multiple methods for doing the same thing. This section covers some basic drawing and editing tasks that should help you get started drawing and editing objects in your vector software. As you work in a program more and more, you'll undoubtedly find other methods for the same tasks. You might even find shortcuts that streamline your workflow.

Drawing Simple Shapes and Lines *LO 7.2*

shape tools—Vector drawing tools that enable a user to draw common, closed-path shapes with ease and efficiency.

Most if not all vector drawing applications feature tools that enable you to easily draw common, closed path shapes with a single stroke or click. In Illustrator, these tools are referred to generally as **shape tools**. In most vector applications, you'll see a range of shape tools such as rectangle tools, ellipse tools, polygon tools, and even star tools. You can normally access these on a main toolbar, although some tools may be hidden behind others. For example, the Rectangle tool is visible on the Illustrator tool panel by default. To access the other shape tools, click the small arrow next to the Rectangle tool and make a new selection from the menu that appears. Table 7.2 details the shape tools available in Illustrator, but you will find similar tools in any vector program. To use a shape tool in Illustrator, select the tool and set the stroke and

Table 7.2 *Basic shape tools in Illustrator.*

TOOL	NAME	DESCRIPTION
▢	Rectangle tool	Draws four-sided closed paths.
▢	Rounded Rectangle tool	Draws four-sided closed paths with rounded corners.
⬭	Ellipse tool	Draws circle and oval closed paths.
⬡	Polygon tool	Draws multisided closed paths with equal sides. By default, draws a six-sided shape; change the number of sides by selecting the tool and clicking once in the workspace to access the options dialog box.
☆	Star tool	Draws closed-path stars. By default, draws a five-pointed star; change the number of points by selecting the tool and clicking once in the workspace to access the options dialog box.

fill options. Then either click and drag to create the shape or click once on the workspace with your mouse and enter the relevant options for the shape in the dialog box that appears. Shape tools in other vector editing programs such as CorelDRAW function similarly. When you draw with a shape tool, anchor points and segments are automatically added along the path of the object.

Most vector programs include other easy-to-use tools for drawing straight and curved open path line segments by clicking and dragging in the workspace. In Illustrator, this is called a **line tool**. Table 7.3 details some of the line tools available in Illustrator. Other programs might use different names for the same type of tools, but they likely function in a similar way. Using a line tool is similar to using a shape tool: Select the tool, set the stroke and fill options, then click and drag or click once in the workspace and set options in the dialog box that appears. Again, some of the tools may be hidden beneath others on the main toolbar in your vector program, so you might need to search out the tool you want if you don't see it on the main panel. As with shape tools, anchor points and segments are automatically added to objects you draw with a line tool.

line tool—Draws open path line segments.

Table 7.3 *Basic line tools in Illustrator.*

TOOL	NAME	DESCRIPTION
/	Line Segment tool	Draws straight, open path line segments.
⌒	Arc tool	Draws curved, open path line segments.
◎	Spiral tool	Draws clockwise or counterclockwise open path spirals.
▦	Rectangular Grid tool	Draws a rectangular grid.
◉	Polar Grid tool	Draws a circular grid.

Drawing Straight and Curved Segments with a Pen Tool *LO 7.3*

Another common type of vector drawing tool enables you to draw objects by placing anchor points one at a time. This is called a Pen tool in Illustrator. Your vector application may call this something else; for instance, it is called a Bezier tool in CorelDRAW. Whatever it is called, it is one of the most useful tools in a vector drawing program, although it may take a bit longer to master than a shape or line tool. With a shape tool, a line tool, or a brush tool (in both raster and vector programs), you click and drag once to create the shape or line. Drawing an object with a pen tool, however, requires a series of clicks. To draw straight line segments with a pen tool, click once on the workspace where you would like the line to begin. This places an anchor point at that spot. Move the insertion point to the spot where you would like the segment to end and click again. Another anchor point appears at that spot and a line segment connects the two anchor points. Continue clicking to add anchor points and connecting segments. To end the path in Illustrator, press Ctrl + click (PC) or Cmd + click (Mac) or simply select another tool from the Tools panel. See Figure 7.6 for an example of this process in Illustrator.

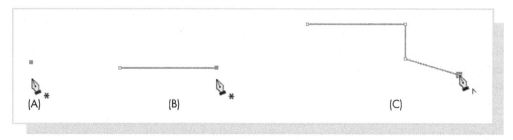

Figure 7.6 *An example of drawing straight line segments with a Pen tool in Illustrator. (A) The first anchor point is set with a click of the mouse. (B) A second anchor point is set with a second click of the mouse and a line segment connects the two. (C) Two more anchor points are set with clicks of the mouse and two more segments are added to the object connecting the points.*

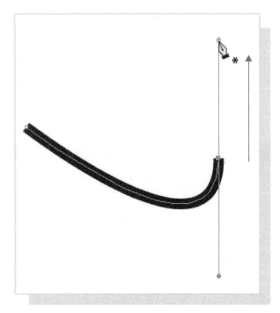

Figure 7.7 *To draw a curve in Illustrator using a Pen tool, click to add the first anchor point, move the insertion point, and then click and drag the mouse to adjust the curve before releasing the mouse button. This curve was created by dragging the mouse up as indicated by the arrow. You'll learn about the long blue line next to this segment in the following section.*

You can also draw curved segments with a pen tool. To draw a curved line segment, click once on the workspace to set an anchor point. Move the insertion point and click again, but this time hold down the mouse button and drag. The line segment you've created will curve. The curve continues to change as you drag the mouse up, down, left, right, or diagonally until you release the mouse button. See Figure 7.7 for an example of drawing a curve in Illustrator. Other vector drawing programs function similarly. Drawing curves may take more practice than using other tools in a vector drawing program, so don't be afraid to experiment. The good news is that if you don't like a curve you draw, you can adjust it without starting over. You'll learn about that in the next section.

You can draw either open or closed path objects with a pen tool. The examples in Figures 7.6 and 7.7 are both open path objects since they begin in one place and end in another. To draw a closed path object with a pen tool, place your final anchor point over the first one. The pen tool icon should change to indicate that it is above the first anchor point. In Illustrator, this is indicated by a small circle next to the icon (see Figure 7.8).

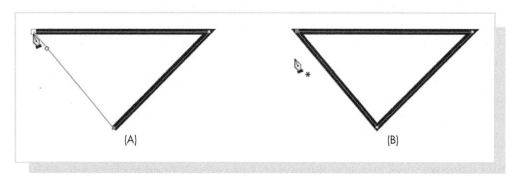

Figure 7.8 *In Illustrator, a small white circle appears when you place the insertion point over the first anchor point (A). Click to add the final anchor point over the first and create a closed path object (B).*

Illustrator and other vector drawing programs include additional drawing tools not described in this chapter. Take some time to explore these tools in your application. Your application's help documentation can be a good source for information about tools you are unfamiliar with. You can also learn about other tools by searching on a phrase that describes your task at hand, using either an Internet search engine or, sometimes more helpfully, the application's help documentation. For example, if you enter "tool to erase line segment" in Illustrator Help, an article describing the Path Eraser tool and how to use it appears.

Editing Objects *LO 7.4, 7.5, 7.6, and 7.7*

At some point while drawing, you'll likely want to move, resize, reshape, or otherwise transform an object. There are so many ways to edit a vector object that it is impractical to cover them all in this book. However, you may be surprised how much you can accomplish with a little bit of knowledge about just a few types of tools.

Using Selection Tools and Bounding Boxes

In vector programs, you can select and transform either a whole object or just one segment or anchor point at a time. To select the whole object, you use a selection tool. In many programs, the Selection tool is represented by an arrow icon on the toolbar. In Illustrator, the Selection tool is the black arrow at the top of the Tools panel. By default, when you click an object with the Selection tool, all of the object's paths and anchor points appear on the screen. For example, all of the objects shown in the Illustrator figures so far have been selected so you can see the blue guidelines representing the paths and anchor points.

In addition, in some vector programs, including Illustrator, a **bounding box** with eight small boxes, called handles, surrounds a selected object (see Figure 7.9). (The bounding box feature is usually active by default in Illustrator, but you can turn it off, too.) You can use the Selection tool and the bounding box to move, **scale** (resize), or rotate an object, as

bounding box—An outline around a selected vector object that can be used to transform the object.

scale—To resize an object to a percentage of its original size.

Figure 7.9 *Bounding boxes are created automatically around a vector object, making it easy to move or reshape it.*

described in Table 7.4. Transforming objects with a selection tool and bounding box is such a useful feature, it is worth exploring similar operations in other vector programs you may use.

Table 7.4 *Using the Illustrator Selection tool and bounding box to select and transform objects.*

TO	DO THIS
Select multiple objects	Hold down the Shift key and click each object or click and drag around multiple images.
Move a selected object	Click and drag the object, releasing the mouse button when it is positioned where you want it.
Scale a selected object	Hover over one of the handles on the bounding box until the pointer changes to a double-headed arrow, and then click and drag to shrink or enlarge. To keep the object's proportions when scaling, hold down the Shift key when you click and drag.
Rotate a selected object	Hover just outside of a handle on the bounding box until the pointer changes to a curved double-headed arrow, then click and drag to rotate in either direction. To limit the rotation to 45-degree increments, hold down the Shift key when you click and drag.
Copy and paste a selected object(s)	Select the object and then use the Copy and Paste commands on the Edit menu.

You can also select one segment or anchor point at a time to edit in most vector applications. In Illustrator, you do this by using the Direct Selection tool, which is the small white arrow just below the regular Selection tool on the Tools panel. (In CorelDRAW, the tool with a similar function is called the Shape tool, not to be confused with the general drawing tool term "shape tool" used in the previous section. In Inkscape, the similar tool is called the Node tool.) With the Direct Selection tool or a similar tool in another program, you can select an individual anchor point or line segment and drag it to reshape the object.

Sometimes you might want to modify an object where no anchor point exists. Helpfully, you can add anchor points to a path in most vector editing programs. In Illustrator you can use the Pen tool to add or remove anchor points along a segment with a single click. Simply hover over the segment where you would like to add a point and click when a small plus (+) sign appears next to the pen icon. (In other vector programs, you may need to use a different tool and double-click a segment to add a point.)

Figure 7.10 shows how some of the tools presented so far in this section can be used to convert a star shape to a rocket shape in Illustrator.

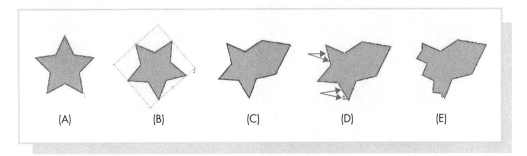

Figure 7.10 *(A) Star shape tool used to create a shape. (B) Selection tool and bounding box used to select the star and rotate it. (C) Direct Selection tool used to pull an anchor point and form the 'nose' of the rocket. (D) Pen tool used to add four additional anchor points (as indicated by red arrows). (E) Direct Selection tool used to pull the new anchor points and reshape the "tail" of the rocket.*

Transforming Curved Segments

Refer to Figure 7.7 and note the long blue line that extends from the right endpoint of the segment. In most vector programs, when you select a curved segment, lines like the blue line in Figure 7.7 appear at the smooth points on that segment. In Illustrator and some other programs, these are called directional handles and they are used to shape curves on a path. The lines on directional handles are called directional lines and are capped at the end with directional points. In Illustrator, you can use the Direct Selection tool to click and drag the directional lines or directional points to reshape and/or resize a curve. Figure 7.11 shows a curve before and after it was adjusted, but the best way to understand how directional handles control curves is to practice with them.

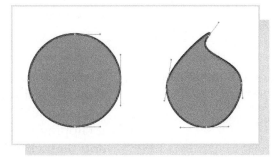

Figure 7.11 *The Illustrator circle on the left was transformed into the teardrop on the right using the directional handles.*

Rearranging Stacked Objects

You can overlap or stack objects in a vector editing program by clicking an object with the selection tool and dragging it over another object. You can also change the order of stacked objects. In Illustrator, you can do this by selecting the object you would like to reorder, choosing Arrange from the Object menu on the Application bar at the top of the workspace, and then choosing an option from the submenu that appears. You can also select an object to reorder. Right-click and choose Arrange from the pop-up menu that appears, and then choose an option from the list. Most vector programs have similar procedures for stacking and reordering stacked objects.

Creating a Clipping Mask

One reason you may want to stack objects is to create a clipping mask (sometimes referred to as just "clip" or "mask" in certain programs).

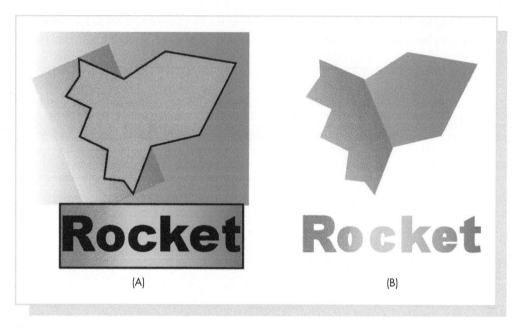

Figure 7.12 *A vector image before (A) and after (B) clipping masks were applied in Illustrator. The rocket clipping mask was created by stacking two colored square objects and the rocket shape (blue at the back, red/orange in the middle, rocket shape on top), selecting all three objects, and then choosing Make Clipping Mask. The word 'Rocket' clipping mask was created by stacking the word over the red/blue square, selecting both objects, and then choosing Make Clipping Mask.*

clipping mask—A vector object used to hide portions of lower objects in a stack.

A **clipping mask** is an object that hides the object(s) below it so that they show through only inside the clipping mask (see Figure 7.12). This is similar to a layer mask in a raster editing program. To create a clipping mask in Illustrator, stack two or more objects, select them, and then choose Clipping Mask > Make from the Object menu on the main Application bar at the top of the workspace. (You can also right-click the selected stack and choose Make Clipping Mask from the menu that appears.) The top object becomes the clipping mask and the objects below it show through just the clipping mask area. The hidden parts of the lower objects are not erased by the clipping mask. You can reveal them again by right-clicking and selecting Release Clipping Mask or by choosing Object > Clipping Mask > Release from the Application bar.

Clipping masks can be used to create all kinds of great effects and also to crop raster images that you place in a vector editing program. To place a raster image in an Illustrator document, choose Place from the File menu on the Application bar. (Some vector programs refer to this as "inserting" or "importing" a raster image. Check your particular software to determine which terminology is used and how to use it.) Once placed in a vector document, the raster image becomes an object you can scale, rotate, move, and otherwise manipulate. Clipping masks are often used with raster images to create interesting fill effects for text or to crop a photo.

checkpoint

What are some ways you can transform vector objects that you draw?

ACTIVITY 7.2 ▶ Creating and Editing Objects

1. Using vector editing software, create an 8.5- × 11-inch artboard.

2. Place the *hydrangea.jpg* image from your data files approximately in the center of the artboard.

3. Turn on rulers and grids and zoom in as needed.

4. Scale the image so it is 5 × 3.75 inches.

5. Using the Pen tool (or your software's equivalent):

   a. Draw a rectangle that is 1 inch larger than the image on all sides, using a complementary color for fill and border.

   b. Add anchor points in the middle of each of the sides.

6. Using the Direct Selection tool (or your vector software's equivalent), select the anchor point on the left side. Pull the anchor point toward the center of the rectangle by clicking and dragging the anchor point. Repeat this on the other sides.

7. Arrange the images by selecting the rectangle drawn with the Pen tool and sending it to the back.

8. Drag the image and the rectangle to the top of the artboard.

9. Place another copy of *hydrangea.jpg* on the lower part of the artboard. Scale the image so that it fits in the remaining space. Leave it large enough to focus on the colors of the flowers and leaves.

10. Using a text tool, in an appropriate font and size, key **Think Pink!** Place the words over any area of the flowers.

11. Select both images, then make a clipping mask.

12. Drag the text with the flower pattern below the flower image as shown at right. Center the text horizontally on the background rectangle.

13. Place another *hydrangea.jpg* on the artboard, scaling it to fit. Draw a star anywhere on the flowers in the image.

14. Select the star and the image and make a clipping mask.

15. Drag the star that now is filled with the flower pattern to the upper left of the background rectangle.

16. Copy and paste the star in the upper right of the background rectangle.

17. Use the Selection tool (or other appropriate tool in your software) to position all of the objects appropriately.

18. Save as *7_Activity2_think_pink* in native file type.

Active Listening

Technical skills and creativity are important to success on the job, especially in digital media careers where a healthy dose of both is helpful. However, one crucial job skill requires no technical know-how or artistic talent: listening. Active listening—really listening and not just hearing—can make you more effective at your job and help you avoid conflict and misunderstandings in the workplace, not to mention gain the respect and admiration of your managers and colleagues.

Active listening not only makes you seem more competent, it can also actually make you more proficient because you'll be better able to meet expectations if you work to understand them when they are communicated to you. Improving your listening skills takes a concerted effort. Try the active listening tips below in your classroom and notice what kind of impact it has. Do you struggle less to understand assignments if you actively listen when the instructor assigns them? Are you able to get right to work on a project without asking for a lot of repeated information? Do you notice less frustration on the part of the instructor? Do your grades improve?

- Most important, give your undivided attention to the speaker. Do not look at your phone, work on your computer, or read while someone is talking to you.

- Let the speaker know you are listening by looking directly at him or her and using nonverbal cues like nodding occasionally, using facial expressions, and interjecting an occasional confirmation, like, "yes" or "I understand." Don't, however, think you can be distracted and absently nod or murmur "mm-hmm." A speaker can tell if you are just going through the motions and not really listening.

- Don't interrupt, but do ask clarifying questions at appropriate intervals. The most important element of active listening is understanding what's being communicated. Asking follow-up questions also lets the listener know you are paying attention and making an effort to absorb the message.

- Resist the urge to form a response in your head before a speaker is done talking to you. Although it is important to think before you speak, you may miss some critical information if you stop paying attention to compose your response.

Many of you may be fantastic artists who can draw anything by hand but find it difficult to replicate your images using only vector drawing tools. Luckily, most vector editing programs include a feature that automatically traces bitmap images and converts them to vector objects. This means you can scan a sketch into a bitmap file, place it in a vector document, trace and convert it to vectors, and then use editing tools to adjust and finalize the image. You can do the same thing with a photo placed in a vector document. In Illustrator, the automatic tracing feature is called Image Trace. Other vector programs have different names for this feature, but they enable you to do the same thing.

A vector tracing feature works similarly in different programs. Some programs offer more controls and options, but the basic idea is the same. To use Image Trace in Illustrator, place a raster file in an Illustrator document. Select the raster object, and then choose Object/Image Trace/Make from the Application bar. You can open the Image Trace panel, shown in Figure 7.13, to modify default settings. Until you are familiar with all of the settings in this box, you may want to experiment with the preset options. You can preview the effect of each preset by ensuring the Preview check box is checked and then scrolling through the list of preset options. When you see an

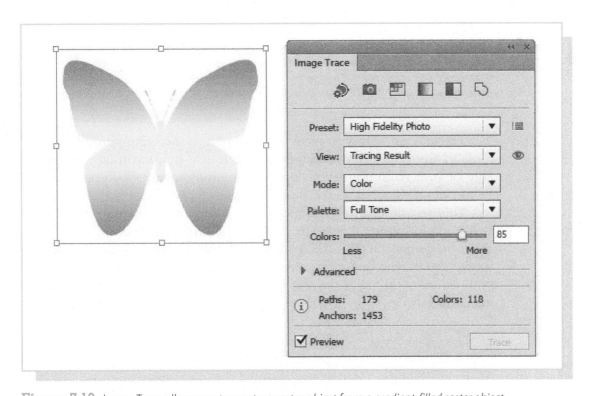

Figure 7.13 *Image Trace allows you to create a vector object from a gradient-filled raster object.*

effect you like, click the Trace button. When you are certain you like the effect, make sure the object is selected and then select Object > Image Trace > Expand from the Application bar. The bitmap is converted to a vector with strokes and fills according to the Image Trace options.

Once you've converted the bitmap to a vector object, you can edit it as you would any other vector object. For instance, Figure 7.14 shows how the butterfly from Figure 7.13 was layered over a rectangle containing an Illustrator pattern fill and converted into a clipping mask. This would not have been possible without first converting the bitmap of the butterfly into a vector object.

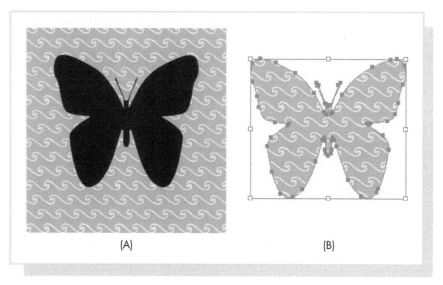

(A) (B)

Figure 7.14 *You can use a raster image converted into a vector image using a tracing feature just as you would any other vector image. In this figure, the butterfly from Figure 7.13 was converted to a simple shape using Image Trace, layered over a patterned rectangle (A), and made into a clipping mask (B).*

Tracing can help you grow accustomed to the editing and drawing tools in any vector drawing application. It also helps you take advantage of your natural artistic talent by providing a way to use your hand-drawn sketches as the basis of digital drawings.

This section covered the most basic elements of tracing. It is well worth exploring the feature in your vector program of choice. However, don't be tempted to use the feature to simply replicate someone else's work. The tracing feature in any vector program is intended to help you use scanned images as the basis of new and original digital drawings and artwork.

checkpoint

What is the purpose behind a tracing feature in a vector editing program?

ACTIVITY 7.3 ▶ Using the Tracing Feature

1. Use vector editing software to create a new 8.5- × 11-inch document.

2. Place the image **apple.jpg** from your data files on the newly created artboard. Resize the image to 3 inches wide. Copy the image and paste it three times on the artboard, so you have a total of four identical images.

3. Select the first image. Use Image Trace (or a comparable tool) and change the Preset to Shades of Gray.

4. Select another image. Use Image Trace to change the preset to 6 Colors.

5. Select another image, trace it, select Low Fidelity Photo, and then change the View to display Outlines.

6. Experiment with other settings for the final image.

7. Save as **7_Activity3_traced_apples** in the native file type.

Impact

lavitrei/Shutterstock.com

Image Effects

In today's world, the impact of images upon businesses has been both a curse and a blessing. Because it is possible to enhance photographs and artwork, more is expected of the images that are used on the Web and in print. No longer is a slightly fuzzy photograph acceptable. No longer is it okay to have the color of a person's shirt not match exactly the intention of the designer. As a result, more time is often required to produce a publication than in the past. The outcome is better but the cost is the same or greater than in an earlier time.

Critical Thinking

1. Is there ever a point where it becomes important to say, "This is good enough"?

2. Has the ability to make images "perfect" actually improved the effectiveness of the message?

Key Concepts

▶ Vectors are defined by open and closed paths, anchor points, and segments. *LO 7.1*

▶ Strokes and fills are what make a path visible. *LO 7.1*

▶ Shape and line tools make it easy to draw objects with a single stroke or click. *LO 7.2*

▶ Certain tools in vector applications enable you to draw a path by plotting anchor points one at a time. *LO 7.3*

▶ Selection tools can be used to select and transform a whole object or one segment/anchor point at a time. *LO 7.4*

▶ Bounding boxes appear around selected vector objects and can be used with a selection tool to quickly transform objects. *LO 7.4*

▶ Directional handles at smooth points on a curved segment control the size and shape of the curve. *LO 7.5*

▶ You can stack and rearrange vector objects. *LO 7.6*

▶ A clipping mask is a vector object used to hide portions of lower objects in a stack. *LO 7.7*

▶ A tracing feature converts raster images into editable vector objects. *LO 7.8*

Review and Discuss

1. Compare and contrast raster and vector graphics. *LO 7.1*

2. Indicate the primary advantages of a vector image. *LO 7.1*

3. Define paths in vector images. *LO 7.1 and 7.4*

4. Define anchors in vector images. *LO 7.1 and 7.2*

5. Explain handles and their purpose in vector graphics. *LO 7.1 and 7.2*

6. Define points and explain how they relate to vector images. *LO 7.1, 7.2, and 7.3*

7. Describe objects in vector drawings. *LO 7.1 and 7.6*

8. Define a bounding box in vector graphics. *LO 7.8*

9. Differentiate between a selection tool and a direct selection tool. *LO 7.1 and 7.4*

10. Identify the tool used to add or remove points along the line or curve in a vector drawing. *LO 7.4 and 7.5*

11. Define a clipping mask and detail how it is used as a cropping tool. *LO 7.7*

12. What can you do with Arrange options? *LO 7.6*

13. Name a tool that can be used to convert raster images to vector images. *LO 7.8*

14. Analyze when it would be an advantage to convert a raster image into a vector image. *LO 7.8*

15. List some of the special effects possibly available in vector software. *LO 7.1*

Apply

1. Create a new 5 x 4 inch image named **7_Apply1_the barn**. Place **barn.jpg** from your data files on the artboard. Scale as needed. Create a clipping mask from the sky area with the text **The Barn Restaurant**. Drag off the artboard. Place another copy of **barn.jpg** on the artboard. Resize to 5 x 4 inches. Drag the text back onto the image. If needed, place a black rectangle behind the text so that it shows better on the image. Arrange as needed and group the image. Save **7_Apply1_the_barn** in the native file type. *LO 7.2 and 7.6*

2. Place **hydrangea.jpg** from your data files onto a 5- x 4-inch artboard. Add a 3-D effect to the image. Resize the image and move to the right half of the artboard. Add the text **Spring Flower Show** on the left with an appropriate text type, size, and color. Experiment with changing the stroke color and size. Add a skew effect to the text. Draw a rectangle the size of the artboard and arrange the rectangle so it is in the back. Add an appropriate color to the rectangle, then group the objects. Save as **7_Apply2_spring_flowers** in the native file type. *LO 7.2, 7.4, and 7.6*

3. Using the Pen tool on an 8- x 8-inch artboard, draw the following three road signs: stop, speed limit, and dead end. If needed, search for official road signs on the Internet and print or take notes before beginning. Fill each with the appropriate color, use appropriate text font and color, and appropriate border color and weight. Use rulers to help draw the image in proportion. Save as **7_Apply3_road_signs** in the native file type. *LO 7.2, 7.3, and 7.6*

4. Find your favorite logo on the Internet or a print copy of the logo. Using what you have learned in this chapter, attempt to draw this logo. Save as **7_Apply4_logo** in the native file type. *LO 7.2, 7.3, 7.4, 7.5, and 7.6*

5. Using an interest or hobby as a topic, locate at least three images that have to do with that hobby. Create a collage of these three images on an artboard that is 8.5 x 11 inches. Convert the images to vector graphics if needed. Make at least three changes to each image using the skills you learned in this chapter. Add text to the scratch area explaining what changes you made to each image. Save as **7_Apply5_my_hobbies** in native file type. *LO 7.2, 7.3, 7.4. 7.5, 7.6, and 7.8*

Explore

1. Pick one of the skills from this chapter and search the Internet for a "how to" video on that skill. Watch the video and learn from it, even if the video is not in the same version as your software or not the software you use. An example would be to search for: **clipping masks Illustrator**. In a word processing document, write a short paragraph on what you learned from the video. Include a reference to the video (in MLA style). Save as **7_Explore1_video**. *LO 7.2, 7.3, 7.4, 7.5, 7.6, 7.7, and 7.8*

2. In a team of three or four students, search for information on using special effects, such as from an effects gallery, or artistic, blur, or brush strokes. (These are only a few examples. View your software to see what is available.) Use an image to try different special effects. You can locate an image on your own or use any from the data files in this chapter. Write a summary of what you learned, including at least two references in MLA format. Include in your summary what type of special effects worked on your image, which ones did not, and why. Save your summary as **7_Explore2_special_effects**. Insert an image example of one good and one bad special effect from your experiment. If time permits, present your summary to the class. Include in your presentation a visual of at least one good example of your image and one special effect that was not effective. *LO 7.4*

3. Search for a current movie that you would like to see. Find one of the official images used in marketing the movie. Save the image to insert in your summary. Write a summary of what this image communicates to you about the movie and analyze what special effects and tools may have been used to create the image. Save as **7_Explore3_movie**. *LO 7.4 and 7.7*

Academic Connections

Communications: With a partner, write instructions to draw a house. Swap instructions with different partners. Using the instructions from the partner and the Pen tool in Illustrator (or comparable tool in your software), draw the house. Save your drawing as **7_AC_communications**. Take a few minutes to share with the class the differences between how the house you gave instructions for looked and what you anticipated it would look like.

Science: Visit the website for the Arizona Science Center, My Digital World series if available. If this site is no longer available, search for another digital world website or on the keywords "digital science." Create a slide show advertising My Digital World for the Arizona Science Center (or for the site you found). The slide show should contain at least six slides and two images. Images should contain a reference in the footer on the slide in which they are used. Save as **7_AC_science**.

UNIT 2 PROJECTS

Independent Project
Creating a Business Identity

Brainstorm and decide on a business name to use for this project. The business name should reflect the type of business that your digital imaging project is going to advertise. Write a tag line for the business. Complete the steps below, documenting the software and photography skills that you are using as you complete each part of the project.

1. Using your camera, take a minimum of 50 digital photographs. Review Chapter 4 on digital photography and the rules and tips that you have learned for good pictures. The topic of the pictures should be what you want to use to build a business identity for your project.

2. Choose 24 of the pictures you have taken to use in the project. These pictures should be ones that will establish and enhance a business identity. Use these images to create at least six marketing items. More than one image should be used in most of these marketing items. Be sure that there is at least one print project and one Web project. Some ideas for marketing include:

   - Mural for an office.
   - Banner for a website.
   - Image for a t-shirt.
   - Billboard advertisement.
   - Logo for the business.
   - Magazine or newspaper advertisement.
   - Images for a brochure.
   - Others specific to business; for instance, a restaurant will need a design for a menu.
   - Cover for a journal.

As you create these projects, save them in the native file format for the software used and save another copy in the format that would be best for its intended use.

3. In your projects, use a variety of both raster and vector graphics, documenting which ones are raster and which ones are vector.

4. Use both complementary and analogous colors in the designs.

5. Use CMYK and RGB colors in different projects.

6. Resize, recolor, and resample as needed. Include this in the documentation for the skills that you have used and the intended use for the project.

7. Save the projects as: *Unit2_m1*, *Unit2_m2*, *Unit2_m3*, *Unit2_m4*, *Unit2_m5*, and *Unit2_m6.*

Portfolio

Create three folders to add to your portfolio: **Unit2_project_images**, **Unit2_business_identity**, and **Unit2_classwork**.

In the **Unit2_project_images** folder, add the images that you took with your camera. Before adding them, be sure that you have resized and resampled them to an appropriate size if you did not do so while creating the unit project.

In the **Unit2_business_identity** folder, add the marketing items that you created—in their native file type and in the file type that is best for their intended use.

Save the documentation for the Unit 2 Project as **Unit2_journal** in the **Unit2_classwork** folder. This should include documentation of the skills that you used in completing this project.

Also, choose at least six class assignments from the end of chapter Apply or Explore activities to add to the **Unit2_classwork** folder. Choose those that you think demonstrate your best work and show a high degree of skill.

iStockphoto.com/Pashalgnatov

FBLA-PBL or BPA

Visit the national website for FBLA-PBL or BPA. Find at least 6–10 items on the website that create an identity for the organization.

www.fbla-pbl.org

www.bpa.org

Summarize your findings by listing the images found and answering the following questions about the images collectively or individually:

▶ Do you think the images are original? Why or why not?

▶ If the image is original, is there anything that the person taking the picture could have done to make it more effective? Include in your discussion any relevant points from the chapter on creating effective images.

▶ Is there more than one image or element included in the finished product? How many? What was used to create each one?

▶ What feelings does the image (or the collection of images) elicit in you when you first view it?

▶ What would you have done differently for the image, both in taking the picture or editing it to place on the Web?

▶ Did you agree with the elements added to it? What would you have done differently?

▶ Are the colors appropriate for Web publishing?

▶ Which images or elements that help create the Web identity could also be used in print publishing? Why?

▶ Overall, do the images build a good business identity? Why or why not?

Print Publishing

8	Print Type
9	Print Graphics
10	Print Design

Career Clusters: Graphic Designer

Interview with Craig, graphic designer at Ramsdell Design

Describe your average day. During a typical day I'm able to spend most of my time designing, which I love. Because my office is in my house, I'm at work as soon as I'm done with breakfast, usually by 8:00 a.m. and I work until 6:00 p.m. most nights. I design books, book covers, and websites, employing photographs, illustrations, and text in my designs depending on the direction I get from consulting with clients. Although I started my career before design went digital, the computer is now part of my everyday design life.

What is the worst part of your job? The worst part of my job is not knowing if there will be work to do when I'm finished with my current projects. And having to pester clients who are late in paying!

What is the best part of your job? Getting to spend most of my time designing and not having to be in many meetings, or doing budgets and other running-the-business kind of stuff.

Employment Outlook In general, average employment growth is expected for graphic designers in the near future, with high competition for jobs, according to the U.S. Bureau of Labor Statistics. Most graphic designers concentrate in a specific area, such as advertising, newspaper design, or website design. More and more, graphic designers with experience in website and animation design have the most employment opportunities as demand for online, mobile phone, and other electronic media content increases.

Skills and Qualifications Most graphic artists hold a bachelor's degree in fine arts, graphic design, or a related concentration. To be most employable, graphic artists should keep up with the latest digital media software and tools. Beyond postsecondary training and natural artistic talent, a graphic designer must possess excellent communication skills, an ability to recognize and willingness to adapt to changing trends, and self-motivation. Since more than half of all graphic designers are self-employed, some basic business know-how is also important for graphic designers.

Job Titles graphic designer, graphic artist, art director

What About You? Graphic design is an appealing career for artistic people, but not the easiest field to break into. Use a search engine to research job openings for graphic designers.

- What sort of qualifications do employers want to see in candidates?
- Do the postings mention any specific software packages job seekers should know?
- How can you maximize your chances of success in a graphic design career?

Chapter 8

Print Type

Lesson 8.1 The Vocabulary of Typography

Lesson 8.2 Making Text Readable

Lesson 8.3 Cleaning Up Typeset Text

When you look at a magazine, a book, a newspaper, a poster, an invitation, or any other printed document with text, you may or may not notice the text on the page. However, whether it's subtle or commands your attention, the text is just as important to a good design as the choice and arrangement of art or photographs. The text selection, position, spacing, size, and more are all an important element of design collectively called typography.

Learning Outcomes

▶ **8.1** Distinguish between typefaces and fonts.

▶ **8.2** Describe the parts that make up a typeface.

▶ **8.3** Understand how typeface, size, and style affect readability.

▶ **8.4** Adjust leading and tracking for readability.

▶ **8.5** Recognize how measure and alignment impact readability.

▶ **8.6** Use common, simple techniques to grab attention with typography.

▶ **8.7** Make documents clean and professional by using a few typesetting conventions.

Key Terms

- alignment
- ascender
- baseline
- curly quotes
- descender
- display typeface
- em dash
- en dash
- font
- kerning
- leading
- measure
- orphan
- point
- sans serif
- serif
- tracking
- typeface
- widow
- x-height

The first lesson in learning about typography, like so many other subjects, is a vocabulary lesson. Very likely you are familiar with the terms typeface and font. However, perhaps you don't know the difference between the two; in fact, you might use both words to mean the same thing. Technically, there's a difference. **Typeface** refers to a set of letters, numbers, and other characters created, like a piece of art, by a typeface designer. For example, Times New Roman is a typeface, and all of the characters in the typeface share certain design characteristics. A **font**, on the other hand, refers to a collection of characters with the same style within a typeface.

The best way to understand this difference is to consider an example: Times New Roman Bold, Times New Roman Italic, and Times New Roman Regular are all fonts within the Times New Roman typeface style. This modern meaning of the term font relates to the computer files used to depict text on a screen and to print text on a printer or press. The data for each typeface style is stored in a separate file. So, if you look in the fonts folder on your computer, you will likely see several files related to the Times New Roman typeface. In Windows, you will probably find Times.ttf (regular), TimesBD.ttf (bold), TimesBI.ttf (bold italic), and TimesI.ttf (italic). Each of these files is a different font, but they all belong to a single typeface. (See the History feature for more information about the history of the term font.)

Beyond distinguishing between the terms typeface and font, knowing some other common typographical terms will help you learn more about typefaces. Figure 8.1 identifies some of these elements, and Table 8.1 describes them in a little more detail.

With these few vocabulary terms, you are ready to move on to what typography is really all about: using text in a design.

typeface—A collection of letters, numbers, and other characters created by a designer.

font—Within a typeface, a set of characters with a specific style.

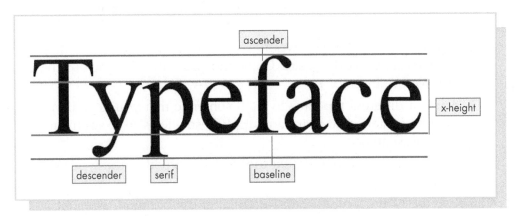

Figure 8.1 *This diagram identifies some of the elements of a typeface. Table 8.1 describes these and a few additional terms in more detail.*

Table 8-1 *Common terminology used to describe typefaces or typeface elements.*

Serif	Typefaces with small decorative strokes or "feet" at the ends of the main strokes that define each letter.
Sans serif	Typefaces with no serifs.
Descender	The part of a lowercase letter that extends below the baseline, as in the letter "y."
Ascender	The part of a letter that extends above the x-height, as in the letter "f."
Baseline	The imaginary line on which the typeface sits.
x-height	In simple terms, the height of the lowercase letter "x" in a given font.
Points	The unit of measure used to indicate the size of type. One point is approximately 1/72 of an inch.

Think About It

Typeface Design and Copyright

Search the Internet to determine if a typeface designer can protect his or her work with a copyright in the United States. Do you agree or disagree with what you discover about typefaces and copyright law?

checkpoint

What is the difference between a typeface and a font?

ACTIVITY 8.1 ▶ Identifying Elements in a Typeface

1. Create a new 8.5- × 11-inch document using your desktop publishing software.
2. Key a sentence that you would use for your current update status on a social networking site. Copy and paste the sentence so there are five instances of it.
3. Apply a different typeface to each sentence that you keyed. Make the first sentence 20-point and apply a smaller size to each succeeding sentence.
4. Use the pasteboard and Text tool to label whether the typeface is serif or sans serif.
5. Use the Notes tool, if available, to label the baseline, x-height, ascender, and descender.
6. Save as *8_Activity1_identifying_elements*.

Granata1111/Dreamstime.com

Fonts Through the Ages

Originally, the term "font" referred to a collection of metal letters and other characters set on a press and used to print a specific size and style of a given typeface. This means that each typeface was associated with many different fonts, one for each size and style of that specific typeface. So, for example, 14-point Caslon Bold was one font and included all of the metal pieces needed to reproduce characters in 14-point Caslon Bold. To produce 12-point Caslon Italic, the press operator had to use another font that included all of the metal pieces for 12-point Caslon Italic.

In the computer age, the metal pieces once used to create type have been replaced by information in computer files called font files. Because computer fonts are scalable, size is no longer relevant in the definition of a font. However, different *styles* of a particular typeface are stored in separate font files. In this way, the legacy of the original metal fonts is reflected in the modern idea of a font.

Lesson 8.2 ▶ Making Text Readable

The primary concern for designers working with text is usually readability, especially when working with blocks of text. Readability means you can easily recognize the letters and words and follow the text along without "losing your place." It also means the text helps visually set the tone for the message. You can make text readable by selecting the appropriate typeface for the subject matter, using the right type size and style for your project, adjusting spacing if necessary, and considering the overall size and alignment of text blocks.

In the professional world, many companies, especially book, newspaper, and magazine publishers, develop their own rules for these typographical elements (Figure 8.2). If you are working on a project for someone else, it's a good idea to ask if they have a set of typographical rules, or type specifications. If not, you can use some basic guidelines presented in this section or consult other resources for more in-depth guidance.

Perhaps the best way to determine what works is to experiment. In some instances, you can try out different typographical design elements using a *lorem ipsum* text file. *Lorem ipsum* is basically a string of nonsensical Latin words that imitate real text. You can obtain a *lorem ipsum* text file easily on the Internet (be sure you trust the source you download from), flow it into your design, and adjust any of the elements described in this lesson to determine which combination works best.

iStockphoto.com/Izabela Habur

Figure 8.2 *Computers are used to assist with the creation of professional publications that have consistent typographical elements.*

Of course, because *lorem ipsum* is nonsensical, it isn't a perfect measure of readability. But it is very useful for determining at the beginning stages of a design whether a certain typeface is a good candidate for your text.

Selecting Typeface, Size, and Style for Readability *LO 8.3*

Choosing a typeface that fits the tone of a project is one way to help text deliver its message to readers. For example, a standard, traditional typeface is appropriate for a medical journal article, while a more playful typeface works for an invitation to a Halloween party (see Figure 8.3).

Although average readers probably don't know the name of a particular typeface, they can recognize the feel it gives to a document (see Figure 8.4). Furthermore, typefaces come in and out of style. If you are headed for a career in graphic arts, start paying attention to the typefaces you see around you every day. You may even want to start clipping examples of typefaces you think are effective so you can review them later when you need inspiration for your own projects.

Figure 8.3 *Which of these typefaces would work better for a medical journal article and which would be appropriate for a Halloween party invitation?*

Figure 8.4 *What do the typefaces in these two posters tell you on first glance about the art exhibits they promote?*

There is some debate in the design world about whether serif or sans serif typefaces are easier to read. For a long time, many people have insisted that serif typefaces are easier to read, at least in printed blocks of text. You'll still hear this idea from many sources. However, research has been unable to prove that either serif or sans serif typefaces improve readability. Most likely, it is a combination of typeface and other factors outlined in this section that makes a typeface more or less readable.

Picking a typeface that fits the tone of a project is important for helping express the text's message, but choosing the right size is even more important to readability, especially in an extended block of text. The best point size for a particular project depends on the typeface, the page size and layout, and the intended audience.

In a block of text, most typefaces are readable for most people at 10 to 12 points, and many books, magazines, and newspapers use that size range. However, that is not a hard and fast rule. In fact, if the text is set in multiple columns, you may find a smaller point size looks better. Or, if your audience is visually impaired (mostly elderly, for example) or beginning readers, you may consider using a larger point size to increase readability. In addition, the larger the print surface, the larger the type size can be. For example, 10-point text on an 18- × 24-inch poster intended to hang on a wall would not be very readable.

It's also important to realize that point size refers only to the height of the typeface rather than its width, so two typefaces with the same point size can be *visually* different sizes (see Figure 8.5). The best way to determine the right size is to start with standard 10- to 12-point type and increase or decrease it until it hits the right mark. The more familiar you become with different typefaces and their varying sizes, the less you'll have to experiment to determine what size is most readable in a particular document.

> This example is set at 11 point.
>
> This example is set at 11 point.

Figure 8.5 *These two different typefaces, both set at 11 point, take up different amounts of space.*

Occasionally, you may want to emphasize certain words or phrases in body text. The best type style to use for emphasis is italic or bold. These two type styles are the least disruptive for the reader and therefore the most readable. Avoid underlines, all caps, and combinations of type styles (bold *and* italic, for example). Be careful not to overuse type styles for emphasis. Extended use of italics, bold, all caps, reversed type, or any special effects such as embossing, engraving, outlining, or shadowing can reduce readability.

Adjusting Spacing to Improve Readability *LO 8.4*

Spacing in a block of text is just as important to readability as choosing the right typeface, size, and style. The space between the lines of text in a text block is called **leading** (pronounced "ledding") and it is measured from the baseline of one line of text to the baseline of the next. Even if the term is new to you, you are familiar with the concept of leading if you've ever changed a block of text to double-spaced in a word

leading—The amount of space between lines of text.

processing program. Double-spacing increases the leading in a block of text. Like type size, leading is expressed in points. The type size and leading of a text block are interrelated and are usually given together. For example, the expression "10/12 point" (read "10 on 12 point" or "10 over 12 point") indicates a 10-point type size with 12-point leading.

Readability is reduced if the leading is too tight or too loose. If the leading is too tight (meaning there is not enough space between lines), the ascenders and descenders of letters can crash, making the text difficult to read. On the other hand, if the leading is too loose (meaning there is too much space between lines), the lines of text may look disconnected.

Most computer applications that set text have an auto leading feature, commonly setting the leading at 120% of the point size. So, for example, a word processing program would automatically assign 10-point text a 12-point leading (10 points × 120% = 12 points). This equation works fine for some typefaces at some type sizes, but is not best for every situation. Different text characteristics and situations require increased leading for the best readability. For instance:

- Sans serif typefaces
- Looser word spacing
- Greater x-height
- Wider text columns

Sometimes, graphic designers drastically alter the leading, making it extremely tight or extremely loose. In these cases, the goal is not readability, but dramatic effect. Like so many other elements in design, trial and error (and experience!) is the best way to determine what works for any particular project. As you experiment with leading in your projects, it may be helpful to begin with the automatic setting and adjust up or down based on the characteristics listed above and, most important, what looks best to you as the designer.

tracking—The amount of space between characters.

The tracking on this sentence is normal.

The tracking on this sentence is expanded (loose).

The tracking on this sentence is reduced (tight).

Figure 8.6 *Adjusting tracking can improve readability in some instances and can also help fit text or address line breaks, but the adjustment should never call attention to itself.*

Tracking, sometimes called letter spacing, refers to the amount of space between characters in a word or line of text (see Figure 8.6). Adjusting this space can affect readability. Condensed or tight tracking (less space between characters) can make text hard to read, especially if the typeface is small. Some typefaces at certain sizes are more readable with a little bit of added space between characters (expanded or loose tracking), but too much space can make words slightly less recognizable and slow down readers.

In a few instances, minimal tracking can be useful to fit text in a certain space or fix problems with the way a word breaks at the end of a line, which will be covered later in this chapter. Once again, this adjustment should be applied on a case-by-case basis. Overall, however, the normal spacing between letters as set by the typeface designer is fine and you should not have to adjust it. If you do, it's best to change it very minimally so that the spacing does not call attention to itself and detract from the meaning of the words.

Tracking is often confused with **kerning**. Whereas tracking refers to adjusting all of the spaces between a group of characters equally, kerning refers to adjusting the space between just two characters to improve the appearance of a word. Sometimes when two letters fall next to one another, the normal, equal spacing can look strange. Adjusting the space between just those two characters—kerning—can improve the appearance. For example, notice in Figure 8.7 that the letters *T* and *y* are proportionally the same distance apart as are all other pairs of letters in the word. After kerning, the letter *y* tucks in under the *T* as shown in the second example.

Kerning can give a more finished look to words, but does not necessarily improve readability. Most modern, digital typefaces automatically adjust kerning when certain letter pairs fall next to one another in a word, so in normal typesetting, you should not have to use kerning frequently. It is mostly used for words in larger type sizes on banners, posters, ads, and occasionally headings.

kerning—Adjusting the space between two characters to improve appearance and readability.

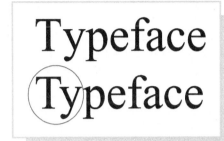

Figure 8.7 *Notice how kerning reduces the space between the "T" and the "y" in the second example in this figure. Kerning certain display typefaces can give the text a more finished look, but you should not have to use it very often.*

Considering Paragraph Width and Alignment LO 8.5

The width and alignment of a paragraph can affect the readability of body text. Lines of text that are too long or too short will slow down readers. But, again, there are no hard and fast rules about what makes the ideal paragraph width or alignment. What works best varies from situation to situation.

The length of a line of text is called the **measure**. The best measure depends to a great extent on the type size. Some designers use one formula or another to get a general idea of what paragraph width will work best in a given design and adjust from there. For example, one formula suggests doubling the point size of the typeface and using the resulting number as the paragraph width (in picas). (Note: Pica is a unit of measure widely used in design. You'll read more about picas in Chapter 10, "Print Design.") According to this formula, 11-point text would have an ideal text width of 22 picas (11 points × 2 = 22 points; use 22 picas wide).

You'll find lots of advice on text width if you search online. In general, however, most advice falls within 45 to 75 characters per line (including punctuation and spaces) for body text on a single-column printed page, with 66 characters per line, seemingly, the ideal.

Another element to consider when setting paragraphs is **alignment**. You are probably already familiar with the different paragraph

measure—The length of a line of text.

alignment—How a line of text or a paragraph is positioned in a column: flush left, flush right, centered, or justified.

alignment choices: flush left, flush right, centered, and justified. (If not, see Table 8.2 for an explanation.) In terms of readability, centered and flush right are the most difficult to read, at least in large blocks of text.

Table 8.2 *Explanation of paragraph alignment styles.*

	Flush left	Each line of text aligns at the left edge of the column and the right side is ragged.
	Flush right	Each line of text aligns at the right edge of the column and the left side is ragged.
	Centered	Each line of text is centered across the entire column and both left and right side are ragged.
	Justified	Spaces between letters and words in each line of text are automatically adjusted so text aligns on both the left and right side of the column.

Center alignment is reserved mainly for titles, stand-alone text such as an equation or a quotation, and sometimes for poetry. Flush right alignment is most useful for tables (like a table of contents), a column of numbers, short display text, or for languages that are read from right to left, such as Japanese. English and other languages that are read from left to right are most readable when set flush left or justified, so when setting a block of text, you will most often be choosing between those two alignments.

There is no conclusive evidence about which of these two makes blocks of text more readable, and both alignments are used extensively in printed material. Your choice will depend on publication style rules (many publications include alignment in their design specifications), on the tone of the project, and on your own best judgment as a designer. When choosing between the two, keep in mind the following general thoughts about the two alignments:

- Flush left is generally considered less formal and more inviting than justified text.
- Justified alignment looks cleaner and more formal than flush left text.
- Flush left produces fewer hyphenated words at the ends of lines and more even tracking, but can leave awkward gaps of white space between text columns.
- Justified text fits more words in a given space, but can produce awkwardly loose tracking on some lines and visually distracting hyphenation at the ends of lines.

Grabbing Attention and Creating Interest with Text *LO 8.6*

Although in most instances the first concern when working with text is making it readable, particularly in newspapers, books, and magazines, another important aspect of typography in design is capturing and directing a reader's attention. This is called display typography (see Figure 8.8).

Display typography can spark interest, set the mood, and help readers navigate text. In addition, this type of typography becomes a part of the overall design scheme and can support good proportion, balance, variety, emphasis, harmony, symmetry, unity, and repetition, all important principles of design that you'll learn about in Chapter 10. Advertisements, magazine layouts, and book covers especially rely on display typography to reinforce a design scheme.

silver tiger/Shutterstock.com

Figure 8.8 *How did the designer use typography to capture interest in this image?*

display typeface—
A typeface used to attract attention to the design of the font as well as to the words.

As mentioned above, choosing a typeface for body text that reflects the tone of the subject matter can help communicate a message. Choosing the right display typeface for headings and other special text elements in a document does the same thing, but with a little more power. A **display typeface** is a stylized typeface usually set at a larger point size than body text. It draws attention and sends a message about the document content. Since a display typeface is used for only a few words and not extended paragraphs, style is more important than readability.

There are many standardized display typefaces, but sometimes graphic designers create their own, even photographing everyday items arranged to form letters and words and adding them to a layout as headings. With virtually endless possibilities, it may be tempting to use several display typefaces in a single document, perhaps a different one for each heading. Resist the temptation. Too many different typefaces are distracting and muddle a design.

In addition to display typefaces, some other common typographical treatments used for display typography include the following:

- **Drop caps.** A drop cap is the first letter of a paragraph that has been enhanced to give it emphasis. The letter may be larger or more ornate to create this effect. Drop caps usually appear at the beginning of a chapter, article, or section. Drop caps are useful for drawing the reader's eye to the beginning of the text and sometimes for indicating a new section. As for all design techniques, use drop caps judiciously. They should never be used for every paragraph on a page.

- **Pull quotes.** A selection of text pulled from the body text and set in a larger type size, pull quotes are useful for breaking up long stretches of text and for highlighting content to catch a casual reader's attention.

- **Color.** Although black or a similarly dark color is almost always best for body text, color applied to headlines, drop caps, or pull quotes is an effective way to draw attention to a layout and reinforce a design scheme. The color may repeat a hue from another graphic element or image or it may contrast with another element to create interest. Be careful when layering colored text on a colored background. Even though colors can create interest, some color combinations can make even display text unreadable.

Figure 8.9 shows a sample layout with most of the typographical elements described above.

The example in Figure 8.9 is fairly conservative, but modern graphic designers do much more elaborate things with typography to enhance designs. Flip through your favorite magazines to get an idea of how professionals use typography to communicate ideas. You'll see simple typographical treatments like those in Figure 8.9 where readability is the main concern as well as more exciting uses of typography.

To see some cutting edge examples of typography, search for "experimental typography" online. In experimental typography, all of the rules are thrown out the window and text is set, not with readability in mind, but for pure dramatic effect. (See the Impact sidebar on the next page for more information about experimental typography's impact on contemporary design.)

Figure 8.9 *Notice how typography is used in this layout to draw attention, set a mood, and add to the design. The display font on the large heading is old-fashioned, slightly nautical, and almost ghostly, reinforcing the image of the old ship and preparing the reader for a chilling tale. The first drop cap draws the reader's eye to the beginning of the story and the smaller one indicates the beginning of a new section while also breaking up a large block of text. Similarly, the pull quote keeps the long columns of text on the second page from looking too heavy and intimidating.*

checkpoint

What elements go into making text readable?

Why don't different typefaces of the same size take up the same space?

ACTIVITY 8.2 ▶ Determining Readability

1. Collect several samples of both good and bad readability. You can find examples of good and bad typography in magazines, mailers, advertisements . . . almost anywhere.

2. With a team of three or four students, identify what makes the "good" articles easy to read. To do this, use a sheet of paper and have each student on the team write something that makes the article easy to read. Pass the paper around several times, giving each team member a chance to identify a couple of items. Using the list on the sheet as a stimulus, discuss specifics of how the article's typography worked.

3. Repeat step 2 for the "bad" typography examples. What makes them more difficult to read?

4. After discussing the examples as a team, each student should create a desktop publishing document that summarizes the discussion. In the summary, demonstrate an example of each of the following: readable typeface, type size, leading, paragraph width, and alignment.

5. Save as **8_Activity2_readability**.

lavitrei/Shutterstock.com

Impact

David Carson and Experimental Typography

This chapter emphasizes the readability of type because communicating a message effectively and clearly is type's primary purpose. However, some graphic designers push typography beyond the limits of readability to great effect.

David Carson is a famous graphic designer who is known for experimental typography, particularly in his work for *Ray Gun* magazine in the 1990s. Working first in surfing sub-culture publications, Carson threw out conventional rules about type and design, disregarding traditional ideas about elements like alignment, spacing, and style. Sometimes Carson's treatment of text made it almost illegible, but his designs excited the design and pop culture world. Because Carson placed no limits on type beyond his own artistic sensibility, it gave his designs an unbounded, free look commonly associated with hip youth culture. As more and more journalists and critics noticed and highlighted Carson's designs, mainstream companies began hiring Carson to lend his distinctive, fashionable look to their products in an effort to appeal to young audiences and customers.

Today, Carson's work and derivatives of his style are seen in countless designs. Use a search engine to find some examples of Carson's experimental typography and then look for examples of his influence in magazines, posters, and television graphics.

Think About It

What typographical "rules" do Carson and other designers like him break? Why does the design still "work"? Describe some situations where the style would be appropriate and some instances where it would be inappropriate.

As referenced several times in this chapter, there are few rules about using typography in design: Typography is more an art than a science. Furthermore, like all elements of design, typography is subject to fads and fashion; what is cool one year is out the next. However, following a few conventions when typesetting text will make your publications appear more professional, whatever the style.

Widows and Orphans *LO 8.7*

After you set the body text in a document, tweaking a few text elements can make a big impact. For instance, address any widows and orphans. A **widow** in typesetting is when the last line of a paragraph falls by itself as the first line of the next page or column. An **orphan** is when the first line of a paragraph falls by itself at the bottom of a page or column or when a single word or part of a word falls by itself on the last line of a paragraph.

To remove a widow or orphan, you can slightly adjust leading on the paragraph or bring a line or two forward or backward so that the offending line is not left alone at the top or bottom of a page or column. To address the second type of orphan, you can tighten or loosen the tracking in the paragraph a tiny bit or force a line break before the hyphenated word that contains the orphan. Be careful, however, if you adjust spacing within a paragraph. The change should be invisible to the reader. When adjusting leading in particular, be sure that adjacent lines of text are aligned properly. For example, the top two columns of text in Figure 8.10 include a widow and an orphan. Adjusting the leading slightly in the first paragraph remedied the widow, but note that the adjacent paragraphs are no longer aligned and the text blocks look disjointed.

Keeping text in adjacent columns aligned, especially at the baseline, keeps documents looking clean and professional. In this instance, adjusting the leading evenly in both paragraphs or even simply pulling one line of text from the first column into the second column and not adjusting the leading at all would work better.

widow—When the last line of a paragraph falls by itself as the first line of the next page or column.

orphan—When the first line of a paragraph falls by itself at the bottom of a page or column or when a single word or part of a word falls by itself on the last line of a paragraph.

Figure 8.10 *Adjusting the leading slightly in the first paragraph fixed the widow at the top of the second column, but the text in two columns is now noticeably disjointed as highlighted by the red arrow. Keeping text in side-by-side columns properly aligned at the baseline keeps documents looking professional.*

Punctuation Marks *LO 8.7*

Addressing a few punctuation matters can also make your documents cleaner and more professional. For example, fine-tuning hyphenation can improve the look of typeset text. When a word breaks at the end of a line, be sure at least two characters remain before the hyphen on the first line and at least three characters carry forward to the next line. Another good practice: Try to avoid hyphenating Web addresses and proper nouns, like names. Finally, avoid more than three hyphenated lines in a row.

Most typesetting programs like Adobe InDesign include hyphenation options to automatically control hyphens in a document, so you can use the guidelines in this section to properly set the hyphenation feature. But some issues can still sneak through. Review the hyphens in your document and address any issues before declaring it finished.

en dash—A punctuation symbol that resembles a hyphen but is longer (normally the width of a capital N in the font and point size in which it is formatted); used in ranges of numbers, letters, or dates.

em dash—A punctuation symbol that resembles a hyphen but is noticeably longer (normally the width of the capital letter M in the font and point size in which it is formatted); indicates a break in thought, similar to parentheses.

curly quotes—Rounded marks used for quotations and apostrophes.

Another note about hyphens: Don't confuse them with en and em dashes. An **en dash** (–) looks like a hyphen but it is slightly longer (normally the width of the capital letter N, in fact). En dashes are used most commonly to indicate a range of dates, numbers, or times and in compound adjectives. An **em dash** (—) is twice as long as an en dash (the width of the capital letter M, usually) and is frequently used to separate a parenthetical thought, much like parentheses. As a graphic designer, you may not be responsible for ensuring the proper punctuation is used in a document, but you should know the difference and be able to insert the correct symbol as indicated by a copy writer, author, or editor.

Similarly, be sure your software is set up to use **curly quotes** (sometimes called "smart quotes") rather than straight quotes for quotation marks and apostrophes, as appropriate. Straight quotation marks should be used only to indicate measure in inches or feet. Straight quotes used where curly quotes should be look amateurish or sloppy. Consult the help system for your particular software to determine how to set up the smart quote function.

checkpoint

Why is it important to clean up widows and orphans and fine tune punctuation marks before declaring your work finished?

ACTIVITY 8.3 ▶ Spacing and Special Characters

1. Open **widows_and_orphans** from the data files for this chapter.
2. Follow the instructions in the pull quote in this file.
3. Save as **8_Activity3_spacing_special_characters**.

Résumé Typography

The same general typography guidelines governing readability in magazines, books, and other print products also apply to résumés. In general, your résumé is not a place to try out unusual or experimental typography. Certainly, the Internet is full of extraordinary résumés from graphic designers displaying their skills through inventive use of typography. But unless you are highly confident in your design ability and going for a job in an environment where you know creativity will be appreciated, it is best to follow convention on your résumé.

The function of a résumé is to provide information about your education, job experience, and skills. The focus should be on content rather than on a flashy appearance. Your goal is to impress a prospective employer so that he or she will consider you as a serious applicant for a job.

In terms of typography, your aim is to create a clean, easy-to-read document. Instead of something outlandish, choose a traditional, legible typeface. It may be acceptable to use one typeface for headings and another for the body of the résumé, but resist the urge to use more than two. Often, judicious use of bold, italic, and varied type sizes is the best approach to résumé design.

Consider the guidelines presented in this chapter when preparing a résumé and always apply treatments consistently. Inconsistent treatment of text on a résumé can make you appear inattentive to details and unreliable. Ultimately, remember that a potential employer should notice your experience and not the typography when reviewing a résumé.

Key Concepts

▶ A typeface is a collection of designed characters while a font refers to a subset of characters with the same style within a typeface. *LO 8.1 and 8.2*

▶ One of the most important goals of working with text is making it readable. *LO 8.3*

▶ Selecting a suitable typeface, size, and style impacts readability. *LO 8.3*

▶ Adjusting the leading, tracking, measure, and alignment can make text more or less readable. *LO 8.4 and 8.5*

▶ Typography plays an important role in capturing readers' interest and directing their attention. *LO 8.6*

▶ Removing widows and orphans and using appropriate punctuation marks can make your documents appear more professional. *LO 8.7*

Review and Discuss

1. Differentiate between the terms typeface and font. *LO 8.1*

2. Describe the difference between a serif and a sans serif font with examples of suggested best uses for each. *LO 8.2*

3. Compare and contrast ascenders, descenders, and baseline. *LO 8.2*

4. Describe how choosing a typeface can set a tone for a project. Give two examples. *LO 8.3 and 8.6*

5. Discuss how two typefaces with the same point size can be visually different sizes. *LO 8.3*

6. Evaluate the best type styles to use for emphasis and type styles that should be avoided. *LO 8.3*

7. Compare and contrast tracking, leading, and kerning. Include how each of them affect readability. *LO 8.4*

8. Apply what you have learned about paragraph alignment by deciding on what type of alignment should be used for a block of text in which you do not want many words to automatically hyphenate at the end of the line. What would be the drawbacks to using this alignment? *LO 8.5*

9. Analyze the use of enhancements in a publication such as display typography, drop caps, pull quotes, and color. *LO 8.6*

10. Describe what can be done to remove widows and orphans within your document. Include information about what you need to be cautious about when making these changes. *LO 8.7*

11. Differentiate between an en and an em dash and provide examples of when each would be used. *LO 8.7*

Apply

1. Create a blank 8.5- x 11-inch document. The document should advertise free pizza to encourage attendance at College Night at the high school. Use skills that you learned in this chapter to enhance the document. Save as **8 Apply1_free_pizza**. *LO 8.3, 8.4, 8.5, 8.6, and 8.7*

2. Create a flyer that is 8.5 x 11 inches. Add a text box for a title at the top of the page. Key **Social Networking Tips** in the text box. Use the following tips in your text: set your profile to private, restrict access to those who view your posts, don't post detailed personal information, be careful posting photos as they can be altered, and socialize only with people you know well. Use information you learned in this chapter to enhance the document. Save it as **8_Apply2_social_networking**. *LO 8.3, 8.4, 8.5, 8.6, and 8.7*

3. Open **free_health_seminar**. Select and copy all text in the document. Using your desktop publishing software, create an 11- x 8.5-inch document in landscape orientation. Paste the text in the document. Resize the text box so that it fits within the margins of the page. Apply an appropriate font size, typeface, and color to the titles and text. Apply leading, tracking, and kerning as needed. In the pasteboard area, write an explanation of why you chose the fonts, sizes, and colors you did as well as where you used leading, tracking, and kerning. Check that there are no widows or orphans in the document. Save as **8_Apply3_free_health_seminar**. *LO 8.3, 8.4, 8.5, 8.6, and 8.7*

4. Work with a partner to search for advantages and disadvantages of using Twitter to communicate. Create a list of at least three advantages and three disadvantages of using Twitter. Each partner should create an 8.5- × 11-inch document and add a title and list of advantages and disadvantages. Apply bullets to each of the lists. Apply appropriate sizes and fonts to all text. Save as **8_Apply4_twitter**. *LO 8.3, 8.4, 8.5, 8.6, and 8.7*

5. A new coffee and yogurt shop (fictitious) is opening in your city. Create an 8.5- × 11-inch document in your desktop publishing software. Use the information in the **blog** document in your data files for the text in this document. Apply appropriate fonts, size, and color to the title and blog information. Save as **8_Apply5_new_shop**. *LO 8.3, 8.4, 8.5, 8.6, and 8.7*

6. Create a new 8.5- × 11-inch page. Add a title that spans from the left to the right margin: **Readability vs. Legibility**. Create two columns below the title. Import **import_text** from your data files into the two-column area. In the left column, make the text readable by choosing an appropriate font, size, and style and then adjusting spacing. If the text does not fit in the column, make adjustments to the font size and/or spacing. In the right column, choose a font, size and style and adjust spacing to make it a bad example of text that is difficult to read. Save as **8_Apply6_readability**. *LO 8.3, 8.4, 8.5, 8.6, and 8.7*

Join the Fun!

- Find Out About
- Financial Aid
- Planning Your Future
- Keys to College Success
- Filling Out College Applications

Free Pizza

October 26
7 PM
BALORA HIGH SCHOOL
BHS Student Center
Bring a Friend - or even your parents!

Explore

1. Search the Internet for font families. Write a 250-word article on font families, including information that may not be in the textbook such as slab serif font. Include at least two references using MLA style. Create a desktop publishing document with an appropriate title for your article as well as font, color, and size. In your document use leading, tracking, and kerning as needed. Save as **8_Explore1_font_families**. *LO 8.1, 8.2, and 8.3*

2. In a desktop publishing document, create four text boxes. Title them: Favorite Title Print Fonts, Favorite Text Print Fonts, Favorite Title Web Fonts, and Favorite Text Web Fonts. Using the information in the textbook and doing some research, list five fonts under each title that you would use the most often. Be prepared to explain why you would choose the ones you chose. Use example fonts to format the titles and text for the lists. Save as **8_Explore2_favorite_fonts**. *LO 8.1 and 8.2*

3. In a team of three or four students, search history of typography. After scanning some of the articles, decide on an article for each team member to summarize. Summarize the article in a word processing document with at least 150 words. Include a reference in MLA style. Each team member should save his or her article as **8_Explore3_your_name**. As a team, create a newsletter with a title and the articles. Use appropriate fonts and formatting for all articles and titles. Save as **8_Explore3_typography_history**. *LO 8.1 and 8.2*

Academic Connections

Reading: Practice reading online. Choose one of the terms in this chapter to research. Locate and read an article related to your chosen term. While reading the article, formulate at least five questions that have been answered in the text. Type the question and the answer. Use more than one article if you do not have five questions when you have completed the article. Key a title and the questions with answers into a desktop publishing document including a reference(s) cited in MLA style. Save as **8_AC_reading**.

Math: In desktop publishing, there will be occasions when you need to reduce either pixels or point size by a certain percentage. It is important, therefore, that you know how to complete the appropriate calculations. Create the following table and perform the calculations to complete the table. Save as **8_AC_math**.

Percentage	Pixels	% of px	Points	% of pt
100%	12		10	
75%	36		24	
50%	48		30	
25%	72		60	

Chapter 9

Print Graphics

Learning Outcomes

▸ **9.1** Use keywords to locate stock photos for projects.

▸ **9.2** Recognize the usefulness and limitations of screen captures and scans in print documents.

▸ **9.3** Source clip art from online collections.

▸ **9.4** Understand the difference between royalty-free and rights-managed image licensing.

▸ **9.5** Resize raster images in a raster editing program.

▸ **9.6** Use limited resampling to manage resolution and file size.

▸ **9.7** Choose an appropriate file type for print graphics.

▸ **9.8** Know the difference between embedded and linked graphics.

▸ **9.9** Distinguish between floating and inline graphics.

▸ **9.10** Utilize text wrapping features for placed graphics.

Key Terms

- clip art
- embedded graphic
- floating graphic
- inline graphic
- license
- linked graphic
- rights managed
- screen capture
- standoff
- stock photo
- text wrapping
- watermark

Creations/Shutterstock.com

You could make an argument that images are the most important element of any multimedia project. Images have the power to capture attention, set a tone, and communicate an idea with no words at all. The right, well-edited image will draw in a reader and send a message of professionalism, but people will pass right by a mediocre, poorly executed image. So it's important to select high-quality images for your projects and employ them effectively. This chapter will describe where to source images, how to prepare them for publication, and how to place them in a document headed for a printer.

So far in this book, you've read a lot about digital images. For instance, you've learned the difference between raster and vector images and what file types and applications are associated with each. You've read about capturing great photos with a digital camera and using raster editing software to alter or improve them. You also learned about creating original vector images using a drawing program such as Adobe Illustrator. Now that you know a little something about image files, it's time to explore how all of that knowledge comes together in a multimedia project, specifically in a desktop publishing project.

Lesson 9.1 ▶ Obtaining Digital Images

Where do good images come from? Many times, if you are working on a project for someone else, the images are provided by an author, a graphic artist, a staff photographer, a freelancer, or some other party. In these instances, it's important to understand the technical elements of an image file so that you can evaluate the art you receive and provide feedback to the supplier if necessary. But if you alone are responsible for providing graphics for your projects, you can get them from many different sources. Any of the following types of images can be used in a desktop publishing file destined for a printer:

- Digital photographs
- Screen captures
- Scans
- Original vector artwork
- Clip art

Sourcing Digital Photographs *LO 9.1*

Digital photos are one of the most common types of graphics in digital media files, and they come from many sources. One great source for photos is your own camera. Using your own photos means you can capture the exact image you need and avoid any copyright issues. However, desktop publishing specialists and other professionals often source photos from other places.

Some organizations, such as certain newspapers and magazines, employ staff photographers to provide photos for projects on an ongoing basis. Even more frequently, digital media professionals and organizations work with freelance photographers on a per-project basis to supply images. But hiring a staff or freelance photographer can be expensive, so many organizations source images from stock photography. **Stock photos** are images made available for use in creative and commercial projects, typically for a fee, but sometimes for free. Although not always cheap, these photos are usually affordable enough that it is more cost-effective to use them than to hire a

stock photo—An image produced and sold by a professional for use by the general public.

professional photographer for a specific photo shoot. You may find stock photos useful for your projects, especially as you are getting started in digital media.

The most common place to access stock photos is from an online stock photo company. Professional photographers contract with these companies to sell the rights to use their images and share a portion of the proceeds. Two of the largest stock photo companies are Getty and Corbis, but many smaller companies also offer fine selections of stock images, and some specialize in certain subject areas, such as science or sports.

Stock photo websites are extensive, so they provide a variety of ways to search for specific images. For example, stock photos are usually cataloged using keywords to describe their content. To identify images that might work for your project, you enter keywords in the website's search feature and all of the images tagged with keywords matching the search are presented for review. For example, Figure 9.1 shows just one of thousands of stock photos that match the keywords

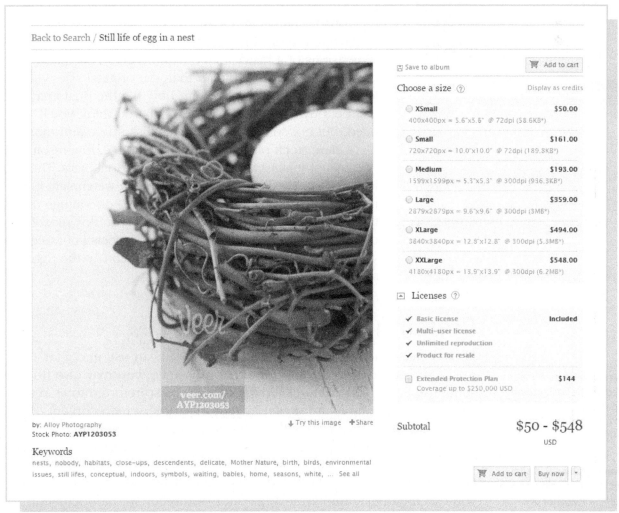

Figure 9.1 *Stock photo websites embed keyword metadata to identify the subject matter in an image and match it to user searches.*

"bird nest" on Veer.com. Note that other keywords associated with the image (shown below the picture) include both literal descriptions like *nests* and *birds* and more conceptual terms such as *waiting*.

Stock photo websites that attach a wide range of keywords to images can be helpful not only when you know exactly what photo you want, but also when you need an image that represents an idea and you're not sure exactly what photo will best convey the abstract concept. To narrow the results of a search, you can use more specific keywords. For example, using the keywords "bird nest robin" on Veer.com returned just 99 images, all of which feature only robin nests. Likewise, searching with the keywords "responsibility high school students" returned 50 images.

Most digital stock photos are available at different resolutions, sizes, and file types. Depending on the intended use, consumers may choose a lower resolution file suitable for onscreen display or a higher resolution that works best for print projects. Generally, the larger the size of the image, the higher the price. You may be tempted to choose the least expensive version. However, recall the relationship between resolution, physical image size, and file size in a raster image. You can reduce the physical dimensions of a raster image with no effect on quality, but you can't make it bigger than the original size without losing clarity. If you are unsure how big the final image will be, buy a file that is bigger than you think you'll need, but not so big that it wastes disk space and money.

Often, stock photo suppliers make free, low-resolution versions of images available to use on a trial basis. These low-resolution versions usually include a **watermark**, a pale image or text embedded in the image, to discourage unauthorized use, as shown in Figure 9.2. If you download one of these trial images and later decide it meets your needs, you can purchase a high-resolution version, at the right size, and without the watermark.

Figure 9.2 *Watermarks appear on stock photos that are available on a trial basis.*

Creating Screen Captures LO 9.2

Photos aren't the only type of raster images you can use in digital media projects destined for a printer. For instance, you may also find some use for screen captures. **Screen captures** (also referred to as screen shots or screen grabs) are digital images of visible screen content . . . sort of like snapshots of what's on the screen at any given time.

Screens can be captured by operating system utilities or by specialized software. For example, on a PC, pressing the Print Screen (Prnt Scrn) key saves a copy of the screen on the Windows Clipboard, which you can then paste into an image editor or directly into a document. On a Mac, the Cmd-Shift-3 key combination takes a snapshot of the entire screen and saves it as a .png file on the desktop. (Other key combinations capture different areas of the screen on a Mac. Consult

watermark—A pale image placed on the background of a page and which is often used for logos or other identification.

screen capture—A digital raster image of visible screen content; a snapshot of a computer screen generated by the operating system or other dedicated software.

Stock Photos

The Internet has made access to stock photos dramatically easier. It used to be that photographers had to send out huge four-color catalogs of their images to prospective customers. These customers would have to flip through page after page looking for the right picture. Once they found a photograph, they would have to purchase the image and have it shipped to them. It was both time intensive and expensive.

Today, these same customers can go to a website, key in a word or two that describes their subject, and then quickly scroll through the photos from which to choose. If they don't find the exact image they have in mind, they can go to other sites and continue their search. When they find the one they want, they can download it instantly and pay for it at the same time.

The result is that professional photographers can more easily reach their audience, and designers of business publications can find the perfect shot for their brochure or newsletter. The quality of these publications is improved and artists have a way to grow their own business.

your user documentation for more information, if necessary.) Specialized screen capture software, such as SnagIt (as shown in Figure 9.3), basically functions the same, but offers far more image setup, editing, and organizing features within the program interface.

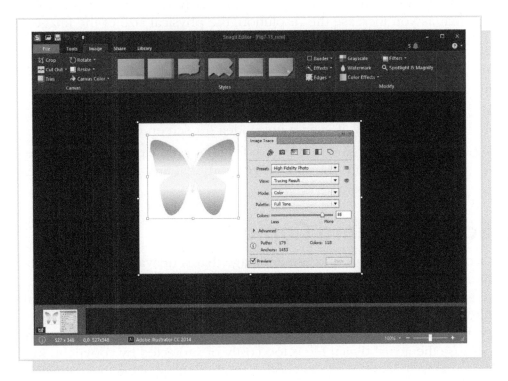

Figure 9.3 *SnagIt is easy-to-use screen capture software with many editing and organizing features.*

Screen captures have limited uses. You should resist the urge to use a screen capture of another piece of art or photo you find online, particularly if your project is eventually headed for a printer. First of all, you run a higher risk of violating copyright if you use a screen capture of an original photo or drawing that has been posted online. Second, a screen capture probably won't yield the quality you want in your printed products. Screen captures are, by nature, low-resolution images. Printing a low-resolution image on a high-resolution printer can produce low quality, fuzzy images. So it is always preferable to use an original, high-resolution image file when possible rather than a screen capture of that image.

Screen captures are useful, however, in software tutorial documentation and other materials where showing the actual computer display is essential to the topic. If you do use screen captures in your projects, keep in mind the following general tips to maximize the image quality in the final product.

- Accept that the final output may not be as sharp as something like a high-resolution photograph. It should be obvious from the content of the screen capture that the image is from a computer screen. Users don't expect the highest resolution from a computer screen, so the final product will probably be acceptable.

- Search online for advice from credible sources. Rapidly advancing technology means best practices change frequently. Often, someone has already figured out how to apply new products and strategies to address the same issues you are facing and has shared tips in technical forums or blogs.

- Process the screen captures in a raster editing program. You can use the program to ramp up the resolution. However, keep in mind that as you increase the resolution, the physical size of the image shrinks. Increasing the resolution all the way to 300 ppi (which is ideal for most printers) may make the screen capture too small to be useful. Most likely, you'll need to strike a balance between sharpness and size. Experimenting can also be useful. Keep in mind that increasing the physical size of images decreases resolution and is rarely, if ever, a good idea for screen captures.

- Use roughly the same resolution for all screen captures within one project. This keeps the screens proportional and improves the overall visual impression.

Scanning Hard Copies *LO 9.2*

Occasionally, you'll want to use an image that is unavailable as a digital file, for example, a vintage family photograph or a hard copy map. In these instances, you can scan the hard copy document to create a digital file. Again, as is the case with screen captures, original digital files are preferable to scans. Don't use scans of hard copy images as a shortcut or because the actual digital file is too costly or protected by copyright. In these cases, it is preferable to choose another image altogether. However, if you have a legitimate reason to scan a hard copy, it is an excellent way to create a digital file as long as you keep in mind the nature of scanning and choose settings that will produce high-quality results.

Essentially, a scanner acts like a digital photocopier by taking a picture of a printed document and transferring the image to a digital file. Once the image is saved, it can be modified like any other raster graphic and used in digital documents. In scanning, the higher the resolution, the more detail in the digital image. Images destined for a printer should be scanned at least at 300 dpi. Many scanners are capable of scanning at much higher resolution, and you should consider using a higher resolution for images you intend to enlarge beyond their original size. But these higher resolution scans mean bigger file sizes and can be a waste of space and detail if your output device discards anything over 300 dpi. Experiment to determine what works best for each situation.

Acquiring Vector Images and Clip Art *LO 9.3*

Digital vector images are another common type of image file used in print products. In the professional world, most original vector images (sometimes called line art) used in print products come from graphic artists. However, like hiring a photographer, hiring a graphic artist can be expensive. In some cases, your own artwork is the best source for line art when you cannot afford to hire an artist. You can create your own art in a vector editing program such as Adobe Illustrator, or you can scan a hard copy of an original sketch and use it as the basis of a vector drawing, as you read about in Chapter 7. Using your own artwork also means you get the exact image you want and you do not need to worry about copyright issues.

What do you do, however, if you are not artistically inclined and can't afford to hire a graphic artist? One option is clip art. **Clip art** is similar to stock photography: It is ready-to-use artwork made available for use in creative and commercial projects, sometimes for free and sometimes for a price.

clip art—A picture or drawing created by someone with the intention that the artwork will be used by others.

Like stock photo sites, clip art collections are searchable using keywords. Styles vary from cartoonish, to realistic drawings, to abstract designs. For example, Figure 9.4 shows a few results from a search on

egg yolk:Kheng Guan Toh/Shutterstock.com; landscape:Elen_studio/Shutterstock.com; chick:onime/Shutterstock.com

Figure 9.4 *Three results of a keyword search on the term egg on a clip art website. Clip art styles vary from simple to complex and from cartoonish to realistic.*

the keyword *egg* at one site. Some clip art is available in both raster and vector formats. Keep in mind, however, that the same principles apply to these raster files as any other, even though their content was originally a vector graphic. Raster clip art files are not fully scalable without compromising image quality. If you purchase line art to use in a print product, it is best to stick with a vector file format that you can resize freely without worrying about pixilation.

Many software programs, such as Microsoft Office programs, make it easy to search for clip art using buttons such as Clip Art or Online Pictures. After you enter keywords, results from a Web search are displayed so that you can choose a clip. These images are often copyrighted, so you must follow proper procedures to get permission to use them. However, there are many other online resources for original, high-quality clip art. When looking for clip art online, be sure to use reputable websites. Some clip art websites offer free images that are actually pirated files. Be sure to evaluate your sources carefully.

lavitrei/Shutterstock.com

Impact

Creative Commons

The Creative Commons is an organization that offers copyright holders a way to grant blanket permission for others to use their copyrighted work with certain restrictions. The permissions granted by a Creative Commons license go beyond Fair Use. With a Creative Commons license, a copyright holder can indicate whether permission is granted for commercial or noncommercial use and whether the work can be altered or must remain unchanged. In each case, the license specifies that the user must attribute the work to the original creator.

Copyright holders can also choose a license that requires users to offer an identical license on any derivatives of the original work. In Creative Commons language, this is called ShareAlike. The Creative Commons also provides tools that allow a copyright holder to release a work into the public domain.

The Creative Commons started when organizers recognized that traditional copyright protection did not fit the actual use of creative material in the Internet age where it's easy and commonplace to share, copy, edit, and post copyrighted material. A growing community of creative people have embraced the idea of Creative Commons, believing that sharing their work, at least to some extent, encourages creativity and innovation for everyone within the community.

Critical Thinking

Visit the Creative Commons website at www.creativecommons.org and read the descriptions of the various Creative Commons licenses. How can a movement like the Creative Commons reduce copyright violation online?

Figure 9.5 *The Wikimedia Commons includes only free images, like this picture of Buzz Aldrin on the moon. However, certain images are protected by Creative Commons licensing requirements that you must be aware of before using them in your own projects.*

One more note about choosing clip art: The old saying "You get what you pay for" seems to apply. The most elaborate, high-quality, and original images are usually the most expensive pieces, while free clip art is generally simpler and less impressive. Be choosy and creative if you use clip art for your projects. Consumers are so accustomed to seeing average clip art that only the best pieces or pieces deployed in an original way will make an impression.

Understanding Licensing *LO 9.4*

When you get images from sources such as stock photo or clip art websites, you must be careful to check and adhere to any licensing restrictions. The very nature of stock photos and clip art is such that they are meant to be used by people other than the original artist. However, that does not necessarily mean that they are free from copyright. When you purchase a stock photo or clip art file, what you are really paying for is permission from the copyright holder to use the image.

license—A legal agreement that gives permission and states detailed conditions for using a copyrighted image.

The permission is referred to as a **license**. Most images traditionally fall into one of two license categories: royalty free and rights managed.

Royalty free means the buyer pays a one-time fee to use the image for an unlimited number of products and for an unlimited length of time without paying any additional fees for each additional use. This does not mean that there are no restrictions on a royalty-free image. The user must follow any guidelines outlined in the royalty-free license agreement. Frequently, these guidelines limit how many times the image can be reproduced. For instance, a royalty-free agreement may grant a user permission to use an image in any type of product like a brochure, a catalog, a book, etc., as long as no more than 10,000 copies of any one product are printed and distributed.

rights-managed—A type of licensing agreement that gives a buyer permission for a specific, limited use of a copyrighted image.

Rights-managed licenses are more detailed than royalty-free licenses. A license that is **rights-managed** may define anything from usage, size, duration, and reproduction, to whether it can be licensed to additional buyers. If the buyer eventually wants to use the image in a way not covered in the original license, he or she must pay an additional fee to cover the new condition.

A rights-managed license not only lets a copyright holder control how an image is used, it can also benefit the buyer by granting exclusivity. Exclusivity means that the copyright holder agrees to limit who else can use the image and/or how it can be used. For example, the seller may agree not to sell the usage rights to someone in the same industry or geographical area as the original buyer or even not to sell the image at all for a certain amount of time.

As you are no doubt well aware, obtaining images online is as easy as clicking, but just because it is simple, doesn't mean it is ethical or legal. It is up to you to ensure that you (and any online companies you use) follow ethical and legal guidelines for images you gather and use in your projects. With so many sources for images, including safe, legitimate sources of free images like the Open Clip Art Library (which provides only nonrestricted image files) and the Creative Commons movement (which encourages copyright holders to grant at least a certain level of rights to the general public for copyrighted works), you should be able to find images that suit your needs without resorting to stealing. (See the Impact feature earlier in this chapter for more information on the Creative Commons.)

Staying Legal

What are some ways you can be sure you are following legal and ethical guidelines when you source images online? How do you know an online source for images is trustworthy and not distributing pirated material?

checkpoint

What is the difference between a royalty-free and a rights-managed image?

ACTIVITY 9.1 ▶ Working with Stock Photos

1. Go to *http://www.veer.com* or another stock photo website.
2. Search for an image of an apple.
3. Download a trial version of an image of an apple.
4. Insert the image into a word processing document.
5. Read about the different image sizes available from the website and then create several copies of the image sized from small to large in the document.
6. If you were going to use this image for a printed brochure on healthy eating, what size would you purchase? Why? Answer these questions in complete sentences in the document with the images.
7. Save the document as *9_Activity1_stock_photos*.

Lesson 9.2 ▶ Preparing Graphics for Publication

Most graphics require a certain amount of preparation before being placed in layout application files. But before you even start working with graphic files, ask the pre-press department at the printer that will eventually print your document about specifications or instructions for image files. The prepress department may give you instructions about variables such as what file types work best with the press equipment, how to handle color in your graphic files, whether to resize images in an imaging program or directly in a layout program, and many more factors that could affect how well your document prints.

Rapidly changing software and technology and the wide variety of software, file formats, and situations makes it difficult to communicate a foolproof plan for preparing image files for publication. However, this section will outline some general tips. Once again, be sure to verify your choices with the service bureau that will eventually print your files.

Prepping Raster Files LO 9.5, 9.6, and 9.7

Whether you are working with raster or vector files, the first thing to do is save a working copy of your files and place the original, unaltered versions in a safe place. The working copy is best saved in the native file format of the image editing program you are working in. The native file format supports the full range of application features and offers the most editing flexibility if you need to make additional adjustments later. Next, develop an image processing workflow, especially if you have a large number of images to process. This will ensure you process the images consistently, which can improve the overall look of your final document. Your workflow might look something like this:

1. Crop image.
2. Adjust colors and convert to CMYK or grayscale, as appropriate.
3. Fix problems and enhance content.
4. Save the working copy again.
5. Resize and address resolution issues, as necessary.
6. Rename, choose appropriate file format, and save a final placement file.

This workflow is just an example and may not work for every situation. For example, after the image is tweaked, you may or may not decide to adjust the resolution and/or size of the image. There are different opinions in the professional community about whether or not to adjust size and resolution before placing image files in another document headed for a printer. Some people prefer to resize images within a layout program because they do not know how big the final images will be in the design until they place the file. However, others think it's better to resize images in a raster editing program before placing them in a layout program for a few reasons:

- Resizing the file before placing it in a layout program can reduce the file size, which makes it display faster in the layout and reduces the overall size of the document. Placing huge, full-size images in a layout program can slow down the responsiveness of the application.
- Raster editing programs are specifically designed to manipulate images so some people contend they produce better results than resizing in layout programs.
- If you supply images separately to the printer at the end of the production, files saved at the size they are used in the layout program can mean fewer problems and faster processing at the printer.

The following guidelines assume you are resizing images and addressing resolution concerns within a raster editing application before placing figures in a layout program. You may find you prefer another workflow, and that is perfectly fine. Much of the information presented here will be useful wherever you end up resizing the images. Learning more about managing graphics and printing will help you make the best decision for your particular situation.

Resizing Raster Images

To resize an image in Adobe Photoshop, follow these steps (the process should be similar in other raster editing programs):

1. Select Image > Image Size from the Application bar.

2. Ensure that the Resample Image checkbox is *not* selected.

3. Enter the predetermined height or width in the appropriate box. (Entering one measure automatically adjusts the other proportionately.)

As you know, the resolution adjusts as the document size of the image changes: As the dimensions of an image increase, the resolution decreases and vice versa. The Image Size dialog box in Photoshop (and other editing applications) clearly illustrates this relationship. Generally, images for print products should have a resolution of 300 ppi, although sometimes lower resolution is okay depending on many factors such as the press equipment, the type of paper used, or the distance from which the image will ultimately be viewed, among other things. (A pre-press representative from your print vendor can help you determine the best resolution range for your particular project.)

After you change the physical dimensions of the image, check the resolution. If it is between 240 and 300 ppi, the image is properly sized and you can move on to the next step in the workflow. Figure 9.6 shows the Photoshop Image Size dialog box before and after changing the document size of the image shown. Notice that decreasing the dimensions from the original 17.78 × 13.33 inches to the desired 4.25 × 3.18 inches increased the resolution from 72 ppi to just over 300 ppi.

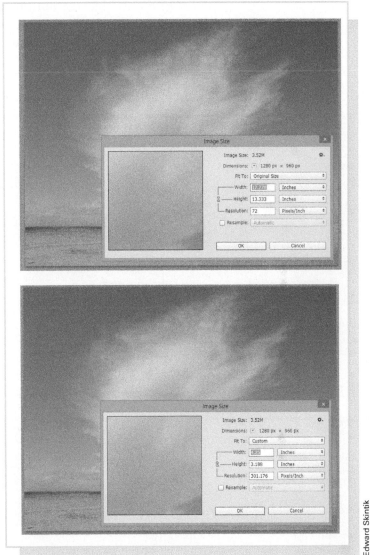

Edward Skintik

Figure 9.6 *For this photo, decreasing the document size to the desired dimensions increased the resolution to 300 ppi—perfect for using in a printed document.*

Resampling Raster Images

The situation doesn't always work out as neatly as it did in the example in Figure 9.6, especially if you are working with photos from a high-megapixel camera. These cameras produce images with high pixel counts and, accordingly, large file sizes and very big print dimensions. You will almost always want to make these images smaller to use in a print product. However, in pictures with very high pixel resolution, reducing the document size to usable dimensions drives the resolution way over 300 ppi, far higher than needed for printer output. For example, review the numbers in the Image Size box before and after changing the dimension sizes for the photo in Figure 9.7. Note the large size dimensions and the file size (9.00 M). Reducing the document size for this image increased the resolution to 630 ppi.

On many high-resolution cameras, you can adjust the image size before taking pictures to save memory space and, with a little planning, you can avoid this situation. However, if you are working with a high-resolution file like the example in Figure 9.7, you might consider resampling the image after you change the document dimensions.

Chapter 3, "Image Files," briefly introduced resampling. When a raster image is resampled, the number of pixels in the image is changed according to a complex formula in software programming called interpolation. Upsampling is an increase in pixels and downsampling is a reduction of pixels. Because pixels represent the details and clarity in an image, adding or removing them can alter the quality of an image, so resampling should be undertaken with caution.

When an image has a very high pixel count and a large document size, you can usually downsample to reduce the resolution to a practical level and still maintain enough pixels to display and print a decent image. Downsampling also decreases the file size, which makes storing, using, and sharing these huge image files more convenient. For example, Figure 9.8 shows the Image Size dialog box after downsampling. The pixel dimension dropped to 975 × 731. Also notice that the file size dropped from 9.00 M to 2.04 M, a much more manageable size.

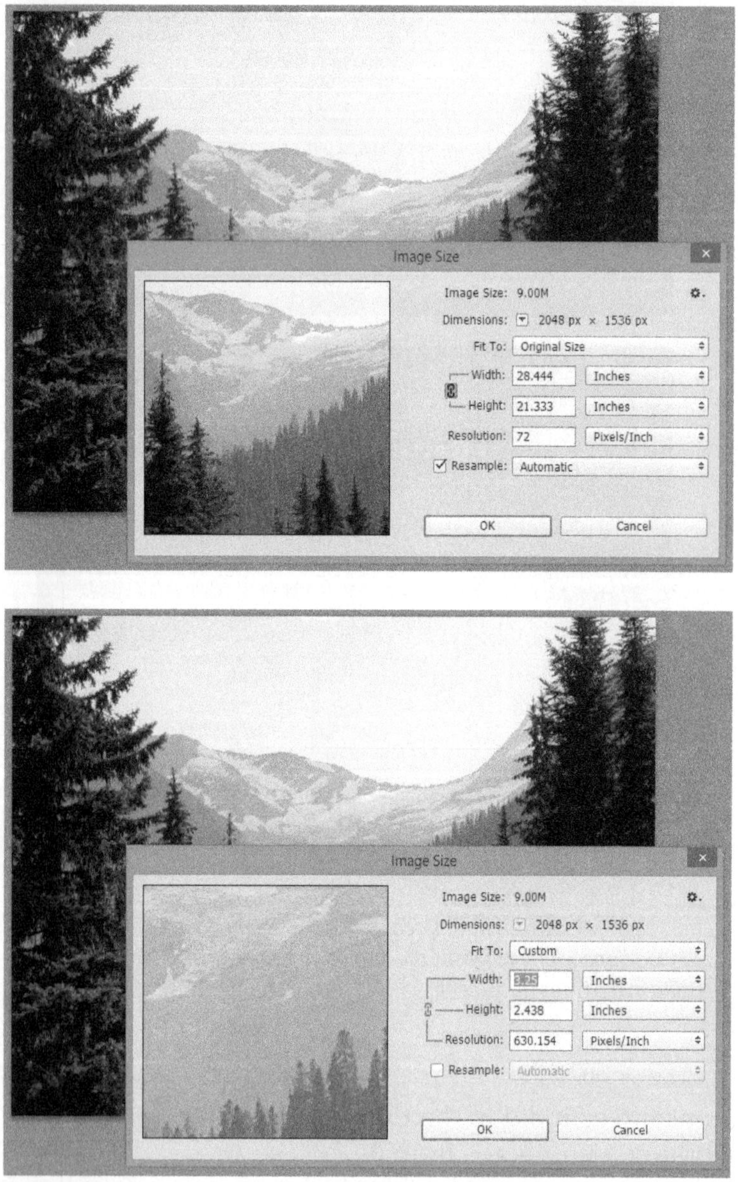

Edward Skintik

Figure 9.7 *Sometimes, reducing the document size of high pixel images sends the resolution far higher than is useful.*

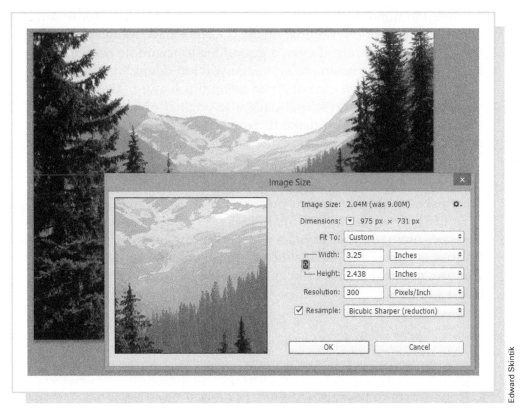

Figure 9.8 *After resampling, the image in this example is sized correctly, has the appropriate resolution for printing, and still retains adequate pixel dimensions for image quality. In addition, the file size is much more manageable.*

To downsample a high-pixel image after you resize it, follow these steps in Photoshop (or a similar set of steps in another raster program):

1. Click the Resample checkbox and, if necessary, the Constrain aspect ratio icon.

2. Select Bicubic Sharper (best for reduction) from the drop-down menu below the Resample checkbox.

3. Change the resolution to 300 ppi. The dimensional size of the image remains the same, but the pixel dimension and file size decrease.

After you click OK and the changes take effect, review the image at print size. If it looks fine, you are done and can move on to the next step in your workflow.

Sometimes, because downsampling changes the number of pixels in the image, the resampled image might benefit from sharpening. In Photoshop, you can choose Filter > Sharpen > Unsharp Mask from the main menu to adjust the sharpness and try to restore some of the quality that was lost in resampling. Other programs have similar sharpening features, and if you will be resampling images, you should learn how to use them. Be careful, however, not to oversharpen.

Keep in mind that not all images are good candidates for resampling, especially if the original image does not have a high pixel count. For example, it's rarely, if ever, a good idea to resample screen captures. Anytime you resample an image you are degrading the quality to some extent, so be careful about using this feature. Also, once you resample an image and save the file, the original pixels are forever changed, so be sure you make these types of changes to a working copy and not to the original image in case you need to start over.

Choosing a Raster File Type for Final Files

The final consideration when preparing files for a print document is what file type to use for the final file. Two of the most common raster file types are native file formats and TIFF. If the raster editing program you use is part of the same suite of applications as the layout program you use, you may consider keeping the file in the native file format (see Figure 9.9).

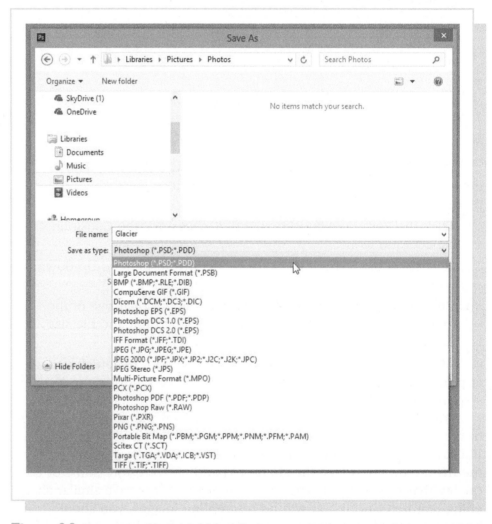

Figure 9.9 *If you are working with Adobe InDesign, you may choose to save your raster images as native PhotoShop files (.psd), but there are many other options as well.*

Native raster files are lossless (unlike JPEG) and preserve all editing features if you need to go back and change something later. In particular, Adobe Photoshop native file format (.psd) is well suited for use in Adobe InDesign. However, native files are generally larger than other raster file types. TIFF is a slightly more flexible raster file type used widely for print graphics, particularly for four-color raster images. A TIFF is basically a lossless file type without compression, and so the files tend to be bigger when compared to lossy file types that use compression like JPEG.

You can choose to use compression when saving as a TIFF, which can reduce the file size, but can potentially degrade the image quality as well, so it is important to understand the trade-offs and implications of compression in your particular situation before applying it to your files. What will work best for your project depends on a wide range of variables such as the software you use, the raster features applied to the files, and the press equipment that will eventually print the final product.

Prepping Vector Files *LO 9.6 and 9.7*

Vector files do not present the same resolution challenges that raster graphics do since they are fully scalable without distortion, so they are generally easier to prepare for print publication. Still, developing a workflow for preparing vector graphics can be useful. Many professionals convert colors, resize, and save final vector files within a vector editing program rather than in a layout program for the same reasons listed above for raster images. Again, you might find you prefer to work differently. However, no matter how experienced you are, it's always best to verify your strategy with the print vendor first to make sure your techniques won't cause problems when you hand off the final files to the press.

As mentioned above, preparing vector files for printing is a bit simpler than preparing raster images, at least for typical line art. Beyond converting colors if necessary and scaling to fit a specific space, the main variable to determine is the final file format. The most widely used file format for vector graphics in print publishing is .eps, although that is beginning to change. More and more desktop publishers are saving vector graphics in their native file format or PDF and using them in layout applications. This is particularly the case for graphics created in Adobe Illustrator and InDesign.

checkpoint

What is the very first step in preparing images for print production, whether you are working with raster or vector graphics?

ACTIVITY 9.2 ▶ **Preparing Files for Print Publication**

1. Using a vector image editing program, open *apple.eps* and *flower.tif* from your data files.

2. Prepare *apple.eps* for use in a brochure by reducing it to a height of 400 pixels, making the height and width proportionate. The brochure will be printed by a commercial print house. Save the file as *9_Activity2_apple*.

3. Prepare *flower.tif* for use in a flyer that will be printed in house on a color laser printer. The image should be 50% of the original size. Save the file as *9_Activity2_flower*.

4. Insert both images into a desktop publishing software and write a paragraph explaining what you did to prepare them for production and why. Save the document as *9_Activity2_production*.

Lesson 9.3 ▶ Inserting Image Files in a Document
LO 9.8, 9.9, and 9.10

No matter the extent to which you prepare graphics beforehand, at some point you need to insert them into a desktop publishing document. When you insert a graphic into a layout, it is either linked or embedded. When a graphic is **linked**, a low-resolution preview of the image appears in the layout. You can move the image, resize it, add special effects, or even delete it from the layout, but none of these actions change the actual image file.

linked graphic—A linked graphic appears in a layout as a low-resolution screen image, but all of its data remains in the individual image file rather than being incorporated into the layout file.

Using a low-resolution preview and keeping all of the data associated with the image in the original file instead of incorporating it into the layout file keeps the layout file smaller and prevents system resources from getting bogged down and slowing your computer. When the document is printed, the software retrieves all of the image information and uses the full range of characteristics, including resolution and color, for the final output. Some applications call this importing, inserting, or placing a graphic.

To make changes to individual elements in a linked file, you must open and edit it in the original image editing program. If the linked file changes or is moved to a different folder, the link to the layout is broken and the layout program will alert you that the link must be updated. Linked files must travel with the layout files. For example, if you send a native layout file to a printer without the individual linked image files, the file will not print correctly because all of the image information is missing.

In contrast, when a graphic is **embedded** in a layout, all of the associated image data is incorporated into the layout file. An embedded graphic appears at its full resolution and, sometimes, can be altered directly in the layout application. However, any changes made to the embedded image within the layout application are not reflected in the actual image file. This can be a problem if the image is intended for use in multiple projects and edits to the embedded file never make it to the master file. Also, copying all of the image information into the layout document drives up the file size. Therefore, it is impractical to embed many graphics into a layout. Although there are some limited situations where embedding is a good idea, linking is the standard method for inserting graphics in layout software.

Whether you link or embed a graphic in a layout, you place it either as an inline graphic or a floating graphic:

- **Inline graphics** (sometimes called anchored graphics) move with the text in a document. That is, as text is added or deleted, the graphic moves up and down the page accordingly. Inline graphics may appear on their own line or they may be anchored to a specific line of text, aligning at the baseline, above the line of text, or below the line of text (see Figure 9.10).

embedded graphic—A graphic that appears in a layout at full resolution, with all of its associated data copied into the layout file.

inline graphic—One that is attached to text and moves with it.

openclipart.org

Figure 9.10 *This is an example of an inline graphic. Notice how when the headline is added in (B), the top of the graphic moves down the page with the text and the top of Humpty's flag is still aligned with the same line of text as in (A). The graphic is anchored to that line of text and moves with it.*

(A)   (B)

opencitipart.org

Figure 9.11 *This is an example of a floating graphic. Notice how the text moves down the page when the headline is added in (B) but Humpty's flag is no longer aligned with the same line of text as in (A). The graphic moves independently of the text.*

- **Floating graphics** are independent of the text. They stay wherever they are placed until you move them, regardless of changes in the text (see Figure 9.11).

Which type of placement you use will depend on the material and the design you are working with. Material with direct references to figures, like a step-by-step instruction manual, for example, will more likely use inline graphics so that images stay with the steps they illustrate. More design-focused material, such as a magazine article, is usually better served by floating graphics.

Layout designs, particularly designs with floating graphics, can benefit from a feature called text wrapping. **Text wrapping** is exactly what it sounds like: Text wraps around a graphic or other object on a page. Most desktop publishing programs offer various options to control how text wraps around another element. For example, text can be set to wrap around an invisible rectangular border between the text and the graphic, or it can be configured to follow the contours of the image, as shown in Figure 9.12. The area between a graphic and the text is called the **standoff**. The standoff can be set wide or narrow and is usually measured in points. Wider standoffs give more importance to the image, but narrow ones create a smoother flow.

Here is an example of text and an image that are wrapped so that both the image and the text are merged. Notice that the text line endings change to accommodate the outline of the graphic. The text wraps around the graphic to save space in the text block.

Edward Skintik

Figure 9.12 *Wrapping text around an image makes it easier to view both the image and text as a unit.*

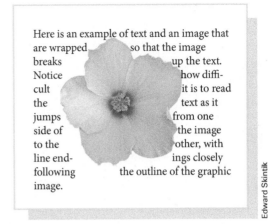

Here is an example of text and an image that are wrapped breaks Notice cult the jumps side of to the line end- following image. so that the image up the text. how difficult it is to read text as it from one the image other, with ings closely the outline of the graphic

Edward Skintik

Figure 9.13 *Images placed in the middle of a text column make it difficult to read the text.*

Avoid placing a graphic in the center of a column of text (see Figure 9.13). Instead, place the image along either the right or left margin of the text, matching the margin of the image with the margin of the text. If you are working with two columns of text, you can place a graphic between the two columns so that it breaks into both columns.

checkpoint

What is the difference between linking and embedding graphic files?

ACTIVITY 9.3 ▶ Linking and Embedding Images

1. Create a new desktop publishing document that is 8.5 × 11 inches. Change the zero point to the left and top margin.

2. Place or insert **squash_text** from your data files into the desktop publishing document.

3. Place or insert the graphic **squash** from your student data files as an embedded image. Move it to the top left margin. Wrap text to the right of the graphic. Change the standoff at the right and the bottom of the graphic slightly so that the image stands out and reading the text is easier.

4. Place or insert the graphic **squash_blooms** as an embedded image from your student data files. Move it to the right margin, aligned with the last line of text. Wrap text to the left of the graphic. Change the standoff slightly to the left and above the image so that the image stands out and reading the text is easier.

5. Save as **9_Activity3_embedded_graphics**.

6. Change the two graphics to linked graphics.

7. Save as **9_Activity3_linked_graphics**. Note the difference in the size of the file. Be prepared to discuss the file size difference in class.

Punctuality

One of the biggest complaints employers have about new employees is their lack of punctuality. Sometimes workers don't show up for work on time—or at all—and don't even call in with an explanation. These workers are telling their employers that they don't care about their jobs. Needless to say, such employees don't keep their jobs for very long.

Being punctual doesn't just mean coming to work on time, though. It means being ready to work as well. It means waiting on customers promptly, being on time for meetings, and completing your work when it's due. Punctuality builds trust: Your coworkers will learn that they can depend on you to do your own work on time and that they'll rarely need to "fill in" for you. As your reputation for reliability grows, so will the importance of your assignments. So avoid the temptation to hit the snooze bar on the alarm clock and get into the punctuality habit!

Skills in Action: Imagine that you are creating a presentation for an important client. A coworker is responsible for providing you with the image files for the presentation. The files were due to you first thing this morning, but you haven't received them yet. The presentation needs to be finished by the end of the day. What will you do? Discuss in class.

Key Concepts

▶ Keyword searches can help identify stock photos and clip art in extensive online collections. *LO 9.1*

▶ Screen captures are appropriate for certain material, but their low resolution makes them less than ideal for print products. *LO 9.1*

▶ Scanning is a useful option for digitizing hard copy documents that are unavailable in electronic format. *LO 9.2*

▶ Understanding licensing structure is critical to using sourced images legally. *LO 9.4*

▶ Royalty-free licenses grant almost unlimited permission to use an image for a one-time fee. *LO 9.4*

▶ Rights-managed licenses grant limited permission to use a copyrighted image, allowing the copyright holder to control how an image is used, and sometimes granting the buyer a certain level of exclusivity. *LO 9.4*

▶ Preparing raster images for print products usually includes sizing the image in an image editing program. *LO 9.5*

▶ Resolution of a raster image is inversely correlated to its document size. As images shrink, resolution rises and vice versa. *LO 9.5*

▶ The target resolution for raster images used in print products is normally between 240 and 300 ppi. *LO 9.5*

▶ Downsampling should be undertaken with caution since it impacts image quality, but it can be useful to manage resolution and file size in high-pixel photos. *LO 9.6*

▶ Native file formats and TIFF are the most common files types for raster images used in print products. Native file formats and EPS are the most typical vector file types for print products. *LO 9.7*

▶ Linked graphics appear in a layout as a low-resolution screen image to be positioned, but the bulk of the image data is maintained in the individual image file until it is called by the software program for printing. *LO 9.8*

▶ Embedded graphics increase file sizes because they bring all of their image data into the layout file. *LO 9.8*

▶ Inline graphics are anchored and move with text on a page; floating graphics move independently of text. *LO 9.9*

▶ Text wrapping is a useful feature for flowing text around objects, particularly floating graphics. *LO 9.10*

Review and Discuss

1. List advantages of using photos from your own camera. *LO 9.1*

2. Evaluate two specific situations in which photos are needed, citing the advantages and disadvantages of using stock photos in these jobs. *LO 9.1*

3. Analyze what should be considered when choosing an image size and resolution in the following scenarios: a) Image will be used on the Web. b) Image will be used in print publishing. *LO 9.2 and 9.7*

4. Identify and describe in detail what most owners of stock photos do to ensure that the stock photo is not used without purchasing. *LO 9.4*

5. Define screen captures and evaluate their use in tutorial documentation. *LO 9.2*

6. Identify when it is appropriate to use a scanned image and when it is not a good idea. *LO 9.2*

7. Explain royalty-free licensing and give examples of what may be included in the licensing agreement. *LO 9.4*

8. Differentiate between rights-managed licenses and royalty-free licenses. *LO 9.4*

9. List some reasons it may be best to resize images in a raster editing program before placing them in a layout program. *LO 9.5*

10. Describe resampling, downsampling, and upsampling in a raster image. *LO 9.6*

11. Compare and contrast the two most common raster file types used for print documents. *LO 9.7*

12. Compare and contrast linked and embedded graphics in a desktop publishing program. *LO 9.8*

13. Differentiate between an inline graphic and a floating graphic, giving examples of the type of material that would use each. *LO 9.9*

14. Describe text wrapping and conclude when and why it should be avoided. *LO 9.10*

15. Describe the effect a wide or narrow standoff can have on the image. *LO 9.10*

Apply

1. Bring a photo from home to scan. This could be of family, pets, or objects such as houses or cars. It could also be of a favorite sunset or other image that you have taken. Scan, edit, and crop the photo as needed, saving it as **home_your_name.jpg**. Write 250 words telling about your family, hobbies, and goals. Save the text in a word processing document as **scanning**. Place, import, or copy the text into an 8.5- × 11-inch, two-column, desktop publishing document. Place the image in the same document. Create a title that stretches across both columns. Decide on the wording and formatting for the title. Place the text in two even columns below the title with appropriate formatting. Place the image either right- or left-aligned using text wrapping. Add a caption to the image. Save the document as **9_Apply1_scanning**. *LO 9.2 and 9.10*

2. Write a 250-word story about the history of a hospital near you. Go to their website or locate a brochure to get your information. Save the text in a word processing document as **hospital**. Create an 8.5- × 11-inch desktop publishing document with two columns. Place the text in the desktop publishing document in the first column. Locate a trial stock photo to use to enhance the document by searching a stock photo website suggested in the textbook. Place the photo in column two with appropriate text wrapping. Add a title across all columns. Format the title and text appropriately. Save the document as **9_Apply2_stock_photos**. *LO 9.1 and 9.10*

3. Place the step-by-step instructions for preparing raster files for print in an 8.5- × 11-inch desktop publishing document. Add a screenshot that clarifies the instructions. Save the document as **8_Apply3_inline**. Change the image to a floating graphic. Save the document again as **8_Apply3_floating_graphic**. *LO 9.2, 9.5, and 9.9*

4. Take a series of pictures using a digital camera. Choose five of the pictures to practice downsampling, preparing them for print. Insert the five images into a desktop publishing document. Save the document as **9_Apply4_downsampling**. *LO 9.1, 9.6, and 9.8*

5. Write a report in a desktop publishing document highlighting what you have learned in this chapter. Add samples of graphics for each new concept learned. Include one paragraph for each section with at least one example of a graphic. The Key Concepts section within the chapter may be helpful in organizing the report. Save the document as **9_Apply5_graphics**. *LO 9.1, 9.2, 9.3, 9.5, and 9.10*

Explore

1. Explore the Internet to locate some newsletters that you may read on a regular basis or some that you may be interested in. Read through a newsletter. Make a list of the skills you learned in this chapter. Find examples of using that skill in the newsletter. Add those examples next to the skill on your list. Note whether they were effectively used or not. Explain what could be different that would be more effective. Use a word processing document to write your 250-word critique, including documentation of your reference in MLA style. Place or import your text into an 8.5- × 11-inch desktop publishing document. Format the text appropriately with a title. Save the document as **9_Explore1_newsletter_critique**. *LO 9.10*

2. Search the Internet for famous logos. Download four of your favorite ones. Insert or place each of the logos in an 8.5- × 11-inch desktop publishing document. Place one in each quadrant of the page. Draw a text box below each one. In it, explain what element or elements in the logo made you choose this logo as one of your favorites. Save the document as **9_Explore2_logos**. *LO 9.2, 9.9, and 9.10*

3. Explore online word art generators. Use your favorite quote or a short quote as the text in the word art. You can explore quotes online as well. Some of the online word art creators may also have a list of quotes that you can select from. Import or place the word art graphic into an 8.5- × 11-inch desktop publishing document. Draw a text box below the word art and write an explanation of why this is your favorite quote as well as what you think it means. Search for clip art or use a stock photo to enhance your document. Save the document as **9_Explore3_word_art**. *LO 9.1, 9.3, and 9.10*

Academic Connections

Reading: Search the Internet for the question: "What is the difference between graphic design and desktop publishing?" Read an article. Write down 5–10 questions from the article. Answer the questions from your reading. Share your questions and answers with a partner. If they have questions that you did not ask, add those to your questions. They should do the same—providing you with questions and answers about an article they read. Below your questions, cite your reference to your article in MLA style. Save your work as **9_AC_reading**.

Math: In desktop publishing, the page is sometimes divided in thirds, fourths, and so on. Math is needed to determine where to place the guide on the ruler. We'll consider the zero point for each of these to be at the left and top margin and that each page has a 0.5 inch margin on all sides. For example, if the page size is 4 × 4 inches, with the zero point at the left margin, where would you place the horizontal guide for it to be at half the page? The horizontal guide would range from 0 to 3 inches (the right margin). Halfway to that would be 1.5 inches. Perform the required calculations and correctly fill in the chart below:

Page Size (Vertical × Horizontal)	Horizontal Guide at half the page	Vertical Guide at half the page	Horizontal Guide at one-third the page	Vertical Guide at one-third the page	Horizontal Guide at two-thirds the page	Vertical Guide at two-thirds the page
4 in. × 4 in.						
6 in. × 8 in.						
5.5 in. × 8.5 in.						
8.5 in. × 11 in.						

Chapter 10

Print Design

Lesson 10.1 Understanding Design Principles

Lesson 10.2 Structuring a Layout

Lesson 10.3 Using PDFs for Print Publications

Dropping clip art randomly onto a page is not desktop publishing. Good desktop publishing skills require you to know where to place images and what effect the placement will have on your page. You have seen in the previous two chapters how to work with text and graphics. In this chapter, you begin to integrate these skills artfully to create a quality desktop published document.

Learning Outcomes

▶ **10.1** Recognize basic design principles: balance, rhythm, emphasis, and unity.

▶ **10.2** Understand the role of white space.

▶ **10.3** Follow preliminary steps to plan a layout.

▶ **10.4** Set up a new document in desktop publishing software.

▶ **10.5** Use a grid to lend underlying structure to designs.

▶ **10.6** Understand why PDFs are important in the print publication process.

Key Terms

- balance
- bleed
- emphasis
- gutter
- layout
- master pages
- pica
- rhythm
- unity
- white space

In Chapter 4, "Digital Photography," you read about how the elements of design and principles of composition can improve your photographs. The same is true for printed materials (and, to a large extent, for website designs, as well). In desktop publishing, designers arrange elements you've read about in previous chapters such as text, graphics, lines, texture, color, and white space to create balance, rhythm, emphasis, and unity in a **layout**, or a designed page. These design principles are what make a layout effective. They help capture attention, guide a reader through a layout, convey a main idea or tone, and generally just make the design appealing.

This chapter will describe a few basic design principles and how you can use certain design elements and techniques to improve print products. It will also cover some more practical aspects of layout design such as structuring a new document, using a design grid, and using PDFs for print publications.

layout—The arrangement on a page of all the key elements without regard to the specific content.

Lesson 10.1 — Understanding Design Principles

The overriding idea behind good design is the relationship between similarity and contrast. Similarity in a design is what helps a viewer navigate and recognize a design as a single unit. Without similarity, a design is chaotic and the message is not clear. Contrast in a design captures, keeps, and directs a viewer's attention. Without contrast, a design can be boring and, potentially, ignored. So a good design needs both. All of the classic design principles seek to contribute either to similarity, to contrast, or to both.

This lesson describes some of the most important design principles that can help you incorporate similarity and contrast in your layouts. Keep in mind that this is just a brief introduction to these topics. If you intend to

pica—A printer's measurement equal to 1/6 of an inch.

Think About It

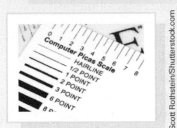

Scott Rothstein/Shutterstock.com

Figure 10.1 *A pica ruler is used by those who work in publishing to determine font sizes and spacing.*

Units of Measure in Desktop Publishing

Before you begin the process of creating a design, it's important to understand the measurement terms used in desktop publishing. In earlier chapters, you might have wondered why font sizes are measured in points. Instead of using inches and fractions, most design professionals use picas and points when making layout designs.

A **pica** represents 1/6 of an inch (that is, there are six picas in an inch) and is used to measure large areas such as page size and column widths. A point is a division of a pica. There are 12 points to a pica or 72 points to an inch. While both terms begin with the same letter, picas are abbreviated by a "p" and points are abbreviated by "pt."

Often you will indicate a measurement that includes both picas and points. For example, a line might be 6p3, which means that it is 6 picas and 3 points long. Using picas and points is awkward at first, but once you get the hang of it, you will find it easier to use than inches. Rather than having to think of a page as 11 inches, you will think of it as 66 picas. Using picas to divide the page into thirds is easy since each third will be 22 picas.

become a designer, you'll need to learn much more about these principles. As you become more familiar with how design principles work, you will be able to decide how you can break the rules to bring a freshness and personal stamp to your work. But practicing the basics first is a good place to start, and knowing just a little bit about design principles can improve the appeal of documents you produce, even as a non-designer.

Balance LO 10.1

Items on a layout—whether text, graphics, lines, shapes, or even white space—have a certain visual weight. The page designer's challenge is to distribute the weight of all the elements across a page to achieve a design principle called **balance**. Balance is important because it is pleasing and restful to the eye. Unbalanced designs can leave a viewer feeling uneasy.

balance—A design principle in which the weight of elements is distributed in a visually appealing way.

To understand balance, consider an imaginary line dividing a layout in half. The design may be divided vertically, horizontally, or diagonally. To achieve balance, a designer must arrange the graphic elements so that all sides of the layout have the same visual weight.

There are three types of balance: symmetrical, asymmetrical, and radial. In symmetrical balance, elements are distributed equally on both sides of the axis, sometimes even in mirror images of one another. In symmetrical designs, the focal point of the layout is often centered along the imaginary axis or an even number of elements are placed on either side of the axis. In asymmetrical balance, the elements on either side of the imaginary axis are not equal or mirrored, but they carry the same visual weight, and, therefore, the overall visual effect is balance. The two flyers in Figures 10.2 and 10.3 show examples of a symmetrically and an asymmetrically balanced layout.

Symmetrical balance is sometimes referred to as formal balance. It is useful for lending a traditional look to a design, and it is easy to achieve by centering elements and/or placing similar objects on either side of a layout. However, you must be careful when using symmetrical balance in your designs. Placing elements so that everything on the page is "even" sometimes creates a boring design.

Asymmetrical balance, sometimes called informal balance, is often more interesting because it involves unexpected arrangements of elements. However,

Figure 10.2 *This layout is an example of symmetrical balance: The shadowed bars on the bottom are a mirrored reflection of the colored bars on top and the heaviness of the centered white type in the bottom evens out the intensity of the colors on the top.*

asymmetrical balance is more difficult to achieve because there is no formula for making it work, and yet you can't simply place elements randomly on the page and call it asymmetric balance either. You have to rely on your artistic eye to determine when an asymmetrical layout is balanced.

There are some guidelines about the visual weight of layout elements that you can consider when creating an asymmetrical design. Here are a few:

- Bigger objects appear heavier than smaller items. However, grouping elements gives an overall impression of more weight, so a group of small objects can balance one large element.

- Objects with a lot of texture (like a large block of text) appear heavier than elements with little or no texture.

- Darker objects appear heavier than lighter ones.

- The position of an object can affect its visual weight: objects placed farther away from the center, or in the top half of a layout, or on the right side of a layout appear heavier.

- Graphics have more weight than text.

- Regularly shaped objects appear heavier than irregular objects.

- Elements isolated from other objects in a layout are heavier.

Radial balance is a bit rarer than the other two types of balance. In radial balance, all of the elements radiate out from a center point, like a starburst. If you've ever looked through a kaleidoscope, you have seen radial balance.

Figure 10.3 *This layout is an example of asymmetrical balance: The weight of the solid yellow block on top is balanced by the texture of the multicolored bars and the text on the bottom right.*

Rhythm *LO 10.1*

Rhythm refers to how a viewer's eye travels through a design. Like rhythm in music, it is the "beat" that a viewer subconsciously recognizes and follows through the layout. Rhythm is important because it connects the individual elements in a design. It is often established by repetition. Repeating an element (lines, shapes, textures, colors, etc.), a series or elements, or a motif (short/long, thin/thick, black/white) establishes a pattern that guides a viewer's eye from one element to the next. Rhythm in a design normally shows up in one of three forms:

- **Regular.** The fixed, even pattern of elements that suggests faster movement.

rhythm—A design principle that connects elements in a design and guides a viewer's eye from one item to the next.

- **Flowing.** A softer, more subtle repetition of elements, often involving curves and rounded patterns, that suggests a slower movement.
- **Progressive.** A more rare form of repetition in which an element is depicted in various stages of progress that suggests movement through time.

Repetition is a good way to control how a viewer looks at your design and can provide a sense of unity (which you'll read about later), but sometimes strict repetition can be boring. To enliven designs, you can add variation to a repeated element as a visual surprise for viewers as long as the overriding rhythmic pattern remains intact.

Review Figure 10.4. Does this design incorporate rhythm? What elements indicate the rhythm? What could be changed to use rhythm more effectively in this example?

openclipart.org

Figure 10.4 *Do you recognize rhythm in this design? What elements contribute to the sense of rhythm?*

Emphasis

emphasis—A design principle in which certain elements in a design stand out more than others.

Emphasis relates to the center of interest in a design. Emphasis in a design is important because it indicates to the viewer where to look first. Also, varied levels of emphasis help a reader navigate a design, moving in order from the most prominent element to the least prominent element. There are three basic ways to establish emphasis in a design: placement, isolation, and contrast.

Creating a focal point in a layout is very similar to creating a focal point in a photograph, as explained in Chapter 4. For example, just as the rule of thirds creates a focal point in a photograph, it can establish emphasis in a layout design. An element placed according to the rule of thirds falls where the human eye likes to rest so it is recognized as a primary element in the design, especially if it is placed slightly above and to the left of the visual center of a rectangular layout. Likewise, isolating an element from other items in a design calls attention to it. But perhaps the most common way designers achieve emphasis is by contrasting the properties of certain design elements:

- **Size.** Larger items attract more attention when compared to smaller items, so using size is an easy way to establish emphasis in a design.
- **Shape.** An element that differs in shape can attract attention. For example, a round image on a page full of square photos will draw a viewer's eye.
- **Color.** Bright colors, in general, stand out when compared to dull colors. Also, varying the color value of an item, making it darker than surrounding items, will attract focus.
- **Orientation.** A vertical object placed in a field of horizontal items will get noticed, and vice versa.

Without emphasis, a design can look chaotic and unsatisfying. Look through some of your favorite magazines to find examples of how emphasis works in page layout. Can you find any examples of designs that lack emphasis?

Unity LO 10.1

Unity in a design means that all of the individual elements of a design look like they belong together. When a design has unity, a viewer can readily see that the headings, text, and graphics are part of a whole. In a series of documents or in a multipage design, unity is also important. Four general areas contribute to unity in a design:

- **Proximity.** Objects grouped closer together are more likely to be recognized as part of a whole than objects placed farther apart from one another. Elements that "float" on the page without any visual connection can seem unrelated.
- **Alignment.** Elements that are aligned look like they go together. Proper alignment helps the viewer move from one element to the next and perceive the design as a single unit. Using a grid, as you will learn in the next section, is a good way to align items on a page.
- **Repetition or consistency.** Repetitive or consistent use of type styles, color palettes, motifs, and spacing can unify a design. Repetition is related to the principle of rhythm, in which repetition creates a connection between elements across a layout.
- **Contrast.** As mentioned above, consistency is an important way to convey unity in a design. However, in some cases, you may want to introduce contrast to a design to bring emphasis to an area or a particular element. Emphasizing certain elements helps establish unity by showing relationships between elements.

unity—A design principle that pulls together all of the individual elements, making the design look like a single unit.

Figure 10.5 *It is interesting how easily the eye can see an object that is even slightly misaligned. In design, you need to be aware of this perception of details and use it to your advantage.*

Figure 10.6 *Using white space appropriately can improve the readability of the text.*

white space—Also called negative space; the blank areas of a design that function like a design element.

As mentioned above, alignment is an important way to convey unity in a design. However, in some cases, you may want to break alignment to bring emphasis to an area or a particular element. When doing so, be sure to make the difference significant enough that it looks intentional. Notice in Figure 10.5 that the pen is just slightly out of alignment. Does your eye want to straighten it?

White Space *LO 10.2*

White space is more of a design element than a design principle, but it is important enough to warrant some specific attention when considering the guiding ideas and goals of design. Strange as it may seem, the areas in which text or graphics do not appear have as much importance as the areas in which they do appear. These areas are called **white space** (or sometimes negative space), and they act as design elements of their own. A block of white space can be used as a means of guiding the eye, as well as of resting it. (See Figure 10.6.)

Some designers believe that as much as 50 percent of a page should be white space. The percentage you decide to use will be determined by the type of publication, but most publication designs can benefit from an increase in white space. You can build white space into your designs in the margins, leading, typeface selection, and spacing between elements. When you consider the overall design, think of white space as an element on the same level as text, images, and graphics. It carries the same force as any of these items.

White space, however, can pose two problems: trapped white space and rivers of white. Trapped white space is just what it sounds like—white space surrounded on all sides by text or graphics. Trapped white space is not nearly as effective a design element as open white space. When designing a page, look for trapped white space that can be "freed." You will not reduce the content of the page, but you will increase its readability and interest. Rivers of white are found most often when text is justified because the extra space inserted in a line can be duplicated on the line above and below. The eye is drawn to the river of white space instead of to the text.

ACTIVITY 10.1 ▶ Design Principles

1. Create an 8.5- × 11-inch desktop publishing document. If possible, change the measurement preferences in your software to points and picas.

2. Place or insert **dog1** and **dog2** from your data files on your scratch area.

3. Review the information on balance, rhythm, emphasis, and unity. Using what you have learned, decide where you want to place these images in your document and place them. (You can move them around later if you decide to do so.) Keep notes on why you placed the image where you did and what design principle influenced your choice. Continue to take notes as you place additional objects from the instructions below and, perhaps, change the location of objects based on the new elements in the design.

4. Add a text box with a large headline font that says **Lost Pet**.

5. Add the following in a bulleted list (in a text box):
   - Answers to JuJu
   - Loves other animals
   - Wearing red collar
   - Very friendly
   - Weighs 40–45 lbs.

6. Add the following to a text box: **FOUND? Call Jennifer Sanchez, 940-555-0123, Reward!**

7. Use some words as art or rotated text; perhaps use the dog's name.

8. Format text and text boxes with appropriate fonts, sizes, and colors.

9. Save the document as **10_Activity1_design**.

Lesson 10.2 ▶ Structuring a Layout *LO 10.3*

Staring at a blank page in your desktop publishing software can be intimidating. The sheer number of choices for arranging elements and the pressure of incorporating design principles can leave your head spinning. So, where do you start? You can make that blank page less daunting by doing some preliminary work before even launching your software. Consider the following suggestions:

- **Gather materials.** Collect all of the text files, images, and graphics that you will place in the design.
- **Brainstorm a design theme.** Think about the message and tone you want to communicate to your audience. Consider who will be looking at your design and how you can best tailor your message to that group.
- **Choose design elements.** Develop the color palette and choose the fonts you think will work best for the design. These elements may evolve as your design progresses, but it's good to have something to start with.
- **Sketch layout ideas.** Consider all of the information you've gathered and sketch some rough layout ideas. Again, these don't have to be final and probably won't be. But having a sketch can be helpful for taking the first step when faced with that blank page.

After you've taken these steps to prepare, you should be ready to launch your software and get started with your design.

Setting Up a New Document *LO 10.4*

When you create a new document from scratch in desktop publishing software, you must specify certain page setup options that will be applied to all of the pages in your document. For example, Figure 10.7

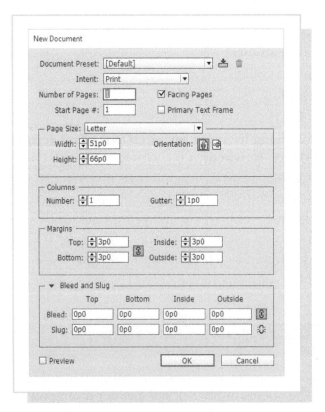

Figure 10.7 *The New Document window in Adobe InDesign offers several options for setting up the basic structure of a new document.*

shows the New Document window that appears when you create a new document in Adobe InDesign. Most comparable software applications offer similar selections.

Here are a few things to consider when making page setup decisions:

- **Facing pages.** Facing pages refers to two side-by-side pages. Two facing pages are also referred to as a spread. If your document will be bound, as in a book or magazine, you will almost always set up your file with facing pages.

- **Number of pages.** Perhaps you are designing a flyer or a brochure that will be only one page. Or perhaps you are designing a multipage magazine. You don't need to know the final page count of your file when setting up a document. However, keep in mind that certain multipage documents sent to a professional printer must be set up in even signatures. See the *Impact* sidebar for more information about signatures.

- **Number of columns and size of gutters.** Columns are non-printing guidelines used to organize and align elements on the page. A **gutter** is the white space between each pair of columns. You'll read more about these elements in the next section.

- **Margins.** When setting the margin widths in a new document, consider the design impact you would like the white space in the margins to have. Wide margins give the eye ample space to rest and can make a design cleaner and easier to take in, but they also mean less content can fit on a page or spread. Narrow margins mean more content can fit on a page but they can make a page look too crowded and chaotic. There is no perfect formula, but some general guidelines can be a helpful starting point when you are setting margins. In general, it is best to avoid equal margins on all sides of a page or spread. Instead, make the bottom margin widest (especially if you will include page numbers or other material at the bottom of the page), the outside margins the next widest, and the top margin smallest unless you have facing pages. In that case, the inside margin (the area where the two pages meet) should be the smallest. (Make sure the inside margin is ample enough that content does not disappear in the middle part of the spread.)

- **Bleed.** A **bleed** is an element that extends through the margin of a page right up to the edge. (See Figure 10.8.) This effect is useful for grabbing attention, suggesting movement in a design, and otherwise making a design impact. An element can bleed off any or all sides of a page or spread. Most desktop printers cannot produce a bleed; only professional presses where pages are printed on huge sheets and then trimmed down to size can produce a bleed. Different printers handle bleeds differently, so it is important to contact your service provider to ask how you should set up a bleed in your files if you

gutter—The white space between columns on a page.

bleed—An element that extends through a margin and off the edge of a printed page.

iStockphoto.com/jfmdesign

Figure 10.8 *Professional presses can produce a bleed off the edge of a page. Can you find the bleed element in this package design?*

lavitrei/Shutterstock.com

Impact

Signatures

The page count for multipage documents that are printed on a press must be even signatures. A signature is usually 16 pages, but it can sometimes be 8, 24, or 32 pages. An even signature is a multiple of the signature number. So, for example, a document printed in 16-page signatures can be any multiple of 16 (16, 32, 48, etc.).

To understand what a signature is, you need to know how these types of documents are printed on a press. The individual pages are actually printed on the front and back of a large, single sheet of paper. For example, in a 16-page signature, eight pages are printed on one side of the large sheet and eight pages are printed on the other. The pages are arranged on the large sheet, not in page order, but in such a way that they fall in correct order when the sheet is folded a certain way. This is called imposition (see Figure 10.9). After the sheet is folded and the pages are in the proper order, the top and bottom are trimmed, forming a group of pages in an individual booklet.

If a document is more than one signature long, all of the signatures are printed, folded, and trimmed individually and then they are bound together. So, for example, if a 112-page magazine is printed in 16-page signatures, there will be seven signatures in the final product. Using signatures saves money because there is less paper waste.

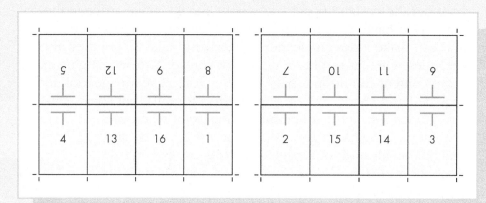

© Cengage Learning

Figure 10.9 *This is the imposition of a 16-page signature. The left side is the front of the printed sheet and the right side is the back of the sheet. After printing, the sheet is folded in such a way that the page numbers fall in the proper order.*

Critical Thinking

Can you create a small signature out of a plain piece of paper? On a rectangular sheet of paper in landscape orientation, draw a horizontal line across the sheet, then draw three evenly spaced vertical lines, dividing the sheet into eight boxes. Flip the paper over and repeat on the other side, matching the lines as best you can. On one side, number each box according to the image on the left in Figure 10.9. Turn the paper over and number each box according to the image on the right in Figure 10.9. (Note: number 2 should be in the box behind number 1, number 15 should be behind 16, and so on.) Fold the paper in half so that number 2 meets number 3. Fold it again so that number 4 meets number 5. Fold one more time so that number 8 meets number 9. Use scissors to trim the top and the side so that the pages can turn freely. Are the page numbers in order? If so, you've successfully created a signature just as a printer would.

intend to use it. Normally, setting a bleed involves extending the element in question beyond the edge of your page by a certain amount. If you simply place the element right against the edge of the page, a gap may show if the printer doesn't trim the sheet precisely.

Using a Grid to Organize Elements *LO 10.5*

A grid is a series of vertical and horizontal nonprinting guidelines on a layout that direct the placement and size of objects on a page. Using a grid reduces the randomness of deciding where to place items on a blank page and how big to make them. Along these same lines, grids can speed up the design and layout process by removing at least some guesswork and trial and error. Placing text, images, and other elements along the lines of a grid ensures proper alignment and helps build cohesiveness, both important contributors to design unity.

In fact, a grid can make it easier to incorporate other design principles as well. For example, the regularity of the grid can be used to create repetition and rhythm; intentionally breaking the repetition of a grid creates emphasis; the even measurements of a grid can help with judging and adjusting for balance. Although it may seem that a grid would limit creativity, it actually enhances it by helping you easily track the extent of similarity and contrast in a design.

The series of vertical grid lines in a layout are commonly referred to as columns. Columns are a division of the space within the margins on a page, separated evenly by the gutters. When you designate the number of columns and the width of the gutters, layout software divides the space between the margins accordingly and displays the nonprinting guides on the page (see Figure 10.10).

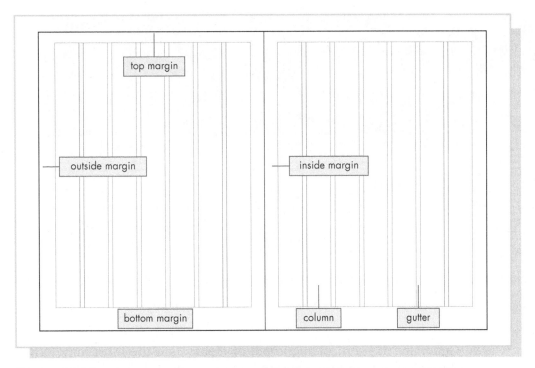

Figure 10.10 *This is an example of a two-page spread set up for a seven-column layout in InDesign. The gutters are each one pica wide. Notice that there are seven columns on each page of the spread.*

The appropriate number of columns for a design will depend on the size of the page and the complexity of the design. Generally, the more complex the design and the more types of elements to be included, the more columns it will need. Think, for example, of a novel with no pictures. The page size is relatively small and the text is set in a single column. In contrast, think of the front page of a newspaper with text, photos, charts, varying size headlines, and more on a fairly large sheet of paper. This broad page size and wide range of elements and content is typically organized into multiple columns.

Keep in mind the following general guidelines when determining the number of columns for your project (see Figure 10.11):

- Two-column grids are useful for narrow pages and simple designs, as long as the column width does not make text line length too wide for comfortable reading. You can add variety to a two-column grid by having some elements span both columns.

- Three-column grids are more flexible than two-column layouts since items can span one, two, or all three columns, and three-column layouts work for almost all page sizes. However, three-column designs are still relatively simple.

- Four or more columns are usually the most flexible choice for page structure. However, the underlying organization can be lost if there are too many columns. Also, odd numbers of columns seem to work best in a design because they allow you to build asymmetry into your designs, an element that produces more exciting layouts. Five- and seven-column grids seem to offer the most options for dynamic, effective page structure.

Figure 10.11 *These examples show a basic design in a two- and three-column layout. Can you see the underlying column structure in each?*

Generally, the vertical alignment of elements is the most important concern in design, and the column feature in most desktop publishing software makes it easy to establish a vertical grid. Establishing consistent horizontal alignment of elements may be a little more involved. Many times, horizontal alignment is determined by how big an element is after you size it to fit the vertical columns. You can position the largest item according to the columns and see how that sizing impacts the depth of the object, then use that depth as a launching point for aligning other elements horizontally.

Another option is to familiarize yourself with the grid feature in your layout software. This feature will automatically add horizontal grid lines, but requires a little more design and page layout awareness than you may have at this point. You can also establish horizontal guides by dividing the page horizontally into thirds, or quarters, or some other common measure.

After you establish the number and size of the columns in your design, you are ready to start placing elements on the page. Keep in mind that you are not limited to the individual columns. Page elements can span two or more columns (see Figure 10.12). The option to span objects across multiple columns is what makes a multicolumn grid flexible. The idea is that an element begins and ends on a grid line, not in the middle of a column and not in the gutter. An exception may be made for rules that separate columns of text or other elements. It is not uncommon to place these in the middle of the gutter.

zurabi/Shutterstock.com

Figure 10.12 *This image shows the InDesign column guides on this 6-column spread from Chapter 8. Notice how the different elements span different numbers of columns and how the picture of the ship actually crosses the inside margin of the two pages, but still aligns with text columns. Do you see any problems with this layout based on what you've read in this chapter so far? How could it be improved?*

Vertical and horizontal alignment is important for establishing order in a design, but just as important is occasionally breaking the order to create interest. For example, bleeding a picture off one or more sides of the page violates the grid structure, but can add interest and excitement to a page. Or rotating one image in a series of similarly sized photos breaks the rhythm, but draws attention to itself, creating emphasis.

As you begin recognizing the grid structure in designs you see every day, you'll also start noticing how designers break the underlying structure to add contrast to their pages. The overriding rule when breaking the grid is to do it for a specific reason: to achieve unity, balance, emphasis, or rhythm. The break will make your designs more dynamic and help strike a balance between similarity and contrast, which is the key to good design.

Master Pages and Templates *LO 10.4*

master pages—Page designs that can be applied automatically to any page within a document.

Because layouts are often repeated from page to page, desktop publishing software provides master page options. **Master pages** are like backgrounds that you can build on top of—anything that appears on the master page will appear on whatever page the master is applied to. Master pages usually include elements that are repeated on multiple pages, such as headers or footers, or even logos. A master page can also contain a basic structure that will be repeated on multiple pages such as columns or standardized text frames. Master pages (as shown in Figure 10.13) are useful shortcuts for standardizing designs across a book series or any document series that shares common elements. This is why they are normally provided by the person who creates the overall design of a project.

Master pages are often incorporated into templates. A design template includes all of the shared elements in a design. When you create a new file based on a design template, the new document opens with the paragraph styles, character styles, color schemes, and master pages associated with the design. In most desktop publishing software, creating a template is as easy as using the Save As command and choosing the template file format. Once a template is saved, you can base a new design on that template.

Some desktop publishing programs provide access to ready-to-use design templates created by professional designers that you can use to create new documents. The template provides the design and you just add content. These are sometimes referred to as "canned." These canned templates can be useful if you are short on time or inspiration; however, the design is

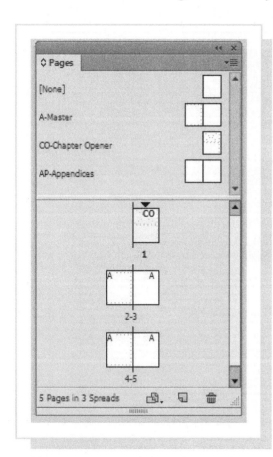

Figure 10.13 *In InDesign, master pages you create are stored in the Pages panel so you can easily access and apply them.*

not unique to your use—anyone can access the same template for their own use. Also, templates are usually generic. You should never use a canned template if you are given a graphic design assignment. That is cheating!

checkpoint

How does a grid contribute to good design?

ACTIVITY 10.2 ▶ Sketching a Layout

1. A new dentist needs a flyer to announce the grand opening of his office. Open **sketch** from your data files. Note that three column guides and three row guides have been created.

2. Design a layout that consists of at least one to two graphics, the company name with a logo, a larger block of text for a short biography of the doctor, and a smaller block of text announcing the time and details of the grand opening.

3. Using the **sketch** data file, label each section as a banner, graphic, larger block of text, or smaller block of text. If you use more than one block on your printout, label across or down more than one third of the grid.

4. Save your completed sketch as **10_Activity2_sketch**.

Lesson 10.3 ▶ Using PDFs for Print Publications

Portable document format, or PDF, is one of the most, if not the most, widely distributed file formats in the world. The versatility and convenience of PDFs offer many benefits to users who share files electronically. The main appeal of the file format is that a PDF created from almost any application on any computer system can be viewed or printed on any other system and will look exactly the same. In a PDF, not only is the original appearance of a document preserved, but also all of the source file information is saved as well. This means that a PDF includes all of the data about fonts, graphics, color, and so on from the native application file. This feature of PDFs makes them particularly well suited to the desktop publishing workflow for printed materials.

Creating and Viewing PDFs *LO 10.6*

When creating files for print publication, you will most likely generate PDFs directly from within your layout program. In these types of programs, PDF technology is incorporated into the native application, making it very convenient to generate PDFs. But it is worth noting that there are some stand-alone PDF applications that might come in handy when you are working with PDFs generated from native applications.

There are two basic tasks associated with PDFs: one is creating PDFs and the other is viewing them. Some PDF software, such as Adobe Acrobat, can both create and display PDFs. Other software, such as Adobe Reader, can display PDFs, but cannot create them. Many applications such as InDesign, Word, or even an open source program like OpenOffice.org Writer, can generate PDFs but cannot view them. (Word 2013, however, can open PDF files so you can edit the text.)

The process of creating a PDF varies from program to program, but normally it's as easy as using the Save As function in whatever software you are working in and choosing PDF as the file type. In some cases, you create a PDF by printing to a PDF driver (for example, you would select Adobe PDF as the printer choice if the software you're using incorporates Adobe PDF technology for creating PDFs directly). Other programs include an Export option for creating PDFs.

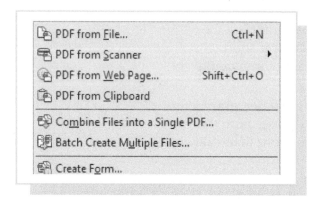

Figure 10.14 *Using the Create menu in Acrobat offers more ways to create PDFs than those available using the Save or Print functions.*

Of course, a PDF creation application creates PDFs from other application files. For example, in Adobe Acrobat you generate a PDF from a wide variety of file types by using the Create menu shown in Figure 10.14. Whichever method an application uses, the result is the same: a PDF of the original file that can be shared across platforms.

No matter what program you use to generate a PDF, you'll want to open it to view it. To do this, you will need a PDF viewer. The most widely used PDF viewer is Adobe Reader, available as a free download. Although some PDF viewers, including Reader, offer some functions beyond just displaying the PDF (you can use tools to add comments to PDFs in some viewers, for example), only full-blown PDF programs such as Acrobat allow you to make fundamental changes and edits to a PDF.

PDFs and Print Production LO 10.6

Before the development of PDF files, sending an electronic document to a press for printing entailed delivering all of the native application files, all of the font files, all of the individual image and graphic files, and any other files used to create the document. Printing from native files left the process vulnerable to all sorts of problems. For example, if the applications and system platform used to create the original files did not match what was used by the print vendor, the document might not print as expected—or at all. Sometimes, even different versions of the same applications or fonts could cause problems in the printing process. Not to mention, the sheer number of items to gather, transfer, and track was a huge task. A single missing image file could stop a print job, costing time and money. But the rise of PDFs smoothed the process. Now, when you send a PDF of your document to a printer, you can be confident that what you saw in the PDF is what will come off the press.

You can create a PDF for the press from almost any application with a wide range of settings and features, which is one of the most appealing aspects of the file format. But to be sure you get what you expect with the fewest roadblocks, it's best to create PDFs using settings verified or supplied by the print vendor. Many times, a print shop will supply these settings and you can manually configure them in your application, optionally saving the settings for future use. Other times, a print vendor will supply a special file that includes the appropriate settings. For Adobe PDF technology, this is called a print options file. When you load a print options file into Acrobat, the proper settings are automatically set and show up pre-loaded in your native application, saving you the trouble of manually adjusting each option.

It is always best to check with your print vendor before creating PDFs. However, sometimes that just isn't possible. In these cases, you can maximize your chances of a smooth printing process by creating PDFs using PDF/X settings. PDF/X settings are a set of standard PDF options developed with the cooperation of publishers and printers. When you create

Granata1111/Dreamstime.com

Digital Publications

In 1971, Project Gutenberg began its mission of making available to the public 10,000 important books and documents by digitizing the Declaration of Independence. Digital publishing can be said to have started with this project, and it has made steady inroads into traditional publishing ever since. The development of computers had a tremendous impact on how publications such as books, magazines, and newspapers were laid out and printed. With the rise of the Internet and especially the Web, many people began to look for their news and features online, rather than in printed magazines and newspapers. It was only a matter of time before national magazines and newspapers saw the benefit of launching their own websites with digital versions of their print content, augmented with in-depth content in the form of breaking news and blogs. Most widely circulated magazines and newspapers now have digital editions that allow them to deliver digital content to a worldwide audience more quickly and inexpensively than they could deliver it in printed form.

The world of book publishing has been similarly revolutionized by digital technology. After the development of dedicated readers that used so-called electronic paper technology, such as the Kindle and the Nook, book publishers began to make digital versions of books available for easy purchase and download through sites such as Amazon Prime and Google Books. By the middle of 2010, Amazon announced that it had sold more eBooks than printed books for the first time. Digital devices such as the iPad (introduced in 2010), other tablets, and smartphones provide additional platforms for people to read books, magazines, and newspapers. Though some people still prefer to read printed books, studies suggest that readers of eBooks actually read more books than people who don't have access to digital readers.

a PDF using a PDF/X preset, the PDF process incorporates a check to ensure the files do not include common problems in printer-bound PDFs:

- Fonts that aren't embedded
- Incorrect color spaces (for example, RGB color in a CMYK file)
- Missing images
- Other production-related issues

PDF/X minimizes the chance of problems once your PDFs reach the press.

Of course, PDFs have many uses beyond smoothing the print publication process. They are essential tools for collaborating and sharing information and can be deployed for web publishing as well.

checkpoint

Why are PDFs so well suited to the print publication process?

ACTIVITY 10.3 ▶ Creating and Viewing a PDF

1. Create a PDF of the flyer you created in Activity 10.2 and save it as *10_Activity3_flyer_pdf*.
2. Exchange PDFs with a classmate via email attachment.
3. Use Acrobat Reader to open and review the PDF. Use the commenting tools to provide feedback on the design elements in the PDF.
4. Return the marked-up PDF to the original creator.

21st Century Skills
CAREER

Flexibility and Adaptability

Conflict can be defined as a disagreement between two or more people. Often, it is caused by differences in values and standards, or by misunderstanding and miscommunication, or simple differences in personalities. Being able to manage and resolve conflict is one of the most important and valued skills you can bring to your job. You can demonstrate your conflict management skills by showing respect and understanding for others, offering alternatives, and avoiding stereotyping and offensive or condescending language. Other conflict management strategies include:

- Intervention, in which an objective third party provides a setting for discussing and resolving the conflict.
- Confrontation, in which the two parties approach each other directly and work together toward a solution.
- Compromise, in which both parties give up something in return for a workable solution.

Skills in Action: How would you handle a conflict between yourself and a classmate? Between you and a teacher or other administrator? Why do you think conflict management skills could make you a stronger leader?

Key Concepts

▶ An overriding idea behind good design is the tension between similarity and contrast: Without similarity, a design is chaotic and unreadable; without contrast, a design is boring and forgettable. *LO 10.1*

▶ Balance is the design principle that says the weight of objects is evenly distributed across a design. *LO 10.1*

▶ In symmetrical balance, elements are distributed equally on both sides of the axis, sometimes even in mirror images of one another. In asymmetrical balance, the elements on either side of the imaginary axis are not equal or mirrored, but they carry the same visual weight. *LO 10.1*

▶ Rhythm refers to how a viewer's eye travels through a design and is often established through repetition of a design element or sequence. *LO 10.1*

▶ Emphasis relates to the center of interest in a design and establishes a visual hierarchy that leads a viewer through a layout. Emphasis is often established through placement, isolation, and/or contrast of design elements. *LO 10.1*

▶ Unity in a design means that all of the individual elements of a design look like they belong together and cause the reader to recognize the design as a whole before noticing its individual parts. Proximity, alignment, and repetition (especially in alignment and structure) contribute to unity in a design. *LO 10.1*

▶ Using a grid reduces the randomness of deciding where to place items on a blank page and how big to make them. *LO 10.3*

▶ The grid is important for establishing order in a design, but just as important is occasionally breaking the order to create interest. *LO 10.5*

▶ Master pages and templates are shortcuts for creating consistent documents that share a similar design and features. *LO 10.4*

▶ PDFs are well suited for the print publication process because they retain all of the data about fonts, graphics, color, and so on from the native application file and minimize issues on the press. *LO 10.6*

Review and Discuss

1. Analyze how similarity and contrast are both needed in a design. *LO 10.1*

2. Describe what makes balance important in a design. *LO 10.1*

3. Analyze the effect an out-of-alignment element on a page has on the human brain and what this can do to the design being accepted. *LO 10.1*

4. Compare and contrast the three types of balance in a design. *LO 10.1*

5. Analyze the effects of bleeding a graphic on a page. *LO 10.1 and 10.2*

6. Compare and contrast master pages and templates. *LO 10.3 and 10.4*

7. Evaluate the uses of PDF file format. What information is useful to obtain from a printer to avoid problems at the press and what is an alternative if that information is not available? *LO 10.6*

8. Evaluate the use of a grid in creating a design. *LO 10.5*

9. Analyze the importance of each of the three forms of rhythm in a design and how it relates to music. *LO 10.1*

10. Defend the use of white space in a publication with an evaluation of some of the pitfalls of using white space. *LO 10.2*

Apply

1. Create a desktop publishing document that is the size of a business card. Most software has business card as a template choice. It should be 3.5 × 2 inches in landscape orientation. Adjust margins to 1/8 inch on all sides and select a bleed of 1/8 inch on all sides. Add a dark background to your business card that extends to the bleed lines. Create a text box with the company name in size 18 font. The company name is Service Learning, Inc. Place the data file ***logo.tif*** to the left of the company name text box and resize as necessary. Create another text box and place near the bottom right. In the text box, include: 432 Distance Learning Blvd., Your City, ST ZIP, 979-555-0432, yourname@sli.org, http://www.yourname.sli.org. Resize the text to size 10. Create another text box and place centered in the space on the right below the company name and the bottom margin. In the text box should be your name and below it Student Advocate. Resize text to size 12. Decide on formatting of all text, including font and colors, to match the logo. Adjust placement of text boxes to create balance and symmetry. Save as ***10_Apply1_business_card***. *LO 10.1, 10.2, 10.3, 10.4, and 10.5*

2. Create an 8.5- × 11-inch desktop publishing document. Using the information from Apply 1, design a formal letterhead that uses a similar design. Save as ***10_Apply2_letterhead***. *LO 10.1, 10.2, 10.3, and 10.4*

3. Create a two-page, 8.5- × 11-inch desktop publishing document in landscape orientation. Design a trifold informational brochure for Business Professionals of America. Use the information in the ***bpa_brochure*** data file. If you need more information for your flyer, search your local BPA in your state or school, or you can search http://www.bpa.org/. Include a source note on the master page that includes bpa.org in MLA format as your source. Locate and save a bpa logo to use on the flyer. Save as ***10_Apply3_brochure***. *LO 10.1, 10.2, 10.3, 10.4, and 10.5*

4. Create a two-page newsletter for a community or school organization. Decide on a theme color scheme and use those colors throughout your newsletter. Use other elements as needed. Include at least three articles

and at least two images that you embed in the newsletter. Supply an appropriate name for the newsletter as a banner at the top of the first page. On the first page, there should be a table of contents for each of the articles with the name of the article and the page number. Use design principles focused on in this chapter and previous chapters. Save as **10_Apply4_newsletter**. *LO 10.1, 10.2, 10.3, 10.4, and 10.5*

5. Open **publishing** from your data files in a DTP or raster editing application Print the document to a PDF file with the file name **10_Apply5_security**. Use the password **2017dim** for someone to be able to open and edit the document. *LO 10.6*

Explore

1. Research the latest technology gadget that is on the market. Create a flyer telling about this gadget. Include on the flyer: name of the gadget and business making the contribution, at least one image, bulleted list of what this gadget can do or a list of the specifications of the gadget, and other elements to add interest to the flyer about this new technology. Review and use balance, symmetry, rhythm, appropriate fonts, and color. Save as **10_Explore1_technology**. *LO 10.1, 10.2, 10.3, 10.4, and 10.5*

2. Explore a career that you may be interested in. Create a half fold brochure with the information that you find. Provide documentation in MLA formatting on the brochure for source of the information. Use at least one image. This can be an image of yourself. Save as **10_Explore2_career**. *LO 10.1, 10.2, 10.3, 10.4, and 10.5*

3. Visit your local Chamber of Commerce or a business in your city. Gather as many samples of brochures, flyers, etc., as you can from the business. Look around on the walls, front of the building, etc. Make a list of everything you saw that requires desktop publishing skills. Include a description of the marketing materials that you found such as brochures, flyers, etc. What did you notice? Give specific examples of skills that you have used and read about in this and previous chapters. Include ideas of skills that were not used effectively. Save as **10_Explore3_marketing**. *LO 10.1 and 10.2*

4. Visit acrobat.com. Explore the website and make a list of what can be done on the website by registering for acrobat.com. Under each item on your list, add a comment on how you think this could be used in business. Create the list in a word processing document, then create a PDF from your file. Save as **10_Explore4_acrobatcom**. *LO 10.6*

Academic Connections

Reading: Read an article on symmetry that has been provided by your instructor or researched. Answer the following questions in a word processing document. What is the author's purpose in writing the article? Write a brief summary of the article using only the main points. How did this article help you to understand symmetry? Give specific examples from the article. What is the main idea from the article? Save your summary as **10_AC_reading**.

Math: Calculate the following picas and points using the inches given. Save your work as **10_AC_math**.

Inches	Picas	Points
1	6	72
1.5		
2		
2.5		
3		
3.5		
4		
4.5		
5		
5.5		
6		

UNIT 3 PROJECTS

Independent Project

Using the marketing items created for your business identity project from Unit 2, create the following:

▶ Flyer advertising the opening of the business. This can be an open house or announcement of an opening date. Use creativity in what to advertise to make a splash in creating excitement about the opening. Save the advertisement as **Unit3_flyer**, both in the native file type and as a PDF.

▶ Two-page newsletter to employees. Use lorem ipsum for text except for one paragraph to get stories started in each placeholder. Use typography for readability and emphasis in headings. Use at least one attention-getter and one element on a master page. Save the newsletter as **Unit3_newsletter** in the native file type, as a template, and as a PDF.

▶ Business card and letterhead to use in the business. Save your work as **Unit3_business_card** and **Unit3_letterhead**, both in the native file type and as a PDF.

▶ Trifold brochure. Save the brochure as **Unit3_brochure** in the native file type and as a PDF.

Note: Alternatively, you can create a new business identity by deciding on a name for your business, a tagline, and a logo. Take photos to use in creating the business identity using your business name, colors, logo, and tagline.

Portfolio

Create two folders to add to your portfolio: **Unit3_project** and **Unit3_classwork**. Place the PDFs of your projects in the **Unit3_project** folder. Choose at least one assignment from each chapter to place in your **Unit3_classwork** folder.

Write a journal to place in your portfolio for Unit 3. Save it as **Unit3_journal** in your **Unit3_classwork** folder. The journal should include an explanation of image, typography, and design choices made in creating your independent project. List specific choices made relating them to principles learned in this unit. Summarize the principles that you have learned in this unit that you believe will help you either in your daily life, now or in the future, or in business.

iStockphoto.com/Pashalgnatov

FBLA-PBL or BPA

Create a template for your local chapter's FBLA or BPA to use for a newsletter to send to the members each month. Save as **Unit3_fbla_template** or **Unit3_bpa_template**. Include the following in your project:

▶ Sketch of your design.

▶ Minimum of a four-page layout using design principles learned in this unit.

▶ A banner designed to use across the top of the first page that includes the name of organization, tagline, volume number, and date.

▶ Story placeholders using lorem ipsum for text with "continuing" notices as needed.

▶ Formatted text in placeholders with an appropriate text type that is readable.

▶ Formatted text in placeholders with spacing in paragraphs and characters.

▶ Effectively placed screen captures for placeholder images.

▶ Two attention-getters.

▶ At least two elements included on a master page.

Using the template, add notations in the text placeholders that highlight the principles used in your design. Leave the lorem ipsum text to fill up the text placeholders with space you do not use for your explanations. Insert images where you have placeholders. Save this version as **Unit3_newsletter** in both the native file type of your software and as a PDF.

UNIT 4

Audio and Video Production

11 Audio

12 Video

Career Cluster: Video Editor

Interview with Cal, Video Editor, McLain Video

Describe your average day. Typical? That depends on whether I'm starting out on a project or getting near the deadline—or bidding for a job or just reviewing raw footage that someone else shot. When I'm in the middle of a big job, though, my day includes many hours of reviewing video, thinking about how it might fit together, and determining how it will tell the story the client wants to tell. I also keep my eye out for very strong images—the expression on someone's face or the perfect lighting—that I might use someplace.

What is the worst part of your job? When the client calls you to tell you to change directions on something you just finished, and you have to do it all over again.

What is the best part of your job? Sometimes, while you're editing, you just know that it's all coming together. The flow of the sequences is just right. The changes in shots are perfect. It's very satisfying.

Employment Outlook The employment outlook for camera operators and video editors vary from year to year. However, many of those in the industry contract with businesses on a freelance basis.

Skills and Qualifications A bachelor's degree in videography or a related field is required for most jobs. Employers expect workers to have a strong visual sense, a creative thought process, the ability to pay attention to detail, good hand–eye coordination, and strong technical knowledge.

Job Titles Video editors, camera operators, film editors

What About You? Does a career in video editing interest you? Use the Internet to find job postings for this career. Research video editing and similar careers using the *Occupational Outlook Handbook* published by the U.S. Bureau of Labor Statistics and available at http://www.bls.gov/ooh/.

- How can you best prepare yourself for a career in video editing?
- What job qualifications should you make sure you have to meet an employer's needs?
- What are the most common technical skills and computer programs listed for video editors?

Audio

Learning Outcomes

▶ **11.1** Distinguish between sampling options for sound.

▶ **11.2** Make choices to reduce the size of sound files.

▶ **11.3** Select an audio file type for the appropriate use.

▶ **11.4** Explain the importance of sound cards.

▶ **11.5** Set up a microphone and record sound.

▶ **11.6** Modify audio files using a wave editor.

Key Terms

- ADC
- analog audio
- channels
- codec
- DAC
- decibel
- digital audio
- Hertz
- MIDI
- ripping
- sample rate
- sample size
- sequencer
- sound card
- subwoofer
- wave editor
- waveform

Sound could be the answer to the riddle, "What is all around us and never seen?" For that description certainly fits for the doorbell that rings, the musical notes, and the car horns we hear every day. The sounds are there, but we cannot see them.

Sound is generated when the air is disturbed, creating vibrations called sound waves. These sound waves travel to our ears, where they cause vibrations in the structures of the middle and inner ear. Our ears change these vibrations into signals sent along nerves to our brain, which interprets them as sound.

Computers and other audio devices can recreate and store these vibrations, allowing us to hear any sound whenever and as often as we would like. In this chapter, you will learn more about this process and what you must know to create successful audio files.

Sound is captured in two ways: in analog or digital form. **Analog audio** is recorded as a series of waves reproducing approximately what the human ear hears. Audiocassette tapes and vinyl records reproduce analog sound. Although audio cassette tapes are basically extinct, vinyl albums are undergoing somewhat of a resurgence. **Digital audio** is created using a series of zeros and ones (bits), with the computer reading the variations to play back what was recorded. MP3 players hold and play digital sound (Figure 11.1).

Analog audio records sound in a continuous wave. These waves have certain properties. One is wavelength, which is the distance between two similar points—such as the two highest points, called crests, or the two lowest points, called troughs—in two consecutive waves (see Figure 11.2). Related to wavelength is frequency, which is the number of times a wavelength is repeated in a period of time. Frequency is measured in **Hertz** (Hz) or thousands of Hertz (KHz). The Hertz value of a sound shows the number of times each second that the wave pattern of sound repeats. Generally speaking, the higher the frequency of a sound, the higher its pitch. The lowest note on a piano has a frequency of 27.5 Hz; the highest has a frequency of 4.186 kHz.

Digital audio records each point along the wave. An advantage of this method is that it becomes possible to manipulate digitally each moment of sound. However, recording each point also creates a huge digital file. Managing the size of sound files requires knowledge of four technical areas: sample rate, sample size, channels, and codecs.

Figure 11.1 *In addition to MP3 players, many small electronic devices, such as smartphones and tablets, can now play digital audio.*

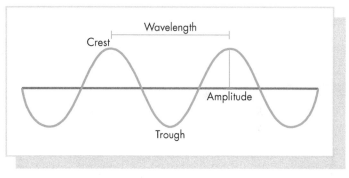

Figure 11.2 *Like all waves, sound waves have three key characteristics—wavelength, the distance between two consecutive crests or troughs; amplitude, the distance between a trough and a crest; and frequency, the number of wavelengths in a given distance or amount of time.*

Sampling

To reduce the size of the file, digital recording software "grabs" sound at set intervals called a **sample rate**.

The higher the sample rate (the more often sound is measured), the better the audio quality. However, the higher the sample rate, the larger the file size. Like frequency, sample rates are measured in Hertz (Hz) or thousands of Hertz (kHz). Sample rates often range from 8 to 48 kHz. CDs sample at 44.1 kHz. One reason this rate was chosen was that it is more than twice 20 kHz, which is generally taken as the maximum frequency humans can hear. The theory underlying sampling says that you should sample at two times the maximum frequency you want to represent. Doing so ensures that the sound is of high quality.

analog audio—Sound recorded as continuous vibrations.

digital audio—Sound recorded as a series of digits.

Hertz—A measurement of the frequency of sound, or the number of times the wave pattern is repeated per second.

sample rate—The number of times a sound is measured.

Sample size is similar to rate, but it reflects the number of bits used to represent each sound sample digitally. The more bits, the more information provided. CDs have a sample size of 16 bits, which provides a clearer, fuller sound than 8-bit sampling, which is closer to the quality of sound you might hear on a phone. Again, the standard sample size on CDs of 16 bits is greater than what is generally taken as the sample size for human hearing, which is 14 or 15 bits. A 32-bit rate has become more common as technology has become more powerful; however, not all sound devices can take advantage of the larger bit rate. In Figure 11.3 the dark horizontal lines represent 8-bit sample points. Together both the dark and the lighter horizontal lines represent 16-bit sample points. From this image you can see that the 16-bit sample size records twice as much information as the 8-bit.

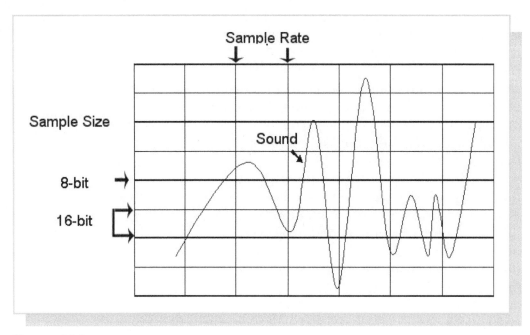

Figure 11.3 *Sound is created as a series of waves. Tracking both the frequency and the height is one way of measuring sound.*

Channels LO 11.1

Channels determine if sound is recorded as monaural (mono) or stereo sound. With stereo, sound is recorded as if coming from slightly different directions, such as would be heard when audible sound reaches two ears. Monaural sound only records a sound from a single side. When a multimedia computer has two speakers, stereo sound is possible but not required. Since stereo audio has more information, files are larger than those for a mono recording.

Codecs *LO 11.2 and 11.3*

Just as you learned in an earlier chapter about modifying an image to make its file size smaller, audio (and, as you will find in the next chapter, video) also can be compressed. The software used to compress sound is referred to as an audio codec. **Codec** stands for compressor–decompressor or, as is also commonly used, coder–decoder. There are a wide variety of codecs, each using a different algorithm. Some audio codecs are designed for speech, which uses a narrower range of frequencies than music. As a result, speech files can be compressed further than can music files. It is important to note that a codec is the main determining factor for quality.

There are many different types of audio file formats. Each format was created to meet a need and may use one or more codecs. Each codec requires specific software to play the sound once it has been compressed. Just as in image compression, sound compression is also described as lossless and lossy depending upon the process used to reduce the file size. Since not everyone has the same software, you will often see music files with several sound options. File formats fall into two categories: lossless compression and lossy compression.

Audio files with lossless compression are essentially copies of the original. They are used by music studios to store music digitally with full fidelity. They are also used for archival purposes. They include, but are not limited to, the following file formats:

- **WAV** (WAVeform Audio Format)—the audio format used primarily on the PC platform

- **AIFF** (Audio Interchange File Format)—audio format used primarily on the Macintosh platform

- **AU** (AUdio)—works on both the PC and Mac platforms, but is no longer very common

In today's audio world, the most popular audio files use lossy compression, of which three are common:

- **MP3** (Moving Picture Experts Group)—high-quality sound based upon the MPEG format used on digital audio players and for music files sent over the Internet

- **AAC** (Advanced Audio Coding)—works on iTunes, iPhones, and other Apple products

- **WMA** (Windows Media Audio)—proprietary to Microsoft but can be played on a number of devices and has both lossless and lossy versions

Files created with lossy compression are much smaller than those created with lossless compression. One researcher tested the differences by copying six different CDs into lossless and lossy files. As lossless WAV files, they ranged in size from 528 to 775 MB. As lossy MP3 files, they were 95 to 140 MB.

> **codec**—An algorithm that compresses sound or video to reduce its file size and then decompresses it when played.

21st Century Skills
CAREER

Organization

Today's workers are asked to do many tasks and can quickly become overwhelmed if they aren't organized and can't work efficiently. Good organizational skills help you stay focused, allow you to be more productive, and prevent you from wasting time. Little things can make a big difference.

- Keep supplies and materials such as headphones and microphones in the same place so you know where they are the next time you need them.
- Give your electronic files and folders descriptive names so that you can find folders and files easily. Audio files are easily lost if they are not given distinctive names.
- Avoid unnecessary complication.
- Break down large tasks into smaller pieces. You can't create the perfect audio file, for example, in one sitting. You have to do it in parts. Script your words, practice them, and be prepared to make several attempts to get the presentation exactly right.
- Create a to-do list to help keep you focused. Check items off the list as you complete them. Keep working methodically and steadily, and you'll soon find that you've finished the large task by taking care of the smaller components.

Skills in Action: Create an electronic to-do list or task planner you can access from your computer or smartphone. Begin using it immediately to improve your organizational skills.

Goodluz/Shutterstock.com

Figure 11.4 *Maintaining an organized workspace allows you to be productive and to work efficiently.*

Sound editing software does not necessarily produce files in all the previously mentioned formats. For instance, Audacity, a free open-source sound editor, does not support the AAC or WMA file formats. One advantage of the MP3 format is that it is portable to many different devices.

Because audio and video are so closely connected, you will find that audio and video extensions are similar. For example a WMA (Windows Media Audio) file is audio only. A WMV file (Windows Media Video), however, is a combination of both audio and video. You will look at video file types more closely in the next chapter.

checkpoint

How are analog and digital audio different?

ACTIVITY 11.1 ▶ Comparing File Sizes

1. Open *introduction.wav* from your data files for this lesson and then listen to the recording.
2. Save the file as an uncompressed .wav file named *11_Activity1_comparison*.

3. Save the file again as a .wmv file with the same file name.

4. Compare the size of the two files by right-clicking on the file name and selecting **Properties**.

5. Write a summary of which file is smaller with an explanation of why.

6. Save your summary as ***11_Activity1_summary***.

sound card—Computer component that allows computers to play or record sound.

Headphones

Thomas Edison made the first recording of a human voice in 1877 using a tinfoil sheet phonograph cylinder. As the sound was played back, people would gather to hear the reproduced sound. As the phonograph, gramophone, record player, and radio evolved, so did the way consumers wanted to listen to recorded information. Therefore, headphones started to be developed. In the 1930s, the first mass-produced headphones appeared on the market. Studio headphones came about in the mid-1950s and were designed specifically for recording and producing sound and music. It wasn't until the late 1980s that noise-canceling headphones became popular. Bose was a major manufacturer of noise-canceling headphones at that time, and they still make very high-quality noise-canceling headphones today. In the late 1990s and early 2000s, wireless headphones increased in popularity. Today, headphones have evolved to be more comfortable and smaller; however, many consumers still appreciate higher-quality large headphones. Prices may range from a few dollars for inexpensive earbuds to thousands of dollars for professional-level headphones.

Dja65/Shutterstock.com

Figure 11.5 *An early headphone set*

Granata111/Dreamstime.com

Lesson 11.2 — Managing Sound Equipment

In order to record or play sound, a computer uses a **sound card**, which may be integrated into the computer's motherboard (the main computer circuit board) or added as an additional component. Sound cards translate digital information stored in the computer or on a CD into an analog wave sound using a **DAC** (digital-to-analog) converter. The analog sound is then sent to speakers or headphones to be heard by the human ear. The sound card reverses the process using an **ADC** (analog-to-digital) converter to change analog sound that has been captured by the computer into a digital format. Usually a microphone is used to capture the sound.

DAC—The acronym used to describe the process of converting sound from digital to analog.

ADC—The acronym used to describe the process of converting sound from analog to digital.

Sound Cards

Sound was a late-comer to the computer world. In the early years, sound cards were not installed on most computers. At that time, only the most expensive computers had sound cards. Sound Blaster offered some of the earliest cards, and its products became the industry standard in the late 1980s. The development of more sophisticated games and other software created demand for higher-quality sound. This attracted more suppliers and convinced computer makers to make sound cards a standard feature. However, all sound cards are not created equal. Low-end cards record and play back sound that often contains additional sounds that make the recording aurally fuzzy. This is the equivalent of a grainy photograph in which details are hard to see. More expensive sound cards combine hardware and software to create a higher-quality sound. As both hardware and software continue to develop, you can expect to hear better sound on even the least expensive computer or tablet.

Speakers and Headphones *LO 11.4*

Speakers for computers come in a wide range of sizes, designs, and costs. Speakers designed for basic use such as warning beeps and short voice pieces can be quite inexpensive. Those designed for a true multimedia experience are much more costly, of course, but also supply far superior sound. These systems—similar to the one shown in the schematic in Figure 11.6—usually have a number of speakers

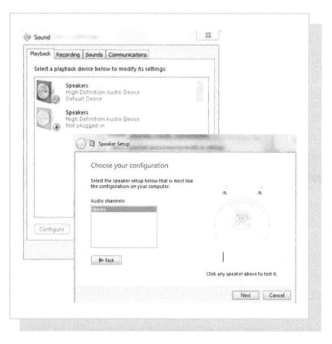

Figure 11.6 *Setting the sound properties and configuring the speakers is essential to establishing good audio playback.*

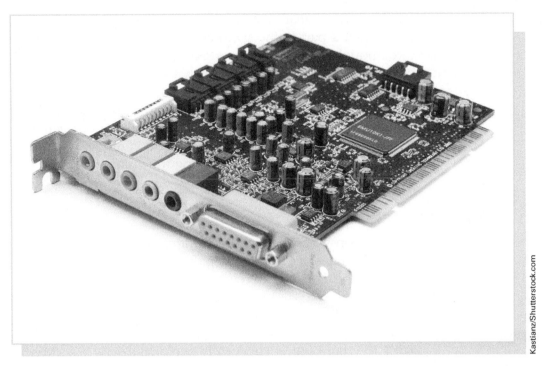

Figure 11.7 *The sound card inside a computer has a series of jacks on the outside used to plug in devices such as a microphone, headphones, or speakers.*

attached to the sound card. A 5.1 system, such as the one shown, includes a **subwoofer**, three front speakers, and two side speakers. An even more elaborate setup, the 7.1, adds two rear speakers. These complex speaker systems are used to create a rich "surround sound" environment.

subwoofer—A speaker that reproduces very low bass sounds.

To connect speakers to your computer you must plug each speaker line into the appropriate jack or connection on the sound card. When using speakers and headphone, it's important to make sure you plug the device into the proper jack. Typically these jacks are color coded to help you select the proper one.

Connections differ in laptops, where microphone and headphone connectors are often on the front or side. Laptops generally do not have connectors for external speakers, although you can get USB speakers that connect to one of the laptop's USB ports to set up a speaker system.

Sound cards are important, as they assist with the input and output of audio signals that are controlled by computer programs. There are many uses for sound cards, but typically we think about sound when using multimedia programs including editing video or audio, watching movies, playing games, or composing music. The better the sound card, either integrated into the motherboard or designed as a plug-in card, the higher the quality of sound.

Speaker Safety

Protecting your speakers mostly requires common sense. While it is difficult to turn up the sound on a speaker so loud that it damages the component, it is possible. Too much volume can cause the cone that vibrates in a subwoofer to tear, making it useless. Too much power can also actually melt a part in the speaker called a voice coil. These events are rare, though, and usually the result of extreme carelessness. Of greater concern, however, is the danger that high volume levels can pose to your hearing and the hearing of those around you, even if they are not so loud as to damage speakers. In addition, if you are listening to audio in a room with others, high volume can also be a distraction—or an annoyance—to those around you. Use your common sense and consideration for others to guide you in setting the volume level.

Headphone Safety

If you are in a location where others are working, it is better to use headphones. Headphones, similar to the pair shown in Figure 11.8, function much like speakers but are close to the ears. In-ear versions of headphones are referred to as earbuds or earphones, shown in Figure 11.9. No matter which headphone type you use, remember that they are really speakers and the biggest concern is personal safety. It is even easier to turn up the volume on headphones or earbuds to a level that can be dangerous to your hearing. Always be careful to limit the sound level. In addition, always check the volume level of the sound before placing headphones on your ears. It is best to turn the sound all the way down before you put the headphones or earbuds on since the sound is often much louder in the confined space of headphones compared to what you hear coming from speakers. Once your headphones are on, gradually increase the sound level. This eliminates the possibility of unexpectedly "blasting" your eardrums and causing hearing damage.

Susan Lake

Figure 11.8 *Some headphones can be used just to hear sound produced by a computer or player. Others such as this one allow you to both hear and record sound.*

Pushish Images/Shutterstock.com

Figure 11.9 *In-ear versions of headphones are called earphones or earbuds.*

Microphones LO 11.5

A microphone is required to record audio files such as voices. There are several types of microphones available on the market: headset (part of the headphone equipment shown in Figure 11.8), lapel (Figure 11.10), handheld, or mounted (Figure 11.11). Some computers, particularly laptops, have built-in microphones. Some newer monitors also have microphones. Special USB microphones attach to a USB port (as shown in Figure 11.12) instead of to the microphone port on the sound card. These microphones often produce higher quality recordings and offer a convenience advantage—USB devices tend to work seamlessly, without the user needing to manipulate settings.

Figure 11.10 *A lapel microphone is designed to be attached to your clothing to make it easy to record hands free.*

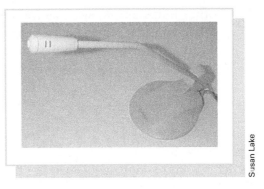

Figure 11.11 *A mounted microphone can be placed between two individuals, allowing both to contribute to the recording.*

Since devices such as computers, monitors, Webcams, and laptops have quality built-in microphones, the user must decide which microphone to use, built-in or external. When recording audio files, it will be necessary for the user to tell the computer which microphone to use.

The quality of microphones differs from one manufacturer to another, as does the price. If your microphone produces a "static" sound, you may need to get one of higher quality. To learn about the performance level of each product, it can be helpful to read product evaluations and reviews before purchasing your microphone.

You should also consider the benefits of keeping the microphone in one position. Microphones that are a consistent distance from the source of the sound will, obviously, produce a more consistent sound quality. For example, a headset microphone will maintain the same distance from the speaker's mouth. In contrast, with a handheld microphone, the distance between the device and the speaker will change if the speaker moves his or her hand.

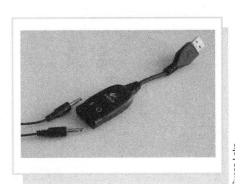

Figure 11.12 *A USB microphone has a special connection that converts the microphone's signal from the USB port to the headphone and back to the computer. This model includes both a headset and a microphone so there are two jacks.*

MIDI *LO 11.5*

Another way to capture music is through the use of a **MIDI** or Musical Instrument Digital Interface. A MIDI is a communication protocol that allows a wide variety of electronic musical instruments, computers, and other devices to communicate with each other. Through a MIDI, "musical messages" can be sent through up to 16 channels. Each channel can be designated for a separate device. The "musical messages" can specify pitch, velocity, volume, and other cues. This data can also be recorded into a software or hardware device called a **sequencer**, so that the data can be edited and played back. This special audio equipment is designed to plug into a musical instrument and record the notes as they are played or to send notes to an instrument. A MIDI doesn't record the vibrations or sounds. It merely records the notes that were played and

MIDI—Communication protocol that allows a wide variety of electronic musical instruments, computers, and other devices to communicate with each other.

sequencer—Hardware device or software application that handles necessary data to record, edit, or play back music.

other information, such as the length of time the note was held. With a MIDI, musical compositions can be written and modified on a computer and then transmitted to a MIDI-connected instrument for playing.

Instructional videos on MIDIs are free and readily available. If you are interested in using a MIDI, search the Internet for reliable sources.

How Important Is Sound?

You've read that sound cards were not included in early computers. Why do you think they were not included? Is audio an essential part of your computer usage? Could you manage without it?

checkpoint

Why are sound cards important?

ACTIVITY 11.2 ▶ Setting up Sound

1. Open **checklist** from your data files.
2. Go to the Control Panel on your computer, open the Sounds dialog box, and determine what speakers and sound card are on your computer.
3. Plug in speakers, if necessary.
4. Plug in a microphone, as provided by your instructor, or use the computer's internal microphone if available.
5. Complete the checklist and save your responses to the checklist as **11_Activity2_checklist**.

Lesson 11.3 ▶ Capturing and Editing Sound

wave editor—Software that allows one to modify or edit audio files.

The ability to capture and edit digital sound requires software as well as equipment. Because sounds are recorded as waves, the software used to edit audio is sometimes called a **wave editor**. There are a wide variety of editors available. Audacity and Adobe Audition are two frequently used audio and sound editing applications. These products, and others, are available for both Mac and Windows machines. Some are free, either because they come with your sound card or, like Audacity, are made available for download. Others must be purchased, and they vary widely in price. Some companies, such as Avid, have created wave editors that can edit most types of sound files. Others are only able to edit a limited number of file types.

Sound Editors *LO 11.6*

Sound editors can be used to convert sound from one format to another. They also provide tools once reserved for complex sound-recording studios, allowing you to add special effects, insert one sound into another, or edit out sound you want to remove. A sound editor is to music and other wave sounds what an image editor, such as Photoshop, is to a photograph.

Recording Audio

Wave editors anticipate that you will want to record sound and they often have a simple tool bar or screen with different buttons for Record, Pause, and Rewind. Figure 11.13 is an example of the recording tool bar, referred to as the Transport Toolbar, from Audacity. As you can see, these controls are similar to those used on other audio and video recording equipment.

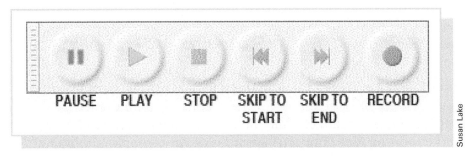

PAUSE   PLAY   STOP   SKIP TO START   SKIP TO END   RECORD

Susan Lake

Figure 11.13 *Recording and playback functions use similar icons regardless of the software editor.*

To record using a microphone, you must first plug its connector into the computer. The connection is typically made through one of the jacks of the sound card at the back of a desktop computer. However, some desktops also have a microphone jack in the front of the computer. As noted previously, laptops may have the microphone jack on the front or side or may have a built-in microphone. Look for a microphone icon or pink connector similar to the one shown in Figure 11.14. If there is no icon, you may need to experiment to find the correct port. You will not hurt the computer if you try a jack/port that is incorrect.

Once the microphone is installed properly, you should verify that the proper sound card and equipment have been selected. There may be a Preferences dialog box, such as shown in Figure 11.15, in which you can make selections.

Susan Lake

Figure 11.14 *On a desktop, the microphone port is typically located on the sound card at the back of the computer, but there may also be a second one on the front of a desktop computer to provide easier access.*

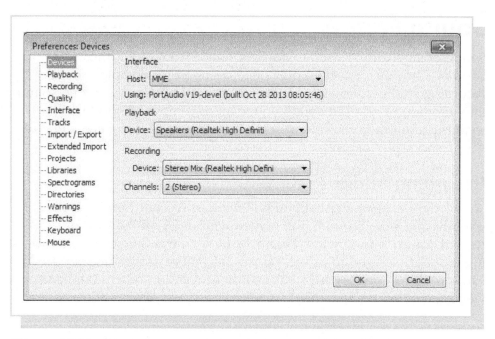

Figure 11.15 *It is important to make sure that the correct recording and sound devices have been selected before recording. These options are often found under Preferences.*

Notice that the Devices link in the dialog box also allows you to choose the number of channels for the recording. Other links allow you set the sampling rate (Quality link) or set standard rules for importing and exporting files (Import/Export link). An example sample rate and type are shown in Figure 11.16. In addition, you can set the input volume level to match your intentions. Once these steps are completed, you can then record and save your voice or other sounds.

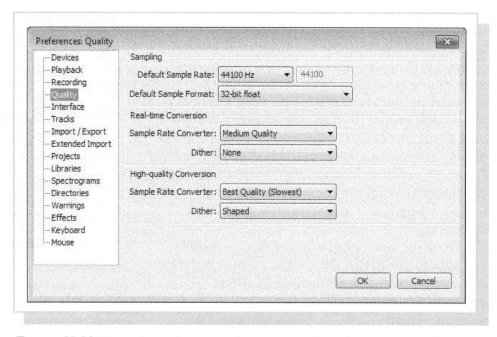

Figure 11.16 *Wave editors often have preference settings that allow you to choose the sample rate such as this one from Audacity. Some programs also let you choose sample size.*

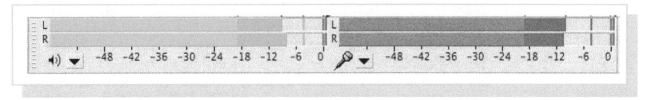

Figure 11.17 *A gauge such as this one in Audacity allows you to see if your sound input is at the correct volume.*

When recording, it is good to leave a second or two of silence at the beginning and end of each recording. This will allow you to make sure that you capture all the sounds you wish to capture and that you do not lose anything that needs to be recorded. If the recording will include speaking, you should have a script. Anyone speaking extemporaneously is generally more likely to add colloquial phrases, insert an *um* or *ah,* and pause for too long, causing a break in the recording. As you are recording, a volume gauge appears (see Figure 11.17) to provide you with a visual measurement of the sound level. Sound pressure and signal level are measured in **decibel** (dB) units. A general rule of thumb is to keep your sound levels between –12 dB to –10 dB. You'll notice the volume gauge is applicable for both the speaker and microphone. The blue lines to the far right of the speaker and microphone sections indicate the Maximum Peak (MP) level. The red lines to the right of the MP line appear when there is a clipping warning. The red lines (Clip lines) appear when four or more consecutive samples of audio exceed the maximum. The Clip lines remain on the volume gauge not necessarily to show that current audio is too loud, but to indicate that clipping did occur somewhere within the recorded track.

decibel (dB)—Unit of measurement for sound pressure level and signal level.

Editing Audio

Once sound has been recorded, you should play it back before doing anything else. Make sure the recording has everything you wanted to record and the sound levels are generally consistent. If you wish to hear a section again, you can fast forward or fast rewind to that part of the recording. You can also navigate within the **waveform** view of the recording to get to a precise point. You'll learn more about that kind of movement shortly.

waveform—A graphical display that represents the changes in recorded sound waves.

To edit your work, you'll use a screen such as the one in Figure 11.18. The wave editor window provides a waveform or a visual reproduction of the audio recording. Because of the digital nature of the recording, you have the ability to correct fractions of a second of sound, much as you could manipulate individual pixels in an image. Some programs may provide special tools to find sounds you want to remove, such as background

iStockphoto.com/Track5

Figure 11.18 *Tools that were once only available to high-end recording studios are now available to anyone with a computer.*

noise or sounds beyond a specific range. You can also add special effects such as boosting the bass notes or fading, which is a gradual reduction in sound, or speed up or slow down parts of the recording. Another useful effect, called Auto Duck, lowers (ducks) the sound in one track when the sound in another reaches a user-set volume. This effect can be used to decrease the volume in a music track when it's paired with a spoken track. The Noise Removal effect allows you to edit out constant background noise that is not part of the recording.

In addition to the original recorded sound, you can insert new sounds or create a spot of silence within a noisy recording. You are not limited to recording a single voice or sound, either. You can take additional recorded tracks and blend them with your original recording. You can copy sections of a different recording or a different segment of the same recording and paste the copied sound into a different location to repeat a sound or a section of sound. The possibilities are endless.

The green rectangle in Figure 11.19 shows the program's time counter, which indicates where, in time, each section of sound is located. In order to find the exact spot you want to edit, you can zoom into the sound file, much as you can do with an image. The red rectangle highlights the Zoom button for Audacity. The placement of this button will vary from program to program, but the function is the same. The yellow rectangle highlights precisely where in the audio file the editing will take place. It is indicated by a vertical line called the editing cursor, which is similar to a cursor in a word processing program. This line moves as the audio is played. You can also move this line to navigate to a specific location in the recording.

Wave editors allow you to select sections of a file to edit in two ways. You can either use the mouse by clicking and dragging or use

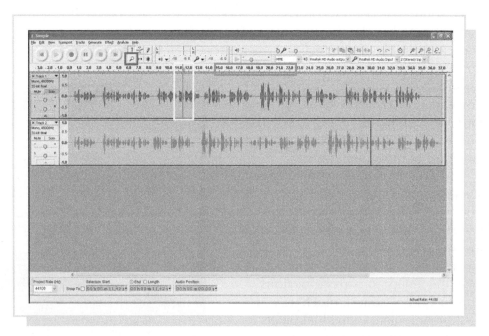

Figure 11.19 *This is an example of two tracks recorded in Audacity. Notice the difference in the wave heights and duration. Each track is a visual representation of the waveform.*

commands from the Edit menu. Those commands will give you the option of choosing the precise times of the beginning and end of your selection. In Figure 11.20, look at the area within the yellow rectangle at the bottom of the screen. The section from 18.40 seconds to 19.00 seconds has been selected. That selection also appears graphically in the window that shows the sound waves (see the red rectangle); its flat appearance in the waveform shows that it is a period of silence. To eliminate the selected section, you would simply click on the trimmer button (highlighted in the figure by the green circle) or press the Delete key on your keyboard. If you inadvertently delete something, or take out more than you wished to, you can use the Undo function to restore the waveform to its previous state.

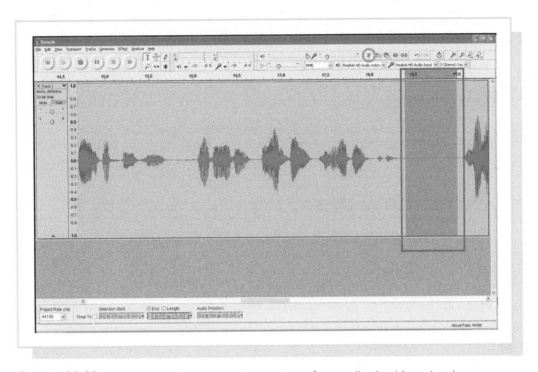

Figure 11.20 *Wave editors allow you to select sections of a recording by either using the wave display or by inputting the start and end times. Once selected, segments of sound can be deleted, copied, or treated with various effects.*

Any segment you want to copy or add special effects to must first be selected in the same way. As with deletions, you can undo these changes if you wish.

You can also add additional tracks to the recording. If you do, be sure to save and name each track separately before importing it into the wave editor. That way if you make a mistake, you can delete the damaged track and go back and retrieve the original. You should also keep the original tracks separate for future use in other projects. Each track in a project should have a separate name to distinguish it from other tracks. Wave editors allow you to synchronize the tracks so that they begin at the same time, making for a more professional sound. See the menu options for syncing in Figure 11.21.

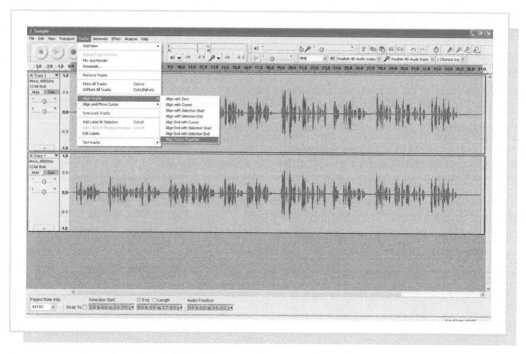

Figure 11.21 *Multiple tracks, such as one for voice and one for background music, can be blended into the same project and synchronized to begin and end at the same time.*

Exporting Files *LO 11.3*

Once your sound is complete, you can export it to the file format you want. Within the wave editor, files are saved in a format read only by the editor. To make them available to others to hear, you need to export the files in one of the formats discussed in Lesson 11.1. Audio files can be used as downloadable podcasts, on websites, and in presentations using software such as Microsoft PowerPoint. The format you select will depend upon the intended use. For instance, if you're creating a podcast and you expect users will download it to portable audio players, you will want to export to the MP3 format that is read by all such players. A WAV file can be read on computers, but not those portable players.

You may wish to include sound from a previously recorded CD. While a computer can play a music CD directly, CDs are created in such a way that it is not necessarily possible to copy individual files to a computer. As a result it becomes necessary to **rip** the tracks on the CD, or convert the information on the CD to a file format that can be read by the computer. There are a number of software options that allow you to convert the CDA files on a CD to MP3 or other format. This process can be used to create an archive copy of a CD you own or to make it easier to listen to your music on your computer.

When thinking about ripping a CD, bear in mind that all copyright laws must be followed. Ripping a CD that you have purchased for your own enjoyment is legal and acceptable. Doing so to provide others with a copy of the music is considered piracy and is illegal

ripping—The process of transferring music from a CD to a computer.

(see Chapter 2 for more on copyright and ethical use of intellectual property). It is considered fair use to include previously recorded music in a school presentation, such as a demonstration of a sound-editing project or a multimedia slide show, provided that proper documentation and referencing is given. However, it is a violation of copyright law to post a multimedia project on a commercial website without first obtaining permission for any previously recorded music used in the project.

lavitrei/Shutterstock.com

Impact

iTunes

One of the significant changes in the digital music world was Apple's development of iTunes to provide an easy, inexpensive way to acquire music without violating copyright laws. Up until the introduction of this form of musical acquisition, illegal file sharing was rampant by people who had ripped CDs and stored the files on personal computers. However, the change in technology has reduced the severity of this issue and will hopefully continue to make it possible for musicians to receive payment for their work. iTunes created a new business model for the sale of music, which was difficult, at first, for many to accept. Apple offered each song at a low price that allowed listeners to buy just a single song instead of a complete album, which was previously the norm. Other companies have now incorporated areas for users to purchase and download music as well. Just a few include Amazon, Rhapsody, Napster, and Walmart. This is a good example of how technology changes the way the world functions. In your future you can expect to see many more such changes, with each one altering the model of what has come before.

checkpoint

Why are the preference settings important when recording sound?

ACTIVITY 11.3 ▶ Recording and Editing Audio

1. Write a script for an audio file that is one to two minutes in length. In the script, you should introduce yourself and briefly explain your short- and long-term goals.

2. Create a new audio file. Set the sample rate and choose the type of channel you desire.

3. Record your script.

4. Save the file as an uncompressed .wav file named **11_Activity3_recording**.

5. Edit the sound file by removing at least one sound in the file and adding one special effect such as reverberation or fading.

6. Save the edited sound file as **11_Activity3_edited**.

Key Concepts

▶ Analog audio and digital audio work in combination. Computers acquire analog sounds and convert them to digital, or read digital files and output them in an analog format. Analog is what you hear. Digital is the means of capturing sounds in software. *LO 11.1*

▶ Audio file sizes are determined by sample size and rate, by the number of channels recorded, and by the codec used for compression. *LO 11.1*

▶ Audio file types consist of two types: those compressed with lossless algorithms and those created using lossy algorithms. Each type serves a different purpose. *LO 11.2 and 11.3*

▶ Speakers and headphones are connected to a computer sound card using a variety of color-coded or icon-identified ports, or jacks. They provide audio output. *LO 11.4*

▶ Microphones are used to capture audio files including voice and music; they are input devices. *LO 11.5*

▶ Sound or wave editors are used to record audio files and then to edit the files. Because files are digital, the data can be edited precisely, just like image files. Editing can include cutting, adding effects, and mixing multiple tracks together into one file. *LO 11.6*

Review and Discuss

1. Evaluate the difference in how analog audio and digital audio are created or captured. *LO 11.3*

2. Compare and contrast sample rate and sample size. *LO 11.1*

3. Write a brief explanation of the importance of sound cards. *LO 11.4*

4. Explain the difference in the file formats WAV and WMA. Which is of higher quality? *LO 11.2 and 11.3*

5. Explain the need for safety when using speakers and headphones.

6. List in order the steps needed to record using a microphone. *LO 11.5*

7. Evaluate some audio editing options possible in sound editing software. *LO 11.6*

8. Distinguish between the MIDI and ripping process of capturing sounds or music. *LO 11.6*

9. Compare the advantages and disadvantages of using a lapel microphone and a mounted microphone. *LO 11.5*

10. Defend the decision to use a codec that is designed for speech audio rather than music audio. *LO 11.3*

11. Justify the use of wave editors in editing a recording. *LO 11.6*

Apply

1. Consider something you know how to do well. Good examples are playing a sport or musical instrument, doing a routine as a member of a dance group, cooking, writing poetry, or any other hobby. Write a script explaining all the steps it would take to successfully complete one action or task in that activity. Record the audio using a device other than the computer. Transfer the audio from the equipment you used to a computer. Edit the audio file to take out any lead time or extra time at the end of the audio. Add at least one effect. Save or export the audio file as **11_Apply1_how_to** as an MP3 file unless your instructor says otherwise. *LO 11.2, 11.3, 11.5, and 11.6*

2. Write a review of one of the sections in this chapter. Choose from managing audio files, managing sound equipment, or capturing or editing sound. Record your voice as you read your review. The audio file should be at least two minutes in length. Save the audio file as **11_Apply2_review** in an appropriate file format. *LO 11.2, 11.3, 11.5, and 11.6*

3. Rip an appropriate song from a CD that you have purchased so that you can listen to it on your computer. Save or export as **11_Apply3_song** with the file type MP3. Create a flyer using desktop publishing software to provide details about the song (e.g., year it was produced, artist's name, and similar information).

4. Assume you are running for an office in an organization, such as the Future Business Leaders of America (FBLA), Business Professionals of America (BPA), or another club or organization. Decide on an office for which you would run. Write a script introducing yourself as a candidate. Include in the script any experience or special talents you have that qualify you for the position. Explain why you would like to serve in this position. Record the script. The recording should be no less than three minutes. Save as a .wma file with the name **11_Apply_4_office**. Edit the recording as needed. Save the file again as **11_Apply4_edited**, also as a .wav file. *LO 11.2, 11.3, 11.5, and 11.6*

5. Write a script to review one of your favorite movies. What do you like about the movie? Give specific examples to explain why this movie is your favorite. You may want to watch the movie again so you can note specific features to use as examples. Record the script. The recording should be at least three minutes. Edit the file as needed. Save or export the script as **11_Apply5_interview** in the default format for your software. *LO 11.2, 11.3, 11.5, and 11.6*

Explore

1. Search the Internet or books for information on how to create a podcast. Write a script for this subject. Record yourself reading the script and create an audio file. Include your sources of information in your script. Save or export the script as **11_Explore1_podcast** with the file format MP3. *LO 11.2, 11.3, 11.5, and 11.6*

2. Working with another student, explore a career choice. Write down five to eight questions to ask about the career. Either interview someone in the chosen career or do research to get answers to the questions. Write responses to the questions. Connect a stand-up microphone to the computer. Record the questions and answers in the form of an interview, with one of you reading the question and the other giving the response. Save or export the interview as **11_Explore2_interview** with the file format MP3. *LO 11.2, 11.3, 11.5, and 11.6*

3. Research and listen to at least three podcasts on subjects of interest to you. Write a summary of what you have observed or noticed about content, voice control, inflection, tone, or any other things you may have learned from listening to the podcasts. Cite specific examples from the podcast—and plan to include audio clips from the podcasts to support those examples. Include the sources in your script. Record the script then edit the recording adding the clips from the podcasts in a separate track. Save or export the script as **11_Explore_3_voice** with the file format MP3. *LO 11.2, 11.3, 11.5, and 11.6*

Academic Connections

Writing: Watch the trailer for a new movie that you are interested in seeing. The purpose of a movie trailer is to pique your interest and make you want to see the movie. Did watching the trailer encourage you to see the movie? How did it make you want to see the movie more? If you answered no, what could they have done to make you want to see the movie? Write a short review of the trailer from your notes. In the written portion of your review, include your sources. Save as **11_AC_writing_text**. Then record the review as an audio file. Save the recording as **11_AC_writing_audio** and export the audio in a format instructed by your instructor.

Social Studies: Listen to a podcast on a specific event in history. Take notes on specific facts given in the podcast. Write, record, and edit an audio including the facts learned and your source of information. Save the recording as **11_AC_social_studies**.

Chapter 12

Video

Learning Outcomes

▶ **12.1** Compare video cameras based upon their specifications and features.

▶ **12.2** Distinguish between various video formats.

▶ **12.3** Describe care and safety precautions when using a camcorder.

▶ **12.4** Write a video script.

▶ **12.5** Create a video storyboard.

▶ **12.6** Select the type of shots to be used in a video.

▶ **12.7** Film and edit a video using transitions and effects.

▶ **12.8** Share a video.

Key Terms

- 4K or Ultra HD
- bitrate
- camcorder
- CCD
- CMOS
- Digital Single-Lens Reflex (DSLR)
- dissolve
- fade
- flash storage
- frame rate
- high definition (HD)
- interlaced
- keyframe
- panning
- progressive
- rendering
- scene
- storyboard
- take
- tilting
- timecode
- transition
- widescreen

Video is the culminating digital media skill that requires knowledge of graphics and sound as well as other artistic skills. Video integrates these activities into a single medium that often requires high-end computer hardware and software such as Adobe Premiere Pro, Apple Final Cut Pro, and Sony Vegas pro.

Less demanding software such as Windows Movie Maker and iMovie for the Mac makes it possible to edit and create video with fewer of the functions found in the more advanced software. Even if you do not have the latest in technology, you can still develop the media skills needed to create effective video.

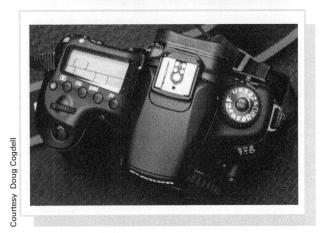

Figure 12.1 *This digital camera's mode dial is set to the video mode. With a resolution of 320 × 240 pixels, it captures 30 frames per second. DSLR cameras shoot 24-30 frames per second (fps).*

Figure 12.2 *Modern camcorders are light and easy to use.*

camcorder—Portable video recorder.

Digital Single-Lens Reflex (DSLR)—A camera that uses a mirror system to capture an image.

Equipment used to create videos has become much more available recently. You are no longer restricted to expensive and heavy **camcorders**. Today digital cameras, like the one in Figure 12.1, can record video. Even smartphones have cameras that can shoot a few minutes of video with little preparation. However, there are also more professional, high-end expensive camcorders with microphones that can capture vivid sound while reducing wind noise. These cameras can record high definition video used to create professional-looking movies. Smaller, less expensive camcorders, such as the one in Figure 12.2, shoot at a lower resolution, but are easy to carry, simple to use, and capable of making a good-quality video.

Digital Single-Lens Reflex (DSLR) cameras are becoming more popular because the user can shoot video at frame sizes similar to film. This results in more detailed, crisp images. DLSR cameras also provide more control over depth in the field so the user can record something in the foreground that is very sharp, yet something in the background can be blurry. This is done frequently in Hollywood-style movies and advertising to help those viewing the movie or ad to focus specifically on one object or person. DSLR cameras also have interchangeable lenses that can be used for a variety of purposes. Your choice of equipment will be determined by the purpose for which you intend to use the video you shoot. If you simply want to record fun times with friends and post the results on YouTube or a similar sharing site, you probably won't need very expensive or sophisticated equipment. If you're making videos for a business, however, you'll want equipment that allows you to create a professional-looking product.

Evaluating Camcorders *LO 12.1 and 12.2*

The first videocassette recorders were so heavy they had to be held on a person's shoulder. They also recorded on tape, with the microphone sometimes picking up the hum of the tape being turned. Those days are in the past. Camcorders today are digital and come in a variety of sizes. They may fit in your pocket or palm, or they may be larger professional-sized models used in the broadcast industry (See Figure 12.3.). Camcorders vary greatly in quality, depending on the resolution, or the sharpness of the image they record, and the aspect ratio. Newer camcorders can also act as projectors. You can display the footage on walls or screens right from the camcorder itself.

Camcorder Formats and Aspect Ratio

Camcorders have evolved from standard definition (SD) to high definition (HD) and are moving toward 4K. New **4K Ultra HD** camcorders have four times the resolution (3840 × 2160 pixels) as previous camcorders. The 4K camcorders may be handheld, cinema, action, or DSLR camcorders.

A standard definition (SD) camcorder typically records images with a resolution in the range of 720 × 480 pixels. That means there are 480 lines of 720 pixels each. SD uses the traditional television aspect ratio of 4:3. That is, for every 4 inches of width to the image, there are 3 inches of height. SD is sometimes referred to as digital video (DV). SD is an older technology, discussed here to give you an idea of resolution and size.

A **high definition (HD)** camcorder records an image of much higher quality, though precisely what level of quality varies from device to device. Blu-ray quality camcorders have a resolution of 1920 × 1080 pixels (simply referred to as 1080). However, others record at the lower end of the HD scale, which is 1280 × 720, often simply labeled 720p. Both kinds of HD camcorders can shoot at the 4:3 aspect ratio but also allow you to record video at the 16:9 aspect ratio that has become the standard on HD television sets. Footage recorded at the 16:9 high-definition resolution must be viewed on an HD television. HD devices (both for recording and viewing) tend to cost more than SD equipment.

Figure 12.4 gives you an idea of the difference between the two aspect ratios. The two bands at the top and bottom of the image are present in the traditional TV image but not in HD or **widescreen** versions of a video. In a technique called letterboxing, these areas are often replaced with black bars when a widescreen image is played on a standard monitor. While it may appear that the 4:3 aspect ratio would provide a better picture, that is not the case. An HD video records more pixels making it a better, sharper image. If you watch HD video on a standard 4:3 TV, you may notice some information or graphics are cut off. This is because when the video editor inserted the information or graphics on the video, they were not placed in the proper area.

Another distinction to be aware of is whether the digital image is interlaced or progressive. If it is **interlaced** (indicated with an i), alternate lines are drawn on the screen. **Progressive** (p) draws one line after another. You will see a video listed as a number such as 1080i or 1080p to indicate which format is recorded. Interlaced video is the standard format used for television broadcasts. While televisions display the image smoothly, without the lines, that is not necessarily the case on computer monitors or other devices. As a result, progressive is considered a better video format. A camcorder should be able to record a progressive image.

Figure 12.3 *This is one example of a professional broadcast camera.*

4K Ultra HD—Describes a camcorder with a resolution around 3840 × 2160 pixels.

high definition (HD)—Describes a camcorder that produces a much higher quality image than SD, which can reach as high as 1920 × 1080, and usually has a 16:9 aspect ratio.

widescreen—Referring to the 16:9 ratio used in HD television and the differing formats used by movies.

interlaced—Video recorded or broadcast as a series of alternating lines.

progressive—Video recorded or broadcast as a series of sequential lines.

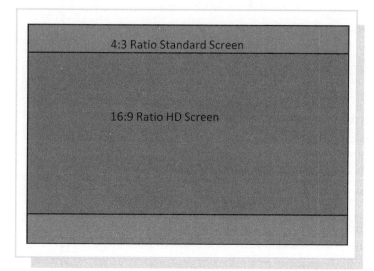

4:3 Ratio Standard Screen

16:9 Ratio HD Screen

Figure 12.4 *The widescreen area is represented by the dark red while the standard screen area is represented by a combination of both the dark and lighter red. Any information in the light red area is lost when viewed on a standard definition TV.*

CCD (charge-coupled device)—A light sensor that records images.

CMOS (complementary metal-oxide-semiconductor)—An image-recording light sensor that is larger and uses less power than a CCD sensor.

bitrate—Video transfer speed.

Two other elements that affect the look and cost of a camcorder include quality of the optical sensor and the bitrate. The quality of the optical sensor is either **CCD (charge-coupled device)** or **CMOS (complementary metal-oxide-semiconductor)**. The names refer to the technology used to record electrical changes on the sensor. The two types are generally equal in quality. CCD sensors were the first type to gain widespread use. CMOS sensors are somewhat larger and tend to draw less power than CCD sensors, and they are being used with greater frequency on HD cameras. Most important is the camera's resolution, which is affected by the number of sensors, expressed in megapixels (millions of pixels). The higher the number of megapixels, the more light is absorbed and the higher the quality of the image. The lens you are shooting through can have an effect on the look of your video as well.

The **bitrate** indicates the speed at which information is transferred to and from the camera. Bitrate is another measure of the quality of a video. Bitrate is measured in megabits (millions of bits) per second. The bitrate will also determine the file size and compression of the video. The lower the bitrate, the lower the quality of the video. In addition, the bitrate affects the delivery or streaming of the video to your TV or computer.

Compare the specifications for two camcorders below to see what kind of information you are likely to encounter when making a decision on which camcorder to use. Frame rate refers to how many images are taken per second of video. You will learn more about this in Lesson 12.3. Recall what you read in Chapter 4 about the differences between optical and digital zoom.

Resolution: 1280 × 720
Sensor: 1.6-megapixel CMOS sensor
Average Bitrate: 8.8 megabits per second
Frame Rate: 30 fps
Zoom: 10 × optical/200 × digital

Resolution: 1920 × 1080
Sensor: 3.32-megapixel CMOS sensor
Average Bitrate: 17 megabits per second
Frame Rate: 30 fps
Zoom: 25 × optical/500 × digital

Storage Media

Camcorders, like digital cameras, must store the images recorded. Because of the huge file sizes required for video, it is important to have enough memory for your projects. Manufacturers employ a variety of storage devices.

- **Hard Drives**: Like a computer, some camcorders have internal hard drives. These drives can vary in size from 32 GB, which will hold up to seven hours of high-quality video, to as large as 240 GB. Video footage is saved in computer-compatible files that can be easily downloaded. This type of media has two disadvantages. First, the hard drives are more delicate than other media. Second, the video files may not be compatible with standard video editing programs. Users may need to purchase and download free transcoding software (e.g., HandBrake, VLC) to convert video to particular editing software. However, camcorders with hard drives generally come with editing software.

- **Flash Memory**: Flash memory is the type found on memory cards used for digital cameras. This type of storage is typically used on the smallest camcorders because the memory is compact, suited to their small size. The amount of video that can be held varies with the size of the flash memory. Some devices have internal flash memory; others use removable cards.

- **DVDs**: Some older camcorders have internal DVD burners, which record the video footage to full-size or three-inch DVDs. However, the industry is moving away from this format. The DVDs hold approximately about 30 minutes of video, so these devices are good only for people who plan to make short videos. Another drawback to these camcorders is that the video cannot be edited by all video editing programs because they cannot read the format, and DVD players are becoming obsolete technology as well.

Important Features

Camcorders (like that shown in Figure 12.5) have several other important features that affect the quality of the video being shot. For instance, they can offer a manual focus option in addition to the automatic focus function. The quality and other functions will come from the sensor and lens used in the camera. Keep in mind that more "bells and whistles," along with manual control functions such as focus, iris, and frame rate, will affect the cost of the camcorder.

The following features are among the most important to bear in mind when choosing a camcorder:

iStockphoto.com/oleg66

Figure 12.5 *Camcorders offer many handy features that enable a person to record exactly what and how they want.*

- **LCD Display/Viewfinder**: You see what you are shooting by using either the Liquid Crystal Display (LCD) or the viewfinder. The viewfinder is the actual location (eyepiece) where the user looks into the camera to view what is being recorded. The LCD provides a larger viewing location on the camcorder. LCD displays can reach up to four inches in size, though they are smaller on pocket camcorders. With many camcorders, the LCD flips out from the body of the device and can be tilted in a wide range of angles. This allows the user to hold the camcorder at different angles to capture the action while still seeing what is being shot. On sunny days, the LCD image can be difficult to read. Using the viewfinder can alleviate that difficulty.

- **Zoom**: Like digital cameras, camcorders have two types of zoom. Optical zoom physically moves the lens to get a close-up. Digital zoom focuses on a smaller area but enlarges the pixels. The result is a more blurry picture. While digital zoom ratings for camcorders vary, using this feature loses image quality. Optical zoom does not lose image quality.

- **Image Stabilization**: The purpose of image stabilization is to correct for the possibility of the user's hand shaking while recording. Here, too, you can have an optical or digital effect, and just as with zoom, optical stabilization is preferable to digital.

- **Microphone and Microphone Jack**: Camcorders have a built-in microphone, usually on the front or top. These are not always of the best quality. If the device has a microphone jack, you can plug in an external microphone that may result in a higher quality audio. Also, many camcorders can handle multiple microphone inputs that plug into a sound board and capture multiple wireless microphones at one time.

- **Low Light Capability**: Camcorders perform at their best in bright sunlight, but many videos need to be captured indoors. A camcorder's ability to take high-quality video in low light is indicated by its lux rating. A lux is basically a measurement of the light falling on a specific subject. A lux rating of 1 lux is approximately equal to the amount of light that falls one square meter from a single candle. A low lux rating will result in poor quality; a rating of at least seven is considered minimal, and the lower the lux rating, the better.

- **Battery Life**: Manufacturers provide estimates for the amount of time you can record on a camcorder's fully charged battery. Several factors can reduce the amount of actual battery time when recording. Using the LCD draws power from the battery, as do zooming and playing back the video to review what videos have been captured. Having a backup battery is helpful, and it is certainly advisable to make sure the battery is fully charged before beginning to shoot video.

- **Input/Output Connections:** There are a variety of connection cables that are necessary. They include component, composite, HD/SDI, HDMI, audio input L/R, etc.

Care and Safety LO 12.3

Many rules for caring for digital cameras apply to camcorders as well. You should protect the lens by keeping the lens cap on when not recording, avoid touching the lens with your fingers, clean the lens with a soft cloth, and avoid dropping the equipment. Avoid forcing the LCD screen open or shut or forcing memory cards in or out of their slots. Also, remember to simply use a damp cloth to clean the body of the camcorder.

These following guidelines are helpful in preventing accidents when filming:

- When not using the camcorder, remember to keep it in a protective case.
- Never videotape when driving or operating any vehicle.
- If you are going to move while filming, be sure to study the area prior to filming. If outdoors, look for changes in terrain such as sloping ground or sudden drops. When filming indoors, check the position of furniture such as desks or office equipment. Clear potential dangers from your path. Image stabilization will be important at this point.
- Be sure that any props being used by people in the video are safe and the actions they will perform will not harm anyone. It's always a good idea to have your actors rehearse their actions so that they know where they are supposed to be in relation to each other to ensure everyone's safety.
- When you are using a professional camcorder, tape down cables to prevent tripping. Accessory bags should also be placed to the side so no one will trip.
- Use your common sense when using this expensive equipment.

checkpoint

Why is it important to understand the features of camcorders?

ACTIVITY 12.1 ▶ Camcorder Features

1. Open **Checklist** from the data files for this lesson.
2. Using the camcorders at school, at home, or from a friend, explain to a partner all the different parts on the checklist. Have your partner check off that you have accurately explained everything.
3. Either scan and upload your checklist or follow your instructor's direction on turning the checklist in. Save as *12_Activity1_checklist* if you scan it.

Lesson 12.2 ▶ Planning and Recording Video

It is important to note that there are guidelines to follow for good quality video images. Of course, video is more complex than taking pictures because it combines moving images with audio and possibly with still images as well. The final product is quite dependent upon the editing that occurs after the footage is saved to the computer.

Iavitrei/Shutterstock.com

Impact

Amateur Video

Amateur film and video has been a staple of family life for several decades. Proud parents record birthday parties, athletic contests, and graduations. Many families have recorded family gatherings. However, amateur videos have also been important in current events as well as historical events. Perhaps the most famous amateur video is the half-minute of film that Abraham Zapruder took on November 23, 1963, that recorded the assassination of President John F. Kennedy in Dallas, Texas. Also momentous was the video footage of Rodney King, an African American, being severely beaten by four white Los Angeles police officers in March 1991. More recently, amateur video of massive demonstrations have affected several countries, and some footage of celebrities in unguarded moments produced a great deal of embarrassment. In a world in which cell phones can capture images or videos that can be uploaded in seconds to social media or other sites, the impact of amateur video is likely to continue to grow.

Before the Shoot *LO 12.4, 12.5, and 12.6*

Planning your video before you shoot is the first step in creating good video. It's tempting to think that you can take your camera, shoot what you see, and then use the video editor to merge all the pieces into a quality production. Unfortunately, shooting without a plan will leave you with a video that lacks focus. Benjamin Franklin said, "If we fail to plan, we plan to fail." This is particularly true when shooting good video.

There are a number of points to consider when planning a video. The most obvious is to decide where the action will take place, what that action will be, and what words will be said to accompany the action. Consider what kinds of shots you will use and whether you will use special camera effects. The best way to plan all these elements is to write a script and create a storyboard.

scenes—A segment of a video that occurs in one location and during one continuous time frame.

Peter Kunasz/Shutterstock.com

Figure 12.6 *Videographers tell a story with the images they record.*

Scripting

Good videographers, or video artists, begin by writing a script. A script helps you determine in advance where and when the action will take place, what shots are necessary, and what will be said. Scripts are written as a series of **scenes** or units of action. Where and when action is taking place is the foundation of each scene. Whenever a location or time is changed, you create a new scene.

Making a video is like telling a story. Whether the story is about a new product being introduced for a sales meeting, a work team engaged on a project, or an executive's strategy for entering new markets, there is a central theme or message you want to convey. Anything that isn't needed to deliver that message, or which obscures that message, does not belong in the video.

Professional screenwriters use a standard format for scripts. Following the standard format will help make certain all essential details are included and also that the length of your film is appropriate. The rule of thumb is that one page of script is approximately one minute of film time. Script writing software provides prompts and formatting guidelines, but you can simply use a word processor and follow the standards.

A new heading marks each new scene. Scene headings are always capitalized and centered. They state the place and time of the scene. Whether the scene takes place indoors or outdoors is indicated by the abbreviations *INT.* for interior or *EXT.* for exterior. A dash separates the location of the scene from the time of day. A blank line space follows the scene heading before the scene description.

Scene descriptions begin at the left margin. Names of characters are written in all capital letters the first time they are used in a description. The names of characters who appear in a scene but have no dialogue are not capitalized. Sounds that the audience will hear—such as the low voices of customer service representatives in a call center—are capitalized. Dialogue is centered on the page under the character's name in capital letters. The character's manner or expression is typed below his or her name in parentheses. These format rules are shown in this example:

```
                INT. OFFICE--MID AFTERNOON

MONICA, in a suit, sits on top of the desk, legs
crossed, holding new sales brochure.


                        MONICA
                  (into the camera)
        We have a new array of investment options to offer
                        clients.
```

Storyboarding

Once a script has been written, the next step is to transfer the action to a storyboard. A **storyboard** is a series of drawings that outline the scenes and production details of the filming (see Figure 12.7). Storyboards may use stick figures or line drawings. They can be created using paper and pen or computer programs such as Illustrator. There's even an iPhone app for making storyboards. A free program designed by Celtx has both script writing and storyboard components, making it easy to work with your project from start to finish.

Storyboards define the entire video visually. They help develop the story in segments that block out the action and identify when techniques like close-ups or unusual camera angles are to be used. While straight-on shots at different zoom levels are standard, camera movement can add interest to a scene. Changing focus or camera angles

storyboard—A visual method of outlining each scene.

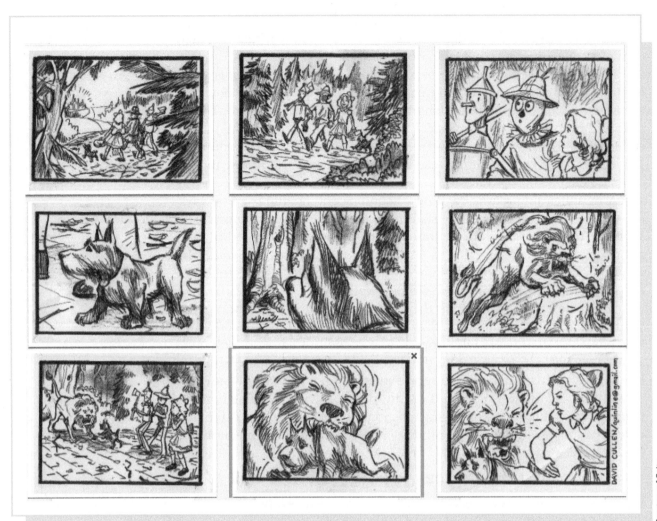

Figure 12.7 *A storyboard demonstrates the action that will occur in a scene but also shows the camera shots to be employed. This is an example of a storyboard developed by Celtx (www.Celtx.com) that guides you through the entire development process of a video segment from beginning to end.*

from time to time also adds visual interest. Keep these guidelines in mind when deciding when to use different types of shots or techniques:

- Begin a scene with an establishing shot to orient the audience. This is generally a long shot—one taken from a distance—that gives a broad view of the scene, showing where the action is taking place. Including a known landmark like the corporate headquarters is a good approach to setting this context.

- Medium shots show the full bodies of one or two characters or several characters from the waist up. They are essentially the standard view in a scene.

- In close-ups, one object fills about three-quarters of the shot. Close-ups of an actor's face heighten the emotion he or she is feeling. Close-ups of an object, like a product, focus the audience's attention on that object.

- Zooming involves slowly moving closer to or farther away from a person or object.

What makes a video compelling to watch?

With the explosion in personal videos on sites such as YouTube, each of us has become a critic. We are quick to click away from a video that does not appeal to us. What makes a video good? What keeps you watching? How can you use your responses to these questions to improve the videos you make?

- Moving the camera to cover a wider area changes what the viewer sees. **Panning** moves the camera from one side to another. **Tilting** moves the camera angle up and down.

- Most video is shot at eye level, but low-angle shots—taken from below and looking up—or high-angle shots—taken from above and looking down—change perspective. Low-angle shots make the object being filmed look larger and more powerful. High-angle shots have the opposite effect.

In planning shots, be careful not to overuse effects. Zooming, for example, is a good technique for focusing on important action, but too much moving in and out is disorienting to the viewer.

panning—Movement of a video camera from one side to another.

tilting—Movement of a video camera angle up or down.

Other Planning

As you continue to plan your video, you also need to think about any necessary costumes or props. If you are going to shoot your video outdoors and want to use a public place like a city park, you should check with the local government. There might be rules about making videos in that public space, and a permit may be required. Also, people in your video must sign release forms giving you permission to use them in your video. Without these permits and release forms, legal difficulties may arise.

During the Shoot *LO 12.6 and 12.7*

Once your script and storyboard are complete and the actors, costumes, and props are assembled, it's time to shoot. Keep in mind that getting the results you want may require several attempts at the same scene. Each version is considered a **take**. You may need a new take if a character makes an error in movement or in speech. You may also wish to shoot the same scene, or part of it, more than once from a different angle or focus to provide choices when editing. Have someone hold up a chalkboard or piece of paper marked with the scene and take number for you to record at the beginning of each take. You will use this as a marker when editing later.

take—Identifies the number of times a sequence has been filmed.

The most important thing to remember when shooting a scene is to have enough light. The light should generally be behind the camcorder and shining on your subjects. This is the most effective way to capture people's actions and expressions, or the details of objects or the setting.

The second important point is to keep your camera steady, avoiding shakiness—a true sign of an amateur. Stand with legs apart and slightly bent. This will help keep you steady. Shoot with your elbows tucked in tightly. When moving the camera to pan or zoom, be sure to keep your feet steady. If you don't, the image will jerk and may make the audience dizzy. Better yet, if possible, use a tripod. Tripods are a good investment, as they are relatively inexpensive and can significantly enhance the quality of recorded video. Camcorders generally come with a threaded hole in the bottom that can be used for mounting the device on a tripod. Many digital cameras have the same feature.

Finally, frame the subject. When framing your subject, you should use the "Rule of Thirds" principle. This principle breaks down an image into thirds horizontally and vertically so that it has nine parts. The theory is that if you place points of interest on the lines and intersections of the grid, then your image will be better balanced. For example, when taking a picture of someone's face, you would want the eyes to be on the upper third line of the grid. See Figure 12.8 for an example. The principal subject of your shot should not usually be directly in the center of the image. Position your camera so the subject appears slightly to the left or right and slightly above or below the center. Be sure, when recording people, to allow headroom—space between the person's head and the top of the frame.

It can be helpful to spend some time shooting what is called "B-roll" footage, or extra video that does not come directly from the script. You can record different views of the setting or take some footage of an important prop. If your video includes an interview, take some footage of the person being interviewed going about his or her daily work or some other significant activity. In editing, you might choose to combine this footage with parts of the interview and treat it as a voiceover.

Figure 12.8 *Note the position of the eyes in this image.*

checkpoint

Why is a script important when creating a video?

ACTIVITY 12.2 ▶ Planning the Video

1. With a partner, start the planning process by writing a script then creating a storyboard for a five-minute video on a topic of your choice. The storyboard can be a frame-by-frame drawing of the video. Consider creating a video about a hobby or one your school could use to encourage more students and parents to attend sporting events at your school.

2. Follow the formatting guidelines given in the chapter for your script and storyboard or download scripting and storyboarding software. Transfer action from the script appropriately to the storyboard.

3. Check with your instructor for instructions on saving or exporting your script and storyboard.

4. Save your work as *12_Activity2_planning*.

Lesson 12.3 Working with Video

Recording video is only half the process needed to create a good movie. The second half requires you to transfer the images to your computer, edit the images, and share the video.

Video Transfer *LO 12.7 and 12.8*

Most video cameras are designed to transfer video from the camera to the computer using a Universal Serial Bus (USB) or FireWire connection. FireWire—sometimes called i.LINK— was developed by Apple, but now also appears on PCs (see Figure 12.9). FireWire has typically been a faster connection than the USB but is more expensive, and USB has become the standard for computers. However, newer cameras have USB 3.0, which is faster (4.8 Gbps transfer rate) than both USB 2.0 and FireWire 800. Intel has also showcased USB 3.1, which features 10 Gbps transfer speed and is backward compatible with USB 3.0 and 2.0. A Thunderbolt cable is utilized in the same way for Mac users. If a camcorder has both FireWire and USB ports, it may use the FireWire to download video and the USB to transfer still images. You will need to consult the documentation for your camcorder to find the specifics of its particular connectors. Camcorders and cameras often come with their own connecting cable, which is needed to transfer to video to the computer.

Figure 12.9 *USB 3.0 cables provide for faster video transfer. It is important to review your camera carefully to identify which cable you should use.*

Courtesy Doug Cogdell

Regardless of the type of connection, attaching the camera to a computer and turning the camera on will create a link between the two devices. Depending on the storage medium, there may be special software that will facilitate the transfer or you may be able to access the camera's memory and copy directly from it. If the recording device has a removable memory card, you can remove the card from the device and insert it into the computer's card reader slot or use an external card reader.

Frames *LO 12.7*

Videos are actually a series of still images linked together along a continuous path with each frame representing a point, much like pixels in a still image. Figure 12.10 shows you how each frame catches a moment in time.

Figure 12.10 *Frames move so fast that it is impossible to pick out each separate movement, so the eye blurs them together, creating an appearance of motion.*

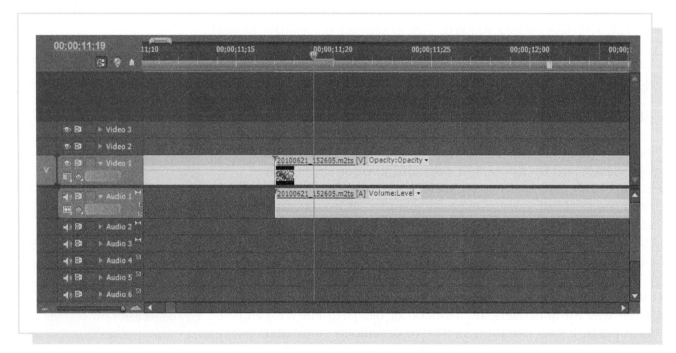

Figure 12.11 *In this screen capture you can see a timecode showing the movement from one clip to another.*

frame rate—The number of frames per second that video records.

timecode—A sequence of numbers digitally encoded to help identify each frame of the video by hour, minute, second, and frame.

keyframe—A software notation of a change in a frame; a mark that indicates where on a timeline an action such as movement begins.

Because each image or frame is projected only briefly, the images appear to be moving. Generally there are 30 frames per second (fps) of video, recorded as a **frame rate** of 30 fps. Just as a comparison, film for movies is typically recorded at 24 fps. Capture video at 60 fps would produce an exceptional video that may also be run in slow motion without distortion.

Each frame is given a specific notation called a **timecode**, which records the hour, minute, second, and frame number of each image. You use this timecode to locate insertion or editing points. It is important to keep track of your start and stop timecode to know what segments you particularly want to change. **Keyframes** in video indicate changes in clips or audio, usually in the form of an effect. A video timeline tracks each second and the changes that occur at keyframes. Figure 12.11 is an example of the timeline used in a video editing program to track events.

Figure 12.12 *Windows Movie Maker is designed for work with short clips such as those you might capture with a smartphone.*

Opening Software *LO 12.7*

What you see when you open video editing software depends on the complexity of the program. Basic packages like Windows Movie Maker and iMovie for the Mac have simple screens (see Figure 12.12) you can use to import video clips as well as still images. In this example, to add video, images, or audio to the movie, you simply go to the Capture Video menu and click the appropriate option. You can drag each item to the appropriate spot on the timeline at the bottom of the window.

If you are using a more advanced program such as Adobe Premiere Pro, Sony Vegas Pro, or Final Cut Pro you have many more options. The more advanced software packages are designed for longer videos than ones created in Movie Maker, and they are designed to save the created files as a project. Within a project, you will have separate sequences that may be scenes.

Figure 12.13 shows the Premiere Pro screen with a number of different editing panels. Each panel has a series of tabs for different functions. The project panel on the upper left lists all the imported files. As with the Movie Maker example, these files can be video, audio, or still photographs. The bottom left panel lists effects built into the program that can be used to change the appearance of these elements. In the top middle is the source panel, which allows you to view and modify a file before inserting it into a sequence. A tab in that panel provides a list of effects already used. The lower middle panel is the sequence mixer into which you place each file you want in your video. The timeline indicating each second appears at the top of this panel. Among the several editing tools in the lower right panel is a zoom tool (the magnifying glass), which allows you to see each second more easily. The

Figure 12.13 *Adobe Premiere Pro offers multiple panels to use as part of the video editing process. Within each panel, separate tabs open additional options.*

Communication

In the workplace, you need the ability to communicate your ideas clearly. Customers and coworkers must be able to understand you. They will have difficulty doing so if you use vague or incorrect language or if you use unfamiliar words and phrases. Video terminology can be very confusing to those not familiar with terms such as codec and timecodes. Learning to translate technical terms into concepts others can understand is an important part of communication.

Communication is also about paying attention to details such as grammar and spelling. Text that appears in video that contains typographical errors sends a message to the viewer that the videographer did not care enough to proofread and be a professional. A company's image can be severely damaged by such careless mistakes. Learning to proofread text is as much a part of communicating as paying attention to words that are spoken.

Skills in Action: Examine advertisements, company signs, billboards, and other business-related communications for spelling and grammatical errors. Create a presentation highlighting your findings. If possible, include scans of the advertisements or digital photos of the signs. Did the errors affect your opinion of these businesses?

upper right panel is the preview panel, which allows you to see the video as it will appear with all the sequences in place.

All panels can be undocked, closed, or maximized if you want them larger. Panels can be moved around to customize your screen. Often video developers work with multiple screens and move one or more panels to a second monitor to make it easier to see the material.

Editing *LO 12.7*

Videos can be edited in interesting ways. Of course, as you would expect, you can cut and paste segments to enhance the effectiveness of your video, as well as to remove unnecessary material. A vertical line is used to move along the timeline allowing you to select the exact spot in which to work. You can add text to video for elements such as titles and credits. Occasionally, text is also used to establish location or other details. Even a simple program such as Movie Maker provides opportunities for you to make editing changes, including the following:

- changing the duration of an image on the screen
- rotating an image
- changing the aspect ratio from standard to widescreen
- changing the volume on audio

Other frequently used editing options include transitions and effects. **Transitions** are used when you move from one scene to another. As Figure 12.14 shows, video editors may have a great variety of transition effects. They can be as simple as a quick **fade** to black or something

transitions—Movement between scenes.

fade—Transition technique that moves from black to the image or the reverse.

Figure 12.14 *Windows Movie Maker provides a variety of options for making the transition from one sequence to another.*

dissolves—Transition technique in which one scene slowly changes to the other.

more complicated. **Dissolves** are one type of transition that causes one scene to slowly become another.

Adobe Premiere Pro has countless ways to edit video. In addition, a video clip can be cropped or even superimposed over another clip by using two tracks. Many of the same functions are available for audio as well. The speed at which a clip plays can be changed, adding interest to a video. As with images, metadata assigning copyright information and other details can be stored in video files.

Although these sophisticated software platforms provide much more editing capacity, it takes time to develop the skill to use them well. Increasing your knowledge of the terminology pertaining to the software will be helpful.

Audio *LO 12.7*

With camcorders, video and audio are recorded at the same time, making synchronization much easier. However, it is still possible to pull apart the video or audio of a recording to use separately. In addition, you can insert audio into a video just as you can still images. If someone is speaking, you must carefully synchronize or match the two so that the movement on screen matches the sound that is heard.

You may think about using music ripped from a CD to add interest to a video. While technology makes it easy to do this, remember that posting to the Web or otherwise distributing a video with this music is in violation of copyright laws. You also need to consider whether the music is really suited to your purpose and audience. You can obtain royalty-free music—and video—from websites that provide material under a Creative Commons license, which allows people to download and use media. Be sure you fully understand exactly what rights a website conveys before using media created by others.

Exporting Video *LO 12.8*

Editing can be time-consuming, and requires care. To be sure not to lose your work, you should save frequently. You might consider saving each editing stage as a slightly different version. That way, if anything goes wrong, you can go back to a previous stage. Each program saves video with its own extension, and movie files can only be opened within that program. Once a video has been completed, save the final version in the native format. Doing so makes it possible to go back and edit that final version, should you wish to do so.

To make the video viewable for others, you must export it from its native format into one that can be read by the anticipated hardware. This conversion process is called **rendering**. It may be quite time-consuming depending upon the size of your video and the processor speed of your computer.

rendering—The conversion of video to a format that can be used with various viewers.

Your choice of export format may be based not only on hardware, but also on the means of delivery. In some instances, it may be necessary to export in a variety of formats to meet the requirements of different viewing devices. There are a wide number of format choices, and as videography is a growing field, this list of choices is constantly developing. It is important to stay current with industry file format standards and frequent changes. A few file formats that are common include:

- **MOV**: Also called QuickTime, a standard developed by Apple
- **WMV**: Windows Media Video, a standard developed by Microsoft
- **AVI**: An older standard for personal computers that still is required by some programs before burning a video DVD
- **MPEG**: A multimedia standard for personal computers and other devices; MPEG-4 is designed for both audio and video
- **FLV**: Flash video played using Adobe Flash player; many are moving away from FLV files as there are issues running FLV files on Macs
- **MP4:** Common digital multimedia format used to store video, audio and other data; it also allows Internet streaming

Each software application you use will give you a variety of options. Windows Movie Maker, for instance, provides five options for saving the movie.

- To run on a computer
- To make a CD

- To attach to an email
- To send to the Web
- To send back to the camcorder, from which it can be viewed on a TV.

When saving to the computer, a pull-down menu lets you choose the type of device so that the program can save the file in an appropriate format (see Figure 12.15).

The export process uses compression algorithms (video codecs) similar to the ones used to create audio recordings. These codecs make the file sizes smaller to increase transmission speed. Compression is important with video. Just one second of uncompressed video can take up as much as 30 MB of space. As with images, you have to decide which format you want, balancing file size with image quality.

The encoding or rendering process can be time-consuming depending upon the type of computer you are using and its capabilities. Some programs, such as Premiere Pro require an operating system that uses 64-bit software in the Windows version. This enhanced software allows the computer to work faster and use more available memory, but not all computers can run that operating system. This is another consideration when selecting your video editing software.

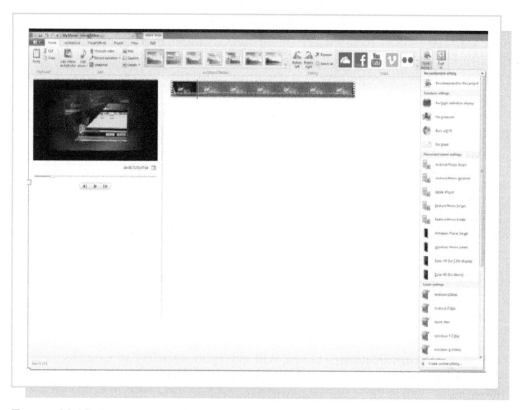

Figure 12.15 *Once you are ready to export your video, you need to know what format it is to be rendered in, such as MP4 (an MPEG-4 file format) or WMV.*

YouTube

YouTube was developed in 2005 to simplify the process of sharing videos online and was quickly bought by Google as it became widely used. YouTube has changed frequently as the technology has matured. Early videos were played in a 4:3 aspect ratio and in monaural sound. Today videos are widescreen in video format with stereo audio. Hundreds of hours of video are posted every day—with no end in sight. Figure 12.16 shows only one example of what you may find on YouTube.

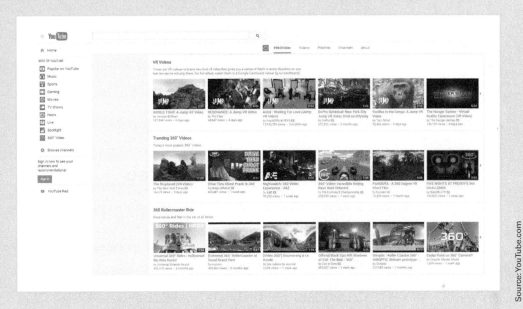

Figure 12.16 *YouTube offers videos in a variety of categories as well as the ability to search and browse among them.*

Sharing Video *LO 12.8*

The point of creating a video is to share it with others in order to convey a message or evoke a feeling. There are a number of ways to make this happen. In the business world, short videos or podcasts can be uploaded to a company's Facebook page or website. By using either of these methods, others can open your video easily.

You can also burn your video to a DVD. DVDs have greater storage capability than CDs, making them more suitable for video. Keep in mind that many are defaulting to other storage devices as DVD players are on the decline. Therefore, this may not be the best option for storage.

Flash storage—A commonly used storage medium for videos that uses a non-volatile memory type.

A commonly used storage medium for videos is **Flash storage**. It is a solid-state storage system that uses a nonvolatile memory type. Flash storage does not require power to maintain the stored data and there are no mechanical parts involved, thus reducing power consumption. Flash storage can store large amounts of data and is fast, efficient, and mobile. Flash storage systems typically consist of a flash controller and a memory chip. The memory chip stores the data and the controller manages access to the storage area on the memory unit.

Another method of sharing a video is to stream the video. Streaming video allows you to view video directly from a server rather than downloading a file to your computer. This is a method that movie distributors are adopting to make it possible to view movies instantly, without having to use a DVD.

checkpoint

What is the difference between saving a movie in a movie-editing program and exporting the movie?

ACTIVITY 12.3 ▶ Editing Video

1. Use a camcorder to record video using the plan created in Activity 12.2.
2. Edit the video with software supplied in class. Include, as a minimum, the following edits:
   a. Text added for titles and credits.
   b. At least one transition added.
3. Export video to a file format given by your instructor.
4. Save as *12_Activity3_editing_video*.

Key Concepts

▶ Video equipment can vary in quality and size from a smartphone to a high-end professional camcorder. *LO 12.1*

▶ When comparing video cameras the following specifications are important to consider: resolution, aspect ratio, sensor, bitrate, storage medium, and features. *LO 12.1*

▶ Most video today is recorded digitally with new 4K Ultra HD camcorders having higher resolution (3840 × 2160 pixels). *LO 12.2*

▶ Camcorders with hard drives or flash memory can store more video. Those that record to DVDs are being phased out by suppliers. *LO 12.1*

▶ Important camcorder features include the size of the LCD display, the optical zoom power, image stabilization, the availability of a microphone jack, low-light capability, battery life, and input/output connectors. *LO 12.1*

▶ There are several care and safety requirements you should consider when using a camcorder. *LO 12.3*

▶ Video scripts follow a standard format that identifies each scene separately and includes information about the location, time, characters, sounds, and dialogue. *LO 12.4*

▶ A storyboard creates a visual guide for use when shooting a video. It gives information on the type of shots as well as the action. *LO 12.5*

▶ Video shots fall into three categories: wide angle, medium, and close-up. Shots can be panned from side to side or tilted up and down. Varying types of shots, angles, and effects can add visual interest to a video, but they should not be overdone. *LO 12.6*

▶ Video is transferred to a computer for editing using a USB or FireWire connection. *LO 12.8*

▶ Video frames are recorded as frames per second and the timecode records each hour, minute, second, and frame. *LO 12.6*

▶ Video can be edited by trimming away parts of a clip, by adding transitions, inserting effects, and by adding text such as titles and credits. Editing programs allow users to edit using a timeline or storyboard. *LO 12.7*

▶ Editing programs save files in a proprietary format. The files must be exported in order to be viewed on different kinds of platforms, or they can be streamed, which makes it unnecessary to download the files. *LO 12.8*

▶ Each export requires the video to be rendered in specific ways for it to play as intended. *LO 12.8*

Review and Discuss

1. Evaluate quality and choice of video equipment. *LO 12.1*

2. Describe the resolution of a high-definition camcorder. *LO 12.1 and 12.2*

3. Compare and contrast the high definition (HD) camcorder and the 4K Ultra HD camcorder. *LO 12.2*

4. Justify the use of the letterboxing technique in videoing. *LO 12.2*

5. Compare an interlaced and a progressive video. *LO 12.1*

6. Evaluate examples of storage media. If you were purchasing a camcorder, which type of storage media would you prefer and why? *LO 12.1*

7. Analyze the uses of a camcorder that would cause the battery life to be less than the manufacturer provides. What measures are used to judge the low-light capability on camcorders? *LO 12.1*

8. Describe the formatting of a script. *LO 12.4*

9. Discuss the process of planning and shooting a video, and provide three tips to ensure success. *LO 12.6*

10. Create two different scenarios in which you would share a video. Describe the content of the video. What methods you would use to share it and why? *LO 12.8*

Apply

1. Using scripting and storyboarding software, plan the creation of a simple five-minute video you would create to encourage others to volunteer for a nonprofit organization. Keep in mind the need to tell a story with a focused theme. Transfer the action from the script to the storyboard. Save as **12_Apply1_volunteering**. *LO 12.4 and 12.5*

2. Write a script and storyboard for a video about a school activity such as a sports activity. Create and edit the video. Save or export scripts, storyboards, and videos as **12_Apply2_school_activity**. *LO 12.4, 12.5, and 12.7*

3. In a team of three students, plan a video of a job interview to use as a good example of interviewing. First, research and find questions that should be asked in the interview. Write at least five appropriate interview questions. Based on these questions, write a script for the video and make a storyboard. Make three videos, with each member of the team getting a chance to participate as the videographer, the interviewer, and the interviewee. Each videographer should also edit the video using supplied software. Save scripts, storyboards, and video as **12_Apply3_interview**. *LO 12.4, 12.5, and 12.7*

4. Open the student data file **orientation.rtf**. Research a business where you would like to do an internship. Fill in the information using your research. With a partner, plan an employee orientation video for your prospective employer. Your partner should video you, and you should video your partner. Record and edit each video appropriately and save as **12_Apply4_orientation**. *LO 12.4, 12.5, and 12.7*

5. With a partner, decide on a new business or product to market in a video. Be creative! This video could be used for an advertisement and should be less than two minutes long. Write a script and create a storyboard for the video, then record and edit the video. Follow your instructor's directions for sharing the video. Save the script, storyboard, and video as **12_Apply5_advertisement**. *LO 12.4, 12.5, and 12.7*

Explore

1. Search YouTube or other websites for good and bad examples of videos. Critique two bad and two good examples and write a summary of what you found, citing specific characteristics you learned in this chapter. Save as **12_Explore1_critiques**.

2. Research video blogging. Write a summary of three different types of blogs that you read about. Choose one type of video blog and work with a partner to create a video blog. Save as **12_Explore2_video_blog**. *LO 12.4, 12.5, 12.6, 12.7, and 12.8*

3. Research how-to videos on an appropriate topic of your choice. Create a list of best tips from your research and from watching a few examples. Summarize what you have learned. Create a how-to video on the topic. Edit the video as appropriate. Save summaries and all plans and videos as **12_Explore3_how_to**. *LO 12.4, 12.5, 12.6, 12.7, and 12.8*

Academic Connections

Communications: In today's global business market, many businesses are turning to video communications to save on business expenses, such as travel to meetings, and to ensure speed of action. Research or interview someone with experience in video conferencing to gather some tips for successful video conferencing. Write a summary of what you have learned. Save as **12_AC_communications**.

Writing: With a partner, write a script on the topic of successful business report writing to be used for a how-to video. The video should be targeted for two minutes in length. Save as **12_AC_writing**. *LO 12.4*

Team Project

With a partner, create a five-minute local news video. Use the following information as guidelines:

▶ Plan the shoot by deciding on the location and gathering any props that may be needed.

▶ Script the video with your partner.

▶ Storyboard the video with your partner.

▶ Shoot the video following the script.

▶ Use video software to edit the video, adding a title, credits, and other enhancements.

▶ Export the video in the .avi format as **Unit4_project_video**.

▶ Share the video with the class.

▶ Critique classmates' videos, giving ideas on what could be done to enhance the video to make it more effective.

FBLA Leadership Positions

Visit the national or local FBLA website. Decide on a national or local leadership position for which you would like to run. Think about the strengths and skills you would bring to this position. Think about what you can include in a video interview to best showcase your strengths and skills.

Script and storyboard to plan your video and make any other plans you need for the shoot. Next, have a partner shoot the video for you so that you are in some of the video shots. You should shoot your partner's video for them. Export as **Unit4_FBLA_video_interview** as an .avi file.

www.fbla-pbl.org

Portfolio

1. Add your video project from the unit projects to your portfolio folder.

2. Write a summary of teamwork. In your summary, define teamwork, explain what it means to you, and describe in detail at least two experiences you have had in working as a part of a team. Include the advantages of being a part of a team as well as disadvantages.

iStockphoto.com/Pashalgnatov

UNIT 5

Web Publishing

Arts, A/V Technology & Communications

Career Cluster: Web Master

Interview with Robin, Webmaster, Pink Bird Design

Describe your average day. First, I check my email to get any updates on any new job requests. Then, I prioritize my work for the day. My workload changes daily. I never know quite what to expect. I need to be ready to adapt and change gears quickly. I may work for one easy hour or 14 very intense hours, depending on the workload and the deadlines involved. I also try to devote some time each day to professional development to keep my skills up to date.

What is the worst part of your job? The deadlines are usually very tight; this can be very stressful!

What is the best part of your job? It's very satisfying when I successfully complete a project and have created work that I am proud of, and the client is happy.

Employment Outlook The outlook for Web Developers and related careers is very good, according to the U.S. Bureau of Labor Statistics. These jobs are expected to grow much faster than the average from 2008 through 2022.

Skills and Qualifications Associate or bachelor's degree in Web development and administration or related field; technical, communication, and problem-solving skills; design sense; ability to work under pressure; attention to detail; commitment to staying up to date with technical changes; possibly certification

Job Titles Web Developer, Webmaster, Web Administrator

What About You? Does a career in Web Development and Administration interest you? Use the Internet to find postings for Web Developers. Research Web Development and similar careers using the *Occupational Outlook Handbook* published by the U.S. Bureau of Labor Statistics and available at *http://www.bls.gov/ooh/*

- How can you best prepare yourself for a career in Web Development and Administration?
- What job qualifications do employers require?
- What are the most common technical skills and computer programs mentioned?

Web Development

Learning Outcomes

▶ **13.1** Describe the difference between Web development and Web design.

▶ **13.2** Explain various methods for developing websites.

▶ **13.3** List three important considerations for Web development.

▶ **13.4** Describe the functions of coding and common tags.

▶ **13.5** Explain the challenges of Web development.

▶ **13.6** Explain how Web developers meet the needs of universal access.

▶ **13.7** Write correct code.

▶ **13.8** Explain the differences between HTML, XHTML, and HTML5.

Key Terms

- attribute
- browser
- Cascading Style Sheets (CSS)
- closing tag
- Content Management System (CMS)
- domain name
- element
- empty element
- File Transfer Protocol (FTP)
- hacking
- Hypertext Markup Language (HTML)
- metadata
- opening tag
- tag
- Universal Resource Locator (URL)
- validate
- Web Content Accessibility Guidelines (WCAG)
- web editor
- web server
- well-formed code
- World Wide Web Consortium (W3C)
- XHTML

Since its first appearance in 1992, the World Wide Web has grown to become a staple of people's lives. People across the world search the Web for information and entertainment, connect with friends and family members through social media sites, shop for goods, and plan vacations. Making it all possible is the work of Web developers, who work on the "back end" of the website. They program behind the scenes and ensure interactions on web pages work effectively. Web developers focus on how a website works and make sure users can do what they need to do. Web developers are responsible for the website's technical aspects. They use several tools to accomplish this work, including a particular kind of computer language that, when implemented, results in the development of the website. Before you can understand effective Web Development, you need to grasp the fundamentals of that language.

It is important to distinguish the difference between Web development and Web design. This chapter focuses on Web development, and the next chapter provides specifics about Web design. Web development involves all of the processes that take place behind the scenes when developing a website. Web development provides the "back end" of the website, including the coding language that ensures the web page works properly. A Web developer can be expected to build a website "from the ground up."

Therefore, Web developers write the code and scripts to ensure interactions on the websites work effectively. A Web developer focuses on how a website works and makes sure users can do what they need to do on the site. Web developers also have an administrative role in keeping the websites up and running.

Technical aspects that Web developers must consider include website performance and capacity. The site's performance and capacity are used to determine website speed and the "traffic" on the website. The website capacity also includes how much content can be handled on the website. Because of the Web developer's responsibilities, successful Web developers are typically logical thinkers who are detail oriented and have excellent programming and technical skills.

Traditionally those who created websites served as both Web developers and Web designers. But with the influx of Web interactivity, animation, video, audio, and enhanced design features, the need for separate Web developers and designers became necessary. Web designers focus on Web graphics and interface design and the appearance of a website. They are more in tune with the design process relating to the front end (client side) of the website. Web developers do not focus on the design and appearance, but create technically sound websites with "clean code." Web developer and Web designer duties may have some overlap, but they have a common goal—to create a website that functions properly, attracts users, and serves the users' needs.

Methods of Developing Websites

LO 13.1 and 13.2

As noted previously, Web developers use special computer language, or code, to build the website. However, there are other ways to build a website. For example, there are companies online that for free or for a minimal fee will allow the user to utilize their website builder program. The user may copy and paste content into the program and/or upload documents and graphics. The builder program then creates the website from the provided information. However, these online programs typically limit the type of content that may be uploaded and the functionality of the website, have limited design features, and limit the amount of content. Consequently, these website builder programs are good for those who need a very basic website (of no more than one to three web pages), minimal functionality, and a general website design.

Another way to develop a website without actually creating the code yourself is to use a template website. The templates available through these types of websites allow you to provide your own content and graphics. However, the templates may have built-in graphics and additional design features. One thing to remember about using templates is that additional customization to meet your specific needs is typically not possible unless you are able to write code yourself. It is always a good idea to view websites that have been built either through a website builder program or a template website to see the function and design before you think about using one yourself to develop your website.

A website can also be developed through the use of a weblog (blog) program such as WordPress. WordPress is a free, open source product many use to assist them in the development of a website. WordPress is also considered a **Content Management System (CMS)**, which is a computer application that allows for content publishing, editing, organizing, deleting, and general maintenance from a central location. WordPress has an intuitive, user-friendly back end that allows users to easily develop content. WordPress also provides plugins for additional functionality. Plug-ins allow you to add elements like shopping carts, maps, forums, and photos.

Another way, as noted previously, to develop a website is to build it yourself. Writing your own code and scripts allows you to customize the website to meet your specific goals and the needs of those who will be using the site. You will learn more about coding in the next section.

Content Management System (CMS)—A computer application that allows for content publishing, editing, organizing, deleting, and general maintenance from a central location.

Hosting a Website *LO 13.1 and 13.2*

It is important to remember no matter how a website is developed, it must be hosted on a **web server** in order to be accessible on the Internet. When using website builders and templates, those companies may provide the additional service of hosting your website and provide you with a domain name for an additional fee. However, some hosting services are free as long as you agree to their name appearing either on your site or as a part of your **Universal Resource Locator (URL)**. For example, if you used Weebly, a free website builder, the URL for your site may be http://yourname.weebly.com.

web server—A computer used to store web pages for browser access.

Universal Resource Locator (URL)—The unique "address" used to access a website.

A **domain name** is a unique name for a website and it becomes a part of the URL. A URL is used to identify specific web pages. It is the actual "address" you use to access the website. Each site has a unique address. If your domain name is "NortonBeanCounters," your URL may be http://www.nortonbeancounters.com. When choosing a domain name, it is important to choose a name that is easily identifiable and related to the purpose or content of your site. Domain names must be formally registered to ensure others are not using the same domain name. There are websites that allow users to search for a domain name to ensure it has not already been taken. You may use a company such as GoDaddy to purchase your domain name and host your website. There is typically a fee to register a unique domain name.

Every domain name uses a suffix to identify whether it is an educational, government, organization, military, commercial business, or

domain name—The unique name for a website, which becomes part of the site's URL and which must be formally registered.

other type of entity. Review the list below to become familiar with commonly used suffixes.

- Commercial business: .com
- Education: .edu
- Government: .gov
- Military: .mil
- Mobile-compatible websites: .mobi
- Network organizations: .net
- Organizations (non-profit): .org
- Small business: .biz

There may be some crossover, for example, if you wanted to ensure that another company's URL does not include your domain name. Therefore, you could purchase www.nortonbeancounters.com, www.nortonbeancounters.net, www.nortonbeancounters.org, and so on. However, you would only actually use the one URL that matched your type of company.

Individual countries also have specific suffixes. A few are provided below.

- Canada: .ca
- China: .cn
- India: .in
- Italy: .it
- Japan: .jp
- Portugal: .pt
- United States: .us

Considerations for Web Development *LO 13.3*

There are many things to consider when you are thinking about developing a website. They are not limited to, but include the following.

- What are your goals for the website?
- What are the needs of those who will be using the site?
- What is the information, service, or product you will be offering through the website?
- How will you develop the website?
- Where will the website be housed?
- What will the domain name be for the website?
- Can you serve as the website developer, designer, and administrator, or do you need other people to help?
- How will you maintain the content and quality of the website?
- What is your timeline for the development of the website?
- How will you secure the website?

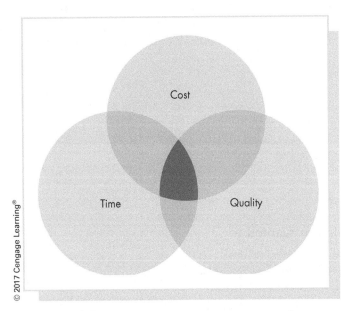

Figure 13.1 *Time, cost, and quality considerations for Web development.*

Asking these questions is an important step to take before the actual development of the website. The answers to these questions typically fall into one of the following three most important considerations for Web development: time, cost, and quality. For example, if you use a builder program, the time you spend may be minimal to moderate depending on how much content you have to build, and the cost may be minimal as well; however, the quality may be low. If you build your own website as you write your own code, the time you spend will be high, cost will be low, and quality will depend on your expertise. Therefore, many argue that you can never have all three: minimal time, low cost, and high quality. You may only achieve two of these three important considerations. The graphic in Figure 13.1 may help you visualize the goal of integrating time, cost, and quality in the development of websites.

The small, dark blue area in the middle is the only place where cost, time, and quality have all been considered. Therefore, you can see how difficult it is to create something in which all components have been considered and met. However, there are larger areas in which cost and quality or cost and time or time and quality have been met.

checkpoint

What is the difference between a Web developer and a Web designer?

ACTIVITY 13.1 ▶ Exploring Tags

1. Conduct research on the Internet and create a list of at least 10 free online Web development tools. These sites can be free or fee-based.

Lesson 13.2 ▶ Writing Code for Web Development

Whether you access the Web through a desktop computer, laptop, tablet, or a smartphone, you will find that whichever of the tens of millions of locations on the Web you visit, each will behave in a similar way. They will behave in similar ways because to display a web page the Internet browser reads and interprets instructions provided through special codes or languages. HTML is one of those languages.

HTML (HyperText Markup Language) is a universal code that allows anyone using a web **browser** to view web pages. Whether you use Google Chrome, Apple's Safari, or other browsers, the browser will display web pages in much the same way on all devices. The browsers do so by reading the HTML code, which tells the browser what to display and where on the screen to display it.

It may seem that HTML files are like the PDF files you learned about in Chapter 10, a standard file format that is interpreted exactly the same way across all platforms. That is not quite the case. HTML files do not have quite the universal constancy of PDF files. All Web browsers do not show web pages in *exactly* the same way. Still, the relatively constant appearance of files formatted in HTML makes a web page look fairly similar around the world and on different devices. In fact, you don't even have to be connected to the Internet to read HTML documents. Web documents can be read on any computer, much like a word processing document. This broad applicability of HTML code makes it a valuable business tool.

Inside HTML *LO 13.4, 13.8*

HTML is a coding language designed to translate text and graphics into a viewable page. HTML gives structure to Web content typically by using parts such as headings, paragraphs, and images. HTML, similar to a software package, has been updated throughout the years. HTML is the basis for two new versions, XHTML and HTML5. **XHTML** is the more current, widely used version and allows for more structured websites. Therefore, as coding is discussed in this chapter, XHTML examples will be provided. XHTML was developed due to a need for providing universal consistency and quality to websites on the World Wide Web. HTML5 has been in existence for a few years, but it is not yet universally accessible through all browsers and devices. However, HTML5 is on the cusp of the coding world and additional information should be investigated about it as well.

Whether you are using HTML, XHTML, or HTML5 to code and build your website, there are three terms you must know: tags, elements, and attributes. **Tags** provide web browsers with instructions pertaining to the look and structure of the web page. Tags are always enclosed with the less than symbol (<) on the left and the greater than symbol (>) on the right. These symbols are referred to as angle brackets. Tags are the secret to HTML's universal means of delivery.

Elements define the structure and content within a web page. Elements are many times referred to as designators that define headings, paragraphs, and other components. For example, XHTML allows for up to six levels of headings, noted as <h1> through <h6>. Elements are written in all lower case. The opening tag for heading 1 is <h1> and the closing tag is similar, but contains a forward slash after the first angle bracket: </h1>. Other examples of opening and closing tags are provided in Table 13.1.

HTML (HyperText Markup Language)—The code used to create web pages.

browser—A computer program that allows you to view web pages.

XHTML—A markup language similar to HTML but with stricter additional options and requirements.

tag—HTML code used to identify an element in an HTML file and instruct browsers on how and where to display the element.

element—defines structure and content within a web page; designators that define elements such as headings, paragraphs, and other components.

Table 13.1 *Basic XHTML Tags.*

OPENING TAG	CLOSING TAG	EXPLANATION
`<html>`	`</html>`	Defines an HTML document. Required for every web page.
`<head>`	`</head>`	Defines the document's head element. Required for every web page. Must be within the html opening and closing tags.
`<title>`	`</title>`	Must be within the head opening and closing tags. Names the page and will appear in the title bar of the browser.
`<body>`	`</body>`	Defines the document's body. Required for every web page. Must be within html opening and closing tags.
`<a href>`	`</a>`	Creates a link to another web page by providing the URL; for example `<a href=http://www.cengage.com</a>`
`<div>`	`</div>`	Defines a separate element on a web page.
`<em>`	`</em>`	Provides emphasis to text. Italics is the default.
`<h1>`...`<h6>`	`</h1>`...`</h6>`	Defines HTML headings of various sizes; h1 is the largest and h6 is the smallest.
`<ol>`	`</ol>`	Defines an ordered (numbered) list.
`<p>`	`</p>`	Defines a paragraph.
`<strong>`	`</strong>`	Provides strong emphasis to text. Bold is the default.
`<ul>`	`</ul>`	Defines an unordered (bulleted) list.
` `	*Self-closing	Results in a line break.
`<li>`	`</li>`	List item.
`<img/>`	*Self-closing	Inserts an image when accompanied with the image source, such as src="logo.jpg"
`<hr/>`	*Self-closing	Inserts a horizontal rule; with attributes, the width, color and size can be specified.

*Self-closing tags are empty elements that do not require a separate closing tag.

attribute—Tag that provides additional information about an element. The format is name="value".

Attributes provide additional information about the element. Common attributes provide identification for the attribute, classify the element, provide a source of embedded content, provide a hyperlink reference, or pertain to the appearance of the attribute. Attributes have two parts and the layout of the attribute is different from the layout of an element. The two parts of an attribute include the attribute name and the value of the attribute. An attribute is contained within the element. It is written in the format of the name of the attribute followed by an equals sign and then the value of the attribute noted within quotation marks. For example, the following are attributes for setting the height and width of an image:
`<img src = "image1.jpg" height = "100" width = "150">`

In XHTML, all pages begin with a DOCTYPE declaration. There are two main declarations used consistently in Web development.

1. Transitional, which means the page is transitioning from HTML to XHTM
2. Strict, which means the page is totally coded in XHTML

The DOCTYPE also indicates the language (e.g., English = EN) in which the web page is written. An example XHTML DOCTYPE is shown below.

```
<!DOCTYPE html PUBLIC "-//W3C//DTD XHTML 1.0
Transitional//EN" "http://www.w3.org/TR/xhtml1/DTD/
xhtml1-transitional.dtd">
```

HTML5 has condensed the DOCTYPE to make it easier to key, but also because the transition from HTML to XHTML is not the issue it has been in the past. The HTML5 DOCTYPE is written as: `<!DOCTYPE html>` For convenience, using an HTML5 DOCTYPE is one tag many developers are transitioning to even when coding in XHTML.

XHTML Basics *LO 13.4, 13.7, 13.8*

web pages have certain basic components. As noted previously, the browser reads the XHTML code to display the information. Each web page begins with an opening `<html>` tag (refer to Figure 13.2). Next is the `<head>` tag, which provides general information about the page but which does not actually appear on the page. The next element is `<title>`, which names the page. Whatever text is placed before the closing `</title>` tag is the text that will appear in the title bar of the browser. The majority of page code is found between the opening `<body>` tag and the closing `</body>` tag. The body of the document in

lavitrei/Shutterstock.com

Impact

lightpoet/Shutterstock.com

World Wide Web

There can be no denying the impact of the World Wide Web. Since it first appeared in 1991, the Web has become the most prominent and widely employed area of the Internet, with hundreds of millions of users accessing billions of pages on hundreds of millions of websites every day. The Web has spawned new jobs and new businesses; vaulted companies like Google into prominence; helped usher in a transformation of the recording industry; contributed to a crisis of survival for newspapers and magazines; and made it possible for people around the world to communicate with one another, enjoy cultural resources that were once inaccessible, and share their unique perspectives on breaking news stories. While the Web did not launch the Information Age, it has become a major part of the information revolution.

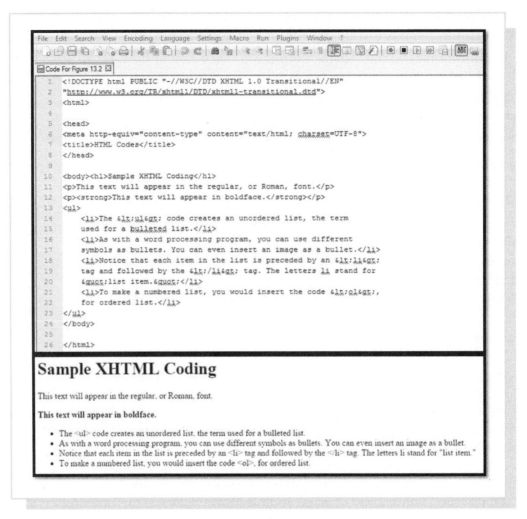

```
File  Edit  Search  View  Encoding  Language  Settings  Macro  Run  Plugins  Window  ?

Code For Figure 13.2
 1  <!DOCTYPE html PUBLIC "-//W3C//DTD XHTML 1.0 Transitional//EN"
 2  "http://www.w3.org/TR/xhtml1/DTD/xhtml1-transitional.dtd">
 3  <html>
 4
 5  <head>
 6  <meta http-equiv="content-type" content="text/html; charset=UTF-8">
 7  <title>HTML Codes</title>
 8  </head>
 9
10  <body><h1>Sample XHTML Coding</h1>
11  <p>This text will appear in the regular, or Roman, font.</p>
12  <p><strong>This text will appear in boldface.</strong></p>
13  <ul>
14      <li>The &lt;ul&gt; code creates an unordered list, the term
15      used for a bulleted list.</li>
16      <li>As with a word processing program, you can use different
17      symbols as bullets. You can even insert an image as a bullet.</li>
18      <li>Notice that each item in the list is preceded by an &lt;li&gt;
19      tag and followed by the &lt;/li&gt; tag. The letters li stand for
20      &quot;list item.&quot;</li>
21      <li>To make a numbered list, you would insert the code &lt;ol&gt;,
22      for ordered list.</li>
23  </ul>
24  </body>
25
26  </html>
```

Sample XHTML Coding

This text will appear in the regular, or Roman, font.

This text will appear in boldface.

- The <ul> code creates an unordered list, the term used for a bulleted list.
- As with a word processing program, you can use different symbols as bullets. You can even insert an image as a bullet.
- Notice that each item in the list is preceded by an <li> tag and followed by the </li> tag. The letters li stand for "list item."
- To make a numbered list, you would insert the code <ol>, for ordered list.

Figure 13.2 *The text sample on the top shows the HTML code written in Notepad⁺⁺, a helpful text editor. The bottom section provides a view of how the codes will make the text appear in a browser.*

Figure 13.2 includes a heading, signaled by <h1>; two paragraphs, each beginning with <p>; and a bulleted list, which has the tag <ul>. At the end of the file, there are closing tags for the </body>) and </html>.

Notice that many tags—from the opening <html> code to the tags for a heading, boldface text, the list, and each list item—appear in pairs. The first tag in the pair, the **opening tag**, identifies the element or a format for the text to follow. The second tag, called the **closing tag**, ends that instruction so it will not apply to any text after it. In the case of the heading and the boldface sentence, the opening tag turns the format (heading, boldface) on, and the closing tag turns it off. In the case of the list items, the paired tags identify each separate list item. Remember that a forward slash (/) indicates a closing tag, the tag used to turn off a format.

You can see that one element, such as the body, can contain several other elements and attributes. As noted previously, some attributes identify the class of objects to which an element belongs, such as the

opening tag—The first tag in a pair.

closing tag—The second tag in a pair.

heading. Some attributes, such as font or color, describe the appearance of an element. Such attributes appear in the start tag, and the end tag for this element would simply be `</h1>`. The attribute need not be "turned off"—it is turned off when the heading is closed.

Some elements are called **empty elements**. They have no content and stand alone. Examples are the line break tag or a tag instructing the browser to insert a horizontal rule or an image. When coding in XHTML, these empty elements are self-closing when written with a space before a forward slash just before the closing angle bracket. For example, line break is written as `<br/>`, horizontal rule is written as `<hr/>`, and image as `<img/>`.

Common XHTML Tags

XHTML works in coordination with **Cascading Style Sheets (CSS)**. CSS is a presentation language that provides for the style, design and appearance of content. Fonts and colors are two components typically involved when working with CSS. CSS will be discussed more in the chapter pertaining to Web design. However, keep in mind that XHTML and CSS are independent coding languages, as XHTML represents content and CSS represents the appearance of that content.

XHTML has dozens of tags, and they cover a broad range of functions. Table 13.1 provides an overview of some of the more common tags.

Remember the following about XHTML.

- XHTML DOCTYPE is required
- `<html>`, `<head>`, `<title>`, and `<body>` are required
- Elements must be properly nested
- Elements must be closed
- Elements and attributes must be in lowercase
- Attribute values must be within quotation marks

Sample XHTML code is provided below.

```
<!DOCTYPE html PUBLIC "-//W3C//DTD XHTML 1.0 Transitional//EN" "http://www.w3.org/TR/xhtml1/DTD/
xhtml1-transitional.dtd">
<head>
<title>Enter Title HERE</title>
</head>
<body>
Enter Body Text Here
</body>
</html>
```

The purpose of the `<html>` `</html>` tags is to tell the browser to read the content as a web page. Under the opening `<html>` tag is a head section `<head>` `</head>`. This section includes the title of the web page as well as other components such as metadata. **Metadata** is simply information about the data. Metadata and other information

empty elements—Elements that do not have any content.

Cascading Style Sheets (CSS)—A presentation language which provides for the style, design and appearance of content.

metadata—Information about the data.

within the `<head>` section will not be visible to visitors to the page. The only exception to this rule is the page title, which will appear at the top of the browser window. Meta elements specify page descriptions, keywords, the document author, date the page was last modified, and other information about the page. Metadata is used by browsers, search engines, and other Web services.

Learn by Reviewing Existing Code

One way to learn to code using XHTML is to visit a website and examine its source code. Those who browse with Safari can view existing source code through the View Source option in the View menu. If you use Google Chrome, you must go to the Wrench menu (the wrench symbol appears by default in the upper right of the main Chrome toolbar), choose the Tools menu, and then select View Source. Regardless of which browser you use, you will see the code for the web page. You can study the codes in conjunction with the text, images, and other design features on a website to begin to understand the effects of various codes. By understanding the effects created by different codes, you can develop pages using the appropriate codes for your needs.

If you take this approach to learning code, try to begin with relatively simple web pages so you do not get too confused. It also helps to focus on just one section of a page at a time to more fully understand the code and its effects.

Another approach to learning XHTML and other types of formatting covered in later chapters in this unit is to use online tutorials. A search for "XHTML tutorial" will produce a list of many tutorials from which to choose. Find one that is clear and easy to follow and start learning at your own pace. The World Wide Web Consortium provides a wealth of information to assist in your learning (http://www.w3schools.org).

The Ethics of Copying Code

It is easy to view the XHTML code created by someone else. It's just as easy to copy it. When you discover an interesting technique, your inclination will be to use that same technique on your own pages. In this way, the Internet becomes a resource for everyone to use for inspiration and encourages the expansion of Web development. However, the ethical decision becomes yours. How much code can you "borrow" before it is no longer your page? Is it important to give credit for innovative techniques? Does this borrowing hinder or encourage development of new ideas? What do you think?

The copyright issue regarding XHTML code is not clear cut. XHTML tags themselves cannot be copyrighted: they can be used by anyone. Nevertheless, in the same way that the development of a book is a creative act that should not be directly copied, the combination of XHTML codes that creates a particular look on a web page should be respected as the creation of an individual, even if it cannot be copyrighted.

Web and Text Editing Software *LO 13.2, 13.6*

Although XHTML is a not difficult to learn, most people find it easier to use a **web editor** such as Adobe's Dreamweaver or any number of free open source programs. You can also write code in a simple text editor like Notepad, Notepad++, or TextEdit for the Mac. Notepad is commonly used as it is free and is included on Windows-based computers. Even a word processing program like Microsoft Word can allow you to save word processing files in HTML format. Writing HTML in a text editor or word processing program has the advantage of letting you focus on the code and then test it, so you gain a better understanding of the code.

web editor—Computer software that creates HTML code automatically as part of the web development process.

Different Ways of Viewing a Site

One advantage of using a text editor like Notepad++ is that it is easy to use, free, and provides some features that will assist you in writing your code. Some features include line numbers, syntax highlighting, WYSIWYG (What You See Is What You Get) printing, word/function completion, and more. Notepad++ also provides a menu for the user to quickly run the code in Google Chrome, Safari, or other browsers.

An advantage of using Web editing software is that it also provides a WYSIWYG interface, making it easy to develop pages quickly. It also provides different panels in which you can work. For example, you may display text in one panel, and the other panel will show how it will appear in a browser. Dreamweaver, like other web editors, gives the user

Websites have become a standard vehicle for communication in the 21st century. Businesses use websites to promote new products, attract customers, conduct purchases, and both announce job openings and receive applications. In a world in which customers, clients, and workers can easily browse for information, it is important for Web developers to create websites that convince visitors to stay and not surf off to another site. Many successful websites immediately capture the visitor's attention, which can be accomplished by loading quickly and by offering text or graphics that visitors find worth their time. Well-done websites highlight key points of the host's message and avoid clutter that obscures those points. Effective websites make use of the interactive nature of the Web, when appropriate, and of the Web's capacity to link the visitor to more information. Using effective techniques to attract and keep Web visitors is clearly an important skill for the future.

Skills in Action: Visit the websites of three different companies. Study several web pages on each site. After your review, write a critique of all three websites, explaining how successful each is in using the tools of the Web—text, graphics, media, and interactivity—to appeal to customers. Identify the specific techniques you believe are effective or ineffective and explain why.

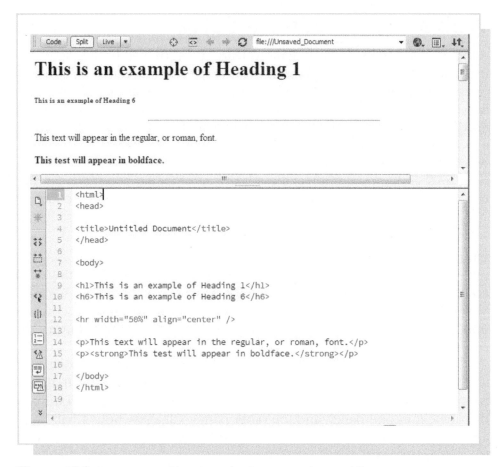

Figure 13.3 *Dreamweaver, like other web editors, gives the user different viewing options that affect whether the html code, the WYSIWYG appearance, or both are displayed.*

viewing options. At the top of the Dreamweaver screen are three buttons that allow the user to toggle the view (see Figure 13.3). Choosing Design means seeing only the WYSIWYG view that emulates what a browser will display. Choosing Code shows only the HTML coding panel. Split displays both the code and how it will appear in the browser. This allows you to work in either HTML mode or a Preview mode, which shows a page being developed as it will appear on the Web. Depending on the viewing mode, different options will be available to the developer.

Features of Web Editors

Generally, web editors provide tools to create many different effects, including these commonly used ones:

- Page backgrounds using color or images
- Text in different sizes and colors
- Wraparound text and other special effects
- Graphics including horizontal rules, bulleted lists, rollover images, and image maps
- Drop-down menus, option buttons, and forms
- Internal and external links

You should look for several key features when evaluating a web editor. Editors like Dreamweaver are full-featured programs that give users a wide variety of tools. Some beginners may feel overwhelmed by these programs, but with practice, users will learn the features and feel comfortable using the programs to develop web pages. As with other digital media software, a key aspect of evaluating web editors is balancing a full array of features with ease of use.

One vital feature is the ability to conduct compatibility checks with different browsers. As noted earlier, all browsers do not necessarily display web pages in exactly the same way, so it is important for Web developers to see how their websites will look in different browsers. A web editing program must have a compatibility check function (see Figure 13.4). Performing a compatibility check helps in isolating and fixing errors when web pages don't display correctly.

Along with ease of use and compatibility checks, you should consider these features in evaluating a web editor:

- **Templates**. Websites often have a set of common elements on most pages. With the templates feature, a developer can create this standardized set of features to ensure they appear on each page in the site in the same way.

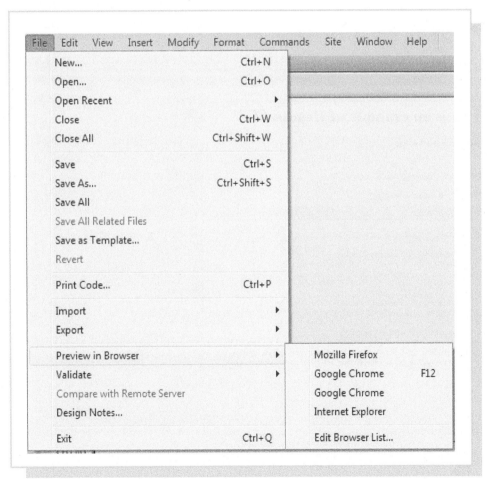

Figure 13.4 *Through the Preview in Browser option, Dreamweaver makes it possible to test a web page with different browsers and different window sizes. Users can add other browsers through the Edit Browser List option.*

- **Media.** A web editor should be able to import video and animation.
- **Interactive elements.** Many websites include elements that require user input. Examples include entering passwords, completing forms, marking checkboxes, adding comments, and selecting options. Some programs have tools that make it possible to drag and drop elements to websites under construction (see Figure 13.5).
- **HTML5, CSS, and JavaScript.** While XHTML code is the building block of websites, other methods of coding, styling, or scripting are in the mainstream, including HTML5, Cascading Style Sheets (CSS), and JavaScript. HTML5 is on the very near horizon. A web editor should have the capability of handling these standard website development tools.
- **Tables/DIV Tags.** Tables have been useful for formatting the layout of a web page. However, CSS and DIV tags are now universally accepted as the layout elements used when creating web pages.

checkpoint

When evaluating a web editor, what are key features to review?

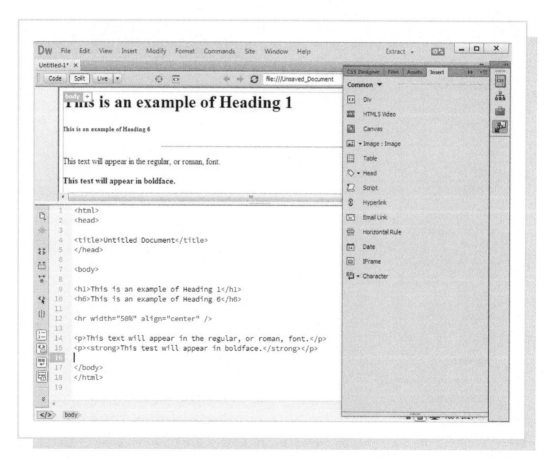

Figure 13.5 *The Forms Control options in Expression, highlighted in red, make it simple to drag and drop interactive elements to a web page. These include boxes for inputting text (the yellow oval), choosing options, or making selections from drop-down menus.*

ACTIVITY 13.2 ▶ Practicing XHTML

Since all web pages are built on the same structure of a DOCTYPE declaration and eight standard tags, it is wise to create these tags in a template file that can be used over and over when creating web pages. Simply open the template file, save as the new filename, and add the page content. This will save time as well as ensure that these basic tags are keyed correctly. This also helps with structuring the web page. So, let's create a template file.

1. Open your web editor.
2. Add the following tags in this order:

   ```
   <!DOCTYPE html>
   <html>
   <head>
           <title>Page Name</title>
   </head>
   <body>
   </body>
   </html>
   ```

3. Save the file in your desired location as: template.html
4. Preview this file in your browser. You should only see the title in the browser tab since there is not content in the body of the page. Now let's use this template file to create a home page for a business that you frequent. Start small but include a heading <h1>, subheading <h2>, a paragraph <p>, some bold text <strong>, some italicized text <em>, a horizontal rule <hr/>, and a list (either ordered <ol> or unordered <ul>). Add two additional tags that are not part of these instructions to individualize your page. Look at Table 13.1 for inspiration. Be sure to save and preview frequently to ensure your page is formatting as you wish. Also, remember that everything will be Times New Roman font, left aligned. This is the default with HTML and we haven't learned styles yet!
5. Open the template.html file if it is not already opened.
6. Click File, Save As and save the file in your desired location as: index.html (index.html is the default filename for the home page of most sites).
7. Change the page title to the name of your business.
8. Click between the open and close body tags and begin creating your page.
   a. Key <h1> Business Name </h1> and press Enter.
   b. Key <h2> Business Address </h2> (make this info up if you don't know it). Press Enter.
   c. Key <p> and add some information about your business </p>. Include some bold and italicized text in this paragraph. Press Enter.
   d. Insert a horizontal rule <hr/>. Press Enter.

e. Create a subheading that identifies a list of information:
   `<h2>List heading </h2>`

f. Create a list of items that your business sells:
   `<ul>`
   `<li>Item 1</li>`
   `<li>item 2</li>`
   `<li>item 3</li>`
   `</iul>`

g. Insert a horizontal rule `<hr/>`.

h. At this point, add to your page some additional content, using two tags that you haven't already used. Keep in mind format and structure. Be sure to add content that enhances your page rather than distracts from it!

i. Save the file and preview in your browser.

Lesson 13.3 > Ensuring Universal Access

The universal nature of web pages means that any web page created in one web editor can be read by any person using a browser to access the Internet. As noted earlier, all browsers do not read all web pages in the same way. However, browser differences are not the only obstacle to accessing web pages.

Obstacles to Universal Access LO 13.5, 13.6

It is possible for everyone to view web pages, but you need to be aware of certain limitations when creating pages. Those limitations stem from the varying capabilities of technological features. These features include the display screen being used, the speed of the computer, the speed of the Internet connection, and the browser being used. A special issue, that combines these areas to some degree, is the question of smartphones or mobile web browsing. Finally, the issue of accessibility for people with disabilities is also important to consider in Web development.

Display

Some computers have larger display screens than others. All displays do not have the same fonts, and some will not be able to display all colors. These and other limitations make it challenging to develop a web page that will appear exactly as you anticipate. Keep this in mind at all times when you are developing a web page so that you can ensure it functions properly. Following these principles will help minimize display-related problems:

- Develop the web page for a lower, rather than higher pixel resolution. While larger monitors capable of 1920 × 1200 resolution have become more common, millions of computer users around the

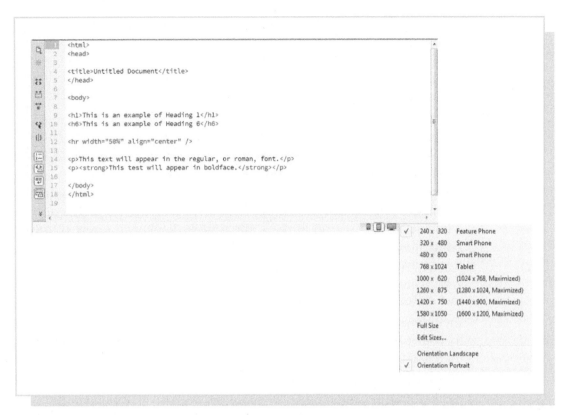

Figure 13.6 *A web page developer can analyze alternative page size options to ensure functionality on various displays.*

world still have smaller monitors. In addition, the integration of tablets makes using a smaller resolution sensible; developing the page for a higher resolution would force users with a smaller screen to scroll left and right or up and down to see key content. Review Figure 13.6 for various screen sizes.

- Avoid font problems in two ways. First, choose common fonts rather than uncommon ones, to make it more likely most computers will have them. Second, specify optional fonts that are similar to each other and provide for the computer to use its default serif or sans serif font if the specified fonts are not present.

Some web editors offer multiple page sizes for viewing web pages (see Figure 13.6). In this case, the developer can ensure the web page functions properly by choosing an alternative page size to see how the page will be displayed.

Download Speed

One of the most important limitations is the speed with which your audience will be able to view your pages. Download speed depends on both the speed of the user's computer and on his or her Internet access. While broadband, or high-speed, access is common, not all users have high-speed Internet connections. In addition, users accessing the Internet from a wireless public Wi-Fi site may be slowed by the amount of traffic on that site, even if the site has high-speed access.

Odds are that your website will be viewed by users with a wide variety of speeds. The best course, then, is to develop your website to be as fast as possible to meet the needs of users with slower computers or connection speeds. After all, if users have to wait for a page to load, they may leave before ever viewing your page. Follow these guidelines to develop faster websites:

- Keep the overall file size of each web page relatively small. The smaller the file size, the faster it will load. Using as few colors and graphical elements as possible helps create smaller files.

- Keep images small and compressed. Specify the height and width of images, which allows the browser to download the image as a background function at the same time it displays the rest of the page. Reusing images helps keep overall file sizes small. If you must have large images, include small thumbnail images on the web page and add a link users can click to display the larger image in a different window.

- Include music, video, and animation only if they are essential to your purpose. These elements all increase file size and thus increase loading time.

- Run error checks on HTML code and CSS styles (which you will read more about in Chapter 14). By fixing errors, you will prevent the user's web browser from being slowed by trying to interpret them.

- Use a host computer that is as fast as possible so that any slowness in loading time is not a problem based on the host, but solely dependent on the user.

Zeynep Demir/Shutterstock.com

Figure 13.7 *With smartphones, people can access the Web virtually anywhere in the world, but the small display can only show a fraction of what is seen on a normal monitor. How can that affect the work of a Web developer?*

Browser

Some compatibility issues are related to browser software. Some functions or formatting commands are not available in all browsers, for instance. This is why it is important when you are developing the website that you check the functionality on various browsers. The web editor may help you by indicating if a particular function is not available to all browsers. Of course, the browser compatibility check previously discussed can help resolve these issues.

Mobile Devices

Display, download speed, and browser type are all factors in the use of smartphones for web browsing (see Figure 13.7). Smartphones have smaller screens than tablets. As a result, mobile devices cannot display as much text as can be seen on a computer screen. Images will be much smaller, too. However, the issue of compatibility goes beyond size. Mobile browsers may have limited capability, such as only being able to interpret a limited set of HTML codes, and load times can be an issue as well.

When developing a website with mobile browsing in mind, follow these suggestions:

- Screen sizes are small, so keeping web pages and images small will help make the page readable and speed access.

- Split large pages into smaller pieces and provide links to additional content.

- Keep content to the essentials, since text can be difficult to read on a small screen; and avoid using animation.

- Limit HTML coding to the basics, such as paragraph and line breaks, heads, strong and emphasis types, unnumbered and numbered lists, and alignment. Many mobile devices can read only a small range of HTML tags.

- Do not use animation. Develop web pages with one column of content, instead of two, for smaller devices. Consider developing web pages with liquid rather than fixed widths. A liquid width specifies the width as a percentage of the user's browser and will resize based on the browser. Fixed column width is specified in pixels and the column does not resize based on the browser.

Accessibility

Many web users have visual, auditory, motor, and other disabilities. These various disabilities can include impaired vision, difficulty hearing, and color-blindness. Designing a web page with these individuals in mind is considered a standard for Web development. The **World Wide Web Consortium (W3C)** has issued two sets of recommendations for accessibility called **Web Content Accessibility Guidelines (WCAG)**. These guidelines call for providing alternatives such as text descriptions for graphical elements; providing adequate contrast between different colors; and providing adequate contrast between text and background. WCAG is primarily for web content developers, web authoring tool developers, web accessibility evaluation tool developers, and others who follow the standards for web accessibility.

Your web development program may have a validation feature that reviews the website design and content for accessibility problems. However, there are also other validation programs you can use. The W3C Validator Service (http://validator.w3.org/) is one example (see Figure 13.8). When you review the notes and potential issues found by the validation program, you are provided with specific information such as line and column numbers and other descriptive text so the issue can be fixed (see Figure 13.9). After you have fixed the issues, you can run the validation program again to ensure the site is accessible. Keep in mind that various coding languages can be checked based on the code used to develop the website. Other codes include HTML5 in experimental mode and HTML for websites with an older version of code. Chapter 17 has more information on Web standards and the accessibility issue.

World Wide Web Consortium (W3C)— Organization that sets standards for the World Wide Web, including such issues as privacy, markup languages, styles, and other issues.

Web Content Accessibility Guidelines (WCAG)— Accessibility standards set by the WC3 for Web developers to follow in order to make websites accessible to individuals with disabilities.

Source: www.validator.w3.org

Figure 13.8 *Expression's Accessibility Checker reviews a website to ensure it is compatible with two sets of W3C recommendations on accessibility. A third option allows the developer to check for compliance with federal government standards.*

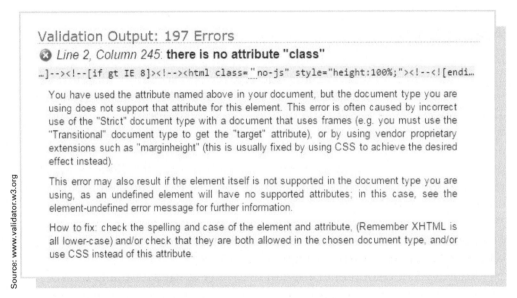

Source: www.validator.w3.org

Figure 13.9 *This is a validation report from an accessibility checker showing errors and how to fix them.*

Dreamweaver, and other web development programs, provide assistance in developing accessible web pages. It is important to consider such assistance when developing websites to meet federal guidelines and to ensure they are effectively designed so that screen readers, for example, can be used. It is important to remember that whatever web development program you use, it cannot completely automate the development process. As the Web developer, you must be careful when coding to make sure you follow the standards and ensure all web content is accessible. This can only be done through careful decision making, planning, development, testing, and evaluation.

Some simple things to consider when developing accessible websites is to make sure you

- use clear visuals and navigation
- supplement audio and video
- develop a site that is keyboard-friendly
- include accessible forms and files
- build in "skip" navigation

When considering your visuals, make sure all images have alternative text in the code or provide descriptive captions. Some browsers refer to this attribute as alt text (alternative text) and some as title text. To supplement audio and videos, closed captioning is essential for videos, and text-based transcripts should be provided as well. Using headings and lists will help with keyboard navigation, and building in "skip" navigation gives the user the option to skip repetitive content and go directly to the content. Screen readers are not the only adaptive technology that may be used. Therefore, ensuring that forms can be completed with adaptive technology is also important for accessibility. Forms should be easily saved as PDF files and aligned with accessibility standards as well. When considering your navigation overall, do not use color as a navigational tool, as screen readers and users who are colorblind will have problems with the navigation.

Ensuring Access by Using XHTML

LO 13.5, 13.6, 13.7, 13.8

To promote improved access on a variety of devices, the W3C has recommended Web developers use XHTML built on the XML (Extensible Markup Language) format. XML is another markup language that offers some options not available in HTML.

The drive behind adopting XHTML is to make code cleaner and more rigorous—to create what is called **well-formed code**, which meets quality standards. The chief difference between HTML and XHTML is that XHTML includes certain rules that were not required in HTML and, therefore, not always followed in documents created using HTML. In approving XHTML, the W3C also *deprecated,* or recommended against using, some tags that had been part of HTML. Deprecated tags include those that browsers interpreted differently or those used for only one browser. By replacing these with codes that all browsers would interpret the same way, the W3C tries to ensure consistency. Learning to adhere to these rules and to use the approved XHTML tags will ensure that any documents you code will meet accepted standards and will remain current and readable in all future browsers.

well-formed code—
Formatting code that meets the quality standards of the coding system.

History

Why is XHTML necessary? HTML arose on a piecemeal basis, and several different versions were developed. While the W3C endorsed some versions of the markup language, developers did not necessarily adopt the most recent recommendations. Many followed tagging practices with which they were familiar, and browsers accepted a wide variety of coding practices. The W3C hopes to make Web access more standardized—and Web coding of higher quality—by adopting XHTML. The W3C first adopted it as a recommendation in 2000.

The key standards of XHTML are the following:

- All documents should begin by identifying the DOCTYPE, which states the markup language in which it is written and the human language in which the content of the web page should be displayed.

- All element and attribute names are lowercase. HTML tags were often a mix of capital and lowercase letters, which could be interpreted differently by different browsers.

- Most start tags must have an end tag. For example, under XHTML standards for well-formed code, any `<p>` tag signaling the beginning of a paragraph must be paired with an end tag (`</p>`). However, as noted in Table 13.1, a few tags are self-closing.

- Tags must be correctly nested, and the order of end tags should mirror the order of start tags. Suppose you wish to format a sentence as both bold and italic. If the start tag for boldface type (`<strong>`) comes before the start tag for italic (`<em>`), then the closing tags should be in reverse order (`</em></strong>`).

- All attribute values should be enclosed in quotation marks. In XHTML, the value would be in quotation marks: `<td colspan="2">`.

validate—To check the code used to generate web pages to make sure it meets quality standards.

Learning to **validate** your pages, as noted previously, for XHTML is one way to make the move from HTML to XHTML or XHTML to HTML5. Validation checks to make sure all code meets the specifications required by the document type.

As HTML5 comes further into the forefront of Web development, it is important to consider some of the new features of HTML5. HTML5 brings about changes with new tags for headers, menus, and navigation. HTML5 does not require a `<head>` tag. By default, browsers will add all elements before the `<body>` tag to the default `<head>` element. HTML5 also provides additional support for audio, video, and other media types, which will eliminate the requirements of media plugins such as Flash. Some of the HTML5 tags are also simpler and compatible with all types of browsers. This, in turn, makes websites developed with HTML5 more compatible for various devices such as smartphones and tablets. There are advantages to both XHTML and

HTML5; however, as a Web developer it is essential for you to stay abreast of changes and updates in the coding environment.

Once a web page or website is completed, you must publish it to make it available to others. The first step in this process is to secure the services of a web server. When users around the world input the URL of your website, they will be loading a copy of your pages from the web server. Remember that the URL is the address of your website and is based on the website domain.

In setting up the web server, you will need a username and password. These security precautions make it possible for only you to access the inner workings of the website, such as uploading files. Having a secure site prevents **hacking**—people gaining unauthorized access to a website. To keep your site secure, you should be sure to keep your login and password secure and use a password that is not easily guessed.

Publishing the website means transferring the files to the server. Typically this is done by means of **File Transfer Protocol (FTP)** software. Some web development software have built-in FTP software. FTP software allows a computer to connect to a remote computer and upload or download files. People who work for the company housing the web server will provide you with the information you need to connect via the server's FTP site. Figure 13.10 shows FileZilla, a common FTP program.

hacking—The unauthorized modification of a website, usually in ways that distort the original purpose of the site or seek to harm the site's owner.

File Transfer Protocol (FTP)—A communications protocol used to transfer files from one computer to another over a network and often used to upload web pages to a web server.

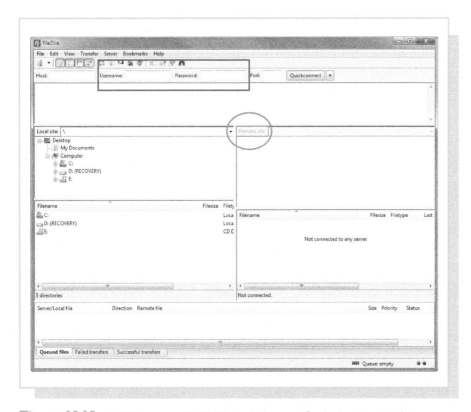

Figure 13.10 *An FTP program like FileZilla includes areas for the user to enter the username and password (highlighted in red). Once connected, the remote site is displayed separately from the local computer. Files on the local computer can be selected and then uploaded to the remote computer or files there can be selected and downloaded to the local device.*

checkpoint

What variables affect how a web page is loaded and displayed, and how can Web developers minimize the difficulties these variables cause?

ACTIVITY 13.3 ▶ **Guidelines for Developing Faster Web Pages**

1. Create a web page that lists the guidelines to develop faster web pages that were identified in this chapter. Use a web editor available in your classroom.

    a. Open the template.html file you create in Activity 13.2. Click File, Save As and save the file in the location of your choice as guidelines.html.

2. Add an unordered (bulleted) list of five or more guidelines that can be used to develop faster web pages.

3. Add a page title that will display in the title bar of the browser.

4. Check the spelling of all text.

5. Run the program's equivalent of the accessibility checker. Report any errors to your instructor or run a report.

6. Preview the file in several browsers. Write down any differences you see.

7. If available, use an FTP software such as FileZilla to upload your page. Get instructions from your instructor on the Web service location and uploading procedures.

Key Concepts

▸ There are differences between a Web developer and Web designer. Web developers are more involved in the back end of the web development process including coding, technical aspects, and functionality. Web designers focus on the front end of the website and deal with Web graphics and interface design and the appearance of a website. *LO 13.1*

▸ There are several ways to develop a website and things to consider throughout the development process. They include website builder programs, template websites, weblogs, and coding it yourself. It is important to consider time, cost, and quality. *LO 13.2 and 13.3*

▸ XHTML and HTML5 are coding languages that identify what and how content will be displayed on web pages. Web browsers interpret XHTML and HTML5 tags to display web pages. *LO 13.8*

▸ Certain tags are needed to mark the opening and closing of various components of a web page. The content of the web page is contained within the two codes <body> and </body>. *LO 13.4 and 13.7*

▸ The body of a document is composed of any number of elements, each of which may be further described by attributes. Some attributes are themselves characterized by values. *LO 13.7*

▸ One way to learn HTML code is by reviewing source code from web pages that have design elements you like. Browsers make it possible to reveal the source code underlying the page. *LO 13.7*

▸ How a web page is displayed depends not only on how it is developed through appropriate coding, but also on the type of device on which the page is being viewed, the speed of the computer and Internet access of the user, and the type of browser. *LO 13.5*

▸ Web developers can take steps to minimize the variations in loading speed and in the appearance of their web pages to try to minimize barriers to access. *LO 13.6*

▸ The proliferation of smartphones, tablets, and other mobile browsing devices raises questions and challenges, as the display on these devices is very small compared to that of a computer. *LO 13.6*

▸ The World Wide Web Consortium (W3C) recommends various practices for making it possible for individuals with disabilities to have access to Web content. *LO 13.6*

▸ The W3C also recommends that Web developers adopt XHTML, a more rigorous version of HTML, to code Web documents in order to make their display more standard across different browsers and devices. However, HTML5 is on the forefront of the coding world. It is important to stay current with changes in coding languages. *LO 13.8*

Review and Discuss

1. Explain how XHTML causes browsers to display web pages in similar ways. *LO 13.5*

2. Describe the components of tags and XHTML. *LO 13.4*

3. Explain the purpose of a closing tag. *LO 13.4 and 13.7*

4. Identify and explain the part of the following code that would be the attribute and that which is the value of the attribute: <h1 align="center"></h1>. Write your own example. *LO 13.7*

5. Differentiate between an empty element and one that is not empty. Give examples of empty tags. *LO 13.4 and 13.7*

6. Create a list of three challenges to Web development. *LO 13.5*

7. Discuss the three features of access to the Internet that may cause limitations in how a web page is viewed. *LO 13.5 and 13.6*

8. Evaluate why a developer should consider creating a web page for a lower pixel resolution as opposed to a higher resolution. *LO 13.5 and 13.6*

9. Summarize how font issues can be avoided. *LO 13.5 and 13.6*

10. Describe what features to consider when designing web pages that may be viewed on a mobile device and explain why. *LO 13.5 and 13.6*

11. Identify and explain the recommendations for accessibility issued by the W3C. *LO 13.6*

12. Justify the change from HTML to XHTML and from XHTML to HTML5. *LO 13.8*

13. Compare and contrast HTML, XHTML, and HTML5. *LO 13.8*

14. Apply XHTML standard formatting to the following HTML code: *LO 13.7 and 13.8*

    <!DOCTYPE html PUBLIC "-//W3C//DTD XHTML 1.0 Transitional//EN" "http://www.w3.org/TR/xhtml1/DTD/xhtml1-transitional.dtd">
    <Html xmlns="http://www.w3.org/1999/xhtml">
    <head>
    <title>Find the XHTML errors!<title>
    </head><body><h1>This could be the Banner for the web page.</h1>
    <ul><li>This is an unordered list.
    <li>This is an unordered list.</li>
    </ul></body></Html>

15. Construct a URL for a website for yourself and explain why you chose the URL and the extension. *LO 13.2*

Apply

1. Open the template file you created in Activity 13.2. Click File, Save As and save the file as lost_dog.html in a folder named **13_Apply1_lost_dog.** Copy the image file lost_dog.jpg into this same folder. From your student data files open the **lost_dog** text file and copy the text between the open and close <body> tags in the lost_dog.html file. Add code to edit the text so that the page becomes an information page about a lost dog. Include at least 10 tags or attributes. Also include the image tag, using the **lost_dog** image from student data files. Don't forget to add alt text to the image. Refer to Table 13.1 for tag examples. Save as **13_Apply1_lost_dog** in a folder named **13_Apply1_lost_dog**. Copy the **lost_dog** image to this same folder. Preview the file in a browser. Correct any coding errors. *LO 13.7*

2. Open the template file you created in Activity 13.2. Click File, Save As and save the file as **13_Apply2_teamwork.html** to a folder named **13_Apply2_teamwork.** Using the Internet, research HTML tags and attributes to create a web page about teamwork. The page should include two paragraphs. Paragraph one should include information on why employers value workers who are good team members. In paragraph two, describe your personal experience with teamwork as either part of a team on the job, at home, as part of a sport or hobby, or in class. Include successes and issues that you experienced while trying to work with a team. Include at least two pictures that demonstrate teamwork. Be sure the images are saved to the same folder as the html file, alternative/title text is included, and that the image filenames are short with no capital letters and no spaces. Choose html tags and attributes to create a well-structured, easy-to-read web page. Consider headings, paragraphs, horizontal rules, and more. Be sure to include a page title and heading. Save and preview your work in a browser and correct any errors. *LO 13.7*

3. Using the Internet, find a local or national service learning organization. Some examples may include a homeless coalition, a women's shelter, or a food bank. Carefully review the design of the website. Summarize what you like and dislike about the website by listing at least three positive and three negative characteristics of the website design. Open the template file you created in Activity 13.2. Click File, Save As and save the file as **13_Apply3_service.html** in a folder named **13_Apply3_service.** Create a web page that includes a title and a heading as well as a paragraph describing the service learning organization. Also include your two separate lists of the positive and negative characteristics. Each list should have its own heading and be separated with a horizontal rule. Include an image with alternative/title text that is a hyperlink to the service learning organization's web page that you reviewed. Save and preview your work in a browser and correct any errors. *LO 13.7*

4. Write a review of a recent event you attended. This could be a sporting event, a concert, or a movie you went to see. It may even be a competition for BPA or FBLA or a leadership conference you attended. Open the template

you created in Activity 13.2. Save your file as ***13_Apply4_event.html*** in a folder named ***13_Apply4_event***. Create a web page for this review. Include the following in your review: date of event, location of event, cost of event (if applicable), a one-paragraph summary of the event, a one-paragraph reflection of your opinion of the event, and other important details. Make sure you include a title and heading for the web page. On your web page, include two appropriate images that enhance your review. Use the width and height attributes to resize the images. Include a hyperlink to a website about the event. Consider appropriate layout and design as you structure your web page. Preview the page in a browser, correct any errors, and then follow your instructor's directions for uploading to a web server. *LO 13.7*

5. Open the template you created in Activity 13.2. Save your file as ***13_Apply5_bio.html*** in a folder named ***13_Apply5_bio***. Create a biographical web page on a computer science innovator; for example, Steve Jobs, Bill Gates, Grace Hopper, Tim Berners-Lee, or others. Format the biography using the tags and attributes you have learned in this chapter. Consider appropriate web page layout and design. Include the following on the biographical web page:

   - Innovator's name
   - Birth date and place
   - Date of death (if applicable)
   - Picture and a hyperlink
   - Summary of why this person is considered to be a computer science innovator Preview the page in a browser and correct any errors. Have one other student review your web page and provide constructive layout and design feedback. Make any necessary changes and then follow your instructor's directions for uploading your page to a web server. *LO 13.7*

Explore

1. Open the template file you created in Activity 13.2. Save the file as ***13_Explore1_deprecated.html***. Search the Internet for a list of deprecated HTML tags and attributes. Using a web editor, create a web page with a list of at least 10 of those tags and attributes. Include a title and a heading for the web page. Include a paragraph with an explanation of what it means to deprecate a tag or attribute. **Note**: In order for the browser to display the greater than and less than symbols as text characters rather than tag symbols, use < and ≶ before and after the tag name. For example, to show the center tag as text in a browser, key: <center≶ *LO 13.5 and 13.7*

2. Search the Internet for a list of essential Web developer job skills. Open the template file you created in Activity 13.2. Save the file as ***13_Explore2_web_developer_skills.html*** in a folder named ***13_Explore2_web_developer_skills***. Create a web page that

identifies at least six of those skills in an ordered list. Include a page title and a heading. Below the list, insert a horizontal rule and add an appropriate image that represents good Web development or design. If necessary, rename the image to a short filename using only lowercase letters and no spaces (e.g., webdesign.jpg). Use the width and height attributes to adjust the image size but be sure to keep the dimensions proportional. Below the image, add a horizontal rule and include hyperlinks to indicate the sources for at least two websites where you found your information. Make sure you provide alternate text for the image. Make sure the hyperlinks are on separate lines. Make sure your image is saved in the same folder as your html file. Preview your page in a browser and correct any errors. *LO 13.5 and 13.7*

3. Project management is one skill essential to Web development. Open *project_management* from the student data files. Use these questions to create an FAQ (Frequently Asked Questions) web page about project management. This web page should include the questions from the *project_management* file and answers you provide to those questions based on your research. As you design this web page, using tags and attributes you learned in this chapter, consider using different formatting options for the questions as opposed to the answers. For example, use a bold format for the headings with a larger heading size and no bold formatting and a smaller heading size for the answers. Consider layout and design as you structure your page. Preview the page and then follow your instructor's directions for uploading to a web server. Save your page as *13_Apply3_project_management.html* in a folder named *13_Apply3_project_management*. *LO 13.7*

Academic Connections

Math: You decide to start a web development business from home. You'll need to save money to get started. You've made the following shopping list: 17-inch color monitor, computer, keyboard, mouse, Web design software, and color printer. You'll also need a scanner and a photo editor. For these items, you have identified the following costs:

Monitor	$299.00
Computer	$950.00
Keyboard and mouse	$39.00
web development software	$650.00
Color laser printer	$799.00
Scanner	$158.00
Photo editor	$450.00

After a careful study, you decide it would be best to purchase a collection of software that includes animation, video editing, and other multimedia editors. Therefore, you won't be purchasing the web development software or the photo editing software separately, but instead you'll purchase an entire collection for $999.00.

What is the total amount you need for all of the purchases? If you have one client so far that has agreed to pay $1,800.00 for you to create his or her web page, how much money will you have made or will you still need to make in order to break even? What would the total cost be with an 8.25 percent sales tax? Save your responses in a document as *13_AC_math*.

Science: Go to http://www.schooltube.com and search for "science fair." Choose three of the videos to watch. Write the steps down for each one of them. Create a web page for each project, summarizing the science projects step by step. Save your web pages as *13_AC_science_project1*, *13_AC_science_project2*, and *13_AC_science_project3* in a folder named *13_AC_science*.

Chapter 14

Web Design

Learning Outcomes

▶ **14.1** Explain the importance of content in web design.

▶ **14.2** Organize content and plan navigation.

▶ **14.3** Describe the differences between designing for the web and for print.

▶ **14.4** Use templates and style sheets to achieve consistent design.

▶ **14.5** Select and incorporate images in web pages.

Key Terms

- alternate text
- banner ad
- cascading style sheets (CSS)
- cell padding
- cell spacing
- hexadecimal number
- home page
- hyperlink
- index page
- navigation link
- rollover
- site map
- template
- thumbnail
- website
- wireframe

Full of hundreds of millions of websites, the Internet displays an amazing variety in how to present and organize content—and presenting and organizing information is the key task of web design. Web designers focus on web graphic and interface design and the appearance of a website. The designer works to make it easy for visitors to understand how to navigate through the website in order to find the information they need.

Think about the websites you have visited. Which ones do you go back to again and again? How efficient is the navigation? Was the website designed with appropriate colors? How does the design of the website help you use the site?

When you're preparing to write a paper for one of your courses, you do not begin by writing the conclusion. You begin by planning and start with an outline that provides a scope of the structure and overall argument of the paper. When a company is designing a new product, it does not begin with the packaging or the color of the product. Instead, designers carefully consider the purpose of the product and how it will function. They then structure the look of the product around its function. The same thing is true when designing a **website**. You have to begin with the big picture and ask these key questions: What content will be provided on the website? What information will need to be gathered to develop the content? How will the navigation work? What fonts, colors, and images will be included in the website? Good web design begins with informational design and proceeds to navigation and interface design. Much planning is involved in the process.

website—One or more web pages linked together in an organized collection.

Figure 14.1 *Planning a website is often a collaborative process requiring the input of several interested parties.*

Fancy/Jupiter Images/Getty Images

Planning Content *LO 14.1 and 14.2*

When designing a website, it is easy to get caught up in the graphic design elements of colors and backgrounds, fonts, and images. Using these elements to make the site attractive can be exciting. However, you should never get so involved in these elements that you forget the most essential element of any website—the content. Without content, any web page is just decoration. Without content, your audience will not be satisfied and will not return to your site. Without content, you have no reason to design a page. Always keep this in mind. Business viewers come to a page to seek information. They want to get information or learn something, and they want to find the information easily. Make this your primary design goal. Continually ask yourself, "Does this feature show how the company can meet the needs of the audience?"

First Things First

The first thing to consider when thinking about a website is the goal of the site. To address this issue, a web designer must ask more specific questions:

- Who is the audience or target market for this website? What are their needs? What are they looking for? What characteristics do they have, in terms of age, income, and interests?

- What product or service does the site make available to this audience? That is, what does the business sponsoring the site want visitors to come away with?

Whether you are designing a site for the company you work for or are creating one for a client, these questions should be central to your design work.

You can begin designing your site by starting a planning document including some initial ideas on what content the site might contain and what information must be gathered to provide appropriate content. You can always add to these later, of course, but it is good to start out with some basics. Figure 14.2 shows such a list for a website for a catering company.

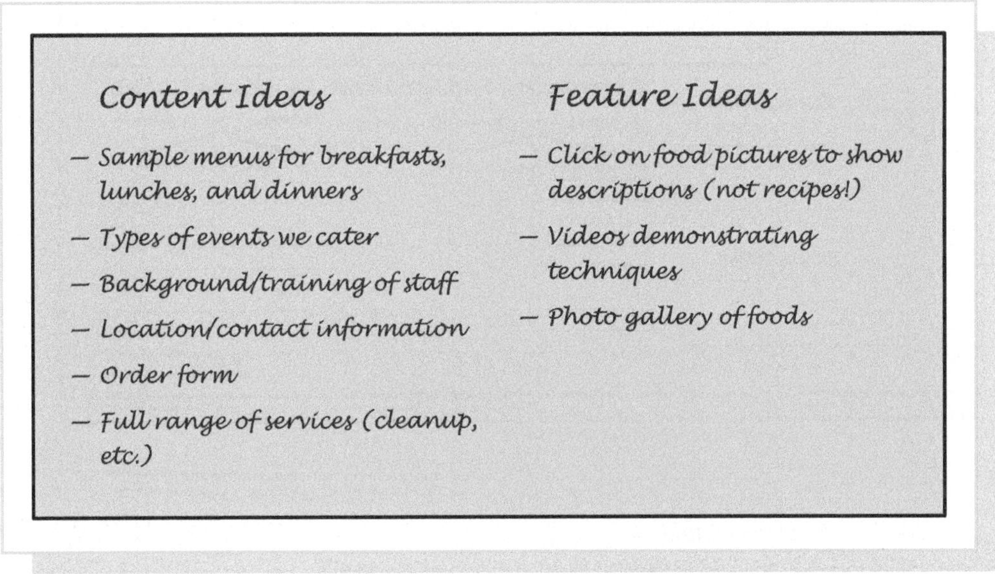

Content Ideas

— Sample menus for breakfasts, lunches, and dinners

— Types of events we cater

— Background/training of staff

— Location/contact information

— Order form

— Full range of services (cleanup, etc.)

Feature Ideas

— Click on food pictures to show descriptions (not recipes!)

— Videos demonstrating techniques

— Photo gallery of foods

© Cengage Learning®

Figure 14.2 *The initial planning document for a website should include some ideas pertaining to the kinds of content that will be included. The final website will not necessarily include all of these items, but it is good to have some basis on which to start.*

Outlining the Site

Once you have preliminary ideas on what content to include in the website, it is time to begin planning in earnest. The first step is to determine the structure for the site's content.

Many designers find it helpful to design web pages using a series of sketches with arrows to linked pages. This visualization process is called **wireframing**. The design of the "skeleton" of a website can be thought of in three ways: information design, navigation design, and interface design. Wireframing is how these components come together to determine the relationship between these components. A sample wireframe is provided in Figure 14.3.

Another way of planning the structure of the site is to use a graphic that shows the hierarchy of pages within the site in a way similar to an organizational chart (see Figure 14.4). Notice that all the main sections branch from the **home page**, the main page of the site (also often referred to as the index page).

wireframing—A blueprint for design tasks; it includes elements a designer will need to consider.

home page—The main page of a website, which is generally the first page visitors will see.

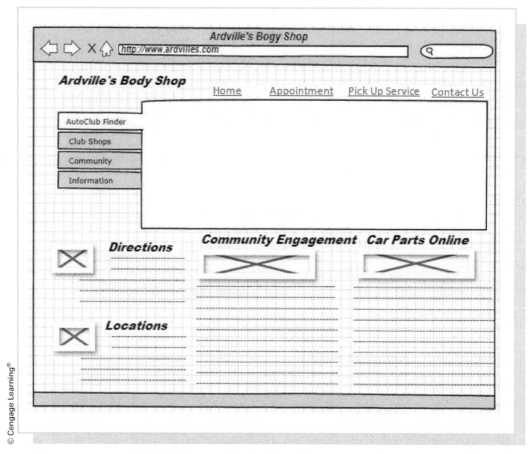

Figure 14.3 *A sample wireframe.*

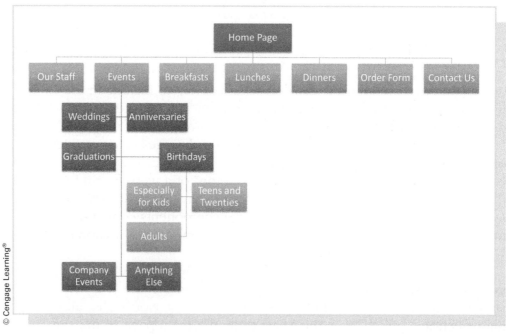

Figure 14.4 *This chart shows part of a possible structure for the website of the catering company. In this format, you can easily see how different pages are related to one another.*

The main headings in Figure 14.4 could serve as major components for the website. In this example, only one of these main sections is broken down further to subsections—six kinds of events that the catering company typically handles—and only one of those is broken down further into sub-subsections—three types of birthday parties. Clearly, though, the other main section headings could be divided further.

When the site is being designed, each section heading would appear on the website's home page and a link that opens the page would be provided. In fact, these main components often appear on every web page in the site, making it possible for visitors to get to the main sections from anywhere in the site. These section headings thus serve as the user's main **navigation links** for getting around the page.

As the content is an important component of an effectively designed website, you must take the time to plan so that your target audience can find information easily. It is important to group similar content together. You are then able to design appropriate components and label navigation properly. Figure 14.5 provides an example of these principles.

navigation link—The means of guiding a website visitor from one page to another within the site.

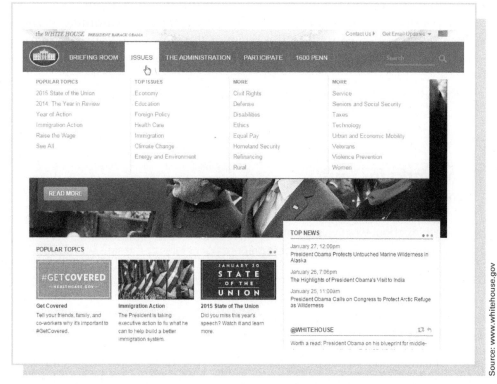

Source: www.whitehouse.gov

Figure 14.5 *The website for the White House has seven main sections in the menu panel across the top, but some—like the Issues section—are divided into many more subcategories. However, the design of the site makes it easy to select the specific issue and find information.*

Supplementing the Navigation Links

Websites typically include two additional tools for helping visitors navigate: a search function and a site map. Links to both should be available on all pages.

You have probably used a search function to try to find specific information on a website, so you recognize the importance of this feature. Web visitors are often busy and want to find what they are looking for quickly. If they cannot find it from the navigation links, they will want to search for it. If they cannot search for it, they will more than likely leave the site.

A **site map** shows all or nearly all the pages in the website, organized to show their relationship to one another. The purpose of a site map is to help visitors see the overall structure of the website so they can more easily find the specific information they want. When you develop a chart like the one in Figure 14.4, this can serve as a model for the site map when all components are included. This chart would then be provided on a single web page. A site map is a secondary resource for visitors, not the main tool for navigating the site. Visitors go to the site map when they are not able to find what they're looking for in the main navigational system. To be effective, a site map should be comprehensive, listing at the very least all the main pages and showing their hierarchical relationship to one another. The site map will not show links across pages that are not part of the same group of pages. Each link on the site map should be a dynamic **hyperlink** that allows the user to click on it to reach the desired page.

If you follow the organization detailed in the chart outlining your website, that structure will be the basis of the site map. Your site map must accurately show the final structure of the website.

site map—A single web page that lists and organizes all the web pages in a site to allow users to find and move to specific pages.

hyperlink—Text or a web object that links to another web page.

What Works for You?

One of the best ways to find effective ways of organizing web content is within reach of your mouse—simply browse the Web. As you go about your everyday web use, think about what you like and don't like about each website you visit. Then, think about how you can apply the best practices principles to the sites you design.

Creating Content *LO 14.1*

After planning the structure of the website, the next step is to create the content—or obtain it from another person who is responsible for the content. Web content should always be focused and concise. People who visit web pages are often looking for information quickly. It is your challenge to provide them with what they want.

Drafting the Text

Writing content for the Web is like writing any other kind of text. The first principle to keep in mind is to remember your target audience. Think about what the audience needs, and write text to meet those needs.

Bear in mind that people who visit websites may be in a hurry. They typically are not interested in reading long pieces of text. The key, then, is to provide information as briefly and effectively as possible. Generally, it is a good idea to keep the text concise on the opening pages of the site or of each section and to place pages with more text deeper in the page structure. Links to those more extensive text pages will make it easy for visitors to find the extended information. If pages seem too dense with text, break the information into one or more pages.

How much text is right for one page? Guidelines typically indicate 250 to 300 words per page is appropriate. Internet search engines can then identify the content and index it properly. However, there are times when there needs to be much more than 250 to 300 words per web page. The key is that every web page should contain enough content to convey the message, but no more. The best approach is to make sure each page focuses on one major topic. If it addresses more than one major topic, break the second topic onto another page and provide links connecting the two. If you have several related topics, consider having a summary page that lists each major topic and links to each separate page.

Figure 14.6 *When planning text for a web page, think about how content is provided on web pages you like and how little you have to scroll or search for the content.*

Godluz/Shutterstock.com

Refining the Text

After writing any content, it is always a good idea to edit it carefully. Read through the copy to make sure it is well organized and clear. Think about your audience's wants and needs and whether the text meets their expectations. Think about what background on the topic your audience might not have and explain any points that need clarification.

Spelling and Grammar Check for the Website

Remember to read all your web copy carefully for errors before publishing. The website presents your company's image to the world. A website with spelling or grammatical errors looks unprofessional and may undermine visitors' confidence in the company's products or services. Most web editors have spell checker options, and word processing programs have both spelling and grammar checkers. Use them to check content before you post the files. However, do not rely on these tools alone. These checks can easily bypass errors such as using "hear" in place of "here" or "their" instead of "there." Consider having someone else proofread your content before you publish, as a fresh pair of eyes can identify problems you may have not seen.

Skills in Action: Visit three different websites and study several pages on each site. Review the content carefully to see if you find any errors in grammar or spelling. Also, make note of any vague or unclear statements. Write a paragraph evaluating the content of each site. Be sure to proofread your evaluations!

Getting Approval *LO 14.2*

Unless you are designing a website for your own business, you are working for someone else. Therefore, there may be someone else who has overall responsibility for the website. This person will have the final say on what should be in the website, how it should be structured, and how visitors will navigate within it. At each stage in the design process, (information design, navigation design, and interface design) you need to get that person's approval of the approach you are suggesting. Show him or her the wireframe, a chart providing an overview of the organization, or the site map before beginning to work with content. If you are writing the content, show it to the person with the authority to approve the site in draft stage and after it has been refined. It is much easier to change the web structure or the content of web pages *before* the actual development of the website rather than after.

Organizing and Naming Website Files *LO 14.2*

You should create a separate file for each web page. Make it a habit to save any files you intend to use on your website into just one folder. Doing so will simplify the gathering process.

The following conventions for naming web files are good guidelines to follow:

- Use lowercase letters only rather than a mix of capital and lowercase.
- Do not use spaces, but use hyphens or underscores between words.
- Use keywords to describe the content on each page in the filename for that page.
- Limit URLs to a maximum of 60 characters.

index page—Another name for the home page, which should be named "index.html" or "index.htm".

You must create an **index page**. This page is the filename of the home page, and is the first page browsers will automatically default to when a domain name is entered. The index page ends with the extension "index.htm" or "index.html". These labels are not displayed by browsers when they display the URL, but they are part of the filename.

Using descriptive keywords is important for getting your website recognized by Internet search engines. These programs use keywords to generate lists of sites as a response to search queries from users. Having the right keywords can help your website show up in these search results.

Several naming guidelines will help ensure that your pages can be viewed by everyone in your audience. The first is related to your extension options. Web pages are saved with .html or .htm extensions. There is no real difference between the two. The .htm extension was adopted originally for computers running under early versions of Microsoft Windows because filename extensions were limited to only three characters. That is no longer the case, so it makes sense to use the full file extension, .html. The web editor you use may be able to set a default file extension so that all files you save will be saved with the same extension.

checkpoint

What are three ways to help users find information in a website?

ACTIVITY 14.1 ▶ Planning a Website

1. Use the data file *planning* to begin planning a website for your new lawn care business. Keep in mind this website can be used for others to find out about your business and possibly hire your services.

2. Add more text boxes as needed, but use the ones given as a minimum.

3. Save the plan as *14_Activity1_planning*.

Lesson 14.2 ▶ Organizing Content and Planning Navigation

In Unit 2, you learned about how to use the principles of design to create attractive and effective print designs. It may seem, then, that discussion of designing for the Web is not necessary as you have already learned about design. However, as you will see, websites present special challenges for web designers that are different from those encountered in print design.

Web Design Versus Print Design *LO 14.3*

Web pages may appear to be like print, but they have major differences. One key difference is that the print designer knows what size the print product will be, how colors will print, and how fonts will appear. Web designers do not have certainty in any of those areas due to the fact that different browsers, different monitor sizes and resolutions, and different operating systems can all affect the size of the web page and the look of colors and fonts. Web designers, then, need to create designs to accommodate these variations.

A second difference is in the tools or design elements available to a designer. Some print products—such as novels and many nonfiction books—have very few elements to design. Pages are filled mainly with simple text. While print products like magazines, brochures, or cookbooks have more design elements, print does not offer the variety of elements available in web designs, which generally include images and interactive elements as well as text.

Another difference is in the attitudes and expectations that the user brings to the product. People are more likely to read an entire book than they are to read an entire website. True, some people may read only a chapter in a book, and others may scan the book's index to locate some specific piece of information. However, with a website, visitors almost always pick and choose which pages to investigate. Website visitors are also likely to make decisions about whether to stay on the website fairly quickly—faster than they might in judging whether or not to read a book. Therefore, web designers need to make designs that are clear, easy to understand, attractive, and appealing. Figure 14.7 shows two promotional pieces for this textbook: a page from a print catalog and a website. Notice how brief the basic information at the website is—and how hot links at the bottom of the page (footer) will take the visitor to additional pages that provide even more information than found in the catalog listing.

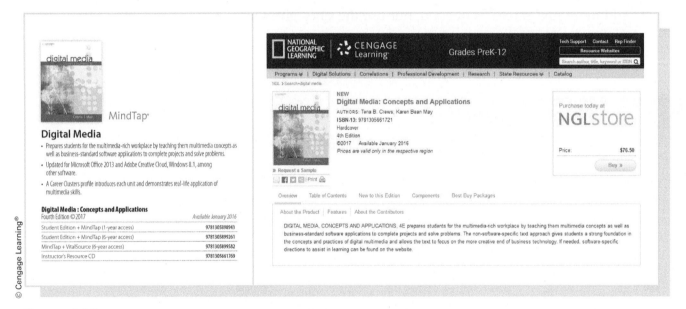

Figure 14.7 *A page from a print catalog (left) and a website for the same product (right).*

Finally, people interact with web and print products differently. With print, people read for information or enjoyment, typically moving one page at a time and generally moving in the same direction, from beginning to end. With a website, the designer does not know where a visitor will first enter the site—it may not be the home page if a search result leads the visitor to one of the pages with detailed content on a particular topic—and the designer does not know how the visitor will move through the site. What the designer can count on, though, is that many visitors to the website will want to interact with the content on the site. They do not simply want to read the information. Many will want to use built in navigation, choosing where to go by making selections within various menus viewing larger versions of images, filling out order forms, or responding to questions. The web designer has to keep this in mind and invite the visitor's interaction.

Organizing Web Pages *LO 14.4*

In Lesson 14-1, you learned about how to organize the website, and you learned about the importance of having main headings that group the website's content into topical areas with subcategories within them. As a web designer, you not only have to think about the organization of the site but also how it will appear on users' screens. Before you can begin to think about issues like fonts and colors, you have to address how the screen will be organized.

Planning Navigation

Planning navigation is essential in designing a web page. The navigation system is the main way of providing information to your audience. One common means of navigation is through a series of menus or other linking components. The navigation is generally found across the top.

Figure 14.8 shows the main headings for the catering website. One rule of thumb for choosing the location of these links is to go by the number of main divisions to the site. If you have ten or fewer main divisions, the panels can fit across the top. If you have more than ten, they may be too crowded along the top and would be better along the left side. Moody's Catering Company, with eight main divisions, conveniently has the links across the top.

Created and captured by Tena B. Crews

Figure 14.8 *You can place navigation links across the top of the page when there are ten or fewer. Notice the home page receives one of the spots in the top navigation links, making it possible for visitors to return to that point from any page.*

Organizing the Page

Typically the top area of a web page identifies the company or group publishing the site and includes very important functions or links. Which functions or links are important depends on the purpose of the site. At the home page of a publishing company, shown in Figure 14.9, a key function is to make it easy for visitors to find a book and make a purchase. Thus, the search function—highlighted in the figure by the red rectangle—is prominent at the top of the page. Generally, it is good to have the search function towards the top.

© Cengage Learning®

Figure 14.9 *This publisher's website shows the branding at the top, two major components, eye-catching images, and additional navigation in the footer.*

The navigational links should be repeated in the footer. The footer also holds the copyright mark and date or links to a separate copyright page. Links to the site map are typically found in the footer, as is a link to contact the organization publishing the site.

The main area of the web page is where the text and graphics will be displayed. As discussed previously, how much text to display on a page is often debated. Web visitors do not expect all the important content to be immediately visible and are willing to accept the need to scroll to some degree. However, the *most* important information should be placed **above the fold**. Above the fold is a web design term that identifies the area users can see without scrolling down. If interesting, informative information is not placed above the fold, users may not scroll down or may even navigate away from your page quickly and not return to your site. If they have to scroll too far, it is best to split the page into two or more pages. Provide links to the other related pages both at the bottom and the top of each page to make it easier for visitors to move among the pages.

However, many websites are designed in a more visual manner. Figure 14.9 provides a glimpse of one such site. Everything shown in Figure 14.9 is above the fold and you can see the branding at the top, two major components, eye-catching images, and additional navigation in the footer. These are all key elements of good web design.

Browse other websites to see how much text they have and how you respond to the amount of text. Look at the way the site divides and organizes topics and provides navigational aids. Adopt the approaches you find most user-friendly.

Futher Organizing your Web Page

In the past, tables were exclusively used to help web designers organize content. They may still be used today, but most designers use <div> tags, which create divisions of content. These add structure and stability to the design and allow for better control of the placement of content.

Web designers used tables because they provided an easy way to organize content. However, when compared to organizing content with <div>, tables are slower to load and not as flexible. However, tables are many times used to organize numerical data. If you are viewing the code for a page using tables, the tag for tables is <table>, the tag for cells is <td>, and the tag for new rows is <tr>. As in a spreadsheet program, tables are made of units called cells. Each cell is the intersection of at least one row and one column. Changing **cell padding** within each cell allows you to set the amount of space that borders the information in the cell. Setting the **cell spacing** determines the amount of space between cells. Cell padding and spacing are important when using CSS and <div> tags for content organization.

The <div>, or division, code is a part of Cascading Style Sheets (CSS) briefly described in Chapter 13. You will read more about CSS in the next lesson. Designers can use the code to split the web page into multiple sections, and nest, images, animation, text, and objects within each division. In fact, you can nest divisions within divisions. As mentioned previously, there are key areas of design to consider: information design, navigation design, and interface design. Information design is the placement and presentation of the information, but it is important to think about how all of that plays into understanding the content. Therefore, the content should be prioritized and presented in a way that enhances clear communication. Navigation design obviously allows the user to move from one web page to another or within a web

above the fold—The area users can see on the web page without scrolling down.

cell padding—The space within a cell that separates or pads the text or image within the cell.

cell spacing—The amount of space between cells.

page. However, the navigation should be integrated with the content so that the user sees the relationship between the links. Interface design is dealing more with elements that facilitate the usability of the website. For example, drop-down menus, check boxes, radio buttons, and action buttons are a few elements of good interface design that allow the visitor to efficiently use the website.

Using Templates LO 14.5

Once you have settled on the overall look for your website, you can make sure the look is consistent by using **templates**. A template has two types of areas. One type is common to all pages—these are the areas that will not change. The other type is the open area where individual page content will appear.

Some web editors make creating templates relatively easy. In Dreamweaver and Expression, templates are called *master pages.* Templates can also be taught in XHTML. Pages are divided into a head area and an area for sections called "Content PlaceHolders." These sections hold all the unique content, the material specific to each page. All design elements that should appear on every page must be placed outside the "Content PlaceHolder" area. Figure 14.9 (Moody's Catering Company) shows the banner and main menu options that would appear on every page of the catering company's website. Figure 14.10 shows how one of the specific pages (Venues) would look.

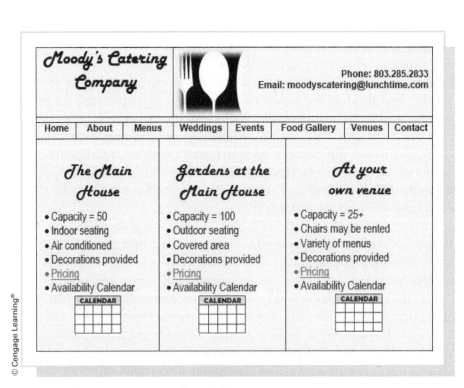

Figure 14.10 *Content that is unique to each page appears in the Content PlaceHolder area. The standard master page comes with one of these placeholders, though the web designer can add more.*

ACTIVITY 14.2 ▶ **Creating a Website Using a Template Program**

1. Create the index page of the lawn care company you made a plan for in Activity 14-1. Use a free online web creation site such as Weebly.com or Wix.com. Sites such as these provide predesigned templates that make creating a well-designed website simple and quick.

   a. Access weebly.com, wix.com or other web creation site and create an account.

   b. Choose a template that complements not only your website purpose, but also your design desires. Make sure the template will also appeal to your target audience.

   c. Create the home page of your website. Include navigation, images, and content as you see fit. Note: You may wish to look at lawn care websites that are already on the Internet to get ideas and inspiration.

2. Once your website has been created, publish the site and submit the site URL according to your teacher's instructions.

Lesson 14.3 ▶ Designing Page Elements

When considering page element design, think about how you want text to wrap, where you want paragraphs to begin, and how you want text aligned. When using CSS, the "word-wrap" syntax allows for text wrap. The default syntax is "normal," which allows words to only be broken at allowable break points. Other XHTML code and CSS syntax can impact text and image alignment as well as paragraph development. One great temptation is to use every design element possible to create pages so that each one has its own personality. However, such an approach would be chaotic. Websites should look coherent, so all pages look similar. This consistency helps create an identity that supports company branding.

A consistent approach has another benefit, too. With a standard layout and the same treatment for design elements recurring throughout each page, visitors to the site know what to expect as they navigate from one page to another. The same design issues apply to printed books such as this text. Notice that elements are similar from one chapter to another, with fonts, sizes, features, and images placed in the same positions each time you encounter them. Those design standards should also be used when designing a website. Consistency of design is one way to make it easy for your audience to find what it is seeking.

Using Design Elements *LO 14.5*

Once you have set the general layout of your web pages, you need to choose fonts, colors, and other elements. While it may be tempting to include as much color and graphics as possible, remember that the purpose of the website is to invite traffic—the right kind of traffic. Your goal is to appeal to visitors who will be attracted to the company's goods or services. Design elements that do not meet the goal are not necessary. Whenever choosing design elements such as fonts, colors, and other features, bear readability in mind. If the content is not readable, it will not be useful to the visitor—even if it is attractive. Another point to remember is that the more colors and graphics, the more time the website may take to load. And, the longer the load time, the higher the likelihood that visitors will surf away from the site.

Fonts

As you should recall from Chapter 13, fonts provide a challenge for web design. You may design a page with a particular font you chose for a specific impact; but if visitors to your site do not have that font, their computers will automatically substitute a generic font that may negate your intended effect and cause issues with your design. The user may also set font preferences that will override your selection.

The best solution is to specify font options so that each visitor's browser can display the text using the option that it has. Web editors organize fonts into groups of similar looking ones to make it easy for the designer to choose with this flexibility in mind. Table 14.1 shows the groups typically available in web editors. The code for the first entry would be written in this way: {font-family: "Arial", Helvetica, sans-serif;}. Browsers will look first to see if they have the font Arial. If not, they will use Helvetica. If they do not have that font either, they will display the text with whatever basic sans serif type face they have.

The best way to style fonts is by using **Cascading Style Sheets (CSS)**. If you have ever used the styles function of a word processing program, you understand the concept of CSS. All text that has the same purpose is assigned the style. Style settings determine the size, color, and line spacing of the text and any other design features specified in the style definition. Every instance of that kind of text across the website then conforms to the style. Therefore, the style remains consistent throughout the entire page and website. Changing the codes that describe the style automatically changes text carrying that style tag everywhere.

If you want to use a custom font, several sites on the Internet provide downloadable custom fonts. You do have to make sure they are licensed for use on the Internet and, if necessary, you must pay for the font. Once you download it, you store it on your web server for use. If you are going to also use the custom font in bold or italics, you'll have

Table 14.1 *Sample Font Families.*

SANS SERIF
Arial, Helvetica
Arial Black, Gadget
Tahoma, Geneva
SERIF
Book Antiqua, Palatino
Times New Roman, Times

cascading style sheets (CSS)—Style sheets that include information on how the page should appear.

to download and save them as well. Custom fonts are just one way to make your website more distinct; however, they are not necessary.

Impact Cascading Style Sheets

When web pages were first coded, text was plain and unadorned. It was not long, however, before code was added that was designed to enhance the look of plain text. Color, attributes, and alignment became common tags. However, content and design are two different page elements. To separate these, web designers began to adopt style sheets that made it easier to code a page. The content was placed in one place and the design information was placed on another. Today, it is expected that style sheets are part of a well-formed site. Using style sheets has several benefits. The page loads faster and a site can be designed with greater consistency and control.

Colors

Font color choices require careful consideration. You want to select both foreground and background colors that offer high contrast, making them easy to read. Yellow on white is a poor choice because there is not enough contrast to make text or design elements stand out. White text will stand out against a black background, but that background may be too stark for visitors to view comfortably in large areas. Therefore, choose colors based upon how well they work together.

It is also important to remember that web page backgrounds do not print. Therefore, if you have a black background and white text and the user prints on white paper, the text will not appear, as it is also white.

Colors are identified with a six-character code called a **hexadecimal number**, or hex code. The first two characters set the red color value, the second two set the green value, and the third two set the blue value. Each character is either a number from 0 (lowest value) to 9 or a letter from A to F (highest value). The pairs of characters together indicate the intensity of the color. Web editors automatically set the hex number for you when you select a color from an array of colors (see Figure 14.11).

There are 140 color names defined for HTML5 and CSS3. However, 17 colors are from the HTML specifications and 123 colors are from the CSS specification. Each color is identified by its hexadecimal number. The 17 colors from the HTML specification are listed in Table 14.2 with their hexadecimal values.

When selecting colors for your web pages, keep in mind a few basic color rules:

- Blue is relaxing and a popular choice.
- Red is visible and powerful.
- Purple gives a sense of importance to a page.
- Yellow and green are well received.
- Brown can be used to simulate wood or leather, providing a sense of dignity.

hexadecimal number (also hex number)—Hex number is use to identify web colors.

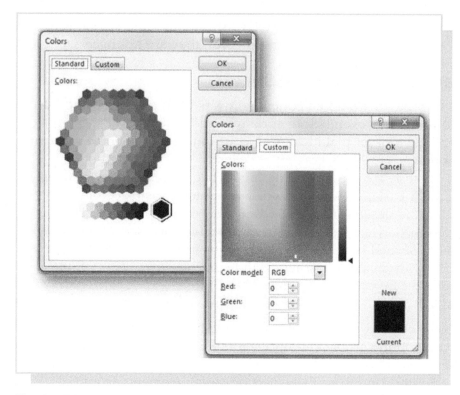

Figure 14.11 *Web editors allow you to choose a color for a panel or other design element from a color array to specify the three RGB values.*

Table 14.2 *List of 17 colors from the HTML specification and identifying hexadecimal number.*

COLOR NAME	#RRGGBB	COLOR NAME	#RRGGBB	COLOR NAME	#RRGGBB
Black	#000000	Aqua	#00FFFF	Silver	#C0C0C0
Navy	#00080	Maroon	#800000	Red	#FF0000
Blue	#0000FF	Purple	#800080	Fuchsia	#FF00FF
Green	#008000	Olive	#808000	Yellow	#FFFF00
Teal	#008080	Gray	#808080	White	#FFFFFF
Lime	#00FF00	Orange	#FFA500		

However, you must work within these general guidelines in an intelligent fashion. On a bright monitor, aqua might not look relaxing. To devise a color scheme for your website, remember what you learned previously about color themes.

Other Design Elements for Web Pages

Web pages offer a host of other design elements. Interactive elements include login input boxes, radio button choice boxes, boxes for inputting comments or other feedback, icons or boxes for rating a product or service, boxes for filling out forms, and icons that open pop-up windows for ordering goods or services. Other elements include icons that link to a company's Facebook, Twitter, or email accounts. All of these elements can add to the interactivity and functionality of a website—but only if they serve the purposes of the website.

checkpoint

How do CSS help web designers manage fonts and colors?

ACTIVITY 14.3 ▶ Choosing Color

While choosing colors for your website is fun and allows you to be creative, it is important to realize that some colors are better to use than others. Choosing colors for your website takes some consideration. You should consider the emotions related to your color choices. Learning about color and emotion, colors that complement, colors that might give a negative vibe, and also colors and culture are all important to consider before choosing the color scheme for your website.

1. Log on to the Internet and go to http://www.mariaclaudiacortes .com/colors/colors.html
2. Work through this Color in Motion website while answering the questions on the handout.
3. Turn in the handout according to your teacher's instructions.

Lesson 14.4 ▶ Selecting and Incorporating Images

Graphics are an important part of many web pages, and they can be effectively used in your website. Some of the skills you need to create and edit graphics for websites are covered elsewhere in the text. You learned in Unit 2 about how to create drawn art and how to edit photos in a photo editing program like PhotoShop. Unit 3 discussed sources of digital art, including issues of rights and cost. Here we will focus on issues involved with saving and placing graphics in web pages.

Saving Images for Web Pages *LO 14.6*

As you learned in Unit 2, the two basic kinds of images are vector graphics and bitmap graphics. Vector graphics, used in drawing programs, use formulas to place points on the screen and then draw lines to connect them. Bitmap graphics describe the color characteristics of pixels on the screen.

Image Resolution

Web editing and manipulation tools can be used effectively to optimize images for the Web. One of the key factors when optimizing images for the Web is to save the image using an appropriate file type. However, this is only one of the best practices to implement. Colors, load time, and image quality are all additional considerations. As you know, visitors to your site will have a better experience if images download faster, rather than slower. However, optimizing images is also important as it saves server space as well because the file size will be smaller. This will help reduce costs, especially if you are paying an Internet service provider to house your web pages.

Vector graphics tend to be saved as bitmap images for display on websites. The SWF format used for Flash files is a vector format, and it is used for animations. JPEG and GIF files are the standard bitmap graphics formats. The GIF format is typically used for rendered art and the JPEG format for photographs.

Bitmap graphics must be saved carefully. They tend to have large file sizes, which results in longer download time. In addition, bitmaps degrade in quality as they are enlarged, but also become distorted as they get smaller. The best thing, then, is to size bitmap images at the size you want in a drawing or photo editing program before saving them. It is better to size them in drawing or photo editing a program rather than in a web editor. Graphic size is determined by the pixel count for the image. Remember that when designing a web page you need to think in terms of a 1200 × 800 monitor. However, all of that size is not available for an image. Some of that space will be used by browser menu bars, tool bars, and other program-related matter. The maximum size for an image, then, should be approximately 600 × 400. Of course, in many cases you'll want a smaller image, which will result in a faster load time (See Figure 14.12.).

Most monitors have a resolution of 72 pixels per inch (sometimes called dpi, for "dots per inch," based on the resolutions in printing). This measure of resolution is separate from the pixel size of the image—it is more about how many bits of information are concentrated in an inch. Images should be saved at one of these resolutions. Photo editing programs typically use 72 dpi as a default.

There are a variety of factors that affect the quality of an image. These factors include size, resolution, and file type. Size includes the physical size of the image and the file size. Resolution is simply the number of pixels in the image. If you are not sure which file type to use, it may be beneficial to save the image as several file types and then compare the file sizes.

Compression

Another issue with images is compression. The higher the compression, the smaller the file size—and the lower the quality of the image. What you lose in quality, you gain in loading speed. Some web editing programs have an 85 percent compression as default. For a photograph

Figure 14.12 *The same image at two different sizes. The image on the left is at 640 × 480 pixels. The one on the right is at 320 × 240.*

sized at 640 × 480, that amount of compression produces a file size of 104 kB. The highest compression rate reduces the file size to 68 kB. The maximum quality level results in a file size of 180 kB.

Placing Images on Web Pages *LO 14.6*

Once your images are formatted and saved appropriately, you are ready to place the image on your web page. Images can serve many different functions but should only be used if they enhance the page. Images can be used in a banner, display a company logo to put its identity prominently on the website, display products, or celebrate company achievements. Whatever the purpose, images should enliven a website.

Placing an Image

Web editors make it simple to place a graphic on a web page. They often automatically write the code needed to insert an image when you click on the appropriate icon or menu option. As you format the image in relation to text and placing additional space around it, code will be added accordingly. Figure 14.13 shows an example of a dialog box that makes all these adjustments very simple.

One step required when placing an image on a web page, which is not required when positioning an image in a print document, is to label the image with **alternate text**. Alternate text (alt text) is a brief descriptor that will appear in a box in visitors' browsers while the image is

alternate text—Brief description of an image that browsers display while the image is loading or if the browser cannot upload it.

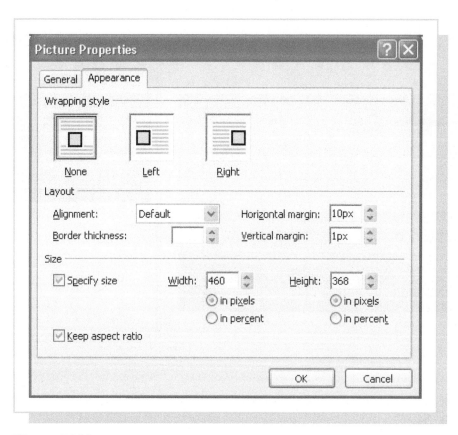

Figure 14.13 *The Picture Properties dialog box allows you to place an image in relation to text, create a margin around it, and change its size. Whatever choices you make are automatically written into the code for the web page.*

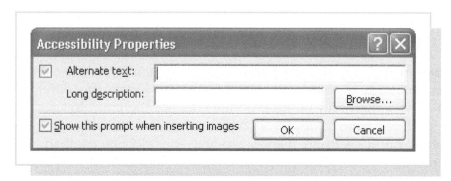

Figure 14.14 *When you insert an image, a dialog box pops up, prompting you to assign alternate text to the graphic.*

loading. It will also show if the browser cannot display the image at all. Alternate text is an example of the accessibility standards being required by the World Wide Web Consortium. Viewers who have visual disabilities may use a screen reader to interpret what is included on the web page. Screen reader software will read the alternate text for that person. To ensure that the web designer does not forget to add the alternate text, the web editor may provide a prompt in the form of a dialog box each time the designer attempts to insert a graphic (see Figure 14.14).

Thumbnails

A standard technique when using large images is to create **thumbnails**, smaller versions of photographs that are placed on the page and, when clicked on by the user, link to the full-size images. Many web editors provide thumbnail capabilities and once you have an image in place, you simply click on the Auto Thumbnail icon and the thumbnail instantly appears, along with an embedded link to the larger version of the photograph. You can then set several attributes as defaults for thumbnail images, including the size.

thumbnail—Small versions of larger images. They speed up the download process by allowing viewers to choose whether they want to see the larger image.

Rollovers

Images can also be used to create **rollovers**. With one type of rollover, the image changes when the mouse rolls over or clicks it. This technique is generally used to indicate that an action is occurring, such as a button being selected.

With another type of rollover, often seen in **banner ads**, a series of images appears in sequence without any user intervention. Rollovers like this are often used to reveal more than one image without cluttering up the page.

rollover—The changing of an image or text when a cursor either passes over or clicks on it.

banner ad—Web ads that often contain a logo and additional business information designed to give corporate identity to a page.

checkpoint

Why are thumbnails useful?

ACTIVITY 14.4 ▶ Thumbnails

1. Create a folder in your home directory (or wherever you save your files) and name the folder **Activity 14**. Inside that folder, create another folder named **images.**

2. Use the Internet or other resource to collect and save, in the **images** folder, 10 images that are all related to each other. Be sure that all ten images are in landscape or all ten are in portrait format.

   a. Rename each image to something short and descriptive.

   b. Make sure each filename is all lowercase and contains no spaces.

   c. Make sure each image is either .jpg, .gif, or .png, and make sure they are at least 500 × 300 in size or larger.

3. Open GIMP or another free graphics editor and follow the directions to batch-process the images into 100 × 75 thumbnail-sized images. (You may need to adjust these dimensions based on your specific images.) Give these images the same filename as the original images but add **–thumb** or **–small** to the filename.

4. Open activity_14_4_thumb.html in your web editor. Save this in the **Activity 14** folder.

5. Insert your images in the web page by changing the filenames of the existing code. Be sure that you are putting the thumbnail-sized images in the image code and the regular sized images in the link code.

6. Add alternative text to each image to describe the image.

7. Save this .html file in the **Activity 14** folder but NOT in the **images** folder. Preview in your browser.

8. Change the embedded styles of the page, including colors, fonts, and alignment, to style the page so it matches the subject matter of your pictures. Refer to the Color in Motion information you learned in Activity 14.3 to help you with your color choices.

9. Submit your finished activity according to your teacher's directions.

Key Concepts

▶ Creating a website begins with planning. Therefore, the first step in planning is to determine the site's purpose and goals, which are based on its potential audience. *LO 14.1 and LO 14.2*

▶ The website should be sketched out in some way (wireframe or organizational chart) and the main sections and related subsections should also be determined. That structure will become the basis of the site's organization. *LO 14.2*

▶ Like any text, the content for a website should be drafted, edited, and then refined. *LO 14.1*

▶ While web pages share some features with print pages, web design is very different from designing for print because of the lack of control the designer has over the look of the final product, the expectations users have on using the Internet, and the possibility of interactive features. *LO 14.3*

▶ <divs> and tables can be used to structure pages, and templates can be used to create common elements on all pages while still leaving space for unique content. *LO 14.2*

▶ Creating options for fonts makes it possible to avoid display issues on different browsers. Using Cascading Style Sheets can help create consistency across a website. *LO 14.4*

▶ Colors are specified using hex numbers and should be selected very carefully. *LO 14.4*

▶ Bitmap graphics such as photographs should be saved to relatively small sizes and in compressed form to help pages load faster. *LO 14.5*

▶ Web editors make it easy to place and format images. Some helpfully remind web developers to add alternate text labels, needed to improve accessibility. *LO 14.5*

Review and Discuss

1. Defend the planning of a website before beginning the design process. *LO 14.1 and LO 14.2*

2. Analyze the ways of sketching or outlining the website that were discussed in the textbook and explain why you are more likely to use one or the other. *LO 14.2*

3. Compare and contrast the differences between a search function on a website and a site map. *LO 14.2*

4. Support the need to know your audience when writing content for your web page. *LO 14.1 and 14.2*

5. Make a list of suggested guidelines to keep in mind when writing content for a website. *LO 14.1*

6. Defend why each stage of the planning process should be approved by the final authority before beginning the design. *LO 14.2*

7. Justify the importance of using descriptive key words in filenames. *LO 14.2*

8. Compare and contrast the differences that should be considered in designing web pages and print publishing. *LO 14.3*

9. Describe the advantages of using a wireframe in planning your website. *LO 14.2*

10. Distinguish between tables and the <div> (division code) as design tools that help you organize content on your web page. *LO 14.2 and LO 14.4*

11. Distinguish between font sizes used in desktop publishing and web design. *LO 14.2 and LO 14.4*

12. Detail the advantages of using styles in cascading style sheets (CSS). *LO 14.4*

13. Describe how red, green, and blue are identified in a hexadecimal number. *LO 14.2*

14. Distinguish between image resolution and compression, and explain the importance of each in using graphics on a web page. *LO 14.5*

15. Compare the differences in thumbnails and rollovers used on a web page. *LO 14.5*

Apply

1. Go to either *http://www.bpa.org* or *http://www.fbla-pbl.org* or to a website suggested by your instructor. Use the data file ***analysis*** to diagram the design of the website. Answer the questions that pertain to the website you are analyzing, and complete the organization chart for the website. Save as ***14_Apply1_analysis***. *LO 14.5*

2. Open the **apply14-2.html** file in your HTML editor. Look in the head section of the document. Some CSS styles have already been embedded into this page by being added in the <head> section of the page. The page needs some work! Some styles need to be added and some need to be edited in order to make the page more attractive. Make the following changes:

   - Change the background of the body to the color lightgray
   - Add a border style to the body that is 3 px solid gray
   - Add a font style to the body; font family Arial, Helvetica, sans-serif
   - Increase the padding of the body to 30 px to add some "white space" around the content
   - Change the font-color of the paragraph to white
   - Change the font size of the paragraph to 14pt
   - Center the paragraph

- Add a style to center the <h1> tag (notice that this also centers the image because the image tag is inside the <h1> tag)
- Right-align the <h6> tag so the footer moves to the right side of the page
- Change the font size of the footer to 8pt
- Add width and height styles of 150px and 100px to the image to make it a bit smaller
- Change the style of the border around the image to 2px solid darkgray
- Add 10px of padding to the image to add some "white space" between the image and the border

Save your changes as **apply14_2_edited.html** and refresh your browser to apply those changes. Submit your document according to your teacher's directions. *LO 14.2, 14.4, 14.5*

3. Pick a model, actress, musician, entrepreneur, or other influential person and create a website about him or her. Plan the website using the **planning** data file. The website should include a home page (index) and two additional pages. The home page will include the "backstory" of your person. The second page should be a list of interesting facts or dates related to your subject. The third page should be a picture gallery of at least 6 images related to your subject. This gallery can be set up in a table structure and the images should be thumbnail sized, similar to what you did in Activity 14_4. Don't forget to add alternate text to all of your images. All your pages should include navigation and appropriate images. To ensure that the structure of all your pages is the same, create an external style sheet and link it to all three pages. Be sure the images are saved in a folder named **images**. Use what you have learned about styles, color, and fonts to enhance the website. Set the site up with appropriate names, copyright information, etc., and then place in a folder named **14_Apply3** *LO 14.2, 14.4, 14.5*

4. Create a website with content from current national news events. Choose at least three news events to write about. Include an index file and a page for each event. Set the site up with a folder. Then save in a named **14_Apply4** with four other pages appropriately named. *LO 14.2, 14.4, 14.5*

5. Use Weebly.com to create a site that is all about you. On your site, create a page for each of the following. Refer to rubric for more details.

- Home Page: One page describing you and your family – give biographical information about each of your family members. A bulleted list works really well here, with each bullet representing a different family member. Use images from the Internet (not actual photos) to represent each family member.
- One page describing your favorite sport or hobby. You can include the colors of your favorite team, pictures, biography of your favorite player, history of the team, etc., or pictures, stats, history, and other interesting information about your hobby.

- One page describing your favorite holiday. Explain why this is your favorite. Be sure to include some historical facts about the holiday. Also include some graphics (or photos) related to your holiday.

- One page describing your goals—what you plan on doing when you "grow up." This should be about the career/college/military options you plan to choose when you finish school. Give details related to this plan. Include related images. Add a button that is a link to a website where we can find out more information about your choice. This could be a link to a website of the college you are planning to attend, the branch of the military you have chosen, or to a career-related site that gives details about your career choice.

- One page describing a place you would like to visit. Where is the place you would like to visit? Write one paragraph that provides some historical information about this place. Also, write one paragraph about why you want to visit this place. Each paragraph should be four to five well-written sentences. Include pictures from the Internet.

- One page on which you create a survey. Create a survey with a minimum of five questions. Use the survey feature of Weebly. The questions should be related to your website or general interest questions. Nothing silly!

- Photo Gallery—include one page where you choose the topic! Include a minimum of five pictures that relate to the topic on the page you choose. Use the gallery feature of Weebly. Include a description for each picture.

Save the files and images as instructed by your teacher. *LO 14.2, 14.4, 14.5*

6. Work as a team to redesign the website provided for the BVCH organization. Use your knowledge of layout and design, including fonts, colors, images, tables, white space, and more, to give an attractive and updated look to this website. After looking over the website as it is currently written, create a redesign plan with your team. Write down all the tasks involved in your redesign and delegate these tasks to each member of the team. The style for this site is inconsistent. Some style is embedded, some is inline, and some is external. There is also some style that is not needed. Move all the styles to an external CSS page and link all pages to this CSS page. This way you only have to edit the CSS page and all edits will be applied to all pages. Some tags are written incorrectly or are not used anymore. These need to be edited, updated, or removed. The layout of the pages of this site is off center. White space is not balanced. Use styles to fix this. The colors and font need to be updated. Choose color palette and font families that appeal to today's audience. Edit the navigation to include only these pages:

   - **index.html**: Includes the "backstory" of the BVCH, the mission, and the goals of this organization

   - **resources.html**: Includes websites and other resource information to help those being served by this coalition

   - **contact_us.html**: Provides contact information for anyone who wants to donate time, talents, or treasures. Include address, phone number, email, fax, and other contact information

- **photo_gallery.html**: Create a photo gallery of BVCH events and activities. Some photos are provided or you can research and find your own images. You can put these in a table and use thumbnails that, when clicked, enlarge the image. Also, include information about the events that the images represent.

Use the Internet to find resources to help with redesigning your site. Some examples include free photo gallery code that you simply download and add to your page; free navigation code that includes animated buttons; a color palette to ensure your colors are complimentary; and more. Check all links to make sure they work; make sure all images have alternate text; check your grammar and punctuation and correct all errors; preview your site in several browsers to check for consistency. Save the files and images as instructed by your teacher. *LO 14.2, 14.4, 14.5*

Explore

1. Websites have different purposes. Working with a partner, explore the goals of informational websites and marketing websites. Using a word processing document, list the goal (informational or marketing) of each website. Work together to compare and contrast the differences that you found. List the differences in navigation, layout, appealing nature, images, etc. Cite at least two resources in the format that your instructor has given you. Discuss what you found with a second set of partners. Include in your final document anything that the other partners mentioned that you had not run compared. Save as ***14_Explore1_purposes***. *LO 14.1*

2. If possible, explore applications available for designing web pages, wireframing, color, and any other web page topic. Create a list of those available and provide a short review of each. Also provide a paragraph about whether you believe you would use the application and explain why or why not. Save your document as ***14_Explore2_apps***.

Academic Connections

Communications. With a partner, find a website that needs some improvement. One partner should explore issues such as navigation, color, layout, etc. with the websites and the other partner should explore the things done right with the websites. Enter into a debate about the website. Ask someone to video record the debate. Save the video as ***14_AC_communications***.

Science. Create a home page about a scientific study or experiment that interests you. Provide appropriate details about the people involved, the purpose of the study/experiment, etc. Save as ***14_AC_science***.

Web Animation

Learning Outcomes

▶ **15.1** Explain why to use animated GIFs and possible advantages and disadvantages.

▶ **15.2** Explain the types of animation and effects.

▶ **15.3** Identify the advantages and disadvantages of DHTML.

▶ **15.4** Use JavaScript or CSS3 to create animations.

▶ **15.5** Describe how using Canvas and SVG would enhance the creation of animations.

Key Terms

- animated GIF
- animation
- applet
- block
- canvas
- conditional statement
- dynamic HTML (DHTML)
- event
- frame
- function
- HTML5 Canvas
- JavaScript
- keyframe
- looping
- morphing
- object
- optimization
- path animation
- rollover
- Scalable Vector Graphics (SVG)
- three dimensional (3D)
- tweening
- two dimensional (2D)
- warping

Have you ever visited a website with a photographic slide show—several images taking turns appearing in a box? Or a website with a moving background? What about a website with a cartoon figure that dances or spins or jumps? Have you been to a website with text that scrolls across the screen? Or one with cascading menus or graphics that move after you click a button?

All these are examples of web animation, ways to make web pages more lively—and, often, more interactive. Adding animation to a website can add an element of fun, but you have to be sure to use it appropriately. Animation is not suitable for every website. It must support the purpose of the website. If it does not, it should be avoided.

Animation is simply a series of still images changing over time and space; thus, in a quick succession, showing movement. Web **animation** can serve several purposes. They draw the eyes of site visitors to a point on the page you want to highlight. Advertisers use animations to get web surfers to focus on something like a logo, the announcement of a special offer, or notice of an important element on the web page. These animations often invite the user to do something—such as click on an offer to learn more about what's on sale or hover over a sale item to see the price and additional details.

animation—Display of a series of images in quick succession to show movement.

Another use of animation is to demonstrate how a product looks, what features it has, or how it works. A computer company might show a 360-degree view of its latest tablet to show just how thin it is. A camera company might use animation to zoom in and out and move left and right to show the key features in its newest digital camera. A luggage company might use animation to demonstrate how to take advantage of all the compartments of a suitcase. A graphic design firm might use animation to demonstrate its design skill.

While animation offers these benefits, it has to be used carefully. To justify whether animation is being used effectively, ask yourself these questions:

- **Does it fit?** Is animation the right kind of thing for the target audience you want to attract to the site? Even if the answer to this question is yes, there is a follow-up question: is this the right *kind* of animation? Placing blinking lights and flashing text on pages aimed at children might catch their eye and entertain them, but these types of animation are probably not appropriate for a business-to-business website.

- **Is it used in the right place?** If you want to attract visitors' attention, make sure you place it in the right area of your website. Focusing attention on a less important part of the site is self-defeating.

- **Does the visitor want animation?** Animated opening screens can show dazzling scenes, such as the beautiful facilities of a spa resort. However, it is important to consider whether the visitors to the site want to see these lush scenes or would prefer to get into the site content itself to find concrete information—or book a treatment at the spa. In most cases, it is wise to give visitors an opportunity to choose *not* to see the animation.

The main point to remember is that if the animation supports and reinforces the web page content, then it is more likely to be appropriate in limited amounts. Too much animation, or animation for decoration only, is distracting and should not be used. There are various types of web animation, not including imported video. Each type lends itself to a particular kind of animation, and each has its advantages and disadvantages.

What Web Animation Works Well?

Think about the web animation you see as you browse Internet sites. What kinds of animation appeal to you or seem particularly effective? Why do they work? Think about how the animation relates to the purpose of the page and what controls website visitors will have over the animation. What examples of animation interfere with your use of a web page? Why do you think they are effective or ineffective? Use your own experience to help you design effective animation for your own website.

Animated GIFs Basics *LO 15.2*

animated GIFs—Several bitmap graphics joined into a single file to give them the appearance of motion.

path animation—Objects that are animated can take new positions along a motion path.

warping—Distorted size or shape of an object.

morphing—An image is transformed from one shape into something completely different.

GIF stands for Graphic Interchange Format. A GIF can be a standard image or can be animated. **Animated GIFs** are the easiest way to create animations. For simple animations, a GIF may be most applicable, as web designers are comfortable with using GIFs and they are relatively easy to animate. Objects that are animated can take new positions along a motion path, which is called **path animation**. This may include things such as rotating, flipping, or changing direction—or color—along a visual path. The size or shape of the object can be distorted, which is called **warping**; or the image can be transformed from one shape into something completely different; that is **morphing**. However, if true dynamic animation is needed, GIFs may not meet your needs. Therefore, advanced methods for animation are discussed later in this chapter.

Animated GIFs are just like a standard GIF image, but with a twist. An animated GIF is a series of images combined into a single GIF file much as a PowerPoint slide show gathers a series of slides into a single presentation. You insert animated GIFs into your web page as you would any other image. Creating them can be easy, and there is a wide variety of software options from which to choose. They include Ulead GIF Animator, a shareware GIF animator software; Adobe Fireworks, a bitmap and vector graphics editor used for creating animated GIFs; and HTML5 Maker, used specifically to develop animated banners for websites.

Animations engage visitors and are typically smaller than videos. To begin to understand how animation works, two important concepts must be explained: frame (or state) and tweening.

Frames or States

frame—Individual image that makes up an animated GIF file.

Figure 15.1 shows a series of images being combined to make an animated GIF. Each separate image is called a **frame** or state. When the animation is played, it cycles through each frame/state, making it appear as if a single image is moving. In this example, when the GIF appears on the screen, the ball seems to roll.

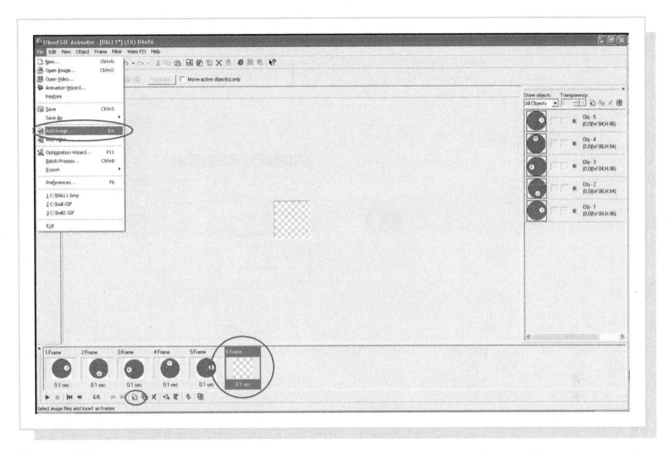

Figure 15.1 *To create animated GIFs, blank frames are added and then images are imported. When all frames are run together, the animation occurs.*

Manipulating a sequence of images, frame by frame, is the basic type of animation. Frames can be added easily to an animation sequence. When a frame is added, it is blank. Image files are then inserted into the frames. You continue adding frames/states and images until all have been added.

To see how the animation looks, you can choose the play or preview option and the sequence of frames will run and the animation will play. If there are any problems with the animation, you can edit the necessary components within the frames and view it again. The option to play or preview the animation in the workspace is shown in Figure 15.1. Each sequence can be set to loop or repeat as often as needed. **Looping** adds length to an animation without increasing file size, though the result does not provide any new animation—it is simply the same images playing over and over again.

looping—Repetition of a series of frames that can be used to add length without increasing the file size.

Tweening

The animation shown in Figure 15.2 is a simple one made of only five art objects. However, animated GIFs may be made up of more frames inserted by the user, or GIF animation software makes it possible to automatically add intermediate stages/frames without

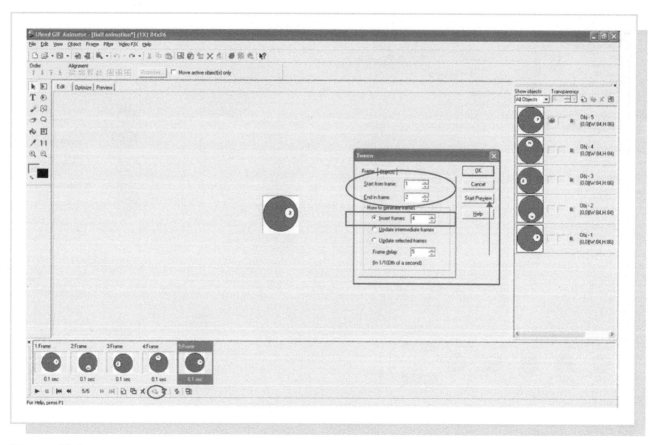

Figure 15.2 *The tweening dialog box allows the user to set specific requirements, and the Start Preview button allows users to see the result of the tweening options before making final choices.*

tweening—The process of making a gradual change in an image by the computer rather than by the user.

going to the labor of creating additional images. The process is called **tweening**, reflecting the fact that it adds a frame or frames *in between* ("*tween*") existing frames to make a series of gradual changes or transformations. For example, if you want an object to grow from small to large on the screen, you can create the smaller and the larger objects and use the tweening function to add intermediate steps. Figure 15.2 shows a Tweening tool dialog box. The options include choosing the two frames between which the images will be inserted, the number of intermediate images (in this case four inserted frames), and the frame delay, which is the amount of time (in thousandths of a second) that each intermediate frame will display.

Figure 15.3 shows the result of the choices in the dialog box—the addition of four frames inserted between the original Frame 1 and Frame 2.

In addition to tweening things like the motion of this rolling ball, you can tween color by adjusting the transparency of the tweened frames and tween position by drawing a beginning and end point in two different places and then tweening intermediate locations.

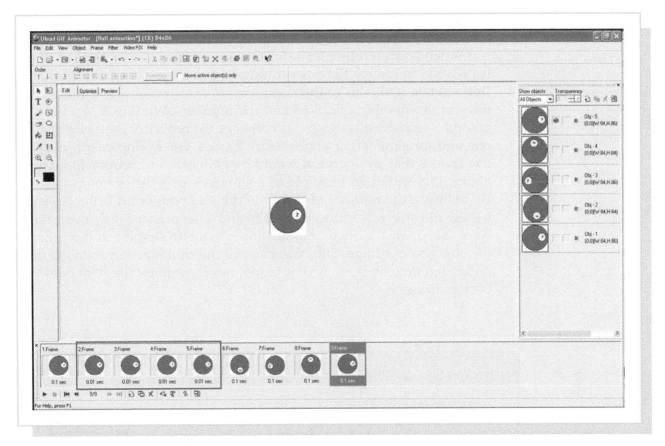

Figure 15.3 *Four frames (highlighted in red) were inserted between the original Frame 1 and Frame 2. In the frame display, they appear to be copies of Frame 1, but they will add intermediate stages to the animation.*

Advantages and Disadvantages of Animated GIFs *LO 15.2*

The advantage of animated GIFs is that basic animations are easy to create. GIF files are excellent choices for graphics with solid colors and with text. The GIF method of compressing color information is to use a code for areas that have the same color. The code instructs the computer what shape to give the color, where to place it, and what color values the area will have. However, this technique is not useful for photographs because of the gradation of colors in photographs.

Animated GIFs have disadvantages too. First, they do not have an extensive color palette. GIFs can only show 256 colors. Second, file sizes can become quite large. There are options to keeping the file sizes of animated GIFs as small as possible. First is to create your animation on a relatively small **canvas**, which is the area within which the animation will be designed. The smaller the canvas, the smaller the file size. The second is to have as few frames as possible while still maintaining a smooth animation. Remember, each frame adds to the

canvas—The area within the workspace where animation will be designed.

file size. The third way to keep animated GIF sizes small is to use as few colors as possible.

When concentrating on using fewer frames and fewer colors, it is possible to reduce file sizes through a process called optimization. **Optimization** is similar to the compression process for a JPG file, which reduces the number of colors and the number of frames wherever possible. Optimization gives you choices for reducing the color palette and for eliminating unnecessary frames. For example, consecutive frames that are identical would be eliminated to reduce file size. Figure 15.4 shows an example of a summary of a file optimization. By reducing the number of colors in the sale banner ad from 256 to 64, the file size was reduced by 28% and 2 seconds of download time were saved. That particular animation was quite simple, so the original file size was not huge. Still, you can see the optimization reduced the download time by 25%. With a larger, more complex file, that could be significant.

optimization—A means of compressing animations to reduce the size of the file.

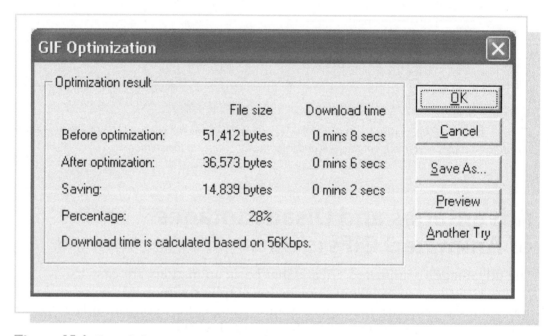

Figure 15.4 *Through the optimization process, file size and download time can be reduced.*

Animated GIFs can stand out from the background of the web page if color is not controlled. Therefore, having the GIF background color the same as the page background color can help blend your animated GIF with your web page. The technique is to set the background color of the animated GIF to full transparency. As a result, when it appears on the web page, you are guaranteed to have no clash between the GIF colors and the web page colors. With an awareness of the basics of animated GIFs, as well as advantages and disadvantages, you can use animated GIFs quite effectively as a means of gaining your audience's attention, making a point, or drawing the visitor's attention to important areas on your web page.

Saving Animated GIFs *LO 15.2*

GIF animation software generally provides options to save files in several different formats, not only as GIF files but also as JPEGs or other editable raster files or as videos. With these approaches, you can then embed the GIF file in your web page. Another approach is to load the animated GIF to a server with its own URL. You then insert into the web page a piece of XHTML code that links to the specific document. The code uses the `<img src>` tag discussed previously, which identifies the animated GIF file as the source of the image.

It is important to note that a GIF file can also be saved as a GIFV file. This file type allows users to upload an animated GIF, compress it into the smaller GIFV file, and use it to animate on social media sites, MP4 video formats, and more. As technology continues to evolve, the file types associated with various graphics will continue to evolve as well.

checkpoint

What are the advantages and disadvantages of animated GIFs?

ACTIVITY 15.1 ▶ Evaluating Animated GIFs

1. Search the Internet for websites showing examples of professional or inspiring animated GIFs.

2. Using word processing software, list at least five URLs to the websites along with a description and a critique of each animated GIF. The critique should include answers to the following questions.

   a. Is the animated GIF effective or ineffective? Why?

   b. What suggestions would you provide to make the animated GIF more visually appealing?

   c. What types of businesses would employ such an animated GIF?

   d. Would there be specific advantages for a business using this animated GIF?

   e. Would there be specific disadvantages for a business using this animated GIF?

3. Use the spelling/grammar checker, read your work carefully, and correct any errors you find. Save your file as *15_Activity1_ animatedgifcritique*.

Keep in mind that many individuals think animated GIFs mainly consist of objects that simply move across the screen. Many think of animated GIFs basically as cartoons or entertaining items on a web page. However, animated GIFs appropriate for professional websites include artistic, visually appealing animations that support the purpose of the website.

two dimensional— Graphics with length and breadth, but no depth.

three dimensional— Graphics with length, breadth, and depth.

Animation typically falls into three categories: **two dimensional (2D)**, **three dimensional (3D)**, and Stop Motion. However, the differences between the categories are beginning to fade as many advanced animation methods provide for the creation of various versions of the same animated image. Hand-drawn animation is typically thought of when 2D animation is mentioned. Examples include various Disney productions such as Snow White or Bugs Bunny cartoons. 2D animation also includes the Simpsons and similar television productions which all have length and breadth, but no depth. The dinosaurs in Jurassic Park and the robots in Transformers are examples of 3D animation. To help clarify the difference between 2D and 3D animation, think of a picture of a globe in which you can only see the front areas displayed on the globe (2D) versus a globe you can spin and see all areas and sides of the globe (3D). The 3D globe has length, breadth, and depth.

A 3D animation can be turned 360 degrees to see all components. Therefore, 3D animation allows you to do or see things you cannot do or see in 2D animation. Lighting can be highlighted differently, textures can be employed, or the shading of colors could be more intense in a 3D animated object than a 2D object. Objects that seem more realistic are probably 3D objects. Stop motion animation is a form of 3D animation and is most commonly seen in "clay-mation" films or videos. Clay-mation is also referred to as object animation and is created by the user physically manipulating the object to make it appear that it is moving on its own. For example, using dolls with movable joints or making inanimate objects seem as though they are animated are two examples of stop motion animation. There are obviously advantages and disadvantages to each category of animation. It's essential you determine which is best and which best supports the purpose of your website. Many require more advanced methods of creating animation.

Animations are typically one of the following types: static, stateful, or dynamic. Static animation, such as animated banners, simply start at one point and end at another point. They have no branching or logic with the animated design. They simply move from start to finish. Stateful animation is said to have at least one "state" or need for input. For example, the user may click to open a window on the screen and then click to close the window. The user could also move the mouse cursor to "hover" over an object and it would change, but once the mouse cursor was moved off of the image, it would revert to its original state. Dynamic animation; however, relies on the user and other variables as well. The other variables may include logic, dragging an item, and anything causing the original state of the object to evolve to an altered state. These are very complex animations. Therefore, as an overview of basic animation, let's first review how to make a static animation such as a banner with animated display text.

Flash

Macromedia developed Flash specifically for creating interactive elements for the Internet. Adobe acquired Flash in 2005 and it became very popular animation on the Web. Flash is a plug-in program which is added to other software, like web browsers, to execute particular types of files. Flash programs run on multimedia files. The plug-ins are written to be relatively small in size, though versatile, so that download times are not long. However, to view items created with Flash, the plug-in is required. Apple products do not come with a Flash plug-in as Apple has adopted HTML5, CSS, and Javascript as open standards for their mobile devices. Many believe that Flash is a part of history.

Banners

GIF animation software make it simple to create a banner with animated display text. Figure 15.5 shows the dialog box for creating a new canvas. Within the Canvas Properties dialog box, you set the dimensions and choose the transparency of the background. Keep in mind the smaller the canvas, typically the smaller the file size.

The next step is to choose to add the banner text. See Figure 15.6. Adding the banner text allows you to key the exact text you want for your banner and format that text. You will be able to choose the font, text color, type size, and other characteristics. Controlling the type of effect for the components of your banner is the next step. Effects include the text appearing or disappearing and such movements as scrolling left, right, up, or down, zooming in or out, rotating while zooming, fading, and dropping down through the bottom of the banner. Frame control gives you control over the speed of the animation.

You can see the results of any animation choice by simply clicking on All Slides the preview button before applying your edits. See Figure 15.7. Once you have the look you want, the next decision to save the banner in the appropriate file format.

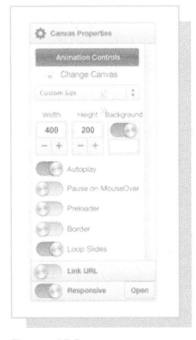

Figure 15.5 *Creating an animation begins with setting the size and transparency of the background. In this case (HTML5 Maker Editor) the choice is a rectangle wider than it is tall, a typical configuration for a banner.*

Figure 15.6 *By simply clicking on Add Text, the Text Properties appear. Choose all appropriate settings.*

Figure 15.7 *Simply click All Slides and then preview the animation.*

Effects

Some GIF animation software make it possible to create many other effects as well. For example, they may include a variety of video effects similar to the transition effects used in editing videos. Figure 15.8 shows the wind effect, which can make an image appear to be accelerating.

The mirror effect, which breaks an image up into multiple pieces during the course of the animation, may also be an effect choice. The pieces created are also images. Through the mirror effect, a reflection of the object is produced. For example, think of looking at a mountain that sits majestically on the other side of a lake and you can see the reflection (a mirror image) of the mountain in the lake.

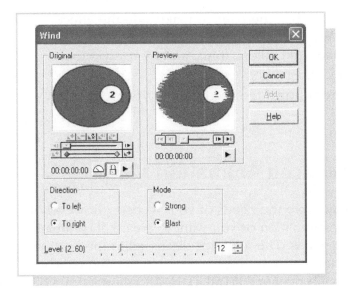

Figure 15.8 *When choosing the wind effect, you can adjust the direction and apparent strength of the wind.*

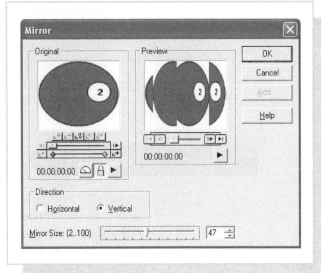

Figure 15.9 *Controls for the mirror effect allow you to distort the image horizontally or vertically and, by adjusting the mirror size, to manipulate the distortion.*

ACTIVITY 15.2 ▶ Fun with JavaScript

1. Create a new web page about your favorite store. Include a title for the browser and a heading that is the store's name. As a subheading, identify where the store is located (the physical location that you visit).

2. Include a sentence or two that discusses why this is your favorite store.

3. Create an unordered list of five or more items you can purchase from this store.

4. Create an ordered list of your top five favorite brands that this store sells.

5. Include an image of the store's logo as well as a link to the store's website.

6. Add horizontal rules between each section of your webpage.

7. Save this as **index.html** in a folder called: **activity_15_2**. Place the image in a folder called **images.**

8. Access the website http://www.javascriptkit.com/cutpastejava.shtml or find some free JavaScript code on the Internet.

9. Search through all the script categories to find some JavaScript that you would like to add to your page. Consider a background that changes based on the time of day, a random pun generator, or a cursor that changes. There are lots of options.

10. Choose one JavaScript feature, follow the directions, and add the code to your index.html page.

11. Preview your webpage. Test the page to make sure the effect works the way you want it to. Make any changes necessary and then resave your page. Add colors, fonts, and more style to the page as you choose.

12. Save the updated **index.html** file according to your teacher's instructions.

Lesson 15.3 > Advanced Animation Methods

Basic GIF animation may serve the needs of your website; however, if you want more dynamic animation or you want to create 3D animation, GIFs will not meet your needs. The methods discussed in this section for creating web animations achieve their purpose by writing code. Some of the effects through dynamic HTML (DHTML), JavaScript, CSS, and HTML5 Canvas and SVG create objects that can only be achieved through higher methods of animation.

Dynamic HTML *LO 15.3*

dynamic HTML (DHTML)— A means of animating text or image elements through the HTML code that determines their placement and appearance.

Dynamic HTML (DHTML) is an efficient way to achieve many animation effects by manipulating the underlying XHTML code. As previously discussed, XHTML is the markup language underlying web pages. It tells browsers where and how to display elements—images or text—on a web page. DHTML creates animated effects by changing how elements are displayed, especially when a site visitor takes some kind of action. For instance, if a user moves the mouse so the cursor is over a particular word, the browser might display that word in a larger type size or a different color. The DHTML code could also instruct the browser to change the position of an image so it moves around the screen.

The advantage of DHTML is that it does not include an image. As a result, it does not require a large file size, which means it loads as quickly as any XHTML file. Instead of creating a moving image and posting it to a server, which requires the browser to retrieve that image, you give the browser the instructions to move the image that is already there. This process saves considerable download time. DHTML does not require users to download any additional software as is necessary with plug-ins.

Of course, DHTML has disadvantages, too. First, like XHTML itself, its instructions will not necessarily be interpreted the same by all browsers. Second, it cannot be used to create very complex animations. Finally, DHTML is not really a standalone tool. Rather, it is a creation of three other tools—XHTML code, Cascading Style Sheets (CSS), and JavaScript. DHTML treats some elements of a web page as objects and lets the tools (XHTML code, CSS, and JavaScript) manipulate those objects. In doing so, the developers can make those objects change in some way—become dynamic. Scripts give developers more capabilities, though, and it is not necessary to place scripts within DHTML code: they can stand alone. For these reasons, JavaScripts are more widely used to create web animations.

JavaScript *LO 15.4*

XHTML code tells a browser where to place elements on a web page and how to display them. The content being displayed is located at a server, a computer remote from the machine where the browsing is being done. While browsing, a user will need to access images, data, and other elements from that server. Each download takes time, slowing the browsing experience, which often leads to frustration for an impatient site visitor. XHTML-coded web pages are also relatively static. Users can interact with them in only limited ways. If the results of those interactions must also be downloaded from the server that holds the website's content, the user experiences more delays, only adding to the frustration level.

These limitations of XHTML led developers to create **JavaScript**, a programming language that can be embedded in HTML documents. JavaScript makes it possible for users to interact with a web page and for the embedded script to respond without needing to access the remote server. The result is a much faster response time and more dynamic, interactive web pages. These JavaScript applications are called **applets**, like the handy mini-applications found on smartphones.

Uses and Elements of JavaScript

JavaScript has many valuable uses. Scripts can be written to change the content or appearance of the web page when users move their mouse or make a choice in a dialog box. JavaScript can be used to perform searches, create pop-up windows, or fill out parts of a form. To get a sense of the variety of things you can do using JavaScript, go to a favorite website and reveal the source code. Scan the code for examples of JavaScript and relate them to the elements on the page in the browser window. You'll see how powerful this programming language can be.

As explained previously, several elements in XHTML code must have beginning and ending tags. JavaScript is no exception. The presence of a JavaScript applet is signaled by the `<script>` open tag; its end tag is the `</script>` tag. Between these tags come the instructions for the Java applet. Within the opening `<script>` tag, the script must identify the programming language of the applet as JavaScript and indicate the text format. The first line of a JavaScript applet, then, should read:

`<script language="JavaScript" type="text/JavaScript">`.

Each statement within the script is an instruction the web browser carries out in the order in which they appear. JavaScript follows many of the same rules as well-formed XHTML code. Commands are case-sensitive, so you must be careful with the use of capital letters. Values (like

JavaScript—A programming language that increases the interactivity of web pages by making it possible for actions to be executed within the browser and without the need to access the server that hosts the website.

applet—An executable program that cannot stand alone but functions only within a web browser.

"text/JavaScript") should be within quotation marks. There are also some coding rules special to JavaScript which are not found in XHTML. For instance, you can group together a set of statements in curly brackets—{ and }. These brackets create a script unit called a **block**, which are all executed simultaneously by the browser. If you're working with a web editing program, you may not need to worry much about the finer points of JavaScript—the web editor will write the code for you.

JavaScript includes several different kinds of tools:

block—A set of JavaScript statements that are enclosed in curly brackets—{ }

object—Unit manipulated in JavaScript, which has both properties and methods.

- **Objects.** JavaScript deals with units called **objects**. Objects can be as large as the entire window visible to the browser and as small as a button on a web page. Objects are analogous to elements in HTML: they are the chunks of meaning that make up a web page. Objects can be nested inside other objects. They have two characteristics: *properties,* which describe them in terms of height, width, name, and URL; and *methods,* which are activities the objects can perform.

function—JavaScript command not executed until an event occurs.

event—An action taken by a website visitor that triggers execution of a script.

- **Functions and events.** JavaScript can delay a command from being executed until something takes place. These delayed commands are called **functions**. The scripts within the functions are triggered by **events**, which are actions taken by a user, such as entering or leaving the page (the events defined as onLoad and onUnload); moving a mouse over an object or area (onMouseover); or clicking a mouse on an object (onClick).

conditional statement—An action taken if certain conditions are or are not met.

- **Conditional statements.** JavaScript also runs on **conditional statements**, such as if/else statements. In such a statement, if a certain condition is met, the script executes a particular command. If anything other than the specific condition is met, it executes another command.

Examples of JavaScript

JavaScript can be used to provide several common interactive functions. For instance, you can create a **rollover**, in which mousing over an image results in a change to the image, which returns to its original state when the cursor moves off of it. You can use this effect to change the appearance of a word by altering its size or color, but you can also use it to swap one image for another. The following example of JavaScript has that effect:

rollover—Changing an image or text when a mouse clicks on it or rolls over it.

```
<html>
<head>
<script type="text/javascript">
function mouseOver()
{
document.getElementById("b1").src ="file:///C://ball-
blue.GIF";
}
function mouseOut()
{
document.getElementById("b1").src ="file:///C://ball-
red.GIF";
}
```

```
</script>
<title>JavaScript image switch</title>
</head>
<body>
<a href="file:///C://" target="_blank">
<img alt="red ball" src="file:///C:/ball-red.GIF"
id="b1" onmouseover="mouseOver()" onMouseout=
"mouseOut()" border="0" width="84" height="86"></a>
</body>
</html>
```

In this example, the two functions, or actions to be executed, are called mouseOver and mouseOut. Notice that one image—the GIF file "ball-blue"—is linked to the mouseOver action, with the other—the GIF image "ball-red"—is linked to mouseOut. The events that trigger those functions appear toward the bottom of the code: the event onMouseover causes the function mouseOver to execute. The event onMouseout executes the function mouseOut. Figures 15.10A and 15.10B show the two images that appear.

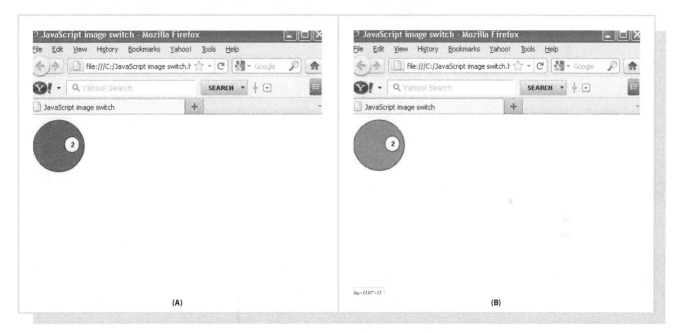

(A)   (B)

Figure 15.10A and 15.10B *The red ball in Figure 15.10A is the normal state for the animation—what the browser will display most of the time. When the mouse pointer is over the image, however, the blue ball in Figure 15.10B will display.*

Another common use of JavaScript is to create a dialog box. These can be used to confirm an action by a user. In the example shown below, the dialog box is used to confirm the decision to exit a site. The initial input goes to a button, described toward the end of the script. The event triggering the pop-up is onClick. When the button is pressed, the dialog box appears with text asking the user to confirm an operation. Notice the if/else conditional statement that follows. If the user clicks "OK," another message appears—*Thank you for visiting*. If the user does *not* click "OK," the "else" conditional applies, and a new dialog box will welcome the user back. Figure 15.11 shows the result of this script.

Figure 15.11 *In the JavaScript applet demonstrated here, the grayed "Press to confirm" dialog box is the original dialog. When the user clicks that button, the secondary dialog box appears to ask for confirmation.*

```
<head>
<script type="text/javascript">
function show_confirm()
{
var r=confirm("Are you sure you wish to exit?");
if (r==true)
  {
  alert("Thank you for visiting!");
  }
else
  {
  alert("Welcome back");
  }
}
</script>
</head>
<body>

<input type="button" onClick="show_confirm()"
value="Press to confirm" />

</body>
</html>
```

CSS3 *LO 15.4*

The name CSS3 indicates that this is level 3 (or version 3) of Cascading Style Sheets. One change from CSS to CSS3 was the introduction of modules. Modules allow instructions or specifications to be completed more quickly as "chunks" (modules) are approved together. CSS3 allows for the animation of most XHTML elements without the use of JavaScript. When coding in CSS3, keyframes must be initially specified. **Keyframes**, written as @keyframes, are used to provide instructions for what styles the element will have throughout the various times of the animation. As CSS styles are coded within the @keyframes property rules, the animation will occur and the styles will change as the timeline of the animation plays out. When setting keyframes within graphic software, the keyframe actually marks the point in time when a change, such as position, color, audio, and other elements, will occur over time.

keyframe—CSS3 statement that provides instructions for what styles an element will have through various times of the animation; a point in time when a change will occur over time.

A few CSS3 animation properties and sample property values include:

PROPERTY	SAMPLE PROPERTY
animation-delay	time: defines the number of seconds (s) or milliseconds (ms) to wait before the animation begins
animation-direction	normal: animation is played in the normal direction reverse: animation is played in reverse direction alternate: animation is played in normal every odd time (1, 3, 5, etc.) and in reverse every even time (2, 4, 6, etc.)
animation-duration	time: defines the length an animation takes to finish
animation-play-state	paused: specifies the animation is paused running: specifies the animation is running

Examples of CSS3

In the following example, the background color of a box (150 pixels × 200 pixels) changes from blue to green and then returns to its original color, blue. Note the blocks of statements indicated by the curly brackets.

```
<!DOCTYPE html>
<html>
<head>
<style>
div {
  width: 150px;
  height: 200px;
  background-color: blue;
  -webkit-animation-name: example; /* Chrome, Safari, Opera */
  -webkit-animation-duration: 4s; /* Chrome, Safari, Opera */
  animation-name: example;
  animation-duration: 4s;
}
```

```
/* Chrome, Safari, Opera */
@-webkit-keyframes example {
  from {background-color: blue;}
  to {background-color: green;}
}

/* Standard syntax */
@keyframes example {
  from {background-color: blue;}
  to {background-color: green;}
}

</style>
</head>
<body>

<p><b>Note:</b> This example does not work in Internet
Explorer 9 and earlier versions.</p>

<div></div>

<p><b>Note:</b> When an animation is finished, it changes
back to its original style.</p>

</body>
</html>
```

One way to learn more CSS3 and other code to use for animations is to search premade animation libraries. CSS libraries, such as Animate. css, allow users to choose an animation of their choice and then download the free CSS code. Figure 15.12 shows an example of some of the possible choices of premade code.

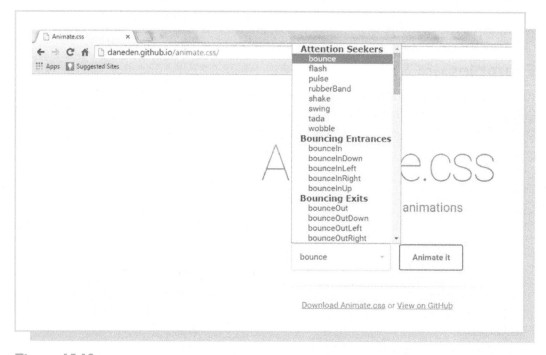

Figure 15.12 *CSS libraries provide free CSS code. It's a great way to learn.*

HTML5 Canvas and SVG

HTML5 allows for dynamic, 2D animation through the coded **HTML5 canvas** element. Written as <canvas>, this element is a container for bitmap graphics in which a script is used to draw graphics. Therefore, canvas is basically a rectangular area (set by the width and height attributes) on an HTML page that has no border and no content. Using script, typically JavaScript, graphics such as boxes, circles, lines, text, and drawn images can be added to the page. The canvas element is supported by several different browsers.

HTML5 canvas—Container for bitmap graphics in which a script is used to draw graphics.

The sample code provided below will draw a diagonal line within a square. When the code is run, the result will be:

Analyze the code below to figure out how big the square is and how long the diagonal line is within the square. Also, review the code to see where the color of the outline of the square is set and review the XHTML code previously learned.

```
<!DOCTYPE html>
<html>
<body>

<canvas id="myCanvas" width="150" height="150"
style="border:4px solid #111111;">
Your browser does not support the HTML5 canvas tag.
</canvas>

<script>
var c = document.getElementById("myCanvas");
var ctx = c.getContext("2d");
ctx.moveTo(5,5);
ctx.lineTo(145,145);
ctx.stroke();
</script>

</body>
</html>
```

Although this example may seem simple, the canvas element can be used for high level, 2D animation. Examples of this high-level animation are Google doodles. Go to www.google.com and see which doodle is online today. Reveal the source code and find the canvas element.

The canvas element may also be used to paint in layers or recreate specific layers within an object. It is important to note that canvas is raster based. Therefore, once an object such as the square and diagonal line is drawn, the system has forgotten the object was drawn. Therefore, if the object is to be used again or moved to another location, it would

Scalable Vector Graphics (SVG)—Vector-based animation used for 3D animation.

have to be entirely redrawn. However, with **Scalable Vector Graphics (SVG)**, which is obviously vector based, the position attributes could simply be edits and the browser would determine how to redraw the object elsewhere. Since you are working with vectors, moving, scaling, repositioning, and flipping, your drawings are easier. Therefore, SVG is used more readily for 3D animation. SVG graphics also do not lose quality when they are resized or are zooming in and zooming out. SVG defines graphics in Extensible Markup Language (XML) format.

XML is similar to HTML: however, HTML was created to display data whereas XML was created to describe data. Therefore, tags in XML are not predefined but must be defined by the one writing the code—hence, self-descriptive. However, SVG may be embedded within an <object> element, or if the element is interactive within an <svg> element. SVG can also be animated with CSS and using JavaScript. Flash is the competitor to SVG, but SVG relies on open XML standards and not a proprietary technology. An SVG file must be saved with a .svg extension. SVG can be dynamic and take on any shape. Like CSS3, libraries are available so that premade code can be obtained on the Internet. Again, the important point is to analyze which type of animation is needed to support the purpose of your website and then select the appropriate methods to create it.

checkpoint

What is one advantage to using each of the following: DHTML, JavaScript, HTML5 Canvas, and SVG?

ACTIVITY 15.3 ▶ Adding Search Using Javascript

1. Open ***javascript.txt*** from your data files for this chapter using Notepad.

2. Read the steps pertaining to adding JavaScript as a page search function from the opened data file and study the code.

3. Select and copy the code for Step 1, which is to add the `<script>` `</script>` tags and the contents within them to the head of a web page.

4. Open ***index.html*** in the web editor you are using. You'll find the file in your data files in the folder ***tbtea***.

5. Find the `<head>` tag and paste the code after that tag into the file.

6. Toggle back to Notepad. Copy the `<form>` `</form>` tags and the script within them. Paste this in your index page above "About Us" in the left navigation pane. Be sure that the `<form>` code is pasted after the `<p>` tag.

7. Save the ***index.html*** file. Create a folder named ***15_Activity2_ javascript*** and move the ***tbtea*** folder into it.

8. Preview your web page. Make any changes necessary and then resave your page.

Key Concepts

▶ Web animations are used to attract customers, demonstrate products, introduce special offers, and highlight specific web page content. They need to be used carefully, though, to make sure they support the purpose of the web page and do not detract from that purpose. *LO 15.1*

▶ Animated GIFs are simple web animations based on graphics created in raster-based graphics programs. GIF animation programs combine individual images called frames or states and use the process called tweening to insert additional frames in order to reduce the amount of time needed to create constituent images. *LO 15.2*

▶ Animated GIFs are easy to create, but they tend to have very large file sizes, which can slow download times. File sizes can be reduced through various techniques, including optimization. *LO 15.1*

▶ Animation typically falls into three categories: two dimensional (2D), three dimensional (3D), and Stop Motion. Two-dimensional graphics have length and breadth, but no depth. Three-dimensional graphics have length, breadth, and depth. Stop-motion animation is a form of 3D animation that is most commonly connected to "clay-mation."

▶ Animations are typically one of the following types: static, stateful, or dynamic. Static animation, such as animated banners, simply start at one point and end at another point. Stateful animation is said to have at least one "state" or need for input such as the user moving the mouse cursor to "hover" over an object that would then change. Dynamic animation relies on the user and other variables as well. *LO 15.2*

▶ Dynamic HTML (DHTML) is a technique that manipulates underlying HTML code to change the way information is displayed on the Web or to create interactive environments for users. However, it has less visual capability than other forms of animation. *LO 15.3*

▶ JavaScript is a scripting language that sits within HTML to create opportunities for user interactions. Because the scripts run through the browser, they do not slow download times. It is a very flexible and useful tool for interactions, but not as visual as GIF animations or flash animation. *LO 15.4*

▶ CSS3 indicates a newer version of Cascading Style Sheets. CSS3 allows for the animation of most XHTML elements without the use of JavaScript. *LO 15.4*

▶ HTML5 allows for dynamic, 2D animation through the coded canvas element. Written as <canvas>, this element is a container for bitmap graphics in which a script is used to draw graphics. Therefore, canvas is basically a rectangular area (set by the width and height attributes) on an HTML page that has no border and no content. *LO 15.5*

▶ Flash is the competitor to SVG (Scalable Vector Graphics), but SVG relies on open XML standards and not a proprietary technology. An SVG file must be saved with a .svg extension. SVG can be dynamic and take on any shape. *LO 15.5*

Review and Discuss

1. Describe two scenarios in which animation might be used. Question whether these are appropriate uses by responding to the three questions listed at the beginning of the chapter to determine if animation is used effectively. *LO 15.1*

2. Identify the options you can use to keep animated GIF file sizes small. *LO 15.1*

3. Explain the process to optimize a GIF file. *LO 15.1*

4. Explain the three types of animation: static, stateful, and dynamic. *LO 15.2*

5. Differentiate between 2D, 3D, and stop motion animations. *LO 15.2*

6. What are the pros and cons of using DHTML to create a complicated animation requiring user input? *LO 15.3*

7. Create a scenario in which DHTML could be used to animate text or objects with justification of use of DHTML for that animation. *LO 15.3*

8. Compare and contrast the use of JavaScript and CSS3. *LO 15.4*

9. Examine the usefulness of using HTML5 Canvas and SVG. *LO 15.5*

Apply

1. Create a single web page titled "Countdown to Christmas." Locate (by searching or obtaining from your instructor) JavaScript code to place in the head and body to perform a countdown to Christmas. Save as *15_Apply1_screen_capture* in a folder named *15_Apply1*. Then make at least two changes to the style by editing the JavaScript. Insert the changed script into the web page. Save the web page in the *15_Apply1 folder* as *15_Apply1_countdown*. *LO 15.4*

2. Copy the folder *15_Apply2* from the data files to your solution folder. Open the file *15_Apply2_javascript_fun* and do the following: add a title to the web page for the browser and a headline on the web page either above or underneath the image; insert the correct folder and filenames (path) for the before and after images so that when you click on the text, the image changes; and center the image and the headline on the page. Add a border around the image. Change the font and size for the entire page. Save the web page in the *15_Apply2* folder as *15_Apply2_javascript_fun*. *LO 15.2*

3. Go to the website animation.css. Explore the various animation effects and watch how they change the title on the webpage. Select the bounce animation effect. Click the download animation .css button. Locate the downloaded file and move it to a folder named **apply15_3anima-tion**. Download the **apply15_3_animation.html** file from the student data files into the **apply15_3animation folder**. Open the .html file in your webpage editor. Copy and paste the following into the <head> section of the web page: <link rel="stylesheet" href="animate.css">. Edit the <h1>tag to read as follows: <h1 class="animated infinite bounce">Example</h1>. Save and test your web page. The words Join FBLA! should bounce infinitely. Now, it is your turn. Choose a different animation to apply to the title and edit your code. Create three more headings on your web page and apply different animations to each. Experiment with the infinite option, removing it to see what the effect looks like as it animates only once. Add font, size, color, and other styles to your page. Submit your files according to your teacher's instructions. *LO 15.2*

4. Create a folder called **apply15_5** and create an **images** folder inside that folder. Create a web page with four pictures of your favorite memes. Make sure they are school appropriate! Include a title for the browser tab and a heading to identify your page topic. Place the images in a two-column, two-row table. Set the height and width of the images so they are not distorted. Adjust the left margin of the table so it will appear centered on the screen. Add a 2-pixel solid black border around your images. Go to www.w3schools.com and study the css3 styles for image borders, text shadow, and background animation. Apply a rounded border to your images. You decide the radius of the border. Apply a shadow, glow, or combination of effects to the heading of your page. Add additional font, color, and layout styles to enhance your page. Add animation to the images so they change from one color to another. Be sure the images are saved in the **images** folder. Save the web page as **apply15_5_CSS3_animation**. Submit your files according to your teacher's directions. *LO 15.2*

5. You've been asked by your instructor to submit three animation projects to be considered for use on your city's website. Take pictures of important sites in your city to use in the project. Place these in a subfolder named *images* within a folder named *15_Apply6*. Create animations using the pictures you have taken and save each of your animations in the *15_Apply6* folder as *15_Apply6_animation1*, *15_Apply6_animation2*, and *15_Apply6_animation3*. Save in the native file type and in a webready file type. Use at least two different animation types described in this chapter. Because html5maker.com will only allow you to save one animation at a time without paying for an upgrade, be sure to download the .swf file before deleting and creating another one. *LO 15.2*

Explore

1. Search for JavaScript code on the Web. Create a JavaScript library of at least five different codes you could find a use for in web design. Copy the head and body code into a word processing document with the source cited for the code. Include a paragraph in which you explain what each piece of code could be used for. Save the document as *15_Explore1_javascript*. *LO 15.4*

2. Search for CSS3 uses. Provide at least three websites as examples. Explain how each may be used and a review of each website, properly citing the website for each instance. Save your document as *15_Explore2_css3*. *LO 15.4*

Academic Connections

Communications: Take an available quiz on communicating effectively to see how well you do. You can use the website provided below or one your instructor provides.

"How Good are Your Communication Skills?" Mind Tools, accessed July 23, 2011, http://www.mindtools.com/pages/article/newCS_99.htm.

Read an article associated with the quiz and create at least one animation demonstrating two things you've learned about communicating in this exercise. Save your animation as *15_AC_effective_communications*.

Science: Search for and watch a video on robotics or use one your instructor provides. Write a summary of what you learned from the video on a web page. Include at least one animation that demonstrates something you learned. Save the web page as *15_AC_robotics*.

Web Media

Learning Outcomes

▶ **16.1** Compare sound formats and determine which are best for web pages.

▶ **16.2** Explain the difference between streaming and downloadable media.

▶ **16.3** Describe the methods for adding media to a website.

▶ **16.4** Follow the necessary steps to add media to a website.

▶ **16.5** Give examples of how podcasts are used.

▶ **16.6** Create a podcast and add an RSS feed.

Key Terms

- aggregator
- embed
- encoding software
- feed
- HTML5
- H.264
- platform
- podcast
- pop filters
- RSS feed
- subscriber
- XML

Lesson 16.1 Adding Sound and Video to Web Pages

Lesson 16.2 Creating Podcasts

As you learned in Chapter 15, a web page can be a multimedia site—home to animation, pictures, and sound. Sometimes the media you want to add to a web page are not animated, but instead are sound or live action videos you record or obtain from another source. A company, for example, might post videos of satisfied customers praising the company's skilled workers and good prices. A car company might want to showcase a new model with a video showing its performance in a road test. Or a university might place audio recordings of key passages from guest speakers on its website.

This kind of rich media can add interest to a web page. It can add effectiveness, too—if done correctly.

Obviously, sound is not visible, yet it should be treated as digitized information. Placing sound on a web page involves several decisions, including appropriate file format whether to make the file streaming or accessible only by downloading, and how to place the sound on the page.

Before considering these technical issues, let's take a moment to discuss choosing appropriate sound. The biggest issue for web page designers who want to use sound, other than file size and download time, is the personal nature of music. The music that appeals to a 20-year-old may not appeal to someone even a few years older or younger. Another issue is the invasiveness of sound in a business environment. Web pages that suddenly begin to play sounds may be a distraction to other workers. As a result, give careful consideration to the use of sound, particularly music, before including it in a web page. Think about the image the business is trying to project to customers through its web page. Be sure to only include sound that is appropriate for and enhances the company's image.

Remember the issue of copyright ownership as well. As tempting as it may be to include high-quality sound recorded by professional musicians, that music is protected by copyright and cannot be placed on a website without permission. Doing otherwise will subject the business to serious legal problems.

Figure 16.1 *Audio and video can enhance the experience of someone visiting a website, but both should be used only when essential to the site's purpose.*

Sound File Formats *LO 16.1*

There are many different formats for sound, which can be categorized into one of two types: those made with lossless compression or with lossy compression.

Lossless compression files are essentially copies of the original source. Common formats for this type of file are the Windows-based WAV (for WAVeform Audio Format) and the Mac-based AIFF (for Audio Interchange File Format). Because lossless compression files are near-copies of the original, they lend themselves to archiving and being used as a master, a source file from which copies are made for distribution. By maintaining the archived file, you have a complete copy of the recording should anything happen to the distribution copy.

Those distribution copies tend to be lossy for the simple reason that lossy files are much smaller. Lossy files reduce the size of an audio recording by eliminating some of the data. For instance, lossy versions of music files typically eliminate the highest- and lowest-frequency sounds, leaving the midrange, where most of the music data lies. The most well-known lossy file format is the MP3 format, but others include WMA (Windows Media Audio), Apple's AAC (Advanced Audio Coding), and RM (RealMedia). iTunes is a popular location to store and purchase music (see Figure 16.2).

Figure 16.2 *Apple's iTunes can be downloaded for free onto either a Mac or PC platform.*

If you plan on including sound on your web page, you should use a lossy compression. Sound files are often quite large and must be downloaded from the web page on which they are stored in order to be heard. Slow connections make the download process time consuming. Therefore, use large lossless sound files with caution. Posting files made with lossy compression will minimize the downloading time. Which format you use depends on several factors, including file size, quality issues, and **platforms** (computers or mobile devices, for instance) that visitors to your website will use. The most universally accepted lossy file format is MP3.

Audacity, like other sound-editing software, provides a large range of levels of quality for creating MP3 files, from 8 kilobits per second to 320 kbps. Remember, though, that this higher-quality version will be much larger in file size—a 192 kbps is nearly twice as large as a 96 kbps file.

Figure 16.3 *MP3 players make it possible for music—or talk—to go almost anywhere.*

Streaming or Downloading *LO 16.2*

Streaming is a process that allows a media file to begin to play before it has completely loaded onto a web page; thus, the sound begins to play more quickly. Therefore, streaming is an excellent choice. In order to stream, the audio file must be converted to a lossy compressed format. You could do so in a sound editor such as Audacity. However, other tools are also available.

platform—The specific operating system of a digital device and the hardware associated with it; among computers, the two main platforms are Windows and Mac.

encoding software—A program that changes media files from one format to another and can be used to create streaming media.

Adobe publishes media **encoding software** called Adobe Media Encoder CC. This program can be used to convert graphics, audio, or video files from one format to another. Figure 16.4 shows the Adobe Media Encoder CC work area. Changing the format of a file is simply a matter of choosing the file that is to be encoded—either one available on the Internet or one saved to a computer and then choosing the desired format.

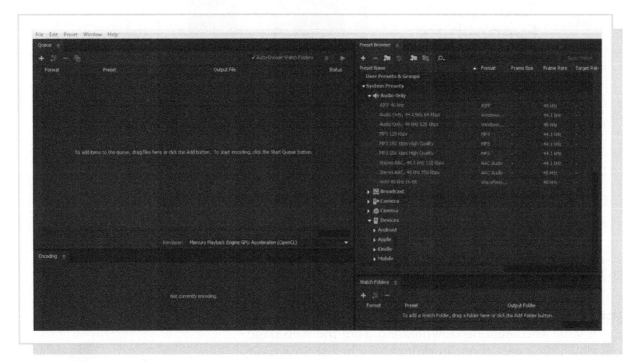

Figure 16.4 *Note the various file formats and devices.*

Granata1111/Dreamstime.com

Streaming to Success and Difficulties

RealNetworks—home to RealPlayer—was the first major player in delivering streaming media. Launching in the mid-1990s, the service quickly became a dominating piece of software. The ability to stream video was important in the early RealNetworks years because the majority of Internet users were still using slower dial-up connections.

It was not until the middle of the first decade in the twenty-first century were most Internet users in the United States connecting through broadband. In addition, due to low bandwidth, users appreciated streaming video because it was faster. Apple and Microsoft, however, quickly came out with their own streaming technologies. In addition, Real had some features that proved annoying to some users, who felt that the software was taking over aspects of their computing experience. RealNetworks no longer has the dominating position it once held.

Early streaming video often consisted of only snippets of media. That has changed in recent years, however. In 2010, Netflix launched a streaming-only option for full-length feature-length movies, with thousands of possible titles available to subscribers. Amazon, Hulu, and Roku have announced similar services.

Placing the Sound on the Page *LO 16.3 and 16.4*

There are two main ways to place sound on a web page: embedding the sound file or adding a hyperlink. There are advantages and disadvantages to each, and different issues are raised with the use of each method. These are discussed within each section below.

One word of caution. The term **embedding** is used here only to indicate that the sound file will reside on the web page. It is not meant to endorse the <embed> tag, which is supported by some browsers. This particular code is one of those tags that the World Wide Web Consortium (W3C) discourages.

embed—To place a media object on a web page rather than on a separate page.

Embedding the Sound File

Have you ever opened a website and found yourself instantly listening to some music? Did you wonder where that music came from? Remember that HTML code is written in different sections, for example, the <head> and the <body>. If you place the sound in the <head> of the page and use the autoplay command, it will play as soon as the page is open, without giving the user any control over the sound.

Because automatically playing sound is unwelcome to many site visitors, this practice is discouraged. One way around automatic play is to include some simple controls for the web visitor to use. With these, he or she can choose to hear the sound or not. The commands are simple:

```
<input type="button" value="Play Sound" name="Play"
onclick="FileName.play()">
```

```
<input type="button" value="Stop Sound" name="Stop"
onclick= "FileName.stop()">
```

The result of this code appears in Figure 16.5: a pair of buttons that give the user control over the sound. Note that this code should be placed in the body of the XHTML code, not the head.

These are functional but not very interesting visually. In a more full-featured web editor program, you can make changes to the styles associated with the buttons to give them more appeal. Consider features such as the font displayed, the size of the button, the positioning of text within the button, the background color of the button, and the size and color of the button border—among several other options.

You can use **HTML5**, supported by the W3C, to include both a sound file and a small audio player on your web page. A basic code for such a player looks like this:

HTML5—A newer version of HTML supported by the World Wide Web Consortium.

```
<audio id="console" src="FileName.wav"
controls="controls" autoplay="false"></audio>
```

In this line of code, four elements are essential. The <audio> tag introduces the object you're trying to place on the page; id is the name for the object, which can be anything you want it to be; src identifies the name of the sound file; and controls stipulates that a control panel should be displayed. By adding the autoplay attribute

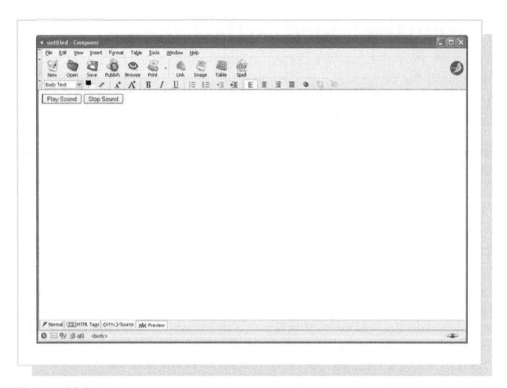

Figure 16.5 *Giving a web visitor control over whether or not to play sound with some simple XHTML commands is more considerate than making the sound play automatically.*

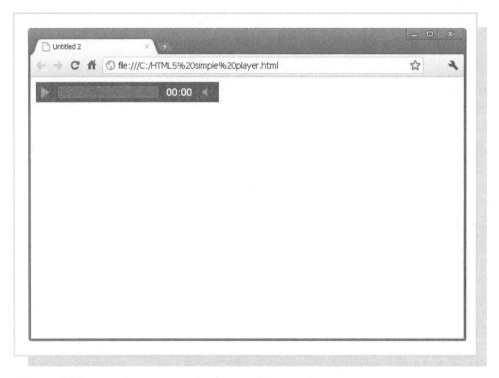

Figure 16.6 *A single line of HTML5 code produces a simple audio player that users can control. Along with the Play command, controlled by the arrow at the far left of the control panel, there is a volume control at the far right.*

and setting the value to false, you ensure that site visitors will have to activate the player to hear the sound, rather than it playing automatically. Figure 16.6 shows what this audio miniconsole looks like in the web browser Google Chrome.

Think About It

Do You Want to Hear Music Right Away?

Have you opened a website and heard music playing automatically? Did you find the music annoying? Were you listening to your own music before opening the page and did you find it annoying to have two melodies going at the same time? Were you in a workplace where you suffered the glares of coworkers—or a supervisor—who were bothered by the sound? When you're placing media in a website, it is a good idea to put yourself first in the position of a visitor to the site. Consider how you would experience a particular feature—the use of media, an interactive strategy, or an organizational scheme—before implementing it. Only include the feature if you think it would truly be appealing or useful to potential visitors.

Using a Hyperlink

Perhaps the simplest method for making a sound file available to web visitors is to keep it on the web server and create a hyperlink within the website. This might be the most considerate method as well because it keeps the audio optional for the user without adding features to the page that might slow down the web visitor's browser. When users click on the link, they will be taken to a new page where they will be able to hear the sound file. On opening the new web page, the site visitor's default audio player will play the sound. The code contains the `<a href>` tag that identifies a hyperlink, the filename and path, and some text that the hyperlink is attached to:

```
<a href="FileName.mp3">Click here to play the
audio file.</a>
```

Notice that this text appears before the `</a>` end tag. That sequence makes the text ("Click here to play the audio file") activate the hyperlink. Figure 16.7 shows how the hyperlinked text will look in a browser window. The precise wording of the text to be displayed can vary. You can also connect the hyperlink to just one word, rather than the whole sentence, by placing only the word "here" within the angle brackets defining the link:

```
Click <a href="FileName.mp3">here</a> to play the
audio file.
```

Video LO 16.3 and 16.4

HTML5 can be used effectively to embed video in web pages. HTML5's `<video>` tag has become widely supported by many browsers. However, if a browser does not support the HTML5 `<video>` tag, Quicktime may be used as a "back up plan." HTML5 code is extremely important for web video compatibility with iPhone and Android users.

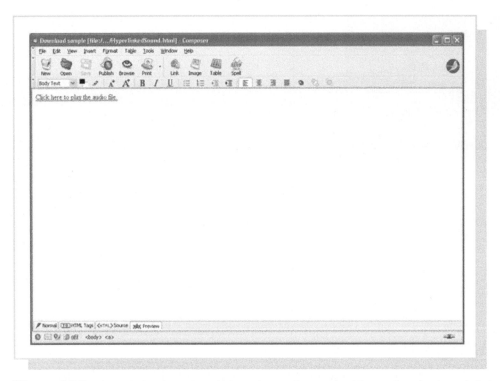

Figure 16.7 *The underlined words and blue color are the standard format for a live hyperlink.*

Many web visitors think of video files as MP4 or AVI files, but actually these are referred to as container formats. You might relate them to a ZIP file which may contain different files within it. They, like container formats, define how things are to be stored, but not what can be stored inside the container. For example, video files typically contain multiple tracks. There may be both video and audio tracks associated with a video file.

Two common video container formats includes MPEG 4 and Ogg (typically with an .ogv file extension). Before you can embed videos on the Web, you must first encode the video in the .ogv and .mp4 containers. The .ogv format is related to video bitstream and used to play videos using the HTML5 <video> tag. MP4 was described in a previous chapter.

Example code to embed a video in HTML5 is as follows.

```
<video width="450" height="230" control>
<source src="folder/video.mp4" type "video/mp4;
codecs="avc4.55E11E, mp4a. 23.1'">
<source src="folder/video.ogv" type "video/ogg;
codecs="theora, vorbis'">
</video>
```

This code specifies the dimensions of the video and adds two source elements which link to the video files. When the browser encounters this type attribute, it then understands which file to load. If a browser does not support HTML5, it will continue reading the code until it finds the <object> tab; however, a Flash video container will then be necessary for the video to run. If a Flash plugin is not downloaded or the video is trying to load on an Apple product, the video will not run.

checkpoint

What are the methods for placing audio and video objects on a web page?

ACTIVITY 16.1 ▶ Playing Audio on a Web Page

1. Search for free music for websites or get music from your instructor. Read the Terms of Use for the music before using.

2. Create a single web page with a hyperlink to the music. Save the web page in a folder named *16_Activity1* as *16_Activity1_linked*. Place the music in the same folder.

Lesson 16.2 ▶ Creating Podcasts *LO 16.5*

An addition to the world of web pages is **podcasting**. Podcasting is a means of providing downloadable audio or video to anyone who wishes to access the media content. The name *podcasting* results from combining the words *iPod* and *broadcasting*, with the iPod being the device that spurred this new form of information delivery—though that device is hardly the only method by which files are accessed. As stored audio files, podcasts are similar to radio shows that people once recorded on audiocassettes, and video files are similar to television shows recorded on videocassettes in the past or on a digital video recorder today. The advantage of podcasts is that site visitors can download the files and then hear or view the broadcast on their own time though a variety of technologies. The files are posted on a web server that is available 24/7, which means they can be accessed any time. Once the user downloads the files, he or she controls when they will be played. The other benefit of podcasts is that users also control the device on which the files will be played. Podcasts may be played on smartphones, desktop computers, tablets, and any number of different portable music players.

Who uses podcasts? Many podcasts are personal projects—individuals' recorded blogs, hobbyists' reviews of movies or video games, and similar examples of self-expression. However, podcasts are also of growing importance in the business world. The websites of media companies are full of podcasts of their programs or of program segments, such as interviews with government officials or notable cultural figures. Businesses post podcasts of important product announcements or other company news. Some financial companies use podcasts to give consumer advice or to publish audio of their investment experts analyzing the week's financial news. Even the federal government has some podcasts like audio files from the Social Security Administration describing various tasks such as how to notify the agency of a change of address or how to file a claim for benefits.

podcast—Audio or video stored on a web page and available for downloading via the Internet.

Discovering Podcasts.

The iTunes Store puts hundreds of thousands of free podcasts at your fingertips. Easily find and enjoy your next favorite on your iPhone, iPad, iPod touch, computer, or Apple TV. From automotive to news, fitness to pop culture, there's a podcast (or more) for everyone.

Figure 16.8 *iTunes does not host podcasts, but it is the most-used outlet for distributing podcasts to the public.*

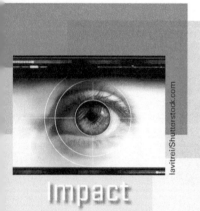

Impact

Podcasts, Blogs—and Shared Media Sites

There is little question that podcasts represent a huge change in information technology. They first appeared in 2004, with the debut of the iPod, and within two years, there were more than 40,000 different podcast sources—more than the number of all the radio stations around the world. By 2010, industry researchers counted nearly 90,000 podcast sites. Today a third of all online activity is spent watching videos, and podcasts could be a viable component of those videos. YouTube is the number two search engine, and many podcasts are housed on YouTube's Video Podcast Network. YouTube has more than 1 billion users, and every day individuals watch hundreds of millions of hours of YouTube videos. Over 300 hours of video are uploaded to YouTube every minute. Amazing!.

Why So Popular?

What makes technologies like podcasts, social networking sites, or media sharing sites so popular? More important, what can a business do to make its offerings stand out in these environments?

Podcasts and XML *LO 16.5*

Podcasts are made available using XML files. **XML** (for e**X**tensible **M**arkup **L**anguage) is a markup language specifically designed to hold and move data. XML holds packets of data; XHTML describes how the data is to be displayed. XML differs from XHTML in several other ways. First, it does not have any set tags, as XHTML does. Instead, the user creates the tags, which might be as simple as `<to>` and `<from>` tags to indicate the recipient and sender of a message, which is the data. An advantage of XML is that it keeps the data separate from the method of presentation. That way, if the data changes, the XHTML code is not affected. XML is also more device independent, meaning the data can be made available to people on different types of computer platforms, mobile devices, and so on. XHTML is a combination of XML and HTML.

XML can be used to hold a wide variety of data, from product catalogs to lists of podcasts. What it cannot do is *display* that data in a useful way. Instead, when you view XML code in a web browser, you see not only the data—or links to it—but also the codes themselves. To show the data in an organized and attractive way, it is necessary to use another language. One option is Cascading Style Sheets (CSS) (see Figure 16.9). The W3C recommends another solution, however—using a styling language called XSLT (for e**X**tensible **S**tylesheet **L**anguage **T**ransformations). Entire texts are devoted to instruction on writing XML code and XSLT style sheets and it is

XML—Markup language designed to hold and move data.

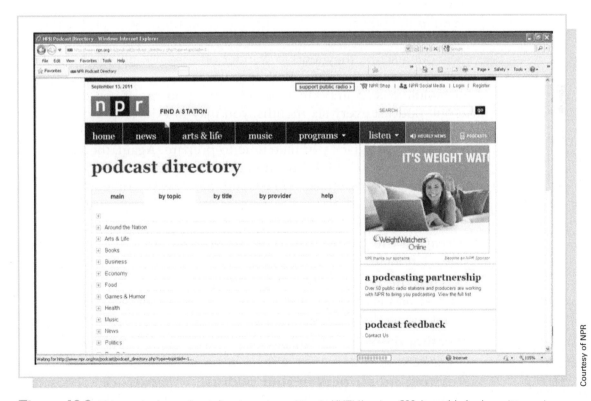

Figure 16.9 *This particular podcast directory was written in XHTML using CSS. It could also be written using XML code and then styled in XSLT.*

beyond the scope of this text to delve into these. Both languages are quite complex. Fortunately, there are easier ways of creating podcasts than writing them in code.

Steps in Creating a Podcast *LO 16.6*

Before you create a podcast, it is important to consider the following:

- format (e.g., formal or informal, all audio or audio and video)
- length (e.g., 15 minutes snippets or 45 minute lectures)
- script (e.g., script your text or talk "on the fly")
- scheduling (e.g., podcasts will be produced once per week or once per month)
- lawyering (e.g., getting artist consent to play songs or use other licensed materials)

Your podcast represents you. The format you choose is how others will begin to relate to you and your material. The format many times depends on the content and how you want to deliver the content.

When considering the length of your podcast, you must include any music you may use as a lead-in or exit to your podcast. Everything you include takes up time. You want the podcast to be short enough to keep the listener's attention, yet long enough to cover the content appropriately.

Scripting can provide a smooth transition into and out of a podcast and helps to ensure all topics are appropriately covered in the set amount of time provided. Scripting is encouraged if only one speaker is involved in the podcast and it is not a conversational-style podcast with multiple participants. When individuals try to simply talk about the subject without a script, they tend to wander off topic or talk too long about a certain portion of the topic. Both lose the listener's attention.

Scheduling is an important aspect of the podcast. If you only produce one podcast every six months, you may not develop a consistent listener base. You also don't want to provide podcasts, perhaps, on a daily basis, as that gives you little time to prepare. Again, the content, and your objective, should drive how often you schedule your podcasts. Lawyering is essential to make sure all creative content used in the podcast is legal to use.

Making a podcast involves four basic steps:

1. **Creating the media file.** Typically podcasts are audio files, but they can include video and even documents.

2. **Saving the file in a downloadable form.** Remember key features of podcasts is that they are downloadable. In this case, you do not want the media to be streaming.

3. **Posting the file to a web server.** There are different options for this step.

4. **Inviting subscribers to your podcast.** Podcasters can choose from among several different tools to increase the visibility of their podcasts and invite visitors to become **subscribers**.

subscriber—Web visitor who accepts notification of any updates to a podcast or a website that has frequently changing content.

Creating the Media File

Some additional points to keep in mind when creating a podcast:

- **Keep the content focused.** Podcasts typically focus on one topic or a few related topics. Participants should agree in advance about the topics to be covered. If the podcast will include more than one speaker, assigning someone the role of moderator to keep the discussion on topic is a good idea.

- **Be prepared before recording.** Being prepared does not mean you necessarily must have a script. Many excellent podcasts are impromptu conversations among people who are well-informed and opinionated about the subject at hand, whether that be investments or the movie industry. However, even these conversations can benefit from some advance planning, such as having note cards with main points or key statistics or, if the podcast is an interview, having the questions written down. If you're shooting a video podcast, being prepared means having all necessary equipment ready. Suppose you're demonstrating how to prepare a one-dish dinner to showcase your catering business. Make sure you have all ingredients and cooking equipment ready before you start shooting. With a video, being prepared also means making sure that all participants are appropriately dressed for the podcast. For a business podcast, they should look professional, not as though they are dressed for a weekend outing (see Figure 16.10).

- **Be sure all participants can be equally heard.** Many podcasts consist of a group of individuals discussing issues in their area of expertise. Be sure that participants and microphones are arranged in such a way that each member of the panel can be recorded at the same level. Test the seating arrangement before beginning the recording and adjust seats if necessary. Use more than one microphone if necessary.

pop filters—used to decrease explosive breath sounds common when recording your voice.

- **Share the microphone.** In conversation, more than one person often speaks at the same time. That doesn't pose a problem usually as we can ask someone to repeat what he or she said if we didn't hear it. In podcasts, multiple individuals speaking simultaneously makes for jumbled, unintelligible sound. Caution people to take turns speaking. If more than one person is speaking, using external microphones will offer better sound and greater flexibility than built-in microphones. It may also be important to purchase an inexpensive pop filter. **Pop filters** decrease explosive breath sounds common when recording voices.

- **Be conscious of your audience.** Think about the background knowledge and interests of people who are likely to want to listen to and/or view the podcast. Tailor the content of the podcast to

Figure 16.10 *One option when recording a podcast is to place a microphone near each speaker.*

Juice Images/Getty Images

that audience. If you're discussing technical material for a knowledgeable audience, you can use technical jargon and may not have to define terms. If you're targeting a general audience, though, you'll have to be sure to explain what those terms mean.

- **Avoid distracting background noise.** The only sounds included in a podcast, whether audio or video, should be the ones meant to be recorded. Keep the room in which the recording takes place quiet. Be sure to tell anyone taking part in the podcast to turn off their cell phones before recording begins!

- **With video, keep the camera steady.** Video in a podcast, like sound levels, should be steady and smooth. Avoid jerky camera movements and unusual angles. However, that does not mean that every shot should be static and identical to all the others. Move the camera to show the new speaker when a different participant joins the conversation—but move it slowly and evenly. If the podcast video includes a demonstration, you might wish to pan down to the person's hands so the viewer can better focus on what is being done. You might even wish to zoom in to show detail. Remember to make these camera movements smooth.

Of course, you can use audio or video editing software to fix some problems that might arise in the course of the recording, such as quiet spots in the course of an audio recording or the need to increase the volume slightly on one participant's voice. The best rule to follow is to keep the podcast simple and straightforward. Avoid using special effects. People tend to seek out podcasts for information, not entertainment. While they may hope for talks to be lively, they generally are not looking for technical wizardry. Remember, as always with web media, to make the style of the presentation suit the image and goal of the company in whose name it is presented.

Presentation Skills

The increasing use of media to communicate means that workers are more likely than ever before to be called on to make presentations. To make them effective, presenters need good presentation skills. Effective oral communication requires you to speak clearly, enunciating words so they are easily understood. You should also use emphasis effectively, stressing the most important words to give the message more impact. Working well with others is important if the presentation includes multiple individuals: Avoid speaking over each other—or interrupting.

Skills in Action: Watch or listen to two business–related podcasts. Take notes on the way participants in the podcast present themselves and their ideas. List examples of both positive and negative behaviors and explain why each is a good or bad practice. Use your list to develop a checklist of pointers for making presentations—and use your checklist to evaluate your own presentations.

Saving the File

Podcasts are saved in the same file formats as other audio and video files meant to be made available on the Web. Since podcasts are meant to reach an audience, it is best to put the files in the most widely available formats. For audio podcasts, MP3 files are the ideal choice since they can play on a range of platforms. They also have the advantage of creating small file sizes. Remember a key to podcasts is that they are downloadable. You want to keep file sizes as small as possible so visitors to the website spend as little time as possible making the downloads.

For video files, it is probably best to save the file in more than one format, such as .MOV for QuickTime and .WMV for Windows Media Player. Another good choice is the **H.264** format that developed from the MPEG-4 specification you read about previously. H.264 is advantageous because it can play on many different platforms, including mobile devices, and compresses video files very efficiently.

H.264—A video format that is highly compressed and can be played across many platforms.

Posting the File to a Web Server

For a podcast to be available to the public, it needs to be posted on a web server. Some companies have their own web servers, which host their websites and they may also have an FTP site. In this case, the information technology staff that manages the server will be able to guide nontechnical staff through the steps in uploading the podcast files to the server. If a company purchases web hosting from a service, its staff will also provide instructions. Either way, posting the files will be similar to the process for posting web pages.

It is possible to create podcasts without having a dedicated web server. The Internet has free podcast media hosting sites, such as soundcloud.com. You may be able to post a podcast on iTunes or YouTube for free or for a fee. Uploading audio files is as easy as saving the file, registering at the site, clicking on an Upload & Share button on the main screen, and then on the Choose Files button to select the file that you have stored. Once the file has been uploaded and transcoded, it is ready to save on the website. By choosing to make the file Public and checking the box for enabling downloads (see the red rectangle and red oval in Figure 16.11), you make it possible to podcast the file.

Another way to post a podcast is by opening a free blog on a site such as WordPress or setting up a blog through Google. Joining usually requires a simple registration process, which involves choosing a display name for the blog, providing a contact email address, and providing a few other bits of information. There are many blogging sites to choose from.

Creating a podcast is quite simple on one of these blogging sites. The particular steps will vary somewhat from site to site; the following steps outline the procedure for Google's Blogger. You begin by creating a free account linked to an email address and protected by a password. Once signed in, you are taken to the Dashboard, which has the overall controls for the site (see Figure 16.12). By clicking on the

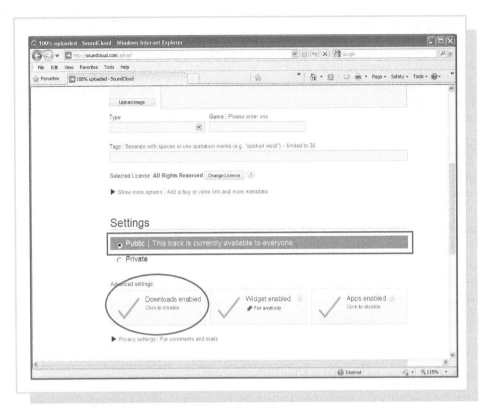

Figure 16.11 *Soundcloud is just one example of a website that hosts audio files that can be stored for podcasting.*

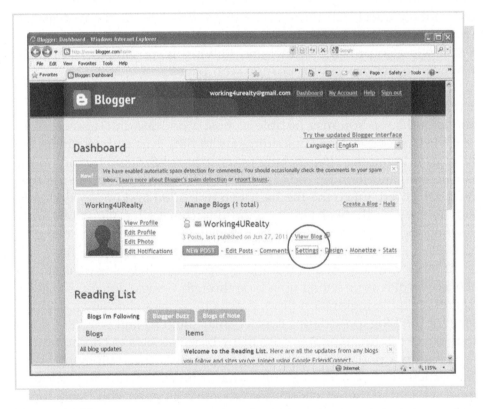

Figure 16.12 *Blogger's Dashboard, or control panel, has a Settings tab that is one step in enabling a podcast.*

Settings tab, you are taken to a screen that allows you various options regarding date stamping, archiving, and similar features. One of these features—the Show Link Fields tab—will enable podcasting if you choose *Yes* in the drop-down menu and then save the settings (see Figure 16.13).

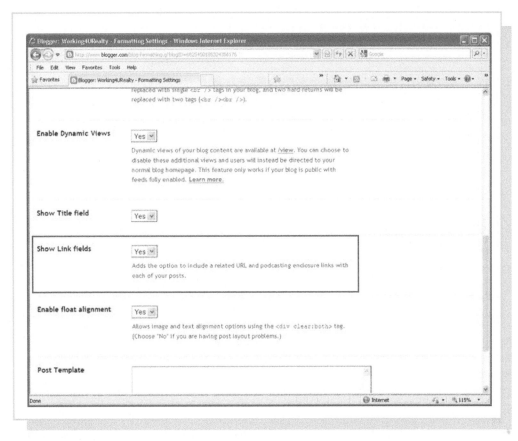

Figure 16.13 *By choosing Yes in the Show Link fields option, available in the Formatting tab, you can enable podcasting.*

The next step to creating a podcast in Blogger is to create a blog post, as shown in Figure 16.14. Notice the field for the URL of a link below the title of the post. You paste or key the URL for your stored audio file in that space. Once the blog is posted, these settings will enable the audio file to be recognized as a podcast. You can provide a description of the podcast contents in the body of the blog post. When you have filled in all the information, simply click Publish Post, underneath the body of the post, to post the podcast.

Inviting Subscribers to Your Podcast

The final step in podcasting is getting your podcast recognized. In the world of the Web, a **feed** is any electronic content and the process by which that content is syndicated, or made available to

feed—Electronic content and the process of syndicating that content.

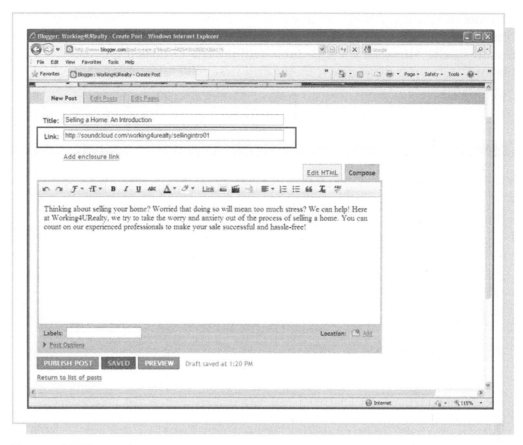

Figure 16.14 *The Link field allows you to insert an audio or video file hosted on another website into a Blogger blog post. Once podcast viewers are notified of the post, that piece of media will be available to them.*

RSS feed—One standard for syndicating web content.

aggregator—Software that collects and lists websites that have been syndicated.

subscribers. You'll need to register your website or podcast site, with a service that will recognize your podcast site and make it public. Depending on where you post your podcast, you may be prompted to choose one of two types of feeds: Atom or the **RSS feed**. RSS (for **R**eal **S**imple **S**yndication) is the older standard; Atom was developed more recently. As yet, RSS has a larger following. Either option allows software called **aggregators** to collect and list syndicated websites. The aggregators show when any of these websites has been updated with a new entry. As a result, subscribers do not have to constantly monitor every site that has podcasts or news updates in which they're interested. They need only check the aggregator to see if there have been any updates and then, if there have, go visit the site or sites. The notice they receive from the aggregator often includes a brief description of the update.

The RSS manager service allow you to enter a category for your podcast so it will be listed in appropriate areas of iTunes and other media RSS aggregators. You can also enter a description and keywords to provide more information about the podcast site, which will make it more likely to be noticed by those people most interested in your subject. Each time you create a new podcast, the RSS manager service will automatically recognize it and make that information available to anyone who subscribes to your site. This feed controller also provides statistics on the number of subscribers, the number of visitors to your site, and the number of downloads.

You can also use the RSS manager service to add icons (called "chicklets" by the program) representing any of several aggregators, as shown in Figure 16.15. At the bottom of that window is an option to add the code for the icon to your website or podcast. If you accept the option, the RSS icon will appear on your website's main page, as shown in Figure 16.16. Before any syndication or aggregator icon can be added to your Blogger page, Blogger asks your permission to include it. Therefore, accepting it is the last step in publicizing your podcast.

checkpoint

What are the steps in making a podcast?

Figure 16.15 *In the Chicklet Chooser screen, the RSS manager service lets you choose which size RSS icon to place on your website or with which other aggregators you wish to list your website.*

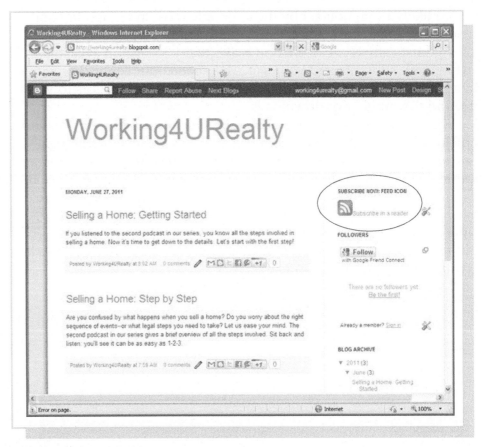

Figure 16.16 *Any visitor to your website can become a subscriber simply by clicking on the RSS icon.*

ACTIVITY 16.2 ▶ Creating a Podcast

1. Go to http://www.podcast.com or another library of podcasts. Listen to at least two podcasts to get ideas for an appropriate podcast of your own.

2. Create a two-minute audio podcast on a topic of your choice. Save your podcast as *16_Activity2_podcast*.

3. With your instructor's permission, post the podcast to WordPress, Blogger, or another similar website. Provide your instructor with a link to the podcast.

Key Concepts

▶ Choosing a file format for audio files to be posted on the Web is a matter of balancing quality, file size, and accessibility. Some file formats are only available on some platforms, or operating systems and devices. The MP3 format, which is data compressed to a small size, is still the file format of choice because it can be played on a wide variety of systems. *LO 16.1*

▶ Media files can be streamed or downloadable. Streaming saves time for the user by making it possible for web visitors to listen to or hear the file before the whole file is downloaded. *LO 16.2*

▶ There are two basic methods for posting media on a website—to embed it by writing the code to place the media in either the head (which will play the media automatically when the page opens) or in the body with buttons or some other controls; or to create a hyperlink that sends the web visitor to another page to obtain the media, using the standard tags for creating a hyperlink. *LO 16.3 and 16.4*

▶ Video should be streamed rather than downloadable because files can be very large. Making the screen size smaller can help keep file size small. *LO 16.2*

▶ Another way to make media available to web visitors is in podcasts, which create downloadable media packets and invite users to subscribe to the service and be notified of updates. Media companies use podcasts to make programs available to listeners and viewers; businesses may post podcasts of important product announcements or other company news or to give consumers information. *LO 16.5*

▶ Preparing for a podcast, whether an audio or video version, helps make a presentation of good quality.

▶ Podcast files should be saved in a downloadable format. They can be saved to a company-owned server or to a web hosting service, whether it free or fee-based. After uploading the file to the server, it is necessary to publish a link to the file, which can be done simply by creating a blog with a link to the media. To make a podcast visible, the podcaster should set up a subscription service like an RSS feed that will be noticed by podcast aggregators and thus notify subscribers of updated content. *LO 16.6*

Review and Discuss

1. Differentiate between lossless and lossy compression. *LO 16.1*

2. Explain why streaming audio or video is better than downloading. *LO 16.2*

3. Justify the use of controls to play sound on a website rather than using autoplay.

4. Evaluate the use of HTML5 to include a sound file on a web page. *LO 16.3*

5. Suppose a company's web design policy states that, for all web pages, code for RealPlayer plug-in should be used. Write a proposal to change the policy with justification for your proposal.

6. Compare and contrast XML and XHTML, and state the advantages of using XML with XHTML.

7. Compile a list of tips for creating a good podcast when a single individual is producing it. *LO 16.6*

 # Apply

1. You are creating a proposal for a potential client who needs sound added to his website. The sound file will be a daily update on two current news topics. Create a sound file with brief summaries of two major news stories in your area. Save as **16_Apply1_sound** in a folder named **16_Apply1**. Create a web page with the code for linking the sound and save it as **16_Apply1_linked**. Be sure the web page and sound file are in the **16_Apply1** folder. *LO 16.1*

2. Create a video of special attractions in your city to use on a city website or use a video that you have already created. Keep in mind the hints learned from the chapter for a smaller file size. Make the video file streaming in either MOV or AVI format or use a format given by your instructor. Save the video in a folder named **16_Apply3** as a file named **16_Apply3_city_movie**. Create a web page that embeds the video with user controls. Save the website as **16_Apply3_city_website** in the **16_Apply3** folder. *LO 16.1 and 16.4*

3. Work with a partner to create a teaching video on a topic of your choice. Think about something you know how to do that you can share with others. Save, export, or encode the video as **16_Apply4_teaching** in a folder named **16_Apply4** as a MOV or AVI file format. Insert the teaching video on a web page as a hyperlink. Save the web page in the **16_Apply4** folder as **16_Apply4_web_instruction**. *LO 16.4*

4. Create a two-minute podcast reviewing a restaurant, a book you have read, a movie you have watched, or a game you have played. Save the review in a folder named **16_Apply5** with the file name **16_Apply5_review**. Upload the podcast to a website such as SoundCloud. Then invite subscribers to the site. Send the link for the website to your instructor. *LO 16.6*

5. In a team of three, respond to the following interview topics.

- Briefly tell about yourself.
- What are your goals?
- What is one of your greatest accomplishments to date?
- What experiences have you had that prepare you to work?

Each team member should take turns shooting the video, asking the questions, and answering the questions. Each student should embed the video of them answering the questions in a web page. Save the video as **16_Apply6_interviewing** in a **16_Apply6** folder. Save the web page as **16_Apply6_interviewing_webpage**. *LO 16.4*

Explore

1. Search for an RSS feed to subscribe to or subscribe to one identified by your instructor. Read at least three of the past posts at the site. Create a short podcast journal for each post, highlighting important things you heard. Introduce the podcast to classmates by identifying the location of the original site and what interested you about the topic. Save as **16_Explore1_podcast1**, **16_Explore2_podcast2**, and **16_Explore1_ podcast3** in the **16_Explore1** folder.*LO 16.6*

2. Locate two websites with sound or video. Find at least one that includes a user control and another that uses hyperlinking. In a document, include the source citation and discuss the method that was used to place the sound or video on the site. You may want to view the underlying code to determine the method used. Was the method used effective? Why or why not? What would you have done differently? Save your document as **16_Explore2_web_review**.

3. Search for "best podcasts." Watch or listen to two of the podcasts. In a word processing document, give the source citation and explain why you thought the podcasts won the award. Did you like it? Why or why not? What would you have done differently? Save your document as **16_Explore3_best_podcasts**.

Academic Connections

Communications. Write 15 sentences explaining points you have learned in this chapter. In each sentence, identify the noun and verb. Save your sentences as **16_AC_communications**.

Science. Search for or get from your instructor the location of two podcasts on science projects. Summarize the projects using an audio notes app or other software available to you. Save your summaries as **16_AC_science**.

Chapter 17

Web Standards

Lesson 17.1 Ensuring Standards and Access

Lesson 17.2 Getting Found

When designing web pages and developing content, interactive features, animation, audio, and video, you always need to keep the purpose of the website in mind. How will visitors perceive and respond to your site? Will they find your site well-structured, easy to navigate, and accessible to visitors with disabilities? Does it follow web conventions? Most important, perhaps, is the question of whether those browsing the Web will even find your site. What techniques will you use to attract visitors? Why do you think those approaches will work?

Learning Outcomes

▶ **17.1** Explain how the W3C creates standards.

▶ **17.2** Identify issues involved in web accessibility.

▶ **17.3** Explain how the WAI and Section 508 try to ensure accessibility.

▶ **17.4** List conventions for web pages.

▶ **17.5** Explain how Internet search engines work.

▶ **17.6** List techniques that can be used to improve a website's standing in search engine results.

▶ **17.7** Explain the purpose and value of web analytics.

Key Terms

- accessibility
- adword
- assistive technology
- FAQs
- keyword
- link exchange
- meta tag
- Robot Exclusion Protocol (REP)
- screen reader
- search engine
- search engine optimization (SEO)
- Section 508
- spider
- validator
- Web Accessibility Initiative (WAI)
- web analytics
- Web Master

Financial institutions must follow state and federal laws regarding financial transactions, communications with customers, credit approval, and many other activities. Airlines have to meet strict safety standards in order to operate. Insurance companies are regulated by many states, and countless other businesses—from grocery stores that have their scales checked by the office of weights and measures to giant pharmaceutical companies that must follow strict guidelines to win government approval for new drugs—work under the watchful eye of government regulators.

The World Wide Web is, in many respects, in a completely opposite situation, as companies and organizations are generally free to say what they want to say, show what they want to show, and do both in the manner they please, taking into consideration legal and ethical constraints. There are, nevertheless, standards that websites are expected to meet.

Figure 17.1 *Corporations that wish to sell stocks to the public must follow certain financial reporting requirements set by the federal government.*

iStockphoto.com/EdStock

World Wide Web Consortium *LO 17.1*

The World Wide Web Consortium (W3C) plays the major role in establishing and promoting web standards. The W3C, in promoting the creation of well-formed code, seeks to ensure that websites appear in similar ways across many browsers and hardware platforms.

Unlike software that is developed and maintained by specific companies, XHTML and other markup languages are not written and owned by specific companies. Instead, the W3C, an independent non-profit organization, oversees and monitors the creation and proper use of XHTML code. The W3C produces technical documents outlining specifications for these markup languages and other web development tools. These documents are developed as part of a long, careful, collaborative process involving professionals from many companies within the industry. Before standards become finalized, committees of these professionals draft versions that are proposed, reviewed and commented on by any interested party, and discussed, revised, and vetted and perhaps revised again. More information about the W3C, its role, and its processes can be found at www.w3.org.

Once the W3C publishes a standard—such as the HTML 5 Specification or the Cascading Style Sheets (CSS) Specification—developers of browser software and websites begin to integrate these modifications into their programs. This means that users with older versions of browser software may not be able to use all of the features that are part of a newer or updated website. For example, older browser versions may not be able to make use of CSS. This is one reason that businesses need to consider the pros and cons of using the most current HTML options and understand what standards are guiding their choice.

Website developers and individuals who direct the work of those creating web pages need to know current W3C recommendations. It is easy to fall behind quickly in the fast-changing world of web design.

Ensuring Access *LO 17.2 and 17.3*

While the W3C is concerned about maintaining stable markup and scripting languages that result in websites that can be used by as many browsers as possible, another set of issues revolves around ensuring that websites are accessible to as many people as possible, regardless of their abilities. There is a growing demand that those who design websites—or oversee web designers—make their sites usable by all users, regardless of their vision or hearing abilities. Two sets of rules govern **accessibility**: those developed by the W3C and the federal government rules provided under Section 508.

accessibility—The principle of making web content understandable and usable by all people regardless of disabilities.

Sir Tim Berners-Lee and the Web

Who better to invent the World Wide Web than someone who had computing in his genes—the son of two computer scientists? Both of Sir Tim Berners-Lee's parents had worked on the Ferranti Mark I, the first computer sold commercially. Berners-Lee began to design software after graduating from college in the 1970s. While fiddling with a program for himself, he invented the key concept underlying the World Wide Web—the idea of hypertext, or links in one file that connected to other files. In 1989, he proposed a system for using these hypertext links to connect documents across the Internet. In the space of few months, he created the code for the first server to store web information and the first browser to access it. He spent the next few years promoting the Web—an idea whose time had come.

Berners-Lee was knighted by Queen Elizabeth II in 2004.

W3C Standards

Driving the W3C's policy of ensuring accessibility is the vision of Sir Tim Berners-Lee (see Figure 17.2), director of the organization and widely regarded as the founder of the World Wide Web. Berners-Lee has stated, "The power of the Web is in its universality. Access of everyone regardless of disability is an essential aspect." To implement that vision, the W3C launched a multifaceted effort called the **Web Accessibility Initiative (WAI)**. The WAI includes the creation of guidelines for website accessibility, support materials and resources for web developers, tools for evaluating accessibility, and even advice on using the Web for those who have disabilities. As part of the WAI, the W3C has issued recommendations for accessibility called Web Content Accessibility Guidelines (WCAG).

Web Accessibility Initiative (WAI)—W3C effort to ensure accessibility by creating accessibility standards and providing resources relevant to the issue.

The WCAG is designed to promote accessibility in four areas:

- Content is *perceivable*, which means that it is made in such a way that individuals with disabilities can perceive the content in some alternative way, such as alternative or title text for images or captions for multimedia, or through the use of **assistive technology**. This category also includes making site content easy to see or hear and creating content that can be presented in different ways without losing meaning.

Figure 17.2 *Sir Tim Berners-Lee, credited with founding the World Wide Web, formed the World Wide Web Consortium to set standards for web developers.*

AP Photo/Elise Amendola

- The website is *operable*, which means that all site functions can be accessed using a keyboard, that users have enough time to read and use content, and that there are navigational and searching aids. This category also includes making sure that the content or presentation of a site will not induce seizures in those individuals with an increased risk of seizures.

assistive technology—Any device or software developed with the goal of helping those with disabilities use and interact successfully with a computer.

- Content is *understandable*, which means the text is readable and clear, that actions and reactions on the site are predictable, and that steps are taken to prevent users from making errors in interacting with the site.

- The site is designed in *robust* ways, meaning that it is, as much as possible, compatible with current technology and adaptable to future technology.

These guidelines call for such practices as providing alternative text descriptions for images. These are needed because many **screen readers** used by the vision-impaired would skip over each image. With an alternative text, the program has something to read to the web visitor. Another example of an accessibility option is to allow keyboard input, rather than mouse movement, for all actions on the site. This aids those individuals who cannot use a mouse. Providing transcripts, or text versions, for recorded speech is a way to make audio such as podcasts accessible to the hearing impaired.

For the inexperienced web designer or website manager, complying with these recommendations may seem a daunting task. W3C helps by providing a host of sample techniques explaining how to tailor site content to achieve these standards. In many cases, it gives several alternatives using different web development technologies, such as XHTML, CSS, and scripting languages. The web designer can thus find help with the type of tool with which he or she is most comfortable. These techniques are specified not only for media elements but also for interactive features on a page, such as checkboxes and radio buttons. The problem with these features is that web assistive technology does not always fully interpret them. Figure 17.3 shows a form that may not be properly interpreted by a screen reader.

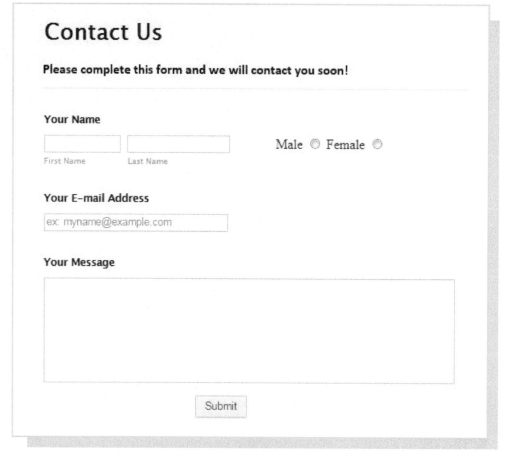

Figure 17.3 *A simple form that requires user input might not be interpreted fully by some assistive technology.*

Analyze the following code a banking institution may use to develop an online form for customers. Think about what this form would look like.

```
<p> <input name="account" id="reg chkg"
value="regular checking"
type="radio"> <label="reg chkg="">Regular
Checking<br/>
<input name="account" id="int chkg"
value="interest-bearing checking"
type="radio"> <label="int chkg="">Interest-Bearing
Checking<br/>
<input name="account" id="svg" value="savings"
type="radio"> <label="svg">Savings</label><br/>
<input name="account" id="mny mkt" value="money
market" type="radio">
<label="mny mkt">Money Market</label><br/>
<input value="Continue" type="submit"></
label="int"></label="reg"></p>
```

In this sequence of code, `type="radio"` instructs the browser to create radio buttons. The codes `id="int chkg"` and `value="interest-bearing checking"` identify one type of account. The text Interest-Bearing Checking shows the text that will be displayed in the list. You could make a similar list showing different choices by changing the id, value, and text label. For instance, a car rental company might use `id="mid"`; `value="midsize car"`; and `Midsize Car` for the label.

Some assistive technology web readers would not be able to read these labels, however, and would thus not convey full information about the list or how to interact with it. The technique used to solve the problem is to insert the word for after the label element. Instead of reading like this:

```
<input name="account" id="reg chkg" value="regular
checking"
type="radio"> <label="reg chkg="">Regular
Checking<br>
```

the code for each line in the button list would read like this (the change is highlighted):

```
<input name="account" id="reg chkg" value="regular
checking"
type="radio"> <label for="reg chkg="">Regular
Checking<br>
```

Simply by adding for, the label becomes recognizable to screen readers that would not recognize the `label` element alone.

Section 508

The W3C recommendations for web accessibility are guidelines but not mandates. That is not the case for the other set of accessibility standards, Section 508 standards. These standards are based on

Section 508 of the Rehabilitation Act of 1973. The section, an amendment to the 1973 law that became official in 1988, requires electronic and information technology offered by federal agencies to be fully accessible to all users. Although the law's requirements do not apply to sites created by businesses, this is a standard to consider so that all members of your audience are included when you are constructing web pages. Several Section 508 requirements are similar to the W3C's accessibility standards.

At the time of this writing, the Section 508 regulations for websites were as follows:

(a) A text equivalent for every non-text element shall be provided (e.g., via "alt," "longdesc," or in element content).

(b) Equivalent alternatives for any multimedia presentation shall be synchronized with the presentation.

(c) Web pages shall be designed so that all information conveyed with color is also available without color, for example from context or markup.

(d) Documents shall be organized so they are readable without requiring an associated style sheet.

(e) Redundant text links shall be provided for each active region of a server-side image map.

(f) Client-side image maps shall be provided instead of server-side image maps except where the regions cannot be defined with an available geometric shape.

(g) Row and column headers shall be identified for data tables.

(h) Markup shall be used to associate data cells and header cells for data tables that have two or more logical levels of row or column headers.

(i) Frames shall be titled with text that facilitates frame identification and navigation.

(j) Pages shall be designed to avoid causing the screen to flicker with a frequency greater than 2 Hz and lower than 55 Hz.

(k) A text-only page, with equivalent information or functionality, shall be provided to make a website comply with the provisions of this part, when compliance cannot be accomplished in any other way. The content of the text-only page shall be updated whenever the primary page changes.

(l) When pages utilize scripting languages to display content, or to create interface elements, the information provided by the script shall be identified with functional text that can be read by assistive technology.

(m) When a web page requires that an applet, plug-in or other application be present on the client system to interpret page content, the page must provide a link to a plug-in or applet that complies with §1194.21(a) through (l).

Figure 17.4 *Assistive technologies, such as this braille keyboard, enable people with various abilities and disabilities to access the benefits of computers and the Internet.*

(n) When electronic forms are designed to be completed online, the form shall allow people using assistive technology to access the information, field elements, and functionality required for completion and submission of the form, including all directions and cues.

(o) A method shall be provided that permits users to skip repetitive navigation links.

(p) When a timed response is required, the user shall be alerted and given sufficient time to indicate more time is required.

The regulations for video and multimedia content include the requirement that these media have closed captions or open captions and that audio descriptions also be supplied.

Testing Sites *LO 17.2 and 17.3*

Web developers may not always be certain that all the features they include in a site meet W3C standards or accessibility guidelines. Various tools are available to check for compliance.

Testing for Valid Code

Many web editors have built-in code validation features that allow web developers to ensure that the code they write is correct. By setting the measure to XHTML or HTML 5, they can verify that the code meets the most current standards supported by the W3C. Even if a web developer does not have such a tool, it is possible to use the organization's various quality assurance tools, including a **validator** that checks four areas: markup language, cascading style sheets, appropriateness to mobile computing, and correctness of RSS or Atom subscription feeds. Other validators are available from other online sources as well.

validator—Software that checks websites under development for compliance with particular standards.

Testing for Accessibility

How do you know if your website meets W3C accessibility recommendations or Section 508 requirements? One way to find out is to use the list of questions provided in Table 17.1.

Table 17.1 *You can use these questions to begin to evaluate the accessibility of a website.*

1.	For all images, is alternative text provided?
2.	For all applets, are alternative text and content provided?
3.	For all graphical buttons, is alternative text provided?
4.	For all image maps, are text links provided for each hotspot in the image map?
5.	For all graphics that convey important information, are long descriptions provided?
6.	For stand-alone audio files, are transcripts provided with words spoken or sung as well as all significant sounds?
7.	For audio associated with video, are captions—transcripts of dialog and sounds—synchronized with the video?
8.	For animations, are alternative text and a long description provided?
9.	For video, are auditory descriptions provided and synchronized with the original audio?
10.	If color is used to convey information, is the information also clear from the markup or text?
11.	Do foreground and background color combinations provide sufficient contrast when viewed by someone with color blindness or when viewed on a black-and-white screen?
12.	Is the web page free from any blinking or updating of the screen that causes flicker?
13.	For scripts that present critical information or functions, is an alternative, equivalent presentation or mechanism provided?
14.	For pages that use style sheets, are the contents of each page structured so that they read appropriately without the style sheet?
15.	Is a "text only" alternative provided, and does it contain substantially the same information as the original page?
16.	Is the "text only" alternative page updated as often as the original page?

Another common way to test for accessibility is to use websites that specifically test for noncompliance, including color blindness. Two commonly used sites including the following:

- A testing tool developed by WebAim.org, a joint effort of Utah State University and the Center for Persons with Disabilities: http://www.wave.webaim.org/

- The W3C has compiled a list of dozens of site evaluation tools, each of which is briefly described here: http://www.w3.org/QA/Tools/

Keying your site address into the appropriate location on one of these sites will return a report with any infractions listed.

Web Conventions *LO 17.4*

Another area in which web designers provide a courtesy to their readers is by designing sites to conform to certain page conventions or expectations. For instance, websites should include a copyright date and indicate the last date that a page has been updated. Pages should also have links back to the home page in the event that a reader has come to a page from a search engine and cannot use the browser's Back function to reach the site's main page. It is also expected that the home page will have a contact link or form so that site visitors can notify the **Web Master** of any technical problems encountered at the site.

In addition, businesses and organizations that have contact with the public should always include information about their physical address (including state and country) as well as a telephone number. Detailed maps indicating a way to reach the business are particularly helpful—and can be useful for attracting customers. Many businesses link to the mapping services of Google or MapQuest to allow visitors to easily find directions from their own location—or a nearby airport or other transportation hub—to the business's location.

Another web convention is to provide a page for **Frequently Asked Questions (FAQs)**. These questions and answers help site visitors locate specific information they are interested in or clarify procedures they are unsure about. With some sites, it may be necessary to have multiple FAQ pages, each focused on a particular set of topics.

It is a convention, of course, to use blue underlined text for active links and purple underlined text for links that have been used. Because web users understand underlining to indicate a link, it is best not to use that formatting for any other purpose. Instead of the blue and purple for links, it is also common to use a contrasting color or text treatment consistently across the site so links stand out among the regular text content and images.

Web Master—Person who administers a website.

Frequently Asked Questions (FAQs)—Answers to common questions about the products or services of the organization owning the site or about the site itself, often with links to appropriate pages on the site.

Think About It

Are Conventions Worth Following?

Have you ever visited a website in which you had difficulty figuring out where to go or what to do to interact with the site? What caused the problem? Were commands, buttons, or links placed in unusual places? Were there fewer navigation aids? How did your experience affect you? Did you visit the site again, or were you so discouraged that you wanted to have nothing to do with it? Keep these experiences in mind when thinking about how to put together your website.

Evaluating Websites

Designing quality web pages requires you to keep many features in mind. Table 17.2 has a checklist with a series of questions designed to help you ensure that you have met acceptable standards and created an effective site. It is also a good checklist to use when evaluating the content and design of other sites.

Table 17.2 *Low scores on this checklist can highlight troublesome areas in a website design.*

	CRITERIA	SCORE
	(For each criterion, assign a score from 1 to 4, with 1 indicating poor and 4 indicating outstanding.)	
1.	Is it easy to navigate from page to page?	
2.	Is it easy to find information?	
3.	Do all pages have a link back to the home page?	
4.	Are links easy to locate?	
5.	Are links useful?	
6.	Do all links work?	
7.	Does the site engage the reader?	
8.	Is the page visually appealing?	
9.	Is the text easy to read with a contrasting background?	
10.	Are opening pages short enough so extensive scrolling is not necessary?	
11.	Is the content on each page identified?	
12.	Is the content on each page useful?	
13.	Are there grammar, spelling, or punctuation errors?	
14.	Are there errors in factual information?	
15.	Does information appear quickly even with a slower Internet connection?	
16.	Are images optimized (reduced in file size) as much as possible to decrease download time?	
17.	Is there alternate text for graphics and image maps?	
18.	Does the home page have a contact person and email address?	
19.	Is there information indicating when the site was last updated?	
20.	Is there information about the site such as a physical address?	
	Record the total score:	

checkpoint

How are WCAG standards and Section 508 standards similar? How are they different?

ACTIVITY 17.1 ▶ Designing for Accessibility

1. Create a single web page for a hotel. Title it **LaZaar Hotel**.

2. Insert **banner** from your student data files. Add alternative text for the banner.

3. Create a form that uses radio buttons for the type of room a guest could choose: queen, queen suite, king, and king suite. Add appropriate labels for the input so that it can be read with assistive technology.

4. Add your name and date at the bottom of the page.

5. Run an accessibility validation report. Correct any errors.

6. Save the web page as *17_Activity1_accessibility*.

Lesson 17.2 ▶ Getting Found

Web developers have to keep in mind another issue as they design their site and create content: how do you get found? The Internet has hundreds of millions of websites, and thousands more are added every day. It serves no purpose to have the finest website offering the most carefully prepared message if no one visits the page. Having your website found can be accomplished in several standard ways. The most obvious, of course, is to advertise. Businesses now regularly publish their website's URL on every ad they place and on all official communications.

MATTHEW STAVER/Landov

Figure 17.5 *Larry Page and Sergey Brin founded Google, which revolutionized web indexing—and became one of the largest, most powerful, and most profitable companies in the industry.*

The next most obvious way of being found is through **search engines** such as Yahoo!, Google, and Bing. To understand how to enhance your possibility of being found by these search engines, you need to understand how they work.

lavitrei/Shutterstock.com

Impact

search engine—Program that searches for user-defined keywords in web documents or in databases that store information about websites and displays lists of sites that contain those keywords.

spider—Program that roams the Internet, searching for information about websites that it then sends to a search engine database.

meta tag—An HTML tag that stores information about a website.

keyword—A word included in a meta tag or header that is meant to indicate the content of a web page.

How Search Engines Work *LO 17.5*

Search engines maintain vast indexes of websites that indicate important words found on the pages and the location of those pages. To find this information, the search engines use specialized software called **spiders** or *bots* or *crawlers*, which continuously roam the Internet and send the results of their encounters back to the search engine's database. Exactly which words the spider returns to the database depends on the search engine. Some index words in titles and headings. Some index every word that is not an article (*a*, *an*, or *the*). Some index the words in the beginning of the web page, but not farther down. Others index the words that occur most frequently throughout the page.

Spiders also look at the page's **meta tag**. This tag, placed in the head section of the HTML code by the web designer, provides the crawler with information about the site, such as a site description and keywords. Since it is in the head, the information does not appear on the page seen by viewers but it does appear in the snippet of text shown in the list of search results in a browser. **Keywords** found within meta tags are specifically indexed so that someone using that word as a search term is likely to be notified of all sites containing that term as a keyword in the list of search results.

Loading the meta tag with keywords is not the secret to getting your website indexed, however. Many web developers in the past did that, and the practice—called *keyword stuffing*—fell into disfavor. In fact, search engines now pay little attention to meta data. Several factors improve the ability of a website to be successfully indexed:

- Using well-formed code, following the practices outlined in Chapter 13.

- Making sure that no links within the website are broken.

- Using simple, relatively short URLs.

- Using very descriptive titles and headings that clearly state the topic of the content they refer to.

- Keeping pages relatively small in size. Microsoft, in discussing its Bing search engines, recommends that text-only web pages should be no larger than 150 KB in size.

- Including a sitemap for the website. This is very helpful if some links within the site are placed within menus or list boxes, which would otherwise make them invisible to the spider. By placing the URLs for those pages in the sitemap, they become noticed and searched.

- Registering the website with search engines like Google, Yahoo!, and Bing.

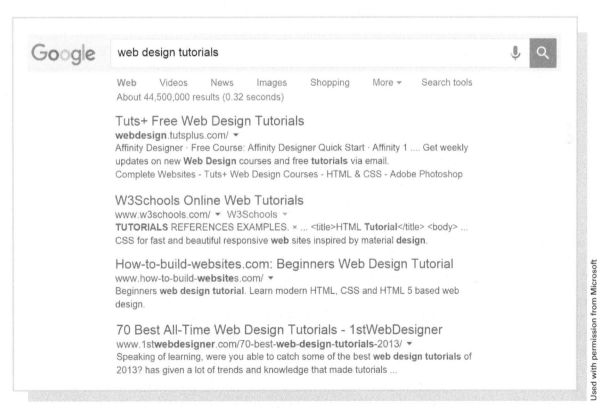

Used with permission from Microsoft

Figure 17.6 *This Bing screen shows an example of search results on the term "web design tutorials." Companies are eager to reach the top of the search results to gain more visibility. Companies that pay the search engine company gain listings on the right and at the top of the result list under the heading "ads."*

Spiders do not index everything on a website. They do not, for instance, index text within images. For that reason, it is very important not to place vital information about a business—such as its name and address—only in a graphical banner or the corporate logo. The website must also include that information in text form in order for it to be indexed.

You can also choose not to have the spider index some information. For instance, you might not wish the spider to index pages showing results of searches within your website. The **Robot Exclusion Protocol (REP)** allows for certain directories or files to be blocked from search engines. The block is carried out by creating a robot.txt file that lists the relevant directories or files in this fashion:

```
User-agent:
Disallow: /directory-name/
Disallow: /file-name
```

Note that each directory or filenames need to be listed separately. The robot.txt file is then uploaded to the website's main directory, where it will be noticed by search engine crawlers whenever they visit the site.

Enhancing Search Results *LO 17.6*

Search engines do more than simply compile long lists of websites that have the same keywords, however. They also list those sites in rank order. One factor affecting the ranking is the determination by the search engine of each site's likelihood of giving the searcher satisfactory results. That is one reason it is useful to enter multiple words when searching—and even to place some words in quotation marks if you want to see only sites in which they are used in a particular order. Both of these techniques narrow the search results.

Three key factors can affect ranking order:

- The frequency and relevance of keywords within the website.
- The number of links to the website from other websites: the more of these links, the higher the ranking. With Google, the higher-ranked the linking websites, the higher the ranking of the sites they link to.
- Purchasing adwords. **Adwords** are keywords and phrases for your site to which you agree with a search engine such as Google or Bing to link an advertisement. When web visitors search on those words or phrases, your ad may be one of those the search engine displays—depending on the value of your bid for the ad space compared to the bids of competing websites who chose the same adwords. These ads display in a specific area of the search results page (typically to the right or at the top of the main search results). The company that purchases the ad only pays the search engine for the listing when users actually click on the ad to visit the company's website.

Robot Exclusion Protocol (REP)—Web standard that allows web administrators to block search engine spiders from indexing certain directories or files within the website.

adword—Keyword or phrase on which a site owner links an ad. Adwords compete with other ads using the same keyword or phrase for special display space when the word appears as a search term.

The practice of trying to maximize these positive factors is called **Search Engine Optimization (SEO)**. Some ways to optimize your website include:

- Sign up with webmaster tools. Google and Bing both offer a suite of web master tools to provide you with valuable information. This information may include your site's health, speed, and many other metrics.

- Carefully consider keywords. Think about words users may use to find you online. Also, review your website analytics to help figure out which keywords are bringing visitors to your site. Such keywords should also be included in your content, title, and headings.

- Create amazing content. Remember that content doesn't always mean text. Amazing content can include videos, free resources, and other items that make your content stand out and attract visitors.

- Make it easy to share. Social media and exchanging content helps get the word out about your amazing website. Make it easy for visitors to share your content with others by providing Facebook, Twitter, email and other sharing exchanges. Make these "share" links obvious and clearly visible.

- Agree to **link exchanges** with other websites. By establishing mutual links, sites increase the rankings of each site.

Another option utilized by some firms is to hire SEO consultants to try to increase the amount of traffic to their sites.

search engine optimization (SEO)—Techniques used in an effort to enhance the ranking of a website in search engine results.

link exchange—Agreement among two or more websites to link to each other in hopes of increasing the ranking of each party in search engine results.

Web Best Practices

The World Wide Web is one of the forces driving information and commerce in the 21st century, and getting recognition can be difficult with the competition of millions of websites. Each year since 1996, the International Academy of Digital Arts and Sciences has given its "Webby" awards to the top websites in dozens of categories. The awards recognize websites that are exceptional in their appearance, interactivity, functionality, or usability.

Skills in Action: Visit the awards (www.webbyawards.com), look for the most recent list of winners, and browse the list of categories until you find one that interests you. Find the websites that were nominated in that category in the last year and visit each site. Take notes on what makes each one effective or interesting. Compare your notes with those of classmates to develop a list of web "best practices."

Web Analytics *LO 17.7*

The way to learn more about traffic to your site is to use **web analytics**, which are statistical reporting tools that indicate the amount and nature of traffic to a website. Google Analytics is one of the most popular web analytic tools, in part because it is free and in part because of Google's broad reach in the Internet. Bing has a similar reporting tool under its Webmaster Tools program. Additionally, there are many, many independent analytics programs available for free as well as for purchase.

These programs can provide a large store of data about website visitors:

- Total number of visitors by day, week, and month
- The number of those visitors who were new to the site or had visited before
- The average amount of time visitors spend on the site in general and on each page in particular
- The bounce rate: the proportion of visitors who leave the site after seeing only one page
- The number of visitors who responded to ads or adwords
- The number of visitors who went on to purchase products or services from the site
- The source of traffic—whether visitors came directly by entering the URL or clicking on a bookmark, by clicking on a link from another website, or by clicking on a search result
- The number of visitors coming from each source

All of this data can be compared to past results so that a website owner can see how the site is performing currently compared to earlier periods. Because the statistics can narrow down to individual pages, it is possible to determine if some pages on the site are receiving little traffic. If that is the case, steps can be taken to revise the content on those pages in the hopes of generating more traffic. Figure 17.7 shows snapshots from different Google Analytics reports that illustrate the way data is presented in that program. Other programs will have their own reporting format.

To use one of these analytic services, you simply sign up or purchase and download the software. In the case of Google Analytics, when you sign up for the program, Google gives you an account number and a snippet of JavaScript code that must be inserted in every web page on which you wish data. The code is inserted between the `<head>` and `</head>` tags at the top of the page.

checkpoint

What is the purpose or usefulness of web analytics?

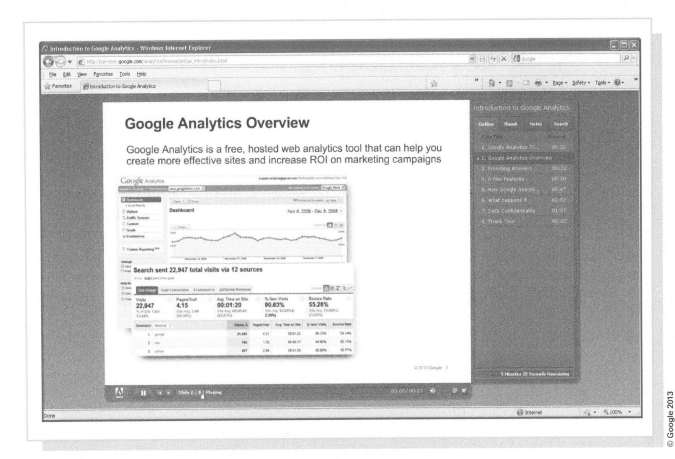

Figure 17.7 *This screen from a Google Analytics tutorial shows two of the standard reports the program generates. The line graph indicates the flow of traffic to a website over time. The chart in front shows the report that details the behavior of visitors who came to the site from each source.*

ACTIVITY 17.2 ▶ **Using Keywords and Web Analytics**

1. Create a single web page, adding a description and keywords as a meta tag.

2. Go to a source given by your instructor to generate code for web analytics. Create a profile for a website named ***17_Apply2.com***. Paste the appropriate code into the head of your web page.

3. Title the page "Finding My Web Page."

4. Insert ***banner2*** from the student data files on the web page. Underneath the banner, write a list of the best ways to make sure your web page will receive proper indexing.

5. Include your name and the date at the bottom of the page.

6. Save the web page as ***17_Activity2_finding_web_pages***.

Key Concepts

▶ The World Wide Web Consortium goes through a rigorous process of proposing, receiving comments on, and revising standards before issuing them as final recommendations. The W3C expects web developers, browser companies, and others to follow the standards. *LO 17.1*

▶ One W3C initiative tries to promote accessibility of websites to individuals with disabilities, focusing on recommendations to make sure that websites are perceivable and operable, that web content is understandable, and that site designs are robust enough to adapt to future technologies. *LO 17.2*

▶ Section 508 of the Rehabilitation Act establishes rules that the websites created for agencies of the federal government must follow to be accessible. While these rules are not binding on non-government websites, they are useful guidelines. *LO 17.3*

▶ The W3C and other organizations offer tools that can be used for testing the validity of a website's underlying code and the degree to which the site is accessible to those with disabilities. *LO 17.3*

▶ Certain practices—such as including update, copyright, and contact information; including navigational links back to the home page and a FAQpage; and using blue underlined type for hyperlinks—have become conventions on the Web, which means web users will expect websites to include them. Doing so is a courtesy and a way of ensuring the goodwill—and enjoyable browsing—of site visitors. *LO 17.4*

▶ A checklist of questions can be used to evaluate a website and highlight issues that may need fixing.

▶ The best way to get a website noticed is to be recognized and given high ranking by search engines. Search engines index websites based on content, which makes keywords important. They rank sites based on the richness of the content, the number of external sites linking to the site, and other factors. Buying ads with the search engine can help boost rankings. *LO 17.5 and 17.6*

▶ Web analytics generate statistics that can be used to analyze the traffic to a site and the behavior of visitors when they reach the site. These statistics can be used to identify pages, links, or relationships that are effective—and those that are not—in generating traffic and in keeping visitors at the site once they arrive. *LO 17.7*

Review and Discuss

1. Differentiate between the development of software by specific companies and the creation of XHTML, HTML5 and other markup languages. *LO 17.1*

2. Outline the process of approval of new standards by the W3C. *LO 17.1*

3. Identify the biggest challenges once new code has been approved by the W3C and integrated by web developers. *LO 17.1*

4. Identify the relationship between the W3C and WAI. *LO 17.2 and 17.3*

5. Identify the four areas promoted by the WCAG (Web Content Accessibility Guidelines). *LO 17.2 and 17.3*

6. Compare and contrast the WCAG recommendations by the W3C and the government's Section 508. *LO 17.2 and 17.3*

7. Analyze how web page conventions affect the design of a web page. *LO 17.4*

8. Describe effective tools to use in getting your web page found in search engines. *LO 17.5*

9. Formulate a plan to ensure that your website will be found using search engines. *LO 17.5*

10. Justify the use of search engine optimization and the need for SEO consultants used in some businesses. *LO 17.5*

Apply

1. Create a FAQ page for your school. Include at least 10 questions that you think would be the most requested. Create a website for the school with a navigation bar including four pages in addition to the FAQ page; the other four pages can be left blank. Include at least two alternate text or label names in the design. Save the pages in a folder named ***17_Apply1*** with the file names ***index.html***, ***contact_us.html***, ***schools.html***, ***calendar.html***, and ***faq.html***. *LO 17.2*

2. Visit a website of your choice or one that the instructor assigns for you to visit. Open ***checklist*** from the data files and check off the items as you find them on the web page. List the name of the website at the bottom of the page. Save your completed checklist as ***17_Apply2_attributes***. *LO 17.2*

3. Create a single web page with a list of at least 10 items to purchase in a specific category. Use an appropriate layout for the items and a form in your design. Use accessibility attributes. Save the page as ***17_Apply3_purchase***. *LO 17.2*

4. Research an animal and create a website about it. The website should contain an index page, a FAQ page, a site map page, and a page with links to get more information. Check all pages for accessibility when finished. Save the pages in a folder named ***17_Apply4*** with file names ***index.html***, ***facts.html***, ***sitemap.html***, and ***get.html***. *LO 17.2*

5. Plan a fund-raising project for a career and technology organization such as FBLA or BPA. Create a web page to advertise your plan. Include accessibility attributes that you learned about in this chapter and run an accessibility report. Include ideas for helping to get your page found. Set up the website so that all the files are in a folder named *17_Apply5*, the main page named *index.html*, and any images are in an *images* subfolder within the *17_Apply5* folder. *LO 17.5*

6. Choose three colleges and design a college website, comparing them. Consider at least three factors to use as comparison points. These three factors should address information that can be found on the web pages for each college. Save the web pages in a folder named *17_Apply6* with the file names **index.html**, *college1.html*, **college2. html**, and *college3.html*. Be creative in using as many skills as you have learned not only in this chapter but throughout the unit on web design. *LO 17.2 and 17.5*

Explore

1. Search for information about elements of web page design that could induce a seizure in a web visitor. Create a single page with a document linked to the page that explains what you have found in your search. Include an email link for contact information with the copyright information and date updated at the bottom of the page. Also, add a link to your resource. Add a banner that you have created in photo editing software that includes text and an image. Save the page as *17_Explore1_seizures*. *LO 17.2*

2. Search for the web page presenting the WCAG. Summarize what you found on the website on a single web page. Save the page as *17_Explore2_wcag*. *LO 17.2*

3. Visit five website that interest you. In a word processing document, make a list of characteristics that the sites contain that make them easy to find on the Web. Include a list of keywords used in your search for the sites. Save the document as *17_Explore3_searchable*. *LO 17.5*

Academic Connections

Communications: Read an article from the *"Journal of Media and Communication Studies"* pertaining to communication via social networking sites or other online communication. Articles are available online at http://www. academicjournals.org/jmcs. Once you have read the article, write a one-page summary. Save the summary as *17_AC_communications*.

Science: Create a one-page website showing the local weather forecast for the next week and comparing it to the national weather forecast for the same time period. Save your website as *17_AC_science*.

UNIT 5 REVIEW

iStockphoto.com/bradwieland

Unit Projects

Partner with a business to create a website for them. Meet with the business to get information needed to begin. Items to research include:

▶ Purpose of the website

▶ Audience for the website

▶ Types of media that will be found on the website

 • Who is responsible for taking pictures and video

 • Media to avoid

▶ Name and contact information for anyone who will give you content for the site

▶ Timeline for completion of website

▶ Desired update schedule for website

▶ Input from those at the meeting about website preferences

As much as possible, demonstrate the skills covered in Unit 5. The website and planning of the website should have as a minimum:

▶ Digital or hand sketch of the website and its navigation

▶ Standard XHTML tags

▶ Banner for the page

▶ Index page set as homepage

- ▶ Three pages linked to the index page with at least one page linked off one of the three pages

- ▶ Navigation bar on all pages

- ▶ Content on pages is appropriately formatted, easy to read and in small sections as learned in the textbook

- ▶ Copyright and date information at bottom of every page

- ▶ Bulleted or numbered text on one page

- ▶ Cascading Style Sheet with at least two styles

- ▶ At least two appropriate images that enhance the website

- ▶ At least one rollover or set of thumbnails for gallery of pictures

- ▶ Search function and/or a site map

- ▶ At least one JavaScript used appropriately to engage the user

- ▶ At least one animation

- ▶ A survey or form using ASP.NET

- ▶ At least one audio or video with a user control embedded on the page

Save the website in a folder as **Unit5_Project**. The website name can be the business name with appropriate file names and titles for each page.

Do a daily podcast journal about your progress on the project. What did you accomplish that day? What obstacles did you run into? When do you anticipate being finished? Include the day in the introduction of each day's podcast. Save your podcast as **Unit5_podcast_journal** with the day of the month after the word journal. For your final podcast journal, dictate an assessment of what you have learned in this unit. Is there a skill that you particularly enjoyed or disliked? Why or why not? Is there one that you would like to learn more about? Why? Save your assessment as **Unit5_podcast_journal_assessment**.

If you do not have a business to partner with, see your instructor to determine a topic for your website. Be ready with some ideas of your own.

Build Your Portfolio

Open your electronic portfolio and assess the best method to add this unit's assignments to the portfolio. Add to your ongoing portfolio:

- ▶ At least one assignment from each chapter

- ▶ At least one academic connection assignment from any of the chapters

- ▶ Your podcast journal from your unit project

- ▶ Your unit project

FBLA or BPA Competitive Events

Website Development

Go to the national website of the organization that you are a member of or that you have at your school. If you do not have one, choose either FBLA or BPA.

Locate information about an upcoming competitive event for website development. Review the event guidelines and rating sheets if they are available. Plan and sketch a website to submit in the competition. Save your sketch as ***Unit5_winning_edge***.

Resources:

- Competitive Event Listing | bpa.org:
  http://www.bpa.org/compete/eventlist
- FBLA Competitive Events: http://www.fbla-pbl.org/docs/ct/fblareferenceguide.asp

Source: www.bpa.org

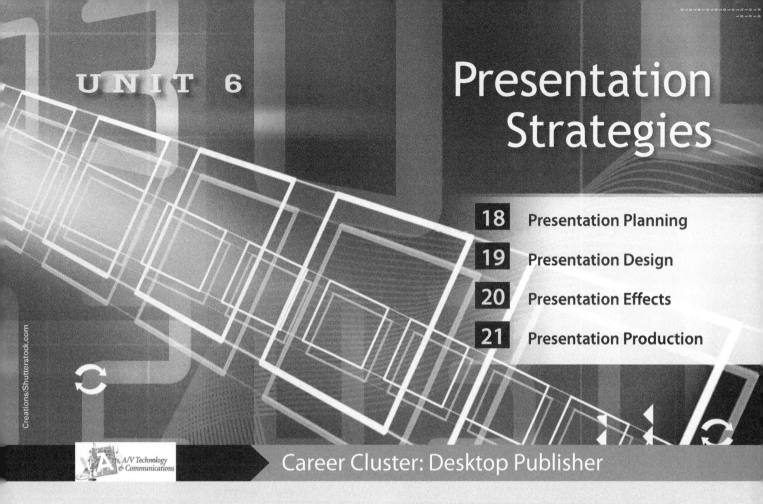

UNIT 6

Presentation Strategies

18 Presentation Planning

19 Presentation Design

20 Presentation Effects

21 Presentation Production

Arts, A/V Technology & Communications

Career Cluster: Desktop Publisher

Interview with Beckie, Clinical Desktop Publisher at Ethicon Endo-Surgery, Inc.

Describe your average day. My typical day begins with a meeting of all team members (clinical trial leader, research scientist, biostatistician, data manager, and myself) for either a new or ongoing clinical study. If the trial is a new startup project, I pull together information from each team member to create a protocol which describes exactly how the trial will be conducted. If it is an ongoing trial, I work with each team member to create supporting documents, safety reports, and presentations. At the end of the trial, I gather information from each team member and use that information to create a final report. This final report, which tells the trial's story from start to finish, is then submitted to an appropriate board or agency, such as the Food and Drug Administration (FDA).

What is the worst part of your job? Trying to keep track of multiple versions of the same document being submitted by all the different team members.

What is the best part of your job? Taking bits and pieces of information to create a solid, coherent, and graphically appealing publication or presentation.

Employment Outlook While desktop publishing has been one of the fastest-growing professions for the past decade, that trend is expected to level off over the next few years. The demand is expected to be highest for those with experience or a relevant certificate/degree.

Skills and Qualifications Associate or Bachelor's degree in Journalism, English, Graphic Design, or Graphic Communications or equivalent work experience; good communication skills; advanced computer and software skills; understanding of printers, scanners, and other office technology; artistic ability; attention to detail

Job Titles Desktop publisher; communication coordinator; technical writer; documentation specialist

What About You? Is a career in desktop publishing right for you? Use the Internet to find job postings for desktop publishers. What job qualifications are employers looking for?

Presentation Planning

Lesson 18.1 **Presentation Basics**

Lesson 18.2 **Preparation**

Lesson 18.3 **Display Features**

Learning Outcomes

▶ **18.1** Research your audience.

▶ **18.2** Plan your presentation using an outline.

▶ **18.3** Structure your presentation's basic points.

▶ **18.4** Use the Notes feature.

▶ **18.5** Effectively arrange your slides.

▶ **18.6** Use appropriate transitions in your slide show.

Key Terms

- audience
- hyperlink
- multimedia
- parallelism
- slide show

Regardless of the career path you choose, there's a good chance that your job will require some level of public speaking at one point or another. For even the most seasoned professional, speaking in front of an audience can be a frightening experience. This fear is often founded on concerns that you will look foolish. What if you forget important points or are unable to clearly express an idea to the audience? Fortunately, you have a great tool that can help you overcome many of these fears—presentation software. With presentation software, your points are visible to everyone, your ideas are structured, and as a side benefit, the audience's eyes are not always on you.

Almost anyone can create a presentation. The challenge, however, is creating a good presentation. That is the goal of this unit.

In order to create an effective presentation, you need to decide on which software program you will use to build your presentation. In addition to traditional, computer-based software options, such as Microsoft PowerPoint, there are other nontraditional presentation software options available. You also need to learn as much as possible about the group you will be presenting to, or your **audience**. Start by researching your audience so that you can be sure to include information that they will find useful. It's easy to become so involved in the production of your **slide show** that you lose sight of the more important aspect of the presentation—the message. The information you gather about your audience will serve as a guide throughout the creation process.

audience—The people who watch or listen to a presentation.

slide show—Collection of slides, or pages, arranged in sequence, containing text and images to be presented to an audience.

Presentation Software

Historically, the term *presentation software* has been synonymous with Microsoft PowerPoint. PowerPoint continues to offer users a multitude of built-in design and display features that are easy to use. With just some basic skills and knowledge, users are able to create compelling presentations with intricate designs. PowerPoint also allows users to add enhancements such as graphics, audio, and video with very little effort.

With PowerPoint, you can share your presentation with other users in person, online, or even via a smartphone (see Figure 18.1).

While computer-based software programs, such as PowerPoint, remain the front-runners in presentation software, there are other options available. Some of the more popular alternatives are online presentation applications such as Google Slides (see Figure 18.2 on the following page) and Prezi. One advantage of using an online application to create your presentation is universal accessibility. As long as you have a computer with Internet access, you can edit, view, or share your presentation from any location. This means that even if you drop your PC down a flight of stairs or destroy your thumb-drive, your presentation is safe and readily available online.

Figure 18.1 *More and more smartphones are providing users with basic presentation capabilities, such as the ability to view, edit, and share presentation files.*

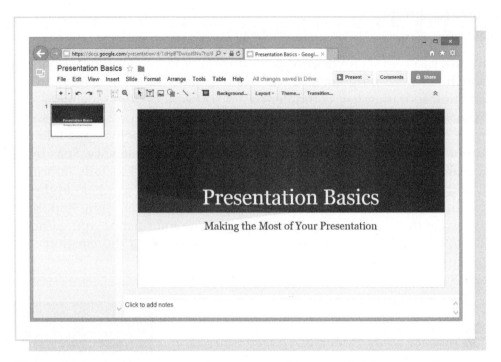

Figure 18.2 *Online presentation software options, such as Google Slides, are providing users with reliable alternatives to traditional computer-based programs like Microsoft PowerPoint.*

Audience *LO 18.1*

The widely used AUDIENCE formula makes it easy to know where to start by presenting a series of questions about the audience and the facilities in which you will present:

- **Analyze.** Who is the audience? How can you "connect" with the members of this audience?
- **Understand.** What is the audience's level of knowledge of the topic you are presenting?
- **Demographics.** What are the different ages, gender, and educational backgrounds represented in the audience?
- **Interest.** Are the members of the audience present because they chose to attend or because they were required to attend?
- **Environment.** Will you have a cordless microphone? Is the platform or podium placed so that the audience can see the projection screen (ideally at least six feet off the floor)? Is your space limited? Will everyone be able to see and hear you? How big is the room? How many chairs will there be in the room?
- **Needs.** What does the audience need or want to get from the presentation?
- **Customization.** What can you do to make the presentation appropriate for this particular audience?
- **Expectations.** What is the audience expecting?

Use the AUDIENCE questions to help you plan ahead. To answer these questions, you may need to get additional information from the person arranging the presentation. Or you may need to contact the individuals planning to attend the presentation, to ask them for answers to some of the questions. As you get the answers to your questions, fill in a chart similar to the one shown in Figure 18.3.

AUDIENCE	
Analyze *Who is the audience?*	
Understand *What is their level of knowledge?*	
Demographics *What are their ages, gender, and educational backgrounds?*	
Interest *Why are they attending presentation?*	
Environment *Where will the presentation be delivered?*	
Needs *What does the audience need/want from presentation?*	
Customization *How can you customize presentation for this audience?*	
Expectations *What is the audience expecting?*	

Figure 18.3 *Use of a chart such as this one makes it easy to keep in mind the essential questions to consider before preparing a presentation.*

Granata1111/Dreamstime.com

The Origins of Presentation Software

Long before the invention of personal presentation software, presentations had to be created by hand. This process was time-consuming and tedious. This began to change in 1973 when NASA sought out General Electric (GE) to develop a computer system capable of creating high-resolution graphics for their Space Shuttle flight simulators. This project laid the foundation upon which computer-generated presentation software would later be built.

In 1982, GE created a new company called Genigraphics that used this newly developed computer system to create custom presentations for large companies, government agencies, and universities across the United States. In 1987, Genigraphics partnered with Microsoft to develop a software application that would be both affordable and user-friendly. The idea was to give individuals a tool they could use to create their own personalized presentations. This new application was called PowerPoint.

checkpoint

How can the AUDIENCE formula help you with your presentation?

ACTIVITY 18.1 ▶ Presentation Planning

1. Think about a presentation that you could offer to make. This could be for an organization on campus or for an outside organization.

2. Open the *planning chart* data file provided for this lesson. Complete the information in the planning chart for your presentation. If needed, interview someone who will be in the audience to get a better idea of the expectations.

3. Save your work as *18_Activity1_presentation_planning*.

Lesson 18.2 ▶ Preparation

Once you have your answers to the AUDIENCE questions, it's time to begin preparing your presentation. Before the introduction of presentation software, this process began with a written speech. Only after the speech was finalized were audiovisual components added to help aid in the presentation of the speech. Today, speakers often use presentation software, such as Microsoft PowerPoint, as a primary planning tool. Though this is a useful technological shortcut, don't fall into the trap of trying to plan your ideas and the **multimedia** elements at the same time—or worse, trying to plan your ideas *around* the multimedia elements. Instead, decide what you want to say and then decide how to enhance that message utilizing the multimedia potential of the presentation software.

multimedia—The combination of sound, animation, graphics, video, and color. In an earlier time, the term audiovisual was used instead.

It's sometimes easy to rush through the preparation process, but this crucial step is essential for creating a successful presentation. Since your audience is more interested in what you are saying than in how attractive your slides appear, the time you spend deciding on what information to include is far more valuable than time spent choosing the perfect graphic. Be sure to consider each of the following four steps during the preparation process:

- Outline
- Beginning
- Structure
- Grammar

Outline *LO 18.2*

The first step in the preparation process should always be to create an outline of how you think your presentation should flow. Use of an outline encourages you to focus on your content before you begin thinking about design issues. As a general rule, a visual presentation should be limited to three main ideas supported by several sub-points or explanations.

The Outline view in PowerPoint and other presentation software lets you easily build a framework for your presentation based on your ideas.

This view also allows you to rearrange those ideas easily until you're satisfied with the organization and flow of each slide. If you use the preset heading styles to create an outline in Microsoft Word, you can automatically generate a set of corresponding slides in a PowerPoint file.

It's important to note that when using the Outline view, special features and shortcuts will only function properly if you have selected a slide type that includes both a title and a text box. For example, if you are in the Outline view in Microsoft PowerPoint and are using an appropriate slide type, a new slide with a new outline point will appear each time you press the Enter key. Pressing the Tab key will convert the title to an outline point. Pressing Shift + Tab reverses this process.

You can also edit text for each slide directly within the pane at the left side of the PowerPoint window. (When you are in Normal view, this pane is called the thumbnail pane.) As the outline points are entered on each slide, PowerPoint translates the information into a series of graduated steps. Notice in Figure 18.4 that the bullets combined with the indenting of lines provide an outline-like view on the slide. If your presentation program does not provide an outline view, you should create a written outline before moving on to the next step in the preparation process.

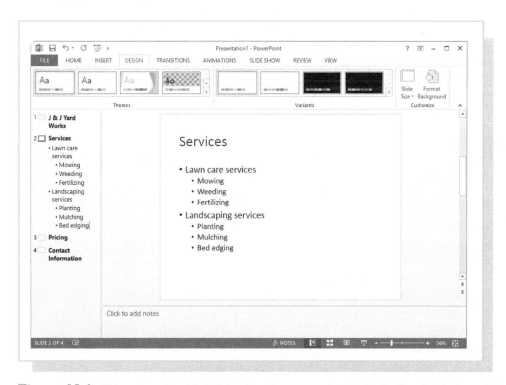

Figure 18.4 *Slides are easily added, deleted, and rearranged using the Outline view in PowerPoint.*

Beginning *LO 18.3*

The second step in the preparation process is establishing the most significant ideas you want to get across to your audience. Record these ideas using the outline feature. At this stage of planning, you may find yourself with a long list of ideas, all of which seem important.

It's necessary to trim this list down so that only key items remain. Otherwise, you may end up with a presentation that is nothing more than a mass of information without focus.

Identify points that can be moved to sub-points or gathered under a common topic. Use the outline feature to juggle ideas until you are satisfied with the outcome. Once you have decided on the major points, add supporting information. It might be tempting to bypass this step, but thinking through your ideas at this stage will help the rest of the presentation process move along more smoothly. It will also help you create a far more effective presentation.

Some presentation designers begin by creating the entire outline on a single slide, and then breaking the points out onto individual slides once the ideas are in place. Other designers prefer to create three slides (one for each main point) and then add their sub-points to those slides. Regardless of the technique you use, once the outline is complete, you should then begin to decide how much information to include on each slide.

As a general rule of thumb, you should limit the number of lines on each slide to no more than six, creating additional slides as needed. Depending on how long your presentation is and how much information you decide to include, you may be able to include supporting ideas on the same slide as their relevant main idea. However, if you need to include more than six lines, you should try to divide the information evenly over two or more slides. For example, say you have one main idea and seven supporting ideas. In this case, you should place the one main idea and first three supporting ideas on slide 1, followed by the remaining four supporting ideas on slide 2.

Play to Your Strengths

In today's technologically focused world, being open to acquiring new skill sets is more important than ever. Those people who resist innovation will be quickly left behind in the workplace, while others who are open to learning new technologies will put themselves a step ahead of their peers. It's important to recognize, however, that not everyone has the same strengths, talents, and abilities. Although your employer might expect you to be familiar with many different multimedia applications, you would be smart to focus on a special area in which you particularly excel. For example, you might be a gifted graphic designer, yet not quite as good at creating presentations or slide shows as a coworker. Maybe you have a special knack for getting the color just right on scanned photos, but your friend's web pages always seem to be just a little easier to use than yours.

In the workforce, as in all areas of your life, it's important that you play to your strengths while continually working to improve your weak spots. Doing so can help you discover new strengths you didn't even know you had. That said, it's also important to choose a field of work where you're confident of your abilities. If you spend your day doing work that you're good at, your level of self-esteem will stay high, you'll be more productive, and you'll likely be much happier on the job.

Structure *LO 18.3*

The third step in the preparation process is forming the structure of your presentation. As you just learned, the basic guidelines of good presentation design limit you to no more than six lines of text per slide and no more than six words per line of text. This means you should keep your ideas brief rather than using long explanations. Complete sentences are generally not necessary or desirable. Figure 18.5 shows you how busy and distracting a slide appears when you include too much text. By reducing this text to include only the most vital words, you improve the overall design and readability of the slide (see Figure 18.6).

Pricing

- Lawn care services
  - We charge $45 per hour for lawn mowing. This includes trimming around all trees and flower beds, as well as blowing grass of driveways and sidewalks.
  - We charge $25 per hour for weeding flower beds and any other areas.
  - We charge $25 per hour for fertilizing lawns, flower beds, or any other areas.

Figure 18.5 *Here's an example of a slide that includes a lot of information with too much unnecessary explanation.*

Lawn Care Services Pricing

- Mowing $45/hour
  - Includes trimming and clean-up
- Weeding $25/hour
  - Any area
- Fertilizing $25/hour
  - Any area
  - Price does not include fertilizer

Figure 18.6 *In this example, the information shown in the previous slide has been reduced and reorganized to follow good presentation practices.*

lavitrei/Shutterstock.com

Impact

Projectors

Digital projectors have become an essential presentation tool. As with other forms of technology, the price of digital projectors continues to drop as the quality improves. Projector quality is usually based on the number of ANSI lumens (the amount of light projected). Another consideration is weight, since projectors are often carried from location to location. Smaller, lighter projectors are usually more expensive than larger ones.

An important point to keep in mind is that projector bulbs are often nearly as expensive as the original cost of the projector. These bulbs need to be protected by allowing them to cool completely before moving the equipment. Projector bulbs are rated by the number of hours they are anticipated to burn, but failing to care for them properly can shorten their life. Newer projectors on the market use LED light rather than traditional bulbs. These have an extremely long life and require less energy to run, so the projectors can be battery powered. Currently, their lumens are fairly low, but the future is bright for this type of projector.

Grammar *LO 18.3*

parallelism—A grammatical term indicating that the basic structure of two or more sentences or phrases is similar. Sentences that are parallel have similar arrangements of subjects, verbs, and sometimes prepositional phrases.

The final step in the preparation process is ensuring that the proper grammatical techniques are used on every slide throughout the presentation. In addition to limiting the number of words and lines on each slide, it's also a good idea to make your points grammatically parallel. This is called **parallelism**, or using the same grammatical structure on all same-level points within a slide.

If, for example, you use a verb and a noun in supporting idea number one, then you should also use a verb and a noun in supporting idea number two. Or, if you capitalize all the terms in idea one, you should do the same in idea two. You do not have to make every statement parallel to every other one—merely to ones that are on an equal level. Attention to this kind of detail gives your presentation a professional look and feel.

checkpoint

Why is the time you spend deciding on what information to include more valuable than time spent on choosing graphics for your presentation?

ACTIVITY 18.2 ▶ Getting Started

1. Open the file you saved from the previous activity: *18_Activity1_presentation_planning*.
2. Determine the three important points you want to make in your presentation. Key these in an outline you create in the presentation.
3. Expand the outline into bulleted points and, if possible, sub-points.
4. Check that all text structure is parallel, that the grammar is correct, and that there are no spelling errors.
5. Save your presentation as *18_Activity2_getting_started*.

Lesson 18.3 ▶ Display Features

Notes *LO 18.4*

Keep in mind that it's not necessary to include every word of your presentation in your actual slides. If that were the case, then you could just hand your audience the printout and walk away without actually giving a presentation. Although this may seem like an appealing choice at times, the main purpose of a presentation is to support and aid a presenter's speech.

Once you have the major ideas and subsequent points in place, you may find yourself with information that doesn't really need to appear on a slide, but would still be helpful to keep in your presentation for reference. Or, as you are organizing your thoughts, points may occur to you that would be good to mention. The Notes or Speaker Notes feature of most presentation software programs is a good place to keep this type of information. You can limit your slide information to the major points and then place additional information you may or may not want to mention in the Notes section (see Figure 18.7). Later, you may want to add even more information as you are completing the design of your presentation.

Figure 18.7 *Information entered into the Notes section, found just below the slide in PowerPoint, can be displayed on your computer without appearing to the audience during your presentation.*

Arrangement and Movement *LO 18.5 and 18.6*

Once the content of your presentation is in place, it's time to think about the order in which the slides appear. As you review your presentation, you may decide the slides need to be arranged in a different order. You can use a feature such as PowerPoint's Slide Sorter view to rearrange slides by simply dragging them to a new location in the presentation.

You can also control the order in which slides display during your slide show using features such as hyperlinks and action buttons. These features allow you to quickly jump from one slide to another, or to a different presentation or location on the Web.

The higher-end presentation applications also allow you to control the way in which slides appear and how quickly they appear during a presentation. Transitions add movement and visual interest to a presentation.

Hyperlinking and Action Buttons

hyperlinks—Text and/or picture that can be used to connect one slide with another or display another presentation or location.

With the use of **hyperlinks** (similar to the ones found on a web page), you can choose to link one slide to any other slide in the presentation. You can also link to another presentation or file, or to a website. Hyperlinks become active when you present the slide show.

Hyperlinks are a good tool to use when you want to refer to information on a previous or upcoming slide during a presentation. For instance, if information on slide 15 is related to something you previously covered on slide 5, you can include a hyperlink on slide 15 that, when clicked, will display slide 5. Similarly, you can include a hyperlink on slide 5 that will return you to slide 15 so you can continue with the presentation. This is a much smoother process than trying to click backwards and forwards through your presentation, searching for a particular slide.

In more sophisticated presentation software, such as PowerPoint, you can use action buttons, such as those shown in Figure 18.8, to add interactivity to a presentation. Action buttons are used to trigger a variety of functions, such as moving to a specific slide, opening a different program, or playing an audio clip. An action can be triggered either by clicking on a button or by hovering over a button with your cursor, called a mouse over.

Figure 18.8 *In PowerPoint, you can use action buttons as navigational tools within your presentation.*

PowerPoint provides a wide array of commonly recognized predesigned action buttons, such as a *Home* icon button, a *Help* icon button, and a *Sound* icon button. Or, you can choose to insert a blank button, then customize it to meet your needs. You can find these buttons on the Shapes gallery.

You select the action the button will perform from the Action Settings dialog box. For example, if you insert an *Action Button: Beginning* shape on a PowerPoint slide, the Action Settings dialog box opens with the hyperlink to First Slide action selected (Figure 18.9).

Transitions

Using the options found on the Transitions tab of PowerPoint or a comparable section of other presentation software, you can choose how each slide will appear during its transition from the previous slide (see Figure 18.10). You can also determine a slide's transition sound and speed from this tab, as well as whether the slide will advance automatically after a set time period or with a mouse click.

Figure 18.9 *From the Action Settings dialog box, you can determine the resulting behavior when a mouse clicks on or hovers over an action button.*

Figure 18.10 *How your slides appear during a presentation or the transition from one slide to the next can be customized using options provided within PowerPoint's Transitions tab.*

You will learn more about the use of transitions in Chapter 20, as well as ways to animate objects on slides to add movement to a presentation.

Think About It

Fact Checking

As a speaker, you have an obligation to be honest with your audience. This means you must check your facts carefully to ensure they are accurate. It's easy to inflate figures and add details you are unsure of in order to make your presentation appear more valuable. Always double-check your facts and incorporate only that information which you can verify. Your credibility will grow and your effectiveness as a speaker will grow at the same time.

checkpoint

What can you do if you find yourself with information that doesn't really need to appear on a slide, but would still be helpful to keep in your presentation?

ACTIVITY 18.3 ▶ Arrangement and Movement

1. Open the file you saved from the previous activity: *18_Activity2_getting_started*.
2. Ensure the slides are arranged in the order in which you want them. Rearrange if necessary.
3. Add notes to the slides, at least one hyperlink, appropriate transitions, and one action button.
4. Save as *18_Activity3_arrangement_movement*.

Key Concepts

▶ It is important to plan your presentation before incorporating graphics and design elements. *LO 18.2*

▶ Planning begins with research—research into which software program to use, your audience, and their expectations. *LO 18.1*

▶ You should record and organize significant points using either the outlining options in your presentation software or a written outline. *LO 18.2 and 18.3*

▶ You can add notes within your presentation software that only you, but not the audience, will see. *LO 18.4*

▶ Presentation software has options to help facilitate movement between slides, such as hyperlinking, action buttons, and transitions. *LO 18.5 and 18.6*

Review and Discuss

1. Explain why is it important to research your audience as a first step to creating an effective presentation. *LO 18.1*

2. Briefly explain what the AUDIENCE formula does to help with creating an effective presentation. List the key terms the acronym stands for. *LO 18.1*

3. Explain how presentation software should be used to plan your ideas. *LO 18.2*

4. Define and explain the first step in the preparation process of a presentation. *LO 18.3*

5. Analyze why a title and content slide works better in Outline view than other slide types. *LO 18.2*

6. Describe the second step in the presentation process for creating an effective presentation. *LO 18.3*

7. Summarize the recommendations for how much information should be on each slide. *LO 18.3*

8. Explain the use of parallelism in the text on a slide show. *LO 18.3*

9. Explain what can be done to information that doesn't need to appear on the slide. *LO 18.4*

10. Discuss how hyperlinks and the order of your presentation slides are related. *LO 18.5*

11. Identify the technique that sets how the slide will appear from the previous slide. *LO 18.6*

12. Other than transitioning a slide show, what other settings can be added to the slide show from the Transitions tab? *LO 18.6*

13. Distinguish between the use of a hyperlink and an action button to move around in the slide show. *LO 18.6*

14. Describe how ethics plays a role in preparing a slide show for a presentation.

15. Explain how the terms multimedia and audiovisual are related.

Apply

1. Plan and create a presentation that outlines the major points in this chapter. Start with an outline, add supporting points, and add notes. If your software allows, include at least one hyperlink, one action button, and appropriate transitions. Save as **18_Apply1_review**. *LO 18.2, 18.3, 18.4, and 18.6*

2. Use the Internet to research information on a vacation that you would like to take. Decide on a destination and the major points that you would like to consider in deciding on where to go for this vacation. Expand on the major points, adding transitions to the slides as well as notes, hyperlinks, or an action button. Save as **18_Apply2_vacation**. *LO 18.3, 18.4, and 18.6*

3. Share with the class a particular skill that you possess by creating a presentation that teaches this skill. It can also be how to do something specific like making a favorite meal. Save as **18_Apply3_teaching**. *LO 18.3 and 18.5*

4. Plan and create a presentation on staying healthy to submit for use in the school clinic. When adding transitions, make the presentation self-running, as the plan is to play it on the monitor for several days a week. Save as **18_Apply4_staying_healthy**. *LO 18.2, 18.3, 18.5, and 18.6*

5. Plan and create a presentation on a business that you are interested in joining or starting. Locate a similar business and create a presentation that contains the following information: history, mission, and vision of the business, tag line, logo, explanation of the product or service, benefits of working for this business, hours of operation, and reasons you are interested in this type of business. Save as **18_Apply5_business**. *LO 18.2, 18.5, and 18.6*

Explore

1. Research types of presentations used in business such as to inform, to persuade, or to build good will. Create a presentation that gives information on at least three types of presentations. Include techniques learned in this chapter. Use at least two resources. Make the last slide a resource slide, citing your resources. Save as **18_Explore1_presentation_types**. *LO 18.3, 18.5, and 18.6*

2. Search the *Occupational Outlook Handbook* for an occupation that you are interested in. Create a presentation about your career to share with others. Include the following major points in your slide show: training and education needed, earnings, expected job prospects, what workers do on the job, and working conditions. Save as **18_Explore2_careers**. *LO 18.3, 18.5, and 18.6*

3. Search for good and bad presentations on the Internet or recall presentations for which you have been an audience member. Write a summary of what you have observed about good presentations and what you observed about what makes a presentation bad. This can include anything to do with a presentation, including the actual presenting of the presentation. Cite at least two sources at the end of your summary. Save as **18_Explore3_good_bad**.

Academic Connections

Reading: Search the Internet using the phrase "reading for details." Read an article about tips or explanations of how to read for details. Pick three major points that you read about and expand those points. Create a presentation on what you have read. Cite your article on the last slide. Save as **18_AC_reading**.

Math: For a special multimedia project, a business is hiring two temporary employees for three weeks. The employees will be paid a regular hourly wage of $15.00. For Week 1, the employees will each work 40 hours plus 5 hours overtime at time and a half. For Week 2, each will work 35 hours. And for Week 3, 30 hours have been authorized for each employee. Answer the following questions:

1. What would be the pay for each employee for Week 1?
2. What would be the pay for each employee for Week 2?
3. What would be the pay for each employee for Week 3?
4. What is the total pay for both employees for all 3 weeks?
5. If Social Security Tax is 6.2%, how much social security would be taken out for each employee for Week 1?
6. At .9%, how much Federal Unemployment Tax would be paid by the employer for all salaries paid for this special project?

Save your answers as **18_AC_math**.

Presentation Design

Learning Outcomes

▶ **19.1** Use pre-defined templates.

▶ **19.2** Incorporate layout elements and options, such as Slide Master settings, slide designs, colors, and backgrounds.

▶ **19.3** Understand the importance of text styling in a presentation.

▶ **19.4** Enhance a message using visual effects.

Key Terms

- background
- media
- slide design (theme)
- slide layout
- Slide Master
- template

Design elements, incorporated correctly, can enhance an already compelling presentation. Used incorrectly, they can easily overpower the ideas you want to communicate. It is pointless for an audience to walk away from your presentation with an appreciation for its design if they failed to follow its message. Whether your design is elaborate or sparse, complicated or simple, it should set the stage for your ideas—not try to steal the spotlight. Whatever choices you make, select elements based upon their ability to help effectively convey your message.

template—A document master pre-designed by professionals who have already chosen the background, font size and color, and bullets to be used.

Once you lay out your message based upon your research and the other preparation steps discussed in Lesson 18, it's time to set the stage for your ideas. The quickest way to add visual effects to your presentation is to use one of the pre-designed **templates** included with your presentation software. These templates contain pre-designed elements, such as backgrounds, font colors, font sizes, and bullets. If time is a critical factor in your design process, the use of a template is an excellent choice. With some presentation programs, such as Microsoft PowerPoint, templates are available whenever you create a new presentation, as shown in Figure 19.1, or available for downloading online, as shown in Figure 19.2 on the next page.

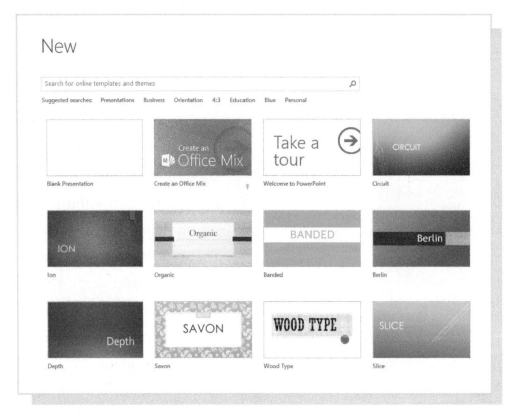

Figure 19.1 *Template designs are pre-loaded with software such as Microsoft PowerPoint.*

Professional Templates *LO 19.1*

Microsoft templates are created by professionals to be attractive and effective. One disadvantage of using a template is that if your audience has frequently attended PowerPoint presentations, they may recognize the template from a previous experience. Your message may be "blurred" by this recognition factor. One solution is to use a template as a base for your design and then modify or personalize it for your presentation. Another possibility is to use third-party designs, but note that you will pay a fee to use many third-party options. Though these

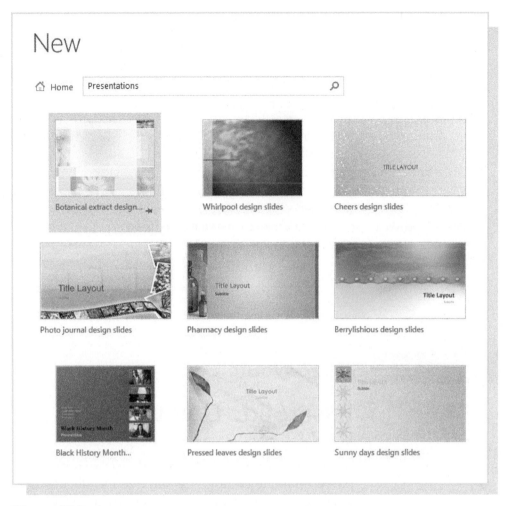

Figure 19.2 *An even larger selection of templates is available online and can be viewed before downloading.*

designs are also created by professionals, your audience is less likely to have seen them as part of a presentation before. As with PowerPoint templates, these designs also include interesting backgrounds, animations, and photos to enhance your presentation.

checkpoint

What is the quickest way to add visual effects to a presentation?

ACTIVITY 19.1 ▶ Using Templates

1. Download a print business card template to create a business card for yourself.
2. Replace the text in the placeholders with your information.
3. Replace the logo if there is one with a logo of your school. Resize and compress as needed.
4. Save your business card as *19_Activity1_templates*.

Time Is Money

Software developers such as Microsoft have discovered that businesses need help in creating professional-looking presentations. Just as desktop publishers learned that it was not easy to produce print documents without specialized training, presenters face a similar challenge. Choice of colors and graphics can be time-consuming and sometimes unsuccessful. With the introduction of high-quality templates to programs such as PowerPoint, the time needed to produce a quality slide show has been significantly reduced. While it can be enjoyable to experiment with all the options available, in a business environment that time lost is valuable. Templates are a way to recover that time.

Lesson 19.2 ▶ Slide Layouts

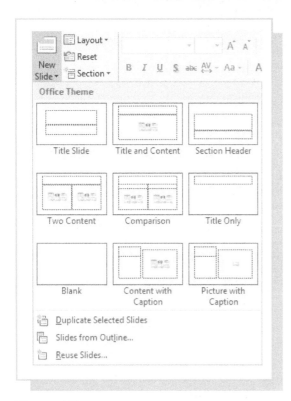

Figure 19.3 *When adding a slide in PowerPoint, you can streamline the design process by choosing a pre-defined layout.*

slide layout—Arrangement of design elements on a slide.

Basic Slide Layouts
LO 19.2

Regardless of whether you decide to use a prepared template or not, you still need to decide what slides to include in your presentation. When you created your outline, you used a slide that contained a bulleted list, so you already have some experience with choosing a **slide layout**. When it's time to begin inserting new slides in PowerPoint, you have the option of choosing from several predefined layouts, as shown in Figure 19.3.

By default, presentations begin with a title slide where you may insert a title and subtitle (Figure 19.4). You can then choose other slide layouts for the body of the presentation.

The most widely used slide layout in PowerPoint is Title and Content, which allows you to insert text content as well as multimedia content such as pictures, tables, charts, diagrams, or videos. Figure 19.5 shows a Title and Content slide with text, and Figure 19.6 shows a Title and Content slide with a chart. Title and content slide layouts are also available in two-column formats for visual variety.

Other PowerPoint slide layouts include section headers to introduce sections of related slides, blank or title-only slides, and layouts for displaying pictures and captions.

Slides that incorporate **media** such as video or sound are discussed later in more detail. A presentation that uses the same layout on every slide is monotonous. Including various slide layouts throughout the slide show makes for a more interesting and appealing presentation.

media—In PowerPoint, media includes sound or video. In other environments, media may include any use of graphical or auditory additions to a presentation, such as a chart or graph.

Figure 19.4 *A title slide typically only contains text with perhaps some graphic/design element.*

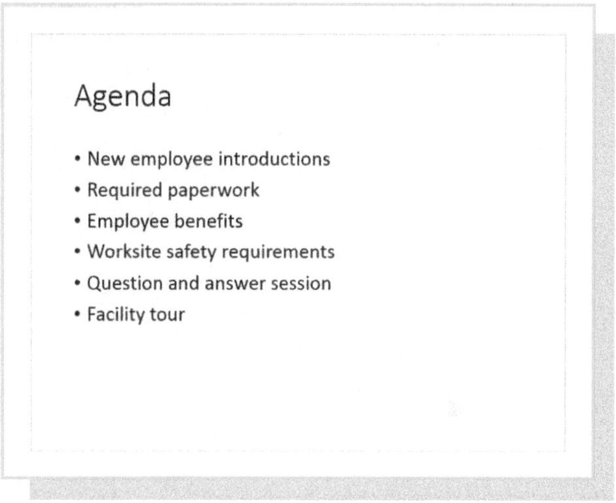

Figure 19.5 *A Title and Content slide layout is a good choice for presenting a main idea along with several supporting points.*

Figure 19.6 *A Title and Content layout can also be used for multimedia content such as pictures, tables, charts, diagrams, or videos.*

Slide Master *LO 19.2*

Slide Master—A single slide that can be designed once and then applied to many slides. PowerPoint allows the creation of multiple masters for use in different situations.

In print design, you work to keep a consistent look, and the same should apply to presentation design. One of the easiest ways to establish consistency is to use PowerPoint's **Slide Master** option, shown in Figure 19.7. This lets you make design choices that apply to all slides. From the Slide Master view, you can choose the font size and style, background, and bullet choices, as well as other details. In addition, header and footer information, such as page numbers, is also included on the master. Although it is tempting to vary these design elements on every slide, you will have a more professional-looking presentation if you stick with consistent elements. Once a master is in place, these consistent elements will automatically appear on each new slide you create. All that is left is to add the details for the individual slides in your slide presentation.

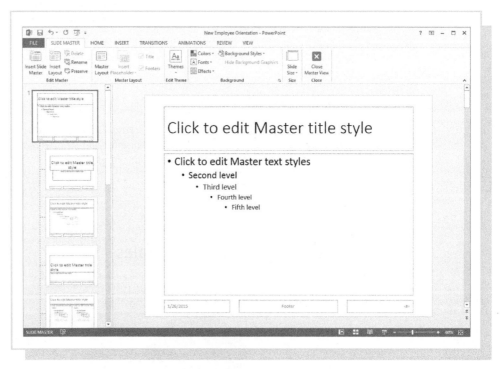

Figure 19.7 *From Slide Master view, you can set features, such as font style and color, across all slides in a presentation.*

Slide Designs (Themes) *LO 19.2*

slide design (theme)—A collection of layouts, colors, fonts, background, and effects that can be applied to a presentation to create a professional, unified appearance.

Presentation applications usually allow you to select a **slide design**, or **theme**, to apply to all slides in the presentation. PowerPoint themes are shown in Figure 19.8. Applying a theme gives a presentation a professionally designed appearance and saves a great deal of time in experimenting with layouts, colors, and fonts.

Figure 19.8 *Themes come in many variations, from formal to playful, and provide layouts, background, fonts, and colors for all slides in a presentation.*

A theme has predefined colors, slide backgrounds, and fonts. Slide layouts may differ from theme to theme. Usually, you can apply a different theme to a presentation and the slides will automatically adjust to show the formats of the new theme.

Color Choices *LO 19.2*

As you learned in Chapter 5, colors have relationships that are characterized according to their location on the color wheel (see Figure 19.9). Complementary colors are located directly across from one another on the color wheel. For example, bright red and dark green are complementary colors. A complementary color scheme has a great deal of contrast. Analogous colors are located right next to one another, such as dark green, light green, and yellow. An analogous color scheme can produce a feeling of harmony.

The use of color in a presentation can do more than simply make your slides look pretty. It can also do the following:

- Increase learning retention and recall by nearly 80 percent
- Increase comprehension by more than 70 percent

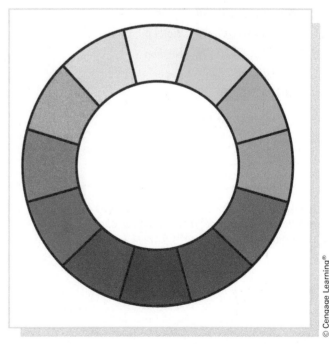

© Cengage Learning®

Figure 19.9 *A color wheel displays the relationship between primary and intermediate colors.*

- Increase willingness to read by up to 80 percent
- Improve selling efficiency by nearly 85 percent

With this much power, color choices cannot be ignored. They should, however, be made carefully. Whether used in the background, as font colors, or as graphic fills, appropriate colors must be selected for maximum impact.

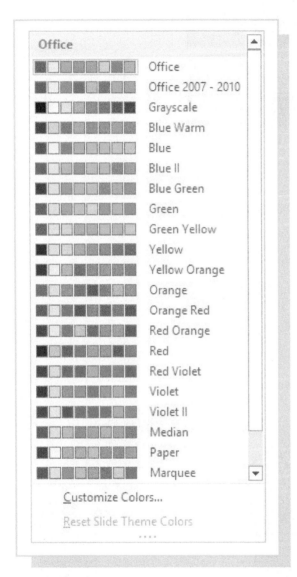

Figure 19.10 *PowerPoint provides built-in color palettes to meet any design need. Or, you can choose to create your own colors.*

Dark blue creates a stable, mature message. It has a calming effect on most audiences. Red or orange can cause excitement or create an emotional effect, which makes these colors good for emphasizing a single word. Green can make audiences feel comfortable.

The most readable colors are yellow with black lettering. This is why school buses and some traffic signs are yellow. Keep in mind, though, that color on a sign is made with paint, while colors on a screen are projected using light. This means that a color that may work well on a sign may not be as effective on a display screen.

Audiences are better focused if the background is a dark color, while the text and drawings are lighter colors. The eye is drawn to the lighter areas, and the use of contrasting colors creates an impact on the audience. Watch for color clashing, however, such as red text on a green background.

Presentation themes include a palette of colors that have been chosen to work well together, with specific colors assigned to elements such as text, background, and graphics. If you do not want to use the default colors for a particular theme, you can select a different color palette from a menu such as the one shown in Figure 19.10. If your presentation covers events at a garden center, for instance, you may want to select the Green or Green Yellow palette. If none of the color palettes supply exactly the right colors, you can customize any color palette by selecting your own colors.

Backgrounds *LO 19.2*

Unlike desktop publishing, where backgrounds are generally white, presentation software gives you free range of background choices. A **background** can consist of a single color, graduated colors, colored textures, or even a photograph (see Figure 19.11). Although it is interesting to see all the possible background variations, use restraint in your selections. The background should not be so overwhelming that the words or the message are obscured. Instead, use a subtle background that supports your message. When making your choice, keep in mind how color influences your audience.

background—The "paper" on which a presentation will be seen by the audience.

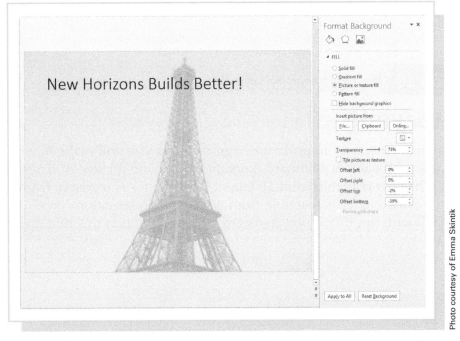

Figure 19.11 *A background picture with a transparency setting of 75% adds to the design of a presentation without overpowering the information you plan to display on each slide.*

checkpoint

How can you easily apply a consistent set of design elements to all slides in a PowerPoint presentation?

ACTIVITY 19.2 ▶ Applying Color

1. Create a new presentation that contains three slides, each with a different layout.

2. Apply a theme that creates a stable, mature message. Change the color palette to Orange Red, or an option that will complement the subject of the presentation (tomatoes).

3. Add a slide at the end of the presentation with a blank layout. Insert the graphic ***tomato*** from your data files as the background. If possible, adjust the transparency of the picture to 50% on the slide.

4. Key **Tomato** as the title for the first slide and your name in the secondary placeholder.

5. From the Slide Master view, insert a text box in the upper-left corner of the slide master and type the file name **19_Activity2_ tomato**. Insert the text box on all layouts you are using. Change the font size on the title for the slides to 60 pt. (Do not change the font size of the title on the title slide.)

6. Exit the Slide Master view.

7. Insert the slide title **Growing Tips** on slide 2. Insert the slide title **Uses of Tomatoes** on slide 3.

8. Use colors from the chosen color scheme for the text on the first slide.

9. Save your presentation as *19_Activity2_tomato*.

Lesson 19.3 ▶ Text on Slides

Text Styling *LO 19.3*

Text styling is the most important design decision you will make when creating a presentation. Billboard painters have a rule for size of letters: A 1-inch letter is readable from 10 feet; a 2-inch letter is readable from 20 feet; a 3-inch letter is readable from 30 feet. A presentation screen is not a billboard, but if 72-point fonts are 1-inch high, then this rule gives

Access and Evaluate Information

The Internet and World Wide Web have given computer users quick and easy access to information on virtually any topic. This can provide you with information you may be seeking as you develop the content of a presentation. But how do you know that the information is accurate, timely, and written by a reliable and knowledgeable source? Following are some tips:

- Verify any information by checking another source.

- Identify the author or organization that publishes or sponsors the site and identify the date the content was created or last updated.

- On the home page, look for a statement or purpose for the site.

- Examine the language of the site. Does it provide facts, opinions, or both? A reliable site should present information in a balanced and objective manner and should be free of spelling and grammatical errors.

Skills in Action: Why is it important to evaluate information you read on the Web? Describe ways in which you evaluate information you obtain in various formats, including the Internet, television, print publications, and in person. Discuss in class.

you an idea how big the font should be to be read by the audience. Actually, you are generally limited to fonts no larger than 96 points.

In PowerPoint, font size is determined by the slide design. If you insert more text in a placeholder than the slide design allows, PowerPoint automatically scales down the font size so the text will fit in the placeholder. You can always manually change the font size, but a better option is to reduce the number of words and lines to keep the font size as large as possible.

Just as you saw in the chapter on desktop publishing, the general font choices consist of serif, sans serif, and display. It is important to choose your font for readability rather than for style. If your audience must strain to figure out the words, they will not be paying attention to your message. Never sacrifice readability for style. Times New Roman may not seem to have enough "splash," but it is a good basic font to use because it is very readable, whether on the pages of a textbook or on a large screen display.

Text enhancements, such as italics and bold, should be used on a limited basis. Underlining is particularly difficult to read on screen and should be avoided. Other choices, such as embossing and shadowing, are also difficult to read. WordArt, which appears to be text, is actually a graphic and should be treated just as you would an image. This means it should only be used if it enhances your message.

Bullets *LO 19.3*

Bullets are used as a standard feature in presentations to draw attention to individual points. Bullets can be standard round dots or more decorative special shapes, such as squares or arrows (as shown in Figure 19.12). The choice is yours, but remember that you do not want the unusual nature of your bullets to detract from the message they are supposed to enhance.

Figure 19.12 *Bulleting is a good tool to use when you want to separate out or emphasize individual pieces of information on a slide.*

Think About It

Every Minute Counts

As a speaker, you have an obligation to provide value for the time your audience invests in your presentation. This obligation means you need to design slides the audience can see easily and understand quickly. It means you must spend your preparation time wisely so that each minute offers your audience useful or important information. Too many slides that have only interesting pictures or too few slides that have condensed text waste your audience's time. If this happens, you have failed to meet your obligation to them.

checkpoint

How should text enhancements, such as bold and italics, be used in presentations? Why?

ACTIVITY 19.3 ▶ Enhancing Text

1. Open the file you completed in the last lesson and save it as **19_Activity3_tomato_revised**.
2. Go to Slide Master view and change the font for all slide titles. Use information you have learned in this chapter as well as the previous desktop publishing chapters to determine what font to choose. Change the label you added to each slide to **19_Activity3_tomato_revised**.
3. Exit Slide Master view.
4. Add bullets to slide 2. Include at least four tips on growing tomatoes.
5. Add bullets to slide 3. Include at least four ideas on how to use tomatoes.
6. Add a text effect such as shadowing to at least one word or title in the presentation.
7. Save your changes.

Lesson 19.4 ▶ Visual Effects

Other than text styling, the most important design decision you will make when creating a presentation is what visual content, if any, to place on each slide. The content could be a table, a chart, clip art, a picture, a diagram, or media in the form of a video or sound. When adding images, such as clip art or a video, it's easy to become so involved in the entertainment aspect of the elements that the message gets lost. When considering what visual effects to include in your presentation, continually ask yourself the following two questions:

1. Does this element clarify the message?
2. Does this element make the presentation more effective?

SmartArt Diagrams *LO 19.4*

The SmartArt feature available in most Microsoft Office applications allows you to create diagrams that convey information in interesting visual ways. Categories of diagrams include lists, processes, cycles, hierarchies, relationships, and so on. Each category offers a wide variety of styles to meet your specific needs. A process diagram shows steps such as in a timeline or series of actions. As an example, Figure 19.13 demonstrates a vertical chevron used to show movement from one step to the next. A hierarchy diagram provides a decision tree or an organizational chart as shown in Figure 19.14. A cycle diagram, as displayed in Figure 19.15, shows a continuous process. A relationship diagram illustrates connections or relationships. Figure 19.16 is a Venn diagram that shows how relationships overlap.

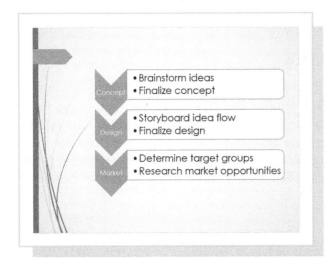

Figure 19.13 *Use SmartArt's vertical chevron list option to graphically display the steps involved in a process.*

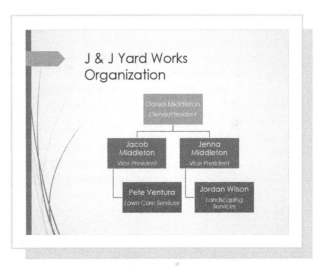

Figure 19.14 *Hierarchies such as organization charts are among the most recognizable SmartArt diagrams.*

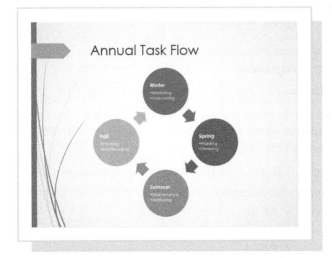

Figure 19.15 *A cycle diagram is used to indicate a continuous flow of events.*

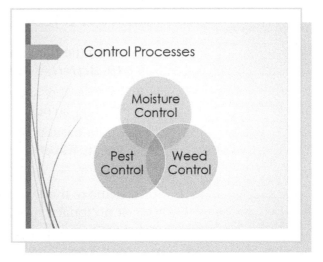

Figure 19.16 *Overlapping relationships are best represented using a Venn diagram.*

Choosing Graphics *LO 19.4*

Be particularly cautious when adding clip art to a presentation. Just as with overused templates, overused clip art can create a ho-hum response from your audience. It is often better to use a simple graphic that you created or a photograph that you have taken instead of work created by someone else. Your own work can have more impact than clip art that everyone has already seen.

Do not forget the drawing tools that are also available to you. Lines and other shapes can provide effective graphics without obscuring your message.

Once you have decided on which visual effect is most appropriate and useful, you can easily insert the element onto a slide and then resize or move it. Just as you limit the number of text enhancements on a slide, you should limit the number of images on a slide to no more than three.

White Space *LO 19.4*

As you have seen, many of the same rules apply for both page layout and presentation design. This applies to white space as well. It means you should not be afraid to leave white space on your slide. This openness will enhance your message and give your audience a breather. Avoid cluttering your slide with too much text, too many graphics, or an excessively busy design. Less is definitely more in presentation design.

checkpoint

What is the most important design decision, other than text, that you will make when creating a presentation?

ACTIVITY 19.4 ▶ Adding Graphics

1. Open the file you completed in Activity 19.3. Save it as **19_Activity4_adding_graphics**.
2. Insert a new slide at the end of the presentation with the Title and Content layout.
3. Add a basic process graphic with the order of growing tomatoes: **Plant**, **Water and Feed**, **Pick Fruit**. Add an appropriate title.
4. Experiment with horizontal rules and shapes on one of the slides.
5. Remove the text box with the filename in Slide Master view so that it no longer appears on any of the slides.
6. Save your changes.

Key Concepts

▶ The use of templates containing pre-designed elements, such as backgrounds, font colors, font sizes, and bullets, help facilitate the creation of professional presentations. *LO 19.1*

▶ Elements and options, such as Slide Master settings, themes, color choices, and backgrounds, are used to enhance a slide's layout. *LO 19.2*

▶ The most important design decision you will make when creating a presentation involves your text styling. *LO 19.3*

▶ Include visual content in a presentation only if it helps make the presentation more effective and clarifies the message. *LO 19.4*

Review and Discuss

1. Evaluate the advantages and disadvantages of using templates in a presentation. *LO 19.1 and 19.2*

2. Discuss the various slide layouts and justify the use of several layouts used most often. *LO 19.2*

3. Discuss the importance of the Slide Master settings in creating consistent presentations. *LO 19.1*

4. Summarize the impact that color can have on the audience. *LO 19.4*

5. Categorize the following colors into complementary or analogous colors: bright red/dark green, orange/blue, blue violet/yellow orange, violet/yellow, and yellow green/green. *LO 19.4*

6. Describe considerations that should be used to decide on text choices. *LO 19.3*

7. Explain when and what type of text enhancement should be used in a presentation. *LO 19.3*

8. Defend the omission of visual effects in a presentation. *LO 19.4*

9. Compare and contrast four categories of SmartArt diagrams. *LO 19.4*

10. Explain why a designer of a presentation would choose to leave some white space on each slide. *LO 19.1 and 19.2*

Apply

1. Use a template to create a presentation of a business plan. Save the presentation as ***19_Apply1_business_plan***. From Slide Master view, insert a text box with **Business Plan** in the top left corner of each slide.

Change the theme and colors to ones that would generate excitement. Review the template, and then choose which slides to delete, leaving only six slides. Leave the title slide, at least one slide with a SmartArt diagram, one with bullets, and three other slides. Replace the subtitle on the title slide with your name. Type new text on the first slide and the SmartArt slide. Save again. *LO 19.1*

2. Create a presentation entitled **Going Green!** Start with a title slide and your name. In Outline view, organize your thoughts and slides. Create a bulleted slide for the second slide with **Tips on Going Green** as the title, another slide with **Effects of Going Green** as the title, and a final slide with an appropriate SmartArt diagram and text. The last slide should be titled **My Plan For Going Green**. In Slide Master view, add an appropriate image in one corner for all slides except the title slide. Make decisions on text choices, visual effects, colors, backgrounds, and bullets. Save the presentation as **19_Apply2_going_green**. *LO 19.2, 19.3, and 19.4*

3. Create a slide show with three slides: one title slide and two with title and content. In Slide Master view, insert the **TechMania** logo from your student data files. Place it at the bottom right of the Slide Master text area. Change the text type and size in Slide Master view for both the Title slide and the Title and Content slide. Change the color palette to one that complements the logo colors. Add a footer with the slogan: **Bring it in!** On the title slide, add the title **TechMania** and apply an appropriate color from the color palette to the title. Save the presentation as a template with the filename **19_Apply3_tech_mania**. *LO 19.1, 19.2, 19.3, and 19.4*

4. Create a blank slide. Insert a cycle SmartArt diagram to represent a basic color wheel. Add shapes as necessary until you have six shapes. Label each in the appropriate position with the colors: **Red**, **Orange**, **Yellow**, **Green**, **Blue**, and **Violet**. Experiment changing shapes and formatting the shape. Add three more slides with title-only content. Use Shapes to demonstrate pairs of analogous colors. Save your presentation as **19_Apply4_color_wheel**. *LO 19.2, 19.3, and 19.4*

5. Create a slide presentation giving information on safe swimming. Embed a video into the last slide, either showing something about swimming or making your points about safe swimming. Save the presentation as **19_Apply5_safe_swimming**. *LO 19.2, 19.3, and 19.4*

6. Create a presentation about a sport or organization within your school. Decide on a theme to use. Add graphics, text enhancements, and visual effects. Save the presentation as **19_Apply6_sport_organization**. *LO 19.2, 19.3, and 19.4*

Explore

1. Visit the website of a local community college. Review the requirements and other information regarding a certificate or degree in Fire Science or EMT (or other Allied Health field if the first two are not available). Use the information that you collect for a five-slide presentation. Choose a slide design that is appropriate to the topic. Add a clip art graphic as a background. Make the clip art transparent enough to be able to read the slides. Insert a slide footer on every slide except the title slide. The final slide should be contact information for the program. Save as ***19_Explore1_fire_science***. *LO 19.1, 19.2, 19.3, and 19.4*

2. Research uses of presentations. Focus on five different uses that you have researched, creating a slide for each use. Demonstrate the skills learned in this chapter on presentations. Save the presentation as ***19_Explore2_presentation_uses***. *LO 19.2, 19.3, and 19.4*

3. Explore templates online for your presentation software. Create a presentation of your choice, using one of the free templates that you found online. Save the presentation as ***19_Explore3_templates***. *LO 19.1*

Academic Connections

Reading: Go to www.dictionary.com and create a deck of 10 flash cards. Put each term on its own slide. Use the following terms: perseverance, accommodate, conscience, mitigate, plethora, reticent, laconic, extant, incipient, and attenuate. Submit the deck of flashcards to your instructor.

Math: You have been asked to create a self-running presentation of eight slides to play for the entryway of the local YMCA. The final slide will have a video that will play for five minutes. If you want the presentation to play at least four times during the hour, what time should each of the other nine slides be set on?

Presentation Effects

Lesson 20.1 Slide Transitions

Lesson 20.2 Animation

Lesson 20.3 Audio

Learning Outcomes

▶ **20.1** Use slide transitions in presentations.

▶ **20.2** Effectively incorporate animation styles, text animation, and motion paths in presentations.

▶ **20.3** Enhance transitions and animations in presentations with audio.

Key Terms

- animate
- animation style
- motion path
- slide transition

Multimedia has transformed the world of communication. Gone are the days when a presenter's options for delivering a message were limited to two or three font choices in black lettering on plain white paper. Today, a presenter can choose to deliver his or her message by way of a digital presentation containing an array of audio and visual effects. When coupled with proper design management, this form of delivery can make for a fun and exciting, not to mention effective, method of communication. In this chapter, you explore the use of digital effects as they relate to presentations.

Once you have outlined your message and selected the appropriate background, text, and images to use in your presentation, it's time to focus on how special effects can be used to enhance your message. Presentation software programs, such as Microsoft PowerPoint, provide several special-effect options you can use throughout your presentation. Presenters commonly incorporate special effects during **slide transitions**, the point in a presentation where one slide closes and the next slide opens on the screen. You can also use a variety of special effects to **animate** text or images appearing throughout a presentation.

slide transitions—The movement from one slide to another that might include some kind of animation.

animate—The application of visual effects to individual items on a slide, such as text or an image.

Lesson 20.1 Slide Transitions LO 20.1

Slide transition describes not only the movement from one slide to another, but also any effects that are used during that transition. The transition between slides can consist simply of moving from one slide to another, or it can be an interesting special effect such as a clockwise spin. In PowerPoint, the movement between slides can occur on a mouse click or after a set period of time. Transitions can also be set to occur with a special sound, set to last for a specific amount of time using the Duration option, and set to occur between all slides by selecting the Apply to All option. You can choose to incorporate any number of transition options from the Transitions tab (see Figure 20.1).

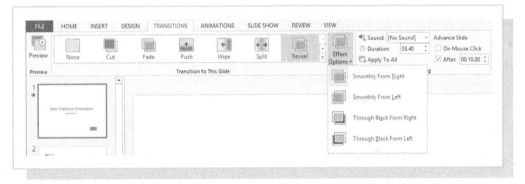

Figure 20.1 *From the Transitions tab, you can incorporate a variety of transition options on a PowerPoint slide.*

Some transitions in PowerPoint have Effect Options (see Figure 20.1). For example, the Blinds transition can be set to appear to open either vertically or horizontally while the Ripple transition can be set to begin movement from the center, top right, top left, bottom right, or bottom left. Similar transition effects are also available in Google Slides (see Figure 20.2), where you can add transitions such as Fade, Slide from right, Slide from left, and Flip. You can also adjust the transition timing to either slow, medium, or fast.

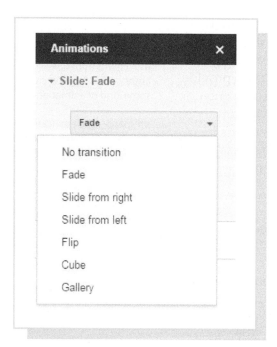

Figure 20.2 *Selecting the Change transition option in a Google Slides presentation displays the Animations menu listing a variety of transition options you can choose from to enhance your presentation.*

As with colors and images, there are questions you must ask yourself before incorporating a special effect in a presentation. Will this effect help clarify your message? Will it make your presentation more effective? While it's unlikely that a slide transition will clarify a message, it may help make your presentation more interesting. Since your goal is for your audience to hear your message, anything you can do to hold their interest will make your presentation more effective. Keep in mind, however, that effects used inappropriately may have the opposite effect. As with color and font styles, sometimes less is more. Too many effects that serve no real purpose may distract your audience. Just because you *can* choose to use a different transition between each slide does not mean it is a good idea. Most of the time, you are better off picking one subtle transition and sticking with it.

The Impact of Animation

In its earliest form, animation consisted of hand-drawn figures depicting scenes on a piece of paper. These scenes, often accompanied by words, were meant to convey a message to viewers. Later, with the introduction of film and television, animation took on movement and sound. While the same story could be told in written form on paper, the addition of movement and sound to an animated message was more appealing to audiences.

In those early years, animation was primarily viewed as a form of entertainment. With the introduction of digital presentation software, other industries soon found animation to be an effective communication tool. Business people and educators, in particular, noted the benefits of using animation in presentations. Today, it's up to digital designers to ensure that these tools are used in creative and effective ways throughout all industries.

checkpoint

What is a slide transition?

ACTIVITY 20.1 ▶ Slide Transitions

1. Search the Internet for "five tips for slide transitions." Make notes on what you find.
2. Create a presentation with a title and one tip on each slide.
3. Add appropriate transitions, using the tips that you have just researched.
4. Save your presentation as *20_Activity1_transition_tips*.

Lesson 20.2 ▶ Animation

Animation Styles *LO 20.2*

An **animation style** is a predesigned animated option that you can apply to text and images on a slide. Depending upon the presentation software you are using, these options are practically limitless and extremely easy to use. In PowerPoint, for example, you can quickly add any one of the most popular animation styles to text or an image by selecting the object on the slide and then selecting an option displayed on the Animations tab (see Figure 20.3).

Or, you can choose an option from the full list of available animation styles. These styles are arranged by category, such as Entrance, Emphasis, Exit, and Motion Paths, as shown in Figure 20.3. This arrangement helps

animation style—A set of animation choices that includes animation, timing, and response.

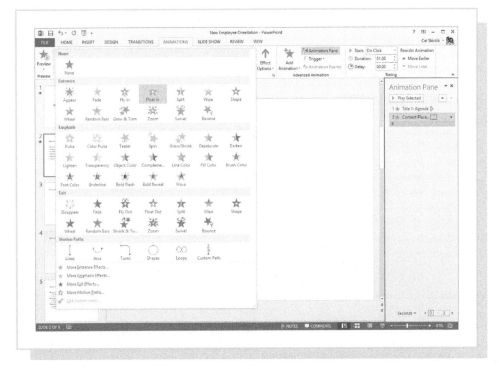

Figure 20.3 *From the Animations tab in PowerPoint, users can quickly add one of the most popular animation styles to text or an image. Animation styles are organized by type, to allow you to quickly browse through all available animations.*

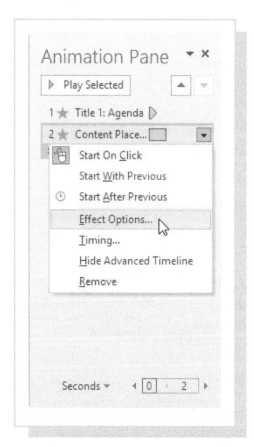

Figure 20.4 *From the Animation Pane, you can customize when and how an animation will appear.*

simplify your decision-making process. You can use the styles as they are designed, or you can modify them in any way you want.

As you select an object on your slide and add an animation to it, you will notice a small number appear next to the object. The first object you animate will have the number "1" next to it, the second object, the number "2," and so on. You can control, adjust, and rearrange the sequence, timing, triggers, etc. through the Animation Pane (see red highlighted rectangle in Figure 20.3), which is accessed by clicking the Animation Pane button on the Animations tab.

From the Animation Pane, shown in Figure 20.4, you can select the drop-down arrow next to any one of the animation effects to see customization options. For example, if you select Effect Options, a dialog box appears from which you can customize the effect, timing of the animation, and text animation (see Figure 20.5).

More unusual and less commonly used animation effects, such as unique motion paths, can also be added to images and text. For example, in Figure 20.6, the Swoosh effect is selected. If added to an image of a paintbrush, the brush will appear to paint on the slide. If the Preview Effect box is checked, you will see how each animation will be applied to the image or text before you click the OK button to make the selection.

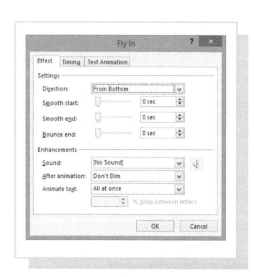

Figure 20.5 *An animation effect's settings—including how and when it will start, the direction it will move, and the speed of its movement—can be changed to meet the needs of any given object within the presentation.*

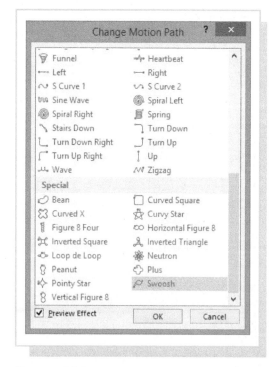

Figure 20.6 *A motion path animation adds emphasis to an image on a slide.*

Time Management

You may not realize it, but you already practice time-management skills on a daily basis. It takes a lot of talent to squeeze homework assignments from three different classes, soccer practice, and your nightly chat room session into one single evening! Your success depends entirely on your ability to plan your time wisely. This is especially true in the workplace.

Time management on the job can be a bit tricky at first. For example, if you've never attempted to add special effects to a 50-slide presentation before, you may not understand how long it will take. Your supervisor will give you some reasonable guidelines, but to be successful you'll soon learn how to size up the work you have to do and what you need to get it done. You'll also learn to set priorities. Which tasks need to be finished first? Don't do the enjoyable work first and put off the less desirable tasks for later. Instead, be proactive in effectively scheduling your time on each and every project.

You can use either the Play From button in the Animation Pane or the Preview button on the Animations tab to preview all of the animations on a slide in sequence. This allows you to check the timing as well as the sequence of all of your animations on a given slide. Any necessary adjustments can then be easily made in the Animation Pane, where even reordering the animations is made easy by either dragging the animation to the desired position or by using the Reorder buttons at the top of the pane.

Text Animation *LO 20.2*

Text can be animated to appear all at once, by word, or by letter using text effects options shown in Figure 20.7. Bulleted points can be set to appear all at once or individually. These are very useful techniques because they mean you can control exactly how much of the text your audience will see and when they will see it. Notice in Figure 20.7 that each item in a bulleted list can be set to appear all at once, by word, or by letter.

The color and style of text can also be animated to add emphasis. For example, text can initially appear on a slide in one color and then change color. Within the Emphasis section of

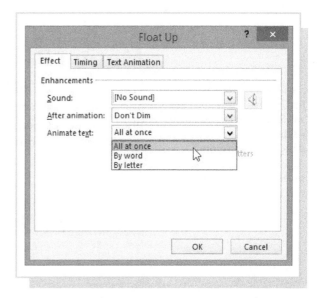

Figure 20.7 *You can have all of the words in a bulleted list appear at once, or have each word appear individually on the screen. You can even set the letters of each word to appear one at a time.*

Figure 20.8 *A variety of effects can be added to emphasize, or de-emphasize, text.*

the Animation list, shown in Figure 20.8, you can choose to have text transition to a darker color, a lighter color, or even a different color altogether. Text animation can be quite effective because it keeps your audience focused on the particular point you are making, while the previous points lose impact.

Again, the decision to use any of these effects must be made with care and should be based on their potential effectiveness. The division of the effects into categories, such as "Subtle," gives you an idea about appropriate situations in which to use each animation. Subtle (or low-key) effects and basic effects can be used in formal situations. Exciting and moderate ones should be reserved for those times when more interesting effects will be appreciated.

As you learned that restraint is often better when it comes to the use of images and text, the same is true for the use of animations. The use of a few animations may help keep your audience's attention, but their overuse will likely overwhelm them and detract from your message.

Motion Paths *LO 20.2*

motion path—The track that animated text or image will follow as it appears on a slide. It can be a simple straight line or a more complicated one with a series of twists or turns.

One of the more enticing animation effects is a **motion path**. The creation of a motion path allows you to produce a flying object or text line that moves across your slide in exactly the pattern you want. It can be quite effective as a means of grabbing attention, and the novelty of creating such paths can be appealing. Figure 20.9 shows the

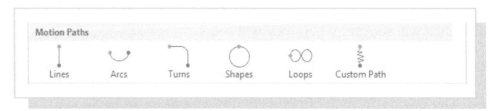

Figure 20.9 *PowerPoint provides several preset Motion Paths, or you can design your own.*

predesigned motion paths available in PowerPoint. Or, you can choose Custom Path, then use your mouse to design your own path.

Once an option has been selected, a preview of the motion path is shown on the slide. Note that all animation effects set for a slide are indicated both on the slide itself and in the Animation Pane displayed to the right of the slide. You can preview all animation effects on a slide at any time by clicking the Preview button in the Animations tab.

Animation Painter *LO 20.2*

Just as you can copy formatting features from one selection of text to another using the Format Painter tool in PowerPoint and other Microsoft Office products, you can also copy animation features from one object to another using the Animation Painter tool. When you copy an animation, you are also copying any settings you've applied to that animation. This makes the Animation Painter a real time-saving tool when enhancing a presentation with animated effects.

Begin by adding the animation effects to at least one object in your presentation. Preview it and check all settings to make sure it is exactly what you want. Then, with the object still selected, click Animation Painter (see Figure 20.10). Your cursor will now appear as a paintbrush and arrow. This means that the animation has been copied. The copied animation effects will be applied to the next object you

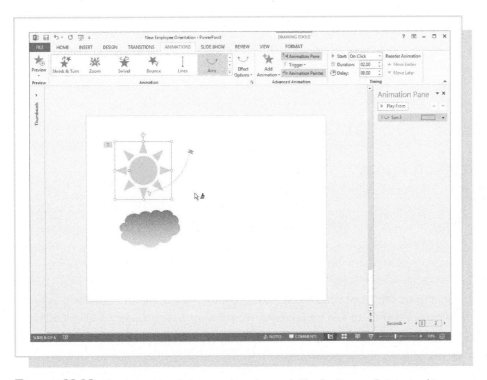

Figure 20.10 *The Animation Painter tool works much like the Format Painter tool in PowerPoint.*

click on. If you have a number of objects to which you want to apply the same animation, double-click the Animation Painter button. You will then be able to click on multiple objects and apply the animation. When you are finished, click on the Animation Painter button again to "turn off" the painter.

checkpoint

How is text animation an effective tool in a presentation?

ACTIVITY 20.2 ▶ Animated Slides

1. Create a slide presentation with four slides, each slide demonstrating one of the following:

   a. Entrance style slide transition added to title slide for both placeholders (title and subtitle) to enter at the same time.

   b. Image of any animal with an appropriate animation added for the movement of the animal.

   c. Motion path added for a title to move somewhere on the slide.

   d. Slide with three bullets with title and bullets animated. Use Animation Painter to add the animation from the title placeholder to the bullet placeholder. (Note that this will cause all the bullets to come on the screen at one time.)

2. Save your presentation as *20_Activity2_animated_slides*.

Microsoft Agent

Microsoft Agent was the software used to create interactive, animated characters, such as the Microsoft Office Assistants. One of the most recognized Office Assistant characters was "Clippy," the animated paper clip with famously large and human-like eyeballs and eyebrows. Clippy was designed to interact with Office Help content and serve as a helpful tool for users. A backlash, however, from those same users ultimately led to Clippy's demise. As a default feature of the program, the character would often appear on screen with annoyingly obvious observations, such as "It looks like you're writing a letter." Microsoft used the anti-Clippy atmosphere to their advantage during the launch of Windows XP. Touting the user-friendly design of Windows XP, Microsoft prominently advertised the fact that Clippy and other Office Assistant characters were no longer needed. According to Microsoft's support site, Microsoft Agent will not be included or supported in future versions of the Microsoft Windows operating system.

Granata1111/Dreamstime.com

Audio in Transitions and Animations *LO 20.3*

In addition to special effects, another option available to you in both slide transitions and animation is audio, or sound. A number of sounds are typically built into presentation software, but you can also add your own sounds that you or someone else has created. Sound can be a significant enhancement if used correctly. A few bars of music attached to an opening slide can set the mood or tone of your presentation. Splashes of sound effects as an animation occurs can draw additional attention to the visual effect, and voice can be used to convey information. Short clips of someone else's ideas or thoughts can be a good way to add credibility to your own ideas.

You can add audio to a presentation slide in two ways. One option is to insert it, much as you would an image from the Insert tab (see Figure 20.11). Using this method, a speaker icon appears on the slide that can be assigned animation options such as timing and visibility. The second option is to attach audio to a transition or to an image or text box you have animated by using the effects options so that the sound plays as the image or text appears on the slide. Your choice depends on your intended use of the sound, but often attaching sound to an object is the most effective use because the sound usually is not the primary focus of the slide.

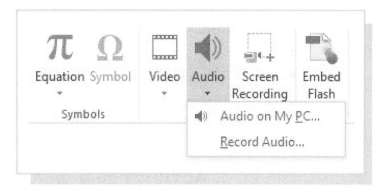

Figure 20.11 *In PowerPoint, you can insert audio from a file or record your own custom audio.*

Recording Sound *LO 20.3*

If you are using Microsoft PowerPoint, a built-in feature allows you to record sound directly from within the program. Figure 20.12 shows the simple recording box that appears when you select the option to record sound.

Regardless of how you intend to use audio, be careful with the use of audio clips provided as part of the software package. Sounds that have been used before in a presentation have the potential to be even less appealing to your audience than reused clip art or templates. Annoying sounds should be avoided. And be aware that noise that sounds interesting in the first few seconds can quickly become irritating to your audience.

Figure 20.12 *The Record Sound dialog box in PowerPoint lets you record and name your own custom sound.*

Think About It

Fair Use of Music in Presentations

It's very tempting to copy music either from a CD or from the Internet to use in a presentation. The fair use rules that apply to schools allow you to use up to 30 seconds of such sound in a school presentation. This same law of fair use does not, however, cross over into commercial use. If you have a need to use music for a business presentation, you must seek permission for its use. Another option is to purchase royalty-free music CDs available at reasonable prices. Royalty free means you cannot sell the music, but you can use it for commercial purposes. It's a good idea to have one or more of these CDs available if you do not want to have to acquire permission each time you want to use music in a presentation.

Keep in mind that although downloadable music on the Internet is frequently advertised as being free for all use, it has often been pirated (stolen), and the site offering it to you does not own the music. Don't put your business or employer at risk by using music that has questionable ownership.

checkpoint

How could a short clip of another person's ideas or thoughts be useful in your presentation?

ACTIVITY 20.3 ▶ Adding Sound

1. Create a four-slide presentation about yourself.
   a. Slide 1 should contain the title **About Me** and your name.
   b. Slide 2 should be titled **Goals**. Include at least three bullets with goals.
   c. Slide 3 should be titled **Interests**. List at least three hobbies or interests.
   d. Slide 4 should be titled **My Family**. Add a picture of your family or yourself.
2. Narrate the presentation if you have access to a microphone. If not, add audio to at least one animation or transition in the presentation.
3. Save your presentation as *20_Activity3_narration*.

Key Concepts

▶ Presentation software programs provide several special effect options which presenters commonly use during slide transitions. *LO 20.1*

▶ Tools such as animation styles, text animation, motion paths, and the Animation Painter can, when used properly, help keep your audience's attention. *LO 20.2*

▶ Audio can be used in both transitions and animations to set the mood for a presentation. *LO 20.3*

Review and Discuss

1. Describe the difference between transitions and animations. *LO 20.1*

2. How do Effect Options allow you to customize a transition? *LO 20.1*

3. Describe the interactive value of using transitions other than just movement from one slide to another. *LO 20.1*

4. Critique the use of a slow clockwise spin transition with sound. *LO 20.1*

5. Compare and contrast the uses of animation styles, the Animation tab, and the Animation Pane. *LO 20.2*

6. Identify the type of animation effect that should be used in formal situations. *LO 20.2*

7. Describe how motion paths can be created. *LO 20.2*

8. Identify ways of putting sounds in presentations and the purposes of using sound. *LO 20.3*

9. Compare and contrast fair use as it applies to business and school use with regard to music.

10. Describe Microsoft Agent and how it relates to animation.

Apply

1. Open ***digital_marketing*** from your data files. Read the content, then create a presentation using the content. Add appropriate transitioning between slides and animations determined by the content. Create a motion path for the last slide. In the Notes section, add details on why you chose the transition and animation effects. Add a design to the presentation. Save the presentation as ***20_Apply1_digital_marketing***. *LO 20.1 and 20.2*

2. Watch a YouTube video on "Death by PowerPoint." Create content for a presentation on what not to do in a presentation. Save your work as **20_Apply2_content**. Add a design, transitions, and animations and save the presentation as **20_Apply2_effects**. *LO 20.1 and 20.2*

3. You work for a travel agency and want to use a self-running presentation about a specific city to visit. Choose a city on which to focus your presentation. Research the city to find out the following: five important facts about the city, five places to see while you are there, and five restaurants you would like to visit while you are there. Place the content in your slides. Choose a style. Add an action button, slide transitions, and animation styles to the content. Use one motion path. Narrate the slide presentation. Use Animation Painter wherever possible. You should have at least five slides in the presentation. Save the presentation as **20_Apply3_travel**. *LO 20.1, 20.2, and 20.3*

4. For future students, the principal has asked you to prepare a slide show about the school. Use information from the school's website to build the content in your slide show. Use a theme that demonstrates your school colors. Use as many of the skills that you learned in this chapter as possible while still making wise choices to best convey your message. Be creative! Save the presentation as **20_Apply4_school**. *LO 20.1, 20.2, and 20.3*

5. Create a presentation comparing three smartphones. The final slide should be your conclusion as to which one is best. Use the notes section to place some of the content so you do not have too much on the slides. Get the audience's attention! Use as many of the skills from this lesson in transitions and animations as possible. Save as **20_Apply5_smart_phones**. *LO 20.1 and 20.2*

6. Create a presentation focusing on one specific car or other vehicle that you are interested in purchasing. Content should be on at least six slides. Choose a design, add transitions and animations, and add sound. Save the presentation as **20_Apply6_cars**. *LO 20.1, 20.2, and 20.3*

Explore

1. Research apps for business productivity. Create a slide show on at least four of the apps that you found in your research that you would consider useful for business productivity. Create one slide on each app, summarizing two good things the reviews said about it and two bad things. Add design, transitions, and animations. Save the presentation as **20_Explore1_apps**. *LO 20.1 and 20.2*

2. Research speaking tips on the Dale Carnegie website. Create a presentation with content about speaking tips. Make the presentation as creative as possible, using skills learned in this chapter. Include at least one special-effects sound. Save the presentation as **20_Explore2_speaking_tips**. *LO 20.1, 20.2, and 20.3*

3. Research at least one presentation software as well as Microsoft Power-Point. Create content in a slide show that compares and contrasts the two software applications. Save the presentation as **20_Explore3_software_comparison**.

Academic Connections

Reading: Read and summarize at least two articles on creating effective presentations or effective speaking skills. Save your work as **20_AC_reading**.

Math: You have been asked to present for at least 45 minutes. How many slides will you need to create if you will spend an average of 5 minutes on each slide with a 5 second transition between slides? Calculate your answer. Be sure to show your work. How many slides would you need if you also plan to allow 10 minutes at the end of the presentation for questions? Save your calculations and answers as **20_AC_math**.

Presentation Production

Lesson 21.1 Communicating the Presentation's Message

Lesson 21.2 Presentation Delivery

Lesson 21.3 Presentation Setup and Packaging

Learning Outcomes

▶ **21.1** Differentiate between presentation types.

▶ **21.2** Recognize presentation delivery options and concerns.

▶ **21.3** Identify presentation setup and packaging options.

Key Terms

- jargon
- kiosk
- Package Presentation for CD

Whether delivering your presentation live to an auditorium full of attendees or digitally to a remote audience of one, you must choose the appropriate media type in order to properly convey the benefits and relevance of your information to each intended audience. An excellent presentation is useless unless delivered in the right media for the message.

Communicating the Presentation's Message

Presentation Types *LO 21.1*

Slide presentations fall into two basic categories: presentations delivered by a speaker to an audience, and presentations recorded in advance to be delivered to individuals either on their own devices or at a kiosk.

Presentations Delivered by a Speaker

Delivering a presentation live allows you to interact with your audience (Figure 21.1). This does not necessarily mean it is delivered in person. You can also deliver a presentation to a widespread audience during an online group meeting that is held live over the Internet. When you deliver a presentation live, you can usually observe your audience's reaction, answer questions as they are asked, and receive immediate feedback about the information you are providing.

AISPIX/Shutterstock.com

Figure 21.1 *When a presentation is delivered by a speaker, all parties involved in the presentation are in live, real-time communication, whether in person or over the Internet.*

Presentations Delivered to Individuals

Although most people think of presentations as being "eyeball-to-eyeball," many more are made available for individuals to browse. A presentation that you are not delivering in person must convey all of your outline points for you, as you will not be there to answer questions, clarify points, or provide additional information. Presentations of this type are often used for training purposes, in which a trainee can view each slide at his or her own speed. You may also find them on websites, as a way to deliver information about products or services.

Kiosk Presentations *LO 21.1*

It's becoming more and more common to see a sales presentation delivered via an interactive **kiosk**. A kiosk is a freestanding computer display that is one of two types: passive or interactive. A passive kiosk display uses software such as PowerPoint that has been designed to run continuously, without user intervention. Each slide is timed to move at a pre-selected pace. Kiosks of this type are used in such places as museums, stores, and visitor centers (Figure 21.2).

Figure 21.2 *A kiosk is a great way to provide information to a broad audience on an as-needed basis. The audience can come and go as they please and no presenter is needed.*

The issue with this type of demonstration is that you must anticipate how fast your audience will read the material, how much material they are willing to read, and how long you can hold their attention. This is an image management situation in which flashy design can be an important addition. Sound and video can also be used effectively as a means of conveying information without requiring the audience to read. Keep in mind, however, that if sound is too intrusive, personnel who work near the demonstration and must listen to it continuously may disable this feature.

Interactive kiosks are considered robotic in nature, as they not only communicate information to viewers, but also interact with them. An interactive kiosk allows users to make selections, often with a touch screen. Your audience can look up information and even print it out. Kiosks of this type are used in places such as libraries, gift registries, and information booths.

Often a focus group—a group of people chosen to provide feedback—will be used to test a presentation that will be delivered to individuals or at kiosks. This allows you to address audience questions in advance and rework your presentation to minimize audience questions.

lavitrei/Shutterstock.com

The Impact of Kiosks

Kiosks have become a way of life. While they can be used to provide information in the form of a slide show, they are useful in many other ways. One of the most common uses is at airports, where boarding passes and flight information are now available at kiosks located throughout the terminal. Not only does this speed up the process of boarding a plane, it also reduces the cost to airlines that do not have to pay for personnel as they once did. Banking kiosks in the form of ATMs are also pervasive. Once again the banks have been able to reduce personnel costs while adding convenience. Most grocery stores now have self-checkout kiosks available for shoppers. And many people regularly carry a personal kiosk around with them—their smartphones. Many smartphones allow users to run slide shows from a file, or even directly from a web page. It's safe to say that kiosk machines will be found in more and more businesses as the technology continues to develop.

Presentation Challenges *LO 21.1*

Your challenge when creating a presentation is to determine how best to convey your message. Remember that no matter what your design choices are, your main objective is to communicate your message, not impress your audience. Viewers will not respond positively because you have the flashiest PowerPoint presentation. They will respond positively because your presentation engages them and provides essential information.

Not every person viewing a presentation has the same needs. A good presenter must discover each person's individual needs. One way is by asking questions while giving a live presentation. You must be comfortable asking and answering questions as they arise, providing intelligent, spur-of-the-moment responses. You can prepare for this by making sure that you know your topic as thoroughly as possible. Rehearsing your presentation in front of a live yet friendly audience (such as coworkers, peers, or family) is also useful. They can ask questions that your real audience might pose, and thus give you practice in answering questions in the midst of your presentation and then transitioning back to continue.

Using Jargon in a Presentation

jargon—Specialized words used within a particular industry, often incorporating acronyms as shortcuts.

It is a good rule to avoid the use of **jargon**, or terms that can cause confusion, when interacting with audience members. Every industry and profession makes use of jargon. Sometimes it is an acronym. Sometimes it is an abbreviated form of a word or several words. And sometimes it is a nickname for a product or process. W3C (World Wide Web Consortium) is an example of an acronym used in the web design community. And "wizzy-wig" is a nickname for the acronym WYSIWYG, which means "What You See Is What You Get," a term commonly used with web design and desktop publishing software.

As has been mentioned several times, it is important to know your audience. This includes being aware of their level of familiarity with the topic of the presentation. Following our examples above, if your audience is a group of people at a web design conference, using the terms "W3C" or "WYSIWYG" would not be a problem. If, however, your audience is made up of students in an "Introduction to Web Design" class, these terms could be problematic for them. If there is any doubt in your mind as to whether the audience will know a particular term, it is always best to avoid the term or to include an explanation.

Global Considerations

In addition, in a global economy, communication is no longer between people from the same region who may have similar needs or similar understanding of context. You must consider the diverse needs of a global audience (Figure 21.3). Language and cultural barriers have to be taken into consideration. Some colors, for example, differ in significance from one country to another. In most Western cultures, white is the color for weddings and represents the "good guys." In many Eastern cultures, white is the color worn at funerals and red is the color for brides and is considered good luck. Because of these differences in use within the culture, these colors can also evoke different emotional responses from an audience, whether conscious or not, and may enhance or cloud your message. Likewise, different images may elicit different responses, depending on the culture of the audience.

Phillip Date/Shutterstock.com

Figure 21.3 *The needs of a global audience can be different from those of a local one.*

When creating your presentations, you must keep all these elements in mind. Ask yourself which images clarify, which colors promote the response you want (and whether that color will work in all cultures), and what type style and size make it easiest for your audience to understand the message.

International Business Etiquette

Do you understand the importance of business cards in Japanese society? Would you know what refreshments to offer—and what not to offer—to a business associate from Saudi Arabia? Do you know whether or not it's appropriate to send a gift to a customer in Germany? Is it expected? What response might you receive if you express annoyance toward a customer from Mexico who arrives late for a business meeting? How hard should you press a client from South Korea for a yes-or-no answer?

More and more companies—particularly cutting-edge, high-tech companies—are doing business with people from other countries. But doing business means different things in different countries. Today more than ever, it's important to understand the expectations of global business communities. Researching and learning the proper way to treat a foreign customer or business associate is not only polite, it's also good business. It builds trust and shows you care enough to make them comfortable. Successful business relationships can be fashioned simply by knowing a little bit about the other person's culture.

checkpoint

What are the two basic categories of presentations?

ACTIVITY 21.1 ▶ Presentation Types

1. Using word processing software, create a list of presentations that you have seen. Divide the list into presentations that were delivered by a speaker and presentations you browsed or viewed at a kiosk. Describe the situation in which you saw the presentation or were involved in the presentation and how you were involved.

2. Label the presentations on your list as passive or interactive. For the interactive presentations, explain how it was interactive.

3. Save your document as *21_Activity1_my_list*.

You may create an exceptional presentation, but if the delivery is poor then the message will not be well received by the audience. A clean, well-rehearsed delivery is the key to getting your point across to an audience successfully. Every presentation can be improved upon simply by being organized. One way you can convey this sense of order in your delivery is to rehearse your presentation, paying particular attention to timing, movement, and even the lighting.

Timing LO 21.2

A presentation's timing can be as simple as when it starts and stops, or it may be much more complex. Timing may encompass details such as planned pauses to ask and answer questions, or the rate at which bullet points and other elements are brought on to individual screens.

If the entire presentation will run without input or prompts from a presenter, the timing of a slide show may be preset using the timing options found in most presentation software programs. If a live presenter will be speaking to accompany the presentation, then what will be said with each slide, the appearance of elements on the slide, and the transition to the next slide must be carefully choreographed and rehearsed. This may take a number of run-throughs and adjustments until the presentation is perfected.

If a presentation is going to be delivered at a kiosk or through some other means where there is no live presenter, then the timing must be set so that the audience has sufficient time to view, read, and understand the content of each slide. Care must be taken, however, not to leave too much time, or your audience may drift away. The ability to record a voice-over to go with the presentation allows you to hold the audience's interest and make sure your message is conveyed, as well as gives you a set amount of time to go by when determining exactly how long each of your slides will stay on the screen and how long the entire slide show will last. For more information on timing, see the Transitions section in Chapter 19.

Granata1111/Dreamstime.com

From Laps to Laptops

Most people take the technology involved in delivering a modern multimedia presentation for granted. While most of us understand that it takes a good amount of time and energy to create, produce, and deliver a quality presentation, can you imagine how much longer it would take to complete those same tasks without the use of modern technology? In other words, imagine trying to create a visual presentation with just the use of pen and paper. Without the invention of computers, presentation software, and digital projectors, those are pretty much the tools you would have to rely on. You might want to keep that in mind the next time you complain that your computer is running a bit too slowly!

Movement LO 21.2

As the presenter, you must consider and plan your movement throughout the delivery of a presentation. This includes details such as the areas within the room which you will use to deliver your presentation, and how you will move to and from each area. You also need to take into consideration your movement around the room if you will be handing out materials. If the projector and/or computer are not within arm's reach of where you plan to stand (see Figure 21.4), you will need the use of a remote control to activate your slides (unless they are set to advance automatically after a certain period of time). Some presentation hardware can also be controlled via applications on electronic devices, such as smartphones or computer tablets.

Movement is more than just moving around the room to pass out materials. More than half of your impact as a speaker depends upon your body language. Body language includes gesture, stance, and facial expression. A strong, positive body language is an essential tool in helping you build credibility and connect with your listeners. It also helps your listeners focus more intently on you and what you're saying. Effective body language supports your message.

Figure 21.4 *While some presenters choose to move freely around the room, others prefer to remain in one area during a presentation, typically near the computer and/or projector.*

Gesture

Although it's common to use your hands to gesture during normal, everyday conversations, you should avoid using your hands in this manner when giving a presentation. On the other end of the spectrum, your hands shouldn't remain on your hips, in your pockets, or folded across your chest either. Instead, your hands should be used as a tool to help emphasize a point or to engage your audience.

Stance

Before you even begin speaking, your stance says something to the audience. For example, a balanced stance with a slight forward lean says that the speaker is engaged with the audience. A slumped stance, on the other hand, says the speaker isn't very interested in the presentation he or she is giving. A good presentation stance might be standing with your feet spread almost shoulder-width apart, pointing straight ahead. Although you can, and should, move around the room, remember that constant repetitive motion, such as swaying, is a distraction that may annoy your audience.

Facial Expression

When you present a slide show, the audience will focus most intently on your eyes. Your eye focus communicates sincerity and credibility. Effective presenters connect with one audience member at a time, focusing just long enough to complete a natural phrase, watching for a moment as the information sinks in.

Other elements of facial expression can convey your feelings, such as a strong interest in a particular subject or concern for the audience. Unfortunately, many people tend to forget about their facial expression when delivering a group presentation. The pressure of the situation often causes presenters to take on a grim, stone-faced expression. To avoid this pitfall, try to relax your face right from the start. It helps to begin your presentation by greeting your audience with a smile.

Total Movement Package

To be honest, standing in front of an audience and delivering a prepared message is not exactly natural. Instead, it's perfectly normal to feel stress and tension at the thought of giving a presentation. While it's easy to say "just be yourself," being natural in this type of situation doesn't always work. Instead, you need to be bigger, more expressive, and more powerful than you would be in a normal conversation. Giving a presentation takes extra effort and energy. It also takes skill and practice. The right body language during a presentation helps ensure that your audience will receive your message as it was meant to be conveyed.

Lighting *LO 21.2*

Lighting is always an important consideration when projecting a presentation. Whenever possible, you should take the time to visit the room in which you will be presenting ahead of time. When doing so, think about which aspects of your presentation may be affected by lighting. Are there windows that do not have blinds that can be closed? Then you will need to make sure that your presentation colors are dark enough and have enough contrast to be seen in a well-lighted room. If windows are not a problem, will you need the lights turned down low because your presentation contains a light color scheme? If so, check to make sure that the lights can be dimmed or turned off and also consider if the audience will be able to take notes or follow along with handouts. If this will be problematic, you should try to adapt your presentation for brighter lighting—perhaps with a different color scheme—or allow time in your presentation for periodic discussion and note-taking with the lights on. If it is necessary to dim or turn off lights, you should make sure you know where the controls are beforehand. As simple as this seems, fumbling for a switch can ruin the best-prepared presentation.

Physical Presentation Concerns *LO 21.2*

In addition to timing, movement, and lighting concerns, you need to consider the following presentation delivery points:

- If you are using a projector, make sure you know how to set it up.

- Locate the power outlets in the room. You may need extension cords to reach them.

- Check to see that the resolution of your projector matches your expectations. Some projectors may not have a resolution high enough to produce the image you expect.

- If you are using a laptop, you may have to toggle between the laptop screen and the projection screen in order to see both displays.

- Check that your presentation can be seen from all points in the room.

- If you are using sound, make sure it is loud enough. Remember that an empty room will echo sound that will be absorbed when people are in the room.

- Make sure all the files needed in your presentation are on your laptop, tablet, or removable drive. A presentation that works fine on the computer on which you created it may not work as well on another if files such as sound are not included.

Think About It

The Ethics of Political Correctness

One issue to keep in mind in any form of communication is political correctness. Political correctness includes use of non–gender-specific terms, appropriate ethnic designations, and non-demeaning age designations. Other areas to be aware of include religious affiliations, political alliances, and socioeconomic levels. Political correctness is often discussed as if it were a contrived response to unnecessary demands. This is not the case at all. Care in use of politically correct terms demonstrates that you respect your audience members and their points of view. Your ability to communicate to any group will be more successful if you are aware of and use politically correct terms.

Laughter is an essential component of all presentations, making your listeners more comfortable and more interested in what you have to say. However, the use of jokes and humor is a particularly difficult area in which to be politically correct. As a presenter, you must measure carefully your audience's response. Avoid laughter at the cost of ridiculing any single group of people.

checkpoint

What is the key to successfully getting your point across to an audience?

1. Using the information in this lesson, create a presentation of at least six slides plus a title slide.

2. Add timings to the presentation. Rehearse the timings and make adjustments.

3. Apply a design that will work well in your classroom without your having to dim the lights.

4. Save the presentation as *21_Activity2_presentation_delivery*.

Lesson 21.3 ▶ Presentation Setup and Packaging

Before a presentation can be displayed or distributed to others, you need to make a series of final setup decisions. How a presentation should be set up and packaged is dictated by the medium from which users will access and view the presentation.

Final Setup *LO 21.3*

Once you've finished creating your slide show, it's time to adjust the presentation's final setup options. To do this, you must first take into account the means of delivery you plan to use for your presentation. For example, if you are preparing a presentation to run on a kiosk, you will want your slide show to run continuously so that no action is required of the viewer. This is just one of the final setup options you can establish.

Figure 21.5 *In PowerPoint, you can set a variety of final slide show options, such as showing all slides or only a portion of the slides, from the Set Up Show dialog box.*

Show Options

If you are using Microsoft PowerPoint, the Set Up Show dialog box (see Figure 21.5) lets you decide the type of show, options for delivery, which slides to include, and how the show will advance.

Resolution Options

The resolution at which your slide show is set to appear is another setup option to consider. Selecting the slide show resolution requires you to know what projector you will be using. Some projectors have a low resolution and the images projected will not be as vivid as your computer monitor. Others will have a higher resolution, but there may be issues with the speed at which your slide show moves. The resolution of your presentation can be set using the Resolution options available in the monitor area of the Set Up Show dialog box (see Figure 21.6).

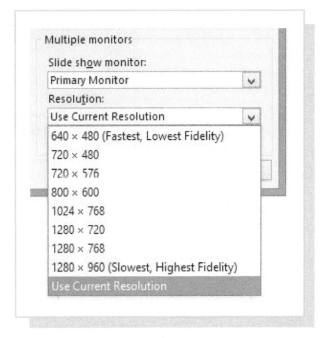

Custom Shows

A helpful feature in PowerPoint is the ability to create custom shows. With this feature, you can give separate presentations to different groups in your organization using one presentation. For example, if your presentation contains a total of five slides, you can create a custom show named *Management* that includes only certain slides and another custom show named *Employees* that includes different slides. Even if you have created a custom show within your presentation, you can still choose to run the entire presentation in order.

Figure 21.6 *The resolution at which your slide show will be displayed is an important factor to consider when finalizing your presentation's settings.*

Package for CD *LO 21.3*

One technology tool available in presentation software such as Power-Point is the **Package Presentation for CD** (or similarly named) feature. By selecting this option, as shown in Figure 21.7, you can use the dialog

Package Presentation for CD—Feature of Microsoft PowerPoint that packages a presentation for ease of transfer to another computer. It may also include a reader so that viewers without PowerPoint can still view the presentation.

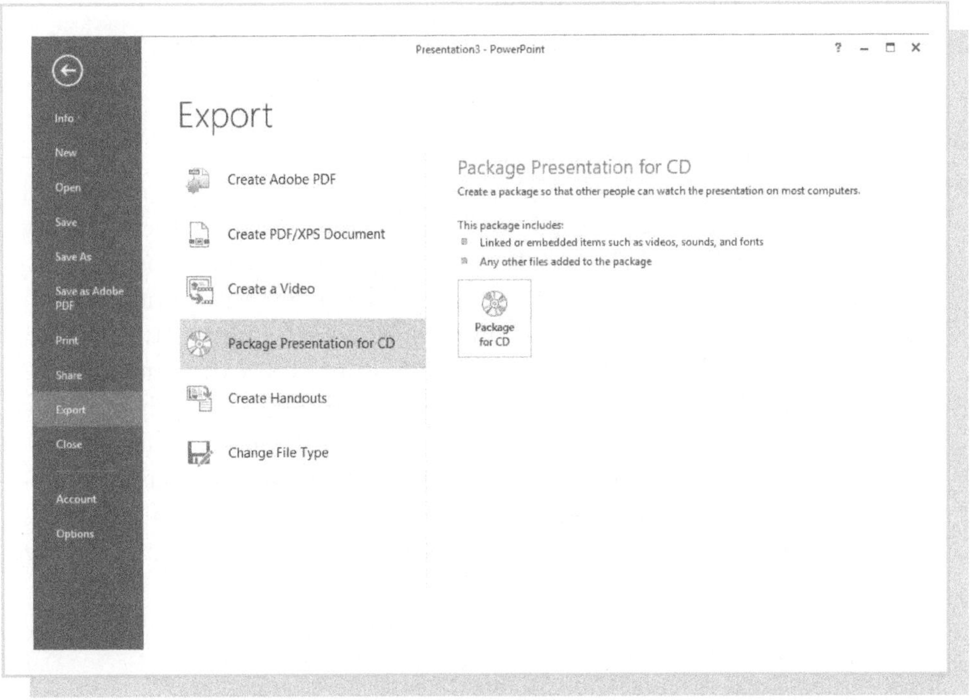

Figure 21.7 *The Export screen, available from the File menu, provides many options for the creation and delivery of a presentation.*

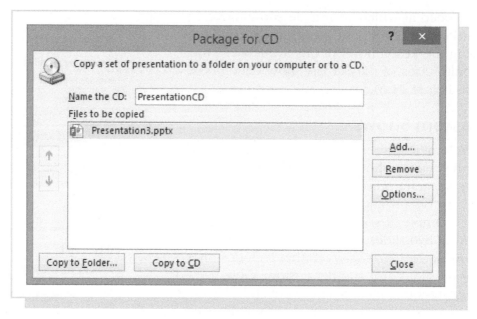

Figure 21.8 *It is easy to transfer presentations to other computers or share them with other users with the Package for CD option in PowerPoint.*

box shown in Figure 21.8 to package the presentation for transfer to media such as a CD, a hard drive, or a USB device such as a flash drive.

Once you are ready to use the presentation, clicking on the "packed" presentation will allow it to play easily, because all essential files such as type, sound, and graphics are included. In addition, a player is included so that it is not necessary for the computer on which it is being displayed to have specific software.

Create a Video LO 21.3

Several third-party software programs can be used to convert a presentation to a video format. Viewers can watch your video file with or without PowerPoint installed on their computer. Unfortunately, most quality video-conversion software must be purchased, and can be costly.

Fortunately, the capability to create a video from a presentation is a built-in feature of recent PowerPoint versions (see Figure 21.9 on the following page). With the Create a Video feature, you can control the quality of the video files you create, as well as the size of each file. Since video presentations are often distributed online, file size is a key factor to consider. While you can record and time voice narration, laser movements, animation, and transitions in a presentation video, you need to remember that these options are likely to increase the file size of a video.

checkpoint

What dictates how a presentation should be set up and packaged?

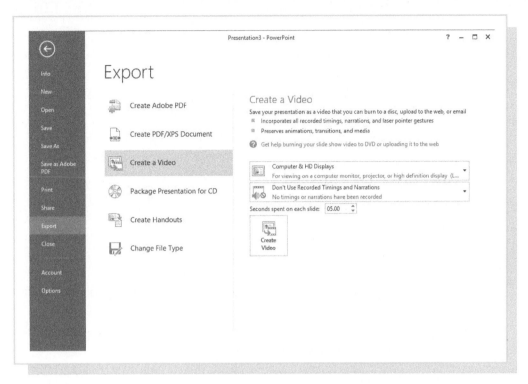

Figure 21.9 *The built-in Create a Video feature in PowerPoint lets users create videos from presentations.*

ACTIVITY 21.3 ▶ Finishing Up!

1. Open *21_Activity2_presentation_delivery* from the previous activity.
2. Use Set Up Show to define that it will be browsed at a kiosk, loop continuously, show all slides, and advance using timings.
3. Save the presentation as *21_Activity3_finishing*.
4. Create a video using the default settings and using the same filename.

Key Concepts

▶ Presentations can be delivered live by a speaker or recorded ahead of time to be browsed by an individual or at a kiosk. *LO 21.1*

▶ Delivery options—such as timing, movement, and lighting—should be taken into consideration when preparing a presentation. *LO 21.2*

▶ The medium from which your audience will access and view your presentation will dictate how you set it up and package it. *LO 21.3*

Review and Discuss

1. How might a presentation designed to be browsed by an individual differ from a presentation that will be delivered live by a speaker? *LO 21.1*

2. Formulate the primary advantage of delivering a presentation live as opposed to setting it up to be viewed at a kiosk. *LO 21.1*

3. Describe the difference between a passive and interactive kiosk. Give examples of each. *LO 21.1*

4. Create a brief list of design considerations needed for both passive and interactive presentations. *LO 2.1*

5. Identify the primary purpose of a presentation. *LO 21.2*

6. Assemble a list of considerations in presenting globally. *LO 21.2 and 21.3*

7. Examine how timing, movement, and lighting can make your presentation more effective. *LO 21.2 and 21.3*

8. Defend why it is important to select your projector's resolution. *LO 21.3*

9. Justify why Package Presentation for CD should be used when presenting on a different computer from the one on which you created the presentation. *LO 21.3*

10. Support the use of video, including some tips to consider when creating the presentation. *LO 21.3*

Apply

1. Create a presentation with a title slide and seven other slides. On each slide include one of your delivery points. Do not add anything to the presentation other than the text required on these seven slides, then save it as ***21_Apply1_delivery_points***. Create a video of the presentation, using either third-party software or the feature in your software. Save or export the file as ***21_Apply1_video***. Add transitions, animations, and at least two graphics to the presentation, then apply a design and save the

whole file as **21_Apply1_delivery_points_edited**. Create a video of the presentation using the same method that you did in the first video. Save or export this file as **21_Apply1_video_edited**. Compare and contrast the two videos for size. Open **21_Apply1_delivery_points_edited** and add a slide to the end that summarizes your findings and then save the file again. *LO 21.1*

2. Choose a specific profession that you are interested in and that you think will require presentation skills. Create a short presentation that describes and lists ways in which you may use presentation skills in that specific career. Interview someone currently working in the career. If you need help with ideas or research, use the online *Occupational Outlook Handbook*. Use narration in the presentation as well as design and a few graphics. Save the presentation as **21_Apply2_career**. Save or export the presentation as a video and upload it to a class website or personal website for review. Save or export the video as **21_Apply2_video**. *LO 21.1 and 21.2*

3. Create a presentation with a title slide and five famous quotes, each on its own slide. On each slide, add an image that enhances the quote. In the notes section, explain why you think the image you selected enhances or clarifies the message of the quote. Enhance your presentation with design, animation, transitions, sound, and graphics. Save your work as **21_Apply3_images**. *LO 21.1 and 21.2*

4. Create a presentation with a title slide and several slides organizing a list of jargon that you think could cause frustration or annoyance in most general presentations. Enhance your presentation with design, animation, transitions, sound, and graphics. Save the file as **21_Apply4_jargon**. *LO 21.1 and 21.2*

5. Choose one of the special features from this chapter (Impact, Think About It, History, or 21st Century Skills). Create a presentation based on the information in that feature. Enhance your presentation with design, animation, transitions, sound, and graphics. Narrate the presentation. Save the presentation as **21_Apply5_feature**. Create a video of the presentation. Save or export it as **21_Apply5_feature_video**.

Explore

1. Interview someone who has presented to a culture other than his or her own. Ask the following questions: What did you do differently to prepare for the presentation? During the presentation, did you have any difficulties? What would you do differently the next time you present to another culture? Create a presentation with a title slide, a slide to introduce the person you are interviewing, and a slide (or slides) with responses for each question. Add design, animation, transitions, graphics, and other elements to enhance the presentation. Make the presentation self-running. Save it as **21_Explore1_interview**. *LO 21.1, 21.2, and 21.3*

2. For a period of one week, keep notes on every kiosk that you encounter and be sure to note whether they are passive or interactive. Share your list with a team of students. Create a presentation with the compiled lists from your team. Save the presentation as **21_Explore2_kiosks** and then share your findings with the class. *LO 21.1*

3. Review Google Moderator with a team of students. Create a presentation outlining how Google Moderator could help you make decisions in the design and content of your presentation to best serve your audience. Save as **21_Explore3_google**. *LO 21.1, 21.2, and 21.3*

4. Research and create a list of third party software that can be used to create a video from your presentation. Input your information into one slide using a piece of SmartArt or a shape. Save the presentation as **21_Explore4_video_software**. *LO 21.2*

Academic Connections

Reading: Open **reading_cloze** from your data files and fill in the missing blanks. Save your work as **21_AC_reading**.

Math: Open **math_fun** from your data files. With a team of students, review the presentation's structure and add additional questions in subjects that relate to business math skills. Save your work as **21_AC_math**. Then play the game to check your work.

UNIT 6 PROJECTS

Independent Project

Complete a research project that you will deliver to an audience. With the assistance of your instructor, choose a topic and an audience to whom you will deliver the presentation.

1. Create an audience planning sheet.

2. Create a presentation that will take approximately 50 minutes to deliver.

3. Save the presentation as **Unit6_Project_presentation_content**.

4. Add speaker notes and check the arrangement of your slides.

5. Save the presentation as **Unit6_Project_speaker_notes**.

6. Add an appropriate slide design to the presentation.

7. Adjust slide layouts for effective presentation throughout.

8. Add at least one element to the master slides.

9. As you work with your presentation, use the following guidelines:

   - Color choices. Adjust color choices for content, audience, and presentation environment.

   - Consider adding a background to at least one slide.

   - Format text type and bullets as needed.

   - Consider the slides that are heavy with text. Add at least one visual element to enhance the presentation.

   - Review your presentation for effective use of white space and balance on the slide. Make adjustments as needed.

10. Save the presentation as **Unit6_Project_complete**.

11. Add at least one special effect such as animation or audio to your presentation.

12. Save the presentation as **Unit6_Project_effects**.

13. Set up the presentation to be delivered live and to be delivered as a self-running presentation at a kiosk.

14. Save these presentations as **Unit6_Project_kiosk** and **Unit6_Project_speaker**.

15. Deliver your presentation to the class, or volunteer to deliver it to an audience appropriate for the topic at a meeting or conference.

Portfolio

▶ Add your saved presentation from the independent project (**Unit6_Project_effects**) to your portfolio: but rename it **Unit6_Project_content_appropriate_name**.

▶ Scan copies of the rubric used for your delivery into one file to add to your portfolio. If you do not have a rubric, create one for your audience to evaluate your delivery. When thinking about questions to place on the rubric, ask yourself what information you would need to do a better job next time. Save the scanned rubrics in one file as: **Unit6_delivery_rubrics**.

▶ Include in your portfolio at least one example from each chapter of a presentation in which you created the content for the presentation.

▶ Journal your thoughts on presentations in a file to add to the portfolio.

- Summarize what you have learned about creating presentations and also about delivering presentations.

- What do you think you will use the most?

- Do you think you will use PowerPoint to deliver a presentation? Why or why not?

- What did you most like about creating and delivering presentations?

- What did you least like about creating and delivering presentations?

▶ Save your journal as **Unit6_journal**.

Winning Edge

FBLA-PBL or BPA

Go to http://www.fbla-pbl.org and click **Multimedia Gallery**. Review at least three of the video presentations found on the website. Write a summary of what you found in the presentations. List at least three things that you thought the presentation did quite well. What do you think the presentation would be used for? Was there anything distracting about the presentation? If so, what was it? How could you have avoided that distraction? Save your work as ***Unit6_Winning_Edge_summaries***.

www.FBLA-PBL.org

Using what you have learned from the presentations, plan a presentation of your own to promote FBLA, PBL, or BPA in your school. Pull out all the stops and use all the tools that you have learned in this unit to create an award-winning presentation. Save your presentation as ***Unit6_Winning_Edge_presentation*** and publish it as a video with the same filename. Be sure to add this presentation to your portfolio.

UNIT 7

Digital Media and the Changing Business Environment

Arts, A/V Technology & Communications

Career Cluster: Development Director

Interview with Dave, Development Director at St. Henry District High School.

Describe your average day. My typical day begins by looking at all email and paper mail that I've received. I then meet with my Development Assistant to review the day's agenda. Most days, my schedule includes multiple meetings with a variety of people, such as potential donors, alumni, faculty, staff, parents, and students. I also manage several team members who are responsible for different development-related areas, such as fund-raising, recruitment, public relations, social media, alumni affairs, grant writing, and more.

What is the worst part of your job? Trying to juggle an extremely busy schedule while also managing team members.

What is the best part of your job? Promoting all of the great accomplishments of our school's faculty, staff, and students.

Employment Outlook According to the Bureau of Labor Statistics, the job outlook for development directors is expected to grow an estimated 14 percent from 2006 to 2016. This is higher than the national average.

Skills and Qualifications Associate, Bachelor's, or advanced degree in Development, Marketing, Communications, Public Relations, Education, or Business Management or equivalent work experience; good communication skills; business management skills; advanced computer and software skills; understanding of nonprofit organizations; grant writing experience; attention to detail; leadership skills

Job Titles director of development, director of business development, director of alumni affairs, academic business manager

What About You? Is a career as a director of development right for you? What skills and abilities do you have that would benefit you in such a job?

Electronic Collaboration

Learning Outcomes

▶ **22.1** Discuss electronic communication.

▶ **22.2** Communicate with cloud computing.

▶ **22.3** Utilize social networking.

▶ **22.4** Participate in videoconferencing.

Key Terms

- cloud computing
- discussion thread
- electronic communication
- email
- email client
- microblogging
- posts
- smartphone
- SMS
- social networking
- synchronous
- wiki

Before the widespread availability of the Internet, messages were primarily conveyed to an intended audience in one of three forms: written communication, person-to-person conversation, or prerecorded video.

Advancements in electronic communication technologies have greatly influenced how people exchange information around the world. More often than not, people communicate with groups or other individuals via an electronic application or device such as the Internet, email, or a smartphone.

Creatons/Shutterstock.com

Reproduced by permission.

Electronic Communication

The ability to send, receive, and respond to a message within minutes, or even seconds, has redefined how people communicate with one another. With simply an electronic device and either Internet or mobile service, you can stay in constant contact with others. This form of communication, known as **electronic communication**, is capable of merging different media types into a single message.

Email *LO 22.1*

Electronic mail, or **email**, is more than just a glorified way of sending mail. It lets you send the same message to one or multiple recipients at the same time. In addition to a written message, you can also send attachments, such as photos, audio recordings, videos, and documents via email. This saves time and money.

Businesses, educational institutions, and other entities often have email accounts associated with their website. For example, if Sally Smith works for Cupcakes and Cookies and the company's website address is www.cupcakesandcookies.com, Sally's email address might be ssmith@cupcakesandcookies.com. This type of email is typically sent and received on a computer through an **email client**, such as Microsoft Outlook as shown in Figure 22.1.

Another option is a free, web-based (cloud) email account. Free email accounts can be set up through services like Google's Gmail,

electronic communication— The electronic transmission of data from one computing device to another.

email— Electronic, or digital, mail sent from one account to another via the Internet.

email client— Computer program used to manage a user's email account.

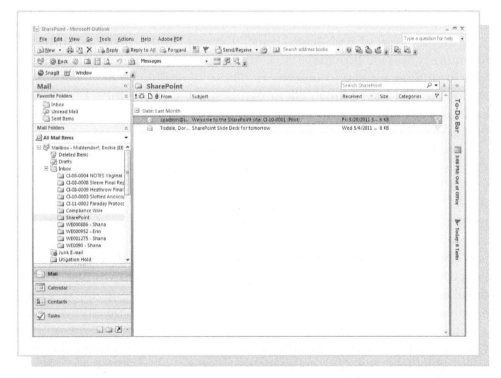

Figure 22.1 *Some software packages, such as Microsoft Office, include email clients that can not only organize your email, but also your contacts, calendar, and tasks.*

Yahoo! mail and others, where the email client appears in a web page, as shown in Figure 22.2. One benefit of using a web-based email service is the ability to access your account at any time, from any computer, as long as you have an Internet connection. Your email messages are stored online through the email service.

Figure 22.2 *With a web-based email client, users can access their accounts from any computer with an Internet connection.*

Another type of web-based email account can be obtained through an Internet Service Provider (ISP). Many ISPs offer "free" email accounts as part of their service to customers. These typically can be accessed through a web-based email client that is specific to the ISP—often accessed through the company's website. The features of these programs vary, but usually include email and contacts as a minimum.

For both the free email accounts and those associated with an ISP, the user chooses their own email address name. This name is followed by the "at" symbol (@) and then the email provider's designated name, such as gmail.com or yahoo.com. Other than possible length restrictions, you are free to choose any name you like, as long as it isn't already in use by someone else. Be cautious, however, about what you choose. Consider carefully whether the name you choose is the image you want to project to all people with whom you will use this email account. For example, while partygirl@gmail.com might be seen as humorous by your close friends, it may raise serious questions with a potential employer and may raise eyebrows with family members. Choose your email names carefully or set up different accounts for corresponding with different people.

Microsoft Exchange is an application that's a hybrid of an email account connected to a business's server and web-based email.

Exchange is part of the Microsoft Servers products and is used by companies that are using other Microsoft infrastructure products. The major features of Exchange include email, calendar, contacts, and tasks. These all work with Microsoft Outlook, but also include remote and wireless synchronization of email, calendar, and contacts using mobile devices or browser-based devices. Exchange allows access to information and support for data storage from anywhere in the world.

Note that email client programs like Outlook allow you to set up multiple email accounts within the system. Therefore, you can use one email client to view and organize the emails from multiple email addresses all in one location. Most email accounts allow you to save a person's name, email address, and other information as a contact. Once a person is set up as a contact, you only have to key their name into the "To" box in the email header to populate their email address automatically. Web-based services such as Google allow you to load your contact information onto some **smartphones** by simply logging into your account on the phone.

Email is an easy way to communicate, but there are some potential issues. Rather than taking the time to sit down and write a well-thought-out letter or note to someone, it's tempting to simply type a quick email instead. This is definitely more convenient, but you should still take the time to carefully consider what you want to say and exactly how you should say it before sending the message. A short, to-the-point message may not be received in the same tone of voice as you intended. Read your message carefully, putting yourself in the recipient's place, before sending any email. Always keep your target audience in mind.

smartphone—A mobile phone that provides traditional digital voice service in addition to a variety of other functions, such as text messaging, email management, web browsing, still photo and video capabilities, MP3 music capabilities, video viewing, video calling, and the ability to run applications, to name just a few.

History

Granata1111/Dreamstime.com

Email

During the 1960s and 1970s, the US Department of Defense embarked on research into the area of computer networks for universities and research laboratories. The result of this project was known as ARPANET, the Advanced Research Projects Agency Network. This was the precursor of today's Internet. In 1971, the first successfully transmitted email message was sent on the ARPANET.

By the mid-1980s, IBM and Apple had introduced a new generation of computer technology—the personal computer. At that time, two users subscribing to the same dial-up service, such as CompuServe, could exchange messages electronically. During this same time, companies began setting up systems that would tie users of in-house computers together, allowing them to send messages to one another.

It wasn't until the 1990s, when the Internet became more readily available, that companies like Microsoft and Apple began offering email programs as part of their standard software packages. Email technology matured, allowing users to attach images, audio, video, and document files to their messages. Today, virtually any technological device can send and receive email remotely from anywhere in the world.

Discussion Threads *LO 22.1*

Message boards, blogs, social networking sites and other websites that allow users to add comments or ask questions typically link messages, or **posts**, to each another. While comments or questions relating to a specific topic remain stand-alone messages, they are electronically connected to one another in a **discussion thread**, like the one shown in Figure 22.3.

Figure 22.3 *Multiple users can share their thoughts and opinions with others regarding an online conversation through a discussion thread.*

In most discussion threads, each new post appears directly beneath the last post. If you want to make a sweeping comment about the overall topic, you can respond to the entire thread. Or, if you agree, disagree, or want to ask a question about one particular post, you can direct your response to only that specific post. If you have a comment or question that is unrelated to an ongoing thread, you can start a new discussion thread with your post.

Cell Phones and Texting *LO 22.1*

Cell phones, once considered a luxury, are now considered a necessity. In fact, according to an FCC report, nearly 90 percent of all Americans own a cell phone. Users are doing more than just talking on their cell phones. Most people use their cell phones to send and receive text messages more often than they do to place and receive phone calls.

A text message is a short, typed message sent between two or more cell phones or other electronic devices. These messages are sent via **SMS** (Short Message Service). An SMS message can include up to 160 characters, including word spaces, depending on the size of the characters. Twitter only allows 140 characters. To make the most of this limited amount of space, people often use acronyms, abbreviations, or other forms of shorthand to shorten an otherwise lengthy message. Figure 22.4 lists some of the more popular shorthand texting terms.

SMS—Acronym for Short Message Service; the texting component of a cell phone or other electronic device.

AFK	Away From Keyboard	K	OK
BFN	Bye For Now	KIT	Keep In Touch
BTW	By The Way	LOL	Laugh Out Loud
EOD	End Of Discussion	L8R	Later
FOFL	Falling On Floor Laughing	MYOB	Mind Your Own Business
F2F	Face To Face	NE1	Anyone
GFN	Gone For Now	NM	Never Mind, Not Much
GI	Good Idea	THX	Thanks
G2G	Gotta Go	TIA	Thanks In Advance
IAG	It's All Good	W8	Wait
IC	I See	WTG	Way To Go
IK	I Know	YW	You're Welcome
IRL	In Real Life	?4U	Question For You

Figure 22.4 *Acronyms or other forms of shorthand save space when typing out text messages.*

Originally, texting on phones was done using the number pad and scrolling through the three or four letters on each key until the correct one appeared. The tedium of this task is another reason that the texting abbreviations became so popular. As with all technology, the practical use of an item often drives the direction that development takes. Since so many people use cell phones for texting as well as email, Internet browsing, and countless other tasks, smart phones now have an on-screen full QWERTY keyboard. On these devices, when the user is keying a text message, a list of probable words appears after the first letters are keyed. If the desired word is in the list, the user can select it or they can continue to key letters and the list is recreated with each new letter added. This makes it easier to enter full words rather than abbreviations and is leading some to return to writing out complete messages. Space constraints are still an issue, but this can be resolved by simply sending multiple texts if everything to be said will not fit into one text message. Alternatively, a phone call can be made.

checkpoint

What are the benefits of using a web-based email service?

ACTIVITY 22.1 ▶ Discussions

1. Visit a blog or other website that uses discussion threads. Post a comment.

2. Take a screen capture showing the discussion thread and your comment. Save your screen capture as *22_Activity1_discussions*.

3. Send an email to your instructor, attaching the screen capture. In the email, briefly explain the discussion thread or blog that you visited. Use an appropriate subject line and make the body of the email at least two paragraphs. Send a copy of the email to another person in your class.

Lesson 22.2 ▶ Cloud Computing

cloud computing— On-demand access to shared data via the Internet.

When stored on a desktop, tablet, or laptop computer, information is directly tied to that one device—leaving the files vulnerable to machine failure or malfunction. With **cloud computing**, information is stored, retrieved, edited, and shared online, and can be accessed from any computer with Internet access, reducing the threat of accidental file damage or deletion. Cloud computing also lets you quickly sync documents, photos, movies, contacts, and emails between two or more computers, smartphones, tablets, or other electronic devices.

File Sharing *LO 22.2*

Sending a file to another user as an email attachment is one basic form of file sharing. Unfortunately, this method has its limitations. For example, some files may be too large to send via email. A better method is to use an online file-sharing service, such as Microsoft SharePoint, Dropbox (see Figure 22.5) or Google Docs.

File sharing is an essential tool when working as part of a team. If you are emailing files back and forth between team members for review, you are bound to end up with several different versions of the same document. This requires you to merge all of the team's edits into one file. A better method is to use a file sharing service that gives multiple users access to the same file. You can even control which users can view a particular file versus which users can edit the file. Users can check out a document, making it unavailable for editing by other users.

Source: www.dropbox.com

Figure 22.5 *Online file-sharing services provide multiple users with access to files from any computer with Internet connectivity.*

Another benefit of online file sharing is the ability to set up a review chain. A review chain sets the order in which you want each team member to contribute, comment, or review a particular file. Once the first member has finished working with the file and has checked it back in, the next team member will be notified via email that the file is available. This allows you to keep all edits and comments within a single file and greatly reduces the risk that a team member might accidentally work from an old or outdated version of the document. Some systems such as Google Docs also allow users to simultaneously work on a document. The document is stored in Google Docs, and each team member can edit and save it. Therefore, the latest document is always available.

lavitrei/Shutterstock.com

Impact

In the Cloud

Did you know that you may already be working "in the cloud" without realizing it? Do you use a web-based email service, such as Gmail? Then you're working in the cloud! A growing number of companies are offering users the ability to store and access information online. Arguably the industry leader in personal computing and entertainment innovation over the past decade, Apple is just one of the companies providing services in the cloud. A storage and computing service, iCloud, lets users store data, photos, and music files on remote servers. The files are then available for download on multiple devices. With iCloud reportedly acquiring 20 million users in less than a week's time upon its launch, it seems a safe bet to assume the future of computing is in the cloud.

Wikis *LO 22.2*

A website that provides users with a tool to create and edit content is called a **wiki**. When you hear the term *wiki*, you probably think of Wikipedia (see Figure 22.6). While that is a popular wiki site, wikis are also used by companies and other entities as a means of promoting communication among different individuals. A wiki is a useful communication tool for collaboration between multiple team members on a project. It can also be used to promote learning and to share information between groups of people.

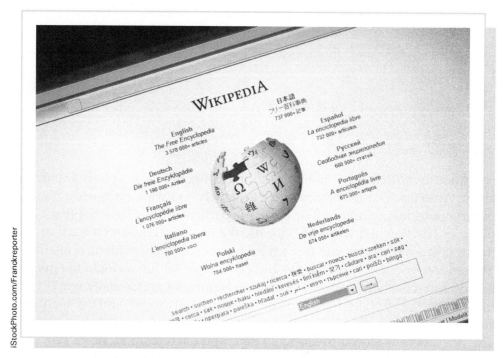

Figure 22.6 *One of the most popular wiki sites is Wikipedia.*

Wikis were names after the Hawaiian word "wiki-wiki," which means "quick." Wikis can be used by businesses as an intranet, for product documentation, and for typical team collaborative efforts. It is, however, important to carefully choose a wiki provider that meets the needs of the business. Some essential questions to ask when starting a wiki include the following.

1. How do you want to use the wiki (e.g., collaboratively with a team, collaboratively with the entire business, for customer information)?

2. Will large files need to be uploaded to the wiki or will audio need to be added?

3. Does the wiki provider give user support?

4. Is the wiki free or fee-based?

5. How long has the wiki provider been in business?

There will be some initial steps to setting up the wiki and making sure all stakeholders have the specific rights they need to create, edit, and/or delete. These steps are typically simple, and you can start to use a wiki right away. All wiki users can see the edits and comments provided by other users. Therefore, wikis work well for collaborative writing and file sharing.

checkpoint

What are the benefits of cloud computing?

ACTIVITY 22.2 ▶ Using Communication Tools

1. Interview at least five business professionals or friends who have used file sharing and/or wikis.

2. Ask interviewees to answer the following questions during the interview: Do you use file sharing or collaborative tools? Which ones were useful? How have you used them? Were they effective? Why? Do you have plans to use them in the future? Save your notes as *22_Activity2_communication_tools*.

3. Meet with a team of three or four students to compare interview notes.

4. Create a wiki to write about what you have learned from the interviews, including some notes from your team collaboration.

5. Paste the link to your wiki in a file saved as *22_Activity2_wiki*.

Lesson 22.3 ▶ Social Networking

The desire to connect with others is a normal human emotion. A popular alternative to face-to-face communication is **social networking**. Social networking sites, such as LinkedIn, Facebook and Twitter, provide users with an avenue with which to instantly share thoughts, ideas, photos, videos, and more with others.

social networking—Online communities that let users instantly share information with other users.

LinkedIn *LO 22.3*

Social networking is more than just a way of communicating your personal thoughts with friends. It's also an effective business tool. Instead of sending out hundreds of resumes to potential employers or running from one job fair to another, professionals can use social media to promote their talents, abilities, and experiences to others.

The most popular professional social networking site is LinkedIn (see Figure 22.7). After establishing an online profile—which includes

Figure 22.7 *LinkedIn is a social networking site for professionals.*

your past work history, education, relevant experiences, and contact information—you can then connect with colleagues and possible employers, as well as other users with similar experiences and interests. You can also explore job opportunities through services provided on LinkedIn.

Facebook *LO 22.3*

Through the use of social networking sites like Facebook, users can instantaneously broadcast personal information—from thoughts and ideas to photos and videos—to other users with whom they choose to be connected. You can also post links to other websites. With Facebook, you can choose how much information you want to share and exactly who will be able to see it. Facebook, for example, lets you set your account so that only those users you've added as "friends" can view your page. You can also leave your account settings open, allowing information on your page to be accessed by anyone. If you leave your account settings open, make sure all posted information is appropriate for all to see. Those that have access to your page can post statements to your wall, leave comments on your personal postings, and tag you in photos. Through a central newsfeed page, you receive a synopsis of your friends' recent activities.

iStockphoto.com/akinbostanci

Figure 22.8 *Social networking sites, like Facebook and Twitter, have become very popular.*

Social Media Considerations

Social media is a great way to share important events, photos, thoughts, and ideas with others. However, if the settings on your social media account are not restricted, this same information can also be seen by potential employers. A simple Internet search of your name can easily lead someone directly to your FaceBook or Twitter account. If you intend to leave your accounts open so that anyone can view them, be conscious of what you post. Also remember that while you may show restraint with the information you share on your account, your "friends" may not. Therefore, it's a good idea to periodically review your account and remove any potentially embarrassing pictures, posts, or comments.

Twitter *LO 22.3*

Twitter combines the broad communication capabilities of social networking with the condensed voice of texting. Through a Twitter account, as shown in Figure 22.9, users can broadcast brief messages, up to 140 characters, to a list of followers. Originally designed as a way for friends to stay up to date with what other friends were doing

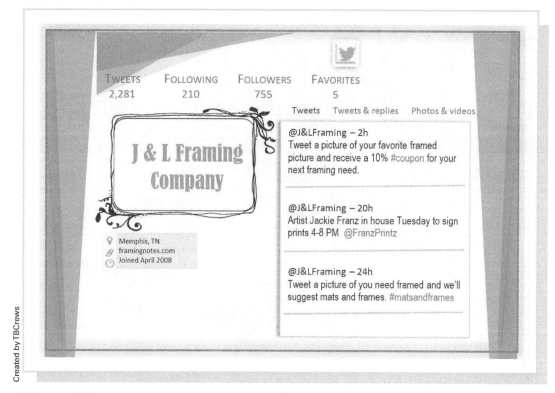

Created by TBCrews

Figure 22.9 *A Twitter account, a type of microblog, lets users send short messages to other followers.*

throughout the day, Twitter has become a popular means for businesses to communicate information to the general public. Messages, known as tweets, are sent and received through a variety of electronic devices, including smartphones and computers. Followers can then reply to tweets, creating a discussion thread as described earlier. Users can also broadcast images and video links through a Twitter account. This form of communication is often referred to as **microblogging**.

microblogging—Online exchange of information through short sentences, images, or video links.

checkpoint

What type of information can be instantly shared with others via social networking?

ACTIVITY 22.3 ▶ Twitter Communication

1. Go to http://www.ted.com/talks/evan_williams_on_listening_to_twitter_users.html and watch Evan Williams discuss the use of Twitter.

2. If possible, participate in a Twitter group by commenting during the watching of the presentation, sharing only positive remarks about what he is saying.

3. Summarize the video with at least 10 key points learned in the presentation about Twitter. Save your summary as ***22_Activity3_twitter***.

In a videoconference, as shown in Figure 22.10, you can conduct synchronous face-to-face communication with individuals in one or more different locations at the same time. **Synchronous** simply means occurring at the same time. When communication can be done synchronously through videoconferencing, it saves people both time and money over traditional conferences, as users do not need to travel for in-person meetings. Participants at one site may gather together in a room, such as a boardroom, or the videoconferencing system may allow them to all be at their own computers participating in the conference. As with other forms of communication, there are important factors to consider when preparing for a videoconference. These considerations include:

- Preparation
- Sound and Movement
- Visuals

Figure 22.10 *Videoconferencing saves money and time by allowing groups of people to meet synchronously. You can display visuals, such as a PowerPoint presentation, as part of a videoconference.*

Andrey Popov/Shutterstock.com

synchronous—occurring at the same time.

Preparation LO 22.4

Before your videoconference begins, you should take time to familiarize yourself with all of the technology tools you will be using, such as the computer, conferencing software, video camera, and audio equipment. If you are leading the videoconference, you should plan on setting up and connecting to your conference at least 20–30 minutes before it is scheduled to start. The camera should be positioned with your body framed from the waist up on the monitor screen.

If you are using a slide show during your presentation, it's a good idea to send a copy of your presentation to all of the participants ahead of time, along with an agenda for the meeting and any other supporting materials. Remember to introduce yourself and anyone else who is participating in the videoconference before you begin. If necessary, be conscious of possible transmission delays during your conference. It's also a good idea to communicate a backup plan with all conference members, in case you lose connection.

Sound and Movement LO 22.4

Since your audience will be able to see and hear you, it's important to communicate both verbally and visually during your videoconference. Act and speak as you normally would and look into the camera. Adjust the microphone settings to pick up your voice at a normal conversational level and remove any distractions from the room.

If at all possible, refrain from making unnecessary movements, such as shuffling papers and rocking your chair. These movements often pull a person's attention away from the subject of the conference. As with sound, some video systems are sensitive enough to pick up on random movements within the camera's frame. If a video camera is motion activated, it will even change focus to capture movement it detects within the camera's range. Even if only for a few seconds, these types of distractions may cause your audience to miss out on important information being presented as the distractions occur.

Visuals LO 22.4

In addition to being able to see the videoconference participants, you can also display visual aids, such as PowerPoint presentations, during a videoconference. Most videoconferencing software programs allow you to switch between different views. You can run a presentation, demonstrate how to use a program on your computer, or display a web page during a videoconference. This capability allows participants to interact with one another just as they would in person.

Considerations

As noted previously, videoconferencing makes it easy to meet with people who are located in other places around the city, state, country, or world.However, there are always things to consider before implementing any system. This is especially true with a videoconferencing system. The following are questions to consider when implementing a videoconferencing system.

- Importance of Quality:
  - Do you need to impress clients you are meeting with and have a clear, high-definition picture in which to conduct your meeting? OR
  - Is your meeting with internal company constituents and you simply need to share information in a casual business environment?
- Need for Multimedia:
  - Are there many supplemental videos and other multimedia components involved throughout the videoconference? OR
  - Can the information simply be provided without any additional multimedia components?
- Need to Record:
  - Is the videoconference something that needs to be recorded for later playback for those who could not be in attendance? OR
  - Is the information simply provided through the videoconference and recording is not a necessity?
- Location of Attendees:
  - Are the participants located around the world? OR
  - Are the participants all in relatively close regional locations (e.g., same time zone)?

Good Netiquette

Just as you are expected to adhere to standard rules of behavior in every other setting of life, there are guidelines that dictate how you should, and should not, behave when interacting with others electronically. Whether you're sending an email message, posting to a blog, transmitting a voice message, or sharing a video, remember to treat others online as you would in person, with respect. Be considerate of people's privacy—the Internet is not private and a message you send to one person can quickly be forwarded to an unlimited number of other people. Some other rules to keep in mind when working online include the following:

1. Do not type in ALL CAPS.
2. If you wouldn't want your mother to read it or see it, don't send it.
3. Be concise. Don't write five paragraphs of information when you can get your point across in one or two sentences.
4. Unless you absolutely need everyone on the original email to see your response, use the Reply button rather than the Reply All button.
5. If you feel attacked by an email, take a break and consider your response before replying. Otherwise, you will likely type something that you will regret.
6. Use good grammar and punctuation in all online written communications.
7. Ask recipients before sending large email attachments.

- Number of Attendees:
  - Will there be hundreds of attendees, which will require high bandwidth? OR
  - Will there be 10 or less attendees, therefore requiring less bandwidth?

checkpoint

What are the benefits of a videoconference versus a traditional face-to-face meeting?

ACTIVITY 22.4 ▶ Videoconferencing Poster

1. Create a poster, using your desktop publishing software, to hang in the videoconferencing room at your school with tips on what needs to be done to prepare for a videoconference.
2. Create another poster with tips for a successful videoconference.
3. Save the posters as *22_Activity4_video_preparation* and *22_Activity 4_video_success*.

Key Concepts

▶ Electronic communications such as email, discussion threads, and texting have redefined how people communicate with one another. *LO 22.1*

▶ File sharing and wikis are forms of cloud computing. Cloud computing reduces the threat of accidental file deletion and lets you quickly synchronize documents, photos, movies, contacts, and emails between two or more computers, smartphones, tablets, or other electronic devices. *LO 22.2*

▶ Users can instantly share thoughts, ideas, photos, videos, and more through the use of social networking sites such as LinkedIn, Facebook, and Twitter. *LO 22.3*

▶ Videoconferencing saves both time and money by letting users conduct face-to-face communication with individuals in different locations at the same time. *LO 22.4*

Review and Discuss

1. Explain how email is more than just a glorified way of sending mail. *LO 22.1*

2. Summarize the benefits of free, online email accounts. *LO 22.1*

3. Summarize some disadvantages of using email. *LO 22.1*

4. Describe Short Message Service (SMS) used with cell phones. *LO 22.1*

5. Explain and justify the use of cloud computing. *LO 22.2*

6. Summarize the limitations of using email attachments for file sharing and suggest a better solution. *LO 22.1 and 22.2*

7. Compare and contrast social networking and tweeting. *LO 22.3*

8. Evaluate the advantages of using videoconferencing for communication. *LO 22.4*

Apply

1. Follow Bill Gates on Twitter for at least one week, commenting each time to what you have read in his tweets. Place the link in a document with your name and save it as **22_Apply1_tweet**. *LO 22.1*

2. Find a free discussion board for a group of four to five students to use to participate in a discussion. For example: http://www.quicktopic.com/. The group or team leader should add the following as the discussion prompt:
Respond to the following questions in some detail:
What did you enjoy learning about the most in this chapter?
What did you enjoy the least?

What topic would you like to see added?

If you could start over, what would you do differently in the class? Each learner should respond to the initial prompt and respond to two other learners' posts. Responses should be specific responses to the topic and not simple comments such as "I like your post." The team should place the link in a document with all team members' names. Save the document as **22_Apply2_discussions**. *LO 22.1*

3. Wordle is an online application that creates word clouds. Go to http://www.wordle.net/ and create a wordle of at least 20 abbreviated terms used in Twitter. If necessary, search for twitter terminology to find words that can be used. Use the Snipping Tool or screen capture software to create an image of your wordle. Insert the wordle into a word processing document and save the document as **22_Apply4_twitter**. *LO 22.2*

4. Post the documents created in the previous Apply activities to Google Docs or another file-sharing service and share them with a team of students. Print the screen showing the documents uploaded into the cloud and insert the image into a Word document. Edit the settings to include sharing the documents with your team. Save the Word document as **22_Apply5_google_docs**. *LO 22.2*

Explore

1. If possible, participate in or observe a videoconference. Write about your observations. Were the participants prepared? How could you tell if they were or were not prepared? Was everyone dressed appropriately? Was sound and movement appropriate? Why? Were any visuals displayed? Describe them. Save your written observations in a document as **22_Explore1_videoconferencing**. *LO 22.4*

2. Explore apps in iTunes or from an iPhone. List at least five apps that you think would be good to use in helping with the changing business environment. Name the app, discuss the review, and discuss how the app is appropriate to the changing business environment. Save your list as **22_Explore2_apps**. *LO 22.1*

3. Search the Internet for blogs/discussions on topics related to the changing business environment and globalization. Participate with an appropriate comment in at least two blogs/discussions. Do a screen capture of each one and insert them into a word processing document. Save the document as **22_Explore3_globalization**. *LO 22.1, 22.2, 22.3, and 22.4*

Academic Connections

Writing. Go to Google images and search for one of the following: mountains, scenery, storm, garden, winter, summer, or fall. Choose one picture and insert it into a wiki that you have created specifically for this exercise. Write one paragraph, creating a story about the picture. Give the link to another student in the class. They should write a middle paragraph, continuing your story. The second person should give the link to a third person, who will write a conclusion. Place the link and all three authors' names in a Word document and save it as *22_AC_writing*. This can be continued by each author participating in three different wikis by writing beginning, middle, and ending paragraphs about three different pictures.

Social Studies. Choose a historical figure and blog about one reason this person is famous. Subscribe to two other students' blogs and post a comment to their blog. Copy the links to the blogs to a blank document and save the document as *22_AC_social_studies*.

Project Development Team

Learning Outcomes

- ▶ **23.1** Form a team
- ▶ **23.2** Understand team activities
- ▶ **23.3** Identify roles within a multimedia development team

Key Terms

- consensus building
- team charter

Lesson 23.1 Team Formation

Lesson 23.2 Team Activities

Lesson 23.3 Multimedia Development Team Roles

Quality multimedia products are not often created by a single individual. You have seen in the preceding chapters that a diverse set of skills is needed, one which requires the work of a team. Teamwork is not simply a matter of gathering a group of people and asking them to complete a task. Functioning as a team requires specialized skills on the part of both the team leader and the team members. Just as it is important to learn how to manage images, perfect presentation skills, and design effective web pages, it is also vital to know how to combine your expertise with that of others in order to produce a professional multimedia product.

In this chapter, you will learn team skills while you explore the impact of technology on business—two areas that will become more important to you when you enter the working world.

While some people consider themselves talented in several areas of multimedia development, most projects require more skill sets than are typically held by any one individual. Therefore, most multimedia development projects require a team approach. Each multimedia development project should begin with the assembling of all necessary team members. This requires bringing together a diverse group of individuals who are able to take direction and work together within an organized team structure.

Stages of Team Development *LO 23.1*

Teams generally go through four stages of development, as shown in Figure 23.1. These stages include forming, storming, norming, and performing. Each stage is fairly predictable, and the issues that arise must be addressed in order for your team to be successful. Forming represents the creation stage, when a team is formed. Storming represents the stage in which personalities begin to mesh—sometimes with initial conflict that will need resolution. Norming represents the stage during

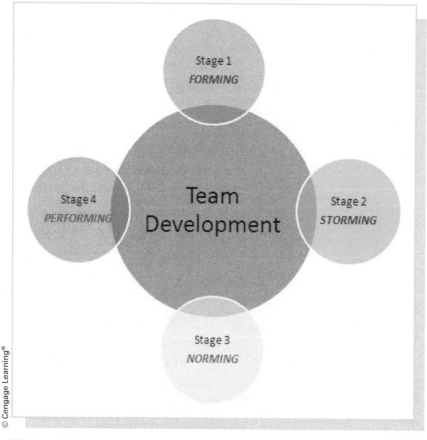

© Cengage Learning®

Figure 23.1 *Typically, team development goes through four stages: forming, storming, norming, and performing.*

which conflicts are resolved and plans are initiated. The last stage, performing, is the moment when the team becomes a functioning productive group. Learning to recognize and work through each stage will help you develop a stronger team.

Forming

As mentioned, the first stage of team development is forming. During this stage, team members meet one another and begin to form ideas about what their roles within the project might be. Although individual responsibilities have not yet been determined at this point in the team building process, you can start to see each person's personality and work ethic. A leader is chosen to provide guidance and direction to the rest of the team. The leader should be prepared to field questions from the team members, such as "What is our team's purpose?" and "What are our team's objectives?"

Storming

The second stage of team development is storming. Team members begin addressing issues during this stage in an attempt to bring clarity to the process. This interaction may result in conflict as each member provides his or her opinion to the group. In most cases, this conflict can be resolved, but without strong leadership a team could easily find itself stuck in this stage of the process. Team members must be willing to compromise during the storming stage and stay focused on their common goals. If not, the team may be unable to move forward in the development process.

Norming

The third stage of team development is norming. The majority of team members have agreed upon a common goal by this stage, and a clear picture of each team member's roles and responsibilities begins to take shape. At this point in the process, the group as a whole has agreed upon all major decisions, while individual members or small groups within the team have dealt with minor issues. Teams begin developing a sense of unity during this stage and may even engage in fun, morale-building activities. While the team leader facilitates discussions, it is up to the team as a whole to mold how the team will work and develop any team processes that need to be followed.

Performing

The fourth and final stage of team development is performing. At this point, the team has a clear idea of its goals and knows exactly what it wants to do and why. While the team leader continues providing support, the team is not reliant upon the leader at this point. Each member is able to work independently or as part of a smaller group within the team. Team members may not agree on every aspect of a project, but they should be able to resolve any conflicts without a great deal of argument and without major changes to any processes. Members may look to their leader to delegate tasks and projects during this stage, but they should not need detailed instructions or a great deal of oversight.

Team Charter *LO 23.1*

As a general rule, groups should be created quickly and begin to work as soon as possible after they have formed. If extended periods of time are allowed to elapse between creation and work, the energy of the team can be lost.

Before a team can begin work on a project, every member must have a clear understanding of the team's mission, purpose, objectives, and time frame. A team with indefinite focus cannot be expected to accomplish much of importance. Part of a team's responsibility is to learn why it was formed. When it knows its reason for existence, then it must establish a **team charter** to specifically identify its goals, its values, and its approach (Figure 23.2).

While officially documenting this information may seem pointless, a team will be more productive in the long run if it initially spends time clearly identifying the path it plans to follow. The following questions cover areas that should be addressed in the team charter:

Figure 23.2 *A clearly defined team charter ensures that members understand the roles they will be playing once a project launches.*

team charter—Specifically identifies the team's goals, values, and approach to handling the task at hand.

- Why was the team created?
- What is the team to accomplish?
- How will the team track its progress?
- What will the team members gain from working on this team?
- What happens when team members need help?

Team Communications

LO 23.1

Communication within a team is essential to the success of the organization (Figure 23.3). Too often fear of ridicule prevents team members from voicing their opinions. Others fear entering into conflict with members of the team. Some members so strongly want to see their point accepted that they refuse to allow others to add ideas. These and other problems of communication can destroy the effectiveness of a team. Members need to find the ways to listen to each other, to be open to the opinions of others, and to be willing to accept a diversity of viewpoints. The team leader is an important component in this process.

Figure 23.3 *Good communication between members is key to a successful team.*

lavitrei/Shutterstock.com

Impact

Can't We All Just Get Along?

Most team members bring various qualities to a project: education, experience, talent, and skill sets. These qualities are what successful teams are built on. Unfortunately, one attribute that every team member brings to a project often leads to a team's breakdown—individual personalities. More often than not, unique personalities lead to disagreements. Remember that even the most cohesive of teams will have varying opinions from time to time. Having the most qualified team members won't do much good if those individuals cannot learn to work together. To be successful, team members must maintain good communication and work through disagreements as soon as they arise.

checkpoint

How long after formation should groups begin to work?

ACTIVITY 23.1 ▶ Creating a Team Charter

1. After forming a team with a project idea, open *team_charter* from the data files for this chapter.
2. With your team working together, complete the information in the team charter.
3. Add all team members' names to the footer of the team charter document.
4. Save your document as *23_Activity1_team_charter*.

Lesson 23.2 ▶ Team Activities

Team-Building Activities *LO 23.2*

Teams are comprised of many individuals, each with different ideas, experiences, and concerns. In order to function as a single entity, teams must gather each person into the group by meshing all of the personalities. One of the best ways for this to happen is to include team-building activities in the functioning of the team. These activities are generally recreational, giving members time to get to know one another and develop trust. Sharing a meal, playing games, and engaging in recognition activities are frequently methods used to build team spirit and help reduce conflict.

Team Meetings

One of the activities that a team engages in is meeting and reporting on the progress and concerns of its members (see Figure 23.4). These meetings should have beginning and ending times and clearly stated purposes. As a good team member, do not keep the others waiting. In addition, do not extend the meeting past the time it is scheduled to end by bringing up unrelated topics or spending too much time on a topic that would be better addressed with another person one-on-one or in a smaller group discussion.

An agenda is the guiding hand at team meetings. With a well-thought-out agenda, members know the subjects to be discussed and the material to have present. Agendas should be delivered before the meeting either as an email attachment or a hard copy, so that everyone is prepared.

Phil Date/Shutterstock.com

Figure 23.4 *Team members meet frequently to update each other on the progress of their project and to discuss any issues in need of resolution.*

Team Decisions

As part of any meeting, decisions must be made by the team. It is during this decision-making process that conflict can arise. Learning to make decisions as a team is a skill that can reduce long-term conflict and increase the team's effectiveness. As part of the decision-making process, everyone in the team should understand the issues related to the decision, including the following questions:

- What are the specific details of the decision to be made?
- What is the deadline for the decision?
- What impact will the decision have on the team?
- Who will be involved in the outcome of the decision?
- How will the decision be made?

consensus building— Process used to reach agreement by a team of people.

There are a number of ways to make a decision. The two most frequently used means of reaching agreement are to gain a consensus or to allow the majority to rule. **Consensus building** requires that everyone or nearly everyone agree with the final decision. Majority rule requires most of the members to agree, but not all. Some decisions are made by small subgroups of team members or by a single member, after the team as a whole has contributed its ideas. Each method of making a decision can be appropriate at various times. Your team must consider each option and its consequences whenever making a decision.

Teamwork

The team concept is becoming the workplace norm. People who have difficulty working with others are at a major disadvantage in the modern workplace. Your communication skills, your willingness to go the extra mile, your positive attitude, your time management skills—all of these elements and more will determine your value as a team member. It is not good enough simply to know how to work with computers. People skills are essential.

Team members must understand their roles and be aware of how they affect the rest of the team. They must also stay in frequent touch with one another to coordinate the work that needs to be done. For example, typesetting on a book cannot begin until the design has been finalized and the text written. The designer and the author cannot spend an excessive amount of time on their jobs and expect the typesetter to work hurriedly in the little time remaining in the schedule at the end. All must work together to ensure that enough time is allotted for each task.

Collaborative Tools *LO 23.2*

Collaborative computing is growing in importance as software is developed to encourage its use as part of a team activity. Brainstorming software such as Inspiration is sometimes used to gather ideas and then to sort them. Microsoft PowerPoint is also used to brainstorm, and its Notes feature can be used to add ideas as they occur to a group using this software. Microsoft SharePoint provides a common resource where team members can share ideas, announcements, documents, and more. Any software that facilitates the gathering of ideas and the tracking of information can be an important collaborative tool.

Technology has provided teams with ways to collaborate even if a team cannot meet in person. You have seen in Chapter 22 how video-conferencing is used to provide people with a means of meeting using a video camera. Teleconferencing using phone lines is another way (see Figure 23.5 on the following page). Google Calendar and Microsoft Exchange are also useful collaborative tools. They allow team members to share their calendars with everyone else on the team, which facilitates meeting planning as well.

Software such as Microsoft Word allows you to create a document, send it on to others for their comments, and then, using the Review tab, accept or reject the suggestions. Figure 23.6 demonstrates how this was done during the creation of your textbook. Notice the revisions within the document, as well as comments on the right side of the document. Each user's edits and comments are tagged accordingly.

There are many tools available on the Internet (some free and others for a fee) that allow you to share and collaborate on documents.

Figure 23.5 *Teleconferencing allows individuals to communicate with voice as well as with expression, gestures, and other visual cues and aids.*

Andreas Pollok/Getty Images

Some, such as Google Slides, have already been mentioned in this text, but there are many others such as Crocodoc and HyperOffice. With collaborative tools such as these, teams can be far more productive than in the past. It is just one way that technology has had an impact on business.

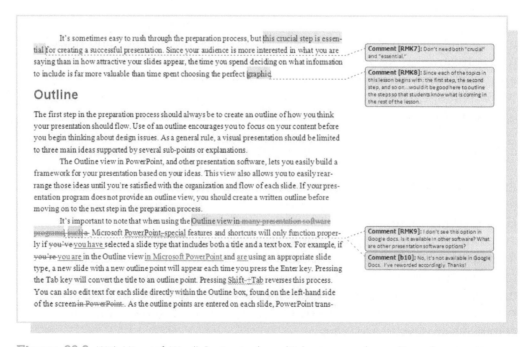

Figure 23.6 *With Microsoft Word's Review tools, multiple users can share edits and comments within a single file.*

ACTIVITY 23.2 ▶ Collaborative Tools

1. Choose a collaborative tool to use such as Crocodoc (at crocodoc.com) or one given by your instructor.

2. Upload the team charter document created by your team in Activity 23.1.

3. Once posted, each member of the team should make at least one comment and an edit in the document.

4. Download the marked-up document and save it as *23_Activity2_collaboration*.

Lesson 23.3 ▶ Multimedia Development Team Roles

A multimedia project is a team effort that requires a host of skilled individuals to fill a diverse set of roles (Figure 23.7). While each role is important on its own, the relationship between roles is equally important. As with any team, a multimedia development team is only as good as its individual members, and their ability to work together as a whole.

Figure 23.7 *Members of a multimedia development team must be able to work as part of a team, as well as independently.*

StockLite/Shutterstock.com

Role of the Client LO 23.3

Even the best multimedia development team is useless without a client. A "client" may be an external client who is paying for a specific product/deliverable or it may be another division, team, or individual within your own company. Regardless of who the client is, however, before the team can begin working, the client must provide them with a clearly defined project. However, the client's role does not end there. Throughout the development of the project, the client must be available to answer questions and provide feedback, ensuring the team is meeting the client's expectations along the way.

Granata1111/Dreamstime.com

Just an Internet Connection Away

In years past, team members often needed to live within commuting distance in order to collaborate on a project. Whether that commute was within walking, driving, or flying distance, it was often necessary for team members to have a "face-to-face" meeting on occasion over the life of a project. Today, with all of the technological advancements we've seen in communication, individual team members on most projects can often live just about anywhere in the world—as long as they have a computer and a decent Internet connection. Gone are the days when a team needed to bring its members to a meeting. Videoconferencing programs, such as Skype, let you bring the meeting to the team members, saving time, money, and energy—a win-win for any team.

Roles of Multimedia Development Team Members *LO 23.3*

Team Leader / Project Manager

Within a multimedia development team, the Team Leader, or Project Manager, must define and coordinate not only the multimedia team, but also the team's projects. A good leader must possess a basic understanding of the multimedia skills required of each team member. While he or she does not need to know exactly how to perform each task, team members want to feel as if their leader at least understands what all of their jobs entail.

Team leaders must have excellent communication skills, as they will often find themselves playing referee between team members with opposing ideas or different work ethics. A good leader must be able to multitask as they negotiate, solve problems, and manage all aspects of each project.

Producer

The producer is responsible for the overall execution of the multimedia project. From the researching of a project's content to overseeing the design and implementation of each phase, the producer works with each team member throughout the life of a project. The producer is ultimately responsible for ensuring that each link in the project fits together correctly, forming a cohesive and professional end result.

User Interface Designer

The user interface designer decides exactly how different multimedia elements within a project will interact with one another and with end users. This person must ensure that the final product is both user-friendly and functional. Therefore, it's important that the user interface designer hold technical and design skill sets (Figure 23.8). The design skill set is essential to developing a multimedia user interface that is appealing, while the technical skill set will ensure that the design is practical enough to actually work. This person must also be able to work with all types of media, including:

- Text
- Graphics
- Audio
- Video
- Photos

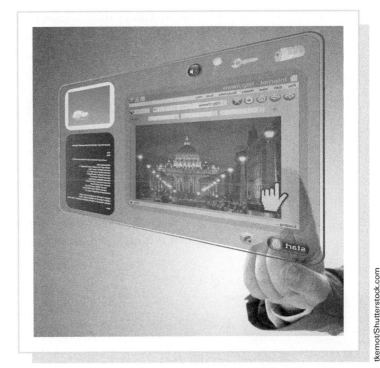

Media Specialist

Media specialists are responsible for creating the content within the project.

Figure 23.8 *Each team member, including the user interface designer, plays a vital role in the success of a project.*

Whether it's the graphics displayed in a presentation or a video on a website, each role is specialized and vital to the overall appeal of the project. In addition to having the individual skills required for each role, media specialists must be able to work well with one another. A graphic artist needs to work with the writer to ensure that the artwork supports what has been written. The motion designer must ensure that any movement he or she adds to the graphic artist's work also matches the intended goals of what has been written, as well as complements the graphic art. There may be up to six different media specialist roles on any given project, including:

- Motion designer
- Graphic artist
- Audio specialist
- Videographer
- Writer
- Editor

Computer Systems Specialist

Using either software programs or programming code, a computer systems specialist ensures that the final product is user-friendly and functional. This person may be a systems architect or a programmer. Whether through the use of a computer software program or individual lines of code, a computer systems specialist is responsible for building a multimedia project's behind-the-scenes computer architecture.

This architecture executes the design initially conceived by the user interface designer. Therefore, in addition to computer programming knowledge, this person must also understand how all types of media interact with one another.

Quality Assurance Analyst

A quality assurance analyst is responsible for establishing a set of guidelines against which he or she will measure each multimedia project. These guidelines should be developed with input from the client, as well as with the team leader and all team members. Once a set of guidelines has been established, the quality assurance analyst must check each and every aspect of the project to ensure that all standards listed within the guidelines have been met.

Think About It

The Ethics of Conflict

Conflict is usually seen as undesirable and something to be avoided. While it is true that physical conflict is not desirable, this is not the case with the conflict of ideas. The importance of teamwork is to bring into the open all possible ideas in order to provide as many solutions as possible. As a member of a team, you have to learn not to see a difference of opinion as a personal attack. If everyone in a team tries to "play nice" by not countering one idea with another, then the team will lose its energy. This does not mean that ideas should be presented in an argumentative manner. Verbal fighting is not the answer. Instead, you must learn to present your ideas and to accept the ideas of others without creating a negative environment for members of the team. This is a difficult ethical challenge for everyone.

checkpoint

What are multimedia development teams useless without?

ACTIVITY 23.3 ▶ Create an Organization Chart

1. Using PowerPoint or other software with organization chart tools, create an organization chart that outlines the team members' roles in a project.

2. Save your organization chart as *23_Activity3_organization_chart*.

Key Concepts

▶ Before starting a multimedia development project, you must first form a team by gathering members who possess all the required skill sets. *LO 23.1*

▶ Team-building activities play an important role in helping individual team members function as a single entity. *LO 23.2*

▶ Multimedia development teams consist of skilled individuals playing diverse roles. *LO 23.3*

Review and Discuss

1. Describe the function of each of the stages of team development and evaluate the results of each stage being well developed. *LO 23.1*

2. Justify the need to create a team charter. *LO 23.1*

3. Explain the need for effective team communication for the success of your team's goals and describe barriers to that success. *LO 23.1 and 23.2*

4. Explain how team-building activities can facilitate the success of the team. *LO 23.2*

5. Describe an effective team meeting and support the need to have regular team meetings. *LO 23.2*

6. Compare and contrast the most frequently used means of reaching an agreement in the decision-making process of a team project. *LO 23.2*

7. Explain how a team can collaborate even when not meeting in person. *LO 23.2*

8. Describe the differences and similarities between the client and the project manager in a team and the characteristics each must possess. *LO 23.3*

9. Describe the function of a producer and the user interface designer in a multimedia project. *LO 23.3*

10. Describe and justify the role of the quality assurance analyst within a team project. *LO 23.3*

Apply

1. Reflect on a past project in this class that had numerous multimedia pieces to it. Write a description of the project. In reflection, create a team charter. Write a brief summary of the specifics in the team development, briefly explaining each area. Explain whether you used consensus building or majority rule or both. List any collaborative tools that you used.

List and define the roles that members played in the project. Correlate them to the roles as listed in the textbook. Save your assessment as **23_Apply1_reflection**. *LO 23.1, 23.2, and 23.3*

2. Research and then create a list of team-building ideas. As a team, choose one of the team-building activities from the list for your team. Submit a list of at least four ideas you found online, with a summary of the one you chose to use and how it worked. Did you feel as if it created more cohesiveness with the team? What would you do differently next time? Would you use this same activity again? Was there one you read about that you wished you had used instead? Save your summary as **23_Apply2_team_building**. *LO 23.1*

3. In a team of three or four students, plan a booklet print project of at least 30 pages with a minimum of three sections. This could be a cookbook with recipes, a collection of poems, or any other collection. Get your idea approved by your instructor. Create an ongoing document to keep notes during the project that will include a team charter, notes on the four stages of team development, details on team meetings, and the roles of each person on your team. As closely as possible, relate your team activities to those described in this text. Save the project as **23_Apply3_project** and the ongoing team notes as **23_Apply3_team_notes**. *LO 23.2*

Explore

1. Interview someone who works in a graphic design firm or has a department with a graphic design team. Compare and contrast the team members as they describe them with those described in this text. Write a summary describing the differences if there are any or any differences described in the tasks assigned to team members. Save your summary as **23_Explore1_interview**. *LO 23.3*

2. Job shadow someone currently employed in a graphic arts field. Spend at least four hours shadowing him or her. Write a summary of what you noticed about working in teams or about project management. If you were unable to observe anything in that area, what did you observe that will be useful information in this field? Why do you think you did not see anything in team or project management on the day that you shadowed? Save your assessment as **23_Explore2_job_shadow**. *LO 23.2 and 23.3*

Academic Connections

Writing. Read an article on Multimedia Transformation. If you are unable to find anything, you might choose to use the following article or ask your instructor for ideas: http://www.edweek.org/ew/collections/multimediareport-2011/index.html

Write a one-page summary of the article. In a team of four students, peer review each other's summaries, using a collaborative tool such as Crocodoc or Google Docs. Peer review for the following: 1) proper paraphrasing without direct quotes; 2) correct grammar and spelling; 3) complete sentences and paragraphs. Download the marked-up file for submission to your instructor, saving it as **23_AC_writing**.

Social Studies. Research the topic of social studies facts that all high school students should know. With a partner, create a presentation or use another software application to create flash cards for 50 questions on these facts (or as many as your instructor directs you to make). Save your work as **23_AC_social_studies**.

UNIT 7 PROJECTS

Independent Project

If you were going to teach how to effectively use electronic collaboration and project management, how would you demonstrate that?

Choose one or more multimedia to demonstrate what you have learned in this unit and from the text as a whole. You can use just one medium or several different mediums (i.e., presentation software, web pages, audio, video, photo editing, etc.).

Practice with or demonstrate your completed project to a partner and then reevaluate your work. Make any changes necessary and rehearse your demonstration again.

Save all parts of your project as **Unit7_Independent_Project**.

Portfolio

Write a journal describing your experiences with various methods of electronic collaboration. If you have not experienced any of the methods, interview someone who has. Include the following in your journal:

▶ Description of the collaboration, when it occurred, and those that were involved.

▶ What were the pros and cons of this collaboration?

▶ What did you learn from it?

▶ When is this a good method to use?

▶ Did it work for your particular situation? Why or why not?

Write a summary of both your best experience working on a team project and your worst experience. If you have had no team project experience, interview someone who has. Include the following:

▶ What made the team project the best experience?

▶ What is it you would like to take from this experience and bring with you to every experience?

▶ What would you not repeat from this experience? Why?

▶ What made the team project the worst experience?

▶ What can you identify as those things to avoid that made it the worst experience?

Save your journal and your summary as **Unit7_Portfolio_electronic_collaboration** and add it to your portfolio.

Add the Independent Project from this unit to your portfolio as well.

FBLA-PBL or BPA

Plan a team project for your student organization. Include the following in your plan:

▶ The methods that will be used for electronic collaboration

▶ A plan for setting up the collaboration

▶ A timeline for when the collaboration will take place

▶ A team charter

▶ Several team-building activities

▶ The roles that will be needed to complete the team project

▶ Details on who will complete all activities and how they plan to do it.

Monkey Business Images/Shutterstock.com

Corporate Capstone

Project Overview

Through the chapters of this textbook, you have studied and practiced taking and managing digital images, print publishing, creating and editing audio and video, web publishing, slide show presentations, and business conferencing. In this capstone project, you will use the skills and knowledge you have gained to increase the effectiveness of a company's communications and enhance its image.

First, you will research and select a company to analyze. One portion of your work will be to analyze many aspects of that company's website. Then you will use digital media to create three products:

▶ Incorporate video, audio, text, graphics, and animated graphics into an existing web page.

▶ Incorporate various digital media into a print document such as a newsletter, poster, or report.

▶ Develop an interactive medium such as a compact disk or digital video disk to display video, audio, and animation products.

Finally, you will present your results in a professional manner. By successfully performing these tasks, you will demonstrate your ability to draw conclusions from your research, implement the new skills you have learned, and practice your presentation skills.

Enjoy this exploration and learn from it. Carry the knowledge you learn from this experience into the waiting business world.

Choose Your Team (or Go It Alone)

Check with your instructor to find out if you will be working independently or as a member of a team. Keep in mind that the number of team members will affect your project management, time management, project scheduling, and project timeline. If you're working on a team, consider using cloud computing technology and software tools to collaborate with your team members. (Even if you are working alone, cloud computing may be useful for storing and working with your files from a variety of locations between home, school, the library, and so on.)

Choose Your Company

Go to the Industries at a Glance site at http://www.bls.gov/iag/tgs/iag_index_alpha.htm and research the different U.S. industry categories, such as Information, Leisure and Hospitality, and Manufacturing. Select a category that interests you and then research the various industries in that category. Research companies in the industry you selected and choose one that most interests you.

Use Yahoo! financial information at http://finance.yahoo.com or a comparable website to locate financial information about the company. You may have to use the Symbol Lookup feature to find the stock symbol for the company. Read about the company and look for any information that indicates a change the company may be experiencing.

Has the company's stock improved or declined over the most recent five-year time period? Has the change been dramatic, with many peaks or valleys, or has it been a gradual change? Using the information provided on the website, is there any indication of what impact technology has on this business? What changes has the company been experiencing or does it anticipate experiencing? In your own words in a word processing document, explain your observations and any conclusions you draw from your reading. Focus on these questions, but include any other pertinent business information. Save your observations as *company*.

iStockphoto.com/Ugurhan Betin

Develop Your Plan

In order to deliver a quality product on time, you must develop a plan.

Break the Project into Logical Parts

Break the project into logical parts and assign each part to a team member based on the team member's strengths and interests. If you're working on a team, be sure that the time requirements for each assignment are comparable. If they are not, break larger tasks into subtasks and assign them to team members who have less demanding tasks to perform.

You should also assign a reviewer to each team member—another team member who can act as a second pair of eyes by proofreading text or checking on layout.

Prepare a Schedule

Prepare a schedule that keeps the project moving at an acceptable rate, allows for revisions, and meets your target end date. If you're on a team, hold regular status meetings during the course of the project and have each team member report on his or her progress toward the project goal. If problems arise, troubleshoot them as a team.

Plan Each Component

For each product, prepare an outline or storyboard that summarizes the information to be presented on each web page, in each section of a report, or in each video frame.

Identify Needed Equipment and Resources

List and locate the various pieces of equipment needed to prepare the products: computers, printers, software programs, scanners, digital camera, and so on. Also, do you need people to act in your video or do voice-overs? Do you need to talk or correspond with outside resources to verify facts?

Analyze the Company's Web Presence

Locate the website of the company you chose. How did you find it? What other addresses might the company have used other than the one you found? Does the company use more than one address? What are the differences?

The name of a website is called a domain name. Domain names are registered to protect the website from use by others. Companies did not always register domain names, and private individuals claimed the right to them instead. As you can imagine, this caused problems for companies who realized too late that their web address had already been registered. Search for information about domain name issues that may have occurred with your chosen company. How do domain issues impact a business? What change does this create in the business environment? Summarize your information and save it as *domain*.

Page Design

Look carefully at the company's home page and consider all the design elements you have studied. Ask yourself the questions listed below and then summarize your observations. Save the summary document as *design*:

- How quickly does the page load?
- Does it have a log-in requirement?
- What colors are used on the opening page?
- What psychological impact or emotional impact do these colors have?
- What font and type size are used on the page?
- What is the primary focus of the page?
- What types of multimedia are used?
- Is there sound on the page?
- Are there navigation tools?
- Does the page use frames?
- Does the page meet disability requirements?
- How effective is the page in keeping your attention?
- Is the page friendly and easy to use?
- Reveal the code used to create the page. Can you tell what software was used to create the page?
- What keywords are included for search engines?
- What is the meta description of the website?

Logo

Is there a corporate logo? How is the logo integrated into the page? What colors are used? What impact do the colors have? Is the logo memorable? Why do you think the logo was designed this way? What file format is the logo saved as? Has technology made any change in the logo? What technology, such as Flash, might impact the logo at a later time? Describe your responses to the logo and save this document as *logo*.

Use raster or vector editing software to duplicate the logo, including the colors. Save your duplicated logo as *logo.gif* or *logo.jpg*. What image tools are most useful in creating the logo?

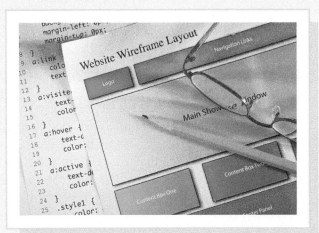

Web Designer

Is there information on the page to indicate who designed or manages the page? Is there a contact email address? Is there information to indicate the most recent update? Does the page appear to be current? If possible, email the site designer to ask for information about his or her credentials, experience, and contributions to the design. Make a copy of the email you sent. If you receive an email response, make a copy of it. Save both as *mail*.

Web Content

Consider the audience that would visit the company's website. Who is this page designed to attract? Why would they come to this site? Would it meet their needs? What is the purpose of this site? Has the company fully used the power of Internet technology?

What information is available on this site? How many links are there? What information appears on these linked pages? Does the opening page provide a site search engine?

Does the site appear to be usable for those in other countries? Which countries? If this site is country specific, can you locate corporate sites designed for another country?

Many corporate websites are created for the purpose of e-commerce, to sell the company's product or services. Is this site designed to market a product or services? How easy is it to use? Does the site content explain shipping and taxes before you have to order? How fast does shopping information load? Do prices appear to be more or less than you would pay in a physical store? Is the site secure? How easy is it to order, make the payment, and track the shipment?

Using the answers to your website content questions, write a summary discussing the usefulness and effectiveness of the pages. Use your knowledge of the Internet and your image management skills to include suggestions about how to improve the page. Include observations of how technology has impacted this business and how the business environment is changing. Save your summary as *content*.

Creating Your Products

Now gather your information and observations to create three products to demonstrate your knowledge of business image management and its impact: a series of web pages, a slide show, and a print document in PDF format. Use the checklists found in the following section to ensure that you include all essential components. Points will be applied based on inclusion of the necessary components and the quality of the information provided.

Web Pages

Your web pages should be saved into a folder titled *chngbus*. Organization of files on the web page will save you time as your website grows. Old files will need to be removed to avoid cluttering both your computer and the server. Create subfolders so that it will be easy to sort through files to locate those that are HTML pages, images, documents, and other file types.

Begin by creating an opening page that includes color, animation, your title, your name, and navigation links. Sound and video are optional. Select colors that will convey the message you intend. Your animation can be created using the corporate logo you re-created as *logo.gif* or *logo.jpg*. The title should reflect your opinion of the site's image management and its impact on the business you chose.

The second page should include an explanation of your overall conclusions. The page should also include links to each of the following pages:

▶ Company information (include *company*)

▶ Domain name (include *domain*)

▶ Page design (include *design*, *logo*, and *logo.gif* or *logo.jpg*)

▶ Mail response (optional—include *mail*)

▶ Content (include *content*)

Slide Show

Use the information you developed for the web pages to create a slide show with a similar design. Set up the presentation to be used as a show that can run independently without intervention. Save the presentation as *changingbusiness*.

Print Document

Use the information you developed for the web pages to create a desktop published document. Save the document as *changingbusiness*. Convert the document to a PDF file and save it as *changingbusiness.pdf*.

Checklists for Evaluating Your Projects

The following checklists will be used to evaluate your projects. You should be sure to review the checklists before planning or executing your projects to ensure that you meet the required criteria.

Checklist for Web Pages

Criterion	Possible Points
Pages saved to a folder called **chngbus**.	5
Opening page contains title explaining how technology has changed business.	5
Opening page contains effective color.	5
Opening page contains navigation links that function correctly.	5
Opening page contains student name.	5
Summary page contains overall conclusions.	5
Summary page contains navigation links that function correctly.	5
Summary page contains links to pages that function correctly.	5
Company information page contains company information.	10
Domain name page contains domain information.	5
Page design page contains effective analysis of website design.	15
Page design page contains logo information.	5
Page design page contains logo graphic.	5
Content page contains content information.	15
Page design demonstrates knowledge of image management.	5
Total for Web Pages	**100**

Checklist for the Slide Show

Criterion	Possible Points
Opening slide contains title explaining how technology has changed business.	*5*
Presentation identifies creator of presentation.	*5*
Presentation uses type effectively.	*15*
Presentation uses color effectively.	*15*
Presentation uses graphics effectively.	*15*
Presentation edits content to slide show format effectively.	*20*
Presentation demonstrates knowledge of image management.	*20*
Presentation requires no intervention.	*5*
Total for Slide Show	**100**

Checklist for the Print Document

Criterion	Possible Points
Title page contains title explaining how technology has changed business.	*5*
Title page identifies author of project.	*5*
Table of contents has all page titles and correct page numbers.	*5*
Document shows understanding of use of typography.	*15*
Document shows understanding of use of color.	*15*
Document shows understanding of use of graphics in print.	*15*
Document includes all content.	*15*
Document demonstrates knowledge of desktop publishing.	*20*
Document converted to PDF file.	*5*
Total for Print Document	**100**

4K Ultra HD Describes a camcorder with a resolution around 3840 × 2160 pixels.

a

accessibility The principle of making Web content understandable and usable by all people regardless of disabilities.

ADC The acronym used to describe the process of converting sound from analog to digital.

additive color mixing Combining three different colors of light at different intensities to produce a whole range of other colors.

adware Software that delivers advertising without the user's knowledge or consent.

adword Keyword or phrase on which a site owner links an ad. Adwords compete with other ads using the same keyword or phrase for special display space when the word appears as a search term.

aggregator Software that collects and lists websites that have been syndicated.

alignment How a line of text or a paragraph is positioned in a column: flush left, flush right, centered, or justified.

alternate text Brief description of an image that browsers display while the image is loading or if the browser cannot upload it.

analog audio Sound recorded as continuous vibrations.

analogous colors Colors that are next to one another on a color wheel.

anchor point A point defining the beginning or end of a segment along a path.

animate The application of visual effects to individual items on a slide, such as text or an image.

animated GIFs Several bitmap graphics joined into a single file to give them the appearance of motion.

animation Display of a series of images in quick succession to show movement.

animation style A set of animation choices that includes animation, timing, and response.

anti-aliasing A raster-editing feature that softens the hard edges of a selection by adjusting the color of the pixels along the outside edge.

aperture Indicates the size of a camera lens's opening.

applet An executable program that cannot stand alone but functions only within a web browser.

ascender The part of a letter that extends above the x-height, as in the letter "f."

aspect ratio The ratio of the width to the height of an image.

assistive technology Any device or software developed with the goal of helping those with disabilities use and interact successfully with a computer.

attribute Part of a tag that further describes or defines an element, which consists of the attribute type and a value for that attribute.

audience The people who watch or listen to a presentation.

b

back lighting When light shines from behind the subject toward the camera, often casting all of the front details of a subject in shadow or silhouette.

background The "paper" on which a presentation will be seen by the audience.

background color The color "behind" a raster image that appears when one erases or cuts a selection from the background layer of an image.

background layer A special kind of layer in raster programs like Photoshop that is always at the bottom of the layer stack and cannot be renamed, moved, deleted, or contain any transparency.

balance A design principle in which the weight of elements is distributed in a visually appealing way.

bandwidth The speed at which a computer can transmit information along a network.

banner ad Web ads that often contain a logo and additional business information designed to give corporate identity to a page.

baseline The imaginary line on which the typeface sits.

bitrate Video transfer speed.

bleed An element that extends through a margin and off the edge of a printed page.

block A set of JavaScript statements that are enclosed in curly brackets { }.

bounding box An outline around a selected vector object that can be used to transform the object.

brightness In the HSB color model, the measure of how light or dark a color is on a scale of 0 to 100%.

browser A computer program that allows users to view web pages.

C

camcorder Portable video recorder.

candid photograph Nonposed, usually informal picture.

Canvas The area within the workspace where animation will be designed.

cascading style sheets (CSS) Style sheets that include information on how the page should appear.

CCD (charge-coupled device) A light sensor that records images.

cel animation The use of transparent pages to create a sense of movement.

cell padding The space within a cell that separates or pads the text or image within the cell.

cell spacing The amount of space between cells.

channels The number of sides from which sound is heard, either mono (one) or stereo (two).

clip art A picture or drawing created by someone with the intention that the artwork will be used by others.

clipping mask A vector object used to hide portions of lower objects in a stack.

closed path A path with no distinct beginning or end, for example a circle, square, or other shape.

closing tag The second tag in a pair.

cloud computing On-demand access to shared data via the Internet.

CMOS (complementary metal-oxide semiconductor) An image-recording light sensor that is larger and uses less power than a CCD sensor.

CMYK color model A color model based on cyan, magenta, yellow, and black pigments used to create full color on printed materials.

codec An algorithm that compresses sound or video to reduce its file size and then decompresses it when played.

color harmony A cohesive and pleasing combination created by a group of colors.

color mode A way to indicate to a computer what color model to use when representing colors.

color model A group of colors identified in a way that computers can understand.

color temperature Measures the type of light shining on an image.

color theme A combination of different hues that work together to create color harmony.

color theory A set of guidelines about how colors communicate feelings and how they combine to create the best look and feel for a project.

color wheel A visual representation of primary, secondary, and tertiary colors that can be useful for understanding and using basic concepts in color theory.

complementary colors Colors that are opposite one another on a color wheel.

compression The process of reducing the size of the image. *Lossy compression* reduces the size of an image file by removing information that is not essential. *Lossless compression* does not change any pixel data.

conditional statement An action taken if certain conditions are or are not met.

consensus building Process used to reach agreement by a team of people.

Content Management System (CMS) A computer application that allows for content publishing, editing, organizing, deleting, and general maintenance from a central location.

contiguous Linked or touching each other (in reference to parts of an image).

copyleft A licensing protection used by those who create open source software.

copyright The term literally means restricting the right of others to copy.

corner point An anchor point along a vector path where the direction changes.

cropping In photo composition, including all wanted elements in a photo and excluding all unwanted elements.

curly quotes Rounded marks used for quotations and apostrophes.

cyber predator A person who uses the Internet to make contact with others (usually with children and teens) in order to harm them.

d

DAC The acronym used to describe the process of converting sound from digital to analog.

decibel (dB) Unit of measurement for sound pressure level and signal level.

deep linking Citing a web address that goes beyond the home or entry page.

depth of field Indicates how much of the image is in focus.

descender The part of a lowercase letter that extends below the baseline, as in the letter "y."

digital audio Sound recorded as a series of digits.

digital media Any combination of audio, video, images, and text used to convey a message through technology.

digital rights management (DRM) Technology that prevents unauthorized copying of a digital work.

digital single lens reflex (DSLR) A camera that uses a mirror system to capture an image. DSLR cameras have interchangeable lenses.

digital zoom The digital enlargement of an image on an image sensor through interpolation of pixels.

discussion thread A chain of individual messages or comments relating to a common topic.

display typeface A typeface used to attract attention to the design of the font as well as to the words.

dissolve Transition technique in which one scene slowly changes to the other.

domain name The unique name for a website, which becomes part of the site's URL and which must be formally registered.

drawing program A general term for graphics software that uses mathematically defined lines to create an image.

dynamic HTML (DHTML) A means of animating text or image elements through the HTML code that determines their placement and appearance.

e

electronic communication The electronic transmission of data from one computing device to another.

element A unit of a web page, defined by start and end tags.

email Electronic, or digital, mail sent from one account to another via the Internet.

email client Computer program used to manage a user's email account.

embed To place a media object on a web page rather than on a separate page.

embedded graphic A graphic that appears in a layout at full resolution, with all of its associated data copied into the layout file.

em dash A punctuation symbol that resembles a hyphen but is noticeably longer (normally the width of the capital letter M in the font and point size in which it is formatted); indicates a break in thought, similar to parentheses.

emphasis A design principle in which certain elements in a design stand out more than others.

empty elements Elements that do not have any content.

en dash A punctuation symbol that resembles a hyphen but is longer (normally the width of a capital N in the font and point size in which it is formatted); used in ranges of numbers, letters, or dates.

encoding software A program that changes media files from one format to another and can be used to create streaming media.

encryption Converting text into an unreadable series of numbers and letters to protect information. Digital encryption uses software that can scramble and unscramble the data.

endpoint A beginning or end anchor point on a path.

end-user license agreement (EULA) A contract software purchasers must agree to before using software.

ergonomics A science that studies the best way to design a workplace for maximum safety and productivity.

ethics Moral choices between right and wrong actions.

event An action taken by a website visitor that triggers execution of a script.

f

fade Transition technique that moves from black to the image or the reverse.

fair use The right to reproduce a small part of a copyrighted work for educational or other not-for-profit purposes, without having to obtain permission or pay a royalty fee.

FAQs (Frequently Asked Questions) Answers to common questions about the products or services of the organization owning the site or about the site itself, often with links to appropriate pages on the site.

feathering A raster-editing feature that softens the hard edges of a selection by adding a border along the outer edge that gradually fades into the background, creating a soft blur.

feed Electronic content and the process of syndicating that content.

file sharing Use of a network to move files between computers, often for illegal purposes.

fill A color or pattern applied to the inside area of a path.

flash storage A commonly used storage medium for videos that uses a non-volatile memory type.

flatten To merge multiple layers into a single layer. Flattening can reduce file size, but should only be done after all editing is complete and is best done on a copy of the original file.

floating graphic A graphic that can be moved around on a page independently of text.

focal point The element within an image on which the viewer's eye focuses.

font Within a typeface, a set of characters with a specific style.

foreground color The color that appears when one paints, draws, or fills an image in a raster-editing program.

frame Individual image that makes up an animated GIF file.

frame rate The number of frames per second that video records; the rate at which each frame is displayed.

framing The use of elements within a scene to visually surround the subject and draw attention to it.

front lighting When light shines from behind the camera and illuminates the front of the subject, producing few or no shadows.

FTP (File Transfer Protocol) A communications protocol used to transfer files from one computer to another over a network. FTP is often used to upload web pages to a web server.

function JavaScript command not executed until an event occurs.

g

gamut The range of colors that can be produced by the primary colors in a particular color model.

GNU General Public License The standard open source contract or license.

grayscale A range of grays from white to black with all the variations in between.

GUI An acronym for graphical user interface. The GUI makes it possible to use a device, such as a mouse, to interact with a computer.

gutter The white space between columns on a page.

h

H.264 A video format that is highly compressed and can be played across many platforms.

hacker A person who finds an electronic means of gaining unauthorized access to a computer.

hacking The unauthorized modification of a website, usually in ways that distort the original purpose of the site or seek to harm the site's owner.

hand tool Navigation tool that moves an image around in a viewing area.

Hertz A measurement of the frequency of sound, or the number of times the wave pattern is repeated per second.

hexadecimal number (also hex number) Hex numbers are used to identify web colors.

high definition (HD) Describes a camcorder that produces a much higher quality image than SD, which can reach as high as 1920 × 1080, and usually has a 16:9 aspect ratio.

highlight The lightest part of an image, which is usually white.

home page The main page of a website, which is generally the first page visitors will see.

HSB color model A color model based on human perception of color that uses hue, saturation, and brightness to define a color.

HTML (HyperText Markup Language) The code used to create web pages.

HTML5 A newer version of HTML supported by the World Wide Web Consortium but not yet fully implemented in all browsers.

hue In the HSB color model, the general color expressed by a value between 0 and 360 degrees. In color theory, another word for color.

hyperlink Text or a web object that links to another web page.

hyperlinks (in PowerPoint) Text and/or pictures that can be used to connect one slide with another or display another presentation or location.

i

illusion of depth In photography, the effect of visual clues that make a viewer perceive an image as three-dimensional in a two-dimensional image.

image map A graphic divided into two or more parts, with each part assigned a different link.

index page Another name for the home page, which should be named "index.html" or "index.htm."

inline graphic One that is attached to text and moves with it.

intellectual property A legal concept that protects a creative work just as if it were physical property.

interlaced Video recorded or broadcast as a series of alternating lines.

ISO A standardized measurement of the speed with which a camera stores an image.

j

jargon Specialized words used within a particular industry, often incorporating acronyms as shortcuts.

JavaScript A programming language that increases the interactivity of web pages by making it possible for actions to be executed within the browser, and without the need to access the server that hosts the website.

jog dial A type of wheel or dial on a camera that makes it possible to scroll through setting options by rotating. There is an indicator for the current selection.

k

Kelvin The measurement, in degrees, of the color temperature of light.

kerning Adjusting the space between two characters to improve appearance and readability.

keyframe A software notation of a change in a frame; a mark that indicates where on a timeline an action such as movement begins.

keylogger Software that tracks keyboard use and transmits it to be used for illegal purposes.

keyword A word included in a meta tag or header that is meant to indicate the content of a web page.

kiosk Term that, when used in conjunction with a computer, describes a freestanding computer used by visitors.

l

layer mask A raster-editing feature that enables one to control what is visible on a layer.

layers A raster-editing feature used to layer editable images individually, make changes, add effects, and make nondestructive edits.

layout The arrangement on a page of all the key elements without regard to the specific content.

leading lines Actual or suggested lines in an image that draw a viewer's eye through an image in a specific direction, usually to the focal point.

leading The amount of space between lines of text.

license A legal agreement that gives permission and states detailed conditions for using a copyrighted image.

line tool Draws open path line segments.

link exchange Agreement among two or more websites to link to each other in hopes of increasing the ranking of each party in search engine results.

linked graphic A linked graphic appears in a layout as a low-resolution screen image, but all of its data remains in the individual image file rather than being incorporated into the layout file.

looping Repetition of a series of frames that can be used to add length without increasing the file size.

m

macro A setting or lens that allows close-ups.

malware The abbreviation for malicious software, designed to damage a computer or steal information.

master pages Page designs that can be applied automatically to any page within a document.

measure The length of a line of text.

media In PowerPoint, media includes sound or video. In other environments, media may include any use of graphical or auditory additions to a presentation, such as a chart or graph.

megapixel A unit of measure equal to one million pixels. On a digital camera, the megapixels on an image sensor react to and record light to produce an image. The number of megapixels indicates the maximum image resolution of a camera.

meta tag An HTML tag that stores information about a website.

metadata Information about a photograph stored within the image file.

microblogging Online exchange of information through short sentences, images, or video links.

MIDI Communication protocol that allows a wide variety of electronic musical instruments, computers, and other devices to communicate with each other.

midtones The middle range of colors in an image.

mode dial A type of wheel or dial on a camera that makes it possible to scroll through setting options by rotating. There is an indicator for the current selection.

morphing Changing one shape into another.

motion path The track that an animated text or image will follow as it appears on a slide. It can be a simple straight line or a more complicated one with a series of twists or turns.

multimedia The combination of sound, animation, graphics, video, and color. In an earlier time, the term audiovisual was used instead.

n

naming convention A set of rules used in the naming of files and folders.

navigation link The means of guiding a website visitor from one page to another within the site.

neutral colors In color theory, black, white, and gray used to change the nature of hues, creating shades, tints, and tones.

nondestructive edit A change made to an image that does not actually alter the original image's pixels.

O

object Unit manipulated in JavaScript, which has both properties and methods.

online backup A means of backing up or storing data using the Internet.

open path A path with a distinct beginning and end; for example, a straight line.

open source Software that allows others to use its code without cost.

opening tag The first tag in a pair.

optical zoom The actual magnification of an image through the movement of a camera lens.

optimization A means of compressing animations to reduce the size of the file.

orphan When the first line of a paragraph falls by itself at the bottom of a page or column or when a single word or part of a word falls by itself on the last line of a paragraph.

out of gamut Refers to colors that are part of the range of one color model but not another.

p

Package Presentation for CD Feature of Microsoft PowerPoint that packages a presentation for ease of transfer to another computer. It may also include a reader so that viewers without PowerPoint can still view the presentation.

paint program A general term for graphics software that uses pixels to create an image.

panning Movement of a video camera from one side to another.

Pantone Matching System (PMS) A standard set of colors and associated inks that make it easy to reproduce a color in printed material consistently.

parallelism A grammatical term indicating that the basic structure of two or more sentences or phrases is similar. Sentences that are parallel have similar arrangements of subjects, verbs, and sometimes prepositional phrases.

patent A property right for an invention that lasts a specified period of time.

path A line that makes up a vector object.

path animation The path along which an animation sequence moves.

perspective In photography, what makes items look larger and closer or smaller and farther away; can be used to create depth and express a story about a subject.

phishing A social engineering activity where the perpetrator uses fake websites or emails to trick a user into providing personal information or passwords.

photographic composition The selection and arrangement of design elements within a photograph.

pica A printer's measurement equal to 1/6 of an inch.

piracy Copying a product (often digital) for profit without authorization from the owner. Music and video products as well as software are frequently subjects of pirating.

pixel Consists of a specific color at a specific location in a matrix or grid. A collection of pixels produces an image on a computer screen or on a printed page.

pixel dimension The number of pixels in a row and column of a raster grid.

plagiarism Copying or otherwise using someone else's creative work and claiming it as your own, usually in an academic or journalistic work, but also more recently in social media.

platform The specific operating system of a digital device and the hardware associated with it; among computers, the two main platforms are Windows and Mac.

podcast Audio or video stored on a web page and available for downloading via the Internet.

point The unit of measure used to indicate the size of type. One point is approximately 1/72 of an inch.

point-and-shoot A camera designed to be easy to use with preset functions.

pop filter Filter used to decrease explosive breath sounds common when recording voices.

posts Published messages in an online forum.

primary color A basic color that cannot be created by mixing other colors.

progressive Video recorded or broadcast as a series of sequential lines.

proprietary A term used for software code that has restricted rights of use.

public domain Creative works whose copyright restrictions have expired. The term may also be used for open source software.

q

quick mask A temporary mask used to make or refine a selection.

r

rendering The conversion of video to a format that can be used with various viewers.

repetitive stress injury Muscle or joint injury that results from performing actions repeatedly.

resampling Adding or deleting image pixels during the process of resizing.

resolution The density of pixels in an image.

retouch tool A tool that enables one to alter the content of an image.

RGB color model A color model that uses red, green, and blue primary colors plus different intensities of light to create colors on an electronic display like a computer screen.

RGB triplet The combination of numbers indicating light intensity for the red, green, and blue primary colors in the RGB color model and representing a certain color within the model. Can be considered the "name" of a color in the RGB color model.

rhythm A design principle that connects elements in a design and guides a viewer's eye from one item to the next.

rights managed A type of licensing agreement that gives a buyer permission for a specific, limited use of a copyrighted image.

ripping The process of transferring music from a CD to a computer.

Robot Exclusion Protocol (REP) Web standard that allows Web administrators to block search engine spiders from indexing certain directories or files within the website.

rollover Changing of an image or text when a cursor either passes over or clicks on it.

rootkit Software designed to keep a computer user from knowing the computer system has been infected by malware.

royalty A fee paid to the person who owns the copyright on a creative work when it is used by someone else.

royalty free A type of licensing agreement that gives the buyer almost unlimited permission to use a copyrighted image for a one-time fee.

RSS feed One standard for syndicating web content.

rule of thirds Principle of imposing an imaginary grid of nine equal spaces (like a tic-tac-toe grid) over a scene to be photographed, then positioning the most important elements of the image along the gridlines, most preferably at or near the intersection of two imaginary gridlines.

s

sample rate The number of times a sound is measured.

sample size The number of bits used to represent the sound in a sample.

sans serif Typefaces with no serifs.

saturation In the HSB color model, the intensity of a hue on a scale from 0 to 100%.

scale To resize an object to a percentage of its original size.

Scalable Vector Graphics (SVG) Vector-based animation used for 3D animation.

scene A segment of a video that occurs in one location and during one continuous time frame.

screen capture A digital raster image of visible screen content; a snapshot of a computer screen generated by the operating system or other dedicated software.

screen reader A type of assistive technology that turns text on the screen into synthesized speech or Braille.

search engine Program that searches for user-defined keywords in web documents or in databases that store information about websites, and displays lists of sites that contain those keywords.

search engine optimization (SEO) Techniques used in an effort to enhance the ranking of a website in search engine results.

secondary color A color created when two primary colors are mixed.

Section 508 Part of a federal law that requires federal agencies to make their websites accessible to all users regardless of abilities.

segment A distinct portion of a path that connects two anchor points.

selection tool A type of tool used to select a portion of a raster image before modifying it.

serif Typefaces with small decorative strokes or "feet" at the ends of the main strokes that define each letter.

sequencer Hardware device or software application that handles necessary data to record, edit, or play back music.

server A computer designed to store files from multiple computers.

shade A hue mixed with black.

shadows The darkest part of an image, which is usually black.

shape tools Vector drawing tools that enable a user to draw common, closed-path shapes with ease and efficiency.

shutter speed Measures the rate at which a camera lens opens and closes.

side lighting Light that shines from the right or left of the camera and illuminates the subject from the side, creating more defined highlights and shadows.

site map A single web page that lists and organizes all the web pages in a site, to allow users to find and move to specific pages.

slide design (theme) A collection of layouts, colors, fonts, background, and effects that can be applied to a presentation to create a professional, unified appearance.

slide layout Arrangement of design elements on a slide.

Slide Master A single slide that can be designed once and then applied to many slides. PowerPoint allows the creation of multiple masters for use in different situations.

slide show Collection of slides, or pages, arranged in sequence, containing text and images to be presented to an audience.

slide transition The movement from one slide to another that might include some kind of animation.

smartphone A mobile phone that provides traditional digital voice service in addition to a variety of other functions, such as text messaging, email management, web browsing, still photo and video capabilities, MP3 music capabilities, video viewing, video calling, and the ability to run applications, to name just a few.

smooth point An anchor point along a vector curve.

SMS Acronym for Short Message Service; the texting component of a cell phone or other electronic device.

social engineering Tricking users into providing information in the belief that a request is legitimate.

social media Websites that allow users to create and exchange information.

social networking Online communities that let users instantly share information with other users.

sound card Computer component that allows computers to play or record sound.

spider Program that roams the Internet, searching for information about websites that it then sends to a search engine database.

spot colors Colors that are generated by a single ink, rather than created by blending ink colors.

spyware Malware that captures information from a computer without the user's knowledge or consent.

standoff The space separating an image from text in text wrapping.

stock photo An image produced and sold by a professional for use by the general public.

storyboard A visual method of outlining each scene.

stroke The visible outline of a path.

subscriber Web visitor who accepts notification of any updates to a podcast or a website that has frequently changing content.

subtractive color mixing Mixing primary pigment colors to absorb different amounts of light and create a range of colors.

subwoofer A speaker that reproduces very low bass sounds.

synchronous At the same time. Synchronous communication is when two people are speaking to one another, either in person or through the use of media, such as a phone, computer, or other electronic device.

t

tag HTML code used to identify an element in an HTML file and instruct browsers on how and where to display the element.

take Identifies the number of times a sequence has been filmed.

team charter Specifically identifies the team's goals, values, and approach to handling the task at hand.

template In Word or other word processing software, a design file that contains the common elements that should appear on all pages; also called a *master page*.

template In PowerPoint or other presentation software, a document master predesigned by professionals who have already chosen the background, font size and color, and bullets to be used.

tertiary color The color created when a primary and a secondary color are mixed.

text wrapping A feature that controls how text flows around a graphic or other object in a layout.

three dimensional (3D) Graphics with length, breadth, and depth.

thumbnail Small versions of larger images. They speed up the download process by allowing viewers to choose whether they want to see the larger image.

tilting Movement of a video camera angle up or down.

timecode A record of each frame of video.

tint A hue mixed with white.

tolerance A setting that determines the range of pixels affected by a raster editing tool's action. In Photoshop, this is a setting for the Magic Wand tool.

tone A hue mixed with gray.

tracking The amount of space between characters.

trademark A word, phrase, or image used to identify something as a product of a particular business.

transition Movement between scenes.

Trojan horse (also called Trojan) Software that appears to be useful but instead allows access to a computer without the user's knowledge or consent.

tweening The process of making a gradual change in an image by the computer rather than by the user.

two dimensional (2D) Graphics with length and breadth, but no depth.

typeface A collection of designed letters, numbers, and other characters created by a designer.

u

unity A design principle that pulls together all of the individual elements, making the design look like a single unit.

Universal Resource Locator (URL) The unique address used to access a website.

v

validate To check the code used to generate web pages to make sure it meets quality standards.

validator Software that checks websites under development for compliance with particular standards.

virus A program that infects a computer without the permission or knowledge of the owner. A virus usually attaches itself to executable programs, allowing it to travel to other computers. Viruses require action by the computer user in order to activate them.

w

warping Distorting a shape, such as stretching it.

watermark A pale image placed on the background of a page and which is often used for logos or other identification.

wave editor Software that allows one to modify or edit audio files.

waveform A graphical display that represents the changes in recorded sound waves.

Web Accessibility Initiative (WAI) W3C effort to ensure accessibility by creating accessibility standards and providing resources relevant to the issue.

Web analytics Tools that analyze and report statistics detailing traffic to a website.

Web Content Accessibility Guidelines (WCAG) Accessibility standards set by the WC3 for web developers to follow in order to make websites accessible to individuals with disabilities.

Web editor Computer software that creates HTML code automatically as part of the web design process.

Web server A computer used to store web pages so that browsers can access them.

website One or more web pages linked together in an organized collection.

Web Master Person who administers a website.

Web-safe colors 216 colors that all users can see, regardless of their computer displays.

well-formed code Formatting code that meets the quality standards of the coding system.

white balance Adjusts an image based upon the color temperature present when an image is photographed.

white space Also called negative space; the blank areas of a design that function like a design element.

widescreen Referring to the 16:9 ratio used in HD television and the differing formats used by movies.

widow When the last line of a paragraph falls by itself as the first line of the next page or column.

wiki Web page content that's open to users for creation and editing.

wireframe A chart providing an overview of the organization, or the site map.

World Wide Web Consortium (W3C) Organization that sets standards for the World Wide Web, including such issues as privacy, markup languages, styles, and other issues.

worm A form of a virus that does not require any action by the computer user. It spreads by using the email functions of the computer. A worm's action overwhelms web servers, often shutting them down.

X

x-height In simple terms, the height of the lowercase letter x in a given font.

XHMTL A markup language similar to HTML but with stricter requirements.

XML Markup language designed to hold and move data.

Z

zoom tool Navigation tool that magnifies or reduces the view of an image.

Index